# PAUL MEIER
## AND ROBERT WISE

## MEGA-MILLENNIUM
### SERIES

THE
### THIRD
MILLENNIUM

THE
### FOURTH
MILLENNIUM

### BEYOND
THE MILLENNIUM

Copyright © 1998 by Paul Meier and Robert Wise

Published in Nashville, Tennessee, by Thomas Nelson, Inc.

The Bible version used in this publication is THE NEW KING JAMES VER-SION. Copyright © 1979, 1980, 1982, 1990, Thomas Nelson, Inc.

Library of Congress Catalog Card Number: 98-75142

ISBN 0-7852-6971-1

Printed in the United States of America

1 2 3 4 5 6 — 03 02 01 00 99 98

# PAUL MEIER

# The Third Millennium

A NOVEL

A
JANET
THOMA
BOOK

Thomas Nelson Publishers
Nashville

# ACKNOWLEDGMENTS

I wish to give special thanks to Robert Wise, a very successful novelist and personal friend, who not only traveled to Israel with me to help complete the political and geographical research for this project but also provided extensive editorial assistance.

I greatly appreciate the historical and sociological research I was able to obtain from a local Conservative Jewish synagogue, as well as from Rabbi Robert Gorelik, of the Adat HaMashiach Temple in Irvine, California, a messianic Jewish synagogue.

I also want to express my appreciation to a now-deceased hero of mine, Jim Irwin, the American astronaut who stepped foot on the moon. My trip to Mount Ararat with a Probe research group to meet Jim Irwin's team in search of Noah's Ark in 1985 and the refusal of the Turkish government to allow us to explore that part of Mount Ararat inspired me to begin the extensive research required for this book.

I have had a rare privilege as a psychiatrist—the privilege to study the spiritual aspects of human beings as well as to study biblical prophecy at Trinity Seminary in Chicago and Dallas Theological Seminary in Dallas. I also had the opportunity to teach at both wonderful institutions while doing research that helped me develop this novel.

The direct or indirect teachings of wise men such as Gleason Archer, John Walvoord, Dwight Pentecost, Robert Lightner, and Charles Dyer were particularly helpful in the development of prophetic themes. Grant Jeffrey's research, books, and telephone assistance are also greatly appreciated, as is the long-distance help I received from Dead Sea Scroll scholars and other scholars who eased my compulsive quest for accuracy and feasibility.

Paul Meier, M.D.
Los Angeles, California

## MEMO: To the Archives of the Hosts of Heaven
## RE: The Final Decade of the Second Millennium
## FROM: Michael, Guardian Angel

Issues have been raised about the fate and final years of planet Earth. A desire has been expressed for study of the circumstances that brought about the ultimate shifts in history and society preceding the third millennium A.D. Therefore, I have undertaken to report the major events of the 1990s (as human beings measure what they call time).

Questions will be raised about my capacity to file this report prior to the occurrence of the actual events. Please be aware that the heavenly Father granted me the unusual privilege of leaping into the future to the year 2001 to complete my personal assignment during this last period.

As a personal guardian angel (G.A.), I have for thousands of years been given responsibility for various human beings, generally of Jewish origin. My work through the centuries has given unique insight into the character and problems of the human race. Of course, I have battled with principalities and powers of overwhelming proportions while completing my work. Therefore, I am also eminently qualified to understand the problems of evil and deception that have constantly been at work distorting the human situation.

During the 1990s, my assignment was the family of Dr. Larry Feinberg. The Feinbergs were a nonpracticing Jewish family living by the ocean in Newport Beach, California, United States of America. The area is almost identical in latitude to that of the Holy Land. The story of Larry, Sharon, and their two children,

Ben and Ruth, will explain the upheavals of the last days of travail.

We will begin midpoint in the decade at the point that the family began to recognize that history was shifting like the plates of the earth over the San Andreas Fault. As we shall see, it was an astonishing time!

This period of explosion and fraud, technical discovery and overwhelming chaos, is surely worthy of angelic scrutiny. The entire globe became as a woman in the last throes of labor. From the fall of the Berlin Wall and the collapse of the Soviet Union to the rise of spirit guides, crystals, and white witches and the distribution of condoms in the public schools, each year passed like the crescendo of a hard rock band increasing in volume to ear-splitting proportions!

Consideration of this period begins on what humans call New Year's Day, 1995, and continues to the end of the year 2000. As we look in on the secret world of my special charges, the truth will be evident.

## New Year's Day, 1995

Howling blizzard winds hurled sleet and snow against the White House. The President of the United States stood silently looking out the Oval Office window, into the darkness. He lingered, waiting to answer the two men who sat in front of his desk as if he enjoyed creating consternation at this secret predawn meeting. Damian Gianardo turned and gawked at his secretary of state. The executive squirmed and looked away.

Gianardo was a tall, distinguished man of commanding presence. Long before the presidency fell into his hands, he acquired the art of walking into any room in a way that immediately demanded everyone's attention. His intimidating black eyes and penetrating stare always produced a disconcerting feeling that he knew what others were thinking. He had an uncanny intuitive capacity to accurately read the intentions and motives of his opponents. Once he grasped the position of another, there were no restraints on Gianardo's pursuit of his own ends.

The president's graying hair was carefully combed over the right side of his head, down across his temple toward his neck. Even hair transplants could not conceal the reminder of the near fatal head injury. His vanity caused him to keep the damaged side of his head toward the window as he spoke.

"Yes, of course, I am completely serious," the president spoke condescendingly. "I want you to implement fully and totally every last directive that I have outlined in my proposal. Got it?" He paused and leaned toward the secretary. "I made the unusual move of calling both of you in so early on New Year's Day because the press and usual observers of my every action wouldn't expect us to be talking this morning." Gianardo crossed his arms and glared at his secretary of state. "There must be absolutely nothing of this conversation in any file or on any tape recording. And timing will be of the utmost importance."

Jacob Rathmarker turned to the secretary of state. "Mr. Clark, I want you to know that in my capacity as vice president I am putting my full support behind the president's objectives. He and I have had full and complete discussions of the matter."

The secretary looked at the outline in his hand and fidgeted nervously. "I have to let someone in," he searched for words, "at least several aides. After all, you are asking me to contact the ten most significant nations in the world. I can't do that entirely by myself. At least a dozen people need to be in on the possible negotiations. You want to change the total alignment of world power. The entire idea is simply mind-boggling."

"You think I'm crazy." Damian Gianardo turned from the window and smiled cynically. "I know what's just run through your mind." The president leaned over the desk and stared fixedly into the eyes of the secretary until the man looked down. "You're thinking that I'm going power crazy." Gianardo enjoyed his uncanny ability to sense the secretary's feelings.

"NO! No." The secretary shook his head defensively. "I wouldn't ever think such a thing of *you*." Clark's instantaneous response was revealingly apologetic. *"Never."*

"You just did." The president winked at Rathmarker. "As easily as I read you," Gianardo continued, "I've foreseen what lies ahead. Mr. Secretary, what seems impossible now will be quite plausible in another year. You will be shocked to see how easily this alliance will fall into place."

The secretary gritted his teeth in frustration. "But you are proposing that ultimately each of these countries would give up its sovereignty to form a confederation with us. If it accepts your idea, each nation would become like one of our states."

"Yes," the president said, slowly picking up a dagger letter opener from the top of his desk. The president's perfectly manicured fingers were long, tapered, and unusually thin. Though they might have been the hands of an artist or a surgeon, the fingers had the disconcerting look of the caricature expected of the undertaker in a horror movie. Damian Gianardo held the sharp weapon between his palms, pushing the tapering point into his hand as if to demonstrate his imperviousness to pain. "You are grasping the implications of what I intend. I spare no expense in meeting my objectives." The president ran his narrow fingertips down the edge of the blade as he laid the letter opener down. "No expense."

"Can you imagine how much power that would consolidate in our hands?" The vice president bore down on the secretary.

"Imagine?" The secretary of state rolled his eyes. "Why . . . ," he fumbled for words, "if this consolidation is accomplished, you would in effect re-create the Roman Empire!"

"Interesting choice of words." Gianardo licked his lips. "Such a possibility had occurred to me."

On the opposite coast, members of a Jewish family were once again preparing for their usual annual observance of New Year's Day. The family of Larry and Sharon Feinberg were irrevocably tied to rituals. In most things they were contemporary to the core, yet vestiges of their Jewish past still demanded a firm grip on the traditions that defined and redefined who they were. Unexpected tension on this fragile linkage was serious business.

New Year's Day had become one such event. Although they seldom observed Passover or Rosh Hashanah, the Feinbergs judiciously guarded their family events on the start of each secular year on the calendar. Sharon expected the entire family to start the year together with bagels and lox, grapefruit, hard boiled eggs served in silver cups, and a side dish of pickled herring. The entire meal had to be consumed before the beginning of the Rose Bowl Parade which everyone watched with at least pretended rapt attention. The annual TV special of the year in review always followed. And then the football games began. A different matter, indeed.

Life with the Feinbergs was supposed to move in well-ordered annual compartments essentially predetermined nearly five decades earlier by the shape of Larry and Sharon's long-displaced rituals of childhood. At least that had once been what was now a fading hope and intention.

"Ruth?" Ben called out. "The football game is about to start. Ruth?"

An endless line of bands and floats paraded across the TV screen until Ben punched the clicker and changed channels to the sports network. "Where in the world is Ruth?" Ben asked his father. "She was here a minute ago."

"I don't know where your sister is." Larry looked mystified. "You know how your mother is about this family stuff on New Year's Day *until* the football games start when she and your sister always get scarce."

"I thought maybe Ruth would watch the game with us since UCLA is playing." Ben's strapping two-hundred-pound frame settled in the chair. He was about the same size as his father, and their hair was an identical dark brown. Ben always looked like the latest page from *Gentleman's Quarterly* even when he dressed casually.

"Maybe Ruth took a stroll down to the ocean." Larry walked to the window.

"We could play chess for a while." Ben pointed to the chess table where their last game was still unfinished. "Maybe Ruth will change her mind and watch."

When Ben was fourteen, Larry had thought it wise to let his son win to boost what the doctor considered a sagging self-esteem. During the last four years, Ben had turned out to be a young master of the computer and reveled in any challenge that demanded strategy. Now that Ben regularly beat Larry, many games were left dangling while Larry searched for a better move before having to throw in the towel. The unfinished game was its own commentary on the subtle tension between the psychiatrist and his son.

"The football widow is leaving now," Sharon called from the hallway. "Jennifer McCoy is meeting me at the movie. I'll be back by the time the game is over."

"You do this every year! Even if she's your best friend, you're blowing it again," Larry grumbled.

"Hey, Mom! Where's Ruth?"

"She went whirling out of here a bit ago." Sharon waved good-bye. "Said that she's meeting Heather and Amy at a movie too. We will all be here for supper."

"You're going to miss watching UCLA stomp Michigan State," Ben chided.

"Please," Sharon shook her head, "we've had enough violence in the last year to last a lifetime. I'm gone." She closed the door behind her and started for the car.

Sharon paused to look at the profusion of flowers around the front walkway, which became a path winding its way down to the ocean. Even in the midst of the mild winter, the flowers lacked nothing in color. The pastel pinks and blues helped Sharon believe that there might still be some peace left in the world. She tried to drink in their colorful reassurance each day before she left the house.

Kind and gentle by disposition, Sharon didn't look forty-seven. She enjoyed teasing Larry that the difference of two years in their ages looked more like twenty. Her glowing olive skin and dark brown eyes added to her natural youthfulness. A little too plump for her own good, Sharon was tall and carried herself confidently. The fussy quality about her elegant clothes betrayed her perfectionistic and controlling tendencies. Sharon always knew where she was going.

From the window, Larry affectionately watched his wife drive away. Their home had become a haven for them against the boiling turmoil of the outside world. Not far from Balboa Island, the family estate backed up to a private beach. Larry could see over to Catalina Island on a clear day. He was fortunate to have been able to get a buy on such a luxurious tract. Larry felt secure in his traditional home contrasting with the more contemporary Mediterranean styles around them. Something about the wood-frame house pleased him. Even though he congratulated himself on being an avant-garde psychiatrist, Larry couldn't suppress a conservatism that more than occasionally popped out. His religious Jewish ancestors had made their indelible mark, which was reflected in the white trim on his gray house. Knowing that he could close the shutters anytime he liked similarly comforted him.

"Kickoff!" Ben called to his father. "Better off watching the game without the women interrupting all the time anyway."

"Strange how Ruth slipped out." Larry turned from the window. "I'll take Michigan State by ten points." He slipped down in his large overstuffed chair.

The TV cameras panned the stadium as the players lined up for the kickoff. "President Gianardo is attending the game today," the announcer's voice boomed across the living room. "Security is incredibly tight, but Gianardo and his wife are in presidential box seats."

"Takes guts for the president to come out in a crowd like that one," Larry noted. "But that man seems to be fearless."

Ben glanced down at the large commemorative magazine on the table. "IN MEMORIAL—1994" was embossed in gold on the cover. He picked up the magazine and began flipping through the pages. Scenes of two caskets pulled by horse-drawn carriages filled the first pages. In the middle were different shots of the White House on fire with the windows blown out. "Gianardo must have seven lives." Ben closed the magazine quickly.

"I still can't believe he survived that terrible head wound when the bomb went off," Larry answered. "The concussion killed the president and vice president instantly. Those other senators died very quickly. How he got out I'll never know."

"He's an amazing man, Dad. Who would have guessed that he was the brains behind that secret agreement the U.S. reached with Israel and the Arabs back in '93 to stop all the hostility? Even though he was the speaker of the House then, he did what the secretary of state couldn't accomplish. He got Israel to make that land deal in order to achieve peace."

"He's certainly cemented relations with the Arabs since then. The emergence of the United Muslim States is an incredible change."

"Yes," Ben agreed, "and with a new capitol in the rebuilt ancient city of Babylon, Arabs are emerging as a world power."

"The seven-year pact Gianardo pulled off protects Israel until the year 2000. I think it was good for everybody," Larry said nonchalantly.

Michigan State kicked off, and the ball bounced on the twenty-yard line. Ben immediately rooted for UCLA while Larry cheered his team. The game would be hard-hitting and close.

Ben reached for a handful of potato chips, but he no longer seemed to be focused on the game. His thoughts abruptly shifted to Cindy Wong. Ben first noticed Cindy at an interstudent council workshop when he was a junior and she was a sophomore. Even though they were from different high schools, Ben had made it a point to find out everything he could about her world. Distance had only intensified his interest.

Ben was drawn to Cindy because she was different. Neither of them was really part of the establishment as Ben saw things. He was Jewish, and she was oriental. The fact that she was both Chinese and blind truly put her in a world by herself. Ben felt an unspoken kinship with her. She was also a displaced person of sorts. Ben thought of his upbringing as being thoroughly American, but he knew that was only marginally true. They were Jews who had come from somewhere else. The Feinbergs could again become outsiders at a moment's notice if the tides of social opinion turned against them. Though Ben had never broached the subject with her, he knew that Cindy would thoroughly understand his feelings and misgivings.

"Hey!" Larry poked his son in the ribs. "You're not even in the game."

"What?" Ben jumped.

"UCLA just scored and you didn't twitch a muscle."

# CHAPTER

## 2

"Are you slick or what?" Jimmy Harrison pulled Ruth closer to him as the Ferris wheel made its final turn.

"I love Balboa Island." Ruth looked out over the amusement park and the ocean that surrounded it. "Most fun place in southern California." As the wheel settled toward the ground, she watched people getting off other rides and entering the little amusement shops around the island. "But I think I like you better."

Jimmy laughed. "How did you shake free of your people on New Year's Day without them blowing a gasket?" He could sense that Ruth liked the warm feel of his hand over hers, and his aggressive flirtatiousness flattered her.

"They think I'm at the movies with my college roommates, Heather and Amy. The old man would blow his mind if he knew I was taking a spin with the guy who sold us my car last week."

Jimmy smiled and bit her ear teasingly, but he didn't like the inference. When the Feinbergs wheeled into the used car lot in their big black '95 Mercedes, Jimmy felt the challenge instantly. He watched the family flash their Rolexes around and immediately knew they would pay top dollar. Halfway into the deal the challenge of seducing a little rich girl gripped him. Jimmy had made the possibility of having a relationship with Ruth as much a goal as getting the most money he could out of Dr. Feinberg, who obviously thought of himself as the supreme negotiator. He couldn't believe it had been so easy to pull off seeing Ruth twice in the last week.

Ruth turned her head sideways and kissed Jimmy eagerly. Only the abrupt stop of the Ferris wheel at the bottom ended the overpowering moment. As she walked away from the seat, she swung her hips carelessly and tossed her long hair over her shoulder.

"You're my kind of woman." Jimmy grinned as they walked out into the park. He watched Ruth's eyes light up when he put a heavy emphasis on "woman." Like her mother, Ruth was tall and could easily slide toward the heavy side. While she had her mother's dark brown hair, Ruth had striking blue eyes. Any possible plumpness was poured into a figure that clearly held Jimmy's full attention.

"Just what's your old man's line of work?" Jimmy put his arm around Ruth's waist.

"He's a shrink," Ruth replied. "He thinks he's God when it comes to sizing up people. Can you imagine that we were barely out of your car lot when he told us that you were some kind of character disorder, con man type? He'd really be steamed if he knew that I was cruising this place with you."

Jimmy's smile hardened. The psychiatrist's diagnosis cut through his façade and made him nervous. Moreover, he felt uncomfortable being a twenty-five-year-old uneducated used car salesman. A six-foot-four-inch blond Nordic weight lifter, Jimmy was the master of creating appearances. The thought of conquering Ruth pleased him. "Let's truck over to my car in the lot. I've got a couple of joints hidden under the seat of my Corvette. How about a little grass to loosen us up?"

"Sure." The pitch in Ruth's nervous voice raised.

Instantly, Jimmy knew that Ruth hadn't ever done

marijuana. She might go for it big and get high quick. On the other hand, Ruth might cough and sputter, and nothing would come of the opportunity. "Well, let's give it a try." Jimmy smiled wickedly.

The couple cut across the park, winding their way past popcorn vendors and men selling balloons, and headed for the parking lot. Straight ahead, the ferry was bringing another load of cars across.

"My father's a real pain!" Ruth suddenly blurted out. "He's so self-confident all the time."

"Tell me about it," Jimmy sneered. "I hate my old man. What a big-time jerk."

"What does he do?"

Jimmy froze. That was the one question he hadn't expected, and the answer might blow everything. Jimmy gazed into Ruth's eyes. She had an innocent, all-accepting look that meant she was really on the hook, but Jimmy knew Ruth was Jewish and that might make everything more complicated.

"Come on, honey," Ruth cooed. "There isn't anything you can't share with me."

Jimmy's eyes narrowed. He let "honey" rattle around a moment. No question Ruth was going for him. "He's a Christian minister," Jimmy answered haltingly. "Has a big church in Dallas, Texas. My old man's a big daddy in Big D."

"Seriously?" Ruth asked incredulously.

"Turns you off, doesn't it?"

"No, no." A sly grin crossed Ruth's face. "I've just never been around preacher types."

"I avoid him at all costs," Jimmy said sternly. "The fanatic spent his whole life saving souls at the expense of me and my four brothers. He was so busy making God happy, Mr. Holy couldn't even take in one of our baseball games. Don't worry. Reverend Big Time has taken care of any interest I'll ever have in God or religion. I don't buy anything the old creep is preaching."

Ruth stopped and abruptly kissed Jimmy passionately on the mouth. She reached up and ran her hands through his hair. She breathed heavily, "I like everything about you. Don't worry about some family hang-up. My world's not any different."

"Really?" Jimmy felt his blood rushing to his face. *This girl's a keg of dynamite*, he thought. At the same time he felt an unexpected sense of caring.

"Look," Ruth took his hand, "my parents got it all wrapped for me as well. They've already got some rich Jewish doctor or lawyer staked out." She paused and tossed her long hair back. "But a long time ago I figured out that my father lives his life by the book. All I ever get out of him is what the latest psychiatric journal party line is. I figure out what he wants to hear, and I just feed it back." Ruth's eyes snapped with fire. "I'm sick of being analyzed by him every time something goes wrong."

She thought a minute. "I'm going to have to go to the movies to cover my tracks. I think I better not do a joint today. Next time."

Jimmy smiled. *Date a shrink's daughter, get psychological excuses*, he thought. "Sure. Next time, we'll make sure that we have plenty of uninterrupted time. I'll call you at your apartment at the university."

"You bet." Ruth put her arms around his neck. "I hate to run, but if I don't, I'm going to get into the movies too late. I have to make sure I don't get into problems with the traffic." Ruth started for her own car and then turned back. "I can't wait for us to be together again. Just maybe I'm falling in love with you, Jimmy Harrison." Ruth ran back, kissed him passionately again, and then ran for her car.

Jimmy stood beside his '89 classic red Corvette and watched her drive away. *Isn't this wild?* he said to himself. *I believe I'm in the home stretch on this one.*

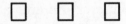

*He's not at all like my father. Jimmy is so deep and feeling.* Ruth's thoughts raced as she frantically drove toward the Fashion Island theater. Jimmy made her feel sexy and alive. Ruth loved the exhilaration. Her face flushed. *Oh, I hope I wasn't too obvious.*

Ruth saw the underground parking entrance to the theater and pulled in. *Amy said the movie was "Marital Fatality,"* she thought as she hurried toward the ticket window.

"Really only twenty minutes are left at most," the girl in the window said.

"I've seen it twice," Ruth lied. 'Just wanted to catch the ending again. Couldn't I just slip in?"

"Who cares?" The girl waved her through the door.

"Owe you one." Ruth waved and hurried inside.

In the dark Ruth found it difficult to adjust her eyes. Finally, she saw the familiar outlines of her two roommates' heads, and she slipped in beside them.

"Hey," Amy whispered far too loud, "how was your little man?"

"Awesome! Just beyond words."

The girls giggled and then settled back to watch the final scenes of the terror on the screen. When the lights came on, the interrogation began.

"Tell me everything you did!" Heather insisted. "Did you make out?"

"You are just too clever." Amy rolled her eyes. "I can't believe the way you're able to snow your—," she stopped abruptly. "Oh, my gosh!" Amy was looking over Ruth's head.

"What in the world is going on here?" A voice came from the aisle.

Ruth turned. "Mother!" she choked.

"I want an explanation of what you think you're up to!"

"Mother, what are you doing here?"

'Jennifer and I changed our minds after we saw what was on at the big Newport theater. We just happened to stop here."

"Great movie." Ruth tried to be casual.

"Yes," Sharon said intensely. "It's too bad you didn't see any of it."

"Wh . . . what do you mean?"

"We got here late," Sharon bore down, "but as soon as we could see in the darkness, we saw Amy and Heather were just in front of us. At first I thought you were out getting popcorn. Then I began to worry about why you weren't here. Several times I almost got up to ask the girls, but I decided that maybe I misunderstood you when you left in such a hurry. When I saw you slip in, I knew something was very wrong."

Ruth looked at her roommates out of the corner of her eye. Nothing that she could say could hide their guilty looks.

"Excuse us, girls," Sharon spoke firmly. "My daughter and I need to talk privately." Sharon took Ruth's hand and started for the lobby. They stopped in a dark corner in the hall. "Have you been lying to us again?" Sharon's voice quivered.

"I'm very sorry." Ruth tried to look regretful. "I didn't think I could tell you the truth, though. I met a boy I knew you wouldn't like."

A look of disgust crossed Sharon's face. "I don't like deceptiveness. Who is he?"

"His name is Jimmy Harrison. I knew you might—"

"The guy at the used car lot? Not him!"

"See! I told you that so—"

"Why can't you find someone of your own class? Really!"

"You are saying *exactly* what I knew you would. And you wonder why I didn't level with you about where I was going?"

Sharon shook her head. "I just don't understand. You and your roommates live like royalty at Pepperdine. You even have a maid to clean your apartment each day. We have given you the best. Yet you keep having these . . . these problems with honesty. When you were at home, we knew of at least five times you crawled out the window after twelve at night. Who knows how many times you really left!"

"You going to throw those incidents up in my face again?" Ruth said indignantly.

"Go home." Sharon began walking away. "I'll meet you there."

"Are you going to tell Dad?" Ruth hurried after her. "Really, he doesn't need the stress."

"Since when did you start worrying about your father's feelings?" Sharon turned and headed for the entrance.

□ □ □

Sharon Feinberg was generally not overly aggressive, but she tended to hover over her family like a mother hen. She carefully chose her confrontations. On the other hand, Larry fussed constantly over what was psychologically appropriate. In fact, the family cringed every time he cleared his throat and suggested "appropriateness." Still, Larry's personal preoccupation added to Sharon's natural tendency to choose her timing well. Two weeks passed before she told him about the movie incident.

"Such a little thing to deceive us about." Larry's neck reddened as he sank down in his overstuffed chair in front of the TV. "Is there anyone more understanding than I?"

"I really thought you overreacted in suggesting counseling. After all, that's a psychiatrist's answer for everything." Sharon threw her hands up in the air. "But now I must agree. I hope that therapy will put an end to her lying to us."

"The counselor is excellent." Larry sounded defensive. "I've known Dr. Ann Woodbridge for a number of years, and I have total confidence in her ability."

"All this talk about being a Christian counselor bothers me," Sharon said. "I'm not sure I'm comfortable with someone tacking her religion on her profession like an advertisement. What would our Jewish parents think about sending our daughter to a Christian?"

"Dr. Woodbridge makes no bones about her values." Larry frowned. "She's an expert on adolescence and character development. I don't think a strong dose of honesty and integrity will hurt our daughter a bit."

"Maybe this psychologist will try to convert Ruth."

"Sharon," Larry pleaded, "the woman isn't an evangelist. Don't you think I know what I'm doing? She and I have had long talks about professionalism."

"I don't know." Sharon shook her head. "The woman's capacity is the question. Something is wrong. We've had Ruth in the best schools. You'd think that by age twenty-two she'd know the difference between the truth and a lie."

Larry opened his mouth to speak and then stopped. "Perhaps," his voice faded.

"We haven't been particularly religious people." Sharon looked at the marriage plaque on the wall. The parchment was in Hebrew with fancy flourishes around the edges. "I went to the synagogue every week when I was a child. Ruth can probably count on her fingers how many times she's been in one."

Larry shook his head emphatically. "We haven't used religion to create guilt. No apologies there."

"But we haven't particularly encouraged religious values either. The Christian counselor makes sense for that reason."

"Perhaps," Larry bit his lip, "we need to look elsewhere. There are good psychological reasons for her behavior."

"The whole world's crazy," Sharon agonized. "I can't even stand to listen to the news anymore. Everything is scrambled. Maybe the times are to blame."

Sharon walked in front of the Hebrew marriage scroll and ran her hands across the edge of the frame. "My father gave us this memento hoping that our children would see it every day. We haven't done well,

Larry. Did you know that Ben is attracted to a Chinese girl whose parents are Buddhists?"

"Really, Sharon. This is the Los Angeles area. We're living inside the melting pot itself."

"Your parents would be just as upset. They wouldn't want our children to assimilate. It's just hard to accept such wide departures from our heritage."

Larry sat up straight in his chair and stuck his chin out. "We are modern Jews. We can't inhibit the natural expressions and interests of our children."

"Then what are we going to do, Larry?"

"I'll talk to her. I'll try to see if I can bring some insight." He added, "At the appropriate time of course."

Sharon stiffened as he finished the sentence. "Perhaps we might try a different approach this time. Let's bring the boy over here. Maybe if we got him out in the light of the day, Ruth would recognize the truth."

"We'll take the secret forbidden quality away." Larry's eyes lit up. "That will kill it! I love to use paradoxical intention like that—encouraging the forbidden so the patient will rebel by doing what is right instead."

"At least we can ask the sort of questions that will clarify who he is."

Larry nodded eagerly. "That's exactly the idea I had in mind!"

# CHAPTER

# 3

**B**eing the guardian angel of the Feinberg family was no easy matter. Because I knew the importance of their role in the divine plan for the future, I had to carefully oversee details that I might have otherwise ignored. No one would have guessed that I placed the advertisement for Jimmy Harrison's car lot in front of Larry, nor would Sharon ever have an inkling that by a similar ploy she was directed toward the same theater on New Year's Day that her daughter was going to attend.

However, trying to make the drama work out right while Dr. Appropriate and Mrs. Hen arranged the props on the set proved to be as challenging as the problems I once had in getting Sisera to drop into Heber's place for a drink and a little nap in Old Testament times.

Jimmy Harrison was invited for dinner several times. A maid was hired for the evening to serve on the Feinbergs' finest china and best linens. The pizza-and-hamburger kid got the message very quickly.

Even though Larry and Sharon subtly slipped in their questions between the salad and the soup, the bludgeoning was obvious. The more the parents whacked the used car salesman, the more Ruth defended. With the parents' help, a relationship that might have lasted a month was becoming a permanent fixture in their home. In their wildest dreams, they couldn't have foreseen that Jimmy Harrison was a part of God's plan for their lives.

Neither did they realize what an important role Cindy Wong would play in the divine scheme of things.

While Ruth and Jimmy struggled with the Feinbergs' attempts at supervision, Ben went relatively unobserved in his pursuit of Cindy. One of his favorite ploys was to *happen* to show up at the Golden Dragon, the Wongs' family restaurant.

One evening in late May, Ben dropped in.

"Cindy here?" Ben asked the waiter.

"Ah . . . you . . . ah . . . know Miss Cindy?" the Chinese server in a black tuxedo asked.

"Good friends," Ben sounded professionally distant. "Social acquaintances. I would like to speak with her if she is here," he said, knowing completely well Cindy was somewhere in the restaurant.

"One moment, please." The man hurried away.

Ben looked around the elegant restaurant. Although the Golden Dragon was in a fairly common shopping center area in Lake Forest, the interior was lavishly decorated. Large tanks of tropical fish lined the walls. The ceilings were covered with gold-and-red dragons, and the tables were made of thickly lacquered black ebony. Linen napkins added the final touch. Ben picked up the ornate silverware to admire the design.

"Name, please," the waiter interrupted his inspection. Cindy was a few steps behind him.

"Cindy!" Ben stood at once. Her skin was smooth like porcelain china—warm olive colored with a blush of color in her cheeks. Her heart-shaped mouth was perfect.

"Ben?" she answered. "Ben Feinberg?" She offered a dainty hand.

"Just happened to be in the area." Ben smiled but sounded obvious. "Thought a little chow mein would be great. Can you sit down?"

"Sure." Cindy felt for the chair, and the waiter helped her find the edge of the table.

"How are things?" Ben liked everything he saw in. Cindy. Even though she was petite, her figure lacked nothing in maturity. Her sightless brown eyes looked completely normal. The only hint of irregularity was in her slightly unfocused look. Jet black hair framed her flawless face.

"School is going quite well. I have been accepted at UCLA next fall."

"Great!" Ben beamed. "Outstanding place!"

"They are going to provide a guide dog, special tutors, everything!"

"Only a very smart girl could pull that off."

Cindy blushed. "I work hard."

"I really admire you, Cindy. You don't let anything get in your way. You never seem to need help."

Cindy's smile froze. "No one will ever need to feel sorry for Cindy Wong. I am quite capable of making my way."

"Oh, exactly," Ben backtracked. "That's what I meant."

"Perhaps I can suggest something for supper." Cindy changed the subject.

"What's your specialty tonight?"

"Ever try Kung Pao Squid? I think you'll find it to be one of our best exotic dishes."

"Only if you eat with me," Ben said slyly.

The smile returned. "Maybe a little hot and sour soup."

"Waiter!" Ben snapped his fingers immediately and waved to the Chinese attendant.

☐   ☐   ☐

As summer approached, Ruth took advantage of her parents' attempts at openness and invited Jimmy over for frequent walks on the family's private beach. The salty mist swept in from the sea over the rocks and up the gentle sloping sandy beach. The waves of the ebbing tide and the tranquil ocean made a swim seem deceptively plausible, but June waters were seldom warm enough.

Ruth stopped and dug her toe into the white sand. "I think I ought to tell you several things," she said slowly. She looked up and watched a sea gull making a lazy, long swoop toward them. A large pelican bobbed up and down on the ocean. "I hope you'll take it OK."

Jimmy realized that his feelings had changed during the past six months. What started as a chase had turned into feelings that he had not known before. "You've decided to push on? Got somebody else in mind?"

"Come on!" Ruth poked him in the chest with her finger. "Silly, you know better. I want to share something with you that is, well, rather sensitive to say."

"Anything is OK as long as I don't have new competition."

Ruth started to walk again. "I've had to face some problems I had before we started hanging out together." She chose her words carefully. "I've needed a counselor to help me get some things straight."

"What do you mean?" Jimmy raised his eyebrows and grimaced. "About us?"

"Got a guilty conscience?" Ruth laughed. "No, I don't talk much about us. I've had to get my act together. The visits have helped a lot."

"So?" Jimmy shrugged. "Why are you telling me?"

"I want you to be happy." Ruth put her arm around Jimmy's shoulder. "I know that your problems with your parents bother you more than you admit. I know that it's hard for you to trust people sometimes."

Jimmy scanned her face. The innocent eagerness he had once seen was still there, but now he realized how much he truly cared for the dark-haired beauty. She was stunning in her black-and-white swimming suit.

Ruth's stylishness reflected taste, savvy, and class. But there was something more powerfully attractive than just her physical appeal. Jimmy saw an inner quality that he had not seen in many women. Her genuineness was the best thing that had ever happened to him. "I *really* do love you." He was surprised at the strength of his feelings.

"I never thought you didn't." Ruth laughed.

But Jimmy knew how far he had come. Only slowly had he come to trust himself with her. Ruth had taught him a great deal in a few months.

"Let's test the waters!" Ruth suddenly pulled away and ran for the ocean. "Dare you to jump in." She kicked her sneakers off and dropped them in the sand. She hopped toward the surf rolling up on the beach and ran into the water.

"You won't last long!" Jimmy called after her. He left his tennis shoes beside hers.

Jimmy watched her. Ruth's virtue had affected him. She had been teaching him a straightforward honesty he hadn't known since childhood. Jimmy had even come to like the feeling.

"Ohhh!" Ruth squealed. "It looks sooo good, but the water feels like it's floating ice cubes."

Jimmy skimmed across the surf as he plunged in up to the top of his ankles. "Good grief!" he gasped. "The current's straight down from Alaska!"

For a few moments they tiptoed around the edge of the sand and the sea before giving up their dance. Ruth splashed the salty water on Jimmy and ran for her shoes with him in full pursuit. He caught up and spun her around.

"You're going to get it!" Jimmy mimicked fierceness and rolled his eyes. Just as abruptly, he kissed her passionately on the mouth.

"Hmmm, you're something else." Ruth gasped for breath. "I've got to sit down." She dropped down on a driftwood log to brush the sand off her feet.

"Thanks for telling about your feelings." Jimmy

helped Ruth back up to her feet. He led her toward the house. "I know that I need to think about my resentment of my dad. I really do try."

"I know," Ruth said simply as they walked up the path toward the house. She stopped at the little gazebo and slipped khaki pants and a loose blouse over her swimsuit. "I know more about you than you think, Jimmy Harrison."

Ruth stepped up on the redwood deck surrounding the back porch. Large pots of geraniums and flowers covered the patio area. She and Jimmy stomped their feet to make sure they didn't track sand into the house. Once inside they made sure no tracks were left across Sharon's immaculate kitchen floor.

Ruth and Jimmy slipped into the den unnoticed because the parents were totally engrossed in watching the news. Jimmy shuffled nervously toward an overstuffed leather chair near the game table covered with onyx chess pieces. Ruth plopped into a plaid colonial chair near the fireplace.

"Oh, come in," Sharon abruptly looked up. "Please sit down," she sounded formal and distant.

"What's happening?" Ruth tried to sound cheery.

"Amazing breakthrough in Israel." Larry pointed to the TV. "They've found that the oil discovery several months ago has turned out to be an extraordinary field. Israel has gone from being an importer to swimming in the crude."

Pictures of elaborate construction work filled the screen. "The new oil money is being used to rebuild the temple of Solomon in a lavish way," Sharon explained. "The cameras are showing the first stages of the new construction that will finish the temple like it was thousands of years ago."

Jimmy's countenance changed. "Really?" He moved to the edge of his seat. "Reconstruction was predicted," he began excitedly and then paused, "in some people's opinion, by the Bible."

Larry looked at Jimmy with a puzzled expression.

"Of course, they're going to kill more animals," Ruth said scornfully.

"As a matter of fact," Sharon answered, "the announcer reported on sacrifices just before you came in. In spite of litigation by animal rights activists and some environmental protection groups, the priests are continuing their work unabated."

"Those people are crazy," Ruth glowered. "They're giving Jews everywhere a bad name."

"The Arabs are certainly getting in on the act." Larry sat back in his chair. "They're protesting louder than anyone. I doubt if they really care that much about the animals being sacrificed, but it's an opportunity to criticize Israel."

"Muslims make me nervous." Jimmy tossed out. "The growth of the United Muslim States ought to worry us. The linkup of Arab countries creates a power bloc of frightening potential. The Bible says . . . ," Jimmy stopped. "I understand the Bible makes references to such a possibility. I'm sure Jewish people everywhere are very sensitive to these issues."

"Absolutely," Larry expressed an unusually genuine interest in Jimmy's opinions. "We have too many strange things happening in the world right now. When too much change occurs, people get a little crazy. They accept ideas they shouldn't and let political leaders easily deceive them. I'm worried by the present political climate."

Jimmy sensed an acceptance that hadn't been there before. Larry was treating him with new respect, and the feeling was exhilarating. "I guess your generation grew up worrying about Russia and the Reds taking over the world. Maybe mine ought to be nervous about the Middle East and the new Arab empire."

"Everything is too interwoven with treaties, computers, banks, economic interest." Larry shook his finger at Jimmy. "Too much like political conditions were just before World War II. Something simple could upset everything! I'm deeply troubled by Gianardo's casual acceptance of assisted suicides and his indifference about euthanasia."

"It's a bad sign." Sharon shook her head. "There's no concern for life."

Larry beckoned Jimmy closer. "The new legislation the president is proposing would essentially allow legal guardians to put severely retarded people and people with physically handicapping conditions to sleep whenever it is convenient. If this bill passes, infants under two years of age with severe disabilities could be terminated with written consent of parents even this year. As a physician, I am very, very alarmed."

"I don't know if this makes sense to you, Jimmy," Sharon's voice was more sincere and personal, "but as Jews, we are deeply committed to life. We fear political intervention in any procedure that would allow the state to kill human beings."

"I hate it!" Larry hit the arm of his chair. "I don't care if public opinion is on Gianardo's side. *All* human life has value. If we don't stand against this trend, the same holocaust that happened in Germany could be repeated here on helpless people and ones with infirmities. It started this way in the Third Reich. First there were abortions on demand, and then one thing led to another."

Ruth shuddered. "This whole conversation gives me the creeps. I know there was a lot of civil rights progress back in the sixties, but Israel isn't very popular right now. Things could get out of hand."

"Not this time!" Jimmy crossed his arms over his chest. "People would rally around the Jews if this nonsense started up. At least I'd be leading the parade!"

The room became very quiet.

Jimmy was startled with the forcefulness of his words. From somewhere deep within him, a stream of conviction had erupted. Values and ideas that had been covered with layers of anger had pushed their way forward. "We must stand above moral compromise," he said quietly.

Larry smiled warmly at Jimmy. "You have encouraged me greatly. Maybe one day we'll need a drum major."

"I know that we don't practice our religion." Sharon looked distressed. "But being Jewish is like having brown eyes. It's always a part of us, noticed or unobserved. We're stuck with who we are no matter which way the political winds blow." Sharon drew her feet up in the chair and wrapped her arms around her legs, drawing into a tight ball. "I can still see my father give the Sabbath toast." She smiled. "He would hold up the glass and say, 'The *chaim,* to life.'"

"We don't know you as well as we should," Larry said. "We need to have these conversations of substance every time you are here. I am very impressed by your moral fiber."

Jimmy retreated back into his chair. "Ah . . . sure . . . sure, any time."

"Jimmy and I will get some Cokes." Ruth stood up and beckoned for Jimmy to follow her. "Let's go to the kitchen." Instead of stopping in the kitchen, Ruth led him out to the patio.

"I can't believe what you said in there." Ruth rolled her eyes. "You certainly knocked them out of their chairs. Did you really mean it?"

"Gosh," Jimmy shrugged his shoulders, "it wasn't that big a deal. But yeah, sure. I meant what I said. My parents did put morality in my head whether I listened to them or not. Even now when I ignore my father's teachings, I know what's right."

Ruth smiled shyly. "I saw every bit of it the first day I met you. You're good in spite of yourself."

Jimmy breathed deeply. The day had vastly exceeded his expectations. He had come to the Feinbergs feeling like a carrier of a social plague invading their antiseptic environment, only to be received as a moral hero. The feeling was better than anything he could remember.

"I saw the truth behind that macho salesman veneer." Ruth kissed him. "The best is yet to be."

Jimmy looked uncharacteristically embarrassed. "I'll try to do my best."

# 4

For several minutes, Jimmy looked at the letter in his hand. He could still hear his words ringing in his memory: *I'll try to do my best.* He opened the letter carefully. The handwriting was so familiar that he didn't need to glance at the return address. The letter kept evoking the sentence running through his mind.

Jimmy walked through the small living room with the letter. Unlike many bachelors, he kept a tidy place. On the front wall was a large poster of James Dean in a leather jacket. On the opposite wall was a framed print of Marilyn Monroe, Humphrey Bogart, and James Dean in a deserted restaurant. The melancholy late-night scene fit Jimmy well. A modernistic couch was pushed against the adjacent wall in front of a TV and VCR unit. Piles of tapes were stacked on an end table. His small desk and files were cramped in the remaining space near the bedroom door.

Jimmy sat down on the bed in his small apartment as the July sunlight streamed in the windows. He had said those very words—"I'll try to do my best"—at least fifty times in the last several weeks, and he didn't like the sound anymore. Each word haunted him. It felt like he had said those identical words every day of his childhood.

*Dear Son,* his mother began as she always did, *your*

*father and I pray for you every day and hope you have found a church to attend by now.*

"Couldn't she have begun some other way?" he lamented out loud. "Why do they always start there?" He felt himself almost say, "I'll try to do my best," but stopped.

*We know you are making good money these days and we are proud of you. But the time is short. Your father just finished another series of teachings on what the Bible says about the end times. I know you don't like to hear what he teaches but please listen to the tapes we are sending. Your father's study of the Bible has convinced us that at any moment true believers could all be called out of this world. We know that God has an important plan for your life, Son. We want to spend eternity with you.*

Jimmy stopped reading and laid the letter on the bed. He walked over to the refrigerator and got a beer. Running his fingers nervously through his hair, Jimmy turned up the volume on the stereo.

*They never stop,* he thought. *I hate that hokey preaching junk my father keeps grinding out! Why can't they just let me be?*

But the words came back to his mind again: *I'll try to do my best.* Jimmy pulled open the drawer on the night stand and pulled out his savings book. The balance read $12,000. He smiled and shut the drawer. Flopping back on the bed, Jimmy began to read again.

*Of all five children, you were always the dearest to my heart. Perhaps your father and I cared too much. Maybe we punished too hard, but you were always so bright, so quick. I wanted to write you something that we've never told you before. Remember when you were two years old and got so deathly sick? Of course, you don't remember, but you heard us tell about the time. I don't think that we ever*

*told you how close you came to dying. The doctor
put you in the hospital because you were so dehy-
drated, but they couldn't get the vomiting to stop.
The nurses believed you wouldn't pull through.*

Jimmy stopped and opened the drawer again. Under
the checkbook and a pile of papers, he found a picture
of his mother and father together. John Harrison was
a tall, handsome man. In the picture he was waving a
cowboy hat. Sally Harrison was holding her husband's
arm and smiling broadly. She looked taller than her
five-foot-seven-inch height. Always in fit condition, she
radiated health. Even though the picture was black and
white, Jimmy could almost see her deep blue eyes and
black hair.

Jimmy brought the picture closer to his eyes. Her
face had a classic profile, and her features were filled
with character. His mother was a striking woman, even
if she looked a bit out of style. The picture caught the
warmth and compassionate glow she always had about
her. Her clothes were simple, but she was elegant in her
unique way.

In the background was their church in Dallas. The
big brick structure had large stained glass windows
and expansive stairs leading up to massive double
wooden doors. The old trees around the front were bent
by years of unyielding plains wind. "With love always,
your parents," was written across the bottom in her
hand.

Once more Jimmy began reading.

*Your father and I came to the hospital late in the
evening. We were terrified that you would die.
Throughout the night, we held you and prayed over
you. We wept, prayed, and paced the floor. You
didn't improve. Around two in the morning, your father picked you up and walked to the window. I can
still see him hold you with outstretched arms. Shaking all over, John told the Lord that if He'd spare*

*you, you would be our gift to Him. Your father put you back in that bed and we knelt on the tile. We wanted you to live more than anything in the world. About thirty minutes later, the fever broke. The next morning you stopped vomiting and that afternoon they took you off all the I.V.s that kept fluid in you. We knew God had spared your life for His purposes.*

Jimmy's hand trembled as he lowered the letter. He took a big drink from the beer can and reached for a cigarette. He started to light up but dropped the cigarette by the side of the bed. He felt a knot forming in his throat.

*Perhaps we should have told you, but we didn't want to coerce you into some life direction that would be of our choosing and not the Lord's. That's the reason your father always preached and pushed you. He knew your life was supposed to be different. I guess we didn't do a very good job, but we believed you were a unique and special child.*

Tears began to run down Jimmy's cheeks. He pulled his knees up against his chest and rested his chin in his hands. From deep down in his stomach he felt a churning pushing its way up. His whole body shook, even before the sound came out. Jimmy had no idea how long he cried before the inner wellsprings dried up. His body sagged against the bed.

Finally, he picked up the letter again.

*Son, I don't care how you make your living. I want you to know that you are still the most significant child in my life. There is a good in you that nothing can stop or hide. I want you to know that my prayers are still with you every day of your life and they always will be. Don't be afraid to let God have His way. Your loving mother.*

Jimmy sighed deeply and picked up the picture again. He stared at the smiling, waving woman, her Sunday coat and hair blowing in the Texas wind. For the first time, he recognized something so obvious that he had completely missed it. Her dark hair, her blue eyes! Yes, they were so much like Ruth's that he hadn't let himself see the resemblance. Something within hadn't wanted him to see, but there was the plain truth. Once again the words came back to him.

"I'll try to do my best," he mumbled. "Oh, yes, I *will* try."

□   □   □

That evening Ruth found Ben on the redwood back porch of their home looking out over the ocean. The large clay pots were filled with blooming flowers. He was leisurely sprawled in a patio recliner. His six-foot-two-inch frame extended far beyond the end of the chair. He was reading a book on computers.

"Bother you a minute?" she asked pensively.

"Got a problem?" he grumbled, turning in the opposite direction. The recliner squeaked beneath his weight.

"Sort of . . ."

"About?" He didn't look up.

"About you and Jimmy."

Ben looked out sourly and shook his head. His brown hair shifted sides.

"I want you to be friends."

He didn't say anything but turned a page.

"Of course, you don't argue, but you don't seem to approve of Jimmy either."

Ben raised an eyebrow but kept looking at the page.

"I don't want Jimmy to feel like an outsider in this family."

"Family?" Ben rolled his eyes. "Things getting that serious?"

"Come on, Ben. You know I care for Jimmy a lot. You

could work harder at overcoming the atmosphere Mom and Dad create."

"Hey, count me out of that battle. If you want to fiddle with the used car man, that's your business."

"See!" Ruth protested. "That attitude is exactly what I mean."

"Don't start putting a bunch of stuff on me." Ben dropped the book onto his chest. "If you want to go with this guy, that's your problem. Frankly, I don't see what you have in common with him, but I'm not pushing the issue."

"And what do you have in common with the little Chinese number you're interested in?" Ruth swung her legs sideways and sat on the edge of her chair.

Ben stiffened. "You quit snooping into my business!"

"Not quite as much fun when two play the game, is it?"

"At least I don't bring her around . . . ," he stopped and then added, "here."

"At least," Ruth repeated him, "I'm honest."

Ben picked up the book and started trying to read again.

"Ben," Ruth pleaded, "I'm not trying to embarrass you, but I know our parents would not really prefer to have an oriental in our family. They would rather that we both marry Jews. You need my help as much as I need yours."

Ben's eyes darted back and forth as if he were reading, but his eyes were focused somewhere else.

"The truth is that we are all outsiders, Ben. That's the really crazy thing that Mom and Dad won't face up to. Jews were the original outsiders. Surely, we can recognize the place that strangers can have in our midst. Haven't we all tried to carve out a place for ourselves?"

Ben looked around their expensive family estate that was in its own way a statement. "Yeah," he said, "I guess you're right. This family seems to be rather preoccupied with being on the inside."

"All I ask is a little help, Ben."

"OK, Ruth, I'll be a good boy and put in a good word for the Corvette man."

"Treat him with respect." Ruth's voice had a sharp edge. "That's all I ask."

"Sure." Ben went back to his book with a decisiveness that signaled an end to the conversation. "Sure." This time his eyes followed the words. After Ruth went back into the house, Ben stopped reading and stared out over the ocean. The sea looked calm enough, but Ben knew that dangerous riptides lurked beneath the surface this time of year.

Cindy Wong was also reading later that evening. She was perched on her favorite stool in the kitchen of the Golden Dragon. Large pots and pans hung from the ceiling. Steaming and shimmering kettles of rice and vegetables were cooking on the big stoves. In one corner crates of lettuce and tomatoes were stacked on top of boxes of oranges. On the counter in front of Cindy was a large, thick book.

"What are you reading?" Frank Wong asked in Chinese.

"Last year in my discussion group at the library, this book was recommended. It is called the Bible." Cindy's fingers ran across the raised dots of the Braille.

"Bible?" Across the table, Jessica Wong began stirring herbs into the special sauce she was making. Her face was wrinkled and worn, but her hair was still jet black. It was pulled back in a tight knot behind her head, making her plain face look uncharacteristically severe.

"Christians believe this is a holy book," Cindy explained. Her small voice matched the petite features of her lovely face.

"Indeed." Frank continued to speak in Chinese. His eyes were so narrow that they were barely slits. Most of his hair was gone, and he was slightly humped forward. "We must always respect such things."

"Especially because we are in a country where the majority are Christians," Jessica added in Chinese. When Cindy had come unexpectedly late in their lives, Jessica had been overwhelmed with the new responsibility. And discovering that the tiny baby was blind had sent her into a panic that occasionally surfaced in her oversensitivity to their ethnic origins. "We must offend no one."

"Are the teachings like those of the Buddha?" Frank stared down at the blank page filled with the raised dots.

"The first part is the history of the Jews," Cindy told her parents. "But in the second section is the teaching of Jesus."

"Jesus is like the Buddha?" Frank asked.

"Sort of," Cindy puzzled. "He was a Jew too. I really don't understand a lot of the story."

"Maybe you should talk to a Jew," Jessica observed. "Do you know any?"

Cindy smiled. "As a matter of fact, I do know a Jewish boy. He is one of our best customers."

"Really?" Frank began dicing the water chestnuts.

Cindy's grin widened. "In fact, you've not been too happy about the time I've spent talking with him when he was here. Remember Ben Feinberg?" Cindy bit her lip to keep from being too obvious. Inadvertently, her overprotective parents had provided her the excuse she had been seeking.

"The big boy?" Frank looked at his wife. "The one who eats the Kung Pao Squid every time?"

"Exactly," Cindy nodded.

"For heaven's sake," Jessica threw up her hands, "why didn't you tell us that you were discussing religion?"

"Indeed!" Frank shook his finger at Cindy. "We highly respect such discussions. After all, we can learn from all religions."

"A Jewish boy," Jessica mused. "How interesting."

"Does the Jewish boy understand the Bible?" Frank asked.

"I must have more discussions with him." Cindy tried to cover the widening grin with her hand. "I hope you will not worry if we have more discussion times."

"Of course not." Frank picked up a handful of mushrooms. "We want our daughter to be as well informed as any American."

"Then I will continue my religious meetings," Cindy said with a straight face.

One of the waiters burst through the kitchen door. "A young man ask for Miss Cindy. Very large boy."

"His name?" Frank's voice became stern.

"Something like Fein . . . Feinberger."

"Ah, so," Frank nodded his head to one side in deference, "a fortuitous moment. You must continue the religious talks with the Jewish boy."

"If you insist." Cindy bowed in respect to her father.

# 5

Damian Gianardo and Jacob Rathmarker stood side by side in the Oval Office listening to the secretary of state make his report. Occasionally, they looked knowingly at each other.

"In summary," the secretary turned his final page and cleared his throat, "your suggestion of a federation of ten nations has been met with total consternation. The idea of a common market and new trade agreements was welcomed. However, the notion that we have a joint military combining all land and sea forces was met by bewilderment. And when I talked of governmental linkage, they ran."

"Thank you, Mr. Clark," the president smiled condescendingly. "Did you bring it to their attention that we have the nuclear attack capacity to make compliance advantageous?"

"Sir," Secretary Clark pulled at his collar, "such a suggestion would have been seen as coercion or an implied threat. I didn't feel that such a course was helpful."

"Not at this time . . . at least." Rathmarker smiled cunningly. "I trust all discussions have been completely and totally confidential."

"Absolutely. I spoke only with my counterparts at the

top level of government. No one wanted a word of these discussions leaked."

Gianardo turned and walked to the opposite end of the office. He crossed his arms and paced back and forth. "Something is needed. A new political climate is required. Some extraordinary event must happen that will cause each of these nations to realize how much it needs my leadership. The world needs a good shaking."

"I don't understand what you are suggesting," the secretary answered nervously.

The president paced with his right side to the wall. "Obviously, I am changing the political face of our country very quickly. People have learned that my leadership is flawless. On the domestic scene we are successfully creating complete dependence on me. We need a good worldwide disaster to accomplish the same thing abroad."

"A *good* disaster?" The secretary swallowed hard.

"Come now, Clark," Damian Gianardo laughed wickedly. "Be a little imaginative. Surely, we can create a nice little crisis that will demonstrate a demand for my proposed alliance."

□     □     □

Through the summer of 1995, Cindy studied the new Bible. Her quick mind was challenged by a new world that began to unfold before her. As her parents worked in the kitchen of the Golden Dragon, Cindy read selected passages to them. Frank commented sometimes, but mostly he said, "Ah, yes, ah, so." Jessica only listened and nodded.

Cindy tried to ask Ben questions about the imposing book. Most of the time he was far more absorbed with Cindy. Yet her fascination with the Bible had its effect on Ben.

"I really don't know anything about the New Testament part," he confessed on a hot July evening as they sat by the ocean in the middle of Laguna Beach. In front of them, a volleyball game was in progress. Just beyond, teenagers were running into the ocean. "The story of the Jewish people is in the first section of the Bible. I know that much." He shrugged. "We call that part the Torah."

The breeze from the ocean swept Cindy's coal black hair back. "In the new part is the story of Jesus," Cindy spoke softly. "He was a Jew too."

"So they tell me." Ben reached for her hand. "Jews have always had a big problem with Jesus."

"But Jesus was a very good man in this book."

"I guess the difficulty wasn't Jesus as much as His followers." Ben let his fingers slide in between hers.

"The story says that Jesus died for us." Cindy didn't move her hand. "Amazing story."

"I've never read the tale." Ben put both of his hands around Cindy's. "Most of the Christians I've known didn't do much for me so I didn't pay any attention to the book. In fact, the Christians persecuted Jews for centuries." Ben leaned forward. "But you are *another* story!"

"What?" Cindy looked surprised.

"You completely hold my attention." Ben put his arm around Cindy's shoulder and kissed her.

☐ ☐ ☐

"Dr. Woodbridge," Ruth said to her therapist, "I'm really frustrated with my parents. You've helped me accept their love and concern, but they just aren't open to Jimmy."

"I thought you'd made progress," Dr. Woodbridge said. She got up from her mahogany desk and walked to the window. The pastel colors in her office added a sense of harmony and order. Pictures of peaceful farm scenes were on the walls. "Communication seemed to be better a few weeks ago."

"Jimmy broke through their stereotypes of used car salesmen." Ruth looked out the fourth-story window with its expansive view of the ocean. "Now, they're terrified that I might marry a Gentile . . . at least Mother is. She knows I'm that serious about Jimmy. No one cared about our being Jewish until I came home with a man whose last name is Harrison."

"Your parents seem threatened?" Ann Woodbridge chewed on the end of her pencil. "And you feel you can't communicate with them."

"Exactly!" Ruth shook her head in disgust. "We can't get past the log jam in our different perspectives."

"What would you think of getting all of us together?" the psychologist suggested. "We could have a family session dealing with communication."

"Dr. Woodbridge, I think you've done it again! I'd also like to have my brother Ben come. For some reason, he and Jimmy seem to lock horns."

"Anyone else?" Ann Woodbridge laughed. "We could rent the Hollywood Bowl for the gathering."

"There's just so much hostility at home," Ruth said thoughtfully. "Dad and Mom are horrified about Jimmy's father. He is a preacher who specializes in Bible prophecy. I believe my parents would run for the ocean if the Harrisons actually flew in from Texas."

"Isn't Jimmy far more accepting of his own father now?"

"You've taught me how to help him." Ruth smiled. "Yes, Jimmy is even talking of attending a church again. I'd go with him if it would help him make peace with his memories of his father."

"As a Christian," the therapist added, "I understand much of what occurred in Jimmy's family. I know his father's reputation. He's an outstanding preacher."

"Really?" Ruth's mouth dropped. "The way Jimmy talks, I thought his father was a sort of nobody . . . a little on the peculiar side even."

"Quite the contrary. Reverend Harrison may not have given Jimmy all the attention he needed, but the minister is an outstanding authority on the Bible."

"I'm really glad to hear that! You can bet I'll make sure Mom and Dad Feinberg hear those facts."

"I hope your contact with our office staff has made you more comfortable with Christians," Dr. Woodbridge said earnestly. "In this office we are believers, but that doesn't mean we're perfect people any more than Jimmy's father is. We simply believe we have found the truth that will help us live in harmony with what God intended from the beginning."

The counselor pulled out her appointment book and began thumbing through the pages of 1995. "I'm going to take a vacation for several weeks. Our get-together will have to be in late September." Dr. Woodbridge ran her finger over the calendar. "Let's go for September 25 and see if we can get everyone in." The counselor stopped and looked at the page more carefully. "The fine print says that day is Rosh Hashanah. Maybe it's a bad time."

"No, no." Ruth stood up. "My parents never observe the Jewish holidays."

"Then I'll see you again on the day of the Jewish New Year."

☐   ☐   ☐

Rosh Hashanah was one of the days that held the two worlds together. On the Feast of Trumpets, as it is called in English, the shofar is blown as the ram's horn tells the world that Jehovah Rafah has provided the world another year of existence. My memory is filled with thousands of these exciting celebration days. I was there when Obed taught Jesse up in the hill country of Judah. Unfortunately, I was transferred just about the time that Jesse's boys got to an exciting age, but this high holy day I was going to be right in the center of the action when the trumpet blew.

Angels revel in holy days. Such times help us keep our bearings as we move between time and eternity. We do not measure as humans do; clocks and calculators do not mean anything to creatures who prefer the imperishable.

On the morning of September 25, 1995, Larry and Sharon had a fleeting discussion about dropping by a synagogue on the way to Dr. Woodbridge's office. Their intentions were good, but anxiety about the confrontation at the counselor's was high. As a result, thoughts of the worship service disappeared as the Feinbergs agonized over what lay ahead.

Ben had been irritated for several weeks about being coerced into the gathering. He considered the entire business Ruth's problem. The fact that he was certain Jimmy was a jerk only added to his conviction that there was no good reason for him to go to a meeting about communication.

That morning Jimmy picked up Ruth from her new graduate-level classes at Pepperdine and headed south on Highway 5 in his red Corvette. "Got to hand it to your counselor," he told Ruth. "I didn't believe she could pull off getting all of us in one room."

"Ben won't be pleasant." Ruth pouted. "He's been such a creep lately."

"I thought I was doing well with your parents." Jimmy stared at the cars in front of them. "Then they started suspecting that something serious was going on, and I went back to the bottom of their list. I guess they just don't want someone with my limitations in their family."

Ruth bit her lip and winced. "Expecting a professional person is their hang-up. You make a very good living, and you've been offered a percentage of a new partnership. You don't have to apologize to anyone."

"Don't kid yourself, Ruth. A college education is everything to them. And also I'm not Jewish."

Ruth said little as they drove south through the pack of cars. Traffic was heavy, and the late September weather was still hot and irritating. Jimmy took the 405 to the MacArthur exit toward Newport Beach and the counselor's office. He pulled into the parking lot in front of the five-story building.

Jimmy turned the key off. "Here goes nothing." He hopped out to open the door for Ruth.

Ruth's parents and Ben were already waiting to enter the conference room on the fourth floor. Their casual greetings were stilted and stiff. Once she ushered the group in, Dr. Woodbridge stood to one side, watching how each person took a chair.

Dr. Feinberg was so nervous he forgot that the psychologist would be observing and immediately claimed a space in the center of the room. Six chairs were arranged in a circle in the plain room. Sharon pointed controllingly to two chairs that she felt Jimmy and Ruth should take. Ben straggled into a corner.

"Why don't we put our expectations on the table?" Dr. Woodbridge spoke pleasantly. "Let's explore the agendas that we brought with us today."

"I'll start," Ruth blurted out. "After all, the meeting is somewhat at my instigation. No one thinks that Jimmy is good enough for me."

"Oh, come now!" Larry protested. "We are very liberal-minded people and, I might say, very accepting."

"Absolutely," Sharon objected. "We have friends from all walks of life." Her dark brown suit seemed unusually severe for her.

"I pride myself on openness." Larry shook his head. In contrast to his usual southern California casualness, he wore a tie and sport coat.

"How do you feel about what you just heard?" Dr. Woodbridge asked Jimmy.

"I know you mean well." Jimmy tried to smile. "But you sound like I'm the gardener you invite in for a sandwich every Christmas."

Sharon's jaw tightened and Ben rolled his eyes.

Larry sat upright and stuck his chin out. "If I have any hidden agenda, it's shaped by what I know professionally. The statistics just aren't good. Ruth's dated only one boy in her life. The odds are even worse for a Jewish girl and a Baptist boy making it work."

"And what are the dangers of a girl with a Ph.D.

marrying a used car salesman with a high-school education?" Ruth added. Defiantly, she tossed her hair sideways.

Larry shrugged. "You know as well as I do. That's strike three."

Dr. Woodbridge kept trying to smile. "At least, we're getting it out quickly."

Sharon cleared her throat. "I don't like what I need to say. I don't even like how it makes me feel to speak up, but I can't be honest if I'm not forthright." She scooted to the edge of her chair. "Maybe it's totally selfish, but I am self-conscious about how my Newport Beach friends will view any future son-in-law who is a used car salesman. After all, we're professional people."

The room became intensely quiet. Jimmy looked down at his feet, and Ruth was obviously pained.

Sharon broke the silence. "Yes, and I feel guilty because I didn't contribute enough of our family background to help Ruth make sure she stayed within our race when she was looking for a spouse."

"I'd like to add a word." Ben pulled himself up to his full height in his chair. "We've always been a close-knit family. We have our little rituals and ways of doing things. It's not easy to bring someone into the inner circle." Ben stopped and smiled unexpectedly at Jimmy. "But I appreciate how it feels to be an outsider. Ethnic differences shouldn't matter if we're as liberal as we profess. All of us need to get over thinking we're better than other people."

"I didn't say that," Sharon bristled.

"In fact, we did." Larry fidgeted in his chair. "It's not flattering, but that's about the sum of what we've said so far."

"I know it doesn't sound like much to your family," Jimmy winced as he spoke, "but I really like selling cars. Sure, it doesn't take much education to be a salesman, but I'm good at what I do. I have an excellent reputation in Laguna Hills. I've done well enough that I've saved $12,000. The boss said that he wants me to manage our new place in Laguna Niguel, and I'll get 10 percent of the profits."

"You sound apologetic," Dr. Woodbridge said thoughtfully, turning to Jimmy. "I sense the conversation is painful for you."

Jimmy smiled weakly. "Can't your Newport friends simply think of me as a businessman? Maybe someday I'll own a chain of car lots."

"Jimmy has been very good for me." Ruth reached out for Jimmy's hand. "He's been the best friend I've ever had."

Ann Woodbridge seemed distracted. Her usually rapt attention faded as if she was hearing something that no one else heard. She turned her head slightly and began looking at the ceiling. The conversation quickly faded.

"Ann?" Larry repeated, "Ann? Are you with us?"

And then it happened. In the twinkling of an eye, Dr. Ann Woodbridge was gone.

# CHAPTER
# 6

For a moment no one moved. Larry stared at the ceiling in shock. Sharon's eyes blinked rapidly while she shook her head. Ben started to point, but his hand stopped in midair. Larry reached out for his wife, but Sharon covered her face with her hands.

"Oh, no!" Jimmy was the first to speak. "No! NO!"

Ruth slid to the edge of her chair. "Ann? Ann! Is this a joke?"

Silence once again filled the room.

"She was right there!" Ben pointed at the empty chair.

"This better not be some kind of crazy psychodrama experiment." Larry stood up.

"It's happened," Jimmy gasped. "Just like Dad said it might. He preached about the Rapture."

"I'm losing my mind." Sharon pressed both hands against her face. "I'm going stark raving nuts."

Larry took several steps toward the vacant seat. "She was right there." He reached out to touch the arm of the chair.

"Mom was right," Jimmy moaned. "The time is at hand."

Larry spun on his heels and raced toward the offices. "What's going on?" he called out before he even had the door open. "Where did Dr. Woodbridge go?" He burst into the receptionist's empty office. For a moment he stared at the three desks.

"Where are they?" Ben stopped behind his father. "The women were here when we came in."

Father and son wandered aimlessly through the unoccupied office. The receptionist's headset was lying on the desk next to her phone. On the other desks, pencils and papers were scattered about as if everyone had abruptly left on a coffee break. The faint sound of a radio playing soft music came from one corner. Nothing was amiss or irregular except everyone was gone.

"Larry?" Sharon called weakly from the doorway. "Wh . . . what's hap . . . pening here?"

"I don't understand," Larry muttered. "It doesn't seem logical."

"Dad, there's just nobody in the whole place. This is real crazy!"

"The whole world is turning into scrambled eggs." Larry marched to the window. "We can't all be having the same delusion at the same moment."

"No delusion." Jimmy held to the door jamb and stared at the floor. "My father preached that this would happen someday. The time has come. He must have figured out that Rosh Hashanah was the key to the timing of the Rapture."

"Rosh Hashanah? Stop it." Larry spun around. "Don't add to the confusion. We've got to keep our heads."

"But they've disappeared," Sharon said. "Gone . . . just vanished into thin air."

"There's got to be a rational explanation." Larry looked out over the ocean. "If Ann Woodbridge is playing some sort of trick on us to force communication, I'll kill her. I'll have her license for this."

"Mother tried to tell me." Jimmy slumped against the door. "She tried to warn me. Dad had figured it all out."

"What in the world are you babbling about?" Larry glared at Jimmy.

"My father called what's happened the Rapture. God's people are taken out of the world. They're with Him."

"Now that is goofy!" Ben shook his head in disgust.

"Would you call this rational?" Ruth took hold of Jimmy's arm. "Do you think what's just happened in this building is logical? Do you have a better idea of what's going on, Ben?" Ruth raised her eyebrows defensively.

Ben turned away contemptuously.

"Look out there." Jimmy pointed out the window. "Do you notice something strange? Several cars have driven off the road and been abandoned there on Pacific Coast Highway and Avocado, causing several fender benders."

"If you're in on this with Dr. Woodbridge," Sharon snapped and shook her finger angrily at Jimmy, still denying what she had seen, "I guarantee you'll wish you hadn't pulled this prank on us."

"Mother, stop it." Ruth protested. "Get a grip on yourself."

"I suggest we all go back to our home." Larry walked decisively to the outside door. "This place is getting to us. I need to contact someone who knows Ann to see if we can get some answers for this behavior. We've got three cars here. We can rendezvous at the house. The drive will help us settle down."

Ruth and Jimmy took the stairs and left through a side door. Once they reached the parking lot, they took off in his red Corvette without waiting for the rest of the family to catch up.

"Jimmy?" Ruth grasped his arm. "What were you talking about up there? What's a Rapture?"

"If I'm right, my parents will have disappeared. There won't be anybody at the church." He veered off the street into a driveway of a convenience store with an outside drive-up telephone. Jimmy punched in the set of numbers followed by his credit card number.

"What are you doing?" Ruth pleaded. "What is this Rapture business?"

Jimmy stared into space as the phone rang. A minute later, he hung up. "This is always the busiest time of day at the church in Dallas. No one is there. No one is left. They are all gone."

"Gone where?" Ruth tugged on his sleeve.

"I've got to get to my father's books . . . the tapes Mother was sending me. They will give us the clues."

"Stop it!" Ruth pounded on the dashboard. "You sound like Columbo! Don't play Dick Tracy with me. What clues?"

Jimmy pulled back into the street and drove the two miles to the Feinberg home, too stunned to even consider stopping to help the other people, crying and wandering along the streets. He ran his hands through his hair and then rubbed his forehead. Finally, he answered, "Many Christians believe that the second coming of Jesus will be preceded by a great conflict. An Antichrist will appear and plunge the world into great tribulation and chaos. Surely, you've heard of this idea."

"Sorta." Ruth frowned. "But I wouldn't listen to such nonsense."

"I thought it was ridiculous, too . . . until this afternoon. My father was an expert on this teaching. For some reason, he really believed these terrible things were about to happen soon and even suspected that they could occur on the Jewish New Year. The whole process starts with God removing His true believers so they won't go through the pain and suffering. The Rapture is a name for their sudden disappearance."

Ruth stared at the sky a few moments before letting go of Jimmy's sleeve. She settled back against the door and silently looked straight ahead.

Jimmy pulled his car into the Feinbergs' driveway. Without saying anything more, he went through the back gate and started down the flower-lined path that led to the beach. Ruth watched him disappear behind the little hill at the bottom and then went into the house by herself. Four or five times, she tried to call Jimmy's parents' home, but no one answered. Even after the other family cars pulled in, Jimmy stayed on the beach. Finally, he noticed the sun was setting and started back to the house.

When Jimmy walked in, his eyes were red and his face drawn. Sharon was placing glasses on the bar in the den. She had already drunk a large glass of wine. Dr. Feinberg was hanging up the phone as Jimmy shut the back door.

"That was Abe Staub," he told Sharon. "Dr. Staub at the hospital. My old buddy who still goes to the synagogue."

Jimmy sat down in the wicker chair by the door unnoticed.

"What did he want?" Sharon threw up her hands. "Someone disappear under his nose too?"

"Yes," Larry said, "they're in trouble at the hospital. About a third of the ambulance drivers just vanished. All the doctors and nurses who attend the weekly Christian prayer breakfast have disappeared. A lot of people have gone up like a puff of smoke. Lots of car wrecks . . . even some plane and boat wrecks. Work accidents too! The hospital is desperate for help."

Sharon raised her eyebrows and shook her head wearily. "What in heaven's name is going on? I can't stand any more of this."

Jimmy listened but said nothing.

"I don't know what's coming down," Ben spoke from the hallway. "Maybe someone will have an explanation. In the meantime, I'm willing to try and help. Maybe I can go with you to Hoag Hospital." Ben stood in the doorway. "After all, I'm a pre-med student now, and I'm certified Red Cross as well. Maybe I could help in the emergency room."

"Abe sounded like they would take anyone with a bit of training right now. I'm going to have to go down to the hospital immediately."

"Heavens!" Sharon leaned on the top of the tile-covered wet bar. "I feel like a character in a 'Star Trek' episode. Sounds like aliens have beamed everybody up."

"If this is widespread," Ben reached for the TV remote control, "there's got to be something on the news channel."

Ruth walked in from the kitchen and sat down next to Jimmy. She put her arm around his shoulders.

A newscaster's voice came on before a picture appeared. "Apparently, about 25 percent of the population has simply vanished," the young man spoke rapidly.

A picture of a man frantically talking to a policeman came on the screen. "A Newport oral surgeon is reporting that his wife vanished from their office while they were working."

"I know that guy." Larry pointed at the screen. "He came here from Oklahoma. His office is just behind Dr. Woodbridge's building."

The policeman was jotting down information. "But I thought I was a believer," the doctor kept telling the police officer. Suddenly, the picture on the screen changed. Notre Dame Cathedral in Paris appeared.

"Europe is reporting about 5 percent losses while virtually no one is missing from Muslim, Hindu, or Buddhist nations," the announcer continued. "This factor is forcing an analysis of a possible religious component in the disappearances."

Ruth watched Jimmy's face while he stared blankly at the television as if he knew what was coming before it was said.

A picture of an empty podium with the seal of the President of the United States flashed across the screen. "Please stand by," the broadcaster spoke very soberly. "We have a statement live from the president."

Damian Gianardo walked briskly to the stand. He appeared nervous and edgy. "My fellow Americans, tonight we are facing one of the strangest crises in

national history. There is no current explanation for the
disappearance of thousands of our citizens. Key military and police personnel are absent without reason.
To ensure orderly process and security, I am now declaring a state of emergency. The National Guard and
reserve units will patrol our streets until further notice. I am asking all medical personnel to stand by,
since we seem to be in a medical crisis created by similar disappearances. Telephone operators will be asked
to work additional shifts to compensate for those who
have vanished."

"At least we're not the only crazy people out there."
Sharon started shaking her head. "The whole world
can't be hallucinating." She stopped and looked at her
husband. "Can it?"

Gianardo shuffled his papers and seemed confused.
"Please do not call the White House at this time. The
switchboards are completely jammed. While we have
no explanations, we are doing everything humanly possible to solve this mystery. I have directed the FBI and
CIA to spare no effort in gathering every possible shred
of evidence. We are quite aware that a couple of African
nations have lost nearly half of their populations. Data
are now being assembled that seem to indicate that
Russia and some Eastern European nations have also
lost large numbers."

The president stopped. He stared abstractly into
space somewhere beyond the camera. Speaking as if
the thoughts were forming as he talked, he said,
"Worldwide unity is required! The world needs our
leadership at this moment as never before. I will immediately dispatch the secretary of state to major foreign
capitals."

"This has got to be an invasion from outer space!"
Ben blurted out. "There's no other possible explanation. We are getting ready to be invaded from some
planet light years away."

Once more the president returned to his prepared
text. "I am discounting early hysterical reports that

correlate these disappearances with fundamentalist Christian teachings. Obviously, many priests, rabbis, and clergypersons are still here, erasing the claim that religious people have been taken. As you know, I have steadfastly resisted the intolerance of reactionary Christian groups who have worked to deny basic human rights in areas such as abortion, homosexuality, and euthanasia. Now is not the hour to capitulate to these same divisive clichés in explaining this current tragedy. This is not a time to revert to superstition."

Jimmy smiled sadly but still said nothing.

The president jutted his chin out and spoke defiantly. "Go back to work! Let us double our efforts day and night until our nation returns to its normal production standards. You can rely on me and my government to protect your interests and guide you through this difficult time. In the name of human goodness, we will gain the inevitable victory!"

"He's wrong," Jimmy said quietly as the picture faded. "This time the head man is completely deceived."

Ruth squeezed Jimmy's hand and grimaced.

"I was a fool not to listen to my father." He paused and added, "And now I can't even talk to him."

"Maybe we should have gone to the synagogue this morning after all," Sharon said aimlessly. "Some way to start the Jewish New Year."

# CHAPTER

## 7

Nothing would ever be the same again. The disappearance of millions of people sent waves of chaos across the world. When Ann Woodbridge could not be located or her disappearance explained, the crisis deepened for the entire Feinberg family.

Larry no longer worried about the "appropriateness" of his comments and conversations. When there was no quick scientific explanation for the phenomenon, his consternation was obvious. The professional exterior crumbled, and he lost the façade that had long been his insulation against anything that made him uncomfortable.

Sharon became very clinging and chattered aimlessly much of the time. Her babbling only made Larry more nervous. She checked out books on Judaism and made several appointments to talk with a rabbi. Nothing gave her much peace of mind. Fortunately, Larry developed a new interest in religious matters and talked with her about her discoveries. In the weeks that followed September 25, Sharon and Larry talked more about what they believed than they had during their entire marriage.

The catastrophe hit hard in Frank Wong's restaurant as well. The Golden Dragon lost many customers and a number of its best employees. Frank and Jessica had no explanation for the disappearances. Consequently, both receded into a comprehensive silence. Most of the time they spoke Chinese and avoided unnecessary conversations with Caucasians. However, Ben considered Cindy's questions about the Bible with new seriousness.

"Amazing numbers of people are converting to evangelical Christianity," Cindy said as Ben consumed Hunan Chicken, the Golden Dragon's special of the day.

"So it seems." Ben ate without looking up.

"I heard one report that also says thousands of people in Eastern Europe and parts of Africa are accepting the ancient faith," Cindy added.

Ben put his chopsticks down and sat back in the black ivory chair. He said, "Apparently, thousands of Orthodox Jews have suddenly embraced the idea that Jesus is the Messiah. Some discovery from a just-released portion of the Dead Sea Scrolls has convinced them. The Essenes, who wrote the Dead Sea Scrolls, had eight copies of the book of Daniel, a book that predicts some of the things that seem to be happening right now. They thought these things would happen in their era."

Cindy swallowed hard. "We've got to recognize that something incredible is going on."

"The Jewish converts have also come to another conclusion," Ben stated. "They expect there will soon be another worldwide persecution of Jews that will be worse than Hitler's holocaust."

"Oh, Ben!" Cindy stiffened. "Those words are too horrible to be said out loud. Don't say such a thing."

Ben looked up at the elegant ceiling. The long figure of a dragon wound its way across the top of the dining room. "We once thought smog was the worst thing in the air. Now a little pollution seems innocuous." Ben began eating silently again.

Ruth struggled in her own way, but the tension was different. She was caught between her parents' discom-

fort about Jimmy's new convictions and her boyfriend's growing faith. The Feinbergs were polite
enough to Jimmy, but they were also bothered by his
firm sense of what had occurred.

In late October of 1995, Jimmy took Ruth's car to
Dallas, Texas, and returned with his father's books and
cassette tapes. The rental trailer provided ample space
to bring back quite a haul.

Jimmy dropped the first box of books on his living
room floor beneath the picture of Jimmy Dean. He
flipped on his stereo and opened the curtains on the
large front picture window. "Been gone too long." He
felt how dry the bonsai tree on the ledge was.

"Do you really understand this stuff?" Ruth looked
at one of the titles as she helped Jimmy unpack the
books.

"It's been a long time." He carried an armful of books
to a bookshelf on the bedroom wall. "But I read part of
a book in a motel on the way back. Much of my father's
teaching is coming back to me."

Jimmy's apartment wasn't large, so the piles of boxes
made it even more crowded to get around. Books were
stacked on the stereo speakers, and the kitchen counter
was lined with cassette tapes.

"I don't know." Ruth shook her head as she thumbed
through the index. "Antichrist, beasts, strange numbers, hmmm. I can't decide how I feel about these
ideas."

"Take it a step at a time," Jimmy called from the
kitchen. "Remember, Christians have been working on
this problem for two thousand years. You can't expect
to get everything in a day."

Ruth sat down on the bed. "This paragraph says that
a world leader will appear who will deceive everyone.
He will become a great enemy and persecutor of Jews.
That's frightening talk! How do I know this author's
not just another nut?"

"Look at the copyright." Jimmy walked in and sat
down on the bed next to her.

"It's 1965."

"OK." Jimmy opened the book to the first chapter. "Thirty years ago, what did this man predict would happen?"

Ruth skimmed down the page. At the bottom she began to read more carefully. Her finger moved slower and slower down the next page. "My gosh!" Ruth looked at Jimmy in wide-eyed astonishment. "The author has perfectly described our experience in September!"

"If he was right about the Rapture, isn't it logical to believe his description of the Antichrist might be on the right track too? You can see that we do have a point of reference from these books."

"Amazing. Simply amazing."

"I'm going to work night and day to see if I can really find what my father discovered. I believe all the clues to figure out what is coming next are in this pile of tapes and books."

Ruth slid up against the headboard of the bed. She pulled a pillow behind her head. "I think I'll read some while you finish opening the boxes."

"Ohhh," Jimmy drawled in teasing tones. "Surely, an honor student from Pepperdine can't be interested in such biblical nonsense."

☐   ☐   ☐

The national security adviser's eyes flashed with anger as he talked with his top-ranking staff member. "Any second now we will have to walk into his office and talk with the president. We don't have the answers we promised him. Do you understand the seriousness of our plight?"

"He's a harsh man," the staffer looked grim. "But we've been unable to find anything but religious answers."

"God help us if you bring that up!" Any further comments were ended when the president's chief of staff opened the door to the Oval Office and motioned for the two men to enter.

"Good morning, gentlemen." Damian Gianardo stood and offered his hand. "Excuse me for a lack of pleasantries. We must get right to business. We are facing an increasing financial crisis across the world. I must quiet public fears. Time is running out. Please give me your report explaining the disappearance of millions of people."

"Sir," the national security chief smiled but spoke haltingly, "we really don't have a written report."

"A verbal explanation is sufficient for now," the president answered sourly. "I promised the world an answer before the end of 1995. A quick synopsis will do."

"The problem is . . . ," the security chief stopped and turned to his assistant. "You tell him, George."

"Mr. President, we have found no rational explanation. We have been unable—"

"You've what?" Gianardo's neck began turning red. "I promised the world that *I* would have an answer. You had best not make me appear to be a fool." His black eyes narrowed and glared as if he could burn holes through the assistant's face.

"The only explanations are religious," the staffer blurted out. The national security chief covered his face.

"Religious!" the president shouted. "You expect me to come out on the day before Christmas and make a religious pronouncement about this disaster? Financial markets are collapsing everywhere, and you want me to offer superstition to reassure the masses?"

"It's all we have." The assistant held up his empty hands.

Damian Gianardo turned slowly to his national security head, looking so fierce that the man was forced to look down. "I would suggest two things. First, you fire this incompetent fool before sunset. Second, you have a plausible answer for me before December 31 or prepare yourself for new employment immediately thereafter. Good day, gentlemen." The president turned back to a letter on his desk and continued reading without looking up as the two bewildered men scurried from the office.

☐ ☐ ☐

1995 ended without the promised explanation about the unusual disappearances that President Damian Gianardo said would be immediately forthcoming back in September. No one—not the FBI, the CIA, the National Geographic Society, or MIT—could unravel the deepening mystery. Uncertainty toned down the New Year's Eve celebrations that welcomed 1996.

The Feinbergs' holiday rituals were somber. Heaviness hung over their house like the Los Angeles smog.

"I don't think that I'll go to a movie this year," Sharon said as she dropped down in her favorite plaid-covered chair in front of the large screen TV. She wore jeans rather than her expensive slacks.

"Really!" Larry looked up from his chess game with Ben.

"Rose Bowl will be on in a while." Sharon sounded unusually detached. "I'll just tough it out."

"The games won't be that great this year," Ben said sourly. He moved his knight into position to checkmate his father. He, too, wore old jeans rather than the usual expensive pleated slacks. "All the good players and coaches are gone. Check," he said mechanically.

"Life is rather gray in a post-Rapture world." Ruth threw a log on the fire and closed the metal screen on the large fireplace.

"I really don't like that phrase." Larry frowned at the chess board. "Then again, what I like and don't like doesn't buy much these days. I guess I might as well get used to the term."

Jimmy turned a page in the book he was reading. He

watched the exchange between father and daughter without comment.

"Jimmy, you've really studied this Rapture idea lately," Ben observed. "You truly believe that's what's happened?" Any hint of competitiveness in his voice was gone.

Jimmy nodded his head but didn't speak. He turned uneasily in the leather chair.

Larry crossed his arms over his chest. "You win again, Ben," he said disgustedly. "I've lost my touch everywhere. Even atheism went out of style this year."

"You've certainly changed your tune." Sharon rolled her eyes. "Aren't you the same man who insisted that religion was the universal neurosis of humankind? How often did I hear you preach that God was a projection of our childhood father-images?"

"I guess the problems of some of my patients confused me." Larry pushed his king over on the board. "I was just too arrogant for my own good. Confusing God with an earthly father doesn't prove at all that there is no God."

Ruth's mouth dropped. She ran her hands through her long hair. "I didn't believe that I would ever hear those words from the mouth of my father, Dr. Larry Feinberg."

"I guess we've all been seriously affected by what happened in September. Your mother and I have had lots of conversations about religion recently. I think it's time for me to be more open."

"What's changed your mind, Dad?" Ruth probed.

"I guess I started paying attention to some of the implications of my medical education. There has to be a Designer behind anything as complex as the human body. We have at least thirty trillion cells—each of which has thousands of components. The odds are against a body simply happening, just evolving from the mud."

Ruth shook her head and stood up. "I've got to go in

the kitchen and get a glass of Coke. I can't believe my ears. Never have I heard such talk from my dad."

Ben pushed Jimmy. "You've decided that Jesus is for real, haven't you? You think He's the Messiah?"

Jimmy nodded and didn't look up from his book.

"You really believe in this Rapture idea, don't you?" Ben asked again.

"I'll help my daughter," Sharon stood up. "I think we all need a cold drink. I'm taking orders. Anyone want some potato chips?"

"Religious talk makes this family very nervous," Ben chided his mother.

"I'll pop some popcorn," Sharon added. "Maybe the game will be interesting after all."

"Not much danger of that," Larry groused. "The talent's gone. I can't believe that UCLA came in last in the PAC-10."

Jimmy closed his book. "The whole world is in such a state of turmoil and confusion that it's hard to get interested in a diversion."

"Jews certainly aren't in style anymore," Ben said as he began repositioning the chessmen on the board. "We have good reason to be sober."

"I can't believe that the Israeli Knesset voted to expel all the Palestinians with less than one-eighth Jewish blood from the small province in the Jerusalem area that was created by that secret treaty back in 1993. The government completely sold out to those right-wing leaders like Yuval Neerman of the Tehiya Party and Reha Van Zeevi of the Moledet Party."

"International reaction has certainly been violent," Ben sighed. "I try to avoid talking politics at school. Other students eat me alive."

"It will get worse," Jimmy said wearily. "Everything is in place."

"What do you mean?" Larry frowned again.

"Israel's been using its tremendous new income from the recently discovered oil strikes to rebuild the temple exactly like it was centuries ago. When it's completed, the next piece of the puzzle will be in place."

"I don't understand the significance of a new temple," Ben acknowledged, "but I understand the implications of the way that Gianardo has sided with the Arabs. He recently expressed regret over signing the seven-year treaty of unconditional support for Israel, even though he is part Jewish and Vice President Rathmarker is totally Jewish. Did you see that picture in the paper last week of him standing with the leaders of the United Muslim States?"

Larry stood up and walked to the windows overlooking the ocean. "The winds are blowing the wrong way. The Muslims have really rallied around their new capital of Babylon. Their fundamentalist clergy predict a future conversion of the world either by persuasion or by a holy war."

Ben smirked. "All we need now is for Israel and the Arabs to start throwing A-bombs around. They could finish off our problem of a shrinking population."

Sharon and Ruth came back into the den and set the colas on the coffee table. "I'll have some popcorn ready in just a second," Sharon interrupted the conversation. "Let's switch to the news channel before the game starts. Maybe we should catch up on what's been going on."

"On New Year's Day?" Ben laughed. "My, but we are edgy."

Sharon snatched the TV remote control from the coffee table and flipped the channel.

The announcer's voice boomed. "Happy New Year to everyone out there. As we begin another year, the top story is fear. Current polls demonstrate that recent unprecedented events have left their mark on every person on the globe. In America the fear of failure, abandonment, and death haunts us hourly. The still unexplained disappearance of multitudes has only heightened the tension."

Cameras panned vacant streets, empty desks, and

unkempt lawns. "Fear has increased extramarital sexual activity. Both homosexual and heterosexual activity has dramatically accelerated across the entire globe. Consequently, the spread of AIDS has also risen. We are now in danger of losing entire populations, especially in Third World countries."

Larry reached for a cola and turned to his wife. "Is this your idea of a little holiday cheer?"

"Oh, dear!" Sharon chewed on her fingernail. "I didn't expect such a depressing report."

A different picture filled the screen. People were crowding and pushing their way forward in a bank lobby. "The sudden loss of population has played havoc with the U.S. economy," the announcer continued. "Hoarding money was common during this past fall. The result sent a tidal wave across foreign markets, causing economic depression and collapse. With the greatest nuclear arsenal in the world, America is still rapidly going bankrupt." Scenes of Wall Street appeared. People were frantically running up and down stairs. "Stock prices fell, sending the prices of gold and silver skyrocketing. Because of the catastrophic decline in the Dole Index, President Gianardo will make a special live address this evening. He is expected to make major changes in the economy to stave off bankruptcy and loss of political leadership around the world. We will bring you that address."

"I think I've heard enough." Larry clicked to a football game. "Rough days are ahead. You might as well get ready. We are looking at tough times in 1996."

"Indeed!" Jimmy answered. "What is before us will exceed our wildest dreams . . . and nightmares."

# 8

Sharon found it hard to pay attention to the football game, so she began to read a novel. Shortly after halftime, Jimmy started reading his book again. Ruth munched on potato chips and curled Jimmy's hair around her fingers. Only Larry and Ben really followed the lackluster Rose Bowl game.

Ben was the first to notice that a car had pulled into the driveway. "Look's like Jennifer McCoy."

Sharon put her book down. "I told her I wasn't going to the movies this year. I'm sure I called her." Sharon hurried down the hall to the front door.

"Hi!" Jennifer hugged her best friend. "I know we called our annual movie off, but I wasn't sure that you really meant no." Jennifer sailed into the living room.

Next to Sharon's five-foot-eight-inch height, Jennifer looked very small. While Sharon tended toward the plump side, Jennifer was thin and slight. "Sorry to barge in," Jennifer chattered in her usual energetic way, "but I just couldn't wait to call." Her movements were quick like those of a little bird flitting from one branch to the next. Sharon had always admired her friend's boundless energy.

"What a surprise." Sharon followed Jennifer across the living room. "No, I had planned to be with the family this year."

"I thought maybe you might change your mind. Anyway I had something very important to tell you."

"Please sit down and tell me what's happening." The TV in the den was barely audible.

Jennifer's countenance abruptly changed. "I hope you won't end our friendship," she stammered. Her short brown hair bobbed from side to side.

"Oh, come on! We've been best friends for over fifteen years."

"Last night . . . ," Jennifer carefully chose her words, "Joe and I went to a New Year's Eve party at Jane McGill's . . . a religious New Year's Eve party. Well . . . a Christian New Year's Eve party." She rolled her bright blue eyes.

"Really?" Sharon furrowed her forehead. "I don't understand the difference."

"With all this Rapture talk, Joe and I wanted to know everything we could about what's going on. You know my parents disappeared." Jennifer's eyes became watery. "I believe we have started to unravel the mystery. The speaker explained that Jesus of Nazareth was really the Messiah and why He is coming back again. The Rapture was tied to His return. Our discussion was simply awesome."

"Jennifer," Sharon frowned, "where are you going with this?"

"When the meeting was over, Joe and I knew we could trust Jesus to be our Lord and Savior. We made a decision to ask Him into our lives."

Sharon's mouth dropped, and she shook her head in disbelief.

"Our children are very upset." Jennifer's eyes pleaded for understanding. "I hoped you would be positive . . . accepting . . . still friends."

Sharon's chest heaved as she sighed deeply. "My goodness! We do have a most unusual New Year's Day at the Feinbergs." Sharon suddenly stood up. "Thank you for coming over, but I must see about the family now."

"Please," Jennifer reached for Sharon's hand, "you're turning me off without even understanding what's happened to us."

"Perhaps I could call you tonight. Maybe after the president's address."

Jennifer followed her best friend to the door. "Sharon! Say something about my decision!"

"I'm stunned." Sharon opened the door. "Obviously overwhelmed. Please, I need time to sort this business out. I'll just have to call you tonight."

Jennifer looked in dismay at her friend as Sharon shut the door in her face.

Long after the sound of Jennifer's car was gone, Sharon leaned against the front door and stared into the vacant hallway. As the rest of the family watched the bowl game, Sharon stayed by herself. Her world had become a lonely, empty place; the solitude seemed strangely appropriate for this New Year's Day.

The game was in the final minutes when Sharon returned to the family room with a plate of sandwiches. Ruth and Jimmy were still reading.

"Who's winning?" Sharon asked.

Ben blinked in surprise. "I guess I lost track. I'm not sure."

Sharon put the sandwiches on the table. Larry and Ben each reached for one, but Ruth and Jimmy remained oblivious as they continued reading.

"I've just had the most amazing conversation," Sharon finally said. "Jennifer tells me that she and Joe have become Christians. Accepted Jesus and the whole bit!"

Larry's jaw slightly dropped and he froze in place. "You're kidding."

"*Now* my best friend believes in the Rapture." Sharon's smile was clearly artificial. "Seems the world is moving in that direction these days."

Jimmy smiled broadly but said nothing.

"Come on," Ben said. "Jimmy, I know that you've got a lot to say on this subject."

"I don't think now is the right time," Jimmy said timidly. "I'm not interested in pushing my convictions on anyone."

"I know you're trying to be sensitive to us," Ben declared as he reached for another sandwich, "but I'm beginning to think we're the people with a problem. No one has come up with a better explanation for the disappearance of these evaporated people than you have. What if we're missing the boat? It's a really scary thought."

Larry and Sharon stared at each other.

No one answered Ben's question. The winds suddenly picked up, and the family could hear the waves pounding the rocks along the beach. Each listened to the unexpected gale that had come in from the sea. The rumbling was foreboding.

Little was said through the rest of the afternoon. After the game ended, Ruth and Jimmy walked down to the gazebo and watched the boiling sea. As night fell a rainstorm blew in, sending them scurrying back to the house. Once again they returned to their reading. Sharon had disappeared, and the father-and-son chess game was back on. An unusual quietness prevailed throughout the house. The unprecedented presidential address was scheduled to begin immediately after the Orange Bowl. By then the entire family had reassembled around the TV. The afternoon sandwiches were still piled high, and the popcorn bowl had been refilled.

"Should be on in just a minute." Larry swirled his vodka and tonic and drank in large gulps.

Sharon sipped on a Bloody Mary, staring silently at the screen.

"And now, the president of the United States," the announcer said. The emblem of office appeared on the screen as the camera zoomed backward from the podium. Damian Gianardo stepped to the stand and began speaking at once.

"My fellow Americans, we start this new year of 1996

with grave problems confronting us. I am taking the unusual step of speaking on New Year's Day because I am proposing a new, dramatic path to recovery. I want you to sleep well tonight, knowing your president is about to turn our deficits into assets."

Larry laughed. "If Gianardo can turn the current financial collapse around, he'll be the financial Houdini of the second millennium A.D."

"The loss of all those people certainly tore a hole in the economy," Jimmy said thoughtfully.

"Congress has just completed an emergency session that I called two days ago." The president stared into the camera. "All foreign assets have been frozen. We will hold hundreds of billions of dollars in assets for a period of six months. The nations that vote to become states of the U.S. will receive their assets back while the obstinate will lose their holdings."

"What?" Larry came out of his chair. "They can't do such a thing. Every principle of international law is being violated!"

"During the past week, Vice President Jacob Rathmarker and I have also flown secretly to the major capitals of the world with leaders of Congress accompanying us. In secret negotiations, I proposed the creation of a new Roman Empire, resulting in a new world order. Though there was some initial resistance, my explanation of the mutual benefits brought some degree of compliance." Gianardo stopped and smiled wickedly at the screen. "Particularly if they wanted their money back."

"Madness!" Larry pounded his chair. "The world wouldn't stand for such blackmail!"

"As I conclude my address, world leaders will begin explaining the new system to their countries. For example, Japan needs our massive nuclear arsenal and military to protect its interests. Of course, we are the reigning military force in the world. The Japanese want the same representation in Congress as our fifty states. In turn, Japan will be divided into ten new provinces, like our own states. Japanese citizens may keep individual savings and holdings. However, as of today, they will be taxed on their earnings for the past year."

"My gosh!" Ben's eyes widened. "In one stroke, the president has eliminated the national debt. Overnight we will be the strongest financial nation that ever existed. Think what free trade in sixty states will do!"

"The Italians have asked for interesting concessions." The president smiled broadly. "Italy will be divided into five states with Rome becoming the European capital of the United States. When the transition is completed, we will change our national name to the New Roman Empire."

"Can he be serious?" Sharon pushed her drink away and tried to clear her head. "I can't believe my ears."

"My family originally emigrated from Italy." Gianardo continued to smile. "Of course, I've overcome the confusion of my Catholic heritage, but I will find considerable satisfaction in presiding over a Roman-based political system. In addition, our close traditional ties with Great Britain will make an easy transition as we create five new states there. Ultimately, the European Economic Community will see the wisdom of joining us, once they realize the power and prosperity of our new seventy-state union. We will retain the American flag with seventy stars and thirteen stripes.

"Israel and the United Muslim States have some apprehension, fearing we might annex them," the president admitted condescendingly. "Negotiations are under way even now with Babylon, the capital of the Muslim world. Naturally, free trade in oil and similar goods would benefit us greatly while we help the Muslims restore their ancient Babylonian Empire. Once again I have single-handedly re-created history, linking a New Babylonian Empire with a Neo-Roman American government in a confederation of cooperation."

Ben pulled at his father's sleeve. "We could be on easy street overnight. Dad, we've got something to celebrate."

"Regrettably, Israel has not understood its opportunity," the president frowned. "Because I helped negotiate the 1993 peace treaty with Israel, we will honor the terms until the year 2000. However, failure to come into compliance with the New World Order can only further isolate the Israelis."

"We're Jews." Larry glared at his son. "This far-flung scheme of Gianardo's could backfire on *us*. Don't be so jubilant."

"An international computerized banking system will be located in Rome for our central banking system. While the dollar remains current, I propose an exciting breakthrough. Cash will soon no longer be needed across the empire. Credit cards will offer speedy business transactions. You will receive a universal social security number along with our fellow citizens in Japan, Italy, and Great Britain. Laser technology will etch the invisible number on the bones in your right hand. The number can also be placed on the forehead if there is a problem with the hand. The method is painless. You wave at a cash register, and the computer will deduct the purchase from your bank account. A completely fair line of credit will be established based on your record of the past three years. A new chapter in economic history is being written."

Larry shook his head. "Universal identification means the possibility of total surveillance. I don't like any of it."

Gianardo was obviously ecstatic. "As a concession to the United Muslim States, we will be using the ancient Babylonian system for numbering names. Common denominations by 6 will be employed since 6 is the number for humanity. For example, the letter *A* would be equal to 6; *B* equals 12; *C* equals 18; and so forth. Using this system produces a numerical equivalent for my full name of 666. Since I am founding the system, I am asking that all social security numbers be preceded by 666 despite the silly superstitions surrounding that number."

"Jews in the death camps were numbered," Larry said as he sank down into his chair.

President Gianardo shook his fist in the air. "Let us affirm the power of humanity; 666 is a triple way of asserting the capacities of a human race set free from old religious superstitions.

"Now I need your endorsement." The president put his manuscript down, folded his hands, and looked straight into the camera. "Do you want an end to our national debt? I am offering an annual surplus. We have the potential to systematically reduce taxes, but I need your approval since Congress has taken an unusual step of calling for an immediate plebiscite by unique means. Those supporting me can register their vote by dialing 1-900-666-6666. Opponents can call 1-900-777-7777. Phones are ready for your immediate response." Numbers flashed across the screen.

Larry folded his arms over his chest. "No country has the right to freeze another nation's assets. Congress buckled out of fear and intimidation. If this man can pull this coup off, there's nothing that he can't get away with."

Jimmy spoke firmly. "There is no hope if you put your faith in the government or the cleverness of men. The end of all things is at hand."

"What do you suggest?" Ben said.

"I'd begin by listening to what your friends the McCoys have to tell you."

An hour after the presidential address, Sharon called Jennifer. The phone rang only once before Jennifer answered. "I'm afraid you caught me off guard this afternoon," Sharon began.

"Oh, I'm so very, very glad you called. Joe and I talked about you all evening."

"Everywhere I turn," Sharon apologized, "I'm hit in the face with so much change that I guess I don't absorb surprises very well anymore. Your announcement was . . . well . . . very unexpected."

"Joe and I have so much we want to share with you. We're not trying to be pushy, but we've found out some incredible facts that you and Larry just have to hear."

"We'd like to get together. Larry wants to know what's happening in your lives."

"Wonderful!" Jennifer sounded relieved. "Since we started studying the Bible today, a whole new world has opened. Along with what we heard last night, we're beginning to make sense out of the craziness going on."

"I'm glad somebody is! That presidential address was another sample of major distraction."

"Sharon, that is *exactly* why we've got to talk immediately. Joe and I were stunned tonight. Did you know that over nineteen hundred years ago the book of Revelation predicted that a world ruler would survive a mortal head wound and the numerical value of his name would add up to 666?"

"What?" Sharon nearly dropped the receiver. "It said 666?" Her voice trailed away.

"Joe spilled coffee everywhere when Gianardo announced that number this evening. But that's just the start."

"There's more?" Sharon leaned against the wall and then slid down to the floor.

"This world dictator will ride on a white horse, implying that the world will see him as a hero, winning battles without bloodshed. Do you know what the president has named Air Force One?"

"No."

"Look at the morning paper. Gianardo has dubbed his private jet *The White Horse*."

"Good grief!" Sharon stared at the floor as she brought her knees up to her chest.

"At the New Year's Eve party we heard something else that we had a hard time accepting until this evening. Prophecy says that first three nations and then seven more nations will join this world ruler before a great war starts, probably between Russia and Israel. Worldwide famines and environmental disasters will occur, then a terrible battle will eventually follow at a place in Israel called Megiddo, or Armageddon. Tonight the President of the United States put that scenario into motion."

Sharon didn't answer for several moments. "You've got to be making this up."

"The teacher at the party taught us that this despot would come from a 'little horn,' a Hebrew expression implying a young country. Do you know of any other nation that came out of the original Roman Empire that is young but ours?"

"Jennifer, I've never heard any of what you are telling me in my entire life."

"I hadn't either." Jennifer laughed nervously. "But here's the clincher. According to the book of Daniel,

exactly 1,290 days before the Messiah returns to earth
to establish His kingdom, the world ruler will stop Israeli sacrifices. Then 1,260 days before Jesus returns,
the world ruler will enter the rebuilt temple of Solomon and declare himself to be sort of a god. Then he
will immediately start a worldwide holocaust against
both Christians and Jews."

"No one could do such a thing!" Sharon protested.

"Think not?" Jennifer answered cynically. "The
whole world is lining up behind Gianardo. Look how
Congress has turned over like a bunch of puppy dogs.
This man can do anything he wants."

Larry's words just an hour earlier came back to
Sharon. *If this man can pull this coup off, there's nothing that he can't get away with.* Sharon cleared her
throat. "Yes, we must talk immediately. I can see why
the party affected you like it did."

"Tomorrow?" Jennifer pushed. "OK?"

"We're booked for the next two days. How about
three nights from now?"

"I don't see why not. And invite your whole family . . .
Ruth's boyfriend . . . Everyone needs to hear."

☐  ☐  ☐

The next morning Larry and Sharon knew the news
report would clarify the scope of the president's power.
Sharon quietly set the box of whole grain cereal next
to Larry's favorite coffee mug.

"You're OK?" Larry asked his predictable first question of the day.

"Yes, thank you," Sharon answered as she had each
morning for the past twenty-five years. "Coffee?"

"Please," Larry automatically answered while turning on the TV. They sat together at the breakfast bar
watching the news.

"The 'morning after' polls indicate that 88 percent
of the American public are strongly behind the presi-

dent's plan for world realignment." The announcer spoke in clipped tones. "Most world leaders report a similar firm backing of the plan in their countries."

As the TV cameras zoomed from nation to nation, there were only small, sporadic protests and demonstrations. The world had simply acquiesced to Gianardo's demands. Fear of America's enormous nuclear and economic powers brought about the effect Gianardo hoped for.

"Never!" Larry shook his head. "Never would I have believed that people would quietly accept what we heard last night. I see no hope for us."

During the next two days, little was said about the fast-moving events breaking in the news. Politicians scurried and parliaments voted. The New Roman Empire was becoming a reality with the speed of a fax machine. An impending sense of doom made it difficult for the Feinbergs to make small talk, and emotional uncertainty made anything else too ponderous to discuss.

The following morning Larry and Sharon once again began their morning rituals.

"You're OK?" Larry remarked perfunctorily.

"Yes, thank you," Sharon answered mechanically. "Coffee?" Sharon held the coffee pot over Larry's personal mug.

"Please," he answered while turning the TV to the usual news channel. Another day began in the never-varying manner of the Feinbergs.

"The presidential press secretary has just released the following information," the announcer read from a script in front of him. "Seven additional European nations have petitioned for membership in the New Roman Empire. Germany, France, Greece, Spain, Portugal, Croatia, and Switzerland are seeking inclusion on the same basis that Japan, Italy, and Great Britain entered. National identities will be preserved while nations become states. English will be the primary language, and each nation will embrace the 666 financial system."

The color left Larry's face. He pushed his coffee mug away.

"The former government of the United States will have control of the newly structured Senate," the announcer continued. "Future presidents must arise from within the geographic boundaries of the former U.S. Previous oil agreements that President Gianardo negotiated with the United Muslim States will guarantee abundant oil supplies for the new international alignment."

"Not a shot was fired," Larry turned to Sharon. "Not a bomb was dropped, and the world was quietly taken by storm. Silently, they marched off to the trains waiting to make the journey to the death camps."

Sharon took his hand. "Our house appears to be built on top of the San Andreas Fault."

"Yes. We seem to be sliding toward an abyss with no rescue in sight. I wonder what our ancestors said at the moment when they stood on the edge."

"I think they would have prayed, Larry."

"Unfortunately, they were better at it than we are. What time are the McCoys coming?"

"About 7:30. The kids will be here as well."

"We must listen well tonight."

□   □   □

The two families gathered in the Feinbergs' living room. In contrast to the cozy warmth of the den, the large room was quite formal. Expensive antiques were interspersed with classic furniture with carved arms and legs. A large oil painting of a castle on the Rhine River was the prominent wall hanging. The McCoys sat down on an expansive silk brocade-covered couch.

For the first hour Joe and Jennifer talked without interruption about their newfound conviction that Jesus of Nazareth was the Messiah. Then they handed out a printed sheet listing the prophecies fulfilled in the first coming of the Messiah. On the back was a list of Scriptures yet to be fulfilled.

"You can see that many of these yet-to-be-completed prophecies are being fulfilled right before our eyes." Joe pointed to key verses describing the Antichrist. "The Bible is the only information we have that can make sense out of what we're watching on our own televisions."

"We believe the next major event will happen this summer on July 25," Jennifer continued. "If the next phase begins on this day, there will be no question that we are racing toward the Great Tribulation at breakneck speed."

"You are exactly right," Jimmy broke in. "My reading clarifies that July 25 will be the ninth of Av, the next Jewish holiday."

"Jewish holiday?" Larry frowned. "I've never heard of a summer holiday."

"The Feast of Tisha Be-Av," Jimmy confirmed.

"Never heard of it," Larry sounded condescending.

"I have!" Sharon corrected her husband. "I'd forgotten about Tisha Be-Av, but my father kept the day. Solomon's temple was burned by the Babylonians on Av 9 in 587 B.C."

"Really?" Larry's eyes widened.

"Few days in Jewish history have been as significant as this one," Jimmy continued. "My father was big on the meaning of this holiday."

Joe slid to the edge of his chair. "Centuries before the temple fell, the twelve spies sneaked into Canaan and returned in terror on Av 9. Their faithlessness caused another forty years of wandering in the wilderness."

Jimmy smiled knowingly. "Titus and the Roman legion destroyed the second temple in A.D. 70 on Av 9. A year later the Romans plowed Jerusalem under on the same day."

"I've been reading Jimmy's books," Ruth joined in. "Because Reverend Harrison underlined so much, it's easy for me to get the high points. Simeon Bar Kochba led the last Jewish uprising against Rome, and his army was destroyed on Av 9, 135. Here, Dad, look for yourself." Ruth handed a book to her father.

Larry turned uncomfortably in his chair. "Are you sure that your information is correct?" he mumbled.

Jimmy opened his Bible on the table. "We've barely scratched the surface. On July 18, 1290, England expelled all its Jews on this same day. France expelled all its Jews in 1306 on Av 9, and later Spain repeated the same injustice on Av 9. Anyone want to guess what year that was?"

"It was 1492," Ben immediately answered.

"Exactly," Jimmy confirmed. "The year Columbus left Spain, the Spanish Empire expelled eight hundred thousand Jews by August 2. Anyone want to guess what day August 2 coincides with on the Jewish calendar?"

Larry shook his head. "Av 9."

Jennifer continued, "Our Bible teacher taught us that World War I and Russia's renewed killing of Jews began on August 9, 1914. Want to guess what day that was?"

"I don't need to," Sharon answered. "My great-grandparents were driven from their village in eastern Russia on Av 9."

"And Hitler and his henchmen made their final plans to kill Jews worldwide on Av 9, 1942," Jimmy added.

"Do you have any idea of the mathematical chances of such a thing occurring?" Joe asked. "Numbers are my world, since I am an accountant. I'd guess that the odds are about 1 in 265 to the eighth power. Literally 1 chance in 863 zillion . . . 863 with 15 zeros after it!"

"Feels like the twilight zone, doesn't it?" Ruth added.

Larry breathed deeply and rubbed his temples. "The whole business is scary, but then everything else in the world is rather terrifying right now."

"Larry . . . Sharon." Jennifer held her hands out. "When we put all the numbers together, the first thing we thought of was your family. Jews haven't fared very well on Av 9. We love you and want to make sure that nothing bad happens this year. We are ready to protect your family from any form of anti-Semitism."

"This page mentions a war with Israel," Larry gestured feebly. "Russia, it says. This book speculates it may happen on the ninth of Av of 1996, which would fall on July 25 this year."

Jimmy opened his Bible to Ezekiel, chapters 38 and 39. "The description of the fall of Russia sounds like a great explosion of fire and brimstone. We know Israel has atomic capacity. We can't discount the possibility."

"We don't know what's ahead," Jennifer pleaded, "but we are your friends. We want you to do everything possible to get ready. You need to study this matter thoroughly in the days ahead. If we're wrong, then write us off as kooks. But if we're not, this is the most important issue in your lives."

"Ben, you're a college math expert." Jimmy pulled a piece of paper out of his Bible and unfolded it on the table. "We worked out these numbers in our Bible study last night. Israel was in captivity in Egypt for 430 years before the Exodus. Turn to Ezekiel 4:4–6 and note what God had the prophet do. He lay on his side for 430 days to signify that Israel would be in another exile for that length of time because of her sins. Jeremiah predicted seventy of those years would be in Babylon from 606 to 536 B.C. Right?"

"I don't get the point." Ben shrugged.

"Watch this!" Jimmy wrote Nisan 1, 536 B.C., on the paper. "That's the date the Jews should have returned from the Babylonian exile when Cyrus released them. Unfortunately, most didn't come back, and that displeased God. Because of their lack of repentance, their punishment was multiplied sevenfold, as Moses had warned it would be in the Torah in Leviticus 26. Sounds strange until you add it to Nisan 1, 536 B.C."

Jimmy wrote out the answer. "I'm going to translate this into the modern calendar." He held the paper. "Anybody recognize the significance of this date?"

"May 14, 1948," Larry sputtered.

"The date modern Israel was born!" Sharon's mouth dropped.

"Precisely," Jimmy said.

"Can you understand why we made our decision for Jesus?" Joe asked quietly.

"I pride myself on being a scientist," Larry answered. "I have to take facts seriously. It's all coming so quickly. I just don't know. I feel like I've been hit by an avalanche. I just can't put it all together this fast. I guess I need some time to think the whole matter through."

"Of course," Joe answered. "Why not study all of the predictions that were fulfilled in the coming of Jesus? They will give you a sense of perspective."

"We want you to know that we are with you no matter what," Jennifer added.

"Thank you." Larry stood. "I'm sure we'll give this entire matter our undivided attention."

Ben offered his hand to Jimmy. "You've been studying a lot more than the *Blue Book* on used cars lately. A lot more."

"There's much more at stake," Jimmy answered. "Money's one thing. Eternity is another."

# 10

For years I had studiously observed the Feinberg family. Angels cannot read human minds, but we are very perceptive about what is in people's eyes, the door to the soul. Having practiced for centuries, we can detect the subtlest changes of thought and motivation. Near the end of the twentieth century, many Americans registered duplicity in their faces. Mouths said one thing while eyes conveyed another.

The Feinbergs began to recover facial coordination when they started saying what they meant. Once the family began to suspect they might have lost their souls somewhere along the way, they began to make progress. Naturally, one would expect congruency from Larry, the psychiatrist, but his problem was not confused emotions. The issue was the state of Larry's soul.

Angels are inevitably entertained with human consternation when people begin to discover the obvious. The Feinbergs were no less amusing. Joe and Jennifer McCoy came to their home on a weekly basis, and Jimmy began feeling the freedom to talk openly about his discoveries. Larry seemed to think he was making unparalleled breakthroughs as he synthesized what had been undisguised forever. From an angelic perspective, things were moving right along.

However, Larry and Sharon had an unspoken tentativeness about final conclusions, pending the coming of Av 9. The Feast of Tisha Be-Av was to arrive on Thursday, July 25. Should Av 9 prove to be a turning point for the world, the Feinbergs knew the day would be the pivotal event in their lives.

That day the bedside alarm went off with irritating electronic precision. Trying to find the off switch without opening his eyes, Larry finally picked up the clock. Once he looked, he knew he couldn't go back to sleep again. The block letters pulsated like the timer on a bomb, THUR.—JULY 25.

"The day," he said as he stared at the ceiling. Sharon reached for his hand.

After showering and dressing, Larry hurried down to the kitchen. Whole grain cereal was already sitting next to his favorite mug.

"You're OK?" Larry routinely asked.

"No," Sharon broke the two-decades-old pattern. "I'm not."

Larry looked at her really for the first time that day. "I love you," he said. They sat down together as he turned the TV on. The coffee pot remained on the stove.

The black screen exploded with color. Soldiers on horseback were riding over rough terrain.

"Last night's report of large-scale movements of Russian troops on horseback now makes sense," the reporter said. "Continuing economic troubles apparently have some bearing on this unusual approach of horse brigades for combat. At this hour Russian troops are in control of the mountains of Lebanon and are bearing down on the state of Israel."

"It's happening!" Larry leaned toward the television.

Columns of troops lumbered down a dusty road. "Libya and Iran have dropped paratroopers on Israel," the reporter continued. "Ethiopian soldiers are reported moving toward Jerusalem at this hour."

An anchorman appeared on the screen. "The State Department is now releasing its assessment of this attack. New hard-liner Russian President Ivan Smirkoff apparently concluded that the current anti-Israeli sentiment would permit a quick strike. Using allies in Iran, Libya, and Ethiopia, Russia evidently had designs on Israel's new oil and gold discoveries. However, world leaders are now expressing their shock. The report of the sudden and unexpected invasion is rocking capitals around the world. The responses point to a serious miscalculation on the part of the invaders. We switch you now to a live statement by President Gianardo, who went to Spain two days ago for unexplained consultations with European leaders."

"Spain!" Sharon gasped. "Oh, no!"

"Fits exactly what Jimmy said." Larry's eyes widened. "He said that Ezekiel predicted that the people of Tarshish or Spain would be surprised."

"And five-sixths of the Russian army will disappear in fire!" Sharon put both hands to her cheeks. "We have already studied what the reporters are going to tell us."

The camera cut away to President Damian Gianardo surrounded by European leaders. "From Barcelona, Spain, a live statement from the President of the New Roman Empire."

"We are outraged at the outbreak of war." Gianardo jutted his chin out as he spoke defiantly. He stood before microphones in a large ballroom of a castle. "We are asking all parties to cease before Israel responds with its quite sophisticated nuclear capacities. While Russia still has some nuclear armaments, we do not want to have an unnecessary exchange from the New Roman Empire." Behind the president, large paintings adorned the wood-paneled walls. "We must honor our treaty with Israel if help is requested. However, at this time, Israel seems quite confident of standing alone. If necessary, we are ready to join with the Israelis in this unprecedented violation of their territorial rights. I will keep you informed as developments progress."

"Get that paper . . . that prophecy sheet . . . the one Joe gave us." Larry shook his head in disbelief. "I'll find a Bible. Hurry."

Sharon grabbed the list of Scriptures and ran back to the kitchen just as Larry found a Bible at the bottom of the bookcase. She pulled her silk bathrobe more tightly around her. Immediately, he looked for the index.

"Chapters 38 and 39 in Ezekiel are supposed to say something about the Russians," Sharon read from the Scripture list. "Look at verse 13 in chapter 38."

Larry read slowly. "Says the people in Tarshish will be surprised all right."

"That's Spain?" Sharon read over his shoulder. Sunlight streamed in on her face, making it look washed out. "Right?"

"The Bible says that Israel will take seven months to bury all the dead Russian soldiers." Larry thumbed the pages. "Let's try this part from the prophet Joel."

Sharon put her finger on the page and started reading, "I will remove far from you the northern army, and will drive him away into a barren and desolate land, with his face toward the eastern sea and his back toward the western sea . . ."

"That description would fit the Dead Sea and the Mediterranean Sea perfectly," Larry interjected.

"His stench will come up, and his foul odor will rise, because he has done monstrous things," Sharon kept reading.

"All Israel would have to do," said Larry as he looked up at the ceiling, "would be to nuke them and leave their radioactive bodies to decay, then this twenty-six-hundred-year-old prophecy will be fulfilled."

"And who's the father of that weapon?" Sharon slowly sank down in a kitchen chair. "A Jew! Albert Einstein! Larry, everything fits."

"We heard every bit of today's headlines last night. Today is the ninth of Av, right on schedule."

"What can we do?" Sharon clutched her husband's arm. "We must do something."

Larry searched Sharon's face, his eyes darting back and forth. "I really don't know how . . . but I think we need to pray."

"You start," Sharon pleaded. "I'll just repeat silently whatever you say."

Larry lowered his head into his hands and closed his eyes. *"Shama Yisrael,"* he recited the words he had heard at the synagogue as a boy, *"Adonai eloheunu Adonai echad.* God of our fathers Abraham, Isaac, and Jacob, please hear us today. Whoever You are, I believe in You. Forgive my arrogance in ignoring You. Please forgive my stupidity in failing to recognize You. I must believe that You intervene in history and that You are sovereign over all things. Whoever You are, please make Yourself known to us."

"Yes," Sharon said softly.

"If Jesus is the Messiah, please show us what to believe. Even if I don't like the truth, I want to see it before my eyes. Help us to know how to help our fellow Jews in Israel. Please help us find our way out of this confusion. Amen." Larry blinked his eyes but didn't move.

"Do you think He heard us?"

"We shall see," Larry sounded weary. "We shall see."

"Why don't you call the office and tell them you will be late?" Sharon suggested. "I think we ought to wake up the kids and talk to them."

"Definitely." After making the phone call, Larry summoned their children to the kitchen. Both slipped on terry cloth bathrobes but stood with bare feet. Ben and Ruth watched the TV in amazement as Larry and Sharon read the passages from Ezekiel and Joel.

"It all fits," Sharon kept saying.

"Just like Jimmy said." Ben stared sleepy-eyed at the CNN report of troops riding out of the Lebanon Mountains toward Israel. "The Russians must be in such bad financial shape that they've gone back to World War I tactics."

"And the Bible really predicted this," Ruth said. She reached for the book and read the passage again.

"Jimmy's been right about everything," Ben told his sister. "I have to give him his due."

"Look up the Isaiah part," Sharon told Ruth. "We need to study everything on this sheet again. Start with verse 3."

Ruth quickly ran down the index to find the right place. Her fingers thumbed through the pages until she found the fifty-third chapter. She started reading, "He is despised and rejected by men, a man of sorrows and acquainted with grief. And we hid, as it were, our faces from Him; He was despised, and we did not esteem Him. Surely He has borne our griefs and carried our sorrows; yet we esteemed Him stricken, smitten by God, and afflicted. But He was wounded for our transgressions, He was bruised for our iniquities; the chastisement for our peace was upon Him, and by His stripes we are healed. All we like sheep have gone astray; we have turned, every one, to his own way; and the LORD has laid on Him the iniquity of us all."

"Isaiah must have been talking about Jesus." Ben asked, "Is it really possible?"

Larry answered, "Yes, children. We must take this possibility very seriously. This morning your mother and I prayed. I've never done anything like that in my adult life . . . not since my Bar Mitzvah. I want both of you to know that I am asking the Holy One of Israel to guide us . . . all of us . . . into the truth. We have to be more open than we've ever been in our lives."

Sharon added, "Sometimes I've treated Jimmy like a second-class citizen, but for a long time I've had the feeling that he was more important to us than we could ever have guessed. Now we must listen to everything he can tell us."

Ruth looked down at the Bible and nodded.

"Our world was once so routine and predictable."

Ben looked out the window toward the ocean. "Things fit together like an equation and could be anticipated. Now . . . ," his voice trailed off, "now nothing fits. I feel like an exile in my own land."

"You've become a Jew again," Larry said poignantly. "In the past the Feinbergs were just another American family chasing the carrot that society dangled in front of their faces. These strange events have made us wander with our father Abraham. We, too, are being called into a strange place of which we know not."

Sharon's eyes filled with tears. "Larry, my father talked like that. You have touched my heart deeply."

"Honey, I'm just struggling. I used to think I was one of the smartest men in the U.S. Now I know that I don't know anything!"

"Never have I been as proud of you nor have you ever been as much a sage as this morning." Sharon kissed her husband's cheek.

"Dad?" Ben bit his lip. "I'm going to pray like you did. I'm going to ask God to show me what is real and true."

"Do you want us to pray with you, Son?" Sharon asked pensively.

"No," Ben withdrew. "I think this is something that I must do by myself. The whole business is too personal."

"But we're all in this together." Larry stood up. "Whatever you need we'll do our best to provide. Well, I must go to the office. I know that each of us has many things to do today. Of course, we want to keep up with what's happening in Israel, but I think we know the end of the story."

"I will call you when Israel drops nuclear bombs on them," Ben said resolutely. "Amazing! Yesterday we had no idea what was going on. Now we are waiting with certainty for an explosion."

"In a couple of years we've seen what people prayed centuries for." Ruth stared at the TV. "Only heaven knows what's next!"

☐   ☐   ☐

The hot July sun beat down as Ben rushed toward the UCLA library with the latest paper under his arm. Cindy was sitting outside on the front steps with her new German shepherd guide dog, Sam, at her feet. Eucalyptus trees swayed in the light breeze. Students walked lazily across the campus.

"Hope you haven't been waiting long." Ben dropped down beside her. "I got held up on the freeway."

Sam sat up. "Par for the course." Cindy reached out for Ben's hand.

"I'm really impressed with your German shepherd. Beautiful dog." Sam looked up casually at Ben but didn't move.

"Very obedient. People don't frighten him at all."

"Well, Cindy, I know Sam will be of tremendous help in going to class.

"I want you to hear what's in the paper." Ben spread out the *Los Angeles Times* before them. "The headlines read 'Russians Vanish in Fireball.' Listen to what the atomic explosion did. Only about a sixth of the Russian army is left after the bomb went off. Many of the survivors rushed toward the Dead Sea, and others ran into the Mediterranean."

"And the earthquake?" Cindy asked. "The big one caused by the explosion?"

"The paper says that the mountains in northern Lebanon shook so badly that the earth cracked open and many Russians were swallowed. They are finished."

"Ben, we've been studying the Scriptures that Joe McCoy gave you. Everything is just as the Bible said it would be. We can't ignore the implications."

"I know. I know." Ben closed the paper. "For the first time in my life I've asked God to show me the truth. I don't want to accept what the McCoys have been telling us, but the handwriting sure seems to be on the wall."

"I've been trying to tell my parents." Cindy patted her

dog on the head. "They listen, but they are more terrified than anything else. Nothing in their background
prepares them to understand. Half the time the news
report terrifies them, and the Bible lessons I give them
leave Mom and Dad in complete consternation the
other half. I feel that nothing is like it was."

"Certainly not for the Russians." Ben rolled his eyes.
"And not for any of my family either. No one has said
it out loud yet, but I think we're all ready to throw in
the towel. How can we ignore the meaning of the total
defeat of Russia?"

"Ben." Cindy looked toward the sky. Her sightless
eyes seemed to be trying to find something she couldn't
quite perceive. "I've been trying to pray like the Bible
says. I have been ending what I ask in Jesus' name. Very
interesting result."

"In what way?"

"I have the strangest sense that Someone is there,
that I'm being heard. I think it's working."

"I thought the issue is what we believe. Having the
right ideas . . . beliefs."

"Maybe it's much more," Cindy pondered. "What if
this whole business is about making contact?"

"That's a new wrinkle."

"Here's another one for you." Cindy smiled mischievously. "I've been having these unusual intuitions.
Hunches if you like."

"And? And?"

"I think the issue is even bigger than you've thought.
I think that God has something very important for you
to do in the days ahead."

Ben jerked. "You've got to be kidding."

Cindy's smile faded, and she became very serious. "I
can't tell you why, but I feel a strong inner sense of
guidance. You have a special task that God wants you
to do."

Ben stared. "Cindy, this is getting way too far-out for
me."

"Well, at least think about it. OK?"

Ben stood up. "Can I walk you back to the dormitory? I've got to get to my next class."

"I need to stay here and study for the next hour. I'm going back inside in a few minutes. See you at lunch?"

"Yeah, sure." Ben backed down the stairs. "Lunch at the usual place." He waved and then realized it looked a little foolish to wave at a blind girl. "Lunch," he called one last time, heading for the parking lot.

Their conversation made him nervous. He had expected the fall of the Russians to be confounding, but Cindy's suggestion was far more disconcerting.

"Take her seriously." The voice came from behind him.

Ben spun around and found a very large man standing behind him. His face looked ancient but did not have any wrinkles. The man's eyes looked young, yet they had such intensity Ben found it difficult to look directly at the man's face for more than a few moments. The wisdom of the ages was in his stare. The big man was an odd blend of antiquity and the present moment.

"Who are you?" Ben recoiled.

"Michael," he said. "I am your friend, Ben."

"I don't know you." Ben retreated further toward the street.

"But I know you. I have known you since the day you were born. Do not be afraid. I bring you good tidings."

"What?" Ben squinted. "What are you talking about?"

The man abruptly reached out and squeezed Ben's hand firmly. He stared deeply into his eyes. "You asked for guidance. Do not be afraid to receive it."

Ben pulled away from the all-revealing stare. Impulsively, he started running down the sidewalk. When he looked back, the man was gone.

Cindy was still sitting on the library steps when Ben came running back. She listened to the approaching footsteps. Her guide dog looked intensely up the sidewalk and barked. "Ben? Ben, that's you? Back so soon?"

"Cindy," he panted, "I just had the living daylights scared out of me. A big guy . . . a strange man appeared out of nowhere. And then he was gone. Disappeared."

"What are you talking about?"

"The guy said he'd known me all my life. I swear I've never seen him before. Maybe I really am going nuts."

Cindy tilted her head and turned her ear toward him. "You're serious. This man really did frighten you."

"He called himself Michael."

"Michael? I know a Michael. Did he have an unusually deep bass voice?"

"Why, yes. Exactly."

"Talk sort of strange?"

"Yes, yes. You've seen him?"

Cindy laughed. "Not hardly. But I have met Michael on a number of occasions. I always thought he was a student. Sort of shows up at very opportune moments."

"Listen, Cindy. This guy is big. Strange. Terrifying."

"Come now, Ben. I've always found him to be extremely considerate."

"You know anything about him?" Ben sounded skeptical.

"Actually nothing. When I've tried to ask questions, he changes the subject. Certainly, he's been no problem. Really, Michael has a knack for appearing when I really need help."

"It was almost like the Rapture experience." Ben ran his hands through his hair. "One minute he was there; the next he was gone. I think I'm getting an overload. Too much happening for me to absorb." Ben looked around the steps and bushes. "I'll see you at noon." He kept glancing over his shoulder as he backed away. "See you at lunch."

"Ben . . . ," Cindy called after him, but he kept trotting toward his car.

# 11

Through the rest of the summer, the headlines were filled with stories of the cataclysmic results of the defeat of the Russians. Their radioactive bodies and the consequent contamination completely fulfilled the predictions of Scripture. Momentarily dumbfounded, most of the world population went on their way without any awareness of the significance of the event. Such was not the case in the Feinberg household.

As the first weeks of September slipped past, I knew that it was time for me to act decisively. The hour had come for direct contact with Ben and Cindy. My assignment was clear. Once again human beings needed an annunciation to prepare for a critical task in the eternal plan. As always, I chose a day dear to the heart of the Father.

I watched Ben walk toward Cindy's dormitory. Cindy was sitting on a bench in front of the dorm with Sam lying at her feet. The German shepherd perked up his ears when he heard the leaves crunch beneath Ben's feet. "Hey, I'm here," Ben called out.

"My hero cometh." Cindy beamed. "Big day for you!"

"Huh?" Ben puzzled. "I don't think I have any examinations today."

"Come on," Cindy chided. "You're not paying attention to the calendar. A girl down the hall is Jewish. She said today's Yom Kippur, the Day of Atonement. Your big day for repentance."

"September 23! I forgot all about it!"

"Naughty boy," Cindy teased. "Now you will have to make double confession."

"Wow!" Ben slapped his forehead. "All the strange things started happening a year ago on Rosh Hashanah. I should have paid more attention to the calendar! Interventions seem to come on Jewish holidays."

"Yom Kippur is a time for getting right with God?"

"Something like that, Cindy. Unfortunately, we didn't pay much attention to our traditions."

Like an actor hearing his cue from backstage, I slipped into the scene from behind the veil of time as only an angel can do. "There are times and seasons appointed for all things," I spoke from behind Ben. Sam barked.

"What?" Cindy turned her head. Sam looked nonchalantly toward the sound.

"You!" Ben jerked.

"These days are your special times," I said.

"Michael?" Cindy asked. "Is that you?" Sam wagged his tail.

"Where did you come from?" Ben stared. "You weren't there a moment ago."

"You are very important people." I stood beside them. "I am honored to be a comrade." Cindy reached for my hand. Her grip was gentle but firm.

Ben was shaking slightly. "Look! We haven't done anything to you. What do you want with us?"

"The issue is what I can do *for* you." I kept smiling. "You are part of a great plan, and I will help you execute your part."

"Why do you keep coming and going?" Cindy asked.

"I have special work to do."

"Who do you work for?" Ben held up his hands defensively. "You're an extraterrestrial? A spaceman?"

"I come from the center of reality itself, but I know

your world exceedingly well, Ben. I have been watching your people from the beginning."

"My people?"

"Are you Jewish?" Cindy asked.

"No. But I do work for a Jewish carpenter." With that I stepped back into eternity and disappeared from their view.

Cindy's fingers around my hand collapsed upon themselves. "He's gone!" Cindy exclaimed before Ben could react.

"My gosh!" Ben choked.

"Where did he go?" Cindy groped around her.

"Right before my eyes! Boom!" Ben stared at the empty sidewalk.

"Ben, we're not crazy. This isn't a hallucination. Michael *was here!*"

"Let me sit down." Ben started walking backward. "Anywhere. Just sit down . . . for a few minutes." He dropped down on the bench. "I must get myself together."

"He wasn't some outer space movie character," Cindy reassured Ben. "When Michael talked, I felt great peace. He said very good things to us."

"I guess so."

"Ben, we were Buddhist before our family came here, but I've been reading my Bible. I know enough to understand what it means to say a 'Jewish carpenter' is Michael's boss."

"What are you driving at?"

"In the Bible there is another person named Michael. I don't know if this guy is the same one or what . . . but I do know that the Michael in the Bible was an angel."

"An angel!" Ben sputtered.

"Well," Cindy held up her hands and shrugged her shoulders, "it makes a lot more sense than spaceman talk."

"An . . . an angel?"

"I read one place in the Bible where it said that many

people had entertained angels unaware." Cindy sounded defensive. "Why not?"

"Listen!" Ben took her hand. "I'm not putting anything down these days. It's just such a mind-boggling idea . . . as if everything else in this past year has been normal."

"Working for a Jewish carpenter?" Cindy beamed. "He had to mean Jesus. The whole thing fits together."

Ben ran his fingers through his hair. "Maybe we're both getting caught up in a psychotic mass hysteria sweeping the country after all of the strange experiences. Maybe—"

"Stop it," Cindy said firmly. "I'm not crazy, Ben, and neither are you. Maybe my blindness is an asset. I have to depend on far more than my eyes to make sense out of things. I know that we have been talking to a real person regardless of how he comes and goes. Let's be scientific about this encounter. If Michael is for real, he'll be back. If he is an angel, Michael wants the best for us."

"How in the world can we set up an experiment with an angel?"

"Doesn't Michael seem to show up around Jewish holidays?"

Ben rubbed his chin and bit his lip. "Seems so," he said reluctantly.

"When's the next special day? Come on, Ben. You're the Jew."

"I think," Ben said slowly, "yes, it's the Feast of Tabernacles! I would have to check, but it's probably coming in a week or less."

"Let's have a date that night!" Cindy's consternation turned to enthusiasm. "If we're on to something, we ought to be able to make contact with Michael then!"

"If I told my father about this, he'd think I'd gone nuts! For heaven's sake, don't let anyone know."

"It's our secret." Cindy reached over and hugged Ben.

☐ ☐ ☐

As a matter of fact, the Feast of Tabernacles fell on Saturday, September 28, five days later. During the week, Ben stewed like a character in an Edgar Allan Poe short story. The words *Jewish carpenter* rolled around in his head with disconcerting frequency. Ben's few developing religious convictions were shaken further. I could not wait for the big evening. I had not had this much fun since I watched John the Baptist's father try to get his voice back.

Ben did not think taking Cindy to a Chinese restaurant was quite the appropriate thing to suggest. They ended up eating at a little corner pizza place two blocks down from the young woman's dormitory, and talking. Ben had not yet realized that conversation with Cindy was the most natural thing in his world.

The corner hangout was a popular UCLA landmark. The walls were adorned with pictures of football triumphs from the past. They laughed, kidded, and joked through a large pizza and endless refills of colas. As the evening passed, other collegians came and went. A couple of students sat in booths studying as if the endless noise and chatter did not exist.

"I guess our little experiment failed," Cindy finally said. "But the evening has still been the best of my life."

Many times that evening, Ben had looked carefully at her. He did not turn from her sightless eyes in the self-conscious way he usually did. Ben's gaze swept across Cindy's lovely olive colored skin and beautifully contoured face.

"You're the most beautiful girl I've ever seen in my life."

Cindy's cheeks turned pink, and she lowered her head.

"I've never known anyone like you." Ben's voice was

filled with emotion. "I don't want to ever be away from you, Cindy."

"We . . . ah . . . better go." Cindy's voice became softer and lower.

"Don't retreat from me." Ben took her hand. "Don't hide from me."

"Please," Cindy's voice cracked, "don't toy with me. I am a very lonely person, Ben. I've learned to accept the fact, but I can't live with false expectations. It would be too painful."

"Oh, Cindy!" Ben took her hand in both of his. "I only want to fill your life with happiness. I would never mislead or use you."

Cindy nodded her head as a tear ran down her cheek.

"You make me very happy." Ben leaned over and kissed her tenderly on her hand. "You can trust me."

"May . . . maybe we should go," Cindy sniffed.

"Yeah," Ben said. "I'm starting to sound like someone on 'As the World Turns.' "

Laughing, they walked out of the restaurant arm in arm. Sam trotted along beside Cindy. Obviously, their preoccupation with each other had pushed thoughts of me completely out of the picture. The timing was perfect for reentry. I watched them walk back to the dorm. Ben stopped behind a tree near the door to the dorm and kissed Cindy forcefully.

"You turned out to be my angel tonight, Ben." Cindy ran her hand down the side of his face.

"You really got shortchanged!" He kissed her again.

This time, I decided that I would at least give a hint before I appeared. I chose a spot about ten feet away to begin walking into time and toward them. Sam immediately picked up the sound and barked.

"Someone there?" Cindy called out.

*"Shalom,"* I answered.

"It's you!" Ben gasped.

*"Shalom Alecheim,"* I responded.

"You did come!" Cindy clapped her hands. "I was right! You are an angel!"

"No." Ben shook his head. "I refuse to believe my own eyes."

"I want you to meet a friend of mine someday." I sounded sincere and serious. "You will enjoy Thomas. He had a problem similar to yours."

"Why are you here?" Cindy was nearly dancing with glee.

"This is a hoax!" Ben was predictably defensive. "You're a fraternity prank. I know it!"

"My Master has a wonderful sense of humor, but I assure you that my reasons for following you are very serious. In fact, it has been my total preoccupation since the day you were conceived."

"Then you ought to know everything about us," Ben said critically. "You should be able to answer questions that no one can know anything about."

"Sure," I answered smugly. "Want to try me?"

"What was my favorite toy as a child?" Ben crossed his arms over his chest.

"You expect me to say a football," I said. "You worked hard at convincing everyone you were going to be an athlete because you knew that would please your father. However, your favorite toy was the stuffed bear you secretly slept with until you were well into grade school."

Ben turned white and his mouth fell open. His arms dropped listless at his sides.

"Good question but not too tough. Cindy, got a really difficult request for me?"

Cindy thought a moment. She was obviously enjoying what was terrifying Ben. "I once had a family keepsake locket that I lost. It was my mother's, and she was very upset when I couldn't find her treasure. It's been years ago, but I would like to have it back. Do you know where it is?"

"Your parents had just started the Golden Dragon, and you helped them put napkins in the holders. You were quite small. Remember?"

Cindy nodded enthusiastically.

"You reached out to find more napkins in the storage cabinet but could not touch anything. When you stretched forward, the necklace fell down inside the cabinet and through a crack in the bottom. If you will move the cabinet, the treasure will be on the floor underneath."

"Wonderful! Wonderful!" Cindy clapped.

"Can you . . . can you read our minds?" Ben's eyes were filled with fear.

"I am your best friend, Ben. You do not have to worry. No, I cannot read your mind. Angels do not do that sort of thing, but we can affect the way you see things. You might say that we influence you for the best. We nudge you in the right direction."

"Please help us." Cindy reached for my hand. "We want to believe the right things. We just can't sort it all out. If you work for a Jewish carpenter, then you must know the truth about who Jesus was."

"Was?" I smiled. "Try 'is.' Ready to find out, Ben?" I watched his eyes. He could only nod.

"His Hebrew name is Yeshua. That's what we all call Him in heaven. Angels know that He always existed. The fullness of God was pleased to dwell bodily in Him. When He died on the cross, He had both of you in mind. He has a most special plan for your lives and has sent me to help you find your place in that destiny."

"This is why you have appeared to us?" Ben asked weakly.

"I have important secrets that I cannot yet fully disclose, but the hour is coming. You will not see me again until Passover of 1997, but I will be guiding you toward the time."

"What are we to do now?" Cindy reached out for my hand.

I clasped Cindy's warm palm tenderly. "Keep yourselves pure. Love each other profoundly but chastely. In the days ahead you will need great moral strength."

"Hard time coming?" Ben asked meekly.

"Pasch, 1997, will be a terrible day for the descendants of Abraham. Cindy, your life will be spent well, and Ben, you shall see the glory of the Lord revealed. Learn now what the love of Yeshua offers, for His love will be your salvation."

I held up my hand in a blessing and then was gone.

Ben and Cindy began to weep. They held each other and swayed back and forth as the darkness of the night settled over them. Periodically, they said something, but most of the time, they huddled together in silence.

Finally, Ben said, "I think I want to pray. I've never really done that . . . I mean in a personal way."

"Me too. You say the words and I'll follow."

"Jesus . . . Yeshua, we're still very confused, but we must place our faith in You. We want to believe the right things and get ready for whatever is ahead. Thank You for sending Michael to warn us. I know I've done a lot of selfish things, and I need Your help. Please forgive me where I've messed up in the past . . . today . . . in the future. Thank You for remembering us on Your cross. We now offer You our lives."

After a long silence, Cindy said, "Amen. Thank You, Yeshua."

# CHAPTER
## 12

### New Year's Day, 1997

**W**hat angel couldn't resist a quiet walk along the beach on a winter morning in southern California? The salty mist sweeps in from the sea, and the pale blue sky's reflection bounces off the tides gently rolling up the sandy shore. The tranquil ocean deceptively makes a swim seem plausible even for this time of the year, but the chilly nip in the air restores perspective. The towering palm trees seem to stand aloof, drinking in the promise of the day and the year ahead.

The winds rolled off the ocean toward the Feinbergs' home. There was no need for a fire in the den fireplace with the sunny, seventy-two-degree weather, but Larry felt the flames in their large stone fireplace were a necessary part of the holidays.

"Great to have Jimmy and Cindy with us today," Larry said casually as he stoked the fire.

"Jimmy's gotten to be a real old-timer at these annual family gatherings," Ben chided. "He's got the day's routine down pat."

"We'll have to break Cindy in," Jimmy acknowledged. We're so glad you're here, Cindy."

"Thank you, Mrs. Feinberg."

"Just call me Sharon. After all, anyone who goes around with my son talking to angels shouldn't be on a formal basis with us."

"If anyone but you had come up with that story, Ben," Jimmy grinned, "I would have bet money the whole thing was a hoax. But when skeptics like you start seeing angels, I know the heavens are about to split open."

"Hey, don't put any stuff on me," Ben rolled his eyes. "You started us down this road with all that prophecy talk you got from your father's books."

"What can I say?" Jimmy laughed. "The more I studied, the more it all came into focus. Just look at all the world history we've watched unfold sitting here staring at your TV. The New Roman Empire, the Russian-Israeli one-day war, the events of Av 9 . . . all were predicted centuries ago."

"I have to admit it," Ben acknowledged. "I came kicking and screaming. The Bible predictions just seemed impossible to swallow."

"Oh, I understand!" Jimmy raised his eyebrows. "Bible prophecy can be very confusing, but once a few pieces fall into place, we can really begin to see where the future is going. We have to remember the different ways in which the Bible calculates time. One thousand human years are but as a day to the Lord. Sometimes a day in the Bible can mean a twenty-four-hour period. Sometimes it is a 360-day prophetic year or even a one-thousand-year period of time. The main thing is to believe that our heavenly Father truly communicates with us and that the Bible is His inspired Word."

"Yes," Larry said softly, "that's what's important. We must believe that God wants to speak to us."

"I've got a hunch we may discover that we've never had a year like the one that's ahead of us," Ben added soberly. "Our guardian angel Michael gave us a stiff warning."

"Wait a minute," Jimmy frowned. "You didn't mention any problems before."

"Perhaps the whole experience was so overwhelming that I've only given it to you in bits and pieces, Jimmy. Yes, on Passover, 1997, Michael said a terrible day would occur in the history of the descendants of Abraham."

The expression on Jimmy's face went flat. "My Bible study group has been studying *exactly* this same possibility. I can't believe what you're telling me. It really fits."

"Fits?" Larry puzzled. "I take everything seriously these days. What fits?"

"What we believe the Bible says," Jimmy spoke deliberately, "is to expect on Passover of this year a repeat performance of what Antiochus Epiphanes did in 168 B.C."

"That's what started the Maccabean rebellion!" Sharon exclaimed. "The temple was defiled and the holy place desecrated."

Jimmy nodded his head and began to speak forcefully. "As bizarre as it may sound, we are convinced that President Damian Gianardo will stop sacrifices somehow on Purim, March 23. Thirty days later, Gianardo will go to Jerusalem, enter the newly constructed temple on Passover, April 22, and declare that he be worshiped as world emperor. He will try to make himself into the god of this world. A worldwide persecution of both Jews and Christians will follow."

Silence fell over the room.

"We could all be killed," Larry finally spoke. "We must take very seriously what both Ben and Jimmy believe they have heard."

"This all makes Gianardo's special presidential address today even more significant. I can hardly wait to hear what he has to say," Ben added.

"I think we ought to turn on the channel right now," Ruth walked toward the TV. "I usually hate this part of the day, but I think I'll pay very close attention this year." She pushed the on button.

"I think we ought to call the McCoys to come over for the president's speech," Larry told Sharon. "They've been such an important part of this journey. They need to be in on anything we can find out."

"Great idea. I'll call them in the few minutes we have left." Sharon reached for the phone.

"If we're right," Jimmy said, "we'll never have another family gathering like today's until Jesus returns."

Larry listened carefully. "What does all of this prophecy mean for us, Jimmy?"

"I believe this will be the year that the Great Tribulation begins. I think that staggering events will begin on Passover."

"I have so much to learn," Dr. Feinberg mumbled. "And so little time left."

☐ ☐ ☐

"Thanks for calling us," Joe McCoy said as he sat next to Jennifer. "We were watching the news when you called. It showed horrible scenes of the famine in Russia. Takes a day's pay there to buy a loaf of bread."

"Well, we still have plenty of chips and colas." Ruth came in with a tray piled high.

"Last year was really wild," Jennifer noted. "Makes listening to the president all the more foreboding."

The group became silent as the image of Damian Gianardo filled the screen. Standing behind the podium with the great seal of office, he began speaking immediately.

"My fellow citizens of the New Roman Empire, I have only a few brief remarks because the state of the country is in such excellent condition. Most of you will find it difficult to realize that one short year ago, we were on the verge of collapse. Today we are enjoying unparalleled prosperity.

"This year will prove to be another time of continued growth of the gross national product. My new welfare system has provided housing and government jobs for anyone who is unemployed or homeless. The many un-claimed houses and buildings left by their vanished owners have been turned into property for the home-less. Previously, the incurably mentally ill accounted for over a third of the homeless, but today we can pro-vide homes for these destitute citizens. The reclama-tion of these properties has opened new ways to help our people. Because of my benevolent concern, this seg-ment of the population is receiving care today.

"I believe the law allowing me to sign a bill into law *before* it goes through needless committees and is stalled in congressional debate is another leap forward. Of course, Congress can still pass laws, but the mem-bers must now have a 75 percent majority to override my veto power or to veto my bills. Your president is per-sonally the guarantor of a system of government that will respond to your every need. As long as I have your total support, you will reap unlimited benefits.

"Let us now turn to the global scene. We are realizing the fulfillment of a dream that has eluded the world throughout this century. I have personally brought about a New World Order. We are at peace with all na-tions, even though they have turmoil among them-selves. Today no nation would dare violate a treaty with us. We have the nuclear superiority for instant re-sponse. No one—from Alexander the Great down to the dictators of this century—has enjoyed the power that I now have to affect the world . . . for good, of course.

"Let me be frank. Israel has taken serious advantage of our nonaggression treaty and must be chastened or else new problems will be created for the New World Order.

"Because Vice President Rathmarker is Jewish, and I am part Jewish, there can be no possibility of anti-Semitism in our position. Unfortunately, Israel's wealth has resulted in distorted thinking and ungrate-ful response to the benevolence I have shown in the past. Israel is insisting on trade terms that are com-pletely unacceptable and certainly not favorable to us.

The New Roman Empire *cannot* allow any group to carve out a better position than we hold. Our superiority must be affirmed and embraced by the world.

"The Israelis are attempting to rebuild their stockpile of nuclear weapons. In the past, other presidents assisted in the acquisition of this weaponry. Now I see clearly that a small nation with neutron bombs can resist the great powers. This capacity must be stopped. The time has come to demand compliance or act accordingly.

"In addition, I am constantly receiving complaints about Israel's outrageous sacrifices. Such barbarism gives us pause and puts the meaning of the country's nuclear capacity into perspective. With all animal lovers, I am incensed. These practices must stop in 1997, or I will be forced to stop them myself!

"Now I must address a serious problem at home. One particular political group continues to create difficulties. Evangelical Christians have always affected the common way of life far out of proportion to their numbers. In the past their value systems were assumed to be of benefit. However, in the last decade their intentions have become clear. This faith is definitely not in the best interest of the New Roman Empire.

"The issue has come to a head with the sect's refusal to comply with our credit-card-in-the-right-hand plan expediting commerce. Their strange superstitions about the number 666 continue to create noncompliance, resulting in such problems as slowing shopping lines, flawing our credit processing systems, and spreading dissatisfaction and dissension. Therefore, by the new authority given me, I have signed my own bill into law today. Businesses can now discriminate against evangelical Christians who refuse to obey social laws and rules for national order. Businesses can refuse to hire or promote anyone who is identified with this faith. Christians without lasered identification can be demoted or fired without compensation for refusal to comply. Persons who cannot pass the checkout test at grocery stores can be refused the right of purchase. Evangelical Christians will line up with the state or suffer the consequences.

"In closing, I have the firmest confidence that our greatest days are before us. There is nothing that cannot be done through human efforts. We are invincible!"

Once again silence settled across the room. No one knew what to say or wanted to comment. Issues were so ponderous that words failed.

"I don't think we need to hear more," Larry reached for the automatic tuner. "Let's turn it off and talk."

"Really!" Ben sat up on his knees. "I'm ready to forget the football games. We've got pressing issues to consider."

"Jimmy," Larry smiled affectionately, "I've really come to respect your opinions. I want to know what you think. You've spent an enormous amount of time studying what the Bible says."

Jimmy picked up a large leather binder and unzipped it. Inside were a Bible, a notebook, and lots of loose pages. "I guess my father's teachings rubbed off on me more than I realized. I didn't think I was paying much attention as a kid, but I absorbed a great deal. It was easy for me to follow his line of thought since he heavily underlined in his books. I could really make up for a lot of lost time quickly."

"You have a fine mind." Sharon was equally warm. "I marvel at how you have put everything together."

Jimmy blushed. "Thank you," he answered softly. He spread out his notes on the floor. "Actually, I have my Bible with me all the time now, so it's not difficult to talk about the meaning of what we're seeing."

"Tell us what you've learned," Larry suggested. "Put things into perspective."

"Remember a prophetic day is 360 days."

"And a *day* can also mean a literal day or 1,000 years," Ruth added.

"Exactly," Jimmy affirmed. "This Antichrist will trample the Jews for 1,260 literal days before the Mes-

siah comes, defeats him, and restores sacrifices. The
Feast of Trumpets on September 29, 2000, is just three
years and nine months from now, which means the
Antichrist will desecrate the temple on Passover *this*
year. That's three and one-half years before the Second
Coming!"

"Good heavens!" Sharon exclaimed. "Jimmy, you're
a genius."

"Feast of Trumpets fits," Jimmy sighed. "I believe
that day is a very probable time for Jesus to return, defeat the armies gathered at Armageddon, and restore
the sacrificial system in the temple. Here's the big
point. Jesus would probably start the sacrificial worship again a few days after His return since the Battle
of Armageddon will probably last a few days and Jesus
will send angels around the world to give individuals
one last chance to trust Jesus as their Messiah and
Savior."

"There's strong evidence to believe that the Antichrist will actually stop the sacrifices 30 days before
Passover, on the Feast of Purim coming on March 23,
1997. Daniel hints that something very significant will
occur 1,290 days before the defeat of the Antichrist and
that there will be a transition period of 45 days after
his defeat until the Millennium officially begins. The
start of Christ's kingdom is 1,335 days after that mystery event on Purim."

"Incredible!" Sharon shook her head. "Absolutely incredible!"

Jimmy pulled a pencil from his leather case and began writing. "From Passover, 1997, to the Feast of
Trumpets, 2000, there are exactly 1,257 days. The war
of Armageddon will probably take 3 or 4 days, which
would take us to October 3, 2000, which is exactly 1,260
days from the time when the Great Tribulation began
and 1,290 days from the Feast of Purim when sacrifices
ceased. It all fits perfectly."

"Astonishing," Ben muttered.

"Here's another mindblower." Jimmy began scribbling quickly. "From the end of the Feast of Purim, 1997, to the beginning of the seventeenth of Heshvan—which is the date that God saved Noah's family—are 1,335 days. On this day in Heshvan, the Balfour Declaration was signed on November 2, 1917, declaring a Jewish national homeland. Just as Noah and as the nation of Israel had a new beginning on Heshvan 17, so will we . . . the third millennium, with Yeshua as ruler, on Heshvan 17, 2000."

"I had no idea the Bible could tell us such things," Larry said. "To think of the years that we wasted when we could have been learning these essential truths . . ."

Joe pointed to a page in his Bible. "Hosea, in chapter 6, suggests there will be a two-day period between the former and the latter Reigns of the Messiah. During these two days, Jews across the world will suffer persecution and great problems, but on the third day, the Messiah will return and heal their wounds. How do you put this together, Jimmy?"

"I equate the former Reign with the beginning of Jesus' ministry. Actually, our current calendar is several years off, and the true date of the beginning of His public ministry is A.D. 28. If I add two thousand Jewish prophetic 360-day years to that date, guess where I come out?"

"My hunch is," Ben answered first, "you're just about on the Feast of Trumpets, A.D. 2000."

"Exactly." Jimmy thumped the pages of his Bible. "If the 'two days' in Hosea 6 are two one-thousand-year periods, then the Antichrist would start persecuting Jews on Passover, 1997, which is almost 1,260 days earlier. Suddenly, all the prophecies fit together."

They all looked around the room at each other, mulling over the implications of what Jimmy had just said.

"What Jimmy has just explained," Joe added, "fits what I've been studying at our church and is what we heard the night of the New Year's Eve party when we committed our lives to Jesus. We *must* anticipate that this Passover will be the start of a terrible persecution."

Ben inched toward Jimmy. "Michael gave us this exact warning."

"I was trained to be a scientist." Larry sat back in his chair. "Probably lots of passages have various interpretations. I think we need real evidence that our conclusions are correct."

"Definitely," Jimmy said. "Everything is conjecture until we see Gianardo enter the temple and demand worship. But once that happens, we'll know that the 1,260-day countdown is on. If that occurs this year, we'll know where we are in the Great Tribulation."

"I don't need to hear more," Larry concluded. "Tomorrow I'm taking a big hunk of our savings out of the bank and putting it into gold bars and cash. I think it's important that we hide some of our reserves and put other cash in a safety deposit box under a false name."

"Maybe we ought to get false driver's licenses," Ben threw in. "I know a place in Las Vegas where you can get new ID's for fifty bucks each. I want one with a name that doesn't sound so Jewish. Ben Jones would do just fine this year."

"Will we ever see the people who were raptured again?" Ruth asked.

"Oh, yes!" Jennifer was enthusiastic. "We learned in our Bible study that they will return with Jesus."

"Will you know your parents?" Ruth asked Jimmy.

"Absolutely," Jimmy reassured her. "I'll know them because the Bible says we will know each other as we were known."

"What an incredible promise!" Ruth hugged Jimmy.

Events moved quickly that winter. Ruth continued in graduate school at Pepperdine pending the outcome of the approaching Passover, April 22. She had not yet found either the courage or the boldness to let anyone know about her faith. Ruth simply avoided revealing that she was not lasered and kept a low profile. Most stores were strict about it, but a few sold things for cash—at higher prices.

Jimmy's situation was easier because his boss had no interest in his religious and political ideas. Jimmy plodded away at the car lot in Laguna Niguel selling everything in sight. Now that he owned 10 percent of the business, his efforts were rewarded well. His savings fund was growing steadily.

Valentine's Day was too significant for the young lovers not to do something romantic. Ben asked Ruth and Jimmy to join Cindy and him at the five-star Five Crowns Restaurant in Corona Del Mar for an elegant dinner. The valet service parked the car, and the couples walked into the Tudor-style restaurant.

"What a place!" Jimmy looked around at the stucco-covered walls and the exposed thick, rough boards. Large beams went across the ceiling. English coats of arms decorated the walls, and hunting trumpets accented the melancholy atmosphere the dark-stained wood created. "Really makes me feel like the king of England to eat in here."

A hostess dressed in garb of English days of old led them across the plank floors to a table next to an antique fireplace. Overhead, a candle-style chandelier lit the table.

The waitress came quickly to take their orders and before long the gourmet meal was served.

"Their prime rib is the best on the coast," Ben talked between bites.

"Oh, I like the walnuts in their special house salad." Cindy squeezed Ben's hand. "You do such nice things for me."

"I don't think we'll be able to come to places like this much longer." Ruth twirled the fettucini around her fork. "I just pray we can all stick together."

"Sure." Jimmy reached over and hugged her. "I'll take care of us no matter what happens."

Cindy ran her sensitive fingers over the fine linen

tablecloth. "We know that God is going to take care of us," she said quietly. "No matter what . . ."

"Things have completely changed." Ben passed the thick-sliced homemade bread around again. "In the past I wouldn't have given much consideration to anything more serious than my next want. Now, we're caught up in a great adventure. I know bad stuff's out there, but I feel alive and part of something very exhilarating. Sure, we have some very formidable enemies, but we're on the side that's ultimately going to win, although the Bible says that vast numbers of believers will die during the Great Tribulation."

"We have Michael watching over us." Cindy cut into her petite filet. The waitress hovered, pouring water and iced tea.

"Our lives used to be flat and overindulged." Ben looked at his sister as he spoke. "We were spoiled rich kids, but that's behind us. I wouldn't go back to the old ways for anything."

"Me too!" Jimmy nodded. "I just didn't realize how important my father's ministry was. He was in the real battle every day of his life."

"And I know how special you are." Ruth took Jimmy's hand. "I don't care if my brother and Cindy are here. You are the best thing in my life and I want everyone to know it. I love you, Jimmy Harrison, and I want to be your wife."

"We ought to come to this restaurant more often," Jimmy told Ben in mock astonishment.

"I don't know how much time we have left together." Ruth's voice was low and intense. "Who knows what tomorrow will bring? We have to make the most of every second."

"Yes," Jimmy said soberly. "I'm afraid you're right. Our great adventure is going to be filled with drastic uncertainties."

"I think we need to take advantage of this very moment," Ruth insisted. "I have the perfect idea for finishing the evening. What better time to get married than Valentine's Day?"

Jimmy started to laugh, but something in Ruth's decisiveness checked him. "You're not kidding."

"No, I'm not. Jimmy, I want to marry you tonight."

Ben and Cindy almost stopped breathing.

"To . . . tonight?" Jimmy stuttered.

"Why not? We love each other and that's all that matters."

"But I thought you'd want a big wedding . . . the white dress . . . the walk down the aisle." Jimmy kept blinking his eyes.

"In a short while we may be dying," Ruth's voice became almost a whisper. "I don't want to face that moment alone. More important, I want us to be together through every step of the way into eternity. What's an expensive wedding with all the fancy flourishes compared to what's happening to us? I say let's go for it tonight!"

"But . . . how?" Jimmy was uncharacteristically befuddled. "Where?"

"Mexico!" Cindy and Ruth said at the same time.

"Sure!" Ben clapped his hands. "Mexico is only an hour and a half from here. For a couple of bucks anything's possible. We could leave right now and have you married before midnight."

"Midnight?" Jimmy swallowed hard and then beamed. "Why not?"

"Let's go!" Ruth stood up. "I'm ready to become Mrs. Jimmy Harrison on Valentine's Day."

I watched the happy foursome speed down Interstate 5 toward Tijuana. Hovering over the car, I made sure nothing marred the trip. A few mental nudges on my part sent Jimmy down the most expeditious side streets, winding up in front of one of Tijuana's less-famous Chapels of Bliss. Before midnight, the foursome were back across the border in San Diego.

Of course, I could listen to both sides of the conversation when Ruth called to break the news to her parents. Sharon shed the predictable tears, and Larry went into his psychiatric father role, dispensing immediate advice. I could easily perceive the loss that both parents felt in not being able to give their daughter the wedding of *their* dreams. In the end, they said the right words and clearly recognized how the times had changed all plans.

The two couples listened to music and said little as they sped north from Tijuana to San Diego. Jimmy and Ruth sat in the back seat cuddled together.

"Incredible. What a night!" Ben thumped the steering wheel. "Hey, there's the exit to your place." Ben turned off Interstate 5 at the Crown Valley exit. "Jimmy, you're the only person in the world I would drive to another country so he could marry my sister. Glad to have you in the Feinberg tribe."

"Well, you can drop me and the missus off at the apartment," Jimmy teased as Ben sped up the winding road. "Think we'll spend the evening home alone."

Ruth giggled and snuggled next to her new husband.

"Don't call me till after one in the afternoon," Jimmy chuckled.

"Sure thing, bro-in-law." Ben wheeled into the driveway. "By the way, congratulations again."

Ben returned to the freeway and headed for Cindy's dorm. "What do you think is ahead for us?"

Cindy felt the window on the door as if rubbing a magic looking glass. "I don't know." She seemed to be peering out into the black night. "The angel said . . . ," she stopped.

"I guess we can't get married." Ben was clearly pained. "I don't understand it. Michael seemed to be clear that we were to maintain a certain proper distance."

"Perhaps we are to develop a perfect love for each

other." Cindy turned toward Ben. "Maybe in heaven . . ."

"I don't want to wait for heaven," Ben groaned. "I want now. I envy Jimmy tonight. Cindy, you'd be enough heaven for me."

"We must trust God to know best." Cindy leaned against Ben. "You have something very important to do in the days ahead, and we must not do anything that could spoil your purpose."

By the time Ben had kissed Cindy good night and gone back to his room, it was three o'clock. In spite of near exhaustion and the late hour, he lay on his bed praying. "What is it You want from me?" he finally cried out. "I don't understand." With that last gasp of frustration, Ben fell into a deep sleep.

Standing in the corner, I listened intensely to both his silent and spoken prayers. "You will know soon enough," I said to myself. "Soon enough."

# CHAPTER

# 13

"Can you believe a month has passed since Jimmy and Ruth got married?" Sharon turned out the light on the nightstand. "I wish we could have given them a proper wedding." She threw back the large downy comforter on their king-size bed. The massive mahogany four-poster bed was covered by a spacious canopy that matched the Victorian furniture.

"Who knows what's proper anymore?" Larry laid down the book on prophecy that Jimmy had given him to read. He got up from his comfortable Queen Anne armchair and began turning down his side of the bed.

"They seem to be deliriously happy." Sharon propped herself up with a pillow. "I have to admit getting married was the right thing for them to do."

"I hope so." Larry pushed himself up on his elbows. "All the strange things that have happened sort of made a shambles of my marriage counseling theories. If they're happy, that's all that counts."

"Do you know what day it is?" Sharon suddenly smiled.

"Sure." Larry frowned. "March 22."

"Not the date, ninny. What holiday started at sundown tonight?"

"What are you talking about, woman?"

"Purim! Tonight and tomorrow are the Feast of Purim."

"Good grief, so it is!"

"My parents always had a little party for us when I was a child." Sharon leaned forward and smiled. "I'd dress up like good Queen Esther who saved all the Jews from evil Haman. Someone dressed up like King Xerxes who fell in love with Esther and made her queen. What great fun!"

"We did that once," Larry reminisced. "I dressed up like Mordecai. I always liked the part in the story where Haman was hanged in the noose he had prepared for Mordecai. Seventy-five thousand Jews were saved in one day along with kindly Mordecai. What a great story!"

"Makes today very special." Sharon slid down next to Larry. "We really need to start remembering these special events in the history of our people. I'm sorry we haven't done a better job teaching our children about their traditions."

"Yes," Larry agreed. "I think that—"

The phone rang.

"Who in the world could be calling us at nearly eleven at night? Really!" Sharon barked. "Let me get the phone."

"Sharon!" the voice at the other end was nearly breathless. "Get your TV on! You won't believe it!"

"Joe?" Sharon pulled the receiver back. "Joe McCoy?"

"Sharon, it's 9:00 A.M. in Jerusalem! TV crews have been out on the Mount of Olives getting the whole thing on film. Call Jimmy and Ruth! Call Ben! Everyone must watch!"

"TV?" Sharon questioned. "Turn the TV on now?"

"CNN!" The phone clicked off.

Larry had already reached for the automatic tuner. "News channel." He punched the button. "I know. It's all starting again."

"President Gianardo and Vice President Jacob Rath-

marker arrived here yesterday for meetings scheduled
to begin at eight o'clock this morning," the announcer
spoke as the picture came into focus. "We have no idea
what their response is to this amazing sight. However,
since they are here in Jerusalem, we will be able to get
a statement shortly."

The cameras covered a panoramic view of the top of
the Mount of Olives. Clouds boiled and swirled as if a
great storm was coming, but there did not appear to be
any wind or rain. In fact, a great calm appeared to have
settled over the area because the trees were not moving. When the cameras zoomed in, two figures seemed
to be emerging from the clouds. The images came and
went from sight.

"For the past forty-five minutes," the announcer
talked in hushed tones, "we have been observing this
phenomenon. The clouds began to gather forty-five
minutes ago, but there was no radar evidence of a
storm. However, the verbal reports from the area were
filled with concern and consternation. Our crews were
first dispatched to Mount Scopus to observe the sky."
The announcer stopped. "Look! There they are again!"

The two figures were much closer to the ground.

"What is going on?" Larry sat up in bed. "Must be a
stunt making it look like people are flying."

"Larry!" Sharon pointed. "They look ancient! Look
at those white beards . . . the long wooden staffs!"

"The two figures appear to be descending," the announcer began again. "Perhaps I might be more accurate to say materializing. They just seem to be coming
out of nowhere. Fortunately, we have this event on tape
since nothing like it has ever been filmed. However,
the experience seems like what many New Agers have
been describing in astral projection and similar phenomena."

"Are they landing?" Sharon puzzled.

"Looks more like they are just stepping out of another dimension into our world."

"We are going to try to get closer," the announcer's

voice returned. "A CNN correspondent has volunteered to make contact. At this moment he is arriving by car at the point that has often been recognized as the traditional site of the ascension of Jesus. Of course, no one took this place as having serious archaeological significance . . . until now. Our cameras are going to try to zoom in to pick up the correspondent's remote mike."

"The brilliance of radiant light makes it very difficult to walk forward." The man's voice boomed as the screen turned white. "Frankly, I am as terrified as if I were walking into the sun, but there is no heat."

Two shapes began to appear on the screen, looking more like photograph negatives. They raised their arms and the long staffs they held. Suddenly, a babble of sound rumbled over the TV.

"We don't have time to get a translation," the announcer explained. "However, I clearly recognize Hebrew."

The intonation changed. Another language came forth.

"Russian!" Another announcer came on, "I can tell they are speaking Russian."

Several times the language changed as the figures became clearer and the dazzling light receded. The two men had shimmering white hair and beards. Their robes were wondrously white. Each man looked as if he carried overwhelming personal authority.

"They are speaking Chinese now," the CNN correspondent explained. "I think I can get a bit closer."

At that moment, the larger of the two men pointed his finger directly at the camera. His dark-set black eyes looked as if they could pierce steel. "Hear me!" he said in perfect English. "We have come that you might hear the final witness of the Holy One of Israel. Listen well, lest your own words become testimony against you. The hour of accounting is at hand!"

"Please excuse me," the correspondent inched forward holding his microphone at arm's length as if it might protect him from the apparitions. "Who . . . who might we . . . ah . . . be . . . ah . . . talking with?"

"Moses!" the huge man roared, and his voice sounded as if it might shake the mountain. "I have come with my heavenly colleague. Behold, Elijah the Tishbite!"

The correspondent fell backward, and the two figures moved past him down the hill.

While Elijah and Moses walked down the Mount of Olives, Larry called Ruth and Jimmy. Sharon got Ben on the other line. After the children were alerted, Larry and Sharon turned back to the TV.

"As best we can tell," the announcer talked rapidly as the cameras followed the two prophets down the hillside, "the two strangers are walking down toward the Kidron Valley as if going toward the ancient walls of the city. Because this event is being carried instantaneously around the world, we are able to register public response as we broadcast. New Age psychics are homing in for readings. We are told now that Gianardo and the Israeli prime minister have been watching for some time. They have left the Knesset and are on their way here at this very moment."

"Look at them!" Larry pointed at the TV. "I can't believe my eyes. Do you truly think we are watching the real Moses and Elijah?"

"They're almost gliding down the hillside." Sharon got out of bed and pulled a chair up close to the television.

The camera switched to the highway that ran in front of the Old City wall. Behind the stone walls loomed the Dome of the Rock Mosque, beside the rebuilt temple of Solomon. Truckloads of soldiers began rolling down the highway and stopping at the bottom. Young men with automatic weapons leaped out and took up positions behind rocks, but the two prophets continued to walk with clear determination toward the convoy.

"Precautionary measures are now being taken before Gianardo and the Israeli prime minister arrive," the announcer continued. "No one appears to know what to do. Amazingly, Gianardo seems to be less apprehensive than his advisers. Sources with the presidential party are telling our reporters that the president seems to be almost fascinated with what is occurring. Apparently, there is a television in the presidential limousine, and CNN is being observed even as I speak."

The television lost the two men as they moved through a grove of trees but picked up a caravan of limousines that pulled up behind the parked military trucks blocking the highway. Almost before the cars stopped, Secret Service agents in plain clothes were forming a protective corridor in front of the cars. Israeli agents carrying Uzis joined them. Suddenly, the ancient travelers came out of the trees onto the highway.

"The figures calling themselves Moses and Elijah have just appeared from behind the Church of All Nations." Another announcer picked up the commentary. "The traditional site of the Garden of Gethsemane is at the bottom of the Kidron Valley. The two men are now walking up toward the presidential caravan. We are going to switch to reporters who have been traveling with the president."

TV cameras caught President Gianardo pushing past his bodyguards who tried to restrain him. He walked toward the approaching figures. The prime minister of Israel appeared to be crouching behind him.

"President Gianardo seems to be seeking a confrontation," the news reporter's voice boomed. "He seems to have some insight into what is happening. The Israeli prime minister is deeply disturbed that such an event is happening on the Feast of Purim. He, too, appears to have some understanding but considerably more apprehension. We have now turned special long-range microphones toward the point where an encounter will occur. We believe that we will be able to pick up whatever is said."

The troops stood up and pointed their weapons at the

two holy men while Secret Service personnel scurried forward with pistols drawn. Moses and Elijah held up their hands as if they could repel anything fired at them, but their pace did not slacken.

An agent with a bullhorn jumped in front of Gianardo. "Who are you?" the amplification echoed off the hillside. "Identify yourselves or we will shoot!"

Moses roared with laughter and tossed his long white hair back. "Can you threaten Adonai?" His laughter rumbled.

"We will take you into custody immediately," the agent insisted.

The prophets kept walking.

The Israeli prime minister seized the bullhorn. "Why have you come?" his voice trembled. "Why on this day?"

"If Ahab did not intimidate me," Elijah responded, "do you think you will give me pause?"

As if hit by a blow, the prime minister dropped the bullhorn to the ground and staggered backward. Gianardo walked past him. "Would you toy with our power?" he sneered. "I understand much more about the supernatural than Ahab would have dreamed of knowing. Don't try and frighten us with innuendos. Tell us clearly. Who do you claim to be?"

"Your ears have not deceived you." Moses thumped his staff on the ground. "Your faithlessness will be your demise."

"Demise?" The president snapped his fingers. "I can blow you back to wherever you came from before lightning can flash."

"Your arrogance has no boundaries," Moses solemnly retorted. "Your blindness will condemn you to eternal darkness."

"Prove it!" Gianardo snapped.

The Israeli prime minister peered from behind Gianardo. "I . . . I . . . I really w . . . want to know."

"Fool!" Gianardo snapped. "Don't indulge these people."

"That you may know," Moses leaned on his staff, "my signs will not be of the earth as they were with Pharaoh, but I shall answer you in the terms of your day. Let your computer experts give you the answer."

"Y . . . yes, say something." The prime minister clasped his hands together and started bowing at the waist.

"You already have my book of Genesis in Hebrew in your systems at the Israel Institute of Technology. Instruct them to remove every twenty-sixth Hebrew letter. You will find that the result will spell the sacred name of God, *E-L-O-H-I-M*. They will find that the word *T-O-R-A-H* is repeated at fifty-letter intervals."

"Really?" the prime minister blinked. "You're serious?"

"Have them look at my description of the burial sites of Abraham and Sarah, and you will also find the words *A-D-A-M* and *E-V-E* there in similar fashion. Let this be a sign! No human could have developed such a system over four thousand years ago. God is God and Moses is Moses!"

Immediately, several aides rushed to the cars. The television announcer interjected, "As best we can tell, Gianardo is now huddling with the prime minister. He seems irritated by the timid response from the Israeli. Gianardo doesn't seem to be confounded by these astonishing figures. We are attempting to get comment on the religious significance of this day because it seems to be a component in these discussions. Look! The Israeli aides are now reporting. The prime minister is pulling away from the president. He's bowing up and down in formal diplomatic posture. Let's see if we can pick him up."

"No question about it. The computers confirm your assertions." The prime minister spoke respectfully. "Why? Why are you here on this day that has such ominous meaning in our history?"

"Do you not know?" Elijah's voice thundered. "Do you not suspect? As happened twenty-five hundred years ago, Haman formed a noose for Mordecai, so does Gianardo draw one for you!"

"Idiot!" Gianardo pushed the prime minister aside. "Don't listen to these apparitions. They are creatures of the lie. Let me deal with them."

"Hear the word of the Lord!" Elijah threw open his arms. "As was true of Haman of old, so shall it be true of you. Within 1,290 days, both of you will surely hang from the rope of your own making!"

"No!" the Israeli gasped.

"Hear us, O world," Moses commanded, "we have come to make the final announcement that Yeshua, whom you crucified, has ascended to the place of all authority and is the Messiah. His return is imminent."

"Good heavens!" the prime minister choked.

Moses turned toward the cameras as if sensing they were trained on him. He began speaking again in low earnest tones that tugged at the heart. "This moment has been chosen because the entire world now has the capacity to hear as if with one ear. Many of you will believe and be saved from the consequences coming on the evil people of this world. Even though you may face death and persecution, you must not yield. The great battle is at hand. Stand with the Lord's people regardless. We will soon give you three signs by which you will know."

"Behold!" Elijah pointed at the sky. "The breaking of the Fourth Seal! A pale horse called Death will ride the skies on Pesach. Passover, Tuesday, April 22, will begin the great unleashing. By Tammuz 17, July 22, one and one-half billion people will have been slain. War, starvation, pestilence, and illness will wipe out one-fourth of the population of the globe. The hard-hearted and the unrepentant will fall because of their own obstinacy. Let him who has ears hear!"

"Another sign!" Moses pointed directly at the president. "A terrible night will sweep across your globe. This Beast will strike and slay one million of God's people who now stand in the Evil Empire. Those Jews who have now come to see the truth about the Messiah will be the major target of this evil war. Behold the terror in your midst!" Moses took a quick, bold step toward Gianardo.

The president covered his face with his arms as the Israeli prime minister fell backward. The TV cameras picked up their terrified faces.

Moses shouted, "From Passover until the Fast of Tammuz, seventy thousand believers will be slain. Their blood will cry up to the sky." The television cameras drew back.

"Larry!" Sharon grabbed her husband. "Do you understand? He could be talking about us! This is the puzzle of terror that Ben and Jimmy were trying to figure out."

Larry put his arm around his wife's shoulder. "Only God can save us," he muttered. "We must get the family together as quickly as we can."

Sharon reached for a pencil. "I've got to write this down."

"Better yet," Larry reached for a tape, "we must catch every word." Immediately they began recording the predictions.

Elijah pointed his staff toward the ocean. "On the seventeenth of Tammuz, July 4, 1776, the Holy One brought forth a new nation that would be greatly used as His instrument in restoring our people. Always a haven for Jews, this country was the primary defender and guarantor when Israel was reborn on May 14, 1948. Once again the gift becomes the curse. You, O America, will be the source of death and calamity!"

Moses roared, "These truths are not hidden to those who seek in faith! You will see that those who have perished will become your intercessors. The martyrs will stand in white robes before the sovereign Lord, crying out for their blood to be avenged. On the day when the Great Tribulation ends at the Battle of Armageddon, it shall be done."

To the consternation of the president's party as well

as the TV cameramen, Moses and Elijah marched forward through the array of men and trucks. The crowds parted before them as if the people were a human sea of water. The camera scurried to line up with the route the two were taking.

"I can't believe my ears." Larry held his head in his hands. "The woes are about to come down."

"But there is so much encouragement here for us," Sharon reassured him. "Just think how hopeless we would be if Jimmy had never come into our lives."

"Maybe we're getting some sense of Ben's place in what's about to start. Oh, God, please help us!"

"He will," Sharon comforted her husband. "I know He will."

"No one has any commentary whatsoever," the TV announcer said soberly. "We have no precedent by which to gauge this message. We are too stunned to even know whether we've been hit with a colossal hoax, an apparition created by spirit guides, or the final truth of history."

"Hoax!" Larry exploded. "He'll eat those words!"

"They're stopping." Sharon leaned forward. "Moses and Elijah are halting before the Western Wall, the wailing wall just on the other side of the new temple."

The two prophets sat down in chairs that Jews had left out for their prayers earlier in the day. Around them, men in yarmulkes and prayer talliths fell with their faces toward the enormous stone wall. Generally, most people backed away in fear. The television cameras switched to pictures of the presidential limousines speeding away from the Kidron Valley. Helicopters appeared buzzing overhead, beginning to circle over the Western Wall. Gianardo's announcement that he had persuaded the Israeli Knesset to outlaw all animal sacrifices as of March 23, 1997, went largely unnoticed because attention was on the two strange ancient ones who descended from the sky in full view of the world's TV cameras.

# CHAPTER
# 14

The whole scene left Larry too disturbed to even think about sleep. He slipped on a sweat suit and went down to the kitchen to prepare a pot of coffee. Suddenly, the doorbell rang. To his surprise, he found Joe and Jennifer McCoy outside. They had barely begun to talk when Jimmy and Ruth drove up. About five minutes later, Ben showed up with Cindy.

"Looks like Jimmy was incredibly accurate." Larry turned the volume down on the large screen TV in the den. "I don't have any idea what's next tonight, but I think I see the outline of the future rather clearly."

"I'm worried for them." Ruth pointed at the two prophets on the screen, sitting calmly as more helicopters filled the sky. "A marksman in one of those choppers couldn't miss!"

"I think they can take care of themselves," Jimmy answered. "Next month will be the critical time," he added. "Now we know that on Passover the 1,260-day Great Tribulation will start."

Sharon held up a faded, wrinkled paperback. "Lots of the 1970s and 1980s prophecy books I found talked about a seven-year tribulation. You're sure about a three-and-a-half-year time of 1,260 days?"

"My dad had a solution to your question. He believed that 2 Thessalonians 2:7–8 taught that the Rapture would occur prior to the Antichrist's being revealed. True Christians were to be spared the worldwide persecution. Revelation 3:10 is an example of this point. I think the Rapture could probably have occurred at a number of different times in the past without contradicting definite prophecies. The real point is that the return of the Messiah will come seven prophetic years after the wicked world ruler signs a false peace pact with Israel. He will return 1,290 days after sacrifices stop and after 1,260 days of terrible tribulation have passed starting when the temple is desecrated. There is clearly a seven-year countdown prior to Yeshua's descending back on the Mount of Olives to destroy the Antichrist, but the Bible doesn't say that the seven-year clock starts with the Rapture."

"That's exactly our conclusion," Joe added. "Daniel 9:27 is very specific that the seven-year time slot is tied to signing the secret peace treaty, which was signed in November, 1993 by many world rulers, including Gianardo, who was only speaker of the House of Representatives at the time. No one could have known then that he would turn out to be the Antichrist."

"No one can be dogmatic," Jimmy affirmed, "until after that single event when he desecrates the temple. Maybe Daniel's 2,200 days were actually 2,300 or 2,400. Our problem is that everything adds up right now. In fact, the evidence is so clear that I believe we've got no time to lose. The sacrifices ceased today."

"We must finalize our survival plans," Larry confirmed. "Those fake ID's are no longer a novel suggestion. Fortunately, I already have a number of gold bars hidden here in the house. I already obtained false passports as well."

"I'm not sure I'll make it," Cindy fretted. "I think Michael hinted that I might not survive."

"Don't talk like that," Ben sounded angry, but his face looked pained. "You're going to survive. We're going to fight this thing through to the bitter end regardless. After all . . . ," his voice became almost inaudible, "you are the best friend I have. You're the most important person in my life."

"But if something should happen to me," Cindy turned to Jimmy, "I will come back with Jesus in 2000. Right? Like your parents?"

"Yes," Jimmy was quite confident, "everyone will return with a new and resurrected body."

"The worst would be like a short separation," Cindy reassured Ben.

Ben ran his hand through his hair and looked disturbed. "I don't know, but I'll protect you regardless."

"Sure!" Jimmy agreed. "My parents taught me that we ought to pray as if everything depended on God while working as if everything depended on us."

"Let's do it. It's time for us to make concrete plans on how to escape and survive." Larry stood up as he spoke. "I think the first logical step is to make sure that we know everything possible about what lies ahead. We can act intelligently only if we are fully informed. I have been studying this matter constantly since I've had my own change of heart and mind. I believe that I've found the only place in the whole world that will be safe. God has ordained a divinely protected area like the old cities of refuge where none of us will become martyrs." He walked over to his desk.

"Really?" Jimmy was amazed. "As hard as I have studied Scripture, I haven't come up with such an area."

Larry pulled a map out of a drawer in his desk and unfolded it on the coffee table. "There is an ancient and almost totally abandoned city in the cliffs that are about four thousand feet above sea level in the mountains of ancient Edom." He put his finger on the map. "The place is called Bozrah. About eighty miles southeast of Jerusalem and approximately twenty-five miles northeast of the ancient city of Petra, the location is in Jordan."

"How did you come up with this conclusion?" Jimmy puzzled.

Larry opened his Bible that was also on the table. "Look at chapter 12 in Revelation. The passage talks about a woman with a garland of twelve stars on her head. She is obviously the nation of Israel. After she gives birth to the Messiah, which is the first coming of Jesus, the red dragon, or Satan, tries to kill the child. That happened right after the birth of Jesus, but God intervened and saved the child. Verse 6 tells us that before the Messiah rules the world, Israel will again flee to the desert where God will protect her for 1,260 days, preserving Israel from the Antichrist and Satan himself." Larry turned back to the Old Testament. "I have studied Isaiah 63 and the book of Obadiah, verses 15 through 21, and discovered that God is going to protect Jews in two cities—Bozrah and Petra."

"Larry," Sharon asked, "can you be sure that you are correct?"

"Micah 2:12–13 confirms my discoveries. Micah makes an amazing play on words in saying that the Messiah will gather the surviving remnant of Israel like a shepherd gathers his flock. The Hebrew word here for 'flock' is *bozrah*. In these passages we have a picture of Jews fleeing from Israel into a desert area when the Antichrist desecrates the temple. There's even a description of escape on 'two wings of a great eagle,' which will probably be some old American transport plane since the eagle is the old symbol of our country. Moses and Elijah will protect everyone for the 1,260 days of struggle before the Messiah returns on the Feast of Trumpets in 2000 and wipes out the opposition. I think that three days later, He will go to Bozrah for His chosen ones and return with them, going through the east gate right into the temple area to start the one-thousand-year millennial kingdom."

"Makes total sense," Joe McCoy agreed. "I think you need to get packing before Passover comes."

"Exactly!" Larry thumped the table. "I need to sell my psychiatric practice, and Jimmy can close out his interest in the car business. You might say that we are in a position to sell at fire sale prices. When we sell the houses, we'll hide the money in suitcases."

Jimmy added, "After we fly to Tel Aviv, we can stock up on camping equipment, canned goods, and survival gear."

"I've already purchased some medical books on mountain medicine."

"There's another reason we need to leave," Sharon spoke up. "You've always been a very compassionate person, Larry. You'll try to help your patients, but if you witness to your new faith, we'll be dead. They'll come and get us. But in Bozrah, there will be Jews fleeing the persecution. They'll be like survivors of Hitler's death camps and will need psychiatric care too."

"OK, family!" Larry shook both fists in the air. "We're on our way."

"I can't go," Ben said soberly. "I think I understand why the angel appeared to us in such an unusual way. Michael knew we'd leave without an early intervention on his part. Cindy and I have a task that we must do right here. No, I have an important job to do in California."

"Oh, my!" Sharon covered her mouth with her hand. The room became very quiet.

"No matter what happens, we won't be apart more than three and one-half years," Ben tried to smile.

Larry turned to Jimmy and Ruth. "And you?" His face was drawn and his eyes deeply troubled.

"Ruth is Jewish and I am married to her. Seems appropriate for us to go."

"Joe? Jennifer?" Larry probed.

"We can't," Joe sighed. "We've already discussed some similar possibilities, but our kids bought Gianardo's philosophy hook, line, and sinker. They hate our Christian faith. Even if it costs us our lives, we must witness to them to the end. We have to do everything we can to pull them back from the abyss."

"I understand." Tears welled up in Sharon's eyes.

"We must pray." Larry hung his head. "We must pray

for each other as we start this journey that will separate us. The battle has already begun for us."

Ben put his arm around Cindy. "We enter a battle we
can't win to gain a crown we won't lose. God will be
the difference."

The families joined hands and bowed their heads.

# 15

Tragedy can spring forth as quickly and unexpectedly as the winds of a summer thunderstorm that tear limbs from trees and smash flowers to the ground. No earthquake or tornado leaves behind devastation like that of human anger and injustice. I watched in horror when the Babylonian hordes tore Judea apart, and I wept in grief as the Romans burned the temple to the ground. Only an angel who has watched the centuries flow past can fully understand how rapidly circumstances trap the unsuspecting and leave the innocent abandoned to the rampaging torrents of unexpected evil.

World events began to move at breakneck speed. Keeping all the pieces together was nearly impossible as the Feinbergs' world started flying apart. Ruth dropped out of her graduate classes in psychology at Pepperdine and quietly faded from her circle of acquaintances. Because of the rapid turnover in the used car sales business, Jimmy's boss was not completely surprised when he quit. Any questions about Jimmy's intentions ended when he agreed to sell his 10 percent of the business back to the boss for 5 percent value. Ben and Cindy stayed in school while they made their own arrangements. Once Ben received his inheritance money, he began systematically hiding the funds for the future. Cindy continued teaching her bewildered parents about the faith of the Bible. The Wongs listened in consternation.

The Feinbergs' premium oceanfront property moved easily and quickly. Larry gave his reason for selling the psychiatric practice as retirement, and no other questions were asked. Once the funds were in place, the family left for Israel on Tuesday, April 15, one week before Passover. Twelve hours later they landed at Ben Gurion International Airport and were soon moving through customs procedures.

"You said their name is Eisenberg?" Sharon asked Larry as they stood in line to clear Israeli passport control.

"Sam and Angie," Larry said quietly. "Jewish believers. Jimmy's father knew them when they were going to Dallas Theological Seminary. They've been coming and going as tourists for some time so no one would detect that they are actually Christian missionaries."

"They know why we're here?" Sharon inched toward the booth where the customs official was checking documents.

"Jimmy was able to get a message to them. We had to code our intentions, but they got the drift I'm sure. They'll meet us after we clear customs."

"I hope they don't think we're crazy." Sharon rolled her eyes as she handed her passport through the window.

Jimmy and Ruth followed behind them. Just on the other side of the luggage check, the family found the Eisenbergs. Sam was a tall, strong middle-aged man while Angie was small with striking blue eyes. Larry didn't speak to them until they were outside. "You got our message?" he said. "Made sense?"

"Of course." Sam nodded pleasantly. "We weren't surprised." The sun had turned his naturally olive-colored skin a deep tan. Ruggedly handsome, he looked like any other sabra, native-born Israeli, walking down the street.

Angie was plainly dressed, like most of the people standing around them. "We understood easily. We've been storing supplies in the area for some time. We've been expecting you."

"What?" Larry looked shocked. "I don't understand. How could you know about Bozrah? About us?"

"It's a long story," Sam explained hurriedly, "but the insight started in Dallas where we once had a successful dry cleaning business. When some of our Jewish friends became believers, we were intrigued and started attending Dallas Theological Seminary. We pretended that we were believers in Yeshua. After the Rapture, we were convinced that the Bible passages on prophecy were true. During our studies, we found out about what was ahead at Bozrah and Petra. But there's another chapter we'll tell you about later."

"You've known all along!" Jimmy set his bags on the sidewalk. "Of course! You were able to read between the lines and understand our intention."

"How are you getting through the border check points?" Ruth asked.

Sam put his arm around Angie's waist and grinned. "We've got a couple of old school buses and a van with tourist signs plastered all over them. I think the border guards have decided that our specialty is dropping Holy Land pilgrims at the historic sites around Petra. They don't even give us a second look now."

"You're a genius!" Jimmy laughed.

"No," Sam said soberly, "God has just protected us well. We've been able to get in a number of shortwave radios and a satellite dish with some battery-operated TV sets and a generator. I think you will be satisfied with the arrangements."

"God has certainly led us to you." Larry shook Sam's hand again. "Now I know that we will be able to make the right connections. We thought that we were the only people in the world who had figured out the divine puzzle about Bozrah."

"We even have Arab Christians with us," Sam continued. "They make contact with the Arab villages in the area. Places like Rashadiya, Dana, Wadi Musa, and Taiyba have Muslim populations. Recent events have made many of them hostile, but in our area Arab and Jewish Christians live together out of their common love for Yeshua."

"Ben will be relieved to know that we can make contact by shortwave," Sharon said thoughtfully.

"We must change your money into gold and Jordanian currency." Sam pointed to a bank down the street. "We'll need some Israeli money for incidentals. After we get the exchange completed, we'll take in some biblical sights along the way to Jerusalem where we have some very special people you will want to meet."

"Pretty scary!" Jimmy raised his eyebrows. "But what an adventure. Let's go!"

The Eisenbergs pulled their van up to the sidewalk, and the new arrivals piled their gear in the back. Jimmy even had a small box of books to complete his studies. As the van wound its way toward Jerusalem, Sam and Angie stopped at significant historic sites. A great sense of awe settled over the group as they stood before the places they had studied in the preceding months. Finally, the old van climbed up the steep hillside toward Jerusalem. Tall green pines bordered the twisting highway. Here and there the burned-out hulks of tanks or troop carriers remained as silent monuments to the battles that had secured the survival of the nation. Suddenly, new high-rise apartments loomed on the tops of the hills. The ancient and the new blended together in the same ocher-colored stones.

"This is our place . . . our land." Larry reached for Sharon's hand. "I had no idea that I would be so deeply touched."

"How proud my father would have been . . . ," Sharon choked. "He would have given anything to have come here."

The van rolled around the final turn and into the city

limits. Jimmy leaned out the window to drink in the intoxicating aroma of the city.

"For the first time I realize that I've never really been at home anywhere," Larry said with astonishment. "I've been waiting for this city to appear all of my life. I am home."

The van turned down Ben Yehudah Street, cutting through traffic, and headed for the walls of the ancient city. Sam found a parking area close to the Damascus Gate and led the party into the Old City. "Stick close," he called back to them. "We're going to take a shortcut through some alleyways, and we need to move quickly and stay concealed as much as possible."

The group walked through dim, narrow streets cramped between high stone buildings for several blocks and then burst through an arched opening.

"The Western Wall!" Jimmy pointed at the huge stones rising up before them.

Sam guided the group along the edge of the building that ran down to the huge wall. Barricades had been erected several hundred feet away, running parallel to the great wall. Troops were poised with guns pointed at the two men sitting calmly at the base of the former boundary to Solomon's temple.

"The troops are terrified of Moses and Elijah," Sam talked rapidly as they walked. "They haven't figured out that all who come in peace will be welcomed with peace. You're about to have the experience of two lifetimes." Sam guided his group forward.

Moses stood and beckoned them to approach. He was a massive man, towering over everyone. A luminous aura surrounded his pure white hair and penetrating eyes. "We have been expecting you." He motioned that they should stand before him.

Larry and Sharon huddled together more in reverent terror than curiosity. Jimmy shuffled forward, holding Ruth's hand.

"Have no fear," Elijah spoke forcefully as he stood up.

"Each of us is part of the heavenly plan. We welcome you as our brothers and sisters."

Larry carefully edged his way forward, clutching Sharon to his side.

"We are going to protect you," Moses' deep bass voice rumbled as he spoke. "We will stand guard over the entrance to Bozrah and Petra for 1,260 days."

"Do not be dismayed when you hear that we have died in these very streets," Elijah explained. "Exactly thirty days later the Messiah will return. During the three days we lie here, the world will rejoice, but you must not mourn. Our deaths will be painless and then resurrection will follow. We will ascend just as Yeshua did nearly two thousand years ago. The world's jubilation will turn to mourning while your trials become pure joy."

"But you must not leave the cities of protection during this time," Moses warned, "unless you are prepared to become martyrs. Half of all believers left in the world will yield up their lives during the Great Tribulation that will be fought everywhere. Within the boundaries of Petra and Bozrah, angels will stand guard at the door.

"Hear me!" Moses held his hand high above his head. "Study Psalm 139! The world has greatly underestimated the unending love and faithfulness of our heavenly Father. His justice endures. He esteems you beyond any measure of your comprehension. As He leads us, so the Father guides your steps."

"Let us bless you." Elijah held his arms upward as he spoke.

Timidly, the Feinbergs, Jimmy and Ruth, and the Eisenbergs knelt before the spiritual giants. Elijah prayed, "Lord Yeshua, open the eyes of their hearts that they may see the spiritual realm."

The six travelers looked up and gasped as they saw hundreds of thousands of angels surrounding the area while other angels raced across the sky in chariots of fire. Frozen in a trance, no one could speak. As they stared, the sight slowly dissolved.

"Go in peace," Moses blessed the group. "Remember what you have seen. As we have the power to open eyes, we can close them as well. Journey with confidence. The times are in His hands."

Sam tugged at Larry's arm and the group began backing away. Only after they had cleared the barriers did they realize that no one had noticed them. Not one soldier asked for identification. The guards were oblivious to the group.

"They can't see us!" Jimmy whispered to Ruth. "God has blinded the eyes of these nonbelievers."

Rather than return to the alleys, Sam led the party through the main gate and out to the street where they found the van. They pulled back on the highway that edged along the walls of the Old City and down the Kidron Valley. At the bottom of the hill, the van started the incline up the Mount of Olives, rounded the top of the hill, and traveled toward Bethany and the Tomb of Lazarus.

No one said anything for a long time. Finally, Larry spoke. "You've done this before? You talked to them earlier?"

"Once." Sam said. "They told us to bring you here when you arrived. We knew you were coming even before your message got here."

"Staggering," Larry mumbled. "Simply staggering. So that's how you knew."

Sharon began to weep. "Why us? We aren't special. We haven't even been good Jews. Why should we be granted such an experience?"

"Grace is like that," Angie answered. "All of us are more special to God than we realize. There is no other answer . . . except His love."

The van lumbered on toward the wilderness and the Dead Sea. The trees and shrubs disappeared as the air became drier and the ground more barren. Most of the remaining eighty miles to Bozrah were spent in silence.

Jimmy kept looking out the window with his forehead on the glass. Finally, he said, "We can't see them, but we sure know that the angels are with us."

"Even the desert blooms," Larry answered, "and the empty places are filled with new life for surely He makes wind and fire to be His messengers."

# CHAPTER

# 16

The president's black limousine pulled away from the Knesset Building and edged toward the broad boulevard that ran from the modern section of Jerusalem to the ancient city. Armed motorcycle troops of the New Roman Empire completely surrounded the car. Only a few people walked down the streets. Jacob Rathmarker rode in a limo behind the president.

"Mr. President," the new aide in a pin-striped suit sounded edgy, "many Jews will hate you for taking this action on the Day of Passover as much as they will resent the invasion itself. We might have waited at least a day longer . . ."

"Absolutely not!" Gianardo snapped. "There's a principle at stake. The world must recognize my absolute power!"

A phone inside the limousine rang. The aide immediately answered. "Yes . . . I understand . . . it's done. Very good." He hung up. "The nuclear facilities have all been secured, Mr. President. Our troops are also poised to take control of the remaining centers where our intelligence indicates atomic capacity might exist. The job is virtually complete."

"Excellent! Any response from the Israeli army?"

"Evidently, they have accepted the order of the prime minister and have not resisted us."

"Did you see his face?" The president laughed
coarsely. "The prime minister's eyes nearly bulged out
of his head. He shook like a frightened puppy when I
told him they would capitulate or we would nuke the
nation off the globe."

"What could he say?" the aide said stiffly. "Their
limited nuclear reserves were no match for what was
hovering over their heads in our planes. He did the intelligent thing. But on Passover?"

"The world must never forget April 22, 1997!" The
president looked out the window at the vacant streets
and the closed shops. "The issue is power. Rare power.
I'm going to do something that will stamp my authority
on this society and convince the world that we are not
to be toyed with." The president pushed a button in the
armrest and the sliding glass window behind the driver
opened. "Straight to the Temple Mount." He pushed the
button and the window slid shut.

"I don't understand," the aide fumbled.

"Of course. I didn't tell you. Now you will understand why we came on a high holiday. We're going out
to their new temple. I've already arranged for live TV
coverage."

"But . . . but . . . isn't that where those two strange
apparitions have settled in? Those two men who keep
making pronouncements? Gives me the creeps."

"Yes, we're going to stop that little charade in one fell
swoop as well."

"Charade?"

"Sure. You didn't believe that hocus-pocus nonsense
was real? Did you?"

"Well . . . I did see the initial television tapes. You
seemed somewhat shaken at the time."

"Nonsense! Just didn't expect the road show. Took
me a while to put it all together. I'm sure the Israeli
prime minister was behind it. Probably created trick
TV tapes, simulated clouds, and holographic images.
Those two clowns sitting down there by the Western
Wall are only a Jewish attempt to use ancient prophecy

to manipulate both Jews and Christians. Today they've been telling Jews to flee to Bozrah."

"Really?" the aide looked incredulous. "What's at Bozrah?"

"Absolutely nothing but tourist ruins and some obscure Arab villages. They've got every Messianic Jew in Israel and every evangelical in our country running around like chickens with their heads cut off. The Israeli Hasidic Jews are equally panicked. Now I'm going to demonstrate to every stratum of opinion that I am the absolute power in this world. We'll show them what frauds those two impostors are. Moses, my foot!"

"What do you have in mind?" the aide asked cautiously.

"I insisted on a news conference in front of the temple, and the prime minister grudgingly said he would be there."

"I see," the aide frowned.

"I could care less about him. It's the TV coverage I want. I intend to extend my control even over the religious community. It's all a matter of principle, my boy."

The aide smiled but sat back stiffly. Nothing more was said as the motorcade wound its way up toward the Old City. Limited traffic made travel easy. Eventually, the Nablus Road stopped before the Damascus Gate in the ancient stronghold. The driver turned left and drove along the wall until he came to St. Stephen's Gate. The motorcade inched its way through the massive stone gate and down the Old City as the back streets became increasingly narrow. Finally, the entourage stopped next to the Monastery of the Flagellation.

"Passover observance helped with security," the aide mused. "The unexpected drop-in has made matters very simple."

"I think of everything," Gianardo said smugly as the aide opened the door for him. The vice-president's limo pulled up behind them.

When the president and his soldiers reached the

Temple Mount, the area was already packed with Israeli security officers and reporters. Cabinet leaders
surrounded the prime minister. Cameras were set up
in front of the new temple. Gianardo walked quickly
through the crowd but did not stop at the entry to the
temple. "Follow me," he demanded.

"You can't go in!" A cohenim priest rushed forward.

"Try and stop me!" Gianardo and Rathmarker
walked in and beckoned for the crowd to follow them.
The horrified priest watched the reporters trample by.

"Enough!" The Israeli prime minister tugged at Gianardo's arm. "Please, we have had enough humiliation
for one day."

Rathmarker pushed him aside and marched up to
the large elegant hanging curtains in front of the Holy
of Holies. The TV cameramen scurried in every direction to record the details. "Set the microphone right
here." Rathmarker pointed in front of his feet.

"The prime minister of Israel has a statement first."
Rathmarker stepped back and pointed at the microphone.

The bent gray-haired man shuffled forward and began reading from a piece of crumpled paper. "The New
Roman Empire called the Knesset into session this
morning and demanded that control of all nuclear capacity be turned over to the empire. Failure to comply
would bring immediate attack upon our country. We
had no choice but to comply and have now done so. Mr.
Gianardo has also demanded that we recognize him as
the supreme ruling power in the world. Failure to do so
would invite disaster. The president of the New Roman
Empire obviously does have supreme authority." The
old man shuffled away.

Rathmarker stepped to the microphone. "Thank you,
Mr. Prime Minister. We are gathered at this place as a
matter of principle. Clearly, the New Roman Empire is
uniting the globe in order to create a more just and
decent world. We are the last hope for a peaceful order.
The empire will insist on nonaggression even at the

price of going to war in order to stop killing. However, global order demands recognition of our authority at every level. History records that religion has been a constant source of strife and conflict. Therefore, we are going to personally put an end to further discord."

Rathmarker whirled around and jerked a section of the huge curtains open, letting outside light flood into the holy place. The priest screamed and the Israeli prime minister dropped to his knees, but Rathmarker marched into the center of the sacred chamber, knocking aside a golden plate of incense that sat on top of the ancient ark of the covenant. Calmly, the vice president returned to the microphone.

"No longer will Damian Gianardo be known as President. As of this moment, his title shall be World Emperor, and I will be Prime Minister. Our authority extends over matters of state *and* religion. As it is treason to resist the secular office, so shall it be sedition to oppose our religious authority. We will not allow anyone in the religious community to stand in the way of a completely peaceful world. Those two impostors by the Western Wall will submit to our rule or face the same penalty." Rathmarker stopped and glared at the Israeli prime minister. "No longer will religious charlatanism be tolerated in any form!"

An ominous quiet fell over the crowd. No one moved. Even some of the TV reporters let their cameras slide to the ground. People stared in terrified awe. Gianardo's twisted smile had a sinister leer of total self-satisfaction. He drank in the moment of stillness with complete fulfillment.

Rathmarker declared, "Today, I will be placing a life-size statue of Emperor Gianardo in the center of the Holy of Holies so no one forgets where ultimate control and authority lie. It's all a matter of principle!"

A reporter held up his hand. "Mr. Vice President?"

"Prime Minister!" Rathmarker barked.

"Yes, sir. Mr. Prime Minister, what if the Israelis resist your control of their religion?"

"I expect some resistance here as well as in America. We have foreseen the possibility. After our troops secure the nuclear sites, they will systematically execute all citizens in Israel who refuse to worship the emperor or attempt in any way to block these actions. In addition, a special task force is now being created throughout the empire to deal with religious disobedience in similar fashion. As is true of all forms of national betrayal, noncompliance must be a capital offense. We will be dispatching troops to take the Bozrah-Petra area under our control to demonstrate that no sanctuaries escape our surveillance. Nothing will stop the establishment of a complete world order of tranquility and harmony. It is a matter of principle!"

"I am completely overwhelmed." Ben turned to Cindy. "We are sitting here in your parents' living room watching everything that we have studied for months unfold on the TV screen. I actually saw the president and vice president walk into the Holy of Holies and declare emperor worship. Did you hear what Rathmarker said? Opposition to their religious ideas will be sedition. They think they are going to be able to attack Bozrah!"

Cindy's sightless eyes were focused somewhere just above the TV set. "He won't get far if he tries to invade God's desert asylum. Jimmy has been right about everything. Now we know that the days ahead are truly numbered."

"I almost wish I didn't know. If the Tribulation is anything like we've studied, I cringe in fear. I don't know if we can stand up to the days before us."

I had been standing behind the couch watching the television, waiting for the right moment to give Ben his instructions. The time had come. Once more I stepped through the time barrier and stood behind the couple.

Sam looked and barked.

"Someone's here!" Cindy jumped.

"Be not afraid," I said softly.

Ben leaped up from the couch. "Michael! You're here!"

"Yes," I said as I walked in front of them. "The moment has arrived for me to give your complete instructions. Events are moving quickly. The next three years will seem like both an eternity and a flash of time. Some days will feel totally unbearable, but in retrospect they will be a blur. I want you to know beyond any doubt that you can and will survive. Long ago you were chosen for these assignments because we knew that your family had the capacity and the ability to endure during these last times."

"My family?"

"The Feinbergs are of the tribe of Levi. Even though you have largely ignored your heritage, you come from the priestly lineage. You carry a godly capacity to stand before the heavenly Father on behalf of others. Once again your family will fulfill their call."

"We're not prepared for such a thing . . ."

"To the contrary! Who has a better analytic mind than you, Ben? You're the family chess master. Your ability to strategize will serve your survival needs quite well."

"But my parents?"

"The Holy Spirit will be drawing multitudes of Jews to Bozrah. Many will need medical attention, but far more will be so traumatized by the catastrophes unfolding around them that their emotional care will be paramount. The members of your family are extremely well equipped for the work. The hand of God will protect the area, and no one will be able to hurt them."

Cindy slowly raised her hand. "You said 'survive.' Sounds like Ben's going to be a general in a war. That's scary."

"Sit down, children. Listen well."

Ben picked up a pencil and a pad.

"Gianardo has committed the ancient sin of Babel, thinking he can stand tall enough to shoot an arrow into the heart of God. Even as we speak, secret security squads are being organized. Nothing is left to restrain this man's arrogance."

"What can we possibly do?" Cindy shook her head. "A blind oriental girl and a Messianic Jew aren't going to make much difference."

"To the contrary, Cindy. You are going to become our counterintelligence operation. In some instances, you will automatically know what to do. At other times, I will direct you to the people you are to contact. You will be bringing hope and insight during these final days. The first point of contact will be with your fellow students at UCLA where you will continue your studies."

"Amazing," Ben sighed. "I'm going from pre-med to mid-Trib! I know that we will be in grave danger but what an adventure!"

"We know you have a heart for the task. Ben, you are one of the 144,000 chosen ones mentioned in the book of Revelation. No one can harm you in any way."

"Please tell us everything you can," Cindy pleaded. "We'll need all the insight you have for us."

"First, I want you, Ben, to move your operation to a more secluded place. I will lead you to an obscure house in the country that will become your center of ministry. Next, you need to share all of this information with the McCoys. They will assist you in your outreach. The four of you will form the core of our activities."

"I can't wait to share your instruction with my parents. We have shortwave contact."

"You must be very cautious, Ben. As soon as Gianardo's secret police are fully functional, they will have the capacity to monitor radio contact. Be cautious what you transmit.

"Although you have been raised in a world of television violence, no one is prepared for what is ahead. All sense of proportion will be lost. People will kill indiscriminately with the ease of swatting flies. They will not hesitate to slaughter anyone who does not have the 666 mark or who negates the so-called world emperor's authority. Treachery will abound and life will be cheap. Do you understand?"

"We will be taking the message of Yeshua into this world," Cindy answered. "Like secret ambassadors?"

"Exactly. You will be surprised to discover how many people will want to hear. You will be equally astonished at how quickly and with total callousness others will betray."

"We will be in constant danger?" Ben laid the pad aside.

"You will not, Ben, because none of the 144,000 will be harmed. But Cindy is volunteering to risk her life with no guarantees of safety. Are you willing, Cindy?"

"Yes, I am!" Cindy replied emphatically but also with some fear. Ben had tears in his eyes at the thought of Cindy's being less protected than he was.

Michael continued, "Let us begin with the first message I want transmitted immediately to your father. You must do so before the radio detection systems are operational. Tell him that there are a million people between Bozrah and Petra. As long as they stay within the protected boundaries of these cities, absolutely nothing can harm them. Should they step outside God's prescribed spiritual fence, little can save them. Jordanian and Syrian troops will soon be directed toward the area. Egyptian and Saudi Arabian troops will go up from the south and the east. Tell your father to pay no attention to these armies, for intervention is impossible. Nevertheless, they should begin building a hospital for the many people who will be coming in from the outside.

"Ben, tomorrow you are to call into the dean's office and report that you are sick. We want to quietly prepare the way for you to ease out of UCLA. I am going to direct you to a house located near Lancaster. Ultimately, that place will become your home and center of ministry."

"What can we expect next?" Cindy reached for Ben's hand.

"The pale horse of the Apocalypse has already begun to ride, my children. The angel of death has been unleashed on the world. War, famine, plagues, and wild animals will be used as vehicles of judgment. The alarm is being sounded, and none will be able to say that they were not warned. You will see great consternation everywhere. Fear not. The Lord Yeshua is with you to the very end of the age. I always stand in the shadows."

Across the city, the McCoys sat glued to their television. As the last words of the emperor's speech faded, Joe turned the set off. "Now, children, do you see the truth? This is exactly what your mother and I have been telling you would happen."

"Great guess, Dad," Joe, Jr., shrugged. "But I had a hunch that religion was the next thing that Gianardo would go for. After all, he's already picked up most of the chips."

Jennifer shook her hands at the ceiling. "Children! This is a life-and-death matter. Don't you understand what's ahead?"

"Sure," Joe, Jr., said forcefully. "I'd shelf all that religion talk you've been into with the Feinbergs. You could get all of us into a lot of trouble."

"Please, Mom," fifteen-year-old Erica begged, "get rid of those Bibles. One of my friends might see them and think that Joe and I approve of what you're doing."

"Children," their father begged with tears in his eyes, "you've got to change your minds. We're not only trying to avoid trouble. Our eternal destiny is at stake. Don't you understand?"

"Let's not get back into this fanaticism thing again," Joe, Jr., said insolently. "Please drop it before we end up in another family fight."

# CHAPTER

# 17

Larry Feinberg urged his horse forward. The desert air was hot and dry. Sam Eisenberg rode quietly at his side. The animals carefully picked their way through the piles of rock. Overhead, the overpowering cliffs were so high that they shut the sun out.

"I thought you'd like to take a closer look at Petra," Sam said. "We really didn't get a good look when you first came to Bozrah. Fascinating place."

"Great idea, Sam. We had to take a break anyway, waiting for that lumber to arrive for the hospital. How much longer are we going to be able to get such large supplies?"

Sam shook his head. "Too many people coming in. We've been able to get around the blockades that the empire's soldiers imposed on the main highway. One of these days they'll find our side roads. Before long, people will be able to take only what they can carry. One day soon Gianardo will unleash his threatened attack on us."

"There's the El Khazneh! The great Treasury of the past." Larry pointed at a huge crevice ahead of them and kicked his horse.

"The Arabs call the entry the Siq. The canyon walls are three hundred feet high at the entry."

Sparks flew as the horse hooves struck the flint

rocks. The two men stopped in front of the massive thirteen-story building carved out of the cliff. Light slipped through from the top, highlighting the red columns and carvings on the overwhelming structure.

"The Nabataeans ruled the desert and controlled the trade routes from El Khazneh." Sam pointed up to the statues that adorned the top level of the building. "At one time, they must have kept a fortune locked inside."

"And you think the apostle Paul stayed here?"

"Many scholars believe the hidden desert years after Paul's conversion were spent in this very place. Maybe he even watched the workmen carve this incredible monument to the power of the Nabataean kings."

Suddenly, the ground began to shake. The horses shied and shook nervously. An ominous rumbling sound arose from the ground. Rocks began to bounce from cliffs.

"Earthquake!" Sam yelled. "Quick, get inside the Treasury."

The horse spun and resisted the hard kicks. When a boulder landed five feet from Larry, his horse bolted forward, nearly hurling him backward out of the saddle. Both men raced between the red stone columns into the black interior of the edifice. They dismounted and tried to quiet the nervous horses, but the shaking floor sent them sprawling. The panicky horses darted toward the back of the huge chamber.

"We'll be killed," Larry gasped. "The building can't stand the strain."

Rocks pelted the earth like hail. Sickening grinding sounds and dust filled the air. After about a minute, the tremor stopped. Both men lay completely still, covering their heads with their arms. The terrified horses beat the ground with their hooves.

"Is it over?" Larry ventured.

"Look's like it." Sam staggered to his feet.

"In all my years in southern California, I never experienced one like that! Only God saved us."

"Let's get out of this building before an aftershock

hits." Sam slowly and cautiously tried to get his horse's reins. "We need to leave this canyon as quickly as possible."

"Immediately." Larry led his horse out. "But I don't think we need to worry. If there ever was a test of God's promise to protect us, we just went through it. There's no other explanation for that mountain of rock not falling on our heads."

"Look up." Sam pointed to the rim of the canyon. "The sky is filled with smoke and airplanes."

"There's an attack going on somewhere." Larry shielded his eyes. "I've got a feeling that we just survived another of God's signs to the world."

"Let's get back to Bozrah as quickly as possible and see what the radio can tell us. By the time we get there, the evening news ought to have some word about what we've lived through."

When the two men rode into Bozrah, the sun was sinking in the sky. Multitudes of people were wandering around the streets and the tent city that had sprung up. After an Arab believer helped with their horses, they went to Larry's house where the transmitter was kept.

Angie saw them coming and ran out to her husband. "Thank God, you're not hurt. We thought the town would fall down around us, but not one building seems to be damaged. We were terrified!"

Sam hugged his wife. "Let's see what Larry can find on the radio. Something big went down today."

Larry flipped the switch of the electric generator and turned on the radio. "I'll try the international station." Larry finally tuned the radio. Other residents of the community crowded around.

For a moment, only static came out. Then an English-speaking voice broke. "Seismographic equipment indicates an epicenter fifty miles north of the obscure and ancient area of Bozrah. The Richter scale has measured a frightening 8. Early reports indicate that as many as five thousand soldiers of the New Roman

Empire patrolling the roads were killed by the tremor. Reports are vague because reconnaissance in the area has not been possible. Equally strange are the radar jamming and confusion occurring in the same locale. For some strange and unexplained reason, jets were flying to attack a target in the same area. Many of these planes crashed into each other. No one is sure of the actual losses since a news blackout has been imposed."

"The Lord *has* saved us. Ben's report and warning were exactly right. Those planes and troops were aimed at us, but we were completely protected."

"Terrible earthquake in Israel earlier today." A girl in Cindy's psychology class leaned over. "Just saw the television news. Lots of casualties among our troops. I'm worried."

"I hadn't heard the report," Cindy said calmly.

"My brother's in the army," the girl continued. "I don't know what in the world we're doing over there anyway. Why can't we leave that little country alone?"

"Israel is strategic in the plan of God."

"What?" The girl blinked. "I don't understand."

"Things are going to get much worse." Cindy smiled. "I hope your brother gets out of Israel before the really big disaster hits."

"Hits?" The girl pushed her closer. "What are you suggesting?"

"These unexpected events are a warning to us. If we heed them, we will be spared the pain that lies ahead."

"Where are you getting this stuff?"

"The Bible predicted exactly what's happening today over two thousand years ago. I simply study the Bible."

"Seriously?"

"Quite."

"Look," the girl whispered softly, "this subject could get us both in a lot of trouble . . . but I'm really worried about my brother. Would you tell me more?"

"I would count it an honor. My name is Cindy. What's yours?"

"Deborah. Deborah Whitaker."

"You've probably noticed that I'm blind. This is my guide dog, Sam." Sam perked up his ears.

"Well . . . yeah."

"No problem." Cindy grinned. "But if you'll wait after class and lead me to a place to talk, I would love to tell you *exactly* what's going to happen."

☐　☐　☐

Many miles to the south of the UCLA campus, Erica McCoy was sitting in a classroom in Newport Union Harbor High School. Students were piling into their chairs, completely ignoring the teacher who was trying to call the room to order. Mary Higbie, Erica's arch rival, sat next to her. Erica kept talking to a boy beside her in order to ignore Mary.

"Please!" The teacher rapped on her desk. "We have a special speaker. We need your unqualified attention for an important announcement."

The students continued talking as if nothing had been said. Erica flipped a paper wad at a boy several rows over.

"Stop it!" The teacher slammed a book on her desk. The boom echoed across the room. "What do I have to do to get your attention. Kill someone?"

Students jeered and applauded the suggestion but quieted down.

"We have a representative of the office of education. Now listen carefully to what he's got to say. Please welcome Mr. Robert Schultz."

A tall, lean man walked to the center of the room with an indifferent swagger. His voice was cold and hard. "I'm here to talk about abuse. As you know, the system takes all forms of abuse very seriously. Anyone who reports sexual, physical, or emotional abuse will receive immediate care and protection. We simply will not allow parents to take advantage of their children."

"Yippee!" A youth in the back row yelled. "Can you come out and work my old man over? He's been short on my allowance lately."

The class roared.

Schultz walked down the row until he stood in front of the youth. Suddenly, he lifted him completely out of the chair. "You have something to report?"

The astonished student's mouth dropped as he silently shook his head no.

"If you have nothing intelligent to say, don't interrupt." Schultz let the student drop back into the chair. His notebook went flying off the desk. "We're not out here playing with the kiddies." Schultz continued walking through the desks. "Abuse is serious business, and we take it seriously. Get it?"

The room was completely silent.

"Today we have identified a new form of abuse . . . religious abuse. Understand?"

No one spoke.

"The leader of our country is now the supreme authority on all religious matters. Noncompliance can be very deadly business. We are not going to allow rampant misrepresentation of religious truth to be disseminated through our society. Should your parents fail to comply, they could be putting you into jeopardy. Such action would constitute abuse."

"I don't understand." Erica held up her hand. "Please give me an example."

"If your parents try to force religious ideas on you that are not approved by Emperor Gianardo," Schultz spoke slowly, "or teach you that any power exceeds that of our leader, you are being put in an abusive situation."

"Do Christian ideas count?" Erica asked hesitantly.

"If they are used to avoid obedience to rules such as the 666 marking law. However, we are increasingly suspect of Bibles. Let us know if they push Bible beliefs on you."

Erica smiled back pleasantly, but her eyes were fixed wide open. As the man continued talking, Erica began making violent scribbling marks on the notebook on her desk. She didn't even realize that he had finished and sat down until Mary spoke in her ear.

"Didn't you say your parents are always putting fanatical stuff on you?"

Erica looked in horror at the smug grin on Mary's face. "Sure," Erica fumbled. "You know we all complain about our parents at home, but I didn't mean anything like this guy was describing."

"You said they were always studying the Bible," Mary bore down.

"Yes, but they read lots of porno too," Erica lied. "Just broad readers."

Mary smirked and looked the other way.

# 18

Ben closed the venetian blinds over the living room picture window before going to the back bedroom. He turned on only the small light on the wall. In the dim light, he carefully took the picture off the wall and set it on the floor. He pulled the old transmitter out of the hole in the wall and hooked up the wires. While he waited a few moments for the set to warm up, he slightly opened a blind over the small back door window in the kitchen so that he could see any movement outside. The radio cracked and hummed as the gauges moved back and forth. He glanced at his watch and saw that it was 2:00 A.M.

"Calling the Woman in the Desert, calling the Woman in the Desert," he spoke softly in the microphone.

"We're here." The answer sounded very distant and faint.

"Dad, that's you?"

"Hard to hear you, Son. Lots of electronic interference in the air since the atomic bombs went off."

"You're OK?" Ben talked low but with great intensity.

"Tired," Larry answered. "In the two months since the earthquake that caught us at Petra, we've nearly worked ourselves to death, but the hospital's coming along just fine. And you?"

"Been wild, Dad. But we're doing very well. The ministry is booming. Cindy brought a girl named Deborah Whitaker to the Lord, and in turn she brought her whole family. We've got over fifty people in our group now. We'll be moving the whole operation very soon to our new location. Can't tell you over the air where it is, but all looks good."

"Excellent, Son. We're praying for you every hour."

"People flocking into Bozrah?"

"Yes. Since the war broke out, people have been terrified. We've got everything here from Jews who were atheists to Hasidim who are now praising Yeshua just to be alive."

Static suddenly boomed with a deafening roar. Ben yanked the headset off and waited until the noise faded out again.

" Ben . . . Ben . . . you still there?" Slowly, Larry's voice became clear again.

"Yes, yes," Ben answered. "I'm back on."

"Radiation will be an increasing problem," Larry explained.

"Dad, that's why I'm calling tonight. We're not sure what's really happened. Gianardo has imposed a news blackout, and no one knows what's hit the United States or from where. We're afraid that a nuclear device may have gone off somewhere in the north LA area. We have no way to tell if fallout is occurring. At the very least a big bomb hit up there."

"We've pieced together reports coming out of Jerusalem, Amman, and some of Europe. Apparently, the United Muslim States, China, remnants of Russia, and the Ukraine revolted against the New Roman Empire. The Star Wars Strategic Defense System destroyed a high percentage of the missiles in the air, but a few must have slipped through. The U.S. has shot back many missiles and blasted these countries. No one is sure what damage has been done to the atmosphere, but it must be extensive. People are terrified of what may be ahead. Famine and disease are sure to follow."

"Got any idea of how many were killed?" Ben asked.

"Early estimates are that as many as half a billion people have perished or will die from the effects of the attack."

"Good grief!" Ben gasped. "No wonder Gianardo doesn't want anyone to know what's going on! What should we do?"

"I wish some of those old Geiger counters were still around, Son. Then again, you might not want to know. Watch the water supply. Food will soon be scarce. I guess it all depends on how bad the States were actually hit."

"Perhaps Michael can give us some clarification when he next appears. July 22 is just a few days away, and that's the Fast of Tammuz. I know he'll show then."

"Any word for us about Joe and Jennifer McCoy?"

"They're doing great! Really got a ministry going to parents of kids who are rejecting Jesus. We meet together several times a week. You and Mom would be very proud of what the McCoys have accomplished. How's everyone there?"

"You wouldn't recognize your mother. I bet she's lost twenty pounds out here in this desert heat. She's really helping with many of the children who have been injured. Jimmy and Ruth are doing a great job at the hospital."

Out of the corner of his eye, Ben saw a figure go past the back window. He jerked the headset off and listened intently. Somewhere out on the street, he heard a car door shut. Ben glanced at his watch again . . . 2:15 A.M. . . . no one should be out there.

"Got to run, Dad. Call back soon."

Without further explanation, Ben hit the toggle switch and shoved the transmitter back into the wall. He pushed the wires on top along with the microphone. Ben leaped from the chair and turned the light out.

In the darkness he put the picture back on the wall

and walked to the living room. Carefully, he looked out behind the large blinds covering the picture window. Across the street, three men were standing and talking. One man pointed to the house and waved his arm. A fourth man abruptly ran out of the bushes next door and darted behind a large tree in front of the house.

"Police!" Ben choked. "I've got to get out of here." He ran for the back door.

Just as he stepped into the kitchen he heard a stick break outside. Instantly, Ben dropped to his knees, huddled against the refrigerator next to the door, and listened intently.

"Now!" A bullhorn blasted from the front of the house. "Hit 'em!"

The back door crashed against the refrigerator as two large men broke in. The black figures flew past Ben into the living room. Glass exploded, sounding like the large picture window was smashed. Ben could hear the front door also breaking open.

"Move and you're dead!" A man shouted in the living room.

Ben realized that he had only seconds before lights would go on and they'd backtrack into the kitchen. He scampered through the open back door on his hands and knees and rolled down the steps. For a moment he scanned the backyard. Apparently, all the police were in the house. He crawled through the grass like a wounded dog heading for the nearest cover. At the back fence, Ben edged his way through the bushes and disappeared into the foliage.

Men continued to shout from the front of the house. Ben could hear doors slamming and more glass breaking. His heart was beating so fast that he felt weak and dizzy. Sweat was running down his neck, and his shirt was damp. He pushed himself backward toward the fence. To his amazement, he felt the boards give. The old wood panels were dangling by a few loose nails. Ben easily knocked them out and wiggled his way into the next yard.

Once he was on his feet he ran straight toward what looked like a gate. Something hit his knees, and he went sprawling into the grass with a metal table landing on top of him. The crash echoed across the yard like a truck hitting a tree. Dogs started barking inside the house.

"Oh, no!" The edges of a wrought iron coffee table ground into his chest. "Got to get out of here." He felt the sting of pain and a trickle of blood run down his shin. Ben hobbled to the gate as a light came on in a back bedroom.

Ben shook the gate hard, but it was locked. Without hesitation he went up the side and over the top. As he hit the ground, he knew a good hunk of his shirt was left on the top spike. A searchlight flashed on in the backyard behind him. He tore out for the street.

Only after running several blocks in the pitch-black night did Ben stop. Nearly exhausted, he fell behind a tree in a vacant lot. The air smelled hot, dingy, and smoky. His leg stung and his back was badly scratched. But at least there were no sounds of cars or men following him. An ominous silence hung over the area.

"Well," he said to himself, "we've got one more transmitter stashed. They haven't got us yet . . . but only *one* more left."

□ □ □

The next morning Ben met with the leaders of his college students' group at the McCoys' home. Jennifer passed out colas as the conversation unfolded. Ben described the details of the chase.

"How did they know you were in the house that we rented for radio transmission?" Isaiah Murphy asked.

"I don't know." Ben pondered the question. "I was sure no one was following me, and I waited until very late at night. I didn't really have the radio on that long . . ."

"They can get a fix quick if they're prepared," Joe McCoy countered.

"I remember looking at my watch. Seems like about fifteen minutes had passed."

"Plenty of time," Joe confirmed.

"We can bet they're on to us now," someone added.

"What do you think, George?" Ben asked a tall, lanky student. "Your father's a retired police officer. Could he give us any insight?"

George Abrams ran his hands through his thick black hair. "My dad doesn't say much these days. I think he's terrified. They went to church when he was a boy, and he knows a lot about Bible teaching, even though he never followed it. He's confused and just doesn't want me to get into trouble."

"I don't think we ought to contact our parents," Mary Chandler added. "We could end up putting people in jeopardy without any intention to do so. Matters are just too serious."

"I agree," Cindy added, "no one knows what the truth is anymore. The news is managed, and the secret police have surveillance equipment that we can't even begin to understand or detect."

"For those very reasons, I think we need to move out to Lancaster at once," Joe insisted. "We can watch what goes on in a small town much easier. The police have all the advantages in the metropolis. Once we're out on the edge of things, we can stay concealed."

"We must carefully cover our tracks," George added. "I don't think we ought to let the parents who meet with the McCoys know where we are. If we keep our two fronts of ministry separate, we'll have an additional safety factor."

"I agree," Joe beckoned for Jennifer to come in from the kitchen. "I think from this point on we need to have only one contact person between the two groups. We just can't take any chances."

"Why not me?" Cindy volunteered. "Since my parents live in the area, I'm a natural link. No one could be suspicious of my coming down here to visit the restaurant."

"I don't know," Ben hesitated. "I don't like the exposure."

"But *you* sure don't need to be wandering around down here," George confronted Ben. "A quick computer check of your family background would reveal that they left with passports for Israel. They'd nail you in a minute."

"In addition, you may have accidentally left some clues back at our meeting house," George reasoned.

"I suppose so," Ben waffled. "I'm just nervous about Cindy being pursued. Only my two very good eyes and the grace of God saved me the other night! I know Michael promised that no one could hurt me, but I'm still human. I get scared sometimes."

"We'll take good care of Cindy," Joe assured Ben. "Let's join hands and commit the plan to the Lord." Joe reached out for Isaiah and another student next to him. "We need to pray for protection for us, our families, and all of our contacts."

The group began praying for each other. Eventually, the prayers ended, and they prepared to leave into the summer night. Some left by the back door while others waited a while before going down the front driveway so they would not appear to have been meeting. After everyone else was gone, Ben, Cindy, and Sam left.

"Drive carefully," Jennifer called after them. "Your lives are precious."

Ben and Cindy talked all the way back to the campus about packing and planning for the relocation. Finally, they pulled in front of Cindy's dorm. Sam sat up in the back seat.

"The work is really going well." Ben smiled. "I'm amazed at how many students you have been able to reach. People seem to be especially attracted to your honesty."

"Perhaps my blindness is an asset. I'm easy to trust."

"Maybe so. I've also been amazed at the response

from the people Michael sent me to contact. The results have been equally exciting. I can't say that I miss the college scene much."

"I worry that the university will try to track you down."

"No, I'm just a person who dropped out of school for medical reasons." Ben opened the car door for Cindy. "I think my tracks are well covered. I don't see how they could possibly locate me unless I let myself get caught like I nearly did last night."

"Don't let that ever happen again!" Cindy mockingly scolded. "You're better at getting me around than my dog. You'd be hard to replace!"

They kissed each other good night, and Ben hurried back to his apartment.

☐ ☐ ☐

I waited until the next morning to talk with Ben. I knew the attack caused him to lose track of time. Without a sound I slipped through the wall of time into his apartment. After turning on Ben's automatic coffee maker, I sat down in a bedroom chair waiting for him to wake up. Shortly, he stirred and reached for the clock.

"Good morning, Ben."

The alarm clock hit the floor. Ben sat straight up in bed. "Who is it?" he shouted.

"I thought you'd recognize my voice by now."

"Don't you ever knock?" Ben looked disgusted. "You scared me silly."

"I apologize. I just wanted to get the day started right for you. Important day, you know."

Ben frowned and reached down to pick up the alarm clock. "Why?"

"It is July 22, 1997. The Fast of Tammuz."

"Already?" Ben blinked. "How did it get here so fast?" He got out of bed and put his pants on. "Let me get a shirt. No telling what's next."

"Actually, nothing you can see today, Ben. Pour yourself a cup of coffee and I will explain."

"Coffee?" Ben stared uncomprehending at the coffee steaming in the kitchen.

"Today a new phase of the Tribulation begins. The Lord Jesus will break the Fifth Seal that John writes about in the Revelation. Seventy thousand saints have died so far during the persecutions and have been kept under the heavenly altar. Today their cries to be avenged will be heard, and the next period of woes begins."

"So, we start again." Ben drank a sip of coffee and sat down at the kitchen table. "The police got very close the other night, Michael. I was really terrified."

"Yes, I know. Perhaps I should clarify some things about your situation. There is no place in the world that is completely protected except the Bozrah-Petra area. Even there, people are still subject to the normal bodily processes like heart attacks, strokes, or injuries. You are living in a genuine war zone.

"You must start now to get ready for what is ahead, and I want you to let your parents know about the next catastrophe. You must also understand what the atomic exchange has done to the world."

"We really *did* get hit?"

"Indeed. Skin diseases will multiply like a plague. You must wash your body often and carefully. Wear long-sleeved clothing and a hat. Expect problems. Crops will fail and food will be in short supply. Animals will go on savage rampages. Wild dogs will roam the streets. Take no chances."

"No kidding!"

"The nuclear explosions have produced large amounts of nitrogen oxides, which are quickly depleting the ozone layer. Great amounts of dirt are beginning to settle into the atmosphere as well. In addition, nuclear fireballs have set many fires around the world. Hundreds of tons of smoke and soot have been released from the burning cities. The nuclear winter is coming that will drop temperatures by an average of thirty degrees in northern Europe, Russia, Canada, and the northern United States. Spring crops will be destroyed next year, and the rains will spread radiation that impedes photosynthesis."

Ben took another long drink of coffee. "What will the results look like when it hits people . . . us?"

"People will feel nauseated and tired, and many will vomit. They will feel better for a while, but they will be developing fewer and fewer white blood cells, antibodies, and platelets. Infections will be hard to fight, and many people will lose their hair. Others will suffer severe weight loss and struggle with internal bleeding. Skin lesions and cancers will be quite common. The degree of injury will depend on how long people are exposed to concentrated radiation."

"And these effects will increase as the days go by?"

"Unfortunately."

Ben set the cup down and looked out the window. "It's going to be a long summer. And what can we expect at the end of the period?"

"In about a month . . . on Tuesday, August 12 . . . Av 9 comes down again. At sunrise in Jerusalem, the Sixth Seal will be broken, and the most violent upheaval the world has ever known will shake the very foundations of creation."

"And I am to tell my parents everything you have said?"

"Yes. They must be prepared for the bad condition people seeking refuge will be in. You must be in a safe location when the earthquakes come, for I tell you nothing of this magnitude has ever befallen the globe."

"I'll get to the transmitter as soon as I can. By the way, Michael, any help you can give me along the way will be appreciated. Something simple would do fine . . . like a warning that the bad guys are coming."

"Fear not, Ben. Great is your reward in heaven."

# 19

It was now the summer of 1997 and the hot August sun blazed down on Ben's car pulling away from the hamburger stand on the edge of the little town of Lancaster. The aroma of relish and onions filled the car. As he drove down Highway 14, Ben described the scenery to Cindy. "Everything's burned up. The grass is brown and even the weeds are dried up."

"Typical summer scene in southern California." Cindy wiped the perspiration from her forehead. "But it seems much hotter now."

"The dust of death is everywhere." Ben sped up as he left the reduced speed zone behind. "Earth's atmosphere has been severely damaged. I've never seen so many dead animals by the roadside."

"Maybe being blind isn't all bad."

"But I wish you could see my little farmhouse. The place is great." Ben slowed down to turn off the highway. "Everything is just like Michael said it would be. I really got a deal. I was able to lease it for almost nothing because of the economic chaos. Perfect for our ministry."

"Can you see the house yet?"

The car bounced on the ruts on the dirt road, sending clouds of dust across the field. "Just straight ahead.

Looks like at least a dozen cars are already there. The gang is helping put the place together."

Ben pulled under a small carport and helped Cindy out. Sam jumped out behind her. Ben picked up the sacks in one arm and then guided Cindy along the side of the house and up the few steps onto the porch of the old farmhouse. "It's sort of faded," he confided, "but it's still white and is over sixty years old. Was built well by some Okies who came out during the depression years. There's a huge oak tree on the other side of the house."

"Welcome home!" Joe McCoy swung the screen door open. "We almost have your things in order."

"Great!" Ben waved at the students working around the house.

Deborah Whitaker stuck her head out of the kitchen. "Place looks like you've already lived here, Ben. The sink is a national disaster area, and the cockroaches are holding their national drag race finals behind the refrigerator. Only a man could cultivate such a climate."

"Now, now, Debbie." George came down the stairs from the second floor. "Don't be a female chauvinist piglet. Ben, we got your bed put together by the window. You can see completely up and down the highway. No one will sneak up on you from that perch."

"Wow! What a job you've done! Cindy and I brought you some hamburgers. Let's stop for lunch."

George bounded over the stair rail and hit the nearest chair before anyone could take a step. "Don't have to say food but once to a growing boy." He sprawled his lanky legs out on the bare wooden floor.

I"m fixing a pitcher of lemonade," Jennifer McCoy added from the kitchen. "I'll call the kids who are working out back."

The small living room was soon filled with college students reaching for hamburgers, fries, and lemonade. They prayed, laughed, teased, and devoured the food.

"We've got the transmitter wired up." Mary Chandler told Ben. "I think we've found a good place to keep it protected when the big quake comes."

Mary pointed upstairs. "We've got all the electronic equipment inside a metal box, and it's surrounded with foam rubber padding. If the house falls in, the equipment will make it."

"What a job you've done!" Ben beamed. "How can I ever thank you?"

"Thank us?" the group echoed.

"How can we ever thank *you?*" Deborah answered. "You and Cindy have brought life itself to us. Without you, we would all be hopelessly entangled in the lies and the destruction devouring the world. You have been our lifeline to eternal survival."

"We are just grateful that God chose to use us." Ben reached out for Cindy's hand. "The truth is that anyone who really desires to be righteous or find the true God will find the way even if an angel has to be dispatched. We owe a great debt to our friend Michael. Actually, we found you because Michael directed us."

George pointed to several students. "We Jews came to the Lord through your witness, Ben. No matter what lies ahead we will live and die with the supreme satisfaction that we found what our ancestors prayed to be. God has surely fulfilled our deepest longings and greatest hopes."

"And we've become great friends," Ben added. "I've found a friendship among you that I've never known before." He stopped and the room became very quiet.

Cindy squeezed his hand. "Why don't we try the radio out?" She broke the awkward silence. "Let's call Bozrah."

"Terrific idea." Mary stood up. "We can show you our handiwork. Let's go upstairs." The group fell in behind her and piled up the steps. Mary led them to a sparsely furnished room with only a table and chair in one corner. At the bottom of one wall was a large metal grate covering the heating duct. "Watch this!" Mary dropped to one knee and pulled the cover off. She slid a metal box out of the wall. "Rather clever, I'd say." She opened the top and lifted the transmitter out. "We're ready to talk to the world."

"We've made a new hookup." George put a small speaker on the table and plugged in the wires. "You won't have to use a headset and we can hear."

"Excellent." Ben carefully fine-tuned the dials. "Calling the Woman in the Desert," he repeated several times. Static crackled over the speaker and humming filled the room. "Come in, Woman in the Desert."

"Hello . . . hello . . . ," the voice sounded low, far away but familiar.

"Jimmy? Jimmy? Is that you?"

"Hey, Ben." Static broke in. "It's me. The old used car salesman."

The group cheered. "You've got an audience here," Ben explained. "The whole gang of believers are with me."

"Can't sell you any cars today," Jimmy's voice crackled. "But I've got a couple of low mileage camels with lots of tread left."

"Save us a couple. How's the family? Ruth? Mom?"

"Of course, it's night here in Bozrah, and Mom has turned in. Ruth is out at the hospital. Ought to be here shortly. Been a busy, hard day, but everyone's healthy. People just keep showing up. The pronouncements by Moses and Elijah are having their effect. More and more are believing."

"People in bad shape?"

"Yeah," Jimmy drawled with his Texas accent. "The world's falling apart and so are the people. Ruth and I work from sunup to sundown, but we love every minute of it. Wouldn't have missed the trip for the world."

"Ready for the earthquake?"

"We think so, but we're not sure what God's special protection will mean. We can only go by the quake

earlier in the summer. We expect to feel effects but not
suffer damage. We are far more worried about you.
Southern California is not a great place for a really big
shake."

"I know, I know," Ben sighed. "The whole group will
be out here with us when it comes. At least we'll be
away from LA where the big catastrophes will happen.
We think we're prepared."

"We'll be praying for you."

"Better sign off," Ben concluded. "Don't want to stay
on too long in case we've got any eavesdroppers. So
long until the next visit."

"Peace!" Static filled the speaker.

Ben switched the set off. Everyone applauded.

"It worked!" Isaiah shouted. "We're beating the system!" Someone clapped. "More lemonade for a toast,"
George demanded. The entourage rushed for the door
and stampeded down the stairs.

"Cindy . . . ," Jennifer stopped at the door. "Could I
ask you for a favor?"

"Of course."

"We can't bring the children out here." Jennifer's face
suddenly looked drawn and sober. "We would only endanger the whole mission. We will have to stay behind
with them."

"Oh, no!" Cindy protested.

"No. Joe and I have already discussed the matter.
They could easily betray us because of their flippant
attitude. We will try to take them to another safe place.
But I was hoping that you might at least witness to
Erica before next Tuesday. It's almost our last hope."

Cindy's brow furrowed. "You know that I would do
anything in the world for you and certainly to help the
children. But . . . it . . . seems only the people that Michael directs us to or that seek our help respond. And
he warned when we go beyond those boundaries we
could be in serious jeopardy. I just wouldn't want to
raise any false hopes."

"Sure, I understand. I guess Joe and I are getting desperate."

Cindy hugged her friend. "I'll see her tomorrow if you'll set it up. Don't give it another thought."

"Well," Jennifer hedged, "maybe we ought not . . ."

"Tomorrow," Cindy insisted. "I'll pray and do my best."

□   □   □

"Ruth!" Jimmy pushed the microphone to the back of the table. "You just missed Ben. Things are going great with them."

"Oh, rats!" Ruth plopped down in a chair. "I've not talked to them in two weeks. Are they ready for the other shoe to drop next week?"

"Sounds like they are. I tried to be optimistic, but I'm not sure that we are. I don't think anyone can really get ready for what's coming."

Larry abruptly walked into the room with exposed studs and rafters. There were no windows; only holes in the siding let the breeze blow through the single room. "Couldn't help overhearing you outside. Sorry that I missed Ben."

"He's moved into the new house. The transmitter worked fine."

"Good." Larry sat down in a simple wooden chair. "I just don't know how we're going to care for this multitude. So many are suicidal. They've lived with stories of the World War II Holocaust all of their lives, and now history is repeating itself. Obviously, Gianardo acts like Hitler reincarnated. It's too much for many of them to bear."

"Is it true that another psychiatrist has come in?" Ruth asked. "I heard people talking at the hospital."

"Yes. Frank Kohl is a Christian who escaped from Germany. Amazing man. I'm sending him to Petra to work with the people camped down there. He's going to help lift the load by treating the psychotic ones."

Jimmy stood up and stretched his legs. "We didn't build the hospital big enough. We're going to need a lot more space. But then again the whole thing may collapse next week."

Larry laughed. "What a gem you are, Son. You've done an outstanding job supervising the men and working with the Arabs. No, I've got a hunch that the hand of God is going to be good to those walls you've put up. Just maybe we'll see the story of Jericho repeated in reverse form."

"I pray so." Jimmy looked at the blisters on his hands. "I'd hate to start over again."

Larry put the chair against the wall. "I think I'll turn in. Dawn comes mighty early around here. You two take care of yourselves and turn out the lights when you leave."

"Sure, Dad." Ruth called after him.

Ruth and Jimmy shut the door behind them and walked out into the brisk night air. The dry heat of the summer day had given way to the cool of the desert night. The sky was filled with stars.

"Great night." Jimmy looked at the silhouette of the black mountains against the dark sky.

Ruth put her arm around his shoulder. "We've come a long way since that summer afternoon two years ago when you made your little declaration of moral principles to my parents. Who would ever have believed it would lead to this place?"

"Seems like a million years ago on another planet."

"It was another time. An age that is gone. Disappeared. Vanished in the twinkling of an eye."

Jimmy looked at the camp fires dotting the hillside. "Sometimes I feel so set adrift. Everything I once held to is gone. Of course, my faith sustains me, but if I didn't have you, Ruth, I think I'd come unglued."

"You make me so very happy." Ruth's eyes filled with tears. "I didn't dream I could find a man who would be so thoughtful and considerate. So loving."

"You're crying?"

"I'm just overcome. I'm so happy. Here I am in the midst of this unmitigated chaos with the world exploding, and I am deliriously happy with you. That's why I'm crying."

"Just don't ever leave me." Jimmy suddenly hugged Ruth. "You are my life."

The young lovers walked toward their little wooden house on the edge of the tent city. People noticed them and nodded respectfully as they passed by.

□　　□　　□

The next afternoon Jennifer drove Cindy to the McCoys' house. As she led Cindy up the walk, Jennifer explained, "Erica and a group of girls are working on cheerleading yells. They should be going home shortly. I'll let you know when I think Erica's friends are gone. There's quite a bunch of them."

"Why have your children been so resistant?"

"Painful question." Jennifer opened the front door. "I anguish over that issue, and I'm not sure that I fully understand the answer yet. Joe and I were good parents even though we were gone a great deal of the time when Joe, Jr., and Erica were small. We couldn't support a southern California life-style on one salary. I guess today you'd label our children as affluent latchkey kids. Perhaps the lack of contact developed their tendency to give more credence to their friends. That's sure the way they are now."

Cindy felt for a chair. "Just pray that I can get through to her today." Sam lay down at her feet.

"I'm going to take you outside to the backyard and let you sit by the gate. A couple of comfortable chairs are there. When the squad leaves, I'll send Erica out with a glass of lemonade."

Noise echoed from fence to fence as the girls yelled, danced, and waved pompoms. Cindy sat in her obscure corner listening. Sam watched the scene intently. In about twenty minutes the rehearsal ended, and the laughing voices drifted away.

"Mother said to bring you this drink," Erica's familiar voice jolted Cindy out of her prayer.

"Erica!" Cindy turned toward the sound. "Sit down. I haven't talked to you in weeks."

"Well," Erica was hesitant and distant, "I have to leave with my friends. We're meeting some guys for pizza. I really can't stay."

Cindy felt the cold glass touch her hand. "Erica, we might never have the opportunity to speak together again. I've got to say several things to you. The hand of God is moving very quickly."

"Please," Erica begged, "we shouldn't be talking about religious stuff. I know you're sincere, but you and my parents are playing with fire."

Cindy set the glass down and took the teenager's hand. "In a few days the earth is going to be nearly shaken out of orbit. We're all going to slosh around like terrified fish in a goldfish bowl. Nothing of this magnitude has ever happened. Most of what you see around you will collapse."

"Look," Erica's voice was hushed, "I'm sure you believe these things, but some of these kids would turn us in to the authorities just for laughs. I have enough trouble making sure my parents' Bibles are well hidden when the girls are over here."

"I understand . . ." Cindy looked down. "I really *do* understand, but your eternal destiny is at stake. Even if something terrible happened to me, I would do everything I could to tell you about Jesus."

"You're a very good person, Cindy. Kind. Giving. I've watched you when you've been here with Ben. But the world doesn't have a place for people like you anymore, and I have to go on living with some of these creeps who call themselves my friends. I must leave religion alone for the good of everybody."

"Erica, no one has much time left. The days are numbered. In a very short while your friends and their opinions won't matter. They *will not* be here. But God has a plan for your life for today and for all of your tomorrows."

"Look." Erica chewed her lip. "After next week, I'll listen. I've got to catch up with the gang now. But I'll talk if you'll just wait until then."

"I'm going to be praying for you. I'll ask God to keep you through what's coming Tuesday. There is no power on earth greater than the Lord Jesus."

Suddenly, the backyard gate swung open. Mary Higbie stepped in and stared at both of them. "I wondered where the God talk was coming from."

"M . . . Mary! You . . . you've been listening!" Erica stammered.

"I came back to find you. The girls are waiting. I just happened to come in the back way."

"Mary?" Cindy asked uncomprehendingly.

"You Christian freaks!" Mary sneered at Cindy.

"I don't understand," Cindy answered vaguely. "Who are you?"

"Really weird conversation, Erica." Mary smirked. "I thought your family was straight. Next thing we know you'll be leading cheers for Jesus." The girl spun on her heels and ran toward the car waiting in the driveway.

"Mary!" Erica darted after her. "Mary! Stop it!" Her voice trailed away as she chased her old nemesis. "Please. Don't make something out of nothing."

Cindy heard the door slam and the car drive away. The backyard seemed intensely silent. "Michael warned me," she said to herself. "He cautioned me about just such a danger."

# 20

Gianardo quickly looked around the Oval Office in the White House and glanced at his watch. He glared at the adviser standing in front of his desk next to Prime Minister Rathmarker. "Monday's a busy day," he snapped. "It's almost five o'clock, and I have things to do this evening. I think this whole idea is nonsense and you are being reactionary."

"Mr. Emperor," the prime minister cleared his throat, "I think we need to consider carefully some hard data in this report."

"Take seriously the prediction by those two Israeli impostors?" Gianardo raised his eyebrows and rolled his eyes. "Been listening to the prime-time show put on by those actors calling themselves Moses and Elijah? I consider their warnings of an impending earthquake to be in a class with Elvis sightings."

"Sir." The adviser handed a stapled report to both Gianardo and the prime minister. "We are not reacting to the press speculations or popular fascination with those men sitting by the Western Wall."

"Then why the sudden investigation of possible earthquakes?" Gianardo snarled. "I'm not about to let the world think that I am even slightly affected by those two freaks. I remain the primary religious authority as well as the political authority. Do you understand?"

"Absolutely." The aide smiled nervously. "We will release nothing but your insights and personal warnings."

"Forget that." Gianardo opened the file. "No matter what you've found, we are not going to appear preempted by those two frauds." The emperor scanned the page. "What's your reading, Jacob?"

Jacob Rathmarker puckered his lips and hesitated. "All the indicators point to the immediate possibility of a massive shift of the Eurasian Plate down to a depth of sixty miles below the surface. Hard facts here suggest the Scotia Plate below South America and the Caribbean Plate would also move. Several scientists including our major adviser, Terbor L. Esiw, are convinced that a corresponding shift would result in the Philippine Plate as well as the Somali Plate off the coast of Africa. A big danger to ignore!"

"Sir." The aide flipped through the pages. "Look at the bottom of page eight. The diagram clearly indicates what could happen in this country. The Juan de Fuca Plate near Mount Saint Helens is likely to move. Of course, the San Andreas Fault would shift. No one can possibly calculate the extent of the chain reaction that would follow."

"But you want me to warn people that something *could* happen in a couple of hours because it coincides with the sunrise in Israel ushering in the ninth of Av!" Gianardo charged. "Impossible. Every religious nut on both sides of the ocean would claim that I'm about to abdicate my position of religious preeminence and have a conversion experience. Anyway, there's nothing here that says exactly when such a shift of the Eurasian Plate might occur. Who knows? Maybe it will happen in thirty minutes or in a hundred years. At best I'll wait until Av 9 is over."

"Our fears are that the recent atomic exchange has created immediate pressure," the aide argued.

"Well . . . ," the prime minister paused. "I'm obviously not going to be seen as reacting to the warnings of Moses and Elijah or whoever they are. We haven't been able to kill the two freaks so they obviously have some sort of supernatural powers. But I'm going to make sure that I'm protected during the next twenty-four hours."

"Like where?" Gianardo shrugged. "If such a big shake comes, there are no guarantees of safety anywhere. Even a cave might fall in."

"We were thinking of calling for a military alert at least," the aide ventured.

"No chance." Gianardo tossed the report aside. "I've got more pressing matters. Come back tomorrow after those two clowns by the Western Wall have been discredited, and I'll talk about future precautions. Let's not forget who is running the world these days." Gianardo pounded the table. "Me!"

□   □   □

The entire UCLA Bible study group worked frantically, making their last-minute arrangements at Ben's farmhouse. Jugs of water were being lined up outside and furniture stacked out of the way.

"What time is it?" George asked.

"It's 7:30 P.M. West Coast time," Mary answered. "We've only got about fifteen minutes left. We need to hurry."

"Put the metal box with the electronic equipment out in the open," Ben pointed to a space in front of the house. "Sure don't want anything to fall on that precious commodity."

Cindy felt her way along the walls. "Is all the food secure?" she called out.

"Got enough for two weeks." Ben passed her, carrying a large sack of cans. "We should be able to wait out whatever comes. I sure hope Michael shows up. A little insight would be really appreciated."

"Since the ninth of Av is almost here, I'm sure he'll visit soon," Cindy added.

"Everybody outside," Ben called. "I want us to sit in a circle out here in the open where we're completely away from anything that could fall. The cars are scattered far enough away from the house that they won't be touched unless the earth opens up."

The students spread blankets on the ground well in front of the farmhouse. Each had a Bible. Even though it was nearly 7:45 P.M., the summer sun was well above the horizon line. Sam began to pace nervously. He sniffed the air and began a low growl.

"I sure wish that the McCoys were with us," Cindy told Ben. "I'm very concerned about them."

"Joe said they were taking their kids out if they had to tie them in the back seat. Maybe the trip will shake some sense into their little heads. I think they were going to drive toward the Sultan Sea and sit out the shake in a flat area."

"I hope they took plenty of food." Cindy sat down on the blanket. "They may have a hard time getting back into the Newport Beach area."

The students huddled around Ben. "In just moments the sun will rise over Jerusalem, and the Lord Yeshua will break the Sixth Seal. When He opens the scroll, He will proclaim judgment on those who have unrepentant hearts. Each of the signs that we have witnessed is a warning to the world to turn from wickedness. Tragically, the sinful are blinded by their own perversity and will not read the warnings that the earth itself is giving us. Even Emperor Gianardo must be using gross denial."

Ben felt unsteady and looked down. The ground moved slightly. Students looked at each other in wonder. "I think it's really happening," someone exclaimed.

"Remember He is with us." Ben looked nervously around the group. "No matter what happens, the Lord Yeshua will not abandon us." Suddenly, he fell backward.

A deafening rumble seemed to be rising out of the earth and from the hills as the ground shifted back and forth. Ben rolled to one side as he reached for Cindy's hand. Sam began to bark and howl. The blankets began to move up and down, and the entire field shifted and turned like a giant carpet being readjusted. The roar increased.

"Look!" George pointed beyond the end of the fence line toward the base of a distant hill. The ground had risen up like a ten-foot wave coming in on a beach. The tidal wave of soil and grass was moving straight toward them in an ever rolling crescendo of motion. The students watched in horror as the grassy field buckled up before their eyes. The blankets and students were picked up as if they were little floating air mattresses in the ocean and thrown behind the incoming surf. Ben clung to Cindy, realizing that she was tumbling over him as they were slung backward off the blanket. Sam's barking turned into a terrified whine.

Ben tried to get to his feet but fell down. He looked up and saw that the swirling motion of the earth was surging. The house, the large oak tree, the cars, and the students had been picked up and dropped in the swift sweeping movement. Kids and blankets were scattered in every direction, but the house was still standing in what looked like relatively good shape.

Cindy clung to Ben's leg. "Help me!" she choked. Sam tried to crawl under her.

"Hold on! Another shock is bound to follow."

The rumbling was ominous and terrifying as the ground continued to shake violently. Cracks split the soil along the road, but none were big enough to be dangerous.

"Look!" Deborah pointed upward. "The sky is exploding."

Gigantic luminous flashes exploded overhead. Fireballs streaked across the sky, and meteorites plunged and disappeared. The darkening sky looked like a gigantic fireworks display. Huge clouds of black smoke began to fill the sunset.

"Electrical inductions," Mary shouted. "I studied the

phenomenon at UCLA." She pushed herself up on her hands and knees. "They're coming from the sources of the earthquakes. The whole atmosphere around the earth is rolling up like a scroll."

The ground was still trembling, but the violent upheaval was slackening. Ben was able to sit upright. "I'm sure volcanoes have erupted by now. Michael said many would parallel the ocean trenches around the Pacific Ocean. The tidal waves have started."

Mary shielded her eyes but kept looking up. "Some of the tsunamis will be a hundred feet high and come in around 250 miles per hour. Thank God, we're on the back side."

"People on every continent must be terrified." Cindy clung to Ben. "Oh, I pray my parents are OK. I tried so hard to get them to come with me."

"Look!" Mary pointed to the west. "The smoky atmosphere is making the sun appear to be black. But look at the moon that's coming up! It's blood red!"

□ □ □

"Emperor Gianardo! Emperor Gianardo! Are you hurt badly?" an aide pulled a big piece of plaster board off Damian Gianardo. "Are you all right, Sir?"

For a few moments the emperor of the New Roman Empire groggily shook his head. The aide pushed another piece of plaster board aside, and Gianardo struggled to his feet. Blood ran over the old scar from his previous head wound. Dust filled his nostrils and he coughed.

"Sir!" The aide panicked. "Can you talk?"

Finally, the emperor cleared his throat. "What happened?" He was barely audible. A few sounds of shifting timber and falling boards came from behind them. There were no voices.

"The complete front of the White House collapsed. Guards are lying under the pillars. You have amazingly escaped alive!"

Gianardo staggered past the bewildered man and then stopped abruptly. What had been the front wall and a window was gone. Up and down Pennsylvania Avenue, trees were toppled, and buildings were in shambles. Cars were scattered as if the hand of a giant had casually tossed them around the landscape. "Ohhh!" the emperor pointed at the sky. "The moon has turned red."

The aide limped beside him, realizing for the first time that a large gash ran down the side of his leg. The arm of his coat was torn, and his face was covered with dust. "Gone." He stared out toward the Mall. "The Washington Monument has broken into pieces."

An errie silence was punctuated by occasional explosions and the noise of water gushing from broken fire hydrants. People were still lying stupefied on the sidewalks and grass. A few sounds of movement came from deep within the White House.

"They were right," the aide muttered. "Totally right. The quake came just as they predicted."

"I wonder how those two Jews set this up?" Gianardo held the side of his head. "How did they figure out the timing?"

The assistant stared angrily at the emperor.

"Got to get to our communications system." Gianardo hobbled back into the crumpled building. "We've got to get to the National Security Building next door."

"Too late now," the aide snapped. "Don't go back in there. The rest of the building may collapse."

"I'm sure the elevator won't work." The emperor rubbed his head again. "Electricity must be off everywhere."

The whole building began to tremble as an aftershock rumbled through the city. "I'm getting out of here!" the aide panicked. "I knew from the first time we were in Israel this was all a mistake. We were warned! . . . We were warned!" His voice trailed away as he ran for the street.

☐   ☐   ☐

Sam Eisenberg scampered up the mountainside with Larry Feinberg right behind him. The sun was just coming completely up over the hills and mountains around Bozrah, spreading a glorious burst of golden glow over the desert.

"I can't believe how well we came out of the earthquake," Larry puffed. "Jimmy's hospital is still standing. You'd think we'd just been through a leisurely Sunday afternoon shake in southern California."

"Yeah," Sam agreed, picking his way carefully along the rocks, "it was like we were on a plate of the earth that just gently floated while everything around it crunched together."

"I heard the soldiers moving last night." Larry pulled out a pair of binoculars. "Sounded like the whole Jordanian army was trying to surround us for a morning attack."

"I'm glad we knew that the surprise was going to be one big surprise on them." Sam reached the top of the rock pile. "I think we can survey the entire area from here."

"Look!" Larry brought the binoculars to his eyes. "Troop carriers littered all over the thirty-mile safety zone." He stopped and looked carefully. "The vehicles are upside down and turned over."

"There are huge cracks in the ground!" Sam pointed to a winding crevasse that split the desert floor. "Soldiers have fallen inside."

"They're trying to retreat!" Larry studied the scene with the glasses. "It looks to me like the entire army is wrecked."

"A rock slide got many of them." Sam pointed to the base of a large mountain across the plain. "Looks like the entire top and side of that bluff slid down."

"Wow!" Larry exclaimed as he lowered the binoculars. "God's really given them something to think about today up in Amman. The Jordanians won't be coming out here for a good while."

The two men sat down on boulders and watched the soldiers crawling around the desert floor. Just then an aftershock rumbled across the valley, and the soldiers fled in every direction. After ten seconds, the movement stopped, and dust started to settle once more.

"Can you believe that we have lived through the greatest earthquake in human history as easily as a robin sitting on her nest in a spring shower?" Sam beamed. "Thank God, His hand has been on us."

"Indeed!" Larry stretched his legs out. "I calculate 1,260 days equaling 180 weeks of Tribulation. We've come through the first 16 weeks in amazing condition."

"We've got a fer bit to go." Sam imitated a Texas accent. "Still, 90 percent of trouble lies down the trail, but I think we'll make it fine."

"Sure thing, partner." Larry laughed as they started back down the hill toward the Bozrah camp. "Thank God, we're the good guys!"

☐   ☐   ☐

I watched the students gather up their blankets and slowly collect themselves. I knew the major aftershocks had passed, and there would be little disruption in the area around Lancaster for the next several hours. The time was right to appear and speak to the entire group. Once more I stepped into human history at a point about ten feet from the front porch of the farmhouse.

"Peace be unto you!"

"Michael!" Ben spun around. "We knew you'd be here!"

"I can see him!" Deborah exclaimed. "I'm actually seeing an angel!"

"It's really him," George pointed. "I can't believe my eyes."

"Today I come to all of you as a sign of favor. Behold, you have found a special place in the sight of God. Rejoice! For as this world passes away, you chose the better portion that is eternal."

"Michael, tell us what has happened." Ben took Cindy by the hand and led her forward. Sam strained on the leash behind her. "Bozrah . . . is everyone OK?"

"God's hand has more than protected. Your family and friends have endured very well, even as their enemies were being swallowed by the earth."

"Praise the Lord!" Ben shouted.

"What about the rest of the globe?" Mary walked forward cautiously.

"Do not fear. Come close and listen."

The students huddled around the farmhouse steps.

"Many people will be ready to receive your witness now. I will send each of you to those who are hungry for hope. Yet be prepared for danger to increase! The times are becoming more desperate with every judgment. People are increasingly treacherous."

"What's happened to California?" a student ventured.

"Judgment has engulfed San Francisco. Their wickedness has been called into accountability. The city is no more."

"LA?" George held up his hand.

"The city is in flames, and many sections have been leveled. Yet other portions in Orange County stand. Railways, overpasses, and bridges have buckled before the glance of the Lord."

"And our people?" Cindy asked. "The Christians? And my parents who are not Christians?"

"Your own parents are alive and well, my child. When you see them next, you will find new receptiveness to your message. But the last sixteen weeks have taken a great toll. Over seventy thousand witnesses have become martyrs. Hundreds of thousands of Israelis who embraced Yeshua as Messiah have paid with their lives. Those who have fled the persecutions of

Gianardo compose a new diaspora. Bozrah has become a haven for these people of the truth."

"What are we to do now?" Ben asked.

"I will talk with each one of you separately. I have many assignments for you to fulfill in the coming months. You will find that the time flies as you complete your mission. Yet for the world, each day will seem an eternity of agony. As the end of this period approaches, you will know what to expect next. Watch the skies, for the next great judgment will come from above. Now come and receive your divine appointments."

Jimmy looked out over the large audience listening in rapt attention to his teaching. The warm sun made sitting outside very pleasant, casting lengthening shadows over the group. Many of the students looked oriental, some were black, while others were fair and European. Some of his class were patients who lived in the large building he had helped construct.

"Now you can see the significance of the lineage of Yeshua in Matthew's Gospel and how the name adds meaning to today's special celebration called Christmas. He was and is the fulfillment of every prophetic expectation for the Messiah." Jimmy picked up an eraser from his portable chalkboard. "Any questions?"

At least two hundred people were scattered across the sand in front of the hospital. The older people were sitting in chairs; many of the young couples sat on blankets on the ground. Many men stood around the back.

An older man held up his hand and waited for Jimmy to recognize him. "I lived around the Christians during my life in Egypt." His clothes looked at least ten years old, worn and dusty. "I don't remember anyone ever explaining that His coming fulfilled Torah prophecy. Your words are wonderful."

"Nor I," a young man called out. "In America, Christmas was a merchant's dream and little more." Others agreed immediately.

"We were all victims of many misconceptions," Jimmy acknowledged. "That's why we are holding these classes. It's important that we get the facts straight. We want your newfound faith to be anchored in Scripture. I think that's enough for today. Everybody back to work."

The group applauded and then dispersed. Jimmy folded up the chalkboard stand and carried it back inside the hospital.

"You're getting quite a reputation as a teacher," Larry called out from across the examination room when Jimmy put the stand down. "People from Petra want to start coming up to hear your Bible studies. Your skill must be hereditary."

Ruth and her mother came in from a corridor of the hospital. "Merry Christmas, everybody," she rushed over and hugged her father. "I'm so glad everybody's here."

Sharon kissed her son-in-law on the cheek. "Must be strange to celebrate the nativity out here in this desert. The whole Christmas experience is new to us since we didn't really recognize Christian customs. Just Hanukkah."

"Sit down." Larry waved to his family. The bare walls smelled of pine. Overhead, rafters ran from one end to the other, making a spartan contrast with the home left behind in Newport Beach. "Gather around the table and let's enjoy ourselves today. Each of you certainly works hard enough." The only furniture was Larry's desk, a table, and six chairs. He opened the refrigerator door. "I have a little gift for each of you. Been hiding this for weeks." He set four cold cans on the table.

"Cokes!" Jimmy clapped his hands. "Wow! How did you ever find these?"

"Believe it or not, they were in the bottom of a box of canned goods Sam Eisenberg brought in several months ago. I hid them for a special occasion."

Ruth popped the metal tab and took a long drink. "I didn't think any of these were left in the whole world. Wonderful!"

"Best Christmas present I've had in years." Jimmy reached for his Coke. "It's amazing how special the common things have become. We certainly took a lot for granted in the old days."

"Not many luxuries left." Sharon laughed. "Hot water's about it. I think I've lost at least thirty pounds."

"Since you mentioned water," Larry observed, "you're the one who keeps up on the logistics, Sharon. How is the water supply holding out?"

"No signs of atomic contamination in the water we desalinate from the Dead Sea, and the water wells are certainly producing at more than acceptable levels. Our irrigation is so efficient that we'll still be harvesting crops after the Tribulation passes. I don't know about the rest of the world, but we won't starve here."

"Simon Assed's factory is turning out dried food like crazy," Ruth added. "How's everything in your department, Dad?"

Larry turned away. "I wish I hadn't brought the subject up." He paused for a few moments. "We're starting to run low on insulin. I'm afraid our diabetics are going to be in trouble soon. I can also see that we could eventually run out of antibiotics. We've got over two years to go, and I don't think our supplies will stretch that far."

"We're going to have trouble with the psychotics," Ruth observed. "The antipsychotic drugs will probably run short too."

Larry ran his hands nervously through his hair. "I just pray we don't find too many AIDS problems. We surely can't cover them, but we can comfort them and give them love and support."

The group silently drank the cold Cokes. Outside they could hear the sounds of people talking and walking down the wooden corridors. Finally, Larry broke the somber mood. "Hey, it's Christmas! This is the day to celebrate the birth of hope. We're sitting in the only protected space on earth. Let's be joyful."

"Absolutely." Ruth set her Coke can firmly on the table. "I almost forgot to tell you why I called this meeting in the first place. In all this gloom and doom, I got sidetracked from the Christmas present I have for all of you today. Are you ready for glad tidings?"

"Of course," Sharon brightened. "This is the season of cheer. What do you have for us?"

"Really, the gift is for Jimmy, but each of you will be blessed in your own special way so I chose a moment to tell you at the same time. I have my own angelic annunciation. Are you ready?"

Everyone applauded.

"I'm going to have a baby."

"What?" Jimmy dropped his empty can. "What did you say?"

"I'm one month pregnant," Ruth said quietly.

"Wonderful! Wonderful!" Sharon clapped.

"Sit . . . sit down." Jimmy rushed to her side.

"I am sitting, silly."

"My first grandchild!" Larry exclaimed.

"Merry Christmas to each of you." Ruth smiled broadly.

"Like Moses," Larry exploded, "a child born in exile. How very appropriate."

Jimmy looked at his watch. "Ben ought to be getting up about this time. Let's call him and spread the good news around the world."

The family darted down the hall to the little office where the radio transmitter was kept. Jimmy threw the switch and carefully set the dials. "Woman in the Desert calling the End Times Prophet. Calling the Prophet. Calling the man."

"Oh, I hope he left the transmitter on last night," Ruth fretted. "We told him that we would call him Christmas Day. I bet he's still asleep."

"Calling the Prophet," Jimmy repeated.

The static popped and the pitch of the humming changed. "Hello . . . hello," a groggy voice answered.

"Ben, are you awake?" Jimmy asked.

"I am now . . . had to get up to answer the radio."

"Merry Christmas!" the whole family shouted in the microphone.

"Sounds like everyone's there," Ben's voice reverberated with a distant roar. "Merry Christmas to you."

"You must have stayed up late partying," Jimmy chided.

"Actually . . . ," the words faded in and out, "went to bed . . . very late . . . police chased us . . . most of yesterday . . . had to hide . . ."

"What?" Sharon grabbed the microphone. "We can't hear you well. You all right?"

The static eased. "Yes," Ben was louder. "No one got caught, but they ran us across the UCLA campus. Only the hand of God saved us. We escaped through some old sewer tunnels."

"Good grief!" Sharon handed the microphone to Larry.

"The McCoys," Larry asked, "how are they surviving?"

"Been tough. But the big earthquake had a decided effect on their children. I think they are beginning to come around. Cindy's made headway with Erica."

"Good. Good," Larry answered. "Tell them to be careful."

"I have a special Christmas card for you," Ruth broke in. "You're going to be an uncle in about eight months."

"REALLY? NO KIDDIN'?"

"Thought that announcement would put a little something in your Christmas stocking this morning, Ben. Wanted you to be among the first to know."

The radio popped and faded, ". . . very happy for . . . Cindy will be very . . . McCoys . . . be here today and I'll . . ." The sound faded away.

Jimmy tried to fine-tune the radio. "We're getting atmospheric interference. Maybe we better sign off."

He spoke loudly in the microphone. "Hope you can hear us. We're signing off. Everyone wishing the End Times Prophet a happy holiday. May God bless you, Ben."

"I do hope he is eating well." Sharon frowned.

"I'd be terrified if I didn't know that Ben had an angel looking over his shoulder." Larry shook his head. "But if anyone is the chess master of escapes, it's my son."

"Find anything else in the bottom of that box?" Jimmy asked his father-in-law. "Like a candy bar?"

"Well, let's go back and see if Santa Claus stashed anything else in the back of that refrigerator."

Everyone stood as the emperor walked briskly into the national security strategy room. The large assembly area was lined with huge maps running up the walls to the top of the high ceiling. Extra telephones and electronic equipment had been placed around the amphitheater-style room. Banks of desks sloped toward a central podium in a horseshoe shape. Damian Gianardo stepped to the walnut speaker's stand and laid a file on the roster. The generals and their aides snapped stiffly to attention.

"At ease." Gianardo motioned for the generals to be seated. "On this January 2, 1998, we face a new year with many severe challenges. We must think together about a common approach to the serious issues that must be resolved. As we all know, recent atomic and natural disasters have destroyed our economic reserves. We are not able to rebuild in many sectors. Even the White House still lies in shambles. The worsening atmospheric situation poses a serious threat to our health. I am here to receive your counsel and guidance. I will begin by asking the chief of staff for his assessment of our military posture."

A large white-haired army general on the second row

slowly rose to his feet. Across his chest were numerous rows of medals. "Mr. President . . . ," General Crose paused. His refusal to say "Emperor" was obvious. "As I warned on many occasions, we have enemies who still have the capacity to strike with nuclear warheads. Another confrontation is certainly possible. Frankly, I don't know if the world could survive another exchange, but our enemies do have the capacity to strike."

"Crose, you've never agreed with any components of my foreign policy," Gianardo interrupted. "But I have prevailed in the face of this lack of support. *Nothing* should have penetrated the Star Wars Strategic Defense System!" The emperor pounded the table. "A major blunder."

"We no longer have the resources or equipment to either repair or improve the system." The general slumped back down in his chair. "We do well to remember these limitations."

"Sir?" A general on the second row raised his hand. "I have been reviewing data on our health care needs and am greatly alarmed."

"Please stand." Gianardo beckoned.

The general thumbed through a thick file. "We are on the verge of collapse. The continuing increase in AIDS and cancer patients was straining our limits *before* the great earthquake. Now we have the additional pressure of fewer functioning hospital units around the country. We must siphon money from the European countries that are part of our federation."

"No! No!" An aide popped up on the front row. "I have the latest polls from Europe. They will not tolerate any further drain on their economies. The empire is increasingly unpopular. We have already gained far too much at their expense."

"Sit down!" The emperor's voice was cold and threatening. "Europe will do what we tell Europe to do. Understand?"

"No." General Crose answered without standing. "Those days are past. The world is in too much chaos.

We cannot command and expect immediate compliance. Face it, these are the new facts of life."

Damian Gianardo's eyes shifted around the room, quickly assessing the cold stares he saw everywhere. The general's obvious defiant attitude made him very nervous. Gianardo bit his lip, fighting back the angry outburst that usually followed such a confrontation. The emperor knew that he could not afford to appear weak in this meeting, but neither could he depose the general in front of his military colleagues. Anarchy might follow.

"Our leadership has cost the world greatly," Crose continued. "Moreover, your obsession with concentrating all religious power in your office has cost us the support of the Muslim world. They still sell us their oil, but Babylon is certainly gouging us with exorbitant prices."

"*Our* leadership?" The emperor forced a smile. "Really? Am *I* the one who directs our missiles toward our aggressors, general? Please don't blame the failures of your planners on me. *You*, not I, designed the Star Wars System."

The room took on a stony silence, and the general's face became crimson. Gianardo walked around in front of the podium, smiling condescendingly. Once the emperor sensed that he was again firmly in control, he continued. "I want to hear the report of the National Aeronautics and Space Administration people. Samuel Goldstein, your report please."

A distinguished-looking man in his forties stood up. Goldstein was wearing an expensive business suit and horn-rim glasses. "Please turn on the overhead projector." The lights dimmed and the large maps lit up. The scientist began projecting a series of slides on the screen behind the emperor.

"For a number of years there has been serious speculation about some comets that appeared to be moving dangerously close to the earth." The scientist clicked the slide machine rapidly. Displays of the solar system filled the screen. "Within the last month we have come to conclusions that we have no qualms about presenting to this group and to the public. We are deeply concerned about the path that the so-called Doran and Whiton Asteroids have now taken. There is no question that they are on a collision course with the world. Both are quite large . . . over a half mile in diameter." A picture of a fiery star came on. "We calculate that one will hit the world around April 11 and the other on Saturday, July 11. A smaller comet we have labeled Comet Wormwood is probably going to hit about August 1. Gentlemen, we are facing another considerable natural disaster."

"Exactly what do you mean?" General Crose's deep voice rumbled.

Goldstein took off his glasses and rubbed his eyes. "Thousands of large asteroids cross Earth's orbit every few years. Any one of them could wipe out a civilization. Smaller ones that have the capacity to destroy entire cities also streak past. Fortunately, we get hit by a large one only every million years or so. A small one may hit every hundred years. A direct hit from a lesser asteroid would be the equivalent of ten Hiroshima bombs."

"But a big one?" The general bore down. "What's the possible effect of this Doran or Whiton Asteroid?"

"Asteroids come in at a speed of about fifty thousand miles per hour," Goldstein continued. "The power of such a collision would be more like a million Hiroshima bombs creating an abyss several miles across. On the opposite side of the world, the earth would actually bubble out and crack. Earthquakes would follow. Dust and debris could clutter the atmosphere so badly that they might even block out the sun and moonlight for a period of time. Just the tail of a comet passing by can create galactic tidal waves."

"But can we do anything?" General Crose threw up his hands. "What's even possible?"

"I suggest that we begin preparing immediately to

shoot nuclear-equipped rockets at these asteroids in hopes of breaking them up before they can penetrate the atmosphere."

"That can't be done," the general barked. "First, we need to be ready for possible future attacks from our enemies. We can't chance a lack of preparedness for retaliation. Second, we both know that trying to hit a foreign object coming in at fifty thousand miles per hour would be like throwing a baseball from a moving car at another car coming from the opposite direction. Wouldn't ever work."

Goldstein looked nervously at the emperor and then at the assembly of military leaders. "Certainly, the task would not be easy. But we must do something. We must try."

"Last time we *did have* warnings about the big earthquake, but we didn't pay any attention." The general looked menacingly at his colleagues, but his remarks were obviously directed at Gianardo. "I suggest that we immediately start work on this problem. This time we don't want any cover-ups."

Damian Gianardo's eyes narrowed, and the muscles tightened around his jaw. He appeared in control, but his hands gripped the speaker's stand with such intensity that his fingernails turned white and his knuckles looked as if they would pop through his skin. He listened silently as the military experts bantered over the possibility of hitting a traveling object in space, but his eyes never left General Crose. Gianardo's face was hard and set.

□　　□　　□

Three days later, Joe McCoy called Ben at the farmhouse. "Calling from a pay phone, Ben. Don't want to chance being tapped."

"Where are you now, Joe?"

"I just dropped Erica and Joe, Jr., off at school. I went around the block and came back to see what was happening. I was shocked to see security police in front of the high-school building talking to the kids on the steps. I'm not sure what to make of it, but I wanted you to be alert. The whole matter may be routine, or we could be in big trouble."

"But I thought Erica had accepted Yeshua and Joe was coming around?"

"Both Jennifer and I believe that we were seeing a change of heart. That's what's really got me scared. I don't think that my own children could deceive us that completely. I'm not sure what to make of any of it."

"Want to come out here?" Ben asked.

"Not yet. After all, nothing's predictable anymore. Did you see the paper this morning?"

"No."

"Another big explosion in Washington, D.C. Chief of Staff Army General Crose's car was blown to pieces. Killed Crose and several other generals. No one can understand how such a thing could have slipped past the vast security network of Gianardo's secret police."

"You're right. Nothing can be taken for granted. We'll be praying for your family. Let us know if we need to meet you somewhere or you need to hide out here."

"Thanks, Ben. You don't know how much it means to know that you are standing with us."

# CHAPTER
## 22

During the following months, the secret police interrogated the McCoys' children several times. Joe and Jennifer suspected there was a leak in their parents' Bible study group, but no one could be sure. The McCoy children were making significant spiritual breakthroughs, but Joe, Jr., had not yet trusted Jesus and was terrified whenever the police cornered him. Each time the police were professional and polite. Their questions were vague and their demeanor non-threatening. Mostly, the investigators asked about the possibility of Joe and Jennifer pushing religious ideas on the kids. They also asked questions about Cindy Wong. Joe, Jr., and Erica answered well enough and tried not to leave openings for further probes.

Although I remained invisible most of the time, I did not cease to watch over Ben and Cindy, and on several occasions I had to intervene. One evening I foresaw the police setting up radar detection to follow the movement of Ben's car. A signal transmitter was attached under a fender. After the police left, I put the bug on the car next to Ben's. Three secret agents nearly lost their jobs for being so incompetent in selecting the wrong car. The officers were totally bewildered by their "error."

In late March the secret police nearly cornered Ben

and George in one of the UCLA dorms that survived the great earthquake. I saw that the police were preparing to surround the building. Ben and George were in a sophomore's room sharing the gospel. We did not have much time to spare so I materialized in the hallway when the rest of the students were in their rooms and I knocked on the young man's door.

"Can I help you?" the puzzled student said as he opened the door. "You're not the one that I thought was coming."

"I believe there is a Mr. Ben Feinberg here."

"Yeah, sure." The sophomore answered uncomprehendingly.

"Michael?" Ben asked from across the room. "Sounds like Michael."

"Yes. Some urgent business has just come up."

"What?" Ben bounded across the room. "What in the world are you doing here?"

"We *must* run. Time is short, *very* short."

Ben stared for a moment and blinked uncomprehendingly. Suddenly, he understood. He grabbed George's arm. "Hey, we'll try to be back tomorrow." He jerked George past the startled student. "See you then." Ben pulled George into the hall and shut the door behind them.

"Michael! What are you doing here?"

"Police are closing in on the building. The student you have been talking to is a plant. The secret security people will be in here any minute."

"What can we do?" George looked panic-stricken.

"We're on the second floor!" Ben looked desperately up and down the hall.

The student's door flew open, and the sophomore ran down the hall toward the stairs at the opposite end.

"Quick! Ben . . . George . . . into the student's room. Lock the door and turn out the light. Get on the ledge outside his window. Give the police time to get in and then drop into the bushes and run for it. I will be your decoy inside the dorm."

Ben and George slammed the door behind them, and I opened a janitor's closet and grabbed a broom. In less than thirty seconds the police were charging up the stairs and pouring onto the floor.

"Stop!" the lead cop shouted. "Who are you?"

"Just one of the janitors. Cleaning up."

"Three men were here. Where did they go?"

"Three men?"

"Two college students and a big guy! About your size, I'd guess."

"Oh, they left. Might have gone up the stairs at the other end."

The first wave of police disappeared, running up the exit stairs to the third floor.

"I'd recognize the other guy." The sophomore's voice was loud and nervous as he bounded up the stairs with the second detachment of police. "Sort of a strange-looking man."

I stepped into the little janitor's closet and back into eternity as the secret police ran up and down the halls.

"Where'd the janitor go?" The leader of the first group came back downstairs.

"What janitor?" one of the second group asked.

"The man sweeping the floor."

"The janitors aren't here at night," the sophomore interjected.

The security officer glared at the college student. "Don't mess with me. I'm not blind. I want to know where the janitor we talked to went." The man swung the closet door open and looked inside. "If this is a college prank . . ." He jerked the sophomore forward by the shirt.

"Hey, I don't know what you guys are talking about. I'm on your side, remember?"

"There's just no one here," a policeman who returned from the top floor reported. "This thing smells like a little joke pulled on us by the boys' dorm."

"Where's the janitor?" the policeman growled in the

sophomore's face. "We'll teach you to trifle with national security personnel."

"No . . . no . . . no." The student flattened against the wall. "Really there were people here pushing religion on me. Honest. HONEST . . ."

"Try this room." One of the policemen reached for the door. "It's locked."

"Can't be." The student fumbled for his keys. He swung the door open. Curtains were blowing gently in the evening breeze.

The policeman ran to the window. "There they go!" He pointed across the campus. "Two guys are running into those trees."

I left the student and the secret police to their discussion and followed Ben to make sure he returned to the farm without any interruptions. The next night I knew that I must remind the group of the instructions that I had given them much earlier.

The group gathered around me in the farmhouse living room. "Let us review our procedures. On what basis do you contact people?"

"You put us in touch with the people whose hearts are open," Cindy answered.

"What went wrong last night?"

Ben and George looked knowingly at each other.

"We've got the message, Michael." Ben looked discouraged. "No one sent us. We thought the guy was open because he was talking about his religious concerns in the cafeteria when we were witnessing to a student you assigned to us. We just jumped the gun."

"Right. You must be wise as serpents and gentle as doves. Assume nothing."

"We won't make that mistake again," George apologized. "Thanks for saving our hides."

"Michael?" Deborah held up a newspaper. "We've not seen you for quite a while. The papers are filled with speculation about the three comets speeding toward the earth. I've figured out that the Doran Asteroid is scheduled to hit on April 11, which is also the day of Passover. Obviously, something big is afoot, and Passover is just days away. The papers are censored and don't report the predictions of Moses and Elijah. What's ahead? Level with us."

"I have not previously revealed anything so that you would study and learn to read the signs of the times for yourselves. You have done well. Yes. On Passover the Seventh Seal will be broken, and God's First Trumpet Judgment will blow. You will remember from the book of Revelation that there are seven "seal" judgments, which have already passed. Now there remain seven "trumpet" judgments and seven "bowl" judgments—the last bowls of God's wrath."

"The meteor is going to smack us?" George asked fearfully.

"No, not directly. But the consequences will still be severe. Even as we speak the National Aeronautics and Space Administration has fired a nuclear missile at the asteroid. Our heavenly Father will allow a direct hit in order to give one more warning to the world."

Mary held up her hand. "Can one bomb really stop something as large as the Doran Asteroid?"

"No, but the atomic explosion will fragment the asteroid. A very large portion will strike one of the isolated Aleutian Islands off the coast of Alaska, causing a large but regional earthquake."

"And the rest of the exploded asteroid?" Ben asked.

"Millions of particles will streak across the sky as they enter the atmosphere. You will see the greatest fireworks show in human history. Thirty minutes prior to the impact in Alaska all wind on the earth will cease. Suddenly, the particles will fall, looking like great drops of blood."

"Earth can't avoid being hit by large chunks of the meteor," Mary probed. "I know damage must result in many places."

"Censorship will prevent a full public accounting, but one-third of all the trees and grasslands on planet earth will burn. Yes, the judgment will be significant."

"What about the other two?" one of the younger students asked. "Will the Whiton Asteroid and Comet Wormwood be a problem for us?"

"The Whiton Asteroid will fall on July 11, and the Second Trumpet will sound. Be ready for the asteroid's impact in the Mediterranean Sea. Ben, you must warn the people in Bozrah and Petra to send out the word for people to stay far above the coastline. A tidal wave will sweep in. Surely, the hand of God shall move and strike until every idol is broken and the world has seen the glory of the Lord. Comet Wormwood will fall on August 1."

"July 11?" Ben snapped his fingers. "That's the seventeenth of Tammuz. The Fast of Tammuz! And August 1, 1998, falls on Av 9."

☐ ☐ ☐

In the predawn skies across the world the Doran Asteroid flashed its bright red tail, scattering millions of burning rock particles over earth's stratosphere. Alaska shook as the remaining central chunk burned its way into a small coastal island. If it had not been for sudden and prolonged rain, the burning forests and grasslands might never have stopped burning. More smoke billowed up into the already polluted atmosphere. In the following days, the night skies were a constant display of showers of exploding and falling stars, but their frequency lessened.

By June most of the unusual night displays had subsided and people were back indoors. The sun was setting much later, and the public's fear and fascination were passing. Erica McCoy took the bold step of inviting her closest friends to listen to her parents explain what was happening in the world. The group of five girls gathered outside around the McCoys' swimming pool.

Joe pointed to the sky. "I'm not trying to frighten you, but these strange occurrences are warnings God is giving the world. We still have another asteroid and a comet headed toward the earth. Unless we repent, a great price will be paid."

Erica's best friend, Melissa, interrupted. "My science teacher says the odds have just caught up with the earth. Sooner or later we were bound to get hit by something big anyway."

"Sure." Joe walked back and forth in front of the group, holding his Bible. "But the real issue is timing. Think. How many things are happening right now that fit the Bible's timetable for the final days of history? And why are so many happening on Jewish holy days? Is it really a coincidence? How can Moses and Elijah predict the precise times and dates so far in advance if God isn't telling them?"

"My parents don't want us to speak about the possibilities at home," another classmate named Paula declared. "But I hear them talking when Mom and Dad think we are asleep. They went to church when they were children and know what you are teaching us is the truth."

"None of us would be here," Melissa added, "if Erica hadn't sworn us to secrecy. I know we're in danger, but I want to know the truth."

Joe, Jr., spoke up. "My sister and I really rebelled against our parents for a long time, but the earthquake changed our minds. My parents told us for weeks that it was coming. When I saw everything falling in, I knew they were right. It's taken me a while to say it out loud, but I know now that what the Bible says about Jesus is the truth."

"We have a special Bible study group for parents," Jennifer said. "We help people like Paula's parents. I think your mothers and fathers would be more open than you think. The police system works by fear. Once you refuse to be intimidated, they've lost their hold over you.

"Girls, that's our story." Jennifer joined her husband and son in front of the group. "Our family has gone from being another southern California wreck to a real unit that stands together. Sure, it's scary, but I wouldn't give anything for the joy that has been restored to us. Even if we were hauled in tomorrow, we have the joy of knowing that we will face eternity together."

"You probably have questions you'd like to ask," Joe added. "Erica, Joe, Jennifer, and I will be here for any response you have. If you don't have any questions, then grab a cola and we'll break up in a bit."

While the girls talked with the McCoys, three cars were pulling up down the street. Plainclothes security officers quietly shut the car doors. A teenager got out of the last car and pointed to the McCoys' residence.

"How do you know they are there?" the policeman in charge asked.

"Because they didn't invite me," Mary Higbie answered indignantly.

"These are the people you told me about several months ago?"

The teenager smiled cynically. "I've overheard a number of conversations in the McCoys' backyard when the Chinese girl was pushing Christianity. I've seen Bibles lying around their house."

"And you'll testify to these facts?"

"Absolutely," Mary said defiantly.

"Got that on tape?" the leader turned to the man behind him.

"Every word of it."

"What?" Mary puzzled.

"We don't want you to back out," the man in charge grumbled. "We've been waiting quite a while to make a big bust, and we're going to hit these people hard. Your testimony is what makes it stick."

"Hit hard?" Mary retreated. "I just want them arrested. Humiliated like Erica treats me . . . but nothing more."

The police drew their weapons and began inserting

the bullet clips. "This isn't some kind of game, kid."
The officer began pointing in different directions and
his men moved quickly. "We're going to make a real example of these fanatics."

"Well, sure," Mary said nervously. "But I don't want
anyone to *really* get hurt."

"Hurt?" The policeman laughed. "Pain is our business. Let's get them, boys!"

Suddenly, the men dispersed into the trees and
shrubs. The first carload of agents charged the front
door. One lone agent held Mary tightly by the arm. "We
want you to identify the suspects."

For a couple of minutes Mary and the policeman
stood under a tree. They could hear distant shouts.
Then an agent came out the front door and motioned
for them to come in. They hurried through the house
and out into the backyard. The teenagers were huddled
together on the ground with police circling them and
pointing their guns. Joe and Jennifer and their children
stood together. Police were aiming guns at them too.

"Identify the traitors," the chief agent ordered Mary,
who stood at his side.

"Mary!" the girls echoed. "How could you?"

"Really," the terrified teen muttered, "I think I've
made a mistake. Yes. This is all a big mistake."

"Identify the McCoys!" the agent demanded. "We already have your accusations on tape."

"I didn't mean for this to happen." Mary tried to pull
away.

"IDENTIFY THEM!" the man exploded.

Mary pointed a trembling finger at the McCoys.

"Get the women first." A policeman grabbed Erica's
wrist while another man reached for Jennifer.

Joe suddenly pushed the first man backward so
forcefully that he fell in the shrubs. Pulling Erica and
Jennifer with him, Joe darted toward the side gate.
"Run!" he yelled to Joe, Jr.

A policeman charged out of the shadows and swung
the butt end of his Uzi into Joe's face, sending him

sprawling in the grass. Two other agents rushed Erica and her mother. One man wrapped his arm around Jennifer's neck in a stranglehold. The other man hit Erica in the stomach with his fist. She doubled up with an agonizing groan.

"Get 'em over here." The policeman pointed toward the edge of the swimming pool. "Line 'em up."

The secret police dragged Joe through the grass and dropped him on the swimming pool tile. Erica was pushed down by his side. A big man held Joe, Jr., by the edge of the water while another agent pushed Jennifer next to her family. The teenagers began screaming.

"Shut them up!" The man in charge motioned to the other police. "We don't need a bunch of crazy girls!"

"Please stop!" Mary pleaded. "I didn't want any of this."

"Stop it!" the policeman in charge yelled. "Or they'll get it right now!" Immediately, the girls became silent.

"The man assaulted us." The policeman with the Uzi kicked Joe's hand aside. "I should have shot him then. Let me finish them off now."

"We don't know about the status of the girls," another man interjected. "Are they witnesses or victims?"

The leader of the secret police walked over to the terrified teenagers. "Do you believe what these McCoys were preaching here tonight? Are their ideas representative of your convictions?"

"No! No!" the girls whimpered and pleaded. "No! Never!"

"OK," the leader snarled. "They're victims. Get their names, addresses, and parents' names, and then let them go. Photograph 'em as well as this backyard."

"And our criminals here?" The policeman pointed his Uzi at Joe's stirring figure on the ground. He tried to sit up but couldn't stabilize himself. Blood was running out of Joe's mouth, and his lips were already extremely swollen. "He tried to escape. So did the girl and her mother."

"You won't get away with this!" Joe, Jr., strained against the man holding him. "God will judge you for what you are doing to us."

"You know our orders," the agent in charge grumbled. "Get these teenagers out of here and then shoot the family."

# 23

**B**en read the *Los Angeles Times* intently.

"Can you believe today is July 10, 1998?" Cindy interrupted him. "The Fast of Tammuz begins here tonight at sundown, which will be dawn of July 11 in Israel."

George pointed at the paper. "Look at the headlines. Everyone is terrified that the Whiton Asteroid is going to destroy the earth. Since the news is so heavily censored, who can believe anything you read in the papers?"

"Michael warned us that an asteroid would land in the Mediterranean." Cindy sat quietly in the living room of the farmhouse. "We know at least some sort of collision is ahead."

"Time is running out." George ran his hand nervously through his hair. "If the entire asteroid hits, the impact will be catastrophic." George returned to reading over Ben's shoulder.

"I'm very concerned about the McCoys," Cindy interrupted their reading again. "No one has heard from them in over a week. My father drove by their house once and didn't see a sign of anyone there."

Ben laid the newspaper down on an end table. "I've prayed continually about Joe and Jennifer. Strange. I just feel a deep emptiness, but I'm not disturbed. I don't know what else to do."

George added, "We certainly don't dare go around their house during the daytime, and making inquiries is dangerous. Since we kept our two groups apart for security reasons, there's no one we can call."

"They know all about Michael's message about the asteroid so we don't have to worry about them being caught by any surprises," Ben concluded. "But if we don't hear soon, I think we ought to make a night run to their house and see what we can find."

"I'm counting on Michael showing up tomorrow," Cindy interjected. "I know he can clear everything up for us."

"Let's see what the radio says." George pointed to the tuner on Ben's stereo set. "It's nearly noon. Maybe we'll get some sort of idea what's really happening."

"OK." Ben punched the power button. "Maybe the announcer is telling the truth today."

As a commercial faded, the radio voice spoke urgently and rapidly. "Ladies and gentlemen, we have just received the latest update from NASA. The Whiton Asteroid's collision course with earth is due completion at midnight East Coast time. The asteroid was over a mile wide with the potential to do overwhelming damage. However, two nuclear missiles have just intercepted the asteroid and successfully fractured its mass. Unfortunately, a portion of the asteroid is still going to collide with our planet. NASA is now anticipating a point of contact near the middle of the Mediterranean Sea."

"Michael was right on target." Ben laughed. "The Second Trumpet Judgment of Yeshua is about to blow!"

"The remaining piece of the asteroid appears to be the size of a small mountain," the announcer continued. "Such a mass could create tsunamis of immense proportions around the entire Mediterranean basin. In addition, similar property damage can be expected comparable to the catastrophe in Alaska. Unquestionably, there will be a great loss of sea life."

"The world is warned," Cindy said sternly. "I don't understand how people cannot see the truth. With blind eyes, even I would be able to recognize that the times are beyond the control of any emperor, president, or man."

"Must be quite a blow to Gianardo's ego," George smirked.

"Expect the night skies to be filled with millions of meteorites," the announcer added. "Be prepared for more fires. No one is sure what this strike will cause. Therefore, earthquakes are possible during the night."

"I'm glad the gang will be here tonight," George mused aloud. "We need to be together in case something unexpected happens. Fortunately, we already know an earthquake's not coming."

"Oh, Michael!" Ben cried out. "Wherever you are, please show up soon!"


The moment had come for me to appear. Once more I stepped into history at about the same place on the porch that I had materialized on my last visit. Everyone continued looking at the sky for several minutes, not realizing that I was present.

"I'm going to find out what the radio reports." George turned toward the house. "Look!" he pointed. "It's Michael!"

"Peace to you on this night of consternation."

"Michael!" Cindy turned toward the house. "I knew you'd be here soon. Tell us what is happening."

"Sit down and listen carefully."

The students quickly assembled around the porch steps.

"First, let me tell you about the condition of the world. The fires of the past months have seriously defoliated most of the forests. There are much less rain and ozone. Rising temperatures last spring hampered crops. Fresh water is diminishing. You must be aware that the decreasing food supply will result in increased violence. Soon guns will be worth more than gold. People will kill for water."

"What's happening to the population?" Cindy asked.

"AIDS and drought have decimated the continent of Africa. Zimbabwe is nearly deserted. In Kenya the soil is baked clay. Drought has spread from the Cape of South Africa to Cairo. Starvation has taken a great toll."

"And South America?" a dark complected student asked.

"El Niño winds have caused drought from South America to Australia. Except for Israel, the whole world is experiencing the full judgment for corrupting the atmosphere. Only Israel continues to enjoy normal production. The hand of God has been heavy while He waits patiently for the nations to turn to Yeshua as Messiah. However, in Israel the land is being prepared for His return and rule."

"What's happening here?" Ben asked. "What is going on in southern California?"

"Even you can feel the effects here tonight. Although air pollution has blocked one-third of the sun and moonlight, nothing is stopping the increase of ultraviolet radiation. Not only skin cancer but incidences of terrible cataracts are increasing. Respiratory illness is rampant. What is occurring in the skies is the Fourth Trumpet of Judgment. Each of you has been affected in ways that you do not feel but have begun to take their toll. It is important that I pray for you and relieve the effects. Even as our Lord did, I am going to lay hands on you that you may be healed of what has accumulated in your systems. Kneel and let me walk among you."

The students bowed on the ground. Some even lay prostrate on the grass with their faces in their hands. Slowly, I moved through them, touching them on their heads prayerfully as the power of the Holy Spirit cleansed and renewed their eyes, revitalized their respiratory systems, and healed their skin lesions. The darkness of the night continued to be broken by thousands of intermediate bursts of meteoric explosions of light.

"Now let me share with you the heavy words that I must bring for this hour." The students gathered once more around the steps. "In the days ahead, nuclear attacks will occur again, and the final woes will be visited on those who have rebelled and been disobedient. The Evil One prowls the earth; he knows that his final hour is at hand, but he is too obstinate to face the implications. You must understand that he is not alive and well but wounded and dying. His final weapon appears to be death, but it is not so. He can use only fear and anxiety to deceive you. Death will come, but you must not be dismayed. Dying is only an unredeemed part of the natural process that continues to work in this world. For the unbeliever, death is terror, but for you, it must be seen as the final means of transformation."

"Why are you giving us this instruction?" Ben interrupted. "Sounds rather ominous."

"You must remember that faithfulness does not exempt you from the consequences of life on this planet."

"Some of us are facing death?" George asked hesitantly.

"All of you have the potential to fall at any time, except Ben, who is one of the 144,000 and is absolutely protected."

"Michael, what are you suggesting?" Ben bore down. "What lies ahead?"

"Remember, martyrdom is the mark of ultimate victory . . . not defeat."

"The McCoys!" Cindy gasped. "You're trying to tell us that something has happened to our friends."

The group became deathly quiet. Ben blinked apprehensively and reached for Cindy's hand.

"Yes. The McCoys have entered into their reward. Let your loss be tempered by the knowledge that they went as a family and now stand together before the throne of God. The faith and patience of the parents ultimately resulted in both children trusting Yeshua."

Cindy's often stoic features froze in place. The absence of any appearance of emotion screamed at the night. Ben bit his lip and closed his eyes. Two of the students gathered around Ben and Cindy, putting their hands on their shoulders.

"They were faithful to the end . . ." Cindy's voice broke uncharacteristically, and she began to weep.

"Such good people," Ben muttered. "Was . . . was the end terrible?"

"Swift and without pain. The bullets came instantaneously, and the McCoy family left this troubled world together."

"We must at least hold some sort of memorial service for them and mark graves for them." Ben pointed beneath a large oak tree next to the house. "We should honor our friends."

"Yes," Deborah agreed. "Let's make crosses out of the old lumber behind the house. We can write their names on the crosses and stick them in the ground as grave markers."

Without anything more being said, the students started preparing a special site under the thick branches of the spreading oak. Some of the youths piled up rocks while others tied two-by-fours together with pieces of rope. Deborah wrote the McCoys' names with an indelible marker she found in her back pack. Soon the four crosses stuck out of the heap of rocks.

After the students gathered around the rocks, Ben began reading from the fourteenth chapter of John's Gospel. " 'Let not your heart be troubled; you believe in God, believe also in Me. In My Father's house are many mansions; if it were not so, I would have told you. I go to prepare a place for you.' " Ben stopped and looked at the little group circled around the four crosses. "Would anyone like to say something?"

Deborah spoke softly. "Without Cindy's testimony, Erica would have perished in her sin. We don't have a choice about living or dying, but we make a decision about where we go. Cindy made that difference in Erica's life."

Silence settled over the group. Finally, Ben read again, " 'I am the way, the truth, and the life. No one comes to the Father except through Me.' " He closed the Bible and the group starting singing in hushed, broken tones, "Amazing grace! How sweet the sound that saved a wretch like me . . ."

Their strong young voices filled the night air as they sang louder with each succeeding verse. Their hymn faded, and they stood quietly beneath the great oak tree, watching the thousands of meteors explode in the black sky. Someone said, "And now the McCoys have joined the heavenly constellation."

# 24

In the summer of 1998, the hot, dry winds of August blew down from the hills and swept over the desert floor. The people in Bozrah and Petra tried to stay indoors during the hottest part of the day. Conditions were increasingly cramped as more Jews poured in after the collision of the last comet—Comet Wormwood—with the earth on August 1, the ninth of Av. Its long trail of gases poisoned a third of the fresh water supplies of planet Earth, resulting in millions of deaths. The environment became so polluted that the amount of light was decreased by a third, both by day and by night.

Larry shut the wooden door of his hospital office behind him and sat down at his desk. He scanned the charts that were left for review. After scribbling several prescriptions, he put the papers in a pile and flipped on the radio transmitter.

"Woman in the Desert calling the End Times Prophet. Woman in the Desert calling." There was no response. Slowly, the sound changed. "Come in," he tried once more.

"The Prophet's answering service," a woman's voice answered.

"Ben? Ben there?" Static became intense and then cleared.

"It's Cindy," the distant answer finally came.

"Cindy, how good to hear you. Is Ben there?"

"I'm not at the farm . . . got another transmitter . . . I'm talking from my room at UCLA."

"Really?" Larry put his ear closer to the receiver. "A new radio?"

"A student smuggled it out of an electronics lab. I can call Ben from here, and it allows us to save on travel time. I was tuning in tonight . . . with students at school. What can . . ." The call faded away.

Larry adjusted the dial. "Cindy? Cindy? Can you pick me up again?"

"Can't stay on long . . . too dangerous. But I hear you better now. How is Ruth?"

"That's why I called. This morning she began having pains. Looks like it could be any time now."

"Wonderful! Ben will be pleased . . . I'm hearing doors . . . slam in the parking lot. I must . . ."

"Cindy, what's happening? Can you hear me?"

"Trouble . . . big trouble . . . police cars are surrounding the dorm . . . I'll . . ." The radio went dead.

"Cindy!" Larry shouted into the microphone. "Cindy! Answer me!"

Larry could hear only empty humming. "God help us," he prayed as he turned the switch off. "I've got to call Ben some way." The doctor slumped back in his chair, frantically trying to think of some alternative to waiting for Ben to call.

The door burst open and Sharon rushed into the room. "Larry! Come quickly. Ruth really *is* in labor. Hurry! I think we have a serious problem."

"What?" Larry bolted out of his chair.

"Ruth started having strong regular contractions about an hour ago. I called for the new Egyptian doctor to check. Dr. Zachery's been delivering babies for thirty-five years. I knew he'd be best."

Larry was across the room and out the door. "What did he say?"

"Looks like the baby is breech."

"Oh, no!" Larry grabbed his temples as he trotted down the corridor. "We don't have equipment to handle such a problem."

Sharon tried to keep up. "Ruth is down the hall in a room by herself. All we have is a regular bed."

Larry shot through the door with Sharon running behind him. Dr. Zachery was bending over with his stethoscope on Ruth's bulging stomach as she writhed in agony. The Egyptian looked gravely concerned. A young Arab woman was sponging Ruth's forehead. The expectant mother's eyes were closed and her jaw tightly clenched.

"What do you think?" Larry crowded at the doctor's elbow.

The doctor beckoned the parents to follow him outside. "We're in trouble," he talked rapidly. "Ruth dilated well and quickly for a first baby, but the baby is in breech position. You understand the seriousness of our problem unless we can get it turned."

Color left Larry's face and he nodded mechanically.

"I cannot find any of the basic medical equipment that we need," the Egyptian doctor wrung his hands. "The contractions are increasing in intensity and rapidity, but without forceps I don't think that I can manipulate the child."

"You've got to try!" Sharon clung to Dr. Zachery's arm. "Please do whatever is necessary."

"Where's her husband?" the doctor asked Larry.

"He's teaching outside."

"He must be informed at once and be here. Sharon, go find him. Dr. Feinberg, you and I will work together. I see no other hope."

Sharon ran for the door. "I'll be back with Jimmy," she called over her shoulder. "I'm going to call for the people to pray."

The two doctors returned to Ruth. An Arab nurse hovered over her, mopping large drops of sweat from her forehead. Ruth moaned softly as another contraction locked in. As the pain increased, Ruth's knees drew up and she cried out.

"We don't have much time, Dr. Feinberg. Talk to her while I get these gloves and gown on."

"I'm here with you, Ruth." Larry held his daughter's hand tightly. "Don't worry. We're praying. The people are praying. Hang in there. Jimmy will be here shortly."

Ruth opened her eyes and tried to smile. She squeezed her father's hand.

"Hold her tightly." Dr. Zachery moved into place at the end of the bed. "I'm going to start applying pressure."

After a few minutes, Jimmy burst through the door and rushed to the opposite side of the bed. "I'm here, dear." He placed his cheek against hers. "Don't worry. We'll get through this together. Even if it takes all night."

Sometime during the next two hours Larry remembered his radio conversation with Cindy and started to tell someone to attempt contact with Ben. At that moment, Ruth began to hemorrhage again, and the recollection was swept from his mind. Sharon returned and alternated between holding her daughter's hand and running reports out to the gathering community. By the end of three hours, everyone in Bozrah was aware of the situation and praying. The Arab nurse was assisted by two Jewish nurses.

But each sweep of the minute hand on Jimmy's wristwatch seemed to take longer and longer as hope slowly faded. Jimmy kept his mouth close to Ruth's ear, quoting from the Psalms and praying. He fought recognizing the red flush of her cheeks and the pale whiteness of her neck. With the deepest reluctance he turned his head toward the end of the bed. Dr. Zachery's gown was soaked in blood as were the sheets and mattress. His father-in-law was listlessly staring at the floor. His eyes were empty and his face marked with despair. Sharon was slumped on the floor against the bed, clutching Ruth's limp arm.

Dr. Zachery straightened up and once again put his stetheocope against the swollen stomach that had become perfectly still. He listened a moment before taking Ruth's hand from her mother. The doctor searched for a pulse for several minutes, then placed Ruth's arm on her chest. The hand slid down to the side of the bed. Mechanically, he placed the stethoscope on Ruth's chest. The Egyptian kept shaking his head until he finally covered his eyes and walked out of the room.

"We can make it, darling," Jimmy insisted. "Together, we can make anything . . ." Only then did Jimmy notice that Ruth's eyes weren't really closed. Her glassy lifeless stare was fixed on some eternal point far above the ceiling.

"No," Jimmy barely gasped. "No." Each negation was more a cry than a word. "It can't be." He slowly stood. Tears were so profuse he could no longer see clearly. "Oh, God," he pleaded, "it can't be! Please, don't let it be."

Larry looked up at his son-in-law but couldn't speak.

"No!" Jimmy screamed at the top of his lungs. "Not Ruth! Not my wife and child!"

Sharon slumped into a heap on the floor with her face buried in her hands.

Jimmy's final cry rang through the thin walls of the room and echoed down the corridors. The door stayed wide open as he ran down the hall and through the crowd that had gathered around the entrance to the hospital. People stood reverently when he rushed past them. He ran without any sense of direction toward the desert sands.

Several times Jimmy fell and staggered to his feet again before he was outside the limits of the city. He clawed his way up the rocks and through the hot sand, running toward the top of some nameless plateau. Only when he reached the top did he stop. The burning sand stung his face as he lay face down. Time lost all meaning. Eventually, his eyes seemed to run dry, and his voice was replaced by a dry hoarseness that no longer made speech possible. His clothes were wringing wet, and his head throbbed with dull, unending pain.

Finally, Jimmy crawled beneath the shadow of a large boulder and stared down on the tent city in the valley. He could see a multitude gathered around the hospital. Many people were on their knees. The entire scene seemed strangely surrealistic, detached, remote.

Unexpectedly, he seemed displaced. Once more he felt like a little boy in Dallas, Texas. For the first time in years, he wanted to talk to his father. The loss of his parents bore in upon him as he thought of his mother.

The desert landscape became a mural he seemed to be observing, a scene from a movie about desert warriors he remembered watching at the corner theater when he was a boy. Everything felt achingly strange and foreign.

A great loneliness engulfed him. Jimmy wanted to die. To be gone. Dispatched. Anywhere in eternity. Never again in this lifeless land. Dissolved. Departed. Dead.

From somewhere down below, Jimmy heard men calling his name. Before long they would find him. He tried to stand, but his legs ached and his hands hurt. Only then did he realize that the knees had been torn from his pants, and his legs were lacerated. His palms were scratched and raw. Feeling was gradually returning. Jimmy took a few steps toward the edge. The men were not far away and kept calling.

One of the searchers saw him and began to wave. Jimmy raised his hand slowly and then let it drop. With no alternative, he started the descent by himself, hoping the group would not catch up with him. When Jimmy arrived at the edge of the camp, he tried not to look at anyone. Hands reached for him, but he walked stoically onward.

The crowd in front of the hospital parted. Jimmy stepped in Dr. Feinberg's office. Larry was bent over his desk, and Sharon sat in a chair next to the wall. Sam and Angie Eisenberg were trying to comfort them. No one said anything when Jimmy shut the door behind him.

"Jewish custom demands a quick burial," Larry said without looking up. "The climate leaves no choice."

"The time of separation will be short," Sam consoled. "The Tribulation won't last many more months, and then we will all be reunited."

The words seemed to fall at Jimmy's feet. He said nothing.

Sharon stood up and looked at Jimmy with deep longing. Suddenly, she rushed forward and threw her arms around his neck, sobbing incoherently. If Angie had not offered physical support, the two would have collapsed on the floor.

"You were the best thing that ever happened to my daughter," Sharon cried. "Thank you for giving my daughter such profound happiness."

The dry wells filled again and Jimmy cried quietly. He did not hear the women walk past the door and down the hall to begin preparing the body, nor did he realize that men were carrying a plain wooden casket down the hall.

"When?" Jimmy eventually asked. "When do we finish it?"

"Tomorrow I think." Sam answered. "Perhaps at noontime."

□   □   □

The long line of mourners followed the family as they walked toward the ancient cemetery of Bozrah. The merciless sun blazed straight down. The plain wooden box was carried on the shoulders of six men. Sam Eisenberg led the way. Carefully, the coffin was lowered into the gaping hole in the ground. As far as anyone could see, a surging mass of people crowded the cemetery and spilled over into the surrounding wilderness.

Jimmy was barely aware of what was happening around him. As the Mourner's Kaddish was recited, the strange sounds of Hebrew made the moment feel even more unreal and detached.

"*Yit-gadal ve-yit-kadash shmei raba,*" the crowd chanted. "*B'alma divra khir'utei ve-yamlikh mal-khutei*" arose toward heaven.

Sam Eisenberg read in English, "Hallowed and enhanced may He be throughout the work of His own creation. May He cause His sovereignty soon to be accepted, during our life and the life of all Israel. And let us say: Amen."

People answered, "Amen," and continued to pray until Sam ended the moment. "He who brings peace to His universe will bring peace to us and to all the people of Israel. And let us say: Amen."

The "Amen" roared across the desert.

Larry stepped forward and threw the first handful of dirt on the casket. Sharon followed the ancient custom. Others dropped in handfuls of dirt and sand, but Jimmy couldn't move. Sharon slipped by his side and filled his palm with sand.

"It is our way," she said simply.

Jimmy stepped to the edge of the grave. The sand trickled between his fingers until it was gone. He wanted to jump in and throw his body over the box, letting them cover him as well. He felt the gentle tug of Sharon's hand pulling him back into the crowd.

Larry locked his arm in Jimmy's, and Sharon supported him from the other side as they started back. A bent little woman stepped in front of him.

Her wrinkled features and sagging eyes made her look ancient. She wore a faded black scarf and a heavy black dress. Most of her teeth were gone. The woman reached for Jimmy's hand. Her fingers bent beneath large, distorted arthritic knuckles. She looked up in his eyes; tears stained her face.

"Fifty-four years ago," the woman said in broken English, "I lost my daughter at Auschwitz. I was pregnant, but the baby was stillborn. I do not know why I lived." Tears again ran down her face. "I still ask the Holy One why He did not take me. I would have preferred to have taken the place of the many who died. Sometimes it is so much harder to stay with the living."

The old woman reached up and kissed Jimmy on the cheek. "Now I know that I was not left alone. The Holy One was always there. Believe in life! *Chaim!*" She shuffled back into the crowd and was gone.

For the first time Jimmy was strangely comforted.

# 25

**B**en Feinberg stood in the shadows of the UCLA building, watching people come and go from the girls' dorm. George reported his findings.

"Deborah is inside talking to some of the girls on Cindy's floor to see if anyone will tell us anything." George talked rapidly. "No one has seen anything of Cindy for at least the last two days. It just doesn't look good."

"I don't understand it." Ben shook his head. "She was going to take radio calls from Israel and stay in her room. No one could have followed her anywhere. I expected to hear from her around ten last night, but I got nothing."

"Deborah has an 'in' with one of the student resident supervisors on Cindy's floor. I think she can get a pass-key to Cindy's room. Look!" George pointed to the side door of the dorm. "Deborah's coming out."

Deborah walked toward the two young men hiding near the large building. She abruptly turned and started down the walkway in the opposite direction.

"Hey!" George scratched his head. "She knows we're over here. Where's she going?"

"Something is very wrong." Ben watched Deborah walk away. "She's making a detour to warn us. Deborah must fear that she's being watched or followed. I think

she must be heading for the parking lot. Let's circle
around behind this building and see if we can head her
off."

Both students ran for the back side of the building
and then cut diagonally across the campus. They
reached the parking area just as Deborah arrived.

"What's happening?" Ben called out.

Deborah waved casually almost as if she didn't recognize her friends. With a fixed smile, she answered
softly, "Get out of here. Meet me at the Pizza Hut down
the street, but watch yourselves. The police may be anywhere right now."

Ben and George sauntered away as if they had just
said hello to an acquaintance. As Deborah sped away
in her Honda, the two friends kept looking in every possible direction. When they reached the end of the lot,
they jumped into the thick foliage. They ran down the
thick row of trees and shrubs until they came out near
a busy boulevard. Immediately, they ran into the traffic
and through the cars. On the other side they trotted toward the familiar Pizza Hut. Deborah was already sitting at a table.

"OK," Ben puffed, "what's up?"

"No one knows all of the details for sure, but here's
the composite I've put together. The girls are terrified
and won't talk about anything, but yesterday the security police suddenly showed up and surrounded the
building. Cindy's blindness made her a very easy catch.
After they ransacked her room, they took her away in
one of the cars."

Ben turned pale and could only shake his head.

"I got into her room. The place was torn apart, and
one thing was clear. The police got the radio. It's gone."
She paused. "I found Sam in the corner." Deborah
shook her head. "He was dead."

Ben bit his lip, swallowed hard, and looked up to the
sky. "God, please help us!"

"We're in this together." George put his arm around
his friend. "Don't panic. God hasn't abandoned us."

"Either she was watched for some time, or she was talking on the radio," Deborah concluded. "The secret police apparently hit like lightning. They clubbed the poor dog to death. No one heard him make a sound."

"They must have known about the radio." Ben's hand began to shake. "I'm sure that's what triggered the raid. I shouldn't have let Cindy keep the thing in her room. It's my fault."

"No, no, Ben." Deborah squeezed his hand. "We've all known that anything could cause one of these attacks. The radio has actually offered security to Cindy. You were able to warn her and keep in contact."

"What am I going to do?" Ben wrung his hands.

"Listen carefully." George took charge. "First, don't make any more calls to Israel for some time. We can't chance that they will find a way to get an instant fix on you. The radio must be silenced. Next, I'm getting the students together. The most important thing that we can do right now is pray.

"Ben, if there's anything that we have learned during these days, it is that God's sovereignty is being vindicated through all of this chaos. The world may be falling apart, but He stands supreme above the flood. The Lord Yeshua is preparing to return as Lord of lords. You've taught us to trust Him for everything."

"Yes . . . yes, that's true." Ben's eyes were misty. "But Cindy is so little . . . and frail. What can she do if they decide to torture her?"

"Ben, you must not return to the farmhouse until we know what's really happened." George was resolute. "Stay with me until we know the police haven't uncovered our base of operation."

"I don't think that I have any choice." Ben's voice was weak and shaky. "I feel like a ship that was just torpedoed."

"Deborah, can you get the word out to the girls to be at my apartment by seven tonight?"

"Sure, George."

"I'll work on getting the word out to the guys. We'll pray this thing through, Ben. You'll see."

"I don't think I'd better go back around the girls' dorm," Ben barely whispered. "They may already know who I am. I feel so helpless. I just don't know what to do. Our only hope is to find somebody who can get inside information on the secret police."

"Fat chance." George shook his head.

□   □   □

Cindy sat quietly in the interrogating room of the LA Police Department. Jack Wilson stood across from her, smoking a cigarette and studying a piece of paper. On the table in front of him was a thick file filled with pictures and papers.

"We've been watching you for a long time." His oily voice was condescending. "We know everything about everyone so you can save us and yourself a great deal of trouble by simply answering the questions."

"If you know all about me," Cindy smiled pleasantly, "then there is nothing for me to tell. You already know."

The plainclothes policeman's eyes narrowed, and he licked his lips. "Don't be cute! We will wring out of you what we want to know one way or the other. Do you understand?" Jack Wilson growled.

Cindy nodded her head. "I am a very small and in many ways helpless young woman. You killed my guide dog; you can kill me. But I know who is in control of my life. Whatever you do will happen because in some way it will lead to the glory of God in the end."

"Oh, how I hate you fanatics!" The man blew smoke in Cindy's face. "You're such fools. Don't act like my ripping out your fingernails will be a picnic for you. I'll yet see you on the floor begging for mercy from *me* . . . not your God!"

"Do you prove how strong you are by hurting a blind girl and killing her dog?"

"Don't try to play on my sympathies." The security

agent eased down on the table in front of Cindy. "I've shot kids younger than you and never blinked an eye. I hate you innocent-looking types most of all."

"How could I possibly harm you? Hurt anyone?"

"You're a pawn. An insignificant blip. But we can't let you or your kind run free or you multiply. If we don't keep a lid on unpatriotic subversives, you'll spread like rats. Don't look for mercy from me. I don't even understand the word."

"But what have I done?"

"I'd show you the pictures, but you couldn't see them." Wilson spread a handful of photos across the table. "Here's one of you with a teenager. Another with the same teen and several of her friends. Then I have several of you with other students who are known enemies of the state. Here's a picture of you and some Jewish-looking guy."

"What do the pictures prove?"

Wilson flipped on a cassette player on the credenza behind him and shoved in a tape. "Listen," he demanded as Cindy's voice filled the room. "We've got miles of these conversations between you and the people in the pictures. We had special listening devices trained on you."

"It must be very disconcerting to be so afraid of what a little Chinese girl might say."

Instinctively, Wilson doubled up his fist and drew back but something seemed to hold his arm in the air. No matter how hard he pushed forward, his fist stayed locked in place. Only as he relaxed his grip could he slowly lower his arm. He quit talking for a moment and stepped backward. Several times Wilson tried opening and closing his fist. As the strange sensation passed, so did much of his impulsive anger.

"As I was saying," Wilson started again, "we know everything about you. Now tell us about the boy. The guy who leads you around."

"You mean Alexander?" A sly smile crossed Cindy's face.

"Alexander?" The policeman puzzled.

"Alexander Bradshaw? He's just a friend."

"Don't give me the friend business. You fanatics only run around with your own kind. There's no such thing as casual acquaintances. We want the man's address."

"I'm not sure what Alexander Bradshaw's address is."

Wilson made notations on a pad. "Come on. What town does he live in?"

"Possibly Anaheim."

The agent reached out with his thumb and forefinger to get a hunk of Cindy's cheek. He squeezed but couldn't seem to close his fingers. Wilson stepped back in astonishment and stared at his hand. "If you're lying to us, we'll soon know. I guarantee you that I will spare no pain in pulling the truth out of you. Do you understand?"

Cindy nodded her head mechanically.

"If you've deceived me, next time I'll hook up electrodes to places on your body that you didn't dream were possible!" The secret police officer pressed an intercom button. "I want a full-scale dragnet on one Alexander Bradshaw from the Anaheim area. Check UCLA records as well. Now take this woman back to her cell."

For the next three days the students met in a house near the campus, fasting and praying. Cindy spent most of the time alone in her cell. Three times different policemen interrogated her about her friends. Each time they bore down on the name of Alexander Bradshaw, threatening her with harm if their search continued to be unfruitful. They had not yet identified any of the pictures of Ben Feinberg.

Cindy knew that time was running out. Although she had not lied, her clever deflection of the secret police's question would soon be exposed. She had simply pulled a name out of the air. By now Wilson would know her identification was only a ploy.

In the small barren cell Cindy knew that there were

no windows and that a single light bulb was never turned out. Her hands had explored every square inch of the cubicle. In one corner was a toilet and opposite were a bunk and uncovered mattress. Strangely, she had not felt afraid or alone during the past four days. And yet Cindy knew escape was completely impossible. Her best guess was, she had been taken to the bottom of the county jail in an old unused section reserved for people the police wanted to keep in seclusion. Cindy sensed from the echoing sounds that there must be other empty cells in the area. She reached up and felt the cold steel bars.

"Heavenly Father," she prayed quietly, "I count it a great privilege to be imprisoned as were Peter and Paul. Should I be called to suffer for the sake of the Cross, I would rejoice in the opportunity to walk in His steps." She stopped and wiped a tear from her eye. "And yet I am weak. How can I stand up against these terrible men? I fear I will break and betray my friends. Please! Should I become too frail, take my life before I say anything that could hurt Ben."

Cindy's prayer was interrupted by an unexpected sound. Her keen ears would have heard footsteps long before anyone reached the cell door. Yet she clearly could tell that the old lock in the door was turning. It was followed by the noise of the heavy metal hinges grinding together as the door opened. Cindy listened intently but heard nothing else.

A man's tight grip clamped around Cindy's arm, and she felt herself being lifted to her feet. "Who's there?" she cried out. "What are you doing?" Instantly, she reasoned they had padded their feet and were preparing to use some form of psychological torture. "I'm not afraid of you," she tried to sound brave. "You're not going to frighten me with some gimmick."

Without a word the man pushed her toward the cell door. His firm grip was not painful, but she couldn't elude the stealthy guard. He led her in the opposite direction from the usual route taken by Wilson. She nearly stumbled going up the steps. The man began walking so fast that Cindy reached out, fearing that she would bump into something, but he forced her hand back to her side.

"Why are you doing this to me?"

The relentless hand only forced her onward. Another door opened, and Cindy could hear people talking in the hall in front of her. Policemen were discussing a car wreck and didn't make any response as she walked past. At the end of a long corridor, Cindy heard an electronic door buzz and then open. A few steps away, the man opened another door. On the other side she could hear many people buzzing and talking. The place sounded like a large waiting room.

"What's happening to me?" Cindy protested again. "Where am I?"

The man said nothing but forcefully moved her right through the middle of the crowd. Cindy felt a very large door open and a sweep of fresh air rushed at her face. The slightly burning, polluted sensation smelled like the usual LA atmosphere. "Are we outside?" Cindy puzzled.

Nothing was said as the man guided her down a number of steps and toward the street. They waited for a moment before Cindy heard a bus pull to the curb. Her captor pushed her toward the bus steps. Cindy gingerly climbed up the three steps and took a couple of cautious steps forward before the guard pulled her down on a seat.

"I demand to know where we are going!" Cindy exclaimed in exasperation.

Abruptly, the talking around her stopped. "We're on the 405," a kindly older woman's voice explained. "You're on the bus that goes by the coliseum. Do you want me to tell you when we're near the campus?"

Cindy's mouth dropped. All she could say was yes.

For a long time she sat bewildered as the bus jostled and lurched down the street and over the freeway. Eventually, her guide pulled her to her feet and shuffled her toward the back exit.

"You're just about there," the woman called after her.

Cindy reached for the safety bars to direct her way but by now was confident that her abductor would not let her stumble. The bus slowed down and the door opened. Immediately, the unseen arm led her down the steps to the street and back up on the curb. Nothing was said as he moved her inside a shelter for bus passengers.

"You did quite well," the deep bass voice boomed.

"Michael!" Cindy nearly shouted. "You've been there all the time."

"For the last four days to be exact."

"You've sprung me from the jail!"

"We walked right past every one of them!"

"I can't believe it!"

"Oh, I have been releasing Christians for nearly two thousand years now. I even helped set Paul and Silas free once."

"I can't believe it! I'm actually out of that terrible place."

"I have materialized now and am going to walk beside you. Follow me and we will catch up with your friends. Ben and the gang are not far from here."

"I just can't believe it! And I feel so good! They didn't feed me much, but I feel so energized."

"Ben and the students have been fasting and praying. You have been receiving the benefits of their intercessions on your behalf."

They hurried down the boulevard and cut down a residential side street, walking as quickly as Cindy could go. Just before they reached the front door of a small, plain stucco house, Michael stopped. "I want you to tell the group several important things. Ben is not to use the radio until I tell him to do so. At the right time, I will explain and tell him how to proceed. The police are now ready to cue in on the frequency you have been using with Israel. Understand?"

"Most certainly!"

"At some time you will wonder why you have been rescued when the McCoys . . . and others . . . have not survived. All these matters have an explanation, but the issues are so complex that you could never fully grasp their significance. God's plan for each and every individual is so vast, interwoven with so many lives, all that is past and present, and with so many options and alternatives, that no computer in the universe could track the eternal dimensions of what happens in time.

"When people tragically lose their lives because of evil or the fallen nature of this world, their family and friends have the choice of succumbing to bitterness or growing in grace. Ultimately, the issue is not what you can understand and explain even to yourself, but your capacity to believe in the sovereignty of our heavenly Father. Remember not to measure events by your standards of justice, but leave the consequences to be tried by grace. Give this teaching to your friends. I am going to leave you now. Just take two steps forward and knock. The group is inside in prayer."

"Oh, Michael! This is the most terrifying, wonderful adventure of my life. I can't wait to tell Ben that I have my own Seeing Eye angel!"

"I cannot wait to watch that little Nazi Wilson explain to his superiors how a blind girl unlocked maximum security and walked right out of the building through the traffic court!"

**D**amian Gianardo sat hunched over his desk in the National Security Building. The emperor grumbled as he read the report Prime Minister Rathmarker handed him.

"Sir," the military chief of staff sitting across the desk sounded professionally distant, "there is no question that the Chinese are still producing nuclear weapons."

"I have threatened them!" The emperor shook his fist. "It is nearly the first of October, and they haven't complied."

The general kept his military posture and avoided eye contact with the emperor. "We estimate that they still have a billion citizens and an army of two hundred million, including reservists. Earthquakes, pollution, and fires have certainly taken a toll but not to the degree we have been damaged. The Chinese don't like paying our high tariffs and have rebellion on their minds."

"I'd burn them like a paper dragon." Gianardo shook his finger at the general.

"The United Muslim States are equally belligerent," the general observed stoically. "Should the Chinese and the Arabs work out a treaty, we would be forced to the wall. We have been able to stomp around the world as if we were wearing steel boots. An alliance in the East would expose our clay feet."

"Don't ever talk like that again in my presence!" The emperor rose to his feet. "I expect optimism. Don't come in here with this nonsense about vulnerability. I am invincible! Now get out!"

The general snapped to attention, bowed his head in respect, and turned on his heels to march out of the room. Gianardo picked up the report and slung it against the far wall of his office. "Send in the next bunch," he barked to his prime minister. "Give me the secret police people."

Rathmarker hurriedly opened the door and three men in suits and ties entered.

"Sit down, gentlemen." The emperor pointed to the chairs in front of his desk. "I want an update."

The men looked back and forth at each other until Sloan, the largest of the three, asked bluntly, "Do you want the truth? Or shall we just make you happy?"

"Level with me," Gianardo said sourly.

"The size of our payroll is dragging us to the bottom. We now have more public employees working for us than any other profession in this empire."

"You should be pleased," the emperor sneered. "I've gotten you everything you want, haven't I?"

"Our reign of terror is the only thing keeping the lid on the country," the second man interjected. "People hate us and don't want to pay the taxes to fund their own surveillance. We've become the target for every form of hate imaginable. The whole operation is becoming counterproductive."

"What about the religious fanatics?" Gianardo pointed at the third man. "Collins? Have you stamped them out?"

"We've tried everything and continue to do so." The security chief pulled at his collar. "Again, the persecution has backfired. In the beginning citizens were glad to turn in the religionists, but now they've become heroes. These believers go to their deaths with a smile on their lips and joy in their eyes. The more we persecute them, the more the Christians reproduce. Right now we're trying to combat a new outbreak of fanaticism in Los Angeles. College kids are turning to Christianity at an incredible rate. Sheer madness has broken out on some of the college campuses. It's their way to rebel against authority."

Sloan added, "Messages keep getting smuggled in from Moses and Elijah in Jerusalem. Unfortunately, their predictions have an uncanny 100 percent accuracy. People are desperate for direction. Those two crazies sitting by that ancient wall are creating a lot of problems for all of us. Can't you do something about them?"

"I think I can solve our mutual problem." Gianardo flipped on his intercom once more. "Call the press," he shouted into the microphone. "I've just fired Sloan, Davies, and Collins as department division heads of national security. New competent appointments will be forthcoming."

"But Mr. Emperor!" Davies jumped up. "You wanted the truth."

"I wanted results," the emperor screamed in the security officer's face. "Now get out of here while you can still walk!"

The three men stumbled backward out of the room as quickly as they could leave.

"Fools!" the emperor ranted. "I am surrounded by nothing but fools and idiots." Gianardo slammed his fist onto his desk. "I'll get rid of those two Israeli actors if I have to kill them myself!"

In the main hospital office Sam and Angie Eisenberg held the hands of Larry and Sharon as they prayed for their friends. "And please comfort Jimmy. Nothing that we say seems to be able to reach him," Sam concluded.

"Each of us needs Your blessing in a personal way. Amen."

"Amen," the three responded.

"Do you know where Jimmy is?" Angie asked.

"He should be back by now," Larry answered. "He goes out to Ruth's grave this time each day. Sometimes he's back earlier." Larry gestured aimlessly. "Sometimes much later."

"No one can comfort Jimmy." Sharon wiped her eyes. "We've talked about the reunion God promises at the end of this terrible time, but nothing helps."

"Facts don't do much for pain," Larry sighed. "Every psychiatrist knows the limits of knowledge to heal the soul. I once read the work of Victor Frankl, the Viennese psychiatrist who survived the Auschwitz death camp. He wrote about the importance of finding meaning in our suffering. I think this is what has made everything so confusing to Jimmy."

The door opened. Jimmy walked in, nodding to each person but not speaking. He walked over to the table and laid a flashlight down, turned, and started out again.

"Mind sitting down with us?" Sam asked.

"I don't think so," Jimmy looked straight ahead. "I have things to do."

"The people really miss your teaching," Angie added. "Every day the immigrants ask when you'll be back."

"Not for a long time," Jimmy's voice was barely audible.

"You have so much to offer," Sam joined in. "You are a truly gifted teacher."

"I'm not sure I believe any of it," Jimmy suddenly turned on the group. "I don't think anything that I told those people is true. In fact, if it wouldn't get me killed to leave, I would be out of here right now."

Angie said, "I know how you feel—"

Jimmy cut her off. "No. You don't know how I feel. You can't possibly know how I feel. You mean well, but you'll leave here with your husband in a few minutes and go home to your kids. Look!" He pointed out toward the camp. "What's so great about being chosen? Most of those so-called chosen people have spent their entire lives on the run because God picked them out to be His special project in history. Big deal! I'd just as well be a happy little nobody who never got any of that divine attention."

"It's hard." Sharon bit her lip.

"Oh, you bet it's hard. I was a happy little man selling cars and making money in LA on my way to the top before I got into this mess. Now I'm out in the desert as isolated as one of those ugly lizards that runs every time a human shows up. If God is in all of this terror and misery doing us some big favor, then please let me out. I'd just as well skip Christmas this year!" He bolted for the door and slammed it, but the wooden door only bounced open again. No one got up to shut it.

"Jimmy doesn't even ask about Ben anymore," Larry lamented. "He's trying to shut the world out."

"How long since we've heard from Ben?" Sam asked.

"Over two months . . ." Sharon clasped her hands together so tightly that her knuckles were white. "Not since the night we heard from Cindy and the radio went *dead.*"

The word sailed through the room like a boomerang. Each person stiffened.

"What if they've got Ben?" Sharon burst into tears. "I don't think I could stand to lose both of my children." She doubled up with her face in her hands.

Larry dropped to his knees in front of his wife, hugging her and crying. Sam and Angie stood helplessly weeping with their friends. The couples silently grieved as time lost all meaning.

At the sound of footsteps, Larry looked up. "Jimmy!"

"I'm sorry." Jimmy stood limply in front of them. "I didn't even get five feet down the hall. I've been so lost in my pain that I didn't even want to hear about Ben and Cindy." He paused and ran his hands through his hair. "He's your son. How could I possibly speak of what this additional loss could mean to you?" Jimmy began silently weeping. "I'm sorry . . ."

Larry struggled to his feet and threw his arms around his son-in-law. "We will always have two sons," he tried to say clearly. "And we will be eternally proud of both of them."

"We can make it." Sharon put her arms around both men. "Yes. Together we can make it. He who is the bright morning star will yet come and shine upon us."

Larry, Sharon, and Jimmy walked together out of the room and down the corridor toward the outside. Sam and Angie watched from the window as the family stood under the stars looking into the night sky.

# 27

During 1999, the year that followed Ruth's death, the world's food supply continued to dwindle. Economic pressure on the large population centers made life increasingly treacherous in the Los Angeles area. As the price of gasoline also escalated, more desperate people were forced to their limits. Violence was common and unpredictable. Ben found his farmhouse to be a haven in the midst of an unstable world.

On Friday, May 21, the Feast of Pentecost or Shavuot, the next woe fell on the world. Gianardo was in his office in the National Security Building dictating to a secretary when he noticed strange insects creeping under his door. The large ugly bugs looked like locusts with scorpion tails.

"What's that?" the emperor pointed to the floor.

"I don't know." The secretary stared, horrified, as more and more insects scurried across the floor.

"Doesn't anybody pay attention to sanitation around here?" The emperor stood up and peered over his desk.

"I've never seen anything like this!" The woman stood up and then tried to stomp one of the pests. The insect made a cracking sound. A putrid smell arose from the floor.

"How is it that I can control the world but can't keep swarming insects from invading my office?" Gianardo threw the switch on his intercom. "Get security in here on the double," he demanded."

"Owww!" the secretary screamed. "They bite! Ohhh!" She began hopping about the room. "No! They sting!"

Gianardo suddenly slapped his pants leg. "Ouch!" he bellowed. "These things are poisonous!"

Two policemen rushed into the room. "What's the problem?" The first man prepared to draw his gun.

"We're being attacked!" The secretary pointed to the floor.

The second man spun around looking in every direction. His feet nearly went out from under him as the scorpionlike bugs squished into a slippery goo under his shoes.

Gianardo plopped down on the top of his desk, slapping at his legs. "I'm on fire," he gasped. "Look!" He pulled up his pants, exposing large red welts up and down his leg.

The first policeman began dancing around the room trying to get the insects off his shoes.

"I demand you stop them!" Gianardo screamed. "I'm the emperor! I run the police! I demand that this stops!"

But it didn't stop. In the following weeks the people of the world, like Pharaoh's subjects in ancient Egypt, found a plague consuming them. No repellent could deter the mysterious bugs that came out of nowhere, leaving infection and unbearable skin irritation in their wake. From coast to coast the infestation became an all-consuming concern. And unlike the temporary severe pain of a normal scorpion sting, the pain from these insects lingered on and on.

The plague did not keep the secret security police in Los Angeles from being relentless, but the growing Christian movement among college students made their job much more difficult. The young leaders Ben had trained during the preceding months began taking new responsibility for meeting the growing requests for spiritual help. Most students had been raised in the wide open permissiveness of the early nineties and naturally rebelled in the opposite direction. The intellectually critical world of the college campus had been the first place to perceive clearly what was ahead for the environment and world politics. Initial hopes that Gianardo had raised for national superiority and economic prosperity were turning into complete disillusionment. The secret police were equally troubled, discerning what was intellectual dissent from religious sedition.

In late summer, mistaken identification resulted in several UCLA professors being shot and a number of politically oriented student leaders being arrested. Government pressure was no longer able to suppress the story, and the scandal rocked Gianardo's administration. For a period of weeks, the police were forced to retreat, but the public embarrassment only spurred on Ben and Cindy's group.

During this time, Ben felt it was safe to attempt radio contact with Israel. Unfortunately, the Feinbergs no longer maintained constant surveillance of their radio. A week passed before contact was established. Ben was overwhelmed when he learned of his sister's death and the loss of the baby. Weeks dragged by as Cindy and the group prayed, counseled, and encouraged their leader.

In Bozrah and Petra the crops flourished. The crosswinds blew polluted air out to sea. Refugees were well fed and healthy. Fortunately, life in Bozrah left little time for private reflection. Jimmy eventually returned to his teaching. Classes grew as the desert population swelled. He plunged into his work with a vengeance, trying to bury his loneliness in the demands the new students made on him.

The scorpion locusts also invaded Israel and inflicted great pain, but nowhere in the world were any believers stung by these pests. When Moses and Elijah warned of other coming woes, the word spread through the country. The heavenly Father stopped the invasion of the painful pests at the edge of the protected zone. As a result, more people poured into the Bozrah-Petra area. Many paid with their lives because the troops stationed around the mountain heights shot them.

On Wednesday, October 27, 1999, the seventeenth of Heshvan, the plague ended, just as Moses had predicted. God chose this date because of its great significance. On this day God spared Noah and his family once the rains began to fall, giving humankind a new beginning. This same day in the Jewish calendar on November 2, 1917, the Balfour Declaration gave Jews a national homeland in Palestine for the first time in nearly two thousand years, another new beginning. The locusts shriveled up, cracked, and died as if their life expectancy was spent. The stench of billions of dead insects around the globe was overwhelming.

Two months later, the next warning of Moses, the Sixth Trumpet Judgment, began to unfold when the military chief of staff and the generals of the New Roman Empire met with Gianardo and Rathmarker in the National Security Strategy Planning Center. It was New Year's Day, 2000.

General Smith stared coldly at the emperor as the reports were given by other military officers. Gianardo listened without any visible emotion as the briefing covered every area that Smith had warned of months earlier. Once the historic context of the problem with China was established, another general switched on the illuminated maps.

"We have carefully pinpointed the new areas of military attack along China's borders. Each of these assaults came last night as part of a coordinated attack on all New Roman Empire forces stationed within China's official boundaries. As best we can tell, the Chinese have obliterated all of our men there. At least fifty thousand soldiers have died, and there is no indication that anyone was taken prisoner. Our current estimate is that

Premier Lei has stationed two hundred million troops along these same border areas. There is no question that they are prepared to attack."

"We must conclude that the Chinese are contemplating hostile action," Prime Minister Rathmarker stated. "I suggest that we plan a preemptive strike at once."

General Smith stood up abruptly. "Just before our meeting began, an aide handed me the following communiqué, which was received from one of our agents placed within the Lei regime. The premier will declare his independence of the empire within the next few hours and then strike against us."

Smith watched the emperor carefully. He could tell Gianardo was avoiding eye contact to keep from acknowledging the fact that he had ignored Smith's warnings, but Gianardo's hands betrayed him. Smith watched as the supreme leader slowly clawed a piece of paper into a tight ball, squeezing it so tightly that the tips of his fingers lost their color. He threw the paper on the floor and stood up.

"Get that worthless little Chink on the phone. Set up the translation so that every word is immediately typed on the television screens overhead. By the time he digests what I have to say, he'll be begging us for mercy!"

Gianardo continued his tirade of threats until the aide returned with the special translator who could type in the responses as he received them. The emperor was delighted with the immediate response from China, assuming that haste signaled respect and fear.

"Lei," Gianardo began without pleasantries or formal recognition of the premier's position, "we will not tolerate any form of resistance to our authority. If the reports of casualties among our troops are correct, we will expect complete and total reparations. Do you understand?"

For a few moments there was total silence in the vast hall. Then the television screen began to fill with words.

"Mr. Gianardo, your arrogance and imperialism are no longer tolerable, nor do we recognize your authority. All ties with the New Roman Empire have ended. In the future all trade agreements will be renegotiated. Your failure to recognize our sovereignty and independence will result only in damage to you and your government."

The emperor blinked uncomprehendingly at the TV screen. "You must have misunderstood him," he murmured to the translator. The man shook his head.

"You tell that worthless yellow-skinned fool that unless he comes into immediate compliance, I am prepared to blow Beijing off the map."

"No!" General Smith bolted from his chair. "You don't dare make such a threat!"

"What?" Gianardo turned around slowly. His intense black eyes squinted into narrow slits. His teeth clenched. "Have you forgotten yourself, General? Do you know who you're talking to?"

"Don't push them!" Smith stammered. "They have the capacity to retaliate. We can't lose our heads and do something rash."

"Unlock the box!" The emperor pointed to the sealed mechanism for sounding a nuclear alert. "I am the supreme power in the world, and I expect complete compliance with every word I utter."

"No, no," the general begged. "Intelligence reports indicate that Lei is unpredictable. Don't push him into a corner."

"Sit him down!" The emperor signaled to a guard standing by the door. "Keep the general in his chair until I indicate otherwise." Gianardo continued giving instructions in shrill tones. "Activate our Star Wars System. I want a missile ready to fire at the moment that I signal."

"We can't take another nuclear exchange," the general begged his colleagues around the room. "The environment can't stand it. The empire will collapse!"

"If the general makes another comment," Gianardo

instructed the soldier, "shoot him. Lack of support in a national emergency is treason."

Across the room men froze at their stations. No one looked at the other.

"Now that we have things under control, I will continue." Gianardo breathed heavily as he spoke. "Tell Premier Lei that he has one minute to signal his acceptance of our authority, or I will wipe out his capital city. NOW!"

The translator talked rapidly into the mouthpiece of his headset as he typed the emperor's message across the screen. No one moved. After ninety seconds the translator began typing again. "We have the satellite capacity to instantly register the firing of any missiles from anywhere in the world. Thirty seconds after any firing, we will detonate a hydrogen bomb that has been smuggled into New York City. For every missile fired, a corresponding bomb will be detonated in another major city of the New Roman Empire."

"Do they have that kind of satellite capacity?" Gianardo turned to the military panel. General Smith nodded his head.

"They couldn't hide a bomb in one of our cities!"

Again the general signaled yes.

"It's a lie," the emperor snarled.

"One last time," the general broke his silence. "We have detected suspicious activity among Chinese agents for some time. Now I understand the full meaning of those intelligence reports. They were assembling nuclear devices."

The soldier guarding the general did not remove his gun. Ignoring the general, Gianardo walked over to the nuclear detonation box. He picked up the receiver and punched in his top secret personal code. "Fire the nuclear warhead programmed for Beijing." The emperor slowly put the phone down and turned toward the TV screen.

Two minutes passed before the translator began typing. "Initial reports indicate that you have fired a missile. We will determine in two minutes if that trajectory is aimed at our country. If the missile continues and is not destroyed within three minutes, we will release an underground hydrogen explosion on Manhattan Island. We will proceed to respond to every missile fired with corresponding destruction of one of your cities. We are prepared to totally destroy what was formerly the United States of America."

"Bluffing!" Gianardo scoffed. "When this is over, each of you will be relieved that your country is in the hands of a man of steel nerves. During this crisis, I want every Chinese citizen rounded up and brought in. No telling who's been collaborating with Lei. Now get to your battle stations!"

Men instantly moved to their emergency positions. Electronic maps flashed on screens around the room. On the two center area overheads, maps of Beijing and Manhattan came up. In the flurry of activity the chief of staff's and the emperor's eyes met. Smith sat emotionless, watching Gianardo's lip curl and his eyes flash disgust at him. This time the general did not flinch or look away. He did not even blink until the emperor finally turned his back on him.

Suddenly, the electronic maps of New York City and Beijing began pulsating simultaneously with concentric circles of radiating light. For a few moments the rings of expanding brilliance moved out across the entire expanse of the cities and then began to fade and with them any indication of population. Everyone stared at the maps.

Smith spoke in somber tones. "They're gone. At least six million people are gone forever from each of the two cities."

By the time the two leaders agreed to a cease-fire, one-sixth of the existing world population was wiped out. In the weeks to come, another sixth would eventually die from the nuclear and environmental fallout. One-third of humankind would be destroyed by two egomaniacs in a matter of weeks.

# CHAPTER
## 28

Cindy Wong sat on a stool in the back of the family restaurant and listened to her father read the newspaper aloud. Her mother continued to stir a boiling kettle on the stove, preparing for their evening customers.

"Say here that emperor make peace with Premier Ching Lei three days after long nuclear disaster. Now that one week pass, it clear that in addition to many millions who die, millions more injured." Frank put the paper down and shook his head. "Craziness. Idiocy. Gianardo is mad man."

"The emperor's losing his grip," Cindy added. "We would never have seen such a story one year ago. He can't censor the press any longer."

"Empire is collapsing!" Jessica shook her finger in the air. "The evil man not stand forever."

The kitchen's swinging doors flew open, and a large man barged in. "Please follow me without saying a word," he commanded.

"Who are you?" Cindy's father dropped his paper.

"We must move quickly. Go out the back door now. Do not make a sound."

Jessica reached for a large chopping knife. "You not rob us tonight!"

"We only have minutes to leave before the security police arrest you."

Before Cindy could speak, the man pulled her off the stool and headed for the rear door. "Follow us," he commanded. "Secret police are coming in the front door this very minute."

The Wongs ran silently behind their daughter. The trio ran down the alley behind the shopping center, following the strange man. Near the back fence line, the large man pushed a piece of the broken fence apart and the Wongs slipped through.

"What happening?" Frank puffed.

"Get across the street!" The stranger took Cindy's hand and waded into the traffic, winding his way among the cars waiting for the stoplight to change. Only after they turned into the first street that ran into a tract house area did he stop.

"Michael!" Cindy exploded. "What in the world are you doing? I recognized your voice in the restaurant."

"Michael?" the parents echoed.

"Listen carefully. The government is rounding up all Chinese citizens tonight. You must hide for several days. Within forty-eight hours confusion and chaos will be so great that the emperor's decision will have to be rescinded and the government will be forced to release all prisoners. However, the police will be double-checking to find any Christians who might have been caught in the sweep. Cindy, they have your picture on file."

"Oh, Michael! You have saved me again."

"We have little time to talk. Listen to what I want you to tell the students that you are discipling. We have less than a year left. The Antichrist will become more desperate as his empire disintegrates. His inability to hold China will result in other nations such as Russia, the Ukraine, and the United Muslim States defying his authority. He will be even more reckless and dangerous. If the police had taken you tonight, you would have been dead before morning."

"Ahhh!" Jessica grabbed her daughter. "Help us!"

"Quiet! Just listen to me. After the next couple of days pass, there will be a period of relative quiet. Governmental leaders will be so involved in trying to handle the disasters in the various nuked cities of the empire that they will leave the Christians and the Chinese alone."

"Cindy tell us about you, Mr. Angel," Frank's voice quivered. "It difficult to believe . . . but we have heard your name often. We are old . . . foolish. But must believe in your Jesus now . . . tonight . . . this moment."

The shrill whining of sirens split the brisk night air. Police cars could be heard closing in from opposite directions.

"They are arresting your Chinese employees right now but do not worry. In three days they will be back to work. Catching Cindy would have been the death blow to all of you."

Frank began bowing up and down in the oriental polite manner. "Mr. Michael, when workers come back, I tell them to believe in Jesus. I tell them His angels never stop their work. Yes, we tell them we believe."

Cindy hugged her parents. "Mom. Dad. I am so relieved. Tonight my prayers have been answered. I thank God for your decision."

"Cindy, even though it is some distance away, you must walk to the McCoys' house. No one has been there for months. The police will not be expecting people to hide in that place because of its reputation for harboring disloyal citizens. I have already unlocked the back door, and there are still canned goods in the pantry."

"Ben will be terrified," she pleaded. "I must let him know that we are OK."

"I will appear at the farmhouse after I leave you. Do not worry. Tonight I must give special assignments to the students for the final months. I will put his mind at peace. Now go!"

"We believe. We believe," Frank kept saying over his

shoulder as the family scurried down the street and
disappeared into one of the dark side streets.

As time passed, my prediction proved to be correct,
and Gianardo backed down on his oppression of Chinese citizens of the New Roman Empire. By early
spring of 2000, the Wong family closed the restaurant
and moved into Ben's ministry headquarters away
from the gangs that had become a significantly greater
threat than Gianardo's secret police had ever been.

In Bozrah, Jimmy sat close to his father-in-law as the
doctor made hasty notations on a pad. Both men listened intently as Dr. Zachery translated the radio
broadcast coming out of Babylon in early spring.

"At least forty million Christians have been killed
throughout the New Roman Empire," the Egyptian
doctor dictated as he pressed the headset against his
ear. "The reporter says that approximately seven million were Jewish believers. Also two million more Jews
were killed. Another twenty million citizens of the New
Roman Empire were executed because Gianardo's men
determined they were unpatriotic in their allegiance to
him."

Jimmy ran his hands through his hair in despair. "No
one in the history of the world has murdered so many
people simply because of their religious and political
beliefs. The man is completely mad."

Dr. Zachery pulled the headset away. "The Muslims
are saying that they have no love for the Christians or
Jews, but no leader so treacherous can be trusted or
tolerated. The announcer says that the time has come
to join with China in a new alliance that will be more
mutually advantageous."

"An announcer wouldn't make such an assertion unless it is the party line. No question but the Muslims
are pulling out," Larry concluded.

"I'm sure that there are no Christians or Jews left in

Babylon," Jimmy added. "The stage is set for the final showdown in the next few months."

"What do you mean?" Dr. Zachery asked.

"Jeremiah 50 and 51 and Revelation 17 and 18 spell it all out." Jimmy pushed his Bible toward the doctor. "The city has both symbolically and literally been the place where God's people have been killed for over twenty-five hundred years. The Bible says that in one hour the hand of God will wipe the place out, never to be built again. We are going to see the destruction happen very soon."

The doctor put the headphones back to his ear. "Now the announcer is saying that it is time for the United Muslim States to renegotiate their oil prices. If the New Roman Empire doesn't accept their terms, then the Arabs are prepared to cut off all oil supplies."

"That's all it will take," Larry stated. "The final battle will be on. The Muslims are cutting their own throats."

□　□　□

Gianardo shut the door behind him. Five young generals sat around a small table in the center of the maximum security chamber. The soundproof room was totally secured against any form of electronic eavesdropping. Detection devices prevented anyone from wearing or carrying any form of recording or transmitting apparatus. No other room in the National Security Building was so totally sequestered. Gianardo sat down at the head of the table with Rathmarker at his right hand.

"Everything said in this room is of maximum secrecy." The emperor looked at each person. "Do you understand? Nothing is communicated to anyone about any detail of these consultations."

The generals nodded their total compliance.

"I am now surrounded by old fools and reactionary idiots. My New World Order is being assaulted by the last vestiges of resistance to my complete control. We must now be ready to crush the enemy without fear of disobedience or resistance from within our own government."

Each officer indicated understanding and agreement.

"Your time of opportunity has come. General Smith thinks that I am not aware of his attempts to thwart me. We must be ready to stop his men at a moment's notice. When the final strike against the Chinese and the United Muslim States comes, each of you must be prepared to assassinate anyone who stands in our way. You may have only one shot. You must not miss."

"You can count on us," one of the young men saluted.

"When this period is past," Gianardo spoke with complete confidence, "you will not only be commanders in this empire but the first military leaders of the entire globe. I congratulate you on a very intelligent decision to stand by me."

Gianardo pushed a file toward each person. "I have already appointed each of you to a new position that will take effect at the moment we strike. Askins will head security. Browning, your command will be the nuclear strike command. Jackson, I have selected you to coordinate all ground and attack forces. I want Imler to oversee domestic coordination of all legislative activities. Salino will handle the final details of surrender after we have humiliated our international enemies."

General Jackson smiled broadly. "We are your servants as together we write the history of the third millennium. What can I do at this time?"

"I want you to create a system that will circumvent the nuclear detonation device in this building. It must be portable since we will be taking it to Rome with us in a few months. We will reassemble our command post there. No one must be aware of what you have done except an expert that I will assign to you. Terbor Esiw will know what to do. He is the secret creator behind this effort."

"Who else is aware of this plan?" Browning asked.

"No one. You will note that my instructions are in my own handwriting. When we meet, you will tell your staff personnel that I have appointed you to an ad hoc task force preparing plans for the rebuilding of this country. Any other questions?"

"Can the world survive another war?" Imler probed. "I'm sure that you have completely covered this option."

"A world with less population will be much easier to manage." Gianardo smiled. "Yes, long ago I recognized the need to reduce population to a level that would be more controllable. In the future we will not have to worry with negative public response or the failure of any form of compliance. I will have completely united religion, politics, and all forms of philosophical thought. Gentlemen! We will be gods."

## 29

On April 5, 2000, Sam Eisenberg pulled his van into the parking lot across the street from the Dung Gate, which led to the plaza beneath the Western Wall. The afternoon sun was covered by storm clouds promising rain. He and Jimmy got out and locked the doors to the van.

"We have only a limited amount of time." Sam talked as they crossed the street. "We must assume security agents have our pictures and names on their computers. If we push our luck, we could be identified."

"Sam, do you really think I could pass for an Israeli?"

"You're concerned?"

"Sneaking out of the protected zone is no small matter, Sam. I just pray that we weren't followed."

"If we had been, the troops would have already caught us. No, Jimmy, we can breathe easy while we listen to Moses and Elijah. They always protect believers in their area. Just walk straight ahead like we're locals."

Jimmy spoke quietly. "Since our contact with Ben has been limited, we haven't received many of the special insights that the angel gives him. We need any new information we can learn from these two giants."

"Time is short. We shouldn't have many months left. I just pray our timetable is correct."

Jimmy looked pained but didn't answer.

The two men hurried past the armed patrol outside the massive ancient stone gate. Metal detectors were along each side of the entrance. Ahead of them they could see a long line of people. The huge throng made it impossible to see what was ahead. Sam edged his way to the railing that kept sightseers out of the excavations along the wall and the Temple Mount. Sam hopped up on a corner post of the railing.

"Good grief! The place is packed. The rumors were true. Jews are flocking in here to listen to Elijah and Moses. The reports of a revival really are right."

"How can we ever get through this crowd?" Jimmy called up to him. "People are packed in here like sardines!" He pointed to the apartment buildings behind them. "People are even hanging out of windows blocks away."

"The loudspeakers will let us hear what's being said," Sam concluded. "We won't have to actually get near to hear it all."

"Listen," Jimmy said firmly, "I risked my life to come in today. I want to get my money's worth. I don't care what it takes, I want to get as close as possible. What about the police and the soldiers?"

"Amazing. They don't even have their guns out. I can see them sitting on the sand bags ready to listen. Things sure have changed since the last time we were here."

"I've got an idea." Jimmy looked over the edge at the archaeological dig. "If the police aren't paying attention, let's drop over the side and work our way up to the other end. We'll just pop up by the wall."

"Here goes nothing." Sam vaulted over the side of the wire fence and dropped five feet into the grass beneath him. Jimmy followed and landed next to his friend.

"Make it fast." Sam started winding through the

stone foundations. "We could still get thrown out if we're seen down here."

"Just think!" Jimmy rolled his eyes. "We are actually walking on the same pavement that Jesus and the disciples traveled going up to the temple. What more appropriate path could we take to talk to two of the greatest men of the Old Testament?"

Sam pointed to the incline ahead. "When we get to the end, we'll have to make a mad dash up the side and over the fence. We'll try to drop down on the women's side of the wall and work our way out of there."

In their mad dash, Sam and Jimmy got separated, but each man worked his way to the next fence that protected the women's division in front of the Great Western Wall. Jimmy vaulted over first, but Sam was close behind. Only after they had waded into the crowd of women did the consequences of their actions become clear.

"What are you doing here?" A woman with her head covered pushed Sam backward.

"You crazy or something?" A small heavyset older woman beat on Jimmy's chest. "Get out of here!"

The women shoved and protested, pushing the two men backward toward the metal rails separating the two sides. Before Jimmy and Sam could completely recover, the irate women pressed them against the partitions. The two men quickly rolled over the railings, falling about ten feet from where Moses and Elijah were sitting.

Jimmy stared. Since their last visit, a wooden platform had been erected so everyone in the area could see the two imposing figures. Their simple chairs had been replaced by heavy wooden thrones. In the immediate vicinity, men were sitting on the ground to allow the people at the back to see even better. A wondrous light hovered about the awesome figures.

Moses turned his head and looked straight at Jimmy. The ancient lawgiver smiled knowingly like a regal head of state conveying recognition to an old friend standing in the midst of an adoring crowd.

Elijah stood up and looked over the assembly. The masses surged forward as Elijah held up his arms. Sam and Jimmy stood in awe.

"Passover is at hand," Elijah said with great solemnity. "This year we celebrate for the last time the meaning of our release from bondage. Never again will we eat the Pasch in anticipation, for within six months our deepest longings will be fulfilled. The Messiah is ready to enter through the Golden Gate to the east."

A great shout arose from the people. Clapping and shouting filled the air.

Elijah again held up his arm for calm. "Yet as the final moment approaches, the man of evil continues his work. The Antichrist's appetite for death is not yet satisfied. You must be ready for more terrible things that are yet to come. As the New Roman Empire crumbles, on the evening of the Passover Supper on the fourteenth of Nisan, the United Muslim States will announce their separation from the evil state. Stand ready! Within twenty-four hours, on the Feast of Unleavened Bread, Babylon the harlot will be severely wounded, then destroyed. In an hour the capital of evil will be silenced for eternity."

"That's April 20," Jimmy whispered to Sam. "In a couple of weeks Gianardo must be going to nuke the Arabs."

"We've got to get the word to Ben," Sam answered. "No telling what kind of chain reaction could be set off. Ben needs to make sure they have enough food stockpiled to last the next six months."

Moses pointed toward Egypt. "The day after the Passover supper, called the Feast of Unleavened Bread, is always on the fifteenth of Nisan because our exodus from Pharaoh began on this day after 430 years of bondage. After the fall of the temple and Jerusalem in A.D. 70, the last brave defenders of the state retreated to Masada. On the fifteenth of Nisan they gave up their lives rather than submit to the forces of tyranny."

Elijah pointed across the plaza toward the Church of the Holy Sepulchre. "On this same day, Yeshua our Messiah laid down His life on a cross for the sins of the world. Therefore, Adonai has chosen this day in the year 2000 for vengeance on the past and present Babylon. So shall the justice of the Lord come on the earth."

"Hear us, O Israel!" Moses shook his staff at the sky. "You have been told these things that you might believe. When the smoke has cleared over Babylon, you will have less than six months left before the final days come. Use them well, for the final chapters of history are being written. Now let us bless the Lord."

Both Moses and Elijah dropped to their knees, and the multitude followed suit. At first, the prophets placed their hands on their faces and wept before the Lord. Then they straightened up and began singing the ancient affirmation of faith: *"Shema O, Ysrael Adonai elohenu Adonai echad."* The multitude echoed the chant. From somewhere in the middle of the crowd an elderly cantor sang out, *"Baruch ata Adonai Elohenu Melech holam."* Once more the people picked up the familiar hymn and sang mournfully.

As the melody faded away, Moses stood up and began reciting the second psalm. "Why do the nations rage, and the people plot a vain thing?" he quoted to the skies. "'The kings of the earth set themselves, and the rulers take counsel together, against the LORD and against His anointed.'"

Rabbis in the crowd began to quote the psalm in Hebrew with the lawgiver: "'Now therefore, be wise, O kings; be instructed, you judges of the earth. Serve the LORD with fear, and rejoice with trembling. Kiss the Son, lest He be angry, and you perish in the way, when His wrath is kindled but a little.'" People began shouting, "AMEN! AMEN!"

Elijah answered with the last line. His voice thun-

dered from the address system, " 'Blessed are all those
who put their trust in Him.' "

A great wind swept down from the Temple Mount,
blowing hats and scarves in every direction. The
mighty gale whistled down the side streets and over the
tops of the apartment buildings at the very back of
the whole area. People began weeping and crying out.
Songs of praise arose with the mournful laments of
people pleading before the Lord. The men closest to the
wall pressed against the enormous stones while others
reached with their hands to touch the rocks.

"Repent!" Moses preached. "The Day of the Lord is
at hand. Repent and believe lest you perish as the people of Babylon are soon to do." Moses then pointed
directly at Jimmy and motioned for him to come close.
He whispered some brief warnings and instructions
for the citizens of Bozrah and Petra into Jimmy's ear,
explaining the seven bowl judgments that remained before Yeshua would return.

"I'm sorry, but we better get out of here." Sam pulled
Jimmy toward the back of the plaza. "Television cameras have been panning the audience. They could be
running a security check right now. Time is running
out."

"Maybe." Jimmy gave a final wave to his new friend.
"But today time has also been fulfilled."

□   □   □

Four days later Damian Gianardo's jet circled above
the Rome airport. *The White Horse* slowly cruised,
waiting for all runways to be cleared for the emperor's
landing. The five young generals sat nervously facing
their leader with Rathmarker at their side.

"Where did this report come from?" The emperor
shook the teletype paper in the air. "The newspapers in
Babylon are warning of an immediate attack on the
city. Only one of you could have known that such a plan
was in motion for a possible assault."

Salino raised his hand cautiously. "They're just guessing. Since our negotiations on oil prices collapsed, they are assuming that our threats might take the shape of an attack, even though the Chinese pledged to stand behind them with nuclear support. Lucky guess."

"Guess? On the very day that the attack is planned!" Gianardo exploded. "The report says that we will bomb the city on April 20! There's a leak!"

"In my new capacity as head of security, I have already checked the matter out," General Askins answered smugly. "An extensive investigation began immediately after this headline appeared."

Gianardo turned slowly toward his young lackey. "Well, he said, "Askins scores again. You managed to put a bullet in the back of General Smith's head at precisely the right moment. You had the other resisters arrested in minutes. Now you tell me that you have the inside on our leak?"

"No leak." Askins smiled broadly. "The source of this story comes from Israel."

"Israel?" Gianardo started.

"Yes. Apparently, Israeli intelligence has found some correlation between our statements and our actions."

"What does that mean?" The emperor frowned.

"Well . . ." Askins paused momentarily.

"Tell me!" Gianardo demanded.

"The only official reports I've received say that Moses and Elijah announced our intentions to the nation at exactly the same moment that we were discussing how a missile attack on Babylon would be conducted and how we would move government control to Rome should China retaliate."

"Moses and Elijah!" Gianardo screamed at the top of his lungs. The generals fell back in shock. The emperor was on his feet, waving the report in the air. "They've done it again! I hate them. They must be wiped out at once. If you can't silence those two impostors, I will kill them myself!"

"I don't understand," Askins fumbled. "All attempts to kill them have failed."

"How dare they undermine my position! The Jews have threatened some of the mightiest rulers of the world from Pharaoh down to Saddam Hussein. Now I have to contend with these freaks from a time warp! I will not allow them to make a fool out of me."

"I don't think we ought to harm them." Askins reached into his briefcase for another file. "Reports indicate an amazing nationwide turning to faith in Jesus as the Jewish Messiah. They call Him Yeshua. We don't understand how, but there's no question that these two figures have effected a major revival in the country."

"How dare you retreat!" Veins on the emperor's neck bulged and his face turned crimson. "How dare you insinuate that we should fear anyone—much less them! How dare you suggest that I retreat from those two apparitions!"

"I'm sorry." Askins's eyes widened as he frantically looked from one general to the other. "I did not mean to imply weakness."

"Where's the code box, Jackson?" Gianardo demanded.

"It's in this special case that Terbor Esiw built. All the controls are there. I have it stored in the back."

"Good. I don't care what the Chinese say. We'll use this story to put additional pressure on them. Tell the United Muslim States they have one final chance. Negotiate or else."

Browning added timidly, "There is the matter of the massive buildup of Chinese troops that might strike if . . ."

"Are you with me or not?" Gianardo screamed at the shocked generals.

The young men's heads bobbed up and down like little boats on a stormy sea. As the men scurried to the back of the airplane, Gianardo stared out the window. He ripped up the teletype report and dropped the pieces on the floor.

April 20, 2000, was a significant day in more ways than one. For believers in Yeshua, it was the Feast of Unleavened Bread and Passover with all the symbolic meaning involved. For Gianardo and Rathmarker, it was the day they broke off negotiations with the United Muslim States. For Babylon, it was the day one of Gianardo's nuclear bombs wiped out half the city, and the surviving half fled for fear of radiation poisoning. And for the United Muslim States, it was the day they changed their minds and agreed to lower oil prices for Gianardo's empire. But they determined that it was only a temporary lull before the storm.

# 30

The depleted ozone layer made it a blazing hot and dirty day in late summer in LA. Ash was visible on this dark afternoon.

Ben raced the car engine, waiting impatiently for the light to change. Isaiah watched out the back window while George looked down the side street. A group of eight men eyed them from the other side of the intersection. The motley crew wore battered clothing, they were unshaven, and their uncut hair was stringy and dirty. The pack studied Ben's car like wolves following a deer in the winter.

"We've got scavengers on our flank." Ben nervously shifted into low. "If they charge, we're going through the intersection regardless."

"The light's changed!" George pointed overhead. "Here they come!"

Ben's car whizzed past the first man swinging a baseball bat. One young man clutched at the door handle, but the car flew by so fast that he was hurled out of the way. The rest of the gang didn't get close.

"Wow!" Ben shifted into second. "I thought the police were bad, but now I wish they were back. It was easier to elude the security people than these gangs that roam the streets everywhere since food has become scarce. There's just no law and order left."

"The nuclear exchange back in January finished everything off," Isaiah said as he watched the men shake their fists in the air. "The bomb that went off in the Van Nuys area finished off the local police. Do you really think that Chicago was completely wiped out too?"

"With censored newspapers and television, it's hard to know anything for sure," Ben answered. "But the few ham operators I've been able to contact are saying that most of Chicago is gone. San Francisco's been fairly well gone since the last earthquake. I get the clear feeling that there's no one left running the country."

"I really appreciate you guys making the dash to pick me up." Isaiah settled back against the seat. "I was able to make all the contacts that Michael assigned me. Either people are turning to Yeshua, or they are turning into animals."

"We need to get out of the Costa Mesa area as soon as we can," George added. "The longer we are here, the more radiation we are exposed to . . . not to mention the danger of attack."

Ben turned the corner and pulled into the parking lot of a store that still accepted cash. "Got to get close to the building so we'll be protected. I'm not going into the grocery store unless the coast is clear." He pulled along the curb in front of a store with dirty windows and faded signs still advertising old specials. The stained posters hung at odd angles from yellowing tape. Beside the entrance men were crouched behind sand bags, training guns on their car.

"We're customers," Isaiah called out. "Don't shoot."

"Leave the car there." A man yelled back. "Walk in with your hands empty. We don't take any chances."

Ben turned the car off and walked slowly toward the door with his palms exposed. Isaiah and George did the same. Inside there were only a few customers, and most of the shelves were depleted. There were no fresh vegetables or meat.

"We don't barter or trade," a rough-looking employee

confronted them. "If you don't have money, don't trouble us."

Ben nodded and kept walking. "Look at those prices!" He stopped and stared at the few cans of beans left on a long shelf. "Ten dollars a can!"

"It's a good thing we stocked up before they nuked Babylon." George picked up some cans of tomatoes. Across the top in black marking ink was the price—eight dollars. "I thank God that we were able to plan ahead."

"We'll just get enough to trade out for gasoline." Ben gathered whatever he could find that they might need for the last two months. "Too bad we couldn't store a little fuel. I figure it will be gone before long. Get some canned meat for us. We aren't likely to see any until the Lord's return."

Shots of gunfire ended their conversation. They hit the floor and crawled toward the cash register. Near the end of the aisle they inched up to look through the large windows. Outside they could see a band of men running toward the store. The guards kept shooting. Two wounded men fell on the pavement; the rest turned back and dispersed. Ben hurried toward the counter.

"Don't worry," the dirty little man waved them forward. "We get these skirmishes every day. Have to shoot one now and then to keep law and order. You got real money?"

Ben nodded.

"Have to scratch out an existence." The checker began adding up the cost on a piece of brown paper. "Not much is left. Without supplies coming through, we have to charge what the traffic will bear. If the trucks run again, we'll drop prices."

Ben studied the man's face. An ugly eczema covered his neck, betraying an outbreak of skin cancer. His eyes were red and matter filled the corners. He looked as if he hadn't shaved in a week.

"Walk all the time now," the cashier rattled on. "Too dangerous to drive. Can't afford the gasoline anyway."

He stopped and looked at the three young men. "I don't think any of us will survive long. If we don't starve, the radiation will get us. It's all over for us and the empire."

"We have a great hope," Isaiah said urgently. "Could we share our faith with you?"

The man looked whimsical for a moment and then turned away. "No. I don't want to hear any religious talk. Don't believe in any of it. Living in this world is like living in hell, and when I die, I imagine that's where I'll end up. I'm consigned to it. Life's nothing but a disappointment anyway."

Ben laid the money out on the counter. "Nine hundred and twenty dollars covers it. Right?"

The man grunted and stuffed the money into his pocket. "Good luck," he grumbled after them. "Luck will get you farther than religion."

The young men walked out with two grocery carts full of supplies. For a moment they stood behind the barrier, looking across the empty shopping center.

"Get moving while you can." The guard lowered his gun. The top of his head looked as if large wads of hair had fallen out, leaving red blotches. On the back of his hand a dark lesion ran up his arm. "You never know when some of those scavengers will turn up. Starvation makes them unpredictable, and desperation turns them into madmen. Hurry up and get on with it."

Ben quickly unlocked the car and loaded his trunk. Even in the short time they had been inside, a thin layer of ash had settled on Ben's old BMW. "We're not going to stop until we get near the edge of town. Watch for a gas station that's away from any houses. We don't want to be ambushed when we stop."

The trio sped on, staying as close to the center of the street as possible. The usual afternoon sun looked dim and very distant behind the layers of ugly brownish haze. Dark smoke-filled clouds drifted overhead, and the air burned their noses. Here and there houses were burning, but no one was responding. Few businesses were left open, and many of the stores had been looted.

Finally, the young men found a station that looked relatively secure. After bargaining for several minutes, a deal was struck and the attendant unlocked a pump. Once the gas tank was filled, Ben started the engine and turned toward the freeway.

"What's that?" George sat up abruptly. "What's out there in the street?"

"Looks like a tanker truck had a wreck." Ben slowed down.

"That's no wreck!" Isaiah pointed to the side of the street. "One of the gangs has deliberately turned that vehicle over to jam the street. They've probably drained the tanks and then set up a road block to raid cars. Watch out! Men will be hiding behind the truck."

"Hang on." Ben shifted into second. "We don't have any choice but to run it."

"Can you see anything coming in the opposite direction?" George braced his feet.

"Yeah." Ben grimaced. "Two cars are coming down the other side. We don't have an alternative. We're going over the curb and around on the right."

When Ben hit the curb, the car bounced up in the air and landed ten feet ahead on the sidewalk, only inches away from a large tree. On his left he saw a blur of faces running toward the car. An awesome thump thundered overhead and the ceiling sagged. Ben abruptly jerked the wheel to the left, sending the car back toward the street. Once again they bounced over the curb and flew out toward the traffic. At that moment a man went sailing off the top of the car, smashing into the street. He rolled wildly toward the tanker, finally landing motionless on his back.

"He dropped out of the tree!" Isaiah stared at the caved-in car roof. "They had a real trap set for anybody who stopped or slowed down!"

Ben shifted into high and hit the gas pedal. "We're not stopping for stop signs until we get out of LA! We don't have any kind of weapon to defend ourselves."

"I hope that angel of yours is paying attention."

George looked quickly up and down the streets. "We're no match for these modern cavemen. Civilization's completely gone. There's nothing left but marauding tribes."

After Ben drove out of the populated area, he began winding up the hillside. The grass was brown and dead. Most of the vegetation was shriveled and blackened. The open space made it easier to detect any movement so the young men settled back in their seats.

Thirty minutes later the winding dirt road to the farmhouse opened before them. Students were carrying wood down from the top of the hill while two fellows stacked the sticks and chunks against the back of the house and next to the great oak tree. Some of the group were hanging wash on the clothesline out back. Ben pulled alongside the house. He could see Cindy's parents busily working away in the kitchen.

Every inch of the living room was taken. Bedrolls and pillows were pushed against the wall. The old farmhouse had become a full-scale dormitory, and the Wongs were the houseparents.

During supper, Ben explained, "We won't be making many more runs into the city. The area's entirely too dangerous now. If someone were hurt in there, we probably couldn't find medical care. We don't need anymore needless pain. Unless Michael appears and gives us assignments, we had best settle in here for the duration."

"Are you sure this will be over by October?" a student asked. "Can our food hold out that long?"

"Only if we stay on our self-imposed ration program," Ben said. "We certainly won't get fat. In fact, some of the time we may feel hungry, but we can make it. With the Wongs' cooking we will be able to use every scrap of food. How do you like their cuisine?"

The room exploded in applause. Frank and Jessica beamed.

"After today's narrow escape, I believe we need barricades around the house and across the road." Isaiah stood up. "If the scavenger gangs find out we have such a large stash of food, they'll attack. I volunteer to oversee the project."

"Here! Here!" rang around the room.

"We must live now as we shall in eternity," Ben instructed. "Tension builds when people live in close proximity. We must use these days to discipline ourselves to be ready for the kingdom of God to break forth. We face a great challenge."

Cindy held up her hand assertively. "Here's your first chance to show your sincerity. I have a chart my mother wrote out for who will be washing the dishes each day."

The students booed and laughed as they continued eating and talking together. Once they were through, the table was cleared for evening worship. Many sat in a big circle on the floor while others sat behind them. A few students sprawled on the steps going upstairs.

Cindy quoted from Psalm 83: "'Do not keep silent, O God! Do not hold Your peace, and do not be still, O God! For behold, Your enemies make a tumult; and those who hate You have lifted up their head.'" She turned around. "Anyone doubt this is the word of the Lord?"

Several students nodded no.

"Is it really true Gianardo has moved the seat of power to Rome?" Deborah asked.

Isaiah answered, "We didn't get much information in LA, but it's clear that no one is in control of anything. The rumor is that not much is left on the Eastern seaboard. They say that the remaining soldiers are being shipped out for a final showdown with the Muslims and Chinese. We heard that the emperor is in Rome to avoid the truth about how bad things are in this country, but they say lots of European cities were wiped out too."

Cindy began quoting again: "'They have taken crafty counsel against Your people, and consulted together against Your sheltered ones. They have said, "Come, and let us cut them off from being a nation, that the name of Israel may be remembered no more." ' Once again we are living in a time of fulfillment of these very words. I would be totally terrified if it were not for the comfort that God's Word gives me."

"We must pray for our comrades who are still in the city," Isaiah added. "Many people are struggling to survive against terrible odds. The revival that we saw on the UCLA campus will dissipate since the school is now closed, but the word is still getting out. We must pray that our friends are able to hold their own."

Cindy stated the concluding lines of the psalm: " 'Let them be confounded and dismayed forever; yes, let them be put to shame and perish. That men may know that You, whose name is the LORD, are the Most High over all the earth.' " She paused for a few moments to allow the words to sink in. "The psalmist prayed for the demise of the enemies of God, and we should do the same. The difference is that we not only know that their days are numbered, we know the number of their days. Let us pray for the victory of our God."

Across the room students bowed their heads. Some knelt with their faces in their hands. Ben watched quietly, feeling a deep sense of satisfaction in knowing that he had played a part in bringing so many of his friends to the faith that was now their literal salvation.

Ben looked at the Wongs who sat with bowed heads. Cindy held her mother's hand as they prayed together. God had blessed the little man and woman with new faith. The students loved the Wongs and encouraged them. In turn, Frank and Jessica had found great gratification in cooking for the kids.

Ben felt overwhelmed, realizing how the hand of God had molded this unlikely company into a community of faith, each now praying fervently for the other. At that moment he thought of Joe and Jennifer McCoy. The faces of Erica and Joe, Jr., drifted before his eyes. He remembered the New Year's celebrations and his family's times together.

And then Ben thought of Ruth. Memories of her and their family rituals swept across his mind. The football games, the teasing, and the family's special New Year's breakfasts. A great loneliness clutched at his heart. Ben looked around the crowded room. Every eye was closed except his, but he felt completely isolated.

Tears rolled down his cheeks, and Ben found it difficult to swallow. For the first time he allowed himself to face the blow Ruth's death was to his mother. He let himself feel the terrible pain that had cut through his Jewish mother's dreams of a grandchild. With great difficulty he prayed aloud, "Let them know that Your name is most holy and high over all the earth."

T he concluding weeks of the summer of 2000 were unusually hot and dry across most of the world. August in southern California was nearly as scorching as the desert heat in Bozrah. Radiation and AIDS continued taking their deadly toll. Old diseases like cholera and bubonic plague reappeared. Animals and crazed dogs ran wild, attacking people, while gangs of thugs and criminals ran in packs far more vicious than anything found in the wild. Many decided erroneously that suicide was the best alternative to a life that was no longer tolerable.

Television and radio were out much of the time. For long periods of time there was no electricity. Blackouts became a way of life. Because refrigeration was unpredictable, lengthy storage of food became impossible.

Ben's crew found their ministry radically changed. Exciting forays into dangerous dormitories were replaced by quiet evenings in the farmhouse. No longer were secret rendezvous possible. The thrill of the chase was replaced by the solitude of nights on an isolated farm. Witnessing was replaced by prayer.

Intercession became a new way of life. The students organized themselves into a continuous chain of prayer, running twenty-four hours a day. A small bedroom was turned into a chapel where each student could take a turn praying for the families in Bozrah and acquaintances in the Los Angeles area. During the afternoons and evenings, the entire group gathered to sing, share, and encourage each other.

As the days dragged by, a slow metamorphosis occurred. The usual collegiate bravado and frivolity were replaced by quiet reflective maturity. No longer was it necessary to be cute or turn everything into a joke. Each person knew a sacred trust had been given and accepted. Every prayer was a moment of standing in the gap for someone who might be on the edge of the abyss at that very moment.

In the Bozrah-Petra compounds, people looked toward September with eager anticipation. Jimmy was teaching every day of the week, helping the new immigrants grasp the significance of what was immediately ahead.

Jimmy looked out over the crowd, which had swelled to a size that strained the range of his voice. Only the intense silence of the immigrants made it possible for him to be heard. "Originally, God intended Israel to divide history into fifty-year Jubilee segments. Every five decades on the Day of Atonement, Jews were to blow horns signifying the cancellation of all debts by the owners. Do you understand?"

The crowd nodded that they had grasped his meaning, even though Jimmy taught in English with a Hebrew translator.

"For financial reasons, the Jews did not keep the plan, but God still honored His timetable. I want you to recognize the wonderful truth that is about to be fulfilled. The year 2000 is a Jubilee year . . . a perfect symbol of Yeshua's atoning love for the sin of the world."

Throughout the gathering, people clapped and applauded.

Jimmy nodded his head enthusiastically. "The whole world gets a special Jubilee new start this year."

Earlier during May and June, Jimmy trained evangelists to leave the protected area and travel throughout the small towns of Israel, sharing their message. More than once the teams were attacked and casualties resulted. Nevertheless, each death only spurred on the new converts in their efforts to share their faith.

In July and August, Jimmy taught the new residents the basic facts of life in Yeshua during the cooler hours of the morning. He held his sessions on prophecy late in the afternoon; most of the people napped during the heat of the day. At night he discussed the meaning of suffering and how to face pain.

Larry and Sharon worked tirelessly, helping the distraught and terrified to bring their emotions under control. They counseled, listened, and often prayed with people who could barely speak English.

☐   ☐   ☐

There was no relief from fear in Rome. The ancient city had become a place of poverty as the fortunes of Europe fell with the demise of the empire. Radioactive fallout had taken a toll in the Eternal City as it had elsewhere. Food was scarce, and people lived in fear of what might next fall on them from the skies. The cheerful, emotional attitude of the Italians of the past had been replaced by apprehension and despair. Heavy smog clouded the normally bright summer sky.

Late summer had always been suffocating in Rome. Now the condition was unbearable. The old papal palace Gianardo had commandeered for a residence was not equipped with air conditioning. His arrogance was repaid with constant discomfort.

The new pope fled the country and was rumored to be hiding in France. Gianardo stopped all worship in Saint Peter's Basilica. Instead he periodically strolled across the chancel and sat on the high altar, proclaiming to any observers his absolute power.

As the United States disintegrated and other countries began pulling away from the empire, Gianardo became even more obsessed with his role as the supreme religious leader of the world. He commissioned bizarre religious inquiries into how religious dignitaries and leaders had designated their positions. Robes were designed and vestments constructed that would blend the symbols of political power and religious authority. Occasionally, Gianardo made public appearances wearing the papal miter. Many of his aides fought to keep from snickering at the strange sight of the emperor walking about in a modern business suit carrying the crosier and wearing the pointed hat of the pope.

In late August, 2000, the emperor summoned the five young generals who now controlled all military operations to the Sistine Chapel. Full-scale maps, drawings, and plans were laid out on long tables beneath the ceiling that was Michelangelo's greatest accomplishment. Each man stood at full attention, making his report of the state of affairs. Gianardo sat against the wall in the golden chair normally reserved for the pope.

"Therefore," Imler concluded, "no longer is there a necessity for any legislative activity. The United States is a country without a center of power. People are not out of control as much as they have been reduced to a meager quest for survival. The entire nation must be rebuilt."

"Good," Gianardo smiled as he talked, "exactly where I want things to be. When the last conflict is over, we will rebuild the old U.S. according to our design. No resistance will be possible because people will be grateful simply to have a means of surviving. I will be unquestioned. In the end, the citizens will recognize me as their source of life. Is this not clever?"

General Imler cleared his throat and smiled weakly. He sat down quickly.

"And the state of the movement of all troops?" Gianardo turned to General Jackson. "Are the troop carriers in motion?"

"Even as we speak, the army and the entire fleet await your direction. You are the only person in the world who knows what we are doing." Jackson looked nervously at his comrades. "Time is running out. We must quickly tell our men where to land. There is a great sense of disarray among the military."

"Excellent!" Gianardo stood up and walked to the table with the maps. "I have personally planned every detail of what lies ahead." He unfolded a map of Israel and began motioning with a pointer. "We are going to land on the beaches near the ancient city of Megiddo. I want to prepare for a drive down the Valley of Jezreel, called by some Armageddon. We will cut the country into two sections."

Browning leaned over and stared at the map. "Armageddon? Why there? In fact, why in the world are we going to Israel of all places?"

"Two reasons," the emperor snapped. "For some unexplainable cause, the Israelis are the only people who have escaped the ecological damage visited on the world by my enemies. They have the only real estate left where we can hope to escape the effects of pollution and radiation. We will govern from Jerusalem until the rest of the world cools off. In addition, their capital has religious significance. In the future, Jerusalem will be a more suitable place for my throne."

"But why is the entire military converging on their shores?" Browning gestured aimlessly. "I mean . . . all our troops?"

"The Muslims have been bargaining with Russia and China. We know the Chinese are moving their hordes toward the Middle East. We are going to meet them in one great showdown that will finally secure the empire."

"This valley is a strange place," the general protested. "Moreover, we are no match for the Chinese army, particularly since the Japanese have joined them. We will be totally overwhelmed."

"Lots of secret military hangars that once housed the Israeli air force are located in this valley. We are going to use them to house the last of our tactical nuclear weapons. Our remaining portable warheads will equalize the numbers quickly."

"But then even Israel will no longer be safe from radiation—"

"I want all forces to be prepared to land by September 1," the emperor cut the general off. "Since they are already at sea, it will only be a matter of telling them where to land. We must be ready to hit the ground running. I suspect the Chinese will be converging on the area quickly. I will personally be on the scene to supervise the final assault when our armies lock in battle."

Browning blinked. His mouth was slightly ajar.

"Some problem with the plan, General?"

Every eye in the room was trained on the general whose face had become rather pale. Browning slowly slid into his chair at the table.

"Jackson, begin immediately to prepare detailed maps of the Megiddo and Armageddon areas," the emperor continued. "I want full-scale reports on all troop movements to our north. In addition, I want television coverage of my personal arrival in Jerusalem. Every radio and TV station is to carry every step of my journey throughout the city. Even though we will work out of the Knesset, I am going to set up a symbolic headquarters in the Holy of Holies in the rebuilt gold-covered temple of Solomon. At that particular place, I will consolidate my position. When I periodically step out of their temple, wearing the vestments of the Christian faith while directing the most powerful army in history, the world will know once and for all that their master has come. Can you not see what a statement we will make for all time to remember?"

No one had time to answer. The emperor stepped back and held his arms up to the painted figures high above him on frescoes across the ceiling. "Behold, ye prophets and saints of the past! I have come! The fullness of time is here!"

On Sunday, September 2, 2000, a helicopter lifted off the ground from the Ben Gurion International Airport in Tel Aviv. Every television camera in the country followed the emperor of the New Roman Empire as he flew across the countryside toward Jerusalem. His helicopter made an enormous sweep of the city before it swooped down over the Old City. Dirt flew in every direction as the chopper settled on top of the Temple Mount.

Soldiers with drawn guns hustled to surround the vehicle as the blades slowed. Damian Gianardo jumped from the open door and immediately was encompassed by troops. The emperor walked briskly toward the gate and steps that led down to the plaza in front of the Western Wall. Generals Askins and Imler trotted behind him.

Even before the entourage had started their descent, the crowd began to disperse. Many Israelis pushed toward the Dung Gate to escape. Other citizens rushed for various passageways into the Old City. By the time Gianardo reached the square, the area had been cleared, except for the soldiers standing behind the sand bag barricades.

Gianardo's men fanned out over the area, forming a protective shield for the emperor. Gianardo did not slow his pace until he was standing directly in front of the two ancient figures who sat passively on their wooden thrones, watching his arrival.

Gianardo turned and faced the prophets. For a minute he studied them as television cameras zoomed in on his face. He seemed more intrigued than dismayed. Finally, Gianardo began edging forward. When he was only ten feet in front of the two giants, he stopped again.

"Why are you here?" the emperor asked sharply.

There was no response.

"The ruler of this world is speaking to you!" Gianardo barked. "Do you not understand the precarious nature of your position?

Again neither Moses nor Elijah spoke, but both men smiled condescendingly.

"I have the power of life and death in my hands." The emperor's voice was menacing. "You nuisances have been allowed to stay only because of my choosing. Do you understand that in a moment I can dispatch you back into the mist from which you came?"

Moses suddenly laughed. Elijah looked sternly for a few moments and then began to smile. Finally, he, too, roared. As the ancients laughed, Gianardo's face turned red. Their laughter turned into an echo, resounding against the plaza. Like no other sound, the laughter rumbled less with frivolity and more with judgment.

Suddenly, Gianardo turned to a soldier behind him and jerked the man's pistol from his holster. The emperor cocked the gun and ran directly in front of the prophets. "Now let the world see who laughs last!" he screamed. "Let every eye see who has the power!"

The emperor swung the gun up and fired two shots directly at Moses' chest. Before the lawgiver had even toppled from his chair, the emperor fired at Elijah. The prophet bolted backward, and Gianardo shot again. The great white head dropped backward. The prophet collapsed and slid from the chair onto the platform.

Gianardo turned around to the stunned multitude behind him. No one moved. Complete silence descended on the holy sight. The emperor's gaze darted back and forth. There was no look of awe or exaltation; only dumbfounded disbelief and dismay covered people's faces.

"I am the most powerful force in the world!" the emperor screamed. "Do you understand? I have exposed these frauds. I have done what even Pharaoh of Egypt could not accomplish." His voice split the silence. No one moved.

"The world thought some abstract idea called God was the power of life and death. I alone am this power. I am the supreme one! Throw away your superstitions! I decree these bodies be left in the city that the world may watch. No one touch them! Watch and see them rot!"

When no one moved, Gianardo threw the gun down and stomped back toward the steps. Soldiers fell in around him. A lone detachment of troops formed a line in front of the thrones. Even before the emperor reached the top of the Temple Mount, the square was empty except for the guards.

Gianardo crawled into the helicopter. The two generals slipped in beside him and buckled their seat belts. "Let's go," the emperor commanded the pilot. "I showed them," he said.

But again no one answered.

# 32

The sun broke over the mountaintops, bathing the far corners of the plaza in front of the Western Wall in arid sunlight. Only a stray dog broke the stillness surrounding the sleeping soldiers. Thursday, September 6, 2000, offered no more promise than the other dog days of that late summer. But then a finger moved. The hand opened and closed and opened again. Slowly, Moses stirred.

For three days the great leader had lain face down on the platform next to the throne. Two jagged holes were ripped open in the back of Moses's robe where the bullets came out. No one had dared to touch his body, but now the man himself pulled his legs together and stood up. The entire front of his robe was covered with dried blood. He rubbed his eyes before he picked up his staff.

Elijah was slumped against the front of his throne. During the previous days, his legs jutted out at grotesque angles. The front of his robe was also stained with ugly brown blotches of dried blood. At first he slowly moved his head from side to side. Once more life surged through his body. Elijah reached for the arm of the chair and pulled himself up. After standing for a moment, he dropped down in the large wooden chair.

The two prophets silently surveyed the strange scene before them; a ring of fully armed troops slept on the stone pavement. Most soldiers rested their heads against wadded-up coats and backpacks. About a hundred feet away other combatants slept in front of piled-up sand bags.

After a few moments of reflection, Moses thumped his staff on the wooden platform. The hollow sound echoed menacingly across the square. One soldier raised his head, blinked, and then lay back against the makeshift pillow. A second later the terrified man was on his feet.

"They're alive!" the soldier scrambled for his gun. "Look!"

Some men grabbed weapons while others could only stare at the two imposing figures looking down on them. "Call the CO!" a soldier yelled from the back.

Moses stepped down to the pavement, paused, turned, and kissed the wall before walking toward the retreating soldiers. Elijah followed. The front row of soldiers dropped their guns and ran toward the rear.

"Do not fear us." Moses waved them back. "Rather fear him who would steal your soul. The time is short. Repent now, for the era draws to a close."

The prophets walked through the parting soldiers and out the gate. Just as they had entered the city months earlier, they now retraced their steps up the Kidron Valley toward the Mount of Olives. As they walked, teams of TV journalists sped toward the ancient hillside but they were too late. The best the reporters could do was photograph the awesome scene from a distance.

Clouds began boiling in the sky, just as they had on the day of the appearing. Once Moses and Elijah reached the site of Jesus' ascension, they held up their arms toward the heavens. Suddenly, the ground began shaking, and a great roaring noise filled the valley. Several television crewmen thought they heard the words, "Come here." Others attributed the sounds to the earth shifting.

Cameras hummed as Moses and Elijah lifted slowly

from the earth. For a few moments they seemed to hover, and then the clouds closed in again. The crew caught the last moments as a swirl of cloud covering wrapped around Moses and Elijah like a billowy quilt of cotton. And then the prophets were gone.

The ground began to shake. Within seconds every building in Jerusalem rumbled. Light fixtures swung back and forth and walls cracked apart. The earthquake split the ground; on the southern outskirts of the city, where Gianardo's soldiers were camped, a huge crevasse opened up through a main street. Whole buildings fell in, and seven thousand of Gianardo's men disappeared as the earth kept shifting, swallowing them alive.

Throughout the rest of the day, aftershocks rocked the city. Cracks in the street closed public access to the Mount of Olives, and rock slides obliterated other roads. Footage of the final moments of the ascent filled the TV screens on an hourly basis. The entire city was in a state of uproar, watching the alternating stories of the earthquake damage and the amazing resurrection of Moses and Elijah. Reporters interviewed the soldiers guarding the Western Wall, but no one could explain how they could possibly have come alive.

The next morning Damian Gianardo sat slumped behind his desk in the makeshift military headquarters set up in the Knesset Building. He stared hollow-eyed at an Israeli commander, who was explaining his soldiers' behavior.

"Our men are good soldiers," the lieutenant in battle fatigues complained. "You are not fair to accuse them of incompetence and irresponsibility. They had no reason not to be asleep. They were ordered to keep anyone from burying two dead men . . . not keep them from walking away."

"Don't be impertinent," Gianardo sneered. "I'm not superstitious. I don't believe in ghosts."

"Perhaps you would recognize that our country has

the highest resurrection rate in the world," the soldier answered coldly.

"Don't push your luck with me." The emperor stood up. "I still want a detachment of troops set up on the site of the ascension. If anything else comes down, I want your men to shoot first and ask questions later."

The soldier saluted and turned on his heels. As he opened the door, General Browning entered.

"I have an update on how the troop landing is progressing." He brushed past the Israeli without acknowledging his presence. "We believe that our units are moving at top speed to secure the entire area near the entrance of the Jezreel Valley." The general stopped and looked out the window. Although there had been no signs of a storm, a bolt of lightning flashed across the sky. A great flash of light filled the room, followed by an explosive roar.

Gianardo and Browning rushed to the window. A large tree across the street was now a smoldering splintered stump. As they watched, an electrical storm broke across the entire sky. Streaks of lightning flew through the air. Terrible popping and crackling sounds bewildered people on the street. They ran for shelter in the closest buildings.

"The earth is coming apart," Browning sputtered. The building shook again. Across the street large rocks began hopping as another earthquake began. "I'm losing it." The general's eyes widened. "Everything is coming unglued."

"Get a grip on yourself, Browning! The environment's messed up from the pollution and A-bomb attacks. Don't go nuts on me."

A file cabinet toppled over, and Gianardo's desk began sliding toward the opposite wall. The general lost his footing and nearly fell. Staggering like a drunk, he tried to reach the door. "I'll try to get some kind of a report for you." Browning ran, not even trying to close the door behind him.

Throughout the rest of the day the Seventh Trumpet of the Lord continued to blow the world apart. It was a warning that God would send, in rapid sequence, the final seven bowls of His wrath on those who refused to repent of their sins against their fellow human beings and against Him. Eventually, a 9.3-rated earthquake in the middle of the Atlantic Ocean sent great tidal waves crashing across the Mediterranean. Many of the empire's ships anchored off the coast of Israel were picked up like children's toys and slung helpless into the rocks and beaches. On the opposite side of the world, the shores of North America were again smashed by corresponding walls of water. Near dusk, polluted hail the size of basketballs fell on many areas of the world. By night the world had once more been warned. Sadly, few understood that the call had come from the Most High.

One week later, the emperor moved his command post north to be closer to the scene of the impending battle. As troops marched, the Bowls of Wrath began to be poured. The First Bowl was terrible sores and boils that appeared on all who were true followers of Gianardo and Rathmarker. They gnawed their tongues from the pain.

On Sunday, September 16, a sailor was the first to recognize the next consequence of global disobedience, the Second Bowl. At first a red coagulation began to cover the surface of the oceans. The seas took on the cast of pinkish blood serum, and all sea animals died. Dead fish and animals bloated and floated on the surface. By the time the seaman's report was registered, other coastal residents noticed the Third Bowl—streams running into the oceans started backing up with the same blood-red covering. As more and more dead sea animals rotted, along with most freshwater animals, the stench was staggering. Within two days, most of the drinking water was in danger of contamination. However, Damian Gianardo wrote off the phenomenon as another result of environmental pollution.

On that Thursday, the Fourth Bowl of Wrath was poured over the atmosphere. The clouds evaporated. Nothing stood between the sun's rays and the ozone-depleted covering around the globe. In a short time the average temperature across the globe rose to 115 degrees at night and 135 degrees during the day. The generals watched as thousands of their finest soldiers dropped from the heat and dehydration.

On Saturday, the terrible sores from the First Bowl recurred, but this time only on Gianardo's inner circle of power players. It was the Fifth Bowl.

Five days later, the latest military reports arrived on each commander's desk. The combination of manipulation of a Turkish dam and the oppressive heat had dried up the Euphrates River. The coagulated blood-red waters left the soil a baked hard red clay. The demise of the environment caused Premier Ching Lei to move his troops prematurely. Lei pressed the remnant of the Muslim world into his conglomerate of Japanese, Russian, and Chinese troops, and the march was on. The massive horde of advancing soldiers rumbled toward the valley known to the ancients as Armageddon. The gathering of the kings of the East down the dry Euphrates River bed to oppose the New Roman Empire of the West was the Sixth Bowl in preparation for the final Bowl: the Battle of Armageddon.

Each of Gianardo's young generals read with increasing alarm the identical report: "At least two hundred million men and women have crossed the dried-up Euphrates River bed. Japanese air and ground forces have joined the drive as well as some contingents of troops from other Asian nations including Korea. We have also been able to identify soldiers from the following countries: Syria, Iran, Libya, Ethiopia, Egypt, Lebanon, Jordan, and Iraq."

General Browning had barely completed reading the top secret dispatch when an aide appeared and handed him another sheet of teletype. Browning scanned the latest data, put the report down, and summoned Imler and Jackson to a conference. Within thirty minutes the three men gathered in the open air just down the hill from the excavations of the ancient city of Megiddo.

"No one should be able to monitor us here," Browning said quietly. "Does each of you understand the significance of the report you received this morning?"

Each man nodded his head gravely.

"We are preparing to enter the greatest bloodbath in history. The numbers of the enemy alone will overwhelm us!"

Jackson agreed. "Even if we nuke a good percentage of their ground troops, I don't think we can stop the air force."

"Atomic response?" Browning's shoulders sagged and he wrung his hands. "If we win such an exchange, I believe the result will truly be the end of the world. What we have seen in the last month is nothing short of the world falling apart."

Browning pulled the latest communiqué from his pocket. "In a few hours you will receive this update. The report you read earlier turned out to be dated. We now have confirmed that Lei's march has passed the Syrian portion of the Golan Heights and is infiltrating the eastern half of the Jezreel Valley. By nightfall I believe they will have established initial outposts from the top of Mount Tabor to Mount Gilboa. The Israeli army is so small now that its numbers are relatively meaningless, but we assume the soldiers will continue to remain under our command out of fear alone. The army has retreated to avoid an initial confrontation, but it is poised to protect its homeland."

Imler looked hard into Browning's eyes. "We're on the western side, and we'll soon be coming across this great valley. At any moment the great battle could start."

Jackson cupped his hand over his eyes and looked out over the rich, fertile valley and the plain at the bottom. Vehicles were moving everywhere. Overhead, the sky was filled with planes. "Could make the Normandy invasion look like child's play," he said cynically. "Bodies will be stacked up out there until the valley is level."

"No question," Browning snapped. "The war will begin tomorrow."

An hour later each man returned to his post and began monitoring his portion of military preparation. As dusk fell, the ground rumbled with the movement of vehicles; the sounds of a mighty army filled the valley. At 8 P.M. Gianardo summoned his military staff.

"Just at the break of sunrise I want our air force to hit them with everything short of nuclear strike weapons. The remaining battleships will lob shells from the ocean. I want the biggest weapons we've got firing point-blank into their positions. After the initial assault, we will unleash the Israelis in a vicious counterattack designed to kill as many of the enemy as possible. We won't win the day immediately, but we will greatly reduce the odds against us."

Gianardo sneered at his generals. "Before this week is over, I will have rewritten the military textbooks. Now implement what I've said."

The generals hurried out to prepare for the dawn assault.

# 33

Well before dawn, the eastern side of the Jezreel Valley exploded with terrific bursts of fire. Phosphoric pieces of smoldering debris hurled through the night. Tracers and flares signaled locations, and shelling immediately followed. The once beautiful hillside was pitted, burned, and torn. At the break of day, bombers dumped their bombs, and the sky filled with fighter jets locked in mortal combat. The earliest light of day was obscured by the smoke that hid the hillside and mountaintops. By ten o'clock, the fallout and dust were so thick that it was even difficult to breathe several miles away along the coastline.

Only after the thick cloud cover of smoke was established did the emperor release his own ground forces. Tanks and armored vehicles sped across the plain to support the assault troops that stung with the force of a million hornets. By noontime, the Chinese made their counterattack. The premier's strategy was relatively simple. He was willing to buy victory at the price of sacrificing any number of troops necessary. By late afternoon, the eastern slopes and the terrain down and out into the valley were filled with dead bodies of Chinese and their allies.

The generals of the empire were sequestered in a bunker deep underneath Megiddo. In a separate room, the emperor had a personal command post where he monitored all decisions and carefully controlled every aspect of the attack.

"What's happening overhead?" Browning called to Imler across the room.

"Stalemate. Looks like we've about neutralized each other's air power. Not much left of either air force."

"Bad news!" Browning hit the table with his fist. "Means the balance of power will shift to their ground forces. They greatly outnumber us."

An allied general hurried into the strategy room. He was covered with dirt and smelled of smoke. The man's face was blackened, and his battle fatigues were torn and grimy. "We're slaughtering them like pigs!" he talked rapidly. "But for every one that falls, two take his place. We're fighting behind piles of bodies, but they won't stop coming. I think we'll run out of bullets before they run out of personnel." The general went to the emperor's quarters to make a personal report.

The afternoon wore on with many identical reports coming in. Near sundown the battle settled into a lull. Heavy artillery fire became more erratic. The sound of airplanes faded; the roaring of the big guns was replaced by the steady fire of infantry rifles and machine guns. Several hours passed before Gianardo summoned the five generals to his quarters.

"What do you think?" Gianardo asked the grim-faced assembly. "Where are we on this Friday night, September 28? If memory serves me right, tomorrow's the big Jewish Feast of Trumpets. Anyone requesting leave for the holidays?"

No one smiled. Finally, Browning answered, "I have always prided myself on being a soldier, not a butcher. Never have I witnessed what has happened out there today. Surely, the carnage exceeds the worst ever seen by the human race."

The emperor dismissed the general's comments by not even acknowledging them. "I'm sure you are wondering where we go next," Gianardo spoke in a monotone. "My plans have gone exactly according to schedule. I have before me a communiqué so secret that not one of you even knew of its arrival. I established contact with Premier Lei without your knowledge. Surprised?" He grinned cunningly at the shocked generals.

The weary group only stared in response.

"Premier Lei has responded to an overture that I made earlier this evening. I lied to him and told him that we were both out of nuclear weaponry, but I told the truth about losing great numbers of our people. I suggested that we cease hostilities and begin negotiations at dawn. He has heartily accepted. Let me share a line or two." Gianardo looked around the room with obvious great pleasure.

" 'The smell of death arises from every continent, and so it will soon be in this place,' " the emperor read aloud. " 'What do we gain? We both have already paid a great price in past wars. I am pleased that you offer peace. We can come to terms. I will expect your next response by morning.' " Gianardo laid the paper down. "Am I not also a man of peace?" He smiled at his leaders.

"What . . . what will you propose?" Browning sputtered. "What will you tell Lei?"

"Listen to some of what I have written." The emperor picked up a scratch pad. " 'I am a mighty man of war, but I am also the prince of peace. In the morning I will bring peace to the globe.' " He laid the sheet down. A smirk crossed his lips and his eyes narrowed. "But this plan I will follow as surely as I live. I will propose that we stop all fighting before dawn and that we both meet on the plain of the battlefield at 9:00 A.M. to settle all differences. But at precisely 8:50 we will hit them with every last nuclear weapon that we *do* have. Because Lei will be in the valley, we'll get close enough to his location to annihilate him and most of his people with the first bombs. When the smoke clears, we will have completely won!"

"You offer peace while planning to totally destroy him

and his allies!" Rathmarker declared proudly. "This will
be the war that ends all wars. World dominion with no
opposition will finally be ours. Let's go for it!"

"Brilliant, is it not?" Gianardo smirked. "This is not
the time to back off."

"You are quite right." General Browning slowly rose
to his feet. "This is not the time to back off."

The late evening hours of Friday, September 28, 2000,
seemed blacker than any night in history. The moon
and stars were completely obliterated by the smoke.
One great cloud appeared to envelope the entire globe.
Months of environmental deterioration were taking a
final toll. Life was being systematically snuffed out. As
dawn approached, an awesome stillness hovered over
Jerusalem.

Just before dawn, a few citizens arose to begin their
preparations for the Feast of Trumpets. Smoke from
the great catastrophe in the Valley of Jezreel rolled in
like a gray mist from the north. From one end of the
Plain of Armageddon to the other, men dug in for a
final assault. The armies of the empire and Ching Lei
were poised to resume attack. Neither side was sure of
the intentions of the other. Fumes and soot were so
thick they could no longer be sure where the battle
lines were drawn. The emperor and prime minister
huddled together, ready to decide what response could
be made to any surprise moves by Lei and his allies.
Vultures hovered overhead, ready for the feast of their
lives.

At the exact moment that the sun started to rise, the
clouds over the Holy City broke, and a great shaft of
light shot through the sky like a beacon light in a
stormy night. The spear of illumination cut through the
murky smog and shot out toward the ends of the globe.

The citizens of Jerusalem awoke to wonderful morning light streaming into their windows. They rubbed

their eyes in amazement at the shimmering daybreak no one had seen for several years. Out in the streets, people looked awestruck toward the sky. The glorious aurora did not blind their eyes but felt soothing and healing. To their astonishment, the continuing glow seemed to swallow the smoke and pollution, imparting a renewed brilliant clarity to the sky beyond what anyone remembered.

The center of the expanding illumination lingered above the Mount of Olives. Suddenly, the Source of the light broke through the clouds on a great white horse. Wearing a golden crown and holding a sharp sickle, the risen and exalted Yeshua once more rode into human history, this time as Lord of the Third Millennium. The magnificent stallion snorted and threw its head back in proud defiance. Across the dazzling white robe of the Messiah was emblazoned in Hebrew "King of kings and Lord of lords." As the Lord Jesus rode, He and the horse radiated the glowing resplendent luster.

On the opposite side of the world, pitch-black night had promised southern California some relief from the heat and ultraviolet rays scorching the earth. Ben and his friends huddled together in a late night prayer meeting in the dim living room of the farmhouse. A few candles placed on end tables were slowly burning down. The unexpected, unprecedented rise in temperatures had pushed the group's water reserves to the limit. The students were praying for water when the sudden worldwide burst of light split the night and shot into the open windows.

In contrast to the day, the night light was not hot but cooling. Immediate relief followed as the glow surged through the house. Brightness filled the room as if it were noon. The moment each student was bathed in the light, the sallow color of the skin turned to a new pink, healthy glow.

"For goodness' sake," Frank Wong looked around the room in bewilderment. "What happen?"

"He's returned," Ben's dry raspy voice was barely audible. "The Lord has returned! Today is a Feast of Trumpet's Day we will all remember for eternity."

"We're saved," Isaiah gasped. "We're going to survive."

"Praise Him!" Deborah raised her hands toward the ceiling. "Praise God! Praise Yeshua, His Son!"

The night had turned into a glorious sunrise. The usual murky gray sky was changing to a brilliant blue. Even the trees and plants were visibly energized and revitalized.

"Oh, thank You, Lord!" Ben ran to the window. "The whole of creation is coming into its own!"

"So *that's* you, Ben!" a small delicate voice said from behind him.

Ben turned. "What? Cindy?"

"You do have a beautiful face!"

"What are you saying?"

"I can see you, Ben. For the first time in my life, I can see."

At that moment angels and archangels broke forth out of the stream of light covering Jerusalem. The heavenly hosts processed into the world, passing on both sides of the Messiah on His white horse. The vast multitude flew forth over the face of the earth as the exalted Yeshua sat suspended in the air. The mighty chorus proclaimed together, "The kingdoms of this world have become the kingdoms of the Lord and of His Christ. And He shall reign forever and ever!"

When the Messiah's horse touched the place of His original ascension nearly two thousand years before, the Mount of Olives broke apart. A great quake split the earth to its center, and the shock wave reverberated to every fault line across the globe, opening a path from the Dead Sea through the Mount of Olives to the Mediterranean. Lightning began flashing across the world, and the skies were filled with a staggering aerial display of color and explosions of energy.

Anticipating the Return at sunrise, well before dawn Jimmy and the Feinbergs had climbed to the top of the highest mountain in the area. Below them in the valley, thousands of Jimmy's students knelt in silent prayer even before the all-encompassing beam of light first shot across the sky. Once the procession of angels began passing overhead, the new believers covered their faces. They knew from Scripture that whenever the Battle of Armageddon was won by Yeshua, He would personally come to Bozrah to gather His brothers and sisters and lead them through the East Gate of Jerusalem to begin the forty-five-day transition into the third millennium A.D.

Jimmy fell with his face to the ground. Larry and Sharon huddled together with their heads bowed. A great chorus of overpowering singing and heavenly praise encouraged them to look again to the sky. They watched, awestruck, as millions of angels appeared in the clouds. An ever-increasing army of martyrs and saints followed, spreading out in all directions. Many in the cavalcade paraded above them, sweeping closer and closer to the ground as they passed by. The group appeared to be coming to Bozrah and Petra now.

White-robed saints waved to the citizens of Bozrah as if they knew them and were reunited with old friends they had been observing for a long time. In turn, the people began waving back. The Jews stood, clapped, held their hands to heaven, shouted, and prayed. They danced and waved to the hosts overhead. They wept for joy.

Jimmy stood mesmerized by the sound. He closed his eyes as his ears drank in the blissful music that exceeded any strain he had ever heard.

"Jimmy." Sharon shook his arm. "Two people are waving at *you*. They are trying to get your attention."

Jimmy opened his eyes. "Oh, thank God! My goodness!" He grabbed the sides of his face. "Look . . . look . . . I can't believe my eyes. There are my father and mother!"

"Jimmy! Jimmy!" Sharon began sobbing uncontrollably. "To your left. Look! In the white robe . . . it's Ruth!"

Open-mouthed, crying, Jimmy reached up on his tiptoes for the sky. The dark-haired beauty in the white robe extended her hand as she slowly descended.

"Ruth! Ruth!" Jimmy called. "It's really you!"

The Harrisons and Ruth steadily moved toward the trio standing on the mountaintop with their hands lifted as high as they could reach.

"A young man is holding on to Ruth's hand." Larry pointed to his daughter. "Jimmy! He must be one of your ancestors. He looks so much like you."

Jimmy found it nearly impossible to see through his tears. He danced from one foot to the other, waving, holding his arms outstretched. "Ruth . . . Mom . . . Dad . . . we're here . . . waiting . . . we've waited so long."

As they moved very close, Reverend Harrison opened his arms. His voice was loud and clear. "Oh, Son, we've been so proud of you. How pleased we are with what you've done!" Jimmy's father took the other hand of the young man standing with Ruth. "We are bringing a very special person with us. Meet my grandson . . . your son."

# APPENDIX

We are about to take a journey into the third millennium since the birth of Yeshūa (Jesus). What kind of journey will it be? Is there really an invisible, supernatural world out there somewhere that must affect our speculation about this journey, or are our ponderings a "universal neurosis of mankind" as Sigmund Freud suspected?

I am a psychiatrist, physician, scientist, and author—not a prophet. Throughout graduate school, medical school, and psychiatric training, I have been steeped in the scientific method and programmed to be a skeptic. But I have come to a few conclusions, after much personal inquiry, about this "journey" and would like to share them with you.

It was in medical school that we learned that the human body is made up of thirty trillion cells and that each cell has thousands of enzymes and other components. We also learned that each of those tiny components is made up of electrons, protons, neutrons, invisible force fields. Did this all bounce together out of nothing?

This skeptic says the only logical conclusion is that a design as complex as the human body requires a Supernatural Designer. To deny this would be the equivalent of claiming that *Webster's Dictionary* came about as the result of an explosion in a printing factory!

If there is a Supernatural Designer of the human body and human spirit, then it seems logical to think that this Supernatural Being probably left us some information—at least some hints about whether it loves us, hates us, or is indifferent to us. Hints about what this being plans to do with us—if anything—in the future. And hints about what type of relationship, if one is even possible, we can have with our Supernatural Designer.

If this Being did give us a form of communication—a

Bible, so to speak—which Bible is His? Which one—if any—
is correct? And if we determine which one is correct, how
do we know how to interpret it?

When we die, do we just die? Or is there life after death?
Just because I hope there is an afterlife doesn't necessarily
make it so! Are we really more than just an amazingly complex body? Are we really spiritual beings who will live forever in modified bodies?

I have obsessed about these questions since childhood.
And in my journey through life, I have come to the skeptical
and scientific conclusions that the God of the Bible is the
Supernatural Being for whom we are searching, and that the
best way to understand His communication to us is to read
the Bible as if we were reading a newspaper article—that is,
take it literally unless the symbolism is obvious.

Because of my compulsive desire to understand the answers to my obsessive spiritual questions, I didn't stop my
education when I finished my psychiatry residency at Duke
University. I continued my studies in theology at two different seminaries until I obtained a seminary degree just before
my 40th birthday.

When it comes to eschatology—the study of potential "end
time" events—I have grown to respect good and sincere
scholars who have a wide variety of views on the end times.
I hope people of all eschatalogical backgrounds have their
lives enhanced in some ways by reading this political/psychi-
atric/eschatological novel.

The Essenes, over 2,000 years ago, waited for the Jewish
Messiah and wrote their thoughts and their scriptures down
in the form of the Dead Sea Scrolls. I believe their Messiah—
Yeshūa—came, but did not conquer the world and make Jerusalem its capital as expected. He was a major disappointment to many people of many faiths.

What most "future-watchers" failed to recognize in the
Old Testament was that it repeatedly predicted *two separate*
visitations of planet Earth by the Creator-God in human
flesh—Yeshūa (Jesus) the Messiah. There would be a *First
Coming* and a *Second Coming,* a *Former Reign* and a *Latter
Reign* of blessings on the Jews and on the world.

The Old Testament had 48 predictions about Jesus' *Former Reign—His First Coming*—including His birth in Bethlehem (Mic. 5:2), His betrayal for 30 pieces of silver (Zech.
11:12), His crucifixion on a cross (Ps. 22:16), and His trium-

phal entry into Jerusalem on a humble foal of a donkey (Zech. 9:9).

The most remarkable prediction about the Messiah's Former Reign was written by Daniel the prophet, more than 600 years before Jesus was born, in Daniel 9:24–27. The Essenes had more copies of Daniel than any other Old Testament book—*eight* copies of Daniel compared to only four of the Torah. And yet Jews today are usually discouraged from reading Daniel. It is seldom read in any synagogues. Why is it withheld?

In Daniel 9:24–27, Daniel says that someday a decree will be made to rebuild the walls of Jerusalem. Sixty-nine prophetic "weeks" after that decree, the Messiah would make His *First Coming*. A prophetic week has always meant seven Hebrew years of 360 days per year. Then He would be *"cut off."* Thus, 69 "weeks" equals 69 × 7 = 483 years × 360 days = 173,880 days. The only major decree to rebuild the walls of Jerusalem recorded in history is the decree of Artaxerxes Longimanus (Neh. 2:1), on May 14, 445 B.C. Add 173,880 days to that date and it comes out to April 6, A.D. 32, the day Yeshūa made His triumphal entry into Jerusalem on a foal. Needless to say, Daniel's prediction over 600 years earlier was fulfilled to the exact day. Messiah was cut off—crucified, resurrected, and ascended from the Mount of Olives. As He ascended into heaven, He promised to *descend* on that same mountain when He returned to Earth for His Second Coming—His Latter Reign—at which time He would conquer planet Earth and make Jerusalem His world capital. The Essenes expected Him to do this the first time.

If we had lived through the Roman oppression, you and I would have hoped as the Essenes did. Even Yeshūa's disciples didn't understand the separation in time between His *Former Reign* and *Latter Reign* until Jesus explained it to them *after* His resurrection.

The timing of Yeshūa the Messiah's Former Reign was specific and clear. Any scientist or common person could have added up the days and gone to Jerusalem's Eastern Gate (which must remain closed until His Latter Reign entry) on April 6, A.D. 32 and waited for Messiah to show up.

But can we predict from the Bible the date of the Rapture of the Church and the Second Coming of Messiah Yeshūa (Jesus)? I believe we can, to some extent, because of what the Bible says, but in a less specific way. The Bible tells us no one knows the *day* or the *hour* of the rapture, but it doesn't say we won't, as that day approaches, know the era.

Allow me to show you another remarkable prediction.

In the Torah, Moses wrote (Lev. 26:18 *and* elsewhere) that in the future, whenever Israel sins greatly as a nation God will allow calamity to come their way. He will however, give them time to repent. If they, as a nation, do not repent after their warning period, then the remainder of their punishment will be multiplied by *seven*.

Over 600 years before the birth of Jesus, God used Ezekiel, a contemporary of Daniel,to show Israel her sin. In Ezekiel 4:3–6, God told the prophet to lie on his side for 430 days to signify the *430 years* Israel would spend in exile for her sins. Another contemporary of Daniel's and Ezekiel's, the prophet Jeremiah, predicted that the first 70 years of that 430 years would be a Babylonian exile (Jer. 25:11). That was Israel's warning period.

Sure enough, as predicted, Nebuchadnezzar came along and transported the Jews from Jerusalem to Babylon in 606 B.C. Then 70 years later, Cyrus the Great of Persia conquered Babylon in 536 B.C. and said he would pay for the millions of Jews to go back to Jerusalem. But the Jews refused. Only 50,000 devout Jews went back. The rest didn't want to interrupt their businesses in Babylon (now Iraq).

This obviously made God angry, so take 430 years of exile, subtract 70 years of warning, and multiply the remaining 360 years times 7, as Moses instructed in the Torah. You will get 2,520 *prophetic* years of 360 days each = 907,200 days from the day Cyrus made his decree to return to Jerusalem, which comes out *(are you ready for a shock?)* to May 14, 1948, the day Israel became a nation.

Read Matthew 24 now, and you will see that Jesus Himself described the terrible events of the Great Tribulation, a 1,260 day, future terrible period in human history that would end when Jesus returned for His Latter Reign (Second Coming). His disciples asked Him when all these things would happen in the future. When people see that a "fig tree" (which commonly refers to Israel in the Bible) buds forth its branches, Jesus said, the generation alive at that time will not all die before these things are fulfilled.

I am still a scientist so I can't be dogmatic. I don't know for sure what "buds forth its branches" means—maybe May 14, 1948. Maybe getting its borders extended in the 1967 war.

Maybe some future Israeli event. I would guess May 14, 1948. I think Messiah Yeshūa will return within 70 or 80 years of that date.

We know that when a world leader goes into a rebuilt Jewish temple in Jerusalem and desecrates it by declaring himself to be a god, our Messiah will return precisely 1,260 days (3½ prophetic days) later. We know that the world ruler (the Bible calls him the antichrist) won't be that until after the Holy Spirit is temporarily taken out of the world. Logic dictates that will most likely occur at the Rapture of all true believers, spoken of in 1 Thessalonians 4. The Bible strongly hints that true believers in the pre-Rapture church age will not go through the great Tribulation, although there are good Bible scholars who disagree and think we will endure the Tribulation.

When Daniel prophesied 69 weeks until the Messiah's First Coming, he also predicted a 70th week—a seven-year period preceding Messiah's Second Coming. Contrary to popular opinion, the Bible *nowhere* predicts that the Rapture will occur seven years prior to Messiah's Second Coming, although it very well could. I believe in a pre-Tribulation Rapture, but the great Tribulation will only last 3½ years, so I believe the Rapture could occur 3½ years *or more* prior to the Second Coming, even 100 years prior to the Second Coming if God so desires.

When the antichrist desecrates the temple, the Second Coming date becomes predictable—1,260 days later. It is only the Rapture that is relatively unpredictable, though many religious personalities may try to convince you otherwise.

Daniel says at the very end of his prophetic book that the Messiah will return 1,260 days after the desecration of the temple by the antichrist, and 1,290 days after some mystery event. (I take the ending of sacrifices and the appearance of Moses and Elijah on Earth literally—but these are my guesses.)

Daniel says in 9:24–27 that the final seven-year countdown before the Second Coming (7 years × 360 days = 2,520 days) will begin with the signing of a peace treaty with Israel by the antichrist. The antichrist, according to Daniel, would be a descendent of the people who would someday destroy Jerusalem and the temple, Titus and the Roman legions in A.D 70. The antichrist will be a future world leader of a new, revived Roman Empire.

Lots of believers think the Rapture *has* to happen seven or more years before the Second Coming because the Bible says that no one will know for sure which world ruler *is* the antichrist until after the Holy Spirit is temporarily taken out of the world and everyone will know who he is when he signs that peace treaty with Israel. I thought that too, until I realized that Israel has signed several peace treaties and will sign more of them—and may have signed a secret one in November of 1993, when the Prime Minister of Israel met with American leaders here in the U.S., 2,520 days before Feast of Trumpets of the year 2000. Several world rulers sign each of those treaties with Israel. I don't think anyone will know for sure who the antichrist is until he desecrates the temple. It is highly unlikely that more than one world ruler will do that.

The first 3½ years of that final seven-year countdown will probably be no worse than our world is right now. One or two of the seal judgments—maybe even three—could happen just prior to the Great Tribulation of 1,260 days (the Seal Judgments are listed in Revelation 6). I believe the Rapture will probably occur anytime from right now until Seal Judgment #1 occurs.

In this novel, I have the Rapture occurring about five years before the Second Coming, but only so my readers will keep their minds open to the fact that good Bible scholars disagree on when it will occur. I taught for 12 years at Dallas Theological Seminary and studied under John Walvoord, whom I consider the world's leading scholar on eschatology. I remember the day Russia invaded Afghanistan—a real shocker to the rest of the world. Dr. Walvoord walked rapidly into the faculty lounge and—with a wink in his eye—said, "I sure hope we're right about this pre-Tribulation Rapture!"

I want to close with a few remarks about why I think the year 2000 will probably be a significant time and the Third Millennium A.D. will bring the Second Coming. Remember that I am a scientist and psychiatrist, not a prophet, so I am *not* saying the Rapture or the Second Coming will occur in the year 2000. My research has turned up some very interesting observations, though, which make me think *something* significant will likely occur then.

1) Hosea 6 is one of those many passages in the Old Testament that contrasts the Former Reign from the Latter Reign. It predicts Messiah's Former Reign, His public ministry which began in A.D 28. He was "raining" His healing, and

His blessings, His teaching, and the gospel on the Jews and on the world—a blessing indeed.

Then Hosea mentions the Latter Reign and discusses what will happen in between the Former and Latter Reigns. Hosea states (Hos. 6:1–3):

> "Come, and let us return to the LORD;
> For He has torn us, but He will heal us;
> He has stricken, but He will bind us up.
> After two days, He will revive us,
> On the third day He will raise us up,
> That we may live in His sight."

The word *day* in the Bible is a vague term. Sometimes it means a literal 24-hour day. Sometimes it means a 1,000-year period (the Old and New Testaments both say 1,000 years is but a day to the Lord). Usually, it means a 360-day prophetic year, but it can't mean that here because nearly 2,000 prophetic years have already passed.

*If* it means 1,000-year periods, which seems logical here, the 2,000 prophetic years after the Former Reign (A.D 28.) will end in the fall of the year A.D. 2000. That's why I think the year 2000 could be a significant year, and I will be carefully studying the events surrounding every Jewish holiday that year if I am alive and ticking! Many Old and New Testament passages say masses of Jews will realize Yeshūa is their Messiah before His Latter Reign (Second Coming). The year 2000 would be a great choice for the Second Coming or the Rapture, but there can be no dogmatism there. The Second Coming *will not* happen in the year 2000, remember, unless Israel signs a peace treaty in 1993 and the eventual antichrist is one of the signators. It also *will not* happen in the year 2000 unless the antichrist desecrates a rebuilt temple of Solomon in Israel in 1997, 3½ prophetic years after the signing of the peace treaty. And remember that even if Israel signs *a* peace treaty in 1993 or 1994, we won't know for awhile whether or not it was the one spoken of by Daniel.

2) A second reason I think the year 2000 may be a significant year is because of another set of astounding predictions by Daniel. Over 600 years before Yeshūa, Daniel predicted that Babylon would be overthrown by a man named Cyrus leading the Persians. Then he said the tiny nation of Greece would eventually defeat Persia. Daniel predicted that when the Greek leader died (Alexander the Great), his kingdom

would be divided into four parts—which is exactly what happened. The Greek Empire would eventually fall to a Roman Empire, then someday the Roman Empire would be revived with ten loosely-held-together nations. The antichrist would come from a "little horn" which could mean a small nation like Belgium, but more likely refers to a *young* nation that descended from Europe, like the United States of America. The United States is currently the greatest military and nuclear superpower, and Daniel and the book of Revelation both predict the antichrist will have such great military powers that he will take over three nations, then seven more without going to war, forming the ten-nation revived Roman Empire.

The prophet Ezekiel spent chapters 40–48 of his book describing the Millennial Temple in Jerusalem when Messiah returns. It also describes some reinstitution of some animal sacrifices, possibly because people will be so loving and good during the Millennial Kingdom that they will need to be reminded that Yeshūa had to die for their sins.

In Daniel's astonishing predictions of future world empires, he makes an astounding prediction. He says one of the four Greek divisions (after Alexander the Great) will be ruled by a leader who will be a "type" of the future antichrist by actually desecrating the temple of Solomon. This prediction was fulflled by Antiochus Epiphanes on December 16, 168 B.C. In Daniel 8:14, Daniel says that leader would stop animal sacrifices (which he did) and that animal sacrifices would be restored in Jerusalem 2,200 days later. (Some versions say 2,300 days; a few say 2,400 days. Jerome, the church father who translated the Latin Vulgate Bible, preferred the 2,200 days. We don't have the original book of Daniel, only copies of it, so we don't know whether 2,200, 2,300 or 2,400 is what Daniel actually wrote.)

The eight copies of the book of Daniel found in the Dead Sea Scrolls are the oldest copies we have, so probably the most accurate. *In all eight copies*, the number is torn out and missing, which seems like an extreme coincidence or an act of deception. Did that number really wear out of all eight copies? I doubt it. Did the Essenes tear it out of all eight copies for some reason? I doubt it. Did the Dead Sea scholars who have been hiding the Dead Sea Scrolls for nearly 50 years tear it out? I don't know. Why would they?

I *do know* that if 2,200 prophetic "days" (or 360 day years) is accurate, then Daniel implied that 2,200 years after Antiochus Epiphanes desecrated the temple and stopped sacrifices, the Messiah would come and restore sacrifices. That 2,200 years (360 day years, remember) will have been completed in fall of the year 2000. Be reminded that "2,200 days" could have a host of other possible meanings. What seems logical to me may seem foolish to another eschatological researcher.

3) A third reason I think the year 2000 may be a very significant year for God to show us some supernatural signs or events is because Jubilee Years were very important to the / Lord. Moses told the Jews to make every fiftieth year a special Year of Jubilee to cancel all debts and set all slaves or workers free of their contracts. It's not difficult to figure out why the Jews never once obeyed this Jubilee Year celebration. It was economically unpopular with the wealthy. God even punished the nation of Israel from time to time for ignoring His Jubilee Year commands.

Significant events in God's timetable occurred on Jubilee Years. For example, the Bible says that Israel crossed the Jordan River and entered the Promised Land on a Jubilee Year (probably 1451 B.C. but this date could be off by a year or two). If 1451 BC. is correct, then Yeshūa also began His "Former Reign" public ministry on a Jubilee Year (28 A.D). And the year A.D. 2000 would be the fortieth Jubilee Year after the Former Reign and the seventieth Jubilee Year after Israel entered her Promised Land. The numbers 40 and 70 are repeated often in Jewish history and prophecy. Jubilee years were to be declared on Yom Kippur of each Jubilee Year. In the year 2000, because of *two* leap days in February of that year, it will fall on October 8.

If you still have any lingering doubts about whether a *sovereign* Supernatural Being is intimately involved with our world and with the Jews in particular, think about this: Moses declared the 17th of Tammuz and the 9th of Av (21 days apart) as special Fast Days of Mourning annually. Zechariah said that in the Millennial Kingdom, however, these Fast Days would become Feast Days of celebration.

Moses broke the Tablets of the Law on a 17th of Tammuz. The 12 spies were sent out and 10 returned with a bad report on a 9th of Av, resulting in 40 years of wandering around in the wilderness.

In 587 B.C., the Babylonians broke through the walls of Jerusalem after a two-year siege and stopped sacrifices for the first time in over 400 years—on the 17th of Tammuz.

Twenty-one days later—on the 9th of Av—they destroyed Solomon's Temple.

In A.D. 70, Titus and the Roman legions besieged Jerusalem and catapulted large stones onto the rebuilt Temple, killing many priests and stopping sacrifices. The historian Josephus records that this occurred on the 17th of Tammuz. Twenty-one days later—on the 9th of Av—they destroyed the Temple and burned it, removing every stone to find the melted gold. One year later, the Romans plowed Jerusalem to make it into a secular city, fulfilling a prediction the prophet Micah wrote hundreds of years earlier in Micah 3:12. The date this occurred? The 9th of Av, A.D. 71.

In A.D. 135, Simeon Bar Kochba led a Jewish uprising against Rome. His army was totally wiped out—which, by the way, was on the 9th of Av that year.

The Crusades began and Jews were killed on Av 9, 1096 A.D., and the Jews were finally expelled from England in A.D 1290. I'm quite sure the British did not know they were declaring this on the 9th of Av that year. France also expelled the Jews on the 9th of Av, but in 1306.

The Jews were expelled from Spain March through August 2, 1492—their final day to get out. It was the 9th of Av. It was also the same day that God manipulated Spain to foot the bill for Christopher Columbus, an Italian of probable Jewish ancestry who kept it a secret, to discover America, where Jews and others would find religious freedom for more than 500 years. A coincidence or a paradox? By the way, America gained her independence on July 4, 1776—the 17th of Tammuz. Polish Jews were massacred on Av 9, 1648. The pograms against Russian Jews began on Av 9, 1882.

World War I broke out in 1914 and the Jews were immediately persecuted in Russia—on the 9th of Av. Hitler and his henchmen met at Wannsee, Germany on Av 9, 1942 to produce their final plans for the destruction of Jews worldwide.

Ezekiel predicted a future war between Russia and Israel in Ezekiel 38 and 39. Remember that he predicted it 2,600 years ago. He also predicted Russia's allies in that war would be Syria (Persia), Libya ("Put") and Ethiopia, among others. Five-sixths of the Russian army would be killed, quite possibly with nuclear weapons. Israel will be surprised because it will come during a time when they have a peace treaty. Israel will spend seven months picking up dead Russian soldiers.

If the Second Coming occurs in the Feast of Trumpets/ Yom Kippur/Feast of Tabernacles season—and I'm quite sure it will some year—then the antichrist would have to desecrate a rebuilt Temple at Passover, 3½ years earlier. Sacrifices would probably cease at Purim, one month before Passover. Seven months prior to Purim will be about the 9th of Av—a good but not necessarily accurate guess for the date of the future Russian-Israeli war.

Russia will also be there again at the Battle of Armageddon, along with 200 million soldiers from China (this number was predicted in the Bible when the whole world population was only a few million). The antichrist, his false prophet, and the revived Roman Empire soldiers will also be there. So will Yeshūa, and He will win the battle. Zechariah (chapter 14) says that peoples' skin and eyes will melt and fall off of their skeletons before their skeletons would have time to fall to the ground. Written under the inspiration of our loving but just, sovereign, communicative Creator-God more than 2,500 years before nuclear weapons were invented, this can *only* be describing the intense heat of nuclear warfare.

How long will humans use gross denial to avoid seeing the obvious? The odds against all of these things being mere coincidence is beyond calculation. Tell Yeshūa this very moment that you are depending on His death and resurrection at His Former Reign to pay for all your past, present, and future sins. He promises He will. He keeps all His promises.

Then tell Yeshūa (Jesus) that you will serve Him the rest of your life, the best you can, while you wait with great excitement for the Rapture and eventually for His Latter Reign—His Second Coming—to set up the *Third Millennium A.D.*

# ABOUT THE AUTHOR

**P**aul Meier, **M.D.**, co-founder of the Minirth-Meier Clinics, has an M.A. from Dallas Theological Seminary and has taught pastoral counseling in seminary. He received an M.S. degree in cardiovascular physiology at Michigan State University and his M.D. from the University of Arkansas College of Medicine. He completed his psychiatric residency at Duke University. Dr. Meier has written or co-authored over thirty books, including *Love is a Choice, Don't Let Jerks Get the Best of You, Happiness is a Choice, Worry-Free Living, Love Hunger,* and *Beyond Burnout.* This is his first novel.

# THE Fourth
# Millennium

THE SEQUEL ■

# THE Fourth
## Millennium

**THE SEQUEL** ▪

# PAUL MEIER
# AND ROBERT WISE

A
JANET
THOMA
BOOK

THOMAS NELSON PUBLISHERS
Nashville • Atlanta • London • Vancouver
Printed in the United States of America

*For all the saints,*
*who from their labors rest,*
*who thee by faith*
*before the world confessed.*

**MEMO: To the Archives of the Hosts of Heaven**

**RE: Conclusion to the Millennial Reign of Yeshua, the Jewish Messiah**

**FROM: The Reverend John G. Harrison**

To satisfy all inquiries about the final phase of history on planet Earth, a concluding report is being filed along with the first report of the guardian angel, Michael, covering the last decade of the Second Millennium, which was presented in The Third Millennium.

His first memo covered the major events at the end of the 1990s as the Tribulation brought devastation and havoc across the globe. Those events centered around his assignment to protect the family of Jewish psychiatrist Dr. Larry Feinberg. The adventures of this family and Jimmy Harrison offered a significant vantage point from which to view the final struggle of good and evil before the return of the promised Messiah.

Because of the additional trauma occurring at the end of the thousand-year reign of Yeshua, which followed the Second Coming, a further perspective on the last days of the human adventure was more than slightly desirable. This report focuses on the activities of Ben Feinberg and my son, Jimmy Harrison, because of their historical significance in Jerusalem during the one-thousand-year period. Researchers may wish to consider the environmental conditions that allowed such persons as Ben and Jimmy to live to extremely old ages, covering many centuries.

Because of my redeemed state as an Immortal, I

was able to have an almost omniscient perspective from which to view this final chapter of the human story.

Inquirers will also want to note the strange mixing of futuristic culture with the tendency of the Middle Eastern cultures to cling tenaciously to ancient customs and dress. As my report will reveal, some facets of the human personality never changed, even when offered the full possibility of redemption. Homo sapiens generally proved to be a perverse lot, always a ripe target for the Evil One.

Using the same technology available at the end of the millennium, I have preserved this report on hologram video recording. Turn the page and the images will unfold in your mind.

Let it roll!

# CHAPTER

# 1

**April 16, 999** N.E. **(New Era)**
**The 1,000th Year of the Millennial Reign**
**of Yeshua the Messiah**

The Egyptian airfoil airliner flew directly into the
Baghdad airport under cover of a total electronic and radar
blackout. Troops snapped to attention and the president
of Egypt hurried down the red carpet stretched from his
airfoil plane to the state limousine waiting to take Ziad
Atrash to his secret meeting with Syrian leader, Rajah Abu
Sita.

Ziad Atrash, a big muscular man with the neck of a bull,
had midnight black eyes deeply set beneath bushy eyebrows
matching his thick ebony moustache. On his fat fingers he
wore three massive golden rings. Ziad purposely chose the
loose-fitting dark brown robe of the desert peoples to
demonstrate nothing had changed with him, no matter
how many centuries separated the president from the first
bedouins who marched up the Mesopotamian Valley. His
large and threatening hands pressed against the window as
he peered in rapt attention at the sights.

Atrash's plans greatly benefited from his longevity,
which resulted from the restored environment after the
final holocaust that ended the Second Millennium. While

people of five hundred to eight hundred years of age were common, Ziad expected to eventually exceed them all. He still looked forty and his dark-tanned skin had few wrinkles. A fanatic exercise enthusiast, he kept his body in prime condition. While he encouraged rumors of bench pressing five hundred pounds, the truth was Ziad could easily clean three hundred and fifty pounds on any day of the week.

Ziad was an extremist. Any appetite or idea that pleased him was pushed to the limit. While he was not long on careful thought, Atrash forcefully and ruthlessly pursued any objective to which he set his mind. Ziad required little sleep and was rumored to spend the early hours of the morning poring over maps and reports.

The battery-driven limousine silently whisked through the streets of rebuilt Baghdad until it turned down the boulevard toward the ancient section of the old city. Ziad Atrash paid little attention to the large rectangular and cubical buildings with functional design so similar to the contemporary buildings all over the world. The new buildings were slick, practical with clean unadorned lines. But once the limousine entered the antiquated streets, Atrash looked with fascination at the hoary granite block buildings over eight hundred years old, the domed roofs, ornate columns, the tall tiled minarets, and the quaint shops.

When the Second Millennium came to a crashing end and catastrophic calamities destroyed much of the world, some of the old city had survived. Syrian rulers at the end of the Old Era made the tragic mistake of joining with forces of the Antichrist, Damian Gianardo, in the long forgotten war against Israel. Atomic explosions, earthquakes, and environmental pollution nearly destroyed the entire globe. Amazingly, some parts of old Baghdad had fared well. When the new sections of the city were reconstructed, life stayed the same along the venerable cobble-stone streets as it had for thousands of years before.

The battery-driven limo floated down the street without making a sound. Ziad watched the people dressed in cos-tumes stretching back to 1000 B.C. Merchants hawked their handmade pots and blankets as their forefathers had done forever. The fabrics were brilliantly colored with hand-woven designs.

"Slow down," Ziad spoke into the car's intercom. "I want to look more closely."

"Yes sir!" The driver slowed the limo down to a crawl.

The Egyptian leader smiled at the long-robed vendors still wearing the Arab headdresses of the desert. As pre-vious millennia hadn't changed their forefathers, modern technology hadn't reshaped these Arabs who still preferred pottery to plastic, camels to shuttles. The passing of the ages had not changed these children of Ishmael and that pleased the Egyptian president.

Women still trudged up the street bent under the load of bushes to be used in a kiln to fire pottery. An old sheik walked along the street with his dog at his heels. The Arab world remained a domain of men, and that pleased Atrash. His people had buckled under to changes dictated by Jerusalem.

The limousine turned the corner and passed the metalsmith shops. Craftsmen hammered away at sheets of copper, turning them into powers and urns. The noise of hammers banging against anvils rang through the air.

Soon the black limousine left Baghdad behind, crossing the Tigris River and heading south. The Fertile Crescent had also changed little. The indigenous peoples preferred to tend their flocks and ride their donkeys across the lush green fields and pastures. The car sped through the streets of Al Musayyib lined with palms and fruit trees.

"How much further to New Babylon?" Ziad barked into the intercom.

"Only about 25 more kilometers," the driver answered. "Would you care for music?"

"None of that religious-sounding elevator junk they ship out of Jerusalem," he growled. "Give me some of the old stuff. The music of my people—the desert music."

Instantly the car was filled with such authentic sound that Ziad could close his eyes and not tell the difference between the new technophonic speakers and a group of Egyptian musicians playing in front of him.

Atrash pushed a button and the seat mechanically reshaped itself into a reclining lounger, elevating the president's feet into a relaxing posture. Built-in vibrators cranked out immediate relaxation.

*I'm tired of our people being at the mercy of those worthless Jews who run everything from Jerusalem,* he thought to himself. *When I get through with the world, the glory of the pharaohs will be rightly returned to my people. The hour is ripe to break loose from these demagogues.* He spit contemptuously on the floor. *The first thing I'll rip out is the religious nonsense and superstition they impose on the world.*

Off in the distance Ziad abruptly saw the replicas of the massive walls of ancient Babylon beginning to rise above the horizon. Ziad immediately pushed the button to run the seat into upright position.

*For years I've longed to see this restored wonder. What a great idea for a theme park! Perhaps, this place ought to be turned into one of the seats of government.* Ziad pushed another button and the window in the car door was replaced by a huge magnifying glass.

The rebuilt walls and the large Yachter Gate rose up before Ziad's eyes. Cut in brick relief, animals with human heads once again depicted the old glory of Nebuchadnezzar, Naboridus, and Belshazzar. In the background Ziad could see the trees lining the Euphrates River. Just ahead inside the walls were the awesome restored Hanging Gardens Nebuchadnezzar first built for his homesick Median queen.

Ziad knew little of ancient history except that some despot named Saddam Hussein started the massive rebuilding of Ancient Babylon at the end of the twentieth century, Old Era. But then Ancient Babylon had been blown into the Persian Gulf at the end of the Old Era, just prior to Yeshua's Second Coming to set up His Millennial Reign. During the reconstruction of the world in the first and second centuries of the New Era, Yeshua refused to allow the rebuilding of a replica of Ancient Babylon. But Yeshua seemed much more passive this past year, His thousandth and final year of His Millennial Kingdom. So Arabs pooled their immense financial resources to begin the rapid, massive building of New Babylon, replicating Ancient Babylon at a nearby site since Ancient Babylon was now underwater in the Persian Gulf. Yeshua never stopped them, so New Babylon seemed to spring up rapidly out of nowhere. Ziad wanted to walk through the replicas of the ancient world rulers' palaces.

The electronic vehicle slowed and Ziad observed tourists flocking to the Ishtar entrance. "Faster!" he ordered through the intercom.

"I have been instructed to take you through the Marduk Gate," the driver answered. "We will avoid the sightseers and enter through a special side entrance in the palace. We will be there in moments."

The limousine shot forward, rising several additional feet off the ground on a cushion of air, veering over the sides of the road. Moving more like a low-flying helicopter, the black car sped past a checkpoint as a soldier saluted. The car once again came down on a road in front of a massive gateway. They slowed to pass the gate and came into the Imgur-Ellil area of the city. The car passed a large golden statue.

"Replica of a statue Nebuchadnezzar ordered everyone to bow before," the driver explained. "On your left is the Marduk Temple. In ancient times there was always a festive New Year's procession as the people brought all the little gods here to pay their respect to Mr. 'Big God' Marduk." The driver sounded amused.

"How do you know Marduk isn't the name of a real god?" Ziad snapped.

"No offense intended," the driver apologized. "Just that no one has suggested such a thing for an awfully long time."

Ziad smiled.

"Down at the end of the street is an exact replica of the building Nebuchadnezzar called 'the Palace at which Men Marvel.' The original palace had been so impregnable no one ever captured it. Generations after Nebuchadnezzer's time the palace fell into foreign hands."

Ziad gawked out the window at the massive walls and high towers.

"To your left is a replica of the Temple E-khul-khul, built to the moon god, Sin of Haran. Belshazzar tried to replace Marduk with Sin, but he didn't really pull it off." The driver laughed. "Sin usually wins."

"Well," Ziad sounded more pleasant, "maybe I'm going to be more successful in my plans."

"The tall building looming over the city is the recon-structed Tower of Babel," the driver continued his expla-nations. "Archaeologists tell us that this is probably not far from the original sight but no one remembers exactly what happened there." Ziad rolled down the window and strained to see the top of the ziggurat reaching up toward the clouds.

The limousine pulled up to a dead end in front of the

great palace walls. Suddenly a section of the wall slid back and the car sped inside. The wall closed behind them.

"We're just about to the side entrance of the throne room," the driver said. "I'll pull up and the soldiers will escort you inside."

Troops stood at attention as the car came to a halt.

*There's old El Khader, the secretary of state, waiting to meet me,* Ziad thought. *Need to puff up and intimidate the old frog.* The president pulled his robe more tightly around his massive chest.

"Your excellency!" El Khader opened the car door. "Welcome to the land of our ancestors."

"And the glory of tomorrow," Ziad shot back.

"King Rajah Abu Sita awaits you in the throne room."

The escort of soldiers fell in around the Egyptian president, and the entourage hurried up back steps and through a concealed door into the massive throne room. Gold covered the walls; the giant throne was inlaid with blue lapis. Atrash paused, overwhelmed by the sight.

"Welcome, brother!" The Syrian king stood in strange long, flowing robes encrusted with gold. He rushed down from the throne with his arms extended. "I have even dressed the part of the ancient kings to surprise you!"

"Rajah!" Ziad opened his arms. "I am staggered by what I see." The Egyptian president kissed the Syrian leader on both cheeks. "The glory of New Babylon exceeds all reports."

Rajah Abu Sita took his friend by the arm and led him toward a massive door at the far end of the hall. "We must look at the Main Court. You will be equally impressed by the anteroom where the mightiest men of the past gathered before entering into the royal presence." Rajah leaned into Ziad's ear and spoke quietly. "And I must take you to my special place where we can talk without possible eavesdropping. You never know where one of those infernal Immortals will turn up."

The high ceilings of the Main Court enhanced the spectacular aura of the elaborate decorations. However, Rajah gave no time for reflection. He walked quickly to a side wall, pushed a knob on the wall, and the panel slid back. The two men disappeared into an elevator.

"I have a lead-lined room five stories down," Rajah spoke rapidly. "I am assured that the latest technology makes intercepting any conversation impossible." The elevator effortlessly dropped downward. *"No one* will be able to find us or hear us."

The metal door opened into a spartan room about fifty feet square. Maps lined the walls; a conference table stood in the center. "No electric wiring of any kind here," Rajah explained. "Lights are battery powered. Couldn't chance any possibility of bugging."

"It must have been hard to build these quarters without observation," Ziad observed.

"We camouflaged the work as archaeology." Rajah pointed to the bottle and glasses on the table. "May I offer a little refreshment to my brother from Egypt?"

"Thank you." Ziad sat down. "Climate control?"

"Battery powered." Rajah poured from the bottle. "The new solar-charged batteries last over a century so we have little need to worry." Rajah smiled courteously.

"You are just the kind of leader I thought you were." Ziad settled back into the chair. "Everything assures me you are the man to help me regain control of the world. The time has come for the sons of Ishmael to cease sitting at the feet of the Jews. Are you ready to overthrow the illegitimate heirs of father Abraham?"

Rajah stopped smiling. He was much smaller than Ziad, thin and weary. He looked his age of two hundred and ten years. His stark white hair matched his white beard, washing much of the dark olive color from his slightly wrinkled face. In one quick sweep he cast aside the heavy imitation robe of the Babylonian kings. Underneath was the usual pullover jersey worn by most of the world population. Only the gold decoration bars on his chest marked Rajah as a distinguished national leader. When he quit smiling, Rajah's face became distinctly unpleasant.

"I have a plan," Atrash continued. "In order to throw off the yoke of the Jerusalem oppressors, we will need Russia and Iran. I know you have special connections with Ethiopia."

Rajah pulled at his beard and looked out of the corner of his eye. "I pondered the suggestions you whispered in my ear when our paths last crossed in Beirut. Yes, my friend, I read between the lines when your diplomatic communique indicated you wished to visit me in this place. But where would we possibly start such a monumental undertaking?"

"We must begin by recognizing the truth about our exalted and glorious leader," Ziad fired back.

The Syrian leader frowned. "I don't understand."

"We have been raised to believe myths about the omnipotent power behind this Yeshua who supposedly is the unique son of God. We have accepted the legends of his magical and invincible power as if he is the only power in the universe. Now is the time to expose the emperor's clothes. Nakedness—not omnipotence—is the truth about him."

"Look!" Rajah thumped his foot impatiently. "The idea of rebelling against the all-powerful Yeshua is madness."

"Oh, don't believe he is omnipotent or omniscient," Ziad purred. "What if Yeshua is only *one* god among *many*?"

"Many?" The Syrian king's mouth dropped.

"You were brainwashed into accepting monotheism as a fact. The Jews tried to corner the world religion market with such claims. But what if many gods are only dormant, just waiting to be called forth by worshipers?" Abu Sita blinked several times. He started to speak but the words didn't form.

"Perhaps other gods rule other planets," Atrash added, "and await our call to return to this planet.

"You've been sitting on the truth all the time." Ziad Atrash gestured forcefully in the Syrian ruler's face. "You are surrounded by the glory of a past that includes many powerful gods. How do you know Marduk wasn't more powerful than Yeshua? Our ancestors knew the secret of calling on the ancient gods to help them control the world. We *can* prevail against the central Jerusalem government with the help of the old gods. Think about it! The source of real power is waiting to be seized by simply learning how the religion of the past operated."

Rajah began pacing the floor and wringing his hands. "Yeshua, just a god among gods? On what do you dare base such conjecture?"

"My friend, how long since you've seen Yeshua on television? In person? Anywhere? Has He even complained publicly about our building of New Babylon? He ruled for centuries with a rod of iron, but now He has become weak and passive."

The old man scratched his head and shrugged his shoulders.

"Something is going on." Ziad feigned a stage whisper. "They want to perpetuate the myth Yeshua is an eternal thirty-three years old as he was at the time of the resurrection." He spoke more forcefully. "But the facts are to the contrary. He is deteriorating just as everyone eventually does and is hiding to conceal the truth. His power is slipping away. We can make ourselves equal with him!" Why else would he have disappeared from public appearances?

"This is dangerous talk." Abu Sita shook his head. "Very dangerous. I will have to study the matter."

"Go to your archives," Ziad demanded. "Study the ancient rituals as I have! The ancient gods are only waiting for us to worship them and then they will join us in the last great overthrow of the Jews."

Rajah pulled at his beard. "But what about the Immortals? Those strange creatures seem to come and go at will, appearing then disappearing like magic. We have always acquiesced to the communiques and edicts they bring from Jerusalem."

"Yes," Ziad agreed. "These strange creatures are a problem. But if we join with the old gods, there will be new legions of spiritual creatures to stand at our sides. I have evidence that spirit guides and demons guided our ancestors."

"But!" Rajah rolled his shrunken eyes. "They say these Immortals are resurrected beings, saints from the ancient past, chosen to rule with Yeshua. We have been taught these beings lived and died before the beginning of this millennium and have returned from the dead or were raptured at the end of the Second Millennium A.D. They certainly have amazing insight and knowledge from the past. Very intimidating."

"Purely psychological warfare!" Ziad slammed his fat fist into the table. "Just nonsense the Jews conditioned us to believe. How do we know they are not simply another form of a spirit guide?"

"Well, we were always taught to . . . uh . . . think . . . ," Rajah stuttered.

"How do you know Marduk wasn't the most powerful god all along, or a being named Sin of Haran?" Ziad stuck his big finger inches from the Syrian leader's nose. "You don't!"

Abu Sita swallowed hard. "You *really* think the time is ripe to strike?"

Ziad Atrash leaned across the table. "From what little I know of history, our people have always had animosity toward the Jews. Do you think it would be very difficult to whip the masses into rebellion?"

Rajah laughed. "Not in this country!"

"Then I suggest we make a pact at once. We can work out terms that are most agreeable to us. After we clarify the details, we'll be in a position to start building a coalition. We can make contacts by personal visits. I will go to Russia and Iran. You see your friends elsewhere." Ziad extended his hand. "Do you agree?"

Rajah Abu Sita squinted and pulled at his beard. "I will carefully explore the ancient archives and review our religious history." He stopped and bit his lip but after a few seconds he extended his hand. "The time has come to act. Give me liberty from Yeshua and the Jews or give me death. You have a deal."

# PART
# ONE

*Then I saw an angel coming down from heaven, having
the key to the bottomless pit and a great chain in his
hand. He laid hold of the dragon, that serpent of old,
who is the Devil and Satan, and bound him for a thousand years.*

Revelation 20:1–2

# CHAPTER

## 2

As this summit in Baghdad drew to a close, a meeting of old friends was about to begin in Jerusalem. Jimmy Harrison walked carefully up the worn steps of the old Internal Affairs building behind the new Knesset. The last few granite steps were worn and slick from centuries of wear. The old man used his cane to steady himself. Even though slow, Jimmy maintained surprisingly good posture for his extreme age.

The original parliament building, constructed during the twentieth century, Old Era, Second Millennium, had long since been replaced by a golden thirty-story edifice with crystal windows and a glowing marble exterior. The Jewish center of government sparkled in the late afternoon sun like a polished gem. In contrast, the Internal Affairs offices were only three stories high, functional and relatively plain.

Once inside, the people mover quickly whisked the old man to the main suite of offices. Lettering emblazoned on the door read Gentile-Jewish Relationships, Internal Problems and Relocation Assistance.

For a moment, Jimmy stared at his reflection in the mirror finish on the glass door. He still liked to think of himself as a six-foot-four blond Nordic weightlifter, but that image was ancient history. His sparse, closely cropped hair had turned snow white centuries ago, leaving no hint of any color. Being thin still caused him to look taller, but aging had shrunk him to a height of barely over six feet. His face was deeply wrinkled, betraying that some time ago he weighed an extra fifty pounds. His double chin had dried up giving him an ancient appearance. The lines around his eyes and neck were deep drainage ditches. He tightly closed his lips and rubbed his chin vigorously as if pushing the loose skin back the way it once was. Failing to change the terrain, he chuckled at his vanity and went inside.

"Ah, Dr. Harrison." The receptionist turned from her computer when the door opened. "We've been expecting your visit. Chairman Feinberg will be glad to see you. Go on back and I'll tell him you're coming."

The white-haired patriarch trudged down the long corridor. A brass plaque on the door at the end of the hall read Ben Feinberg, Chairman. Just as he reached for the doorknob a voice commanded him to enter.

"You've still got ears like a deer, Ben." Jimmy closed the door behind him.

"Not bad for an old codger of 1,034 years." Ben laughed. "Just chalk it up to superior genetics."

"You ought to have hearing aids in both ears." Jimmy pushed on the small electronic piece in his left ear. "Are you sure you didn't get the cochlea transplant so many people are trying these days?"

Ben Feinberg got up to walk around his desk. "Don't be jealous, Jim." He laughed. "The truth is without the ultrasonic sound vibrator in my chair, I probably couldn't stand up half the time. When it comes to getting around, even with a cane, you've got me beat hands down."

The two men exchanged affectionate hugs and sat down in large office chairs that immediately readjusted to the contours of their bodies, providing instant support and comfort. Both men had snow white thin hair, and Ben's long flowing beard was equally colorless. His long hair was pulled back and tied in a ponytail. Ben was almost four inches shorter, but centuries of physical exercise had kept their bodies firm and toned. Age had given their faces a wrinkled sameness, making the two men look very much like brothers.

A second look, however, revealed the two brothers-in-law actually looked quite different. Ben had once been a two hundred pounder tending to the fleshy side. Time had moved much of the weight toward his middle, leaving a significant paunch. Ben kept his bulbous shape in tow with a tight black belt that looked like a rope around a shifting sack of flour. His neck spilled over his collar and had long since been absorbed into his chin and jaw line. When he was tired, dimples appeared on the sides of Ben's mouth and gray circles surrounded his dark black eyes. Age had flattened Ben's nose and rounded his formerly finely chiseled features. Even though nearly everyone wore contact lenses, Ben had stubbornly stayed with metal-rimmed glasses that looked like rejects from a museum. The thick glasses made his piercing eyes look twice their size.

"Sometimes I look in the mirror and have no idea who's staring back." Jimmy dropped into the chair. "In my wildest dreams I would never have believed either of us could live a thousand years."

Ben nodded his head vigorously. "Remember when the world was falling apart? I thought we weren't going to last another six months. Thanks be to God everything changed. When Yeshua returned and cleaned up the environment, he really put things back into place. The increase in ozone, decreased radiation levels, and pure food have done tremendous things for the body, and those leaves from the Messiah's Trees of Life are absolutely incredible! They rejuvenate and keep one going."

"Definitely." Jimmy shook his fist in the air. "But what a job you've done through the centuries, Ben. You've helped so many of your Jewish people relocate and find their way into the new order. You're no small part of why this old city ticks so well."

"Thanks, old friend. How are things going in your end of town?" Ben asked. "Got the public transportation system spinning like a top?"

Jimmy scratched his head. "Well, you know how it is. Get things running right on one end and they fall apart on the other. I've been too busy to look for pictures. Since we completed the underground subway system from Tel Aviv to downtown Jerusalem, we've been able to streamline commuter trips to the Ben Gurion International Airport. Traveling on a jet stream of air gets trains there almost faster than people can read the front page of *The Jerusalem Post.*"

Ben nodded. "Really needed that improvement. We've just got too many people buzzing around in those blasted anti-gravity compact shuttles. In spite of computerized radar, people simply have too many close calls. Fools drive like maniacs!

"Incredible changes in the last ten centuries. Sometimes I almost forget what it was like way back in the good ole days when we drove those awful gasoline propelled cars. Remember when you sold those death traps in Southern California?"

Jimmy laughed. His teeth had been replaced with porcelain implants giving him the radiant smile of a thirty year old. "I sure loved those old smog makers with the shiny paint. Remember that classic '89 red Corvette I once drove? I really thought I was quite the hot dog."

Ben smiled and peered out of his thick glasses. "Was in another lifetime, my boy! Sometimes the memories are just like yesterday; other times it feels like we've been traveling in a time machine. Who would ever have believed we'd end up leaders in the new era God brought to the world?"

"I was quite a rebellious young man." Jimmy grinned mischievously. "And I thought your sister was the living end." His face fell and his eyelids drooped. "You know . . . I didn't think I would survive her death. The truth is, I've never adjusted to Ruth coming back as an Immortal after Yeshua's return." He sighed. The pouch under his chin dropped, making his chin line disappear into his neck. "I've never really liked or accepted this new sisterlike relationship we must have now. I'd go back to the way it was in a heartbeat. By the way, how is your wife?"

"Quite well," Ben answered. "Cindy recently left for the Far East to deliver a series of lectures to her own people on the meaning of the Kingdom of God. The Chinese have always been apt students, and Cindy's Oriental heritage gives her instant acceptance as a teacher. She will be back in another week."

"People have forgotten the troubles of the past." Jimmy's voice sounded more serious. "After we replaced the debris and rubble of the Great War with new cities and buildings, terror and strife disappeared. People take the good things for granted without acknowledging everything Yeshua provided for us."

"Dangerous business to forget history," Ben interjected. "In fact, that's why I called you to come over."

"Oh?" Jimmy scratched his head. "What's up?"

Ben pulled a remote control from his pocket and clicked one of the buttons. A screen dropped at the far end of the room. He hit another button and a computer printout appeared on the overhead. As he punched other buttons material scrolled rapidly down the screen. Finally a heading appeared across the top: Confidential: Top Secret.

"Little larger, please." Jimmy squinted.

"Need my glasses?" Ben chided. He pressed a control button and the picture expanded.

Recent reports from the Los Angeles area of the United States of America and Central Africa indicate a reappearance of HIV. Not since the end of the second millennium has the highly infectious disease been identified; it was presumed extinct. In order to prevent panic, formal acknowledgment is being momentarily withheld. In addition, rapid spread of this disease suggests wide-scale immorality, which is equally unexpected. The time has come for immediate investigation by all agencies and formal discussion with Yeshua.

In the meantime, it is imperative that every level of leadership join in the search for pertinent information. This report is to be considered sensitive and available only to the highest levels of security clearance.

Ben clicked the picture off and glowered at his friend. When he squinted, Ben's shaggy white eyebrows concealed his view, like bushes concealing the eyes of a fox. "See what I mean? Forgetting history can be deadly." He shook a thick, pudgy finger at his friend.

Jimmy settled back in his chair and wrung his hands. "Terrible news." His eye folds dropped leaving only narrow slits. The creases around his mouth deepened. "When did this report come in?"

"This morning. I wanted you to know immediately."

Jimmy slowly stood up and began to pace. His naturally rounded back became even more bent as he shuffled around the room. "We've had problems through the years," Jimmy confessed. He shook his head. "Heaven knows there is no vaccination or medicine to prevent sin! We've always had to struggle with human selfishness." He held up both hands in a gesture of despair. Jimmy's arms were thin, the skin on his hands tight and paper thin. "Sure, lust has gotten out of hand on many occasions but we have not had a natural disaster to contend with all these centuries." He ground his bony fist in the palm of his hand.

"Keep talking." Ben gestured for his friend to continue. "You've always had a nose for understanding the theological implications of such matters."

"The appearance of this plague means something different is going on in the world. For the first time in recent memory, paradise is really threatened."

"Exactly!" Ben slapped the arm of the chair. "I knew you'd see the seriousness of the situation. I need your help. We comprise a rare compilation of knowledge."

Jimmy slowly rose from his chair and picked up his cane. "I think I'll check some other departments of government and see if anything else is brewing."

Ben followed him toward the door. "I'll be speaking at Hebrew University tomorrow and will have time to access the special computer system they use in archaeological research. As soon as I have other information, I'll be in touch."

Jimmy stopped at the door and asked one final question. "I wonder if anyone has discussed this material with Yeshua himself. We haven't seen Yeshua in any public appearances lately, you know!"

Hebrew University had been completely rebuilt in the fourth century N.E. as a center for creative thought. Its archaeology program was recognized as the best in the world. Located on the gentle slopes of Mt. Scopus, the school had a commanding view of the city. Buildings were designed in the architecture of ancient Jerusalem, making the campus look like an oasis of the past in the midst of the contemporary buildings of the new city.

Dr. Meir Lau called his graduate political science seminar to order. Each student used a personal wristwatch cam recorder to tape the Ben Feinberg lecture. A few final stragglers hurried to their seats and quiet settled over the room.

"By now you should have completed your reading assignments, which survey the history of the infamous twentieth century," Dr. Lau addressed the audience. He glanced around the room quickly, assessing the large number of students. "I trust you reviewed the Holocaust literature as well as the special studies on the Messianic Jewish movements. To complete our study of this unit we are delighted to present a representative of the period. Benjamin Feinberg lived through this era and became a Messianic Jew. Every resident of Jerusalem is aware of his outstanding efforts to help our people find their place in Israel. Please greet our guest lecturer."

Students clapped as Ben walked toward the podium. He nodded appreciatively. "Thank you, Dr. Lau. I am delighted to be with you. I want to begin by giving you a quick overview of the changes of the last one thousand years.

Ben began writing on an electronic pad. Immediately his writing was reproduced in typeset sentences on a large overhead screen behind him. Students pushed a button and reproduction copies came out at their desks.

"The beginning period covers the first two centuries of the New Era." Ben wrote, Rebuilding the World. "Our initial task was to re-create the support systems and infrastructures of life and commerce to fit the new global ecological system. Worldwide re-education began under the direction of the Immortals. They disassembled all military machinery and instituted a government, based on an Old Testament model, centered here in Jerusalem."

Ben scribbled another heading. The computer printout read: Second Period—New Technology.

"From the third to the seventh centuries, we were able to create many of the technologies that make extraordinary longevity possible. I'm sure most of you aren't particularly impressed with what people of my generation consider incredibly long life. Our accomplishments are accepted today as routine."

The students made no response, and many looked bored.

"Of course, global prosperity returned during this phase of recovery." Ben wrote again on his electronic tablet. "I call the present time 'The Period of Complacency.' You are the children of affluence. Unfortunately, it is hard to maintain perspective on the meaning of achievement when you were not part of overcoming the obstacles of the past." He stopped and looked carefully at the class. Ben sensed a growing hostility. "Perhaps, I can be more helpful if I talk about issues you encountered in your reading. Would someone like to begin?"

A tall black-haired young man stood in the second row. "Mr. Feinberg, is it really true that most Jews didn't believe in Yeshua in the old days? I find it hard to understand how any Jew wouldn't believe such an obvious fact."

Ben smiled. "You, your parents, your grandparents, your great-grandparents, and far beyond have always lived in the world as it is today. You naturally accept King David as the mayor of Jerusalem who manages our local daily affairs. On television and holograms you see Yeshua as normally as you watch the weather report. Perhaps it would surprise you to learn that when I was your age the weathermen on television were wrong about as many times as they were right."

The class laughed politely.

"But it is true. Many Jews thought Christians were their enemies, and they even believed Yeshua was responsible for anti-Semitism. The truth was veiled from our eyes because most of us had never studied the Torah and the books of the former and later prophets, much less read the book called the New Testament."

A young woman at the back raised her hand. "We have never known war. Even the idea is repugnant. Were you frightened?"

Ben turned and looked out the window. He could see down Mt. Scopus toward the walls of the old city. The sun glistened brightly off the gold of the restored Temple. "Frightened?" he answered. "Terrified is a better word."

Ben's mind drifted back to a Pizza Hut just off the campus of UCLA. A college student named Deborah was sitting across from him. She had babbled hysterically, "The girls at the dorm are too scared to talk about anything, but yesterday the security police suddenly showed up and surrounded the building. Cindy's blindness made her a very easy catch. They ransacked her room, clubbed her guide dog Sam to death, and took Cindy away in a police car. They found her secret radio for receiving calls from Israel."

"We never knew when Antichrist Gianardo's men would descend on us," Ben continued. "My wife was once saved by the intervention of an angel named Michael. She was blind then . . . ," his voice trailed off, "before she was healed when Yeshua returned."

"Were angels like Immortals?" another student asked.

"Somewhat." Ben shook his head. "At least they looked the same to us. They could come and go, then disappear just as Immortals do. But Immortals weren't on earth then. The Immortals are God's people who have been redeemed from death and given a resurrected body just as Yeshua has; they are perpetual thirty-three-year-olds. Wasn't easy getting used to the presence of Immortal saints after the New Era began. Finally, we began to see Immortals as another order of creation. Immortals are a special race of redeemed creatures above us. Because we trust Yeshua to forgive our sin, we'll become Immortals when we die."

"You must have lost many friends," another student observed.

Ben immediately thought of his sister. Ruth had died in childbirth, hiding out in the desert at Petra. Her loss cut to the quick and nearly destroyed Jimmy Harrison, her husband. Ben answered, "During the years of the Great Tribulation forty million Christians were killed by the Antichrist. Fourteen million were Jewish believers. Another twenty million citizens were executed because Gianardo's men thought them to be unpatriotic. Of course, billions died because of the wars, famines, and plagues."

Another memory gave him pause. Ben had not thought about Joe and Jennifer McCoy for a long time. He remembered the children Joe Jr. and Erica . . . and the night the entire family was executed in their own backyard for believing in the Messiah and for sharing the Bible with neighbors.

"We didn't understand many things you take for granted." Ben sounded irritated. "Each death was a very painful loss. You are fortunate to live in a time when the sting has been removed. With the help of a redeemed and reconstituted environment, medicines brought to earth from the Trees of Life, and continually improving technology, you know little about pain. You grew up without the *slightest* idea of how difficult grief can be."

For several moments no one spoke.

Finally one student inquired, "Did everyone really have guns?"

"You are very fortunate Yeshua commanded all weapons, especially nuclear weapons, to be destroyed," Ben answered. "The worst retaliation you'll ever experience is someone hitting another person. Unfortunately, violence was as common as shopping in a grocery store."

"Why?" the tall young man asked again. "Why were all those people so stupid?"

The class laughed but Ben didn't smile.

"The Evil One is also something about which you know nothing," Ben snapped. "You were spared a great source of chaos."

An older man with a white beard raised his hand. "I am Zvilli Zemah. I'm finishing my second Ph.D." He sounded arrogant and condescending. "Do you really expect us to believe in this old superstition about a personified evil called the devil? After all, no one has seriously discussed such an idea for centuries."

"What are you suggesting?" Ben glowered.

"In this university we study the ancient myths of Egypt, the Canaanite peoples, the Baals, and other forms of superstitious thought used by the ancients to explain what they could not understand. Wasn't the idea of Satan nothing more than a way to talk about collective evil? Simply a scapegoat method of blame." The man twisted his face and mimicked a child. "The devil made me do it." The class roared.

Ben looked around the room, dismayed at the lack of seriousness and concern. Their faces looked soft and naïve. "You accept the gifts of the Kingdom of God as Americans once took for granted the benefits of freedom. You enjoy your rights but aren't particularly impressed with responsibilities." His voice had an edge.

"Sorry." Zvilli shrugged. "We generally don't confuse superficial religious ideas with the more profound sociological insights into human behavior."

Ben shot back. "You don't have the slightest idea of what you are babbling! *I* lived in a world where evil was rampant. *We* paid a great price for our foolish ignorance of the diabolical designs of Satan to destroy all who came in the name of God."

Zvilli Zemah looked with satisfaction at the students around him. "Obviously, Mr. Feinberg, you are a politician, not a student." Dr. Zemah sat down.

"You naive young traitor! Don't you understand that all the 'gods' from Egypt's Osiris to Babylon's Marduk on to the Baals, these fraudulent imitations were only masks worn by the devil? He always used wicked rulers like chessmen in a game of world power! Damian Gianardo and Jacob Rathmarker were nothing but the last in a long line of dupes." Ben pounded on the desk. "Don't confuse political theory with theological fact."

Zemah smirked and rolled his eyes. The students were obviously impressed by his defiance.

Ben walked around to the front of the podium, crossed his arms over his chest, and stared at his opponent through his thick glasses. "The primary strategy of evil was always to persuade people it didn't exist. Satan's most insidious work was carried on in the minds of people who denied his existence."

"Are you saying the devil is still at work?" Dr. Zemah raised his eyebrows in mock amazement and looked around at his friends in amusement.

Ben tried to choke back his anger. Zemah was using this lecture to increase his standing with his peers and Ben knew he was being manipulated for the student's personal gain. Before he could check himself, Ben blurted out, "You pseudo-intellectual! The likes of you fried when the rest of creation moaned in those final moments of conflict as the third millennium began. On the dawn of the Feast of Trumpets, September 28 of the year 2000, people like you awoke to the blackest day this world has ever seen. Smoke rolled in from the Valley of Jezreel, and the smog of war and nuclear fallout covered the world. I know . . . I was there!" Ben was nearly shouting.

"Uh . . . thank you . . . Mr. Feinberg," Dr. Lau interrupted. "Your talk has been most informative." The professor sounded embarrassed and uncomfortable.

"No," Ben continued. "You hear me out! On that day when the Lord of Lords and King of Kings returned, the devil was cast into the bottomless pit and Yeshua chained him. If Yeshua hadn't gained this victory not one of you would be sitting in this room. You have been protected from an evil you don't even understand."

"Yes, yes." Dr. Lau took Ben by the arm. "You have certainly put everything into perspective for the students. We thank you for taking your valuable time to be with us."

Most of the students clapped politely. As Ben was escorted out of the classroom he heard Zemah say to students gathered around him, "Silly old fundamentalist." Dr. Lau kept talking rapidly as if he didn't want to give Ben a chance to respond until he had him away from the lecture hall.

"Just a minute," Ben pulled away. "What is going on here? Why are you afraid to let me speak my mind?"

"Oh, never!" the professor assured Ben. "We just know how limited your time is."

"Are you teaching these people that the devil was only a myth?"

"Mr. Feinberg, the academic world is so different from the routines of everyday life. We have to consider many options not talked about in the more mundane discussions of the business world. Thank you for helping us understand how the ancient people thought." The professor shook his hand and hurried away.

Ben walked slowly to the exit. "I can't believe it," he muttered to himself. "I've just been displayed like a relic from the past to demonstrate how old fools did things! These people don't understand. They just *don't* understand."

# CHAPTER

## 3

Far below the palace Rajah Abu Sita sat at the far end of the long table in the secret conference room, watching his secretary of state assemble documents at the other end of the table.

"No effort was spared," El Khader explained. "We checked the memory banks of every computer system and searched through the reserved books in the royal archives. A very interesting passage surfaced from the book the Jews call the Old Testament. In the sixth chapter of the first section of Genesis, it reads, 'There were giants on the earth in those days, and also afterward, when the sons of God came in to the daughters of men and they bore children to them. Those were the mighty men who were of old, men of renown.' Maybe the Jews do know something they haven't told us."

Abu Sita pulled at his beard and smiled.

The secretary of state pushed a book forward. "However, success was achieved through an inter-library exchange with the great Jerusalem library which survived the destruction at the end of the last millennium."

Blackened from years of intense sun, El Khader's face was like the desert people's, giving his skin the texture of shoe leather. His lips were thin and appeared about to crack open any moment. He wore a perpetual frown.

"Did anyone connect your inquiry with me?" Rajah snapped.

"No one," the diplomat answered. "Our request was made through the department of archaeology under the guise of a search for additional material to be used in restoring statues in New Babylon."

"You are sure?" Rajah growled.

"Without question." El Khader carefully unrolled one particular aged scroll. "Because the study of cuneiform has been my hobby, I obtained one of the most ancient accounts of this book and translated the work myself."

"What is it?" Abu Sita drummed on the table with his finger tips.

"During the ancient New Years' festivals, our ancestors chanted this poem in honor of the greatest of the gods. The records of Assyriology call the verses *Enuma Elish.*"

"Hmm . . ." The king leaned forward. "What does it mean?"

"It is the Babylonian account of the creation of the world, the story of the rise of the god Marduk to supreme power over all other gods."

"Really?" Rajah opened his eyes wide in astonishment. Though seldom seen underneath his heavy drooping eyelids, the king's eyes were faded brown with a yellowish ring around the cornea, giving him an eerie appearance. "Tell me more."

"At the beginning of this early period, Babylon was an insignificant city-state and Marduk was known only as a minor god." El Khader stood, beginning to lecture like a college professor. "A most interesting coincidence follows. As Marduk's fortunes rose, so did Babylon's. Once Marduk was recognized as all-powerful, Babylon suddenly burst onto the world scene as a mighty power. I know because I checked the dates carefully."

Abu Sita's eyelids dropped again and his eyes sank back into the dim. "I am amazed," he said more to himself. "Amazed! Maybe Ziad Atrash knows what he is talking about after all."

"Each New Year's Day our fathers celebrated the victory of Marduk over the competing god Tiamat, proclaiming the world a place of violence." El Khader continued, "The ancients believed only the most powerful can prevail on this earth."

"Read some of the verses to me," Rajah commanded.

The secretary of state picked up the cuneiform and read slowly but deliberately:

> "At the using of this name, Marduk, let us bow down in reverence; upon the opening of his mouth be all other gods silent. His command shall be preeminent above and below. 'Be exalted our son, even he who avenged us.' Let his authority be supreme, be it second to none: and let him act as the shepherd of mankind, his creatures, who, unforgetting to later ages, shall ever tell of his deed. He is almighty god."

Rajah pushed himself up from the chair. "Tell me," he asked with the greatest gravity, "is there any formula or ritual for calling this god forth?"

"I am working on the rest of the New Years' worship documents," El Khader answered. "Soon I will have the ancient incantations translated."

"Will they let us contact the god?" Rajah walked around the table.

The old secretary of state's mouth twitched nervously. "Sir, we are playing with fire. The Jews would call such experimentation 'idolatry.'"

Abu Sita cursed violently. "Nothing will stop my search! I don't care what they think."

"But what if an Immortal should show up and . . ."

"Are you defying me?" Rajah pounded the table.

"Never, my king." The old man made obeisance. "I simply raise the questions that a faithful adviser must ask. Nothing more."

The king looked miffed but shook off his indignation. "I must make contact with Marduk. Do you understand? I must know if Marduk still speaks. No other assignment in your entire career of three centuries begins to compare to the urgency of this matter. I want to break into the spirit world."

El Khader nodded his head. "I understand."

"The moment you have the worship instructions ready we will assemble in this room or, better yet, in the Temple of Marduk itself. I will do whatever is necessary to call him forth." Rajah shook his finger in the old man's face. "But time is of essence. We must contact the god quickly."

"Your wish is my command, O Great One." El Khader began backing toward the elevator. "I leave these translations for your study."

Rajah dropped into the chair El Khader had used and began poring over the documents. The secretary of state disappeared into the elevator and was gone.

For over a day Jimmy Harrison pondered the implications of his conversation with Ben Feinberg. Each time he came to the same conclusion: More information was needed. In late afternoon he set up an appointment with old friends in Los Angeles. Because they were eight hours behind him in time, the conversation would be a morning call in California.

Jimmy hurried from the office to his apartment in the

suburbs of Jerusalem. Even though he complained at times, he still drove an anti-gravity compact shuttle because the transportation was so quick. He could speed over the tops of the buildings and fly in a straight line to his destination. Radar and computer settings guided the one-person craft so well that navigation was never a problem. The internal guidance systems even compensated for bad weather and high winds, making the ride like gliding on a cloud.

Preoccupied with recollections from the past, Jimmy didn't notice the other crafts whizzing past. He was thinking about Isaiah Murphy. Jimmy's first contact with Isaiah had come when the teenager was a busboy in Cindy Wong's family restaurant in Lake Forest, California. Because The Golden Dragon was a favorite of the Feinberg family, he and Ruth had dined there often.

Isaiah, a talented black athlete, went on to UCLA. In time he had become a significant member of Ben's college group. Isaiah had been a Christian since early college and was naturally accepting of Jimmy's insights about the Rapture and the return of Jesus, as they were called back in those days. The youth hid out at the old farmhouse with the rest of the gang during the worst days of the Great Tribulation. He and Deborah Whitaker had helped keep the group fed and housed during those terrible hot August days.

Jimmy's shuttle automatically settled down gently on the roof of his house. Built into the side of a cliff, with most of the dwelling completely underground, the home was kept cool in the summer and warm in the winter by the earth. A two-person elevator dropped him from the landing pad roof to the bottom floor in moments. He stepped into his office and walked straight to the communication equipment.

Because of his special government status, Jimmy received the latest technological advances before the general citizenry of the city. For years he had used his hologram phone to place calls throughout the world. During the first two centuries N.E., video telephones became common. However, the big breakthrough came in the fifth century when Terbor Esiw, an electronic wizard from the late second millennial period, perfected light projection transmission. Instead of seeing the caller on the screen, an image was projected in front of the viewer. The caller appeared as a one-foot-high, three-dimensional column of light.

Jimmy turned on his new phone machine, which had only been installed a month. Recent hologram improvements allowed the caller to be projected in full life-size dimensions. Only by touching the creation of light could Jimmy tell the image was just an illusion.

Once he was seated in front of his transmitter, Jimmy punched in the Los Angeles phone number. He flipped the light switch and shot light down on the small black platform directly in front of him. The phone rang twice.

"Hello?" The voice came over the surround system speakers, making it impossible to tell the difference from someone talking in the room.

"Isaiah?" Jimmy threw the projection switch.

"Jimmy!" An image began to form on the platform. "Old friend! It's been far too long." Suddenly a white-haired black man appeared in the room.

"Hey, buddy!" Jimmy almost got up to shake hands. "Haven't heard from you for . . . I don't know . . . has it been fifty years?"

Isaiah laughed. "You know how it is. The older we are, the more quickly time seems to go. Anymore fifty years feels more like a couple of months."

Jimmy studied his old acquaintance. Isaiah had been unusually tall and an outstanding basketball player. With the passing of the centuries, he had become much thinner, making Isaiah look even taller. His face was long and lean.

Isaiah's muscles had become more sinewy and rippled under his skin like rubber bands. His bushy eyebrows looked like rows of cotton stuck above his deep-set dark eyes.

"Look who else is here." Isaiah extended his arm and a woman appeared next to him. "Say hello to Deborah."

Jimmy absentmindedly waved. "Deborah Whitaker! I bet no one has called you by your maiden name for a thousand years. How have you stayed married to that old coot?"

The white-haired woman chuckled. "Living in Los Angeles century after century will certainly make you broadminded."

"Don't push your luck," Isaiah chided. "You don't look like a spring chicken yourself, old man.

"Your E-Mail communique indicated you needed to talk with both of us. Sounded serious. What's up?"

"Are you still running the public health department in Los Angeles?" Jimmy asked.

"Well, sort of," Isaiah rolled his eyes. "You know I was chief administrator for a couple of centuries, and then I shifted back to working with children. But after my back got a little stiff I switched to research. Been doing lots of computer work lately."

"Excellent!" Jimmy gestured at the figure, completely forgetting he was only talking to a column of light. "Deborah, last I heard you were working with the hospitals in the area, right?"

"Yes. As you will remember Yeshua suggested the Los Angeles complex be rebuilt in many villages and burroughs so people would never again be lost in the anonymous character of metropolitan life. Today we have thousands of towns stretching from Santa Barbara to San Diego. We've kept medical care on an individual basis with only a few major technological centers. I help run the complexes."

"Good. My records are correct and up to date," Jimmy acknowledged. "Sure wish we could sit down together for an evening of fun. Is it true they changed all the McDonald's hamburger stands to McDavid's with a specialty in Kosher food?"

"Got one down the street," Deborah answered. "Why not fly over, and we'll see if we can find some of those nasty old greasy, cholesterol-loaded fries we once loved."

"Maybe when we get this problem solved." Jimmy's voice changed and sounded more professional. "Tell me, what's the spiritual condition of Los Angeles like these days?"

Isaiah and Deborah looked knowingly at each other. She answered, "How interesting you'd ask. Recently we were in a meeting with an old acquaintance of yours. Remember Dr. Ann Woodbridge?"

"Remember her! The Christian psychologist? Good grief! I was sitting in her office in a knock-down, drag-out fight with the Feinbergs when she was raptured right before our eyes. I could never forget Dr. Woodbridge."

"Of course, Ann is now an Immortal and looks even younger than when you saw her in her Newport Beach office so long ago," Deborah continued. "She has the celestial oversight of emotional well-being in our area. Dr. Woodbridge just met with a group of us to express profound concern over the sudden moral deterioration throughout the whole West Coast region.

"Of course, we've always had problems," Deborah added. "We all know people sin, but I thought mortals were in better shape than they apparently are. Dr. Woodbridge warned us that a wave of divorce is on the way because of an epidemic of adultery."

"Distressing!" Jimmy shook his head. "Anything else going on?"

"For the first time in years," Deborah added, "psychiatric wards are full. I don't remember a time when so many people have been clinically depressed."

"Does this make any sense to you, Isaiah?"

"Not really, Jimmy. But I can tell you that I'm amazed how angry many people are. Even in the grocery stores you sense a hostility I'd almost forgotten. Genetic engineering has produced fruits and vegetables of incredible size. Cockroaches, mosquitoes, and ants no longer exist. Opportunity is unlimited, and yet people seem very agitated."

Jimmy thought out loud. "So . . . you're seeing spiritual problems, emotional difficulties breaking out like . . . like . . . an infection."

"I think you could put it that way," Isaiah answered.

Jimmy got up from his chair and walked across the room. "I need your help."

"Hey, where'd you go?" Deborah exclaimed.

Jimmy turned and stared at the empty space in front of his computer console. "Sorry! I walked out of transmission range." He hurried back to the desk and immediately the Murphys appeared on the platform again.

"Please put your ear to the ground," Jimmy continued. "If you hear of or see any suspicious or unusual diseases, call me at once. Help me get some insight into why people are going off the tracks."

"Sure," Isaiah answered. "We will also get an appointment to talk with Ben's father. Dr. Larry Feinberg is a spiritual overseer of psychiatric practice in this area as well. I know he still works with Ann Woodbridge. We'll call you in a week or as soon as we know something."

Travel between the Internal Affairs building and the new Knesset was quick and easy through the connecting underground tunnel reserved for use by government employees. The people mover conveyer belts enabled even elderly persons to make the trip in minutes. Ben stepped into his office elevator and minutes later was on the twenty-ninth floor, occupied by the Jerusalem city administration.

Due to the late hour most of the personnel were gone. A remaining secretary was clearing her desk when Ben walked in. "Ah, Mr. Feinberg. His Majesty has been waiting for you. Please go in."

Replicas of the gates leading to Solomon's Temple lined the massive wooden doors to the mayor's office. Ben timidly pushed one of the doors open and stepped in.

"Feinberg," the powerful voice called out from the other end of the enormous office. "Do come in."

"Thank you for seeing me at this hour of the night, excellency," Ben answered. "I'm sure King David has more pressing matters than talking with the chairman of Gentile-Jewish Relations."

"Absolutely not!" David walked from his desk to a more informal area with couches and chairs. "Such a fine servant of the people is welcome night or day. Come, let us reason together." David walked with the regal bearing and confident stride expected of a king. As all Immortals, he was thirty-three years old. A strapping specimen of a man, his long black hair was pulled back over his shoulders and blended into the handsome beard that edged his face. He looked straight at Ben. "Sit down and share your concerns, my son."

Ben approached timidly. "Being the mayor of Jerusalem is just one of the many things you do, I know. I'm sure there is so much more work of which I know nothing."

David smiled warmly and patted Ben on the shoulder. "People are often intimidated by me. Killing giants seems to give some pause. Please don't be put off. Remember, you know of all my great mistakes, as well. Just consider me a friend. Sit down."

"I suppose I can't get a certain image from the start of the New Era out of my mind," Ben began. "I can still see you standing on the Temple Mount with Yeshua, announcing the inauguration of His reign. What a totally overwhelming sight! Of course, each year I watch your oversight and participation in the Feast of Tabernacles. It leaves me rather taken aback."

"Ah, yes. Sukkot! The fifteenth of Tishri!" David laughed with a hearty roar. "How I love that day. The feast reminds us of how God provided for our people during the forty years of wandering in the wilderness. Of course, my son Solomon's Temple was dedicated on this day in 1005 B.C. I do make a great deal of the festival."

"We often call it the Feast of Booths," Ben added. "My family always gets together on this day for quite a celebration."

"I'm going to tell you a little secret." David leaned forward with a smile on his face. "People of your era celebrated Yeshua's birthday on December 25. And the date worked well since it converted a pagan nature festival into a Christian holy day, but everyone knew it wasn't the actual birth date. Know when it was?"

Ben shook his head.

David grinned mischievously. "Remember the Gospel John wrote? In the first chapter, the fourteenth verse, John gave everyone the big clue about the birth. John wrote that Yeshua became flesh and dwelt among us." David thumped on the table with his finger. "Know what *dwelt* implies in the original Greek?"

Ben again shook his head.

"It means 'tabernacled among us.' Get it? John was writing between the lines, telling the world Yeshua was born on the Feast of Tabernacles, which means the Holy

Spirit conceived Him in Mary's womb nine months earlier on about December 25th."

Ben blinked in amazement. "I'm astonished. No one has ever pointed that out before."

"Since we don't make much of birthdays anymore that fact slipped away. People live so long, birth dates aren't nearly so important. But I thought you'd find the idea to be very interesting."

"That fact alone adds new meaning for me this year, Sir. I will make all of my family and friends aware. For centuries we've had an extraordinary gathering and celebration during the seven days of Sukkot. We came to call these outings our Trumpet Parties."

"I want you to try a new drink perfected up north." David poured two glasses of an amber-colored liquid from a crystal decanter. "We've developed an extremely high protein drink with an unusual grape taste using a new hybrid from the Galilean hillsides. We're planning to unveil it at the next festival." He held up his glass in a toast. "To us, Ben, and the coming Trumpet Party."

"Ah, Sir." Ben looked at his glass. "One of the reasons I am here is a concern over something I just noticed in checking records relating to this past Sukkot festival. Each year Yeshua calls representatives of the nations to Jerusalem for the festival. Everything is so exciting and has gone so well through the years, little attention is paid to attendance. But in double checking the record I find that no representatives came from Egypt this year. Isn't that rather strange?"

David's gaze was intense but conveyed no emotion.

"I . . . uh . . . mean," Ben stammered. "Isn't ignoring the Feast a snub to Yeshua? Shouldn't attention be given to the matter?"

David looked at Ben with great admiration. "You are a good and faithful servant. Your Master is well pleased with you. Let us drink." He extended his glass with a forcefulness that suggested no further questions should be asked.

Ben mechanically clicked his glass with King David's and drank. He still felt as though he had stepped into a mystery. He wasn't getting a straight answer.

David put the glass on the table. "A divine golden taste."

"Yes, excellency. Extraordinary." Ben put his glass next to David's. "One further issue. I'm sure you are aware of the HIV outbreaks."

David shook his head yes, but again his countenance revealed nothing.

"I am working on this problem," Ben said slowly, "as I am sure all agencies of the government are. Apparently, even medicine from the Messiah's Trees of Life aren't affecting the virus."

Again David shook his head yes.

"I'm sure Yeshua must be aware of the report." He paused but David indicated absolutely nothing. "In this regard, I couldn't help but reflect that no one has seen our Lord in a long time. I can't remember the last time I saw Him on television or hologram. Is there some reason for His absence?"

David stood up abruptly. "What a man of integrity you are, Ben Feinberg." David took his arm and led him toward the door. "Your service will never go unnoticed. Do you remember what I wrote? 'Blessed is the man who walks not in the counsel of the ungodly, nor stands in the path of sinners, nor sits in the seat of the scornful; but his delight is in the law of the Lord.' You are such a man, Ben."

"But, Sir, about Yeshua's status . . ."

"You have probably wondered about the injustice of some of us being Immortals," David continued, "while others of you must live in unredeemed bodies. Let me tell you it is to your advantage. You have the opportunity to perfect your faith and character to a remarkable degree as you persevere in your journey. You will shine with even greater glory at the ultimate day, Ben. Stay your course, my man. God has a great purpose for you." David shook his hand forcefully and shut the door.

Ben found himself standing alone inches outside the great door, staring at the design. His hand still extended, Ben turned slowly and shuffled through the empty offices and down the vacant corridor.

*I've just been given the door,* Ben said to himself. *What in the world is going on?*

# CHAPTER

## 4

The large banner over the Marduk Gate proclaimed in four languages: Welcome Delegates to the International Archaeology Conference. New Babylon's buildings were covered with streamers and flags. Limousines and caravans of flag-decked cars poured into the city. Even though only two weeks had passed since their first meeting, Ziad Atrash, the king of Egypt, and Rajah Abu Sita, the king of Syria, had obviously been busy and successful.

The two leaders stood on the steps of the Tower of Babel and watched the entourage flowing into the city. "We have done well." Atrash smiled wickedly. "They are all coming."

"The prime minister of Russia arrived last night and has been sequestered at Perepolis; however, he is on his way," Sita observed.

"We have the heads of state from Ethiopia, Egypt, Syria, Iran, Italy, France, Russia, and Jordan." Ziad Atrash pounded his palm. "And China! Fong is the most aggressive of the lot."

Rajah leaned over the rail and looked far out to the farming plain that stretched across the Fertile Crescent.

"The idea of a study conference is the perfect cover. The Immortals never pay attention to such matters since they already know the details of the past."

"The security room beneath the palace is prepared?" Atrash asked.

"More than ready. El Khader will welcome each delegation and start them on a quick tour of the city, ending in the throne room of the Palace. After a sumptuous feast in the main court, the leaders will be ready for our meeting in the lead-lined room."

Atrash stroked his beard and looked extremely pleased. "I gave only the briefest overview to most of the heads of state, but I found immediate acceptance for the idea of revolt. China has already taken significant action."

Rajah Abu Sita nodded. "My experience was exactly the same."

"Fong was enthusiastic to form the alliance. The Chinese have extraordinary historical memories and are still smarting from their enormous defeat at the hands of Yeshua in the Armageddon debacle a millennium ago."

"Then everything is ready. In only three weeks we have been able to bring the world to sit at our feet." Atrash crossed his arms over his chest and stood with his feet apart, looking every inch like an ancient pharaoh. "Let us go welcome our guests."

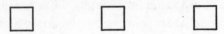

Servers hurried around the long tables in the main court, making sure each dignitary received maximum personal attention. Costumed in the servant's dress of the era of Sargon, the waiters wore short battle skirts with swords by their sides. Sandals were laced up their calves and their hair had been braided and cropped into the square, flat look of the ancient Assyrians. Similarly dressed guards stood at attention around the room, holding spears, shields, and bows.

The carefully planned banquet reflected the same details of a feast from the days of Sennacherib. Huge gold plates were piled high with roasted pheasants and desert quail. Racks of venison roasted on a spit in the mammoth fireplace. Each ruler drank from an embossed golden goblet. Servers poured vintage wines from gold pitchers taken from museums. As the leaders dined, women in lacy veils danced to music from harps, lutes, and cymbals.

"Have they had enough?" Atrash whispered into Rajah Abu Sita's ear.

"If they haven't, they are bigger gluttons than we ever imagined."

"Then let us begin."

Abu Sita nodded to El Khader. The old secretary of state clapped his hands and immediately fifty trumpeters put their instruments to their mouths and blew a fanfare, filling the stone walls with overwhelming sound.

"Glorious leaders of all creation." El Khader's raspy voice echoed down the stone corridors. "Welcome to this conference for the recovery of the glory of the ancients. Great discoveries lie ahead for you." He bowed and turned to Rajah Abu Sita as a slave gives obeisance to his master.

"Noble leaders of vision," Rajah began, "the magnificence of the past shall only be a prelude to the greater achievements of the future. In order to see the greatest treasure of all we must adjourn to our hidden storeroom. Unfortunately space allows only the head of each government to attend. If you're ready, El Khader will lead you."

The secretary of state immediately marched to the secret panel in the wall, pushed the hidden button, and waited as the panel opened, revealing the elevator door. "Follow me," he announced. "You will not be disappointed."

When the entourage stepped from the elevator, they

immediately saw maps and charts lining the walls. Glasses and decanters, note pads, and pencils sat on the conference tables, a single document and pen in front of each chair. In contrast to the palace, the security room looked like the inside of a metal cube.

The plain space quickly filled as the leaders assembled around the tables. Each head of state said little to the other as they sat down. A small man, Fong was completely bald headed with deep-set eyes. Black spindly Ali from Ethiopia looked like a giant next to the Chinaman. Alexi Chardoff, a sullen man, had on the typical Russian version of the universally worn jersey-knit suit. The Russian's thick ruffled hair looked like he had just gotten out of bed. Kahil Hussein, Jordan's king, wore a kaffiyeh headdress dating back thousands of years. Similarly the Iranian president was covered with the traditional robes of the desert. Maria Marchino wore the latest Italian fashion but Claudine Toulouse wore a French version of the jersey uniform. Each face was stoic, impassive, not betraying thought or intent.

Rajah Abu Sita stood at the end of the head table. "The hour has come to fully explore the possibilities of our meeting. You can rest assured no one can intercept our conversations. A foot of solid lead covers the ceiling, floor, and walls. The elevator door is also lead lined." Rajah pointed to a small black box on the table in front of him. "Should anyone have any form of electronic transmission device, it will be detected and an alarm will sound. Similarly, *any* form of transmission attempted during this meeting will be discovered. Only what you write in your own hand or carry in your mind will leave this place. Are there questions about security?"

The leaders looked at each other but no one spoke.

"We must agree to a promise of complete diplomatic secrecy," Rajah Abu Sita continued. "No one will reveal any portion of these discussions unless all agree. For the sake of mutual protection, we have prepared the simple agreement that is before you. If any party cannot agree, he should leave now. On the other hand, if terms are agreeable, we will begin by signing the accord." Sita picked up the document in front of him, glanced at the copy, and immediately signed.

Delegates surveyed their copies. The battery-operated lights set from many different angles in the walls and ceiling filled the room with the illusion of sunlight. One by one the delegates initialed the forms before settling back in their chairs to look at the maps and charts on the walls.

After the final diplomat signed, Ziad Atrash spoke. "Each of us has chafed under the domination of the central government. Our own political agendas have been hindered by the constant intervention of overseers and intruders from Jerusalem. You are justly offended and frustrated. Even though you have not spoken out publicly for fear of reprisal, you desire change. Am I not correct?"

Each diplomat stared straight ahead.

"Until recently upheaval did not seem possible," Atrash continued. "No one dared stand against what seemed to be an impregnable system. But I, Ziad Atrash, ruler of the upper and lower Nile, have found a way. Revolution *is* possible!" He slammed his fist on the table.

"We share a very important fact," Atrash continued. "Each of us was born in the last several hundred years. We are people of the second half of this millennium, leaders of this time. Correct?"

The heads of state looked at each other and nodded.

"We were carefully shaped, trained, and manipulated by educational processes designed in Jerusalem. We were given a version of history written by Jews. The past was defined and described in terms of their successes and our failures." Atrash's voice dropped to an almost inaudible level. "Do you understand?" he whispered. Atrash suddenly pounded on the table and screamed. *"We have been duped!"*

Abu Sita fired back from the other end of the table. "How do we know there is only *one* god who controls this world? This idea is nothing but the religious propaganda of the Jews. We are stooges of Yeshua, controlled and molded by a view of reality concocted in Jerusalem."

"We have simply accepted the superiority of the Jews and their leaders as reality," Atrash returned the verbal volley. "But the party line has been nothing but a lie."

The room became silent.

"Don't look so worried," Atrash chided. "The solution is simpler than you might think." He pointed to a chart on the back wall. "As you drove down these ancient streets, you saw the replicas of Marduk and Sin of Haran. They have counterparts in the gods of Egypt and the Baals of ancient Canaan. Even though these gods seem different, they are really identical—just different in names. All of our countries had female fertility gods as well as gods of war." He pointed at the figures on the chart. "The names aren't important; their function is."

"You don't actually believe there is a god?" Ali of Ethiopia rubbed his long, narrow chin.

Atrash shrugged indifferently. "The issue isn't *a* god but *gods.* There are spirits. Maybe they are even spirits of the dead . . . but yes, there are spirit guides. In fact, we are currently researching ancient Egyptian religious customs to discover the original techniques of the priests of Osiris in order to receive spirit guidance."

"Spirit guidance?" Fong chuckled. "Is such a thing possible?"

Rajah Abu Sita smiled. "You might be surprised at what I get through my meditation sessions based on the practices of the priest of Marduk."

Atrash cleared his throat forcefully. "The point is we can

replace the authority of Yeshua at every level. After we explain his mystique, the new religion will be offered. By the time the central government reacts, armed troops will converge on Israel. My friends, we are on the verge of military victory!"

"Just a minute," Chardoff interrupted. When the rumpled Russian stood, his rotund girth made his knit clothes look ill fitting. "Everyone knows Yeshua *is* a god." He looked around the room and cursed. "Of course we are controlled! Yeshua is a supernaturally powerful, perpetual thirty-three-year-old. He never ages and has ruled with a rod of iron for nearly a thousand years now. Who can stand up to such a being?"

"When did you last *actually* see him? Has he been on television lately?" Ziad asked.

"Well . . ." Chardoff scratched his head. "I don't exactly remember."

"Yeshua has not been seen live for over a year," Rajah answered. "We checked all of the stations throughout the world. Everything has been replays."

"What are you driving at?" Chardoff crossed his arms over his chest.

"Yeshua is in trouble," Atrash said. "We believe he kept himself propped up for some time. Something is happening to him and he cannot control the fact that he, too, is either aging or growing weak for some other unknown reason."

"We have tested his power." Atrash pointed to Fong. "This year Egypt refused to attend the Feast of Tabernacles celebration and no one said a word. The Chinese expelled all its officials from the central government and nothing happened. Our brave chairman of the people has succeeded in defying the central government!"

Fong smiled arrogantly.

Rajah Abu Sita smiled wickedly. "Yeshua claims to be the supreme son of God, but he is a clever impostor. The truth is he is *one* among *many* gods, some greater than he. For some reason we don't yet understand, his power has begun to slip and he can no longer maintain his preeminence. If our countries are united and we have help from the gods, we can throw off the yoke of bondage and be free to do as we please."

"Stop!" Maria Marchino demanded. She pointed a long bony finger at Atrash. The president of Italy was a tall, imposing woman. Her black eyes could pierce steel. "Who has not had one of those blasted Immortals suddenly appear in the middle of a planning session?" She looked around the room and cursed. "Of course we are controlled. Even if Yeshua is slipping, he's supported by bizarre characters who pop up like summer frogs on the Nile."

"What if we have learned the secret of the Immortals?" Rajah's question sounded oily and sly.

"Secret?" Ali frowned.

"Do you see any Immortals in this room?" Ziad Atrash cupped his hand over his mouth and called out, "Yeshua, we are betraying you. Come and get us!" Atrash laughed and threw his arms open. "If you and the Immortals can get through the lead lining, we are yours."

The stunned leaders looked nervously around the room.

"Nothing!" Atrash spit in contempt. "You see, our omnipotent, omniscient, omnipresent masters are powerless when they and their bugging devices can't get through our shields." Ziad laughed diabolically.

"You are saying the Immortals have limits?" Chardoff sank back into his chair.

"Yes," Atrash said slowly, "and we can avoid their intrusions by planning in rooms such as this. Even modern-day monitoring devices depend on X-ray technology and they can't penetrate lead, so it is possible to escape their surveillance and surprise appearances."

Chardoff shook his head in astonished disbelief. His fat

jowls shook back and forth. "No one has ever challenged the Immortals before."

"Exactly!" Ziad Atrash pounded the table again. "We have attributed more power to them than they actually have." With a sweeping gesture of acquiescence, the Egyptian deferred to the Syrian king. "Even more significant, we now have the secret of producing our own protectors."

"What?" Claudine Toulouse said. The small blonde woman leaned forward. "You jest."

"Can't be!" the Jordanian king gasped.

"Are you serious?" the Iranian diplomat asked.

"My friends," Rajah rose on his toes for additional height. "After consulting the ancient manuscripts, we have found the way to receive guidance from other gods, maybe even the greatest of all the gods."

"Monotheism has been the only way of life we've ever known," the Iranian insisted. "Even before this millennium my people believed in Allah as the one true god. We rejected polytheism as primitive, superstitious."

"But isn't polytheism the oldest religion?" Ziad Atrash asked. "Is it possible monotheism is actually a degenerate form of the greatest truth because the Jews have persuaded us monotheism is superior?"

"Yes," Rajah interrupted, "with my own eyes, I have seen the truth."

"Show us," Claudine Toulouse demanded.

Rajah Abu Sita beckoned for El Khader. The old man reluctantly shuffled forward. "Sit down." The king of Syria pointed to his chair and the diplomat dropped down.

"Through the New Year's ritual of Ancient Babylon, we have learned how to turn men into channels for divine communication. My secretary of state offered himself. He has become the voice of the god Marduk." Rajah Abu Sita put his arm around El Khader. "Although not an Immortal, he is an equally significant conduit to the gods." The king condescendingly patted the diplomat on the shoulder. "Show the people," he said to the old man.

"Your wish is my command." The old man's voice shook and squeaked.

The secretary of state placed both hands firmly on the table and lowered his chin until it bumped his chest. He mumbled under his breath and his chest began heaving. A low groan rolled out of his mouth. El Khader slowly raised his head, his eyes closed.

"Hear me!" The diplomat's voice, loud and firm, seemed to emanate from new vocal chords. "Listen to my words and live." The sound was low and forceful, disconcerting and primitive. "I will guide you down ancient paths to find the better way. The hour at hand is pregnant with divine possibility! Dare to seize the moment. As I defeated ancient challengers, so will I prevail in this last time of confrontation."

El Khader's eyelids opened slightly revealing only the whites of his eyes. His lips did not move but the words came from his mouth. The old man's arm became rigid, his fingers stiff. His frightening demeanor was catatonic.

"I hold rights to the kingdoms of this world. I give thrones and palaces to whom I choose." El Khader spoke as if from the bottom of a cave. "You rule because of my choice. The world rests in the palm of my hand. Bow before me and reign supreme!"

The secretary of state abruptly fell forward; his face bumped into the table. For several moments he didn't move. Finally he blinked and asked in his usual frail voice, "Where am I?"

The delegates stared. No one spoke for several moments.

"You would not toy with us?" Ali of Ethiopia finally asked.

"What you have seen is only the beginning," Rajah Abu Sita assured. An exhausted El Khader hobbled away. "Believe me!" the Assyrian king demanded. "Only the surface has been scratched."

"In Egypt we have found similar means of divine guidance," Ziad Atrash insisted. "Friends, the days of control by the Immortals are numbered. Besides, many of the Immortals quit appearing here on earth about a year ago— the same time Yeshua quit making public appearances. That's why we risked our countries' fortunes to build New Babylon as rapidly as is humanly possible, even in our age of such advanced technology."

The king of Jordan rose slowly, looking every inch an ancient desert sheik. "Let us concede for the moment that everything you say is true. Possibly we have seen an amazing discovery. Nevertheless, all power is still consolidated in the central government. After hundreds of years people are conditioned to accept Jewish authority. No one uses force anymore." The king shrugged. "We have known nothing but peace for many centuries."

Ziad Atrash walked to the maps on the wall, turned, and smiled as if fully anticipating the question. "Peace will be our instrument of war. No one anywhere is equipped, trained, or prepared for violence, and therein is our opportunity." He kept smiling and waited for his conclusions to sink in.

"Don't stop now," Ali the Ethiopian demanded. "Make your point more precisely."

"In the world of the blind, the one-eyed man is king," Atrash continued. "When there are no weapons, the man with a stick is to be feared. Even the most primitive knowledge of assault gives the attacker total advantage. Strike the Jewish rulers with a rod of iron, and they will scream like wounded water buffaloes."

The Ethiopian frowned. "Revolt will require more than men running around swinging children's batons."

"I spoke metaphorically," Atrash answered condescendingly. "We have located long forgotten manuals of instruction on the martial arts. Under the guise of creative recreation, we have already begun training karate instructors to be sent to your countries to develop military personnel. We can quickly assemble a vicious strike force whose bodies will be their weapons." With his finger Atrash traced lines on the map from each of their countries to Israel. "No one in Jerusalem today is even vaguely prepared to defend themselves against such physical attack."

Rajah Abu Sita added, "In our libraries we have found elementary books on making gunpowder and small bombs. Even though ammunition makers are now extinct, we believe crude weapons will be quite sufficient to take out the Jews, who have no weapons whatsoever. Each of your countries has other ingredients needed to round out our arsenal of basic weaponry. Do you see the ingenuity in this plan?"

The leaders looked around the room at each other. Here and there men and women nodded in agreement.

"The newly created batteries have great voltage." Aba Sita pointed to the battery-operated lights in the ceiling. "We know how to turn this power into stun guns, which can knock a person cold in a flash."

Chardoff stood up once more and glowered at the group. "This may be the craziest idea I have heard in the last fifty years." The Russian's bushy eyebrows lowered and his puffy red face darkened. He slowly looked around the room. "And then maybe it is the best idea in over a hundred years." He ran his hands through his mop of hair. "At least it's worth pursuing. In our state museum the old weapons are preserved as examples of our barbaric past. But no one knows that beneath the basement of this museum are crates of guns and ammunition. If the equipment can be reconditioned, we have considerable fire power at our disposal."

Ziad cheered and suddenly the group broke into enthusiastic applause. Diplomats began shaking hands and congratulating each other on *their* new plan.

"I have reserves of nitrates in Ethiopia," Ali of Ethiopia shouted above the uproar. "We will be able to make excellent gunpowder. No one will suspect what we are doing!"

Fong held up his hand. "In China we have great reserves of sulphur and ammonia. We can create many varieties of explosives."

Again the group applauded.

"What more could be needed?" Hussein of Jordan asked.

"To the restored World Order!" Ziad Atrash called out.

"To our success!" the group answered.

Two hours later as the delegates returned to their elegant suites in the palace, Fong pulled Chardoff aside. "Come with me," he grunted.

The two men stepped into a small exhibit hall. Fong moved into the furthest corner and began talking rapidly in a low whisper. "Well, Mr. Prime Minister, what do you really think of this plan?"

Chardoff nodded his head soberly. "It makes sense."

Fong bore down. "Only one thing is amiss."

"Yes?"

"Our two great countries combined are the largest land mass and the most populous in the world. An alliance between us would be quite natural and could bring the final consolidation of power. Why should these dogs of the desert dictate to us the terms of the future? Let them march at the front of this conspiracy but after the smoke clears we can make our move to seize the reigns of power. We can rule the world together." Fong stared intensely into the eyes of the Russian. "Something to think about, Mr. Prime Minister."

Chardoff's stoic countenance showed no emotion for several moments. Finally he said, "A most intriguing idea." For the first time, Chardoff smiled.

The electronic identification system flashed Jimmy Harrison's picture on screens throughout the Feinbergs' home. Computer memory instantly identified him and the outer door opened automatically, letting Jimmy into a waiting area.

Ben's voice came over a speaker, "Jimmy, glad you're here. Come on in."

The front door silently slid open and Jimmy entered Ben and Cindy's living room. Decorated to reflect the ancient Israelite setting, the plain stucco walls and simple decor gave the house an understated elegance and classic Jerusalem design. Artifacts and archaeological treasures accented the room, as well.

"Welcome!" Ben Feinberg entered from across the living room. "Good of you to come over so quickly."

"Just got your call." Jimmy extended his hand.

"Look who's here," Ben gestured over his shoulder. A small Chinese woman with white hair pulled back in a tight bun followed him. Small and frail, her quick, sure pace denied the fragile appearance. "Cindy came home early."

"Ah!" Jimmy threw his arms open. "Our little lotus blossom. I thought you'd be gone for another week." He hugged the little woman.

"I returned to make sure Ben wasn't being a naughty boy." Cindy laughed. Olive skin and few wrinkles added to a misleading appearance of youthfulness.

"At his age?" Jimmy Harrison rolled his eyes in mock consternation. "Fat chance."

"Sit down, please." Ben pointed to the chairs. "We need to talk."

"Indeed!" Ben shuffled toward the armchair. "Got some surprising things to tell you."

"Cindy is back," Ben began, "because of unexpected negative conditions in China. Her discoveries add a strange new twist to our inquiry."

"Really?" Jimmy frowned. "What's happened?"

"Without any warning or explanation," Cindy Feinberg began, "the Chinese government demanded that all personnel from or related to the central government in Jerusalem leave the country. I was expelled!"

"What?" Jimmy leaned forward. "I can't believe my ears!"

Ben nodded his head. "In addition, our people in Russia had a similar experience. Jerusalem officials were simply sent packing."

"Why . . . such a thing is without precedent. How dare some government snub us!"

"No one has an explanation," Ben continued. "We are completely mystified.

"Déjà vu," Cindy added. "For a few minutes I thought I was back in the twentieth century. Soldiers and uniformed police showed up at my room and escorted me to the airport. Boom! Before I could even consider what was going on, I was on my way back to Jerusalem."

Russia?" Jimmy scratched his head. "China? What's going on?"

"I thought maybe your investigations would have turned up some clues," Ben Feinberg said.

"Not on this front." Jimmy shook his head. "But I do have some distressing news from Los Angeles."

Cindy brightened. "My true homeland! How is everybody in the south land?"

"Apparently not too well," Jimmy continued. "I talked with Isaiah and Deborah Murphy by phone. They tell me things aren't going so well in Los Angeles."

Ben looked at Cindy. "How long since we've taken a trip to L.A.?"

Cindy shrugged. "We haven't been back in literally decades. But what a great time! Everything is green and new since it's the first of May."

"Maybe it's time we all took a little vacation," Ben suggested. "Any reason you couldn't take several days off, Jimmy?"

"What a great idea. I'd love to visit old friends. I think the time would be well spent."

"We could take the new ultra-glide shuttle that makes nonstop trips from Tel Aviv to Los Angeles," Cindy said. "They say you barely have time to get into the stratosphere before you start down. I think we could be in L.A. in three to four hours."

"Exactly," Jimmy Harrison confirmed. "Three hours and twenty-five minutes. Hardly enough time to have supper and enjoy a good hologram movie."

"I don't think we should wear our government uniforms," Ben added. "Let's just look like average citizens. Perhaps we can learn more."

"I agree," Jimmy answered. "Why don't I go back to the house and pick up a few things? I will meet you at the subway station and we can use my new underground tram to get us to the airport."

"My?" Cindy smiled mischievously. "Getting a little possessive these days, aren't we, Harrison?"

Jimmy laughed and slowly got to his feet. "I do have a little personal investment there. You know how I always loved anything vaguely related to cars."

Ben Feinberg chided, "You've got to be the only person left in the world who still thinks those awful old relics are wonderful."

Jimmy started to the door. "Maybe somebody in L.A. will have a tip on some museum that might let me drive one of those . . ."

The gigantic ultra-guide slowly descended into the traffic pattern of the Los Angeles Interglobal Telaport. The boomerang-shaped craft carried four hundred people and provided every luxury for the traveler. Special express flights between major cities on different continents allowed maximum contact with every corner of the world in record time. The crafts flew in giant sweeping arches and were often used as space shuttles flying into outer space.

"Isaiah and Deborah will be here to meet us," Jimmy said. "They made arrangements for our visit and are planning a little reunion with old friends. Should be a great time."

"Excellent." Ben switched on a ground scope screen and adjusted the range. "Let's take a look at the area." Instantly the landscape of the south coast appeared on the screen.

"Amazing how everything has been rebuilt," Cindy observed. "Wasn't much left after the Tribulation."

"Building subways," Jimmy insisted, "was one of the best ideas. Sure got rid of those old problems with freeways."

Ben agreed. "Yes, your part in changing the freeway

system was very significant. I think your name is still on the plaque in the central station."

"Wouldn't know." Jimmy feigned ignorance.

"Look at the new harbor." Cindy pointed to the screen. "The earthquakes destroyed the old harbor network."

"Filled up the old Long Beach pier with rocks," Jimmy grumbled.

"What a marvelous reconstruction," Cindy added. "And I love the large green belts between each little town, guaranteeing urban sprawl will never occur again. We've come a long way."

"Please prepare for immediate landing," the flight attendant announced overhead. "Activate your air protection systems now."

The three travelers pushed buttons on the armrest and immediately a gentle column of air surrounded them. As the craft slowed, the column of air increased in their wraparound seats, ensuring them of a firm blanket of protection against jolting as they landed. The trio quickly gathered their belongings and hurried toward the exit door. Within moments they were inside the telaport.

Standing just beyond the exit gates was a tall, thin black man and his small white wife. "Greetings strangers!" Isaiah called out. "Welcome to the thousandth-plus-a-few-years class reunion of the celebrated class of 1997 A.D."

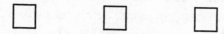

Isaiah and Deborah Murphy had decorated their living room to look like a south-of-the-border fiesta. Candy-filled piñatas dangled from the ceiling. Plates piled with nachos, salsa, and other spicy foods filled serving tables. Streamers hung from the walls and banners welcomed the fifteen delegates to the 1,003rd-year reunion. Encased in plastic for preservation, yellowing pictures from college days lay around the tables.

The first two hours of the reunion were spent swapping stories and updating the group on life in Jerusalem. Finally a lull in the conversations settled around the room.

Jimmy Harrison clapped his hands. "Please gather around. I want to share our reason for coming."

The old gang drifted around the couch, some sitting on the floor while others pulled up chairs. "Lay it on us," someone called out.

"We can't thank Isaiah and Deborah enough for such a fun time," Jimmy said. "In our kosher world, we don't get to enjoy cheese enchiladas often."

The group laughed.

"Actually we came to get a serious report on how things are faring in your world," Jimmy continued. "We've lived through the worst and the best together. Your opinions are always invaluable."

"I tried to contact Dr. Ann Woodbridge," Isaiah reported, "but we couldn't find her anywhere. Ben, we also wanted to invite your father and mother but they couldn't be found either. Rather strange."

Ben nodded appreciatively. "Thanks for trying. Regardless, tell us about the religious and moral climate in Los Angeles these days."

"I hate to say," George Abrams began, "but people are spiritually indifferent. With the glorious mountains behind us and the magnificent ocean before us, pleasure seems to be the number one pursuit. Religion, church, and worship are boring to most folks. I've even seen horoscopes reappearing, as well as psychic readings."

Deborah Murphy shook her head. "Generations have never known anything other than the order and stability of Yeshua's government. No one has ever worried about losing a job or going broke. Everyone has everything they could want."

"Affluence breeds apathy," Mary Chandler added. "People don't care. They exist without passion. I'm afraid many of my neighbors are in the spiritual doldrums. People are once again concerned with status and possessions. Greed is now 'in.'"

"Perspective has been lost," someone said.

"Oh, I think matters are much worse," Isaiah insisted. "People don't stay neutral long. When they are not committed to something, they quickly fall for anything. We are seeing a resurgence of sexual sin like we've never known. Professional white-collar crime is also on the rise."

"Strange," Mary added, "we've become like the children of Israel wandering through the wilderness. God has provided everything we could ever need and we're not even grateful. I hadn't thought about the problem this way before, but we are just about as faithless as they were."

"I'm afraid . . ." Ben stopped and thought for a moment. "Let me put it this way. We have evidence some of the old diseases may be recurring. The matter may be very serious. Sounds like Los Angeles is part of the problem."

"I'm rather surprised this problem wasn't brought to our attention by the Immortals," Isaiah said. "In fact, I haven't been in any meetings lately where anyone from Jerusalem showed up. The Immortals have always helped before big problems get out of hand. I would have expected their intervention."

"I can't find my parents," Ben mumbled to himself, "and I can't get Ann Woodbridge to answer her phone. Very strange . . . something *is* going on."

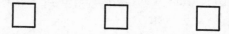

On the other side of the world, it was nearly midnight. King Abu Sita hurried into the Temple of Marduk. The artificial lighting had been shut off and the moonlight turned the reconstructed temple into a place of shadows and dark corners. Flickering candles and torches provided the only light.

The huge temple's long flat roof was supported by massive marble columns. Red and blue frescos etched with gold designs bordered the ceilings. In the front of the great hall six-foot-high candlesticks and a smoldering copper brazier five feet in diameter added a glow. At the top of a row of marble steps a twenty-foot statue of Marduk dominated the temple.

El Khader waited at the front of the sanctuary with two women and an ensemble of musicians. Guards barred all entrances.

"They've all been sworn to secrecy?" The Syrian king pointed around the room.

"On the threat of their lives," the secretary of state answered. He was dressed in a long robe of brilliant blue and a breast plate dotted with jewels hung from his neck. El Khader wore a cylindrical domed hat with a large strip of embroidered cloth hanging from each side. "The designers of my priest robes have been equally sworn." He looked at the two women and the musicians. "We have practiced the ceremony many times so we can do everything with precision. Your wish is our command."

Abu Sita looked critically at the women's transparent gowns. Glistening in the torchlight the filmy veils concealed little. "Do they understand the ancient dialect?"

"No, Glorious One," El Khader explained. "But they can pronounce the words correctly and sing the melodies of worship as they were originally intended. We believe the women will be sufficient."

"The priestesses were dressed like *that*?" Rajah Abu Sita pointed and raised his eyebrows.

"Yes, according to the archives and the writings of the Temple Chronicles," El Khader insisted.

"Then let's get on with it," the Syrian king barked.

The secretary of state snapped his fingers and the musicians began. The women started to hum. He tossed fluid into the copper brazier and flames leaped, sending white columns of smoke toward the ceiling. El Khader dumped a cup of incense into the fire. The pungent smell of frankincense and myrrh filled the night air. Then the old man raised his arms in worship before the menacing statue above him.

Marduk was seated on a throne of gray granite. He had long hair and a flat beard styled in ripples that hung to mid-chest. A turban swirled around the stone head and the god held a rod of iron. The black eyes had the look of a devouring lion. At his feet on the first step lay a small golden goblet and an open silver container filled with white powder.

El Khader handed the king a scroll. "The poem is translated into contemporary Syrian. Read as the women sing and I will call the god up from the other world."

The women slipped into a slow-moving dance while singing, their gowns floating in the evening breeze. Their bodies swayed back and forth as if to seduce Marduk.

Rajah Abu Sita began, "I have cast thee a spell, make thee all great in the gods' assembly. The scepters of the gods given into thy hand: yea, supremely great shall thou be."

El Khader poured more incense into the fire. White smoke completely covered the front of the statue. "Louder!" he commanded the Syrian king. "We must demonstrate sincerity."

The women clicked finger cymbals, gyrating and swaying as if drifting into a trance. The drums picked up the tempo and the flute played furiously. The scene took on an unearthly aura.

Rajah read in time to the music. "The heavens rain oil. The wadis run with honey. Marduk raises his voice and cries: I shall sit and take my ease, for Marduk the Mighty is alive, for the prince, the lord of the earth, exists."

El Khader had already climbed up the stairs on his knees, his hands held upward in praise. "Greatest among the gods! Victor over the god Tiaman! Ruler of the Underworld! We offer you our lives, our fortunes, our empire. Take my body as your vehicle! My voice as your mouth."

Rajah felt his heart thump to the rhythm of the drum beat. The sounds and the smell of the incense were intoxicating and he felt light-headed. Uncharacteristically emotional, he cried, "Blessed Marduk! I worship you with all my heart. Come forth!"

El Khader seized a glob of hallucinogenic powder from the silver cup on the top step. He plunged his tongue into the drug and washed the paste down with the bitter brew. The women rushed toward the bottom step and cried out, "Habu Habu! Isma ya mo lay. Shay-la-har-mar. See-har-ba!"

El Khader stiffened and grabbed his chest as if struck by a seizure or a heart attack. He tumbled forward, the headdress crashing against the top step. The old man inched down the steps and rolled sideways as if dead.

"What's happened?" Rajah Abu Sita cried out. The dancers and musicians stopped. The king stared, more in consternation than fear. When the women backed away, the king crept forward.

Abu Sita peered down at the unconscious diplomat. "Are you alive?"

El Khader blinked but didn't open his eyes.

"Speak to me," the king demanded.

His eyes shut, a low guttural growl like the sound of a mad dog rolled up from the old man's throat. Suddenly he shrieked like a rabid cat. White saliva foamed at the corners of his mouth and ran down his beard. The king took a step back and the women ran out of the building, the musicians hurrying behind them.

"Listen to me!" The words came from El Khader's mouth but his lips didn't move. "I am your guide on the path to all truth. Hear me." The sound was low, deep, dominating. "I am the voice of Marduk. Hear him. The greatest of all the gods!

"My hour has come again." The words flowed from El Khader's mouth as if they had a life of their own. "If you hear me and obey, I will return the glory of this place. I will make my worshipers to walk over the heads of their enemies. I will speak through my servant to those who listen." El Khader's head raised slowly and then fell back against the marble floor.

Silence filled the great hall. King Rajah Abu Sita looked around, realizing the musicians and the women were gone. The guards were standing behind columns near the entrance. When he looked back, his secretary of state had rolled over on his side and was sitting up. El Khader wiped his mouth and stared at the dribble on the front of his robe.

"What happened?" the diplomat's voice returned. "Where am I?"

# CHAPTER
## 6

The Murphys' living room was still cluttered with glasses and plates from the party the night before. Isaiah was picking up some of the dishes when Jimmy came downstairs. "Hope you had a good time," Isaiah called out to his old friend.

"Tremendous," Jimmy answered. "Fabulous to see all the old friends."

"You really look rested. The antijet-lag pills must really work."

"One of the great modern advances." Jimmy Harrison dropped down on the couch. "One tablet before leaving Jerusalem and immediately the ole brain amines started readjusting to the change in sleep patterns. Right now I can't even feel a time difference."

"I've already tried to find Ann Woodbridge and the Feinbergs this morning," Isaiah continued. "I called on the hologram phone, tried their offices, and even tapped the Internet computer system to no avail. As bizarre as it seems, the Immortals seem to have disappeared off the face of the earth."

Jimmy laughed. "The last time that happened to me was the Rapture. Terrified me to the core. At least we know they're either here on earth or in the spiritual realms."

"It's almost like they are intentionally avoiding us," Isaiah Murphy mused. "It just doesn't add up."

"I had the same experience with King David." Ben Feinberg entered from the guest room adjacent to the living room. "Didn't mean to eavesdrop, but I was coming out when I heard your conversation."

"Well, good morning," Jimmy answered. "Cindy's still sacked out?"

"She's just behind me." Ben walked into the room. "Jimmy, I didn't tell you about my experience with our illustrious mayor of Jerusalem. While meeting with him recently, I was distinctly brushed off and ushered out of the room. Things don't normally work that way."

"Ben, do you have any special way to contact your parents?" Isaiah asked.

"No, just the usual ways. Never been a problem before. For ten centuries they've responded immediately. Perhaps I ought to see if I can use Jerusalem's special connection system to the Immortals."

"Actually . . ." Jimmy rolled his cane between his hands. His eyes took on a mischievous twinkle. "You see . . . well . . . I had hoped to locate a museum that might let me drive one of those old Mustangs. Now, I know this is a wild . . ."

"Wild idea?" Cindy said from the bedroom door. "Sounds like a great idea to get killed. Driving one of those antiques today would be like riding a bicycle on a freeway a thousand years ago."

"I tried that once," Jimmy said to himself.

"Nearly got you killed, I'll bet," Cindy shot back.

"Yeah, but what a thrill!"

"Let's go for something a little more on the immediate and practical side." Isaiah punched in numbers on his computerized wrist watch. "Take a quick look at the news and see what's brewing out there. Who knows? We may be missing some important explanation for where the Immortals are."

Isaiah pushed the enter button, and the north side of the wall instantly became a life-size television screen. As the picture came into focus, they saw people running in every direction. A camera crew zoomed in on a man standing in front of the Los Angeles County Courthouse.

"This is Don Blevins with Channel 6. Details are just now becoming available," the announcer's message was clipped. "Apparently a large group gathered to hear the judge's verdict on a petition from Newt Baez, a Southern California resident and activist who was asking the court to set him free from any and all restrictions imposed by the central government in Jerusalem. Judge McCalhenney ruled in favor of the state and ordered Baez to stay in compliance with current law. The group supporting Baez was prepared for this decision and immediately denounced the judge, turning the courtroom into a shambles. Baez and company rushed out of the courthouse to tell the news to followers waiting on the steps. A full-scale riot erupted."

The camera spanned a crowd rampaging in front of the legal center. While a police vehicle was being turned over, a dozen other protestors set a police anti-gravity shuttle on fire. Without weapons, police could only push and pull the rioters away. The police were vastly outnumbered for the battle.

"Discontent has been fermenting for some time," Blevins began again. "While unnoticed by most observers, a movement has been building to demand complete separation from the central government. Matters have clearly taken an ugly turn."

Suddenly a building across the street from the courthouse burst into flames. Mobs of people ran through the streets while rioters shouted, "Down with Jerusalem!"

"Matters are deteriorating quickly," the announcer continued. "The judge's decision seems to have ignited social gasoline." Someone pressed a piece of paper into the announcer's hand. "I have just been informed," Blevins read from the paper, "Judge McCalhenney has been seriously injured after being thrown out of a second-story window."

A camera angle from a flying shuttlecraft filled the screen. Flames shot out of other buildings around the courthouse as people ran in every direction. Another picture of a large crowd pushing unarmed policemen to the ground and trampling them filled the screen.

"Please tell us what is happening," the announcer's voice broke in. Two men stood next to him with hands on their hips, chests heaving up and down from running. "Why has this situation erupted and become volatile?"

"The time has come to revolt!" The smaller man shook his fist at the television camera. "Throw off the oppressors!"

"What are you talking about?" Don Blevins glowered.

"We are going to attack any and all representatives of the government in Jerusalem," the second man shouted. "We'll throw the dictators in the ocean."

"You are targeting government officials?" the announcer gawked. "Are you serious?"

The small man grabbed the microphone. "Join with us, fellow citizens, and assault anyone who tries to restrain you."

"Give me that!" Blevins grabbed for the mike.

Suddenly the second man hit the announcer in the face, knocking him to the street. Television personnel leaped into the fray and the picture faded back to the main studio.

"Channel 6 is carefully monitoring these developments in downtown Los Angeles." The new announcer's voice shook. "Obviously no one has *ever* seen anything like what we are witnessing. We have called for police assistance to help Don Blevins but matters are now completely out of control. Because policemen have not been armed for centuries, no one is prepared for the full-scale revolt occurring in our city. Please stay tuned and we will keep you updated as the story continues to unfold."

An aerial view of smoke and fire from the area around the courthouse again filled the screen.

"Good heavens!" Isaiah exclaimed. "I can't believe my eyes! They are after people like *you*." He pointed at the Feinbergs.

Cindy wrung her hands slowly. "I didn't think I would ever again see people attacked in the streets of Los Angeles." She sank down into a chair.

"Don't worry, dear." Ben Feinberg took his wife's hand. "Yeshua's protection took us through one terrible time. He will do it again."

"I think it's important to get you out of here," Isaiah Murphy insisted. "Maybe we're watching a bunch of nuts at work, and then again we could be facing a full-scale rebellion. Who knows where all of this might lead? We need to get you to the international telaport immediately and put you on the next flight back to Israel."

Jimmy Harrison turned slowly from the screen. "Let's think about what we are seeing for a minute." He began pacing. "In a very short time we have witnessed a three-pronged attack on world stability. The threat of disease was accompanied by spiritual disintegration. Now we look at this screen and discover political instability in America. Such problems haven't existed for nearly a thousand years." He looked around the room. "What's left to attack?"

"One more thing," Ben answered. "Faith in Yeshua."

☐          ☐          ☐

Night had fallen in Jerusalem when students at Hebrew University on Mt. Scopus gathered around television sets to watch the crisis in Los Angeles. The groups looked in shocked silence as the riot continued to spread across the city.

"What do you make of it, Dr. Zemah?" one of the younger students asked.

Zvilli smiled condescendingly. "We are seeing an example of group dynamics at work. Individuals with poor impulse control are being swept away by mob psychology."

Another student observed, "This is unbelievable. We've never seen anything like this riot."

Zvilli Zemah shook his head. "We can expect such phenomena to occur periodically. Social combustibility is the product of the creation of a critical mass of hostility. Californians have always been a rebellious lot."

The television screen was filled with pictures of people attacking another federal building down the street from the courthouse. Glass was strewn across the pavement and computers were being dumped out of the windows.

Rivka Zachary started crying. "I've never witnessed violence before." She dabbed at her eyes. "The sight is horrible."

"Stay rational," Dr. Zemah warned. "The only way to comprehend deviant behavior is by applying social theory. The explosion is a rare opportunity for us to study the psychology of nationalism."

"Death to the Jews! Kill the oppressors!" rioters screamed at the police. TV cameras zoomed in on hate-filled faces. "Throw the yoke off our necks!"

"Listen!" Rivka put her hands over her ears. "They are attacking *us*!"

"We must not personalize a foreign spectacle," Zemah pontificated. "Remember, we are dealing with Gentiles whose reactions lack impulse restraint."

"Kill the Jews?" the girl muttered. "The words are terrible."

The picture switched to the L.A. International Teleport. Crowds were overrunning the parking lot. An announcer said, "The reaction against foreign control has spilled over to the command centers of the city. We are witnessing nothing less than a full-scale insurrection. Apparently rioters are attempting to prevent foreign government officials from leaving the city."

"Weapons will be needed," Zemah added, "unless the Immortals intervene quickly, but even they aren't armed. A frightening dilemma!"

"Some of our people could be in that area," Rivka agonized. "I think we should pray."

Zvilli looked at her out of the corner of his eye and frowned. "Whatever."

Isaiah's battery-propelled car flew into the parking lot of the L.A. teleport and shot toward the end closest to the terminal entrance. "I can't believe there are so many people out here today. Look at the crowds."

"You should have just dropped us off at the arrival gate," Jimmy said.

"Not on your life! Isaiah stays with his old buddies to the last moment." He swung into a parking place. In front of them was an enclosed causeway to the airport.

"Look at those people over there," Cindy pointed out the window. "Looks like they are running. What strange behavior for such a large group."

"Seems more like they are chasing someone," Ben observed.

"Good grief!" Jimmy exclaimed. "I think they are rioters!"

Isaiah quickly leaped from the car. His six-foot five-inch

height allowed a quick survey of the parking lot. "They are coming this way! We've got to get out of here."

At that moment another group appeared near the entrance to the parking area. Cindy gasped, "We can't get out now!"

Ben Feinberg jumped out of the front seat. "We'd better make a run for the terminal." He grabbed Cindy's hand. "We don't have an alternative."

Jim piled out behind them. "Good thing we didn't wear any government insignias or uniforms. Surely they won't bother elderly people."

"We can't chance it." Isaiah grabbed Cindy's overnight bag. "Make a run for it."

The four friends trotted as fast as they could toward the crosswalk. Just as they reached the steps someone yelled out, "Look! Old people. Trying to escape!"

"The old ones work for the government!"

"Get 'em!"

The mob surged toward the steps. Jim and Ben each took one of Cindy's arms and helped her up the steps. Jimmy used his cane to keep from slipping. Isaiah blocked the doorway with his large frame. "Run!" he called after them. "I'm going to slow these crazies down if it kills me. Don't stop."

"No!" Jimmy called back. "Come with us."

"Just don't slow down," Isaiah yelled.

The Feinbergs and Jimmy were halfway across the bridge when the rioters hit the door. Isaiah leaned into the first wave but was immediately pushed to the cement floor. The people didn't even pause but trampled his body. A few rioters tripped and fell but the surging mob was barely slowed.

When the trio came to the other end, Ben pulled Cindy toward him. "Split up, Jimmy. Maybe they'll be confused and decide we're just tourists if we're not together." Ben pushed up his glasses with one hand and jerked Cindy forward with the other.

"I'll run toward the domestic flights," Jimmy called over his shoulder. "Get into the international area before they catch you." He hobbled toward the left of the entry hall.

The Feinbergs found an elevator just around the corner. The elevator door opened and two people got off. Ben pulled Cindy in and hit the up button. The door slid shut with their attackers only moments away. In an instant Ben and Cindy shot upward.

Across the hall, Jimmy slid around a wall and smashed into a porter carrying an armload of luggage. The attendant tipped backward and sent Jimmy hurling into the wall. He bounced off and fell face forward onto the floor. Jimmy's head thumped on the concrete with a sickening thud. His cane rolled across the marble floor. He went limp.

When the elevator door opened, Ben and Cindy saw the Israel ticket counter only fifty feet away. Ben punched the emergency stop button, keeping the elevator and the pursuers from following them. "Run for the desk." He pulled Cindy behind him.

"Maybe they can hide us." Cindy sounded terrified.

Ben ran for the ticket desk. "Help us," he cried out. "People are chasing us."

Without looking up, the youthful agent opened a swinging counter door and let the Feinbergs in. "Hide behind the desk." He kept his head down. "Keep low. I'll prepare the tickets to get you out of here." Without a word the young man began punching information into the computer.

"Please make out an extra ticket." Ben held Cindy tightly. "Hopefully our friend is just behind us."

Three stories below Jimmy lay on the floor, his eyes closed. The sounds of rioting filled the arrival hall. A strong hand reached down and lifted Jimmy up by the wrist. In one quick sweep, the man pulled Jimmy across the floor toward an office. A woman opened the door and the rescuer slipped Jimmy inside. The woman shut the door behind them and locked it.

Jimmy could only faintly hear their voices. "Is he all right?" the woman's voice seemed to echo in his head.

"I think so," the man said louder, "just a bad bump is all." "Oh, dear! Bless him," the woman answered.

Jimmy felt her warm touch on his forehead. Energy surged through his body. After a couple of abortive attempts, Jimmy opened his eyes but couldn't yet focus on anything. At first all he could see above him was the outline of two young people around thirty years old. He slowly sat up and held his head. "Oh," he groaned. "What happened?"

"You tried one of those Batman tricks you used to do as a boy," the man said. "Bad mistake at your age."

Jimmy instantly looked up and blinked several times. "Dad!" he exclaimed. "How did you get here?"

"We Immortals always keep an eye out for our own," Reverend John Harrison said to his son. "A little help every now and then doesn't hurt a thing."

Jimmy tried to get up. "Make sure you're ready," the woman said. Jimmy looked to the other side and stared.

"It's me, Ruth! Remember? I was your *wife*."

"Dear . . ." Jimmy reached out to the Immortal. "Good grief! I can't believe my eyes."

"Your father's right. You are our constant concern."

Jimmy took his former wife's hand. "I think I can stand up now. Please help me." John Harrison supported Jimmy's other arm and pulled him to his feet. He could hear people running past the locked door. "Now I remember. Ben and Cindy may be in trouble!"

"You don't think I'd let my brother and sister-in-law go

unattended," Ruth teased. "I think you'll find everything is covered."

Ruth put her arm around Jimmy's shoulders and gave him a big hug. "I carry you in my heart every moment." She kissed him on the cheek.

Jimmy looked into Ruth's eyes. He remembered youthful days running along the beach behind the Feinbergs' former home in Newport Beach. Ruth was as beautiful now as she was then. Her resurrected body kept her in total health at a perfected thirty-three years old.

Jimmy suddenly remembered the day in the Bozrah desert when Ruth died, giving birth to Jimmy Jr., their stillborn son. For a moment profound pain cut through his heart like a knife.

"I still love you so very much." Jimmy kissed his wife tenderly. "I miss not seeing you every day of my life."

Ruth held him close and patted his back. "How dear you are, Jimmy. And so very good. Such a man of character. I take such pride in telling other Immortals you were my husband in that other life."

"I still wish that . . ." Jimmy's voice trailed off.

"My love for you is perfected." Ruth squeezed his hand. "Nothing has been lost."

"That's easy for you to say." Jimmy shook his head. "From my side the matter certainly feels different."

"Look," John Harrison interrupted, "this is about as romantic as Immortals are allowed to get. If you will remember, we are not exactly here for an ocean cruise."

"Yes." Ruth's smile took a bittersweet twist. "We need to get you on the road home."

"I can't go out there." Jimmy pointed to the door. "And Ben and Cindy . . ."

"Follow me." John was already leading the way through the office. "There's a freight elevator at the back of this room." The minister looked up at the ceiling as if seeing through the tiles and observing something happening far above them. "You will find everything in order at the other end. But quickly. Your shuttlecraft is loading right now."

The freight elevator opened at the third floor. John and Ruth Harrison hurried Jimmy toward the gates. "What in the world is going on?" Jimmy asked Ruth. "Tell me why the world has gone crazy."

"All in due time," his former wife answered. "Right now we need to get you on your way."

"But help me make sense of this bizarre turn of events."

"Look." John pointed straight ahead. "I think you know those people."

"Ben, Cindy!" Jimmy yelled, They were standing with a young man in front of the entry platform. The couple looked unusually relaxed and at ease.

"Hey!" Jimmy called out. "I'm okay."

The young man with the Feinbergs turned around. "Didn't think we would let you down, did you, Dad?"

"Jimmy Junior!" The old man gawked at his son. "You're in on this rescue, too?"

"Sure," the young man threw his arms around his father. "I couldn't let Mom and Granddad have all the fun."

"Absolutely amazing," Cindy observed. "When John and Jim Junior stand side by side they look like brothers."

"The shuttlecraft is nearly loaded," Jim Junior broke in. "We don't have much time to spare."

"Please," Jimmy begged his father, "tell us what has happened to the world."

John Harrison put his hand on the old man's shoulder. "Blessed are they who enter a battle they cannot win to save a life they cannot lose."

"I don't understand." Jimmy searched his father's face. "What do you Immortals know that we don't?"

Ruth took Jimmy's wrinkled, liver-spotted hand. "Be

loved, don't be surprised at the fiery ordeal which has come upon you to prove your faithfulness."

"Ruth," Ben pleaded, "don't talk in riddles. We need to know what to do."

"Tend the flock of God," Ruth answered. "You will not see us again for a long time."

"On your way now." John beckoned for the trio to follow him. "Here are your tickets." He handed cards to each one. "They won't wait much longer for you to board. Jimmy, your cane will be at your seat."

Ben pointed to the flashing light overhead. "I guess we have no choice but . . ." When he turned around John Harrison was gone.

"Ruth . . ." Jimmy called out but no one was standing there.

"Jim Junior's gone, too," Cindy said. "I wonder where they went."

"I think just maybe they are taking care of Isaiah right now," Ben conjectured.

Guards stood at attention as Ziad Atrash and Rajah Abu Sita followed the prime minister through the national Russian museum located inside the rebuilt Kremlin Walls. One wing had mementos from the days of the czar, another the remnants of the Communist era. Corridors were lined with portraits of former heroes and heads of state. Alexi Chardoff pointed out various items of interest as they walked along.

"You must understand," Chardoff explained, "that most of the past was destroyed a thousand years ago. Many of these relics have been re-created."

"How did the weapons survive?" Atrash asked.

"Well-intentioned, former Communist leaders built concrete tunnels beneath the Kremlin and at various bases around the country. Guns were stockpiled for exhibit after the Battle of Armageddon, but for centuries people didn't want to see weapons of destruction. With time the stash was forgotten except by the curators."

"Fortunate indeed!" Abu Sita observed.

"Since our Babylon summit, my best people have worked

hard to restore the guns." Chardoff punched in a secret code to open a locked side door. "You will be pleased at the speed with which we have been able to make these weapons operable. We even have machine guns that can be fired."

Chardoff led the two men down a long, dark hall surrounded with ancient overhead pipes. Cobwebs hung from the ceilings and walls. "The big problem is getting the ammunition ready," the prime minister said as they walked on.

"Our friends in Ethiopia and China are hard at work on this problem even as we speak," Atrash answered. "The problem for our rebellion will be time—not supplies."

Abu Sita nodded his head. "Yes, we must strike quickly before the Immortals get a whiff of what we are planning and come back to earth from wherever they have disappeared."

"Careful," Chardoff warned as he descended winding stairs. "Sometimes the floors get slick in here."

The stairs ended at another door at the bottom. The prime minister inserted a card in the lock and the door slid into the wall. Before them loomed a large warehouse-type area nearly the size of a football field. Workmen and soldiers polished and assembled rifles, pistols, machine guns and other weapons. When the prime minister entered all activity ceased as men snapped to attention.

"As you were," Chardoff commanded. "Continue." Immediately the men returned to their work. The Russian leader pointed to the crates stacked around the room. "See. The supply is substantial."

"Superb!" Ziad Atrash cracked his knuckles. "Even better than I might have hoped. Yes, you are well underway."

"Excellency!" a uniformed man hurried toward the three men. "A special satellite report just came in. We felt you should know at once."

Chardoff eyed the man critically. "General, I was not to be interrupted."

"We felt your guests would want to see the news report from America."

The prime minister looked at the other two leaders and shrugged. "Let's look." He turned back to the soldier. "This better be good."

The general led the trio into a spartan command center. A map of Russia covered one wall; on the opposite wall an inch-thick television set hung like a painting. The screen filled with pictures of smoke and fire pouring out of buildings.

"The news report was just brought to my attention," an aide reported. "The matter seemed urgent."

"What is it?" Chardoff barked.

"Riots have broken out in America," the general stood at attention as he spoke. "Early reports indicate a large-scale rebellion is underway."

"Rebellion?" Ziad Atrash pushed the aide aside. "I can't believe my eyes." He stared at the scenes of chaos in Los Angeles.

"People are protesting control by the Jerusalem government," the general continued. "Leaders of the rebellion are calling for the ouster of all external authority."

"Astonishing!" Atrash ground his hand into his palm. "Our calculations have proven correct." He watched with rapt attention as five youth tore the Israeli flag apart.

"Are you sure it's a revolt?" Chardoff stared at the picture of people rampaging through the streets.

"We reported exactly what the announcer said to date," the general answered.

"Did either of you have any part in instigating the riots?" Chardoff asked the other two heads of state. "What do you know about the chaos?"

"Nothing!" Rajah Abu Sita insisted. "We are seeing a spontaneous rebellion."

"The time *is* ripe!" Atrash waved his big thick arms in the air. "Yes! The gods have given us the exact time for our strike!"

"The gods?" Alexi puzzled.

"Let us counsel together." Ziad Atrash waved the general and aide toward the door. "During my first meditations months ago before the god Osiris, I felt an inner voice urging me to act immediately. I received divine direction to conquer the world." He pointed to the TV. "Now we see the reason for the divine leading."

Chardoff shook his head in amazement. "I thought that spirit guide business with your secretary of state was only a show, nonsense to get our support. You are really serious?"

"Of course!" Atrash barked. "The next step is to implement our new religious system to undermine Yeshua's control. We are totally earnest."

"What do you propose?" Chardoff slowly lifted his hands in consternation.

"We now have absolute evidence of being able to predict the future through communication with the gods." Atrash's speech was quick and clipped. "We must teach more people how to channel and receive supernatural power. We will liberate the world population from the tired morality that has kept us in a straightjacket all these centuries. Once our people know there is an alternative, the rest will be easy."

Chardoff ran his fingers nervously through his hair. "Get on with it."

"Worship Marduk," Rajah Abu Sita insisted. "He is the great god we must listen to."

☐          ☐          ☐

Even before their shuttlecraft landed in Tel Aviv, Jimmy and Ben had a plan of action in mind. After Cindy was safely home, the brothers-in-law hurried to the Knesset and sought an immediate audience with the Apostle Paul.

"I know you are both very important people," the receptionist explained. "But you must understand how pressing matters have been lately. The apostle hasn't been seeing anyone for days. I am sorry."

"You don't understand," Jimmy tried another angle. "We have just returned from witnessing one of the worst disturbances the world has seen in centuries. Surely the Immortals will want a firsthand account of what we personally experienced."

Ben jumped in. "I don't doubt the pressures of Paul's constant oversight of the Gentile world, but we have hard information of spiritual deterioration that demands his immediate attention. Please. You've got to let us in to see him. Try one more time."

The secretary shook her head. "Really! I have my orders."

Jimmy's shoulders dropped and he shook his head. "What more can we do?"

"Don't worry, boys," a strong resonant voice answered from across the room. "Always good to see the likes of you."

"Paul!" Ben exclaimed. "We've been trying to contact you."

"It's all right, Elizabeth." The apostle beckoned Ben Feinberg and Jimmy Harrison to follow him. "I'll work these brothers in." Paul was a small man with an unusually high forehead. Even with his restored body, he was slight and wiry. The beard around his chin added dignity to an otherwise plain face.

"But you said . . ." the secretary protested.

"Don't remind me I'm a man of the law," the apostle chided her. "Sometimes we have to make adjustments."

Ben and Jimmy followed the Overseer of Gentile Affairs into the inner office. The three men sat down in simple chairs around a corner table.

"The world is going crazy!" Jimmy exploded. "We just escaped from the upheaval in Los Angeles. The spirituality of many people seems to be disappearing."

The apostle listened with disconcerting intensity. His piercing black eyes made him appear to be able to read their minds.

"Surely *you* are aware of a change in the hearts of many people." Ben waited but Paul said nothing, and his face didn't convey any emotion.

"We believe the time has come for new teaching on what the Scriptures have always said," Jimmy continued. "Yeshua must come forth and bring revival to places like Los Angeles. The hearts of the people must be called back to the Lord."

Paul held up his hand and made the sign of the cross. "You are good men and your hearts are pure. Such is a great blessing!"

Jimmy looked at Ben. "Thank you," Jimmy stammered. "But we are concerned for the problems of the world. Yeshua must act quickly!"

Paul nodded his head knowingly. "What can *you* do to change the spiritual climate?"

"*Us?*" Jimmy's eyes widened.

"You've been quite effective in the past," Paul answered matter of factly.

"B-u-t," Ben protested, "we need the Immortals to guide us. Yeshua must discipline these renegades. Where is He?"

Paul gently massaged his chin. "There is a time to work by sight and there is a time to walk by faith. Perhaps you've come to depend too much on your leaders."

Jimmy stared, dumbfounded.

"We wouldn't know what to do," Ben reiterated.

"Please," Jimmy pleaded, "be more specific."

"The time has come for you to attack this problem with the power of your witness," Paul said. "If the people will not believe the Immortals, they will not be helped with more signs and wonders. They already live in an age of holograms and electronic illusions. The time has come to offer the plain and simple truth."

"But everyone knows the truth," Ben answered. "For centuries we have received God's highest and best. What more is there to tell them?"

"Remember the Book of Judges in the Old Testament?" Paul asked.

"Yes," Jimmy said slowly. "But . . . it's been a long time since I even looked at the Bible."

"Why?" Paul asked.

"Well," Jimmy shrugged, "everything in the Scriptures is past history. What relevance would it have for today?"

"Really?" Paul raised his eyebrows in mock consternation. "You have so completely mastered God's speech you have nothing left to learn?"

"No." Jimmy squirmed. "That's not quite what I meant."

Paul smiled mischievously. "What do you remember about that ancient period?"

Jimmy thought for a moment. "As I remember, every person did what was right in his own eyes."

"Sound like the problem today?" Paul asked.

"Yes!" Jimmy snapped his finger. "That's right."

"And what created the big problem in Israel?"

Ben raised his hand slowly. "One generation forgot the lessons God taught their forefathers. Instead of staying true to the Law, they went their own way."

"Exactly," Paul agreed. "Because you live longer today you have forgotten that the length of a generation is also extended. You and Jimmy have become what Moses and

Joshua were to the ancient period of the Judges. You must take responsibility for the lives of those who have erred."

"But Jimmy and I are just administrators," Ben argued. "We've always depended on the Immortals to give us direction."

"Y-e-s," Paul drawled, "both you and the masses of confused people have a similar problem. You have allowed others to take responsibilities that are rightfully yours. The time has come for the confusion to change." Paul stood up. "I have total confidence you will know how to proceed." He walked to the door.

Jimmy and Ben reluctantly followed the apostle out of the room. "Could you give us another hint?"

Paul opened the door and pointed toward the reception-ist's office. "I'd dust off that antiquated, irrelevant Bible and see if there just might be something important you missed." As he closed the door behind them, he concluded, "God *will* bless and guide you."

The two brothers-in-law trudged silently down the hall toward the elevator. The door opened, they entered, and quietly descended.

"The Bible?" Ben finally said. "I thought the law was written in every person's heart."

"We've missed something important, Jimmy. I think the whole world has overlooked some basic principle, and we've been given the responsibility of finding what the truth is. You were always the Bible scholar. The time has come for you to go to work again."

"How can two old fogies like us make a dent in anything as big as this?"

"I don't know." Ben lowered his head. "But we don't have any choice but to find out. I'll ask Cindy to help me with some heavy-duty prayer. You study the message and I'll ponder the method."

"Déjà-vu." Jimmy laughed. "Once upon a time, a long

time ago we were at this very same place. Time to get to work. I'll call you tomorrow."

☐ ☐ ☐

Alexi Chardoff waited for the hologram phone line to connect with China. In a few moments, Fong's image materialized in front of him.

"Mr. Prime Minister," the Chinese leader acknowledged the Russian respectfully, "you are looking quite prosperous. How did your meeting with Ziad Atrash and Abu Sita go?"

"Quite well. They were impressed with my weapons and are already on their way back to Babylon."

"Good."

"Any repercussions from the central government for your expelling their people?"

Fong shook his head. "None. Atrash seems to be right. So far Yeshua has only proven to be a paper tiger."

"What do you make of this religion business the Arabs are pushing?"

Fong smiled. "A most useful idea."

"But do you believe it?"

Fong shrugged. "The ancients of China believed they could contact the spirits of the dead. The Chinese have a long tradition of worshiping ancestors. Some people saw it as respect; others believed in spirit contact. In recent years some people have tried to synthesize those old ideas with faith in Yeshua. Of course, the whole business has been forbidden and clandestine."

"Then you do believe in other gods?" Chardoff pressed.

"I suppose I'm more inclined toward believing in the spirits of the dead making contact with us. Who knows? Maybe old El Khader has become possessed with the long-dead spirit of Chairman Mao." He snickered.

"This is no laughing matter," Alexi growled. "We are playing with fire."

"The trouble with you Russians is your long history with the Russian Orthodox Church. You've got the Christian thing in your genes. We're different," Fong boasted. "Don't worry so much. Regardless of what the truth is about Yeshua, I am convinced that we have the fire power on our side. Yet if it will make you happy, I'll look into talking with the departed spirits."

"Humph!" The Russian settled back into his chair. "Strange business. Strange indeed!"

Fong smiled. "The Arabs still think they are going to take over the world?"

"Atrash certainly does. You should have seen his eyes when he saw the weapons. He licked his lips like a wolf closing in on a lamb. His only question was, 'How fast can you get the artillery operational?'"

"I have just completed conversations with the Ethiopians. We will have no problem supplying the sulphur and nitrates. In fact, I have already arranged for massive shipments of both to be sent to you immediately. Under the guise of providing fertilizer and medicines, we have diverted all of our normal shipments from other countries to Russia."

"Is there any problem in making such an arrangement?"

Fong shrugged again. "We will probably create a temporary shortage of both items for a period of time. If you will put out a news report of crop failure, we can cover our tracks well enough."

"How soon will the chemicals be here?"

"I think significant shipments can reach you in a week. The next will follow."

Alexi smiled for the first time. "We will be ready to manufacture when they arrive."

"In the meantime, I will see if any of the spirits of my

ancestors are waiting around to talk." Fong laughed. "Who knows? Maybe they will have a message for you."

☐       ☐       ☐

Deborah Murphy watched her husband working feverishly at his desk. He still had a bandage around his head and his left eye was black and blue. After a few minutes she asked, "You're sure you feel all right?"

Isaiah leaned back in his chair. "Pretty stiff." He rubbed his neck. "If I walk slowly, I'm fine."

"Those baboons could have killed you!"

"Then you'd have got me back with one of those glorious thirty-three-year-old bodies."

"I wouldn't have gotten you back at all!" Deborah protested.

"Thankfully Ben Harrison put me in my car and Jim Junior drove us home. When those maniacs ran over me, no one even looked back. I guess they thought they'd put me completely out of commission. Little did they know you can't stop a UCLA man."

Deborah looked at the big bruise on Isaiah's hand. "I shutter to think how long it would have taken me to find you if the Harrisons hadn't intervened."

"Saved my bacon, Deborah."

"Isaiah, I don't want to put my nose in where it doesn't belong, but I have to ask you. I overheard your conversation with Ben and Jimmy about this AIDS problem. What *is* going on?"

"Honestly, no one seems to know. The epidemic is still a secret and you must not tell a soul. I'm trying to access old data to get some clues for any information on treatment that might still be around. I'm even checking what's out there in places like Africa."

"Nothing makes any sense." Tears filled Deborah's eyes. "Life was so stable and predictable but now we're back in the center of chaos. I want Yeshua to come on television and straighten everything out!"

"While we're waiting, I am going to see what I can get the computer to scoop up. Don't worry about me. I feel better when I'm busy."

Deborah shook her head and walked out of the room. "I just don't know," she muttered to herself.

Isaiah turned back to his computer. For the next hour he tried accessing all the medical systems in Los Angeles to no avail. He settled back in his chair and thought aloud. "With the advent of the Messiah, the disease seems to have just disappeared. No record of a cure anywhere. But there must be something."

After another thirty minutes, Isaiah switched to data for Africa but made little headway. On a wild hunch he began cross-referencing systems for data on medicines. He tried every angle that offered even a shred of hope but nothing clicked.

"Maybe I ought to stop and try tomorrow," he said to himself. At that moment the Internet system filled the screen with a strange message. For several seconds Isaiah stared at the image. He punched the button for an instantaneous printout and then started tracing the data back to its source. In a couple of minutes another pattern appeared and Isaiah ran off a second printout. He carefully compared the reports and then switched programs. Within five minutes he had before him a strange collection of information.

"This just doesn't add up," Isaiah mused. "There's got to be more to the story . . ." He stood up and walked around the room. "No question. I'm on to something." He stopped. "Busted up or not! I'm going to check this out." Isaiah quickly returned the computer to the beginning position and tucked the printouts under his arm.

"Deborah," Isaiah called out, "you won't like this but I need you to help me pack in a hurry. I've got to do a little continent hopping . . . immediately."

*"You're going to what?"*

Jimmy sat across the dining room table in the Feinbergs'
home, watching Ben and Cindy carefully read his report.
"During the last week since our talk with the Apostle Paul,
I've done nothing but worry about what we can do to stem
the tide of rebellion and spiritual lethargy sweeping the
world. I think I have developed a good outline of what
people must hear."

"Well," Ben sounded irritated, "Paul might have given
us a *little* more help. For reasons beyond my grasp, the
Immortals seem to have packed up and taken a vacation.
Not that I'm complaining, you understand."

"Of course not." Cindy rolled her eyes. "Excellent start,
Jimmy. I think you will be pleased with the results of my
inquiries. Ben's television idea of three days ago is a definite
go."

"The worldwide network hook-up is really possible?"
Jimmy asked.

"Cindy used our connections with the Apostle Paul's
office not only to get an agreement for air time but also to
use old recordings of events occurring just after Yeshua's

triumphant entry a thousand years ago. We've got every-thing necessary to proclaim the truth to the nations."

"Do you really think anybody will listen to us?" Jimmy shook his head. "The students at Hebrew University didn't pay much attention to Ben. Could I do any better?"

"Apparently the apostle thought so," Cindy insisted. "You've just lost the sense of how significant your witness is. What we've got to do is package your message in a format that will grab the attention of even the indifferent."

"Here's what is promised." Ben laid a schedule on the table. "In a week the inter-continental television and hologram system is ours for thirty minutes. The program will be synchronized for airing at prime time everywhere."

"Excellent." Jimmy beamed. "Couldn't ask for more."

"Cindy will oversee the development and use of the recordings and edited segments for visual effect," Ben continued. "By coordinating what we say with the images from the past, we can have a maximum impact. Maybe we can even do better than we think."

"Listen," Cindy said firmly, "Paul's message was clear. We've got to take responsibility for our world. We prayed and this door opened. I'm ready to tackle the problem."

"What a woman!" Ben beamed. "Jimmy, I believe your notes captured the heart of the message the nations need to hear. I've arranged for a production consultant to help produce the program. In seven days we will have our own evangelistic crusade underway."

"I'm also developing a network of spiritual counselors to stand by in every city and town," Cindy added. "Paul's computerized list of ministers makes it easy to complete worldwide contact in a few hours. We will have people ready to minister to the repentant who respond to the number on the screen."

Jimmy nervously pulled at his beard. "I'm totally overwhelmed. Never in my wildest dreams would I have seen myself on television—much less preaching!"

"Time is short," Cindy urged. "We'd better get to work immediately."

During the next seven days Jimmy and Ben were in constant prayer. They reviewed Cindy's TV clips and carefully pored over their Bibles. Jimmy found his old notes on prophecy and reread the complete Old and New Testaments. Most of the time he worked at the Feinberg house, laying his notes out on the living room table.

Late Thursday afternoon Jimmy told Ben, "We really made a mistake in recent centuries. We should never have neglected the Scriptures."

Ben pushed back from the table. "No question about it. There is power in every page. Simply studying the book has been a new source of inspiration. In fact, I'm more encouraged now than I've been since this whole intrigue began."

"We've really underestimated how easy it is to take God's blessings for granted." Jimmy shook his head. "Human beings have a strange blind spot when it comes to being grateful. During the Israelites' wanderings through the desert toward the Promised Land, they had everything anyone could have wanted and they still didn't trust God."

"And here we are in the special 'promised time' and the people of the world can't seem to keep on track. Jimmy, I think self-centeredness is a fatal disease to be fought every moment of our lives."

Jimmy nodded. "The cancerous disease may go into remission but it sure makes a comeback in the form of indifference and spiritual slothfulness. The problem creeps up when we least expect it!"

"Preoccupation with one's self devours our love for God. We lose interest in worship."

Jimmy sighed. "Yes, even in this nearly perfect time indifference and lethargy have returned. I suppose affluence tends to spawn apathy. I just pray we can say something effective enough to jolt complacent people back to life."

The Inter-Continental Space Shuttle slowly pulled into the gate of the Addis Ababa terminal. Isaiah Murphy gathered up his things and hurried through the gate and down the corridor. Even though he had gone halfway around the world, the structure of the building wasn't different from the Los Angeles telaport, except for the pictures and decorations on the walls. He quickly disappeared into a sea of black faces.

In a few minutes the people mover delivered Isaiah into the main departure lounge. He slowed down and looked carefully across the expansive foyer. Soon he saw a man standing by the front door. Isaiah waved.

Hosni Gossos immediately walked forward. A small man, the Ethiopian was slightly bent over. Although elderly, his kinky hair was still black, making him look younger. He immediately offered his frail hand.

"Old friend," Isaiah exclaimed. "Wonderful to see you again." They shook hands. "You never change."

The Ethiopian snickered. "Your compliments are always like the tail of the pig. They don't mean much but they certainly tickle the ham."

Isaiah laughed. "Hosni, you remain a man of profound sense of humor. I trust they are treating you well."

"Well enough." Gossos took Isaiah's arm and steered him toward the door. "Are you sure no one followed you from Los Angeles?"

"What?" Isaiah stopped.

"Keep walking in case we are being watched." Hosni continued toward the doors.

"You've got to be kidding?"

"A diplomat never jests about such things," Hosni spoke softly. "No one asks such questions without being on to this thing that's coming down. You know better than I what a dangerous place we are in right now."

Isaiah blinked several times but walked out of the building in silence. The air was hot and muggy with the smell of the tropics. Intense indirect lighting planted underground lit a space six feet off the ground as bright as day, leaving the illusion of walking down an illuminated tunnel without a ceiling or walls.

Once inside the diplomat's solar-powered car, Isaiah looked straight into Hosni's eyes. "What are you talking about? Being followed . . . a dangerous place?"

"You are testing me." Gossos showed no emotion. "Good ploy. Even though we have worked on international problems for three decades, this is no time to take anything for granted. I want you to know I have nothing to do with this conspiracy." Hosni turned on the motor. The vehicle silently inched out of the parking place. "I can speak to you freely because my conscience is clear."

Isaiah swallowed hard. "Why don't you start at the beginning and go from there?" He tried to cover any hint of uncertainty.

"First I must ask you one question." The Ethiopian switched on the automatic pilot, which locked him into his pre-chosen travel route. He swung the seat sideways. "How did you find out what our government is up to?"

Isaiah tried to look passive as his mind raced to answer a question he didn't understand.

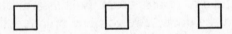

"And now from Jerusalem," the announcer's voice boomed over the television, "a special historical review, celebrating the past and recognizing the glory of the present." Television screens across the world filled with a fast-moving collage of pictures of the Holy City. The three-dimensional effect made the pictures appear to leap from the television sets. Faces of biblical heros momentarily flashed on the screen only to be replaced by placid scenes of the Galilee. "Your hosts for tonight," the announcer said, "are two special men who have lived through every minute of this story." Drums rolled and a band played loudly. "Meet Ben Feinberg and Jimmy Harrison." To the sounds of applause, the two brothers-in-law walked out on a stage erected on the top of the Mount of Olives.

"Welcome to Jerusalem," Ben began. "We are glad to be coming to you live from this exciting historical city. We want to remember where the New Era began."

"Those were amazing days," Jimmy responded. "Let us take you back to the early moments when we were over-powered by the glory of God. Remember the Feast of Trumpets in that first year?" he asked Ben. "The sight was dazzling. Return with us to the first day of the first month, the month of Tishri, as the saints and angels gathered after the final battle of Armageddon."

Pictures of an angel-filled sky flashed on the screen. The angels held brilliant candles of light. The blast of the archangel Gabriel's trumpet sounded in the background. Jimmy kept talking as the old clips of the past continued. "The Feast of Trumpets had often been called the Feast of the Last Trumpet, and on this day it was truly so. Yeshua honored the many saints who had written Scripture for a period of several thousands of years. These great men of God led us through the best and worst times. Their words inspired our hearts."

The scene returned to Ben. "Recently we took another look at what those giants of faith accomplished and were fascinated to reconsider their writings long before their prophecy was fulfilled. Here's your opportunity to share in our discoveries of how accurate their predictions were. Remember Joel?"

The prophet Joel appeared from the films of the archives, mounting the stairs of the original platform on the Mount of Olives nearly a thousand years earlier. Carrying a staff and dressed as he did in 700 B.C., Joel proclaimed, "Rejoice in the Lord your God. As I prophesied, Yeshua gave His *former rain* of blessing during His public ministry two thousand years ago. And now as I predicted, Yeshua is beginning in the month of Tishri His *latter rain* of blessing, His thousand-year kingdom. God has kept faith with His Holy Word."

As the picture faded, Jimmy continued, "No greater prophet came from Israel than Hosea." From another film clip Hosea spoke after Joel finished. Like Joel, Hosea wore the robe and sandals of his time. "I, too, proclaimed the promised Messiah would come twice. I foresaw a former rain of Jewish dispersion and great trouble for our people, lasting two of God's days, two thousand years. But I also proclaimed healing and spiritual revival for Jacob's children, coming as a latter rain on the third day." He cupped his hand to his mouth and yelled out across the Kidron Valley. "The rain is falling."

The prophet Zechariah slipped next to Hosea. "In the tenth chapter of my writings I was referring to this very day when I called on the people to pray for rain: spiritual, emotional, and physical showers of blessing during days of the latter rain. God has once again proven Himself consistent. We must trust Him with our whole hearts."

Ben turned to Jimmy. "We have been the fortunate recipients of these overflowing blessings. The rain of goodness has flooded our villages, towns, and cities across the globe. Our inheritance has been beyond the prophets' dreams. We take for granted what the centuries longed to see."

"Yes," Jimmy responded, "few of you have known the world of chaos and violence out of which we came. You have been spared the terrible experience of war and carnage. Instead of beginning each day asking Yeshua to deliver us, we can gratefully greet every dawn with praise and gratitude."

As Jimmy finished, a picture of the prophet Daniel appeared. In contrast to the Israelite dress of the other prophets, Daniel wore the silks of Babylon. Standing in front of the Temple Mount, he was reading from the second chapter of his own writings. "Blessed be the name of God forever and ever; for wisdom and might are His. He gives wisdom to the wise and knowledge to those who have understanding. He reveals deep and secret things."

Daniel looked up from the scroll. "Over 2,600 years before the fact, I predicted Yeshua, the rock of King Nebuchadnezzar's dream, would smash the ten toes of iron and clay, the ten nation confederacy of the unholy Roman Empire. Through the power of the Holy Spirit I was able to proclaim the truth." Daniel again read from the scroll, "In the days of these kings the God of heaven will set up a kingdom which shall never be destroyed; and the kingdom shall not be left to other people; it shall break in pieces and consume all these kingdoms, and it shall stand forever" (Daniel 2:44). He lowered the scroll. "Today we behold the victory of our God," he exclaimed.

From behind Daniel, a man dressed in royal robes stepped forward. His long rippling black beard was cropped in a straight line beneath his throat. His hands folded, he stood looking at the ground.

"Listen to the voice of one who knows." Daniel turned to the man. "King Nebuchadnezzar once ruled the world as the mightiest of men. He is an ultimate witness to the truth."

Even with a chastened demeanor, the king carried himself with great authority. He was a large man, naturally commanding attention. "Because the Babylonian Empire stretched across the world, I thought I needed neither God nor man, though I did worship false gods to try to manipulate them to give me power. There was no limit to my arrogance." The king hung his head. "Then I became psychotic for seven years and I learned otherwise. God graciously restored my mind and empire and I repented of my presumptuousness. Of all men I can testify to the graciousness of our God and the depth of our need for Him."

Daniel put his arm around the king's shoulders. "I included his confession in the fourth chapter of my prophecy," Daniel said. "The king's apology is instructive for us today." Daniel read from the scroll. "I thought it good to declare the signs and wonders that the Most High God has worked for me. How great are His signs, and how mighty His wonders! His kingdom is an everlasting kingdom, and His dominion is from generation to generation." The prophet cleared his throat and spoke even more loudly. "He does according to His will in the army of heaven and among the inhabitants of the earth. No one can restrain His hand or say to Him, 'What have You done?'"

Nebuchadnezzar held his hands up in praise and shouted, "Amen."

The hosts of heaven responded with an "Amen" that resounded across the earth.

Ben spoke directly into the camera. "My friends, I was standing there watching when these great things happened nearly a thousand years ago and will always carry their memory in my heart. I saw the whole of creation bend in praise and adoration before the victory of our God. Periodically it is important to stop and remember the meaning of the words of the King of Babylon. We owe all that we have and all that we are to our great and glorious God."

The scene changed and Moses appeared, holding the tablets with the Ten Commandments burned in the granite. His long beard and hair were brilliant white and his eyes sparkled with an unearthly light. "Lord, you have been our dwelling place in all generations." Moses' voice was remarkably quiet in contrast to his overwhelming appearance of authority. He quoted part of the ninetieth Psalm with calm gentleness. "Before the mountains were brought forth, or ever You had formed the earth and the world, even from everlasting to everlasting, You are God. For a thousand years in Your sight are like yesterday when it is past, and like a watch in the night. Let the beauty of the Lord our God be upon us, and establish the work of our hands for us; Yes, establish the work of our hands."

As the picture faded, Ben spoke. "I have a confession to make to the world. Unfortunately, I've taken this heritage for granted. I've let the immediacy of these words of instruction and exhortation slip from my mind. The busyness of simply living from one day to the next tends to blur what is truly important. Tonight I want to again say thank you to our great God and to His Messiah. Yeshua, I recommit my life to you." Ben bowed his head.

"Perhaps, each of us needs to make the same confession," Jimmy continued. "Just as the world was cleansed of all sin by the powerful intervention of Yeshua, we also need times of cleansing and healing. Many of us have slipped back into old patterns of indifference and sin. We have forgotten that our lives are not our own but were bought with a price. If it were not for Yeshua bearing the pain and suffering of death on a cross, none of us would have any hope."

Ben raised his head, opened his eyes, and extended his hand. "The Word has already been written on our hearts. Now we need to release what the Holy Spirit has previously placed in our spirits. Perhaps this is a moment of decision in your life. Have you slipped into self-destructive patterns? Has the closeness of your spiritual connectedness diminished? Today you can climb out of that unproductive rut and start down a new road. Right now, wherever you are, is your appointment with destiny. A number is now flashing at the bottom of your screen. People in your area are standing by to help. If you would like counsel about the guilt you are feeling, or help in finding spiritual direction, don't hesitate to call. Let us pray together." Ben bowed his head again.

"We recommit ourselves to You," Jimmy led the prayer. "We affirm that you are our God and we love You. Once again we yield our lives into your keeping."

Across the world multitudes of people were glued to the scenes of the past. Some were weeping. Others were kneeling before the hologram images filling their living rooms. Young children stared in amazement as the incredible scene of angels filling the sky with light ended the program.

Deborah Murphy turned to the groups of friends gathered in her living room. "Wasn't that awesome? I was deeply moved." People nodded silently. "I hope Isaiah was able to watch . . . wherever he is right now."

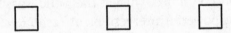

The Addis Ababa hotel was small and obscure—a good place to hide. Isaiah flipped off the TV set in his dingy room and turned to Hosni Gossos. "Can there be any doubt in your mind who is in control of this world?"

The little black man stared at the floor. "What can I say? My eyes do not deceive me."

"Hosni," Isaiah spoke softly, "you've been tricked into believing nonsense about Yeshua. Ali and his pack of quislings have manipulated you into a difficult position.

But tonight you can change your mind and start over. Whose side do you want to be on? God or man?"

Gossos buried his face in his hands and wept.

☐          ☐          ☐

At Hebrew University Rivka and her friends gaped at their television sets. With a slight turn of the head they could see the area of the Mount of Olives. "The two men are right," she said quietly. "We've forgotten how important the Feast of Trumpets *really* is. We've taken too much for granted. I'll confess that my attitude has been flippant. I am going to repent right now." Rivka lowered her head and closed her eyes. Her friends did the same.

Dr. Zvilli Zemah watched in his study office in the upper floor of the large library. He pulled at the ends of his white hair and pursed his lips. "Why couldn't they have been more scholarly?" He crossed his arms over his chair and leaned back against the wall. "We don't need all that emotionalism. A good solid erudite presentation would have made more sense."

Miles away in New Babylon, Rajah Abu Sita grabbed a paperweight from his desk and hurled it across the room. The highly polished piece of jade smashed into the wall, leaving a jagged dent. "How dare those idiots demean Nebuchadnezzar, trying to make him look like a fool!" He screamed at the top of his lungs. "This is a plot to make the people of Babylon appear to be subservient, mindless fools." He pounded on his desk.

The hologram line kept buzzing. Finally the Assyrian king pushed the On switch. "Yes!" he yelled into the microphone. "How dare you put a phone call through right now."

"Sorry," the aide grovelled, "but you said always to respond when the leader of Egypt calls."

"All right," Rajah growled. Immediately the image of

Ziad Atrash materialized before him. "Did you see the little sideshow from Jerusalem?" Rajah began at once.

The veins in Atrash's bull like neck were extended, his eyes intense. "No question this is a setback for us. Who were those two old idiots babbling down memory lane?"

"I never heard of them! Local Jerusalem relics of some order or other. What are we going to do?"

"Obviously someone is trying to create new international heroes by flashing their prune faces across the world." Atrash spoke in quick staccato thrusts. "Presenting themselves as eye witnesses gives that old TV footage credibility. They've got to be stopped."

"What do you suggest, Ziad?"

"Two things. We must begin an immediate counterattack to discredit their message. Each point they made has to be refuted. Perhaps we can even use their method of digging through the archives as evidence of fraud." Atrash doubled his fist and shook it at Rajah. "Second, those two old creeps must go. I suggest assassination."

T hree days had passed since the worldwide television extravaganza. The secretaries in the offices of Gentile-Jewish Relationships, Internal Problems, and Relocation Assistance were working at a feverish pace to process the responses. Wendy Kohn, Ben Feinberg's personal secretary, had just finished piling up the printouts of E-Mail and was carrying the load down the hall. With her foot she pushed open the door marked Ben Feinberg, Chairman.

"Wow, boss! The whole world is writing you."

Ben looked up from reading the previous stack of communiques. "I am totally amazed. People in Africa and Australia are saying the same things. We truly did some good."

The secretary placed the E-Mail on the corner of the large olive-wood desk. "We just got a report on Bible sales. The publishers are going crazy trying to print more Bibles. No one's sold many copies for centuries. Now the shelves are empty. In addition, copies of the Bible on computer disk are selling faster than they can be produced. We should have bought stock in one of those companies."

Ben laughed. "Wendy, I didn't even believe anyone would listen more than five minutes. That's the level of foresight I had."

"You've obviously become the man of the hour." The secretary beamed. "I'm really proud of you."

Another woman burst through the door. "We're getting requests from several nations for you to speak to their national parliaments and congress," Esther Netanyahu said. "I don't know how to schedule your time.

"You and Jimmy Harrison have become the only ones around who seem to know what's happening," Mrs. Netanyahu continued. "You know . . . we haven't received any guidance from Yeshua in months. The weight has fallen on your shoulders, Ben."

"Don't look at me. I sure don't understand what is going on." Ben shook his head. "Frankly, I'd like to go up to the Galilee for a little fishing."

"Not this week!" Wendy laughed. "You haven't even scratched the surface of what is piling up on us."

"I have no choice but to organize the staff to respond," Ben concluded. "We will have to make some executive decisions on how to divide up labor to keep the mail and computer responses from becoming a major logjam."

"As you asked earlier this morning, I have contacted Jimmy Harrison," Wendy Kohn added. "He should be here anytime. He's had a similar avalanche of response at his place."

"And Cindy is still coordinating the work of the spiritual counselors," Ben added. "I know her hands are full."

"Keep up the good work, boss." Wendy started back to her office. "We will return with a shovel and another stack of mail shortly."

For the next thirty minutes Ben spoke rapidly into his auto-dictation machine, which instantly turned dictation into letters that were proofread and corrected for perfect grammar and syntax. A built-in computer notepad at his right allowed Ben to make organizational notes for his staff. As he scrawled his thoughts on the plastic sheet, another computer turned his illegible writing into typed directions for the staff.

"Ben!" a voice echoed down the hall.

Startled, Ben jumped in his chair and looked up. Jimmy burst through the door, waving a pamphlet in his hands. "Look what's all over the streets in California and most of Europe." He slapped the small brochure on Ben's desk. "Just got this faxed to me thirty minutes ago."

Banner headlines proclaimed, "The Fraud Unmasked." The printing quality was high. Ben opened the first page and read aloud: "Once again through the use of trick photography and the manipulation of facts, the government of Yeshua is practicing mind control on the masses." Ben stopped and put on reading glasses. "I must be misreading," he mumbled.

Silently Ben read further, "The recent so-called Celebration of the Past filled your television screen with more of the lies the central government has used for centuries to imprison the minds of the nations. Advanced technology allows the Jerusalem government to mass-produce these fabrications of history. Harrison and Feinberg are not eye witnesses as much as dupes of Yeshua and his Jewish conspiracy." He stopped and laid the pamphlet down.

Jimmy nodded his head. "This material just surfaced all over the world. No one knows the exact source, but tons of this trash seem to have come through the teleports. Flip to the last pages and look at how this little epistle concludes."

Ben slowly thumbed through the leaflet and started at the top of the final section. "The greater truth is to be found in polytheism, the oldest religious system in the history of humanity. A relatively recent idea, monotheism is an impostor pushing the other gods aside by insisting on the supremacy of Yeshua. Do not be misled. A greater god waits to lead us on to a better day of more freedom. Put your trust in the Restored World Order." Ben's mouth dropped.

"Cleans out your sinuses, doesn't it?" Jimmy sat down across the desk. "Sort of like a whiff of ammonia."

Ben shook his head and read on. "Spirit guides will lead you to the greater way. Be prepared for the unveiling of the greatest of gods who is even now returning to his proper throne of power."

"The timing is no accident," Jimmy added. "This material is an obvious response to our television broadcast. We've struck a bigger nerve than we knew."

"This garbage makes absolutely no sense to me." Ben shook his head. "I thought we were battling the sin and indifference of disobedient people. I've assumed from the beginning that what happened to us in Los Angeles was nothing but a radical display of rebelliousness. But this—"

"Remember when we identified a three-pronged attack on world stability?" Jimmy asked. "You said there was only one more thing left to be discredited."

Ben shook his head.

"Faith in Yeshua," Jimmy concluded. "Now we are seeing a clear-cut assault on religion itself."

"But this is lunacy," Ben argued.

"Not to whoever put it out," Jimmy countered. "Defiance is one thing. Apostasy is another. We've got a much larger enemy than we thought."

Ben took a deep breath. "The world is clamoring at our doorstep for guidance, and I don't even know where my head is. Let's go to my house and sit down with Cindy. The three of us need to do some deep thinking and praying."

The two men hurried through the front office. "Ben—" Wendy Kohn called after him but he waved her away.

"Be back shortly," Ben called over his shoulder. "Don't

slow down or they will descend on us like flies," he whis-pered to Jimmy. "Once we get in the elevator we can get away."

The door closed and the elevator shot toward the bot-tom of the building. Just as they reached the bottom Ben turned to Jimmy. "I think we ought to . . ." The elevator made an unusually bumpy landing and hesitated a moment before anything happened. Just as the door began to open slightly, an overpowering blast exploded somewhere out in front of the Internal Affairs Building. Glass and debris blew through the cracked door. Smoke and dust filled the ele-vator shaft. Sounds of timbers splitting and walls collapsing thundered into the small compartment. Ben smashed into Jimmy and the two tumbled to the floor.

For a long time neither man moved. Finally, as the dust settled and silence filled the elevator, Ben pushed away from his friend and sat up. "What . . . happened?"

Jimmy rolled over and reached up for the rail. "I . . . don't . . . know." He slowly got to his feet. "Where am I?"

Ben pushed against the edge of the doors, and they slowly opened. The lobby was gone. Through the smoke he could see only one large support column standing. "We've got to get out of here." He grabbed Jimmy by the coat. "This place could collapse." Ben pulled his friend over the rubble and out onto the street.

"Look!" Jimmy pointed upward. "The face of the build-ing has been destroyed." He looked around. A few feet away the charred shell of some sort of vehicle was still smoking. "There's been an explosion!"

People began pouring out of the exit doors and the street-level windows. Most seemed all right but a few were limping. Much of the face of the building was black; small fires ignited in a few of the windows.

"If that door had been completely open," Ben stammered, "we'd have been hit by the full force of the blast. Our lives were spared."

"Nothing like this has occurred in this city during the whole New Era, Ben. Could this have been aimed at us?"

Ben turned slowly and stared at his friend. "Us?"

Both men looked at the smoking building again. Crowds of people were gathering and emergency vehicles were pulling in. Wendy Kohn appeared out of a side exit with Esther Netanyahu. Both women looked shaken but were not hurt.

Ben waved. "We're all right," he shouted above the noise of the crowd. "Don't worry."

Esther waved back.

By the time the two men arrived at Ben's house, Cindy had already heard the news report and was very upset. "We go to Los Angeles and there's trouble." She threw her hands into the air. "We come home and there's a bomb. What's next?"

"That's exactly what we've got to figure out," Ben answered. "We need more insight than we have."

"And the Immortals can't be found anywhere," Jimmy added. "I've tried everything I know. King David's office is shut down and the Apostle Paul's people won't even return my calls. I even put in another contact to Los Angeles. My parents, Ruth, Dr. Woodbridge . . . they've all checked out."

"I don't know where to turn." Ben slumped down in his chair.

"I'd suggest both of you go through the vacuum area to get the dust off your clothes and hair," Cindy said. "If it works to get the sand off after a trip to the ocean, it'll help get you so you don't look like you've just come out of World War IV."

The two men shuffled into the small room between the garage and the house. The walls were covered with small holes for suction machines, which completely drew all the dust and dirt from Jimmy and Ben. Once they'd gotten themselves together, they returned to the living room.

"I've been thinking," Cindy said. "You remember our old friend, Sam Eisenberg?"

"Sam?" Jimmy said. "Sure. Sam and Angie were Christian missionaries to Israel back before the Tribulation. They figured out the meaning of Bozrah and Petra even before we did. They knew that's where Jewish believers could safely hide during the Great Tribulation until Yeshua came to deliver them himself."

"Did you know that the Eisenbergs still live in Petra?" Cindy said.

"Really?" Jimmy looked amazed. "I didn't realize anyone was still there."

"Sam truly loved the Scriptures," Cindy said. "All these years they've lived a quiet life in those rugged surroundings. I understand Sam has continued to study the Scriptures to such an extent he is a walking-talking Bible. Maybe we ought to take a little trip down to Petra and let Sam help us."

Ben nodded his head thoughtfully. "We need to get some distance from everything that's happened. The dust *truly* needs to settle."

Jimmy's shuttlecraft shot across the ruggedly beautiful terrain of the eastern slope of the Dead Sea rift. Antigravity capacity allowed the four-person shuttle to both take off and land in a very limited space. Shaped like a slick car, the shuttle's aerodynamic body curved to a pointed nose for maximum flying efficiency. The top had a bubble dome allowing a complete view of the landscape. The highly polished black surface was sleek and glistened in the bright sunlight. Without wings, the shuttle could make abrupt turns and extraordinary maneuvers.

Deep gorges cut across the gray-yellow windswept sandy crags on which nothing could ever grow. Far beneath sea level, the blistering summer temperatures sucked the life out of all but the most primitive plant forms. The shuttle's guidance system swung Jimmy and the Feinbergs over the top of lofty peaks and onto friendlier hillsides around Aaron's shrine on Jabal Haroun.

"Moses buried Aaron there." Jimmy pointed to the white shrine resting like a pearl on top of the brown-and-black pile of desert rocks. "After Moses and Aaron defeated the residents of Petra, nearly 4,500 years ago, Aaron knew his death was at hand. He asked to be buried where his she-camel rested. By legend, the mountains shook so severely when Aaron rode by, the camel couldn't stop until she reached the very top of the peak where Aaron died."

"A million stories are hidden in the cracks of the rocks around this ancient place," Ben added. "For centuries Ad-Deir, the monastery where the Eisenbergs live, was used for everything from pagan funerals to a shelter for the early Christians."

"Even the Apostle Paul was rumored to have lived here during the three hidden years after his conversion," Jimmy noted.

The shuttle sailed down above the royal tombs carved into the foot of the al-Khubtha Mountain. The outline of the ancient vaults and columns whizzed past.

Jimmy pointed out the window. "There's the Urn Tomb." The largest and most imposing of the structures carved out of sheer rock stretched up the side of the red-and-pink rock-striated cliffs. Bedouins were still herding their goats along the edges of the valley.

The craft lifted up and then swooped over the monastery, the most prodigious of all the rock facades. The majestic columns with the ornate circular and square domes still left viewers in awe. Jimmy took control and guided the shuttle up Colonnaded Street, the main thoroughfare of ancient Petra.

"I wonder if anything is left of the structures we built during the Tribulation," Jimmy said as he peered out the window.

"Surely my father's field hospital disappeared long ago," Ben answered.

"Look!" Jimmy pointed along the valley. "There are some of the foundations of the buildings."

"Amazing." Ben shielded his eyes from the brilliant sunlight. "That's where . . . where Ruth . . .," he stopped.

"Where Ruth died," Jimmy finished the sentence.

The craft swung back around and settled gently in front of the massive monastery, which looked five times larger from the ground. Two elderly people came running out of the gigantic entrance of the sandstone-colored edifice.

"Ben, Cindy!" Sam waved as he ran, his robes of the desert bellowing out at his side. "Jimmy, welcome back to Petra." Sam was still tall and looked strong. Small blue-eyed Angie followed him, dressed in a similar dark-brown affakyn.

"You really live inside?" Jimmy asked.

"Can't beat the old place for climate control." Sam pointed upward. "Been operating since before the first century B.C. and it's still going strong. Come on in and let's get something to drink."

With the passing centuries new rooms and corridors had been carved into the solid rock, providing a dwelling of extraordinary dimensions. Even with the electronic devices and lighting provided by the technology of the tenth century N.E., the Eisenbergs' home had the spartan feel of an ancient sanctuary.

One room in the center was carpeted with wooden

paneling on the rock walls. The cave was transformed into a cozy den with a large hologram television built into the farthest wall.

"Why have you stayed here?" Ben asked as the group settled into the den.

Angie smiled. "We like the clean primitive feel of desert life. Sometimes the shadows of the mountains even seem to be filled with the sounds of the caravans and armies that marched through this place centuries ago."

"We feel closer to Yahweh, our heavenly Father," Sam added. "After all, Moses first met the Creator out in the desert, not so very far from here. In every sunrise and sunset, the majesty of God is tangible in these mountains."

Ben studied Sam's face and demeanor. Wearing the robes of the bedouins made Sam look like the abbot of a medieval monastery. Wisdom and insight were etched in his wrinkled face. "We understand you spend countless hours studying the Word and praying," Ben said.

"I have soaked up the Scriptures like a desert Arab's skin absorbs the sun." Sam smiled. "Most of the books of the Bible are now completely committed to memory."

"Then let me get right to the point," Ben bore down. "Something extraordinary, unusual, unexplainable is happening to our world and . . ."

Sam held up his hand for silence. "Unusual, yes. Unexplainable, no."

"What?" Ben's eyes widened.

"We have been expecting the confusion we now see on television," Angie explained. "Sam actually predicted these upheavals years ago."

"But how?" Jimmy pressed.

"Through prophecy," Sam continued. "The problem is explained in the Bible."

"Wait," Jimmy protested, "I just got through reading the entire Bible and I—"

Sam broke in. "The treasures of the Word are not unlike gold buried in the ground. You can't discover God's prize gifts by rushing on to holy ground like children picking up seashells on the beach."

Jimmy grimaced and said nothing.

"We saw your television special," Angie continued. "You were most impressive but we sensed your call to repentance was part of the final conflict."

"Final conflict?" Cindy sat up. "What are you saying?"

"You were right again," Angie said to Sam. "They have come as part of the writing of the last chapter."

"For the end of all things," Sam continued, "we must go to the last book of Scripture." He tapped in a code on the control panel built into the end table next to his chair. The television instantly became a giant computer screen. "I want to point out something from the Book of Revelation."

The twentieth chapter filled the wall. Sam scrolled through the pages until he found the exact verses he was seeking. "Read with me." He aimed a laser pointer at the lines, tracing the words until he came to the key sentence. "Do you see what is happening?" he asked.

Ben reached for Cindy's hand. Jimmy read with his mouth open. No one spoke as they absorbed the meaning of what they were seeing.

"Now you understand just how serious matters are?" Angie asked.

# PART
# TWO

*... and he cast him into the bottomless pit, and shut him up, and set a seal on him, so that he should deceive the nations no more till the thousand years were finished. But after these things he must be released for a little while.*

Revelation 20:3

# 10

**June 19, 999** N.E. **(New Era)**

The coalition of mutinous national leaders gathered in a long flat building located between the Sphinx and the great pyramid of Cheops. Soldiers were stationed around the alabaster-covered desert pavilion. The pyramid loomed above the chalk-white building that glistened in the relentless June sun. A special banner over the entry proclaimed, "Welcome to the Conference on World Order." Delegates gathered in the massive lobby.

Fong slipped next to Alexi Chardoff and spoke quietly, "Did you know anything about the bombing in Jerusalem?" Fong wore the simple blue jacket of the ancient Chinese.

"Created quite a stir, didn't it?" the Russian grinned. "The people of Jerusalem thought they were above such little problems. Worldwide consternation only served to further undermine confidence in Yeshua."

"But did you have any part in the matter?" Fong pressed.

Alexi widened his eyes in mock consternation. "Me? I was at home in the Kremlin sleeping in my bed."

"What happened?" Fong sounded impatient.

"The high quality nitrates you shipped us have tremendous fire power," Alexi answered. "Rather easy to plant since no one has paid any attention to security for centuries."

"How did you do it?" Fong persisted.

"One of our people slipped a detonation device the size of a pinhead into the pocket of one of those meddlesome old jerks while walking into the building. The device was set to trigger the bomb when he came back out."

"Clever," Fong observed. "Where were the explosives?"

"In a crate delivered in front of the building. We thought we might be able to hit the man coming out and also get the other old geezer inside the building. Much to our surprise, both men came down together. Would have killed both of them if the elevator door hadn't jammed." Chardoff shook his head. "Strange."

"Are any world leaders bragging about this little caper?"

Alexi shook his head. "Atrash won't acknowledge any responsibility, but his men brought the crate in from Egypt. At least we learned we have the capacity to make successful explosive devices."

The two men strolled into the conference room. "We must not spend much time together," Fong spoke under his breath. "No one must be given a hint of our coalition."

Alexi brushed his greasy hair out of his eyes and nodded.

The men walked into the meeting and moved to different sides of the room just as Ziad Atrash called the meeting to order.

"Welcome friends and world leaders," the Egyptian bull began. Instead of the usual jersey pullover suit, Atrash wore a military general's uniform, reminiscent of the twentieth century. Although no war had been fought for a thousand years, rows of medals were pinned over his chest. "Welcome to the land of mystery." He stood behind a large podium. Behind him were giant posters and pictures of the ancient tombs of the pharaohs. "Egypt has been about the business of world conquest for incalculable centuries. We have listened to the gods from the other world and have been guided by their intervention even before the Jewish race existed. That old beggar father Abraham even came here seeking the scraps under our table." Atrash paused, smirked, and pointed at a large mahogany table in front of him. "Our only mistake was feeding the Jews so well that they wanted loose from the bonds of slavery."

The group laughed and applauded. "Now's your chance to get what they owe you back," Ali of Ethiopia barked.

"We no longer feel any need to meet in secret," Atrash continued. "The first stage of armament production has been achieved. If the Immortals show up, we'll blast them back to where they come from."

The Arabs stomped their feet and clapped vigorously. Atrash snapped his fingers and a group of armed soldiers marched quickly into the room, laid their rifles and pistols out on display tables in front of Atrash, and marched out again.

"These weapons are prototypes of guns being tested in the desert even as I speak. Age has not reduced their effectiveness." He paused, searching for the right words. "We . . . uh . . . also know . . . we have perfected the capacity to explode bombs." The Egyptian president snapped his fingers again and another group of soldiers hurried in front of the dignitaries. "I want you to see our martial arts instructors at work. We can thank Chairman Fong for providing additional Kung-Fu experts. Demonstrate," he ordered the soldiers.

The men immediately paired off into a fast brutal demonstration of attack and counterattack maneuvers. Fists, arms, and feet flew through the air like missiles. The fierce fighting continued until one of each pair lay motionless on the floor.

"You can imagine how effective the assault forces will

be against unprepared citizens," Atrash continued. "Following our conference, the instructors are prepared to return with you to your countries to begin immediate training of your young men. In addition, the weapons shipments are already sailing toward each of your countries."

The group again clapped enthusiastically.

Rajah Abu Sita followed the Egyptian at the podium. "Our propaganda response to the international television fiasco worked. We acted at once to counter the unexpected success of those two old frogs. Consequently, we moved without consultation with each of you and spread pamphlets all over the world. Timing was of the essence."

Khalil Hussein, the king of Jordan, stood up. "Unfortunately, the results of the television program were quite dramatic in my country. Many, many people listened. The government monitored the calls to the special counselors and discovered an alarming number of people responded." He sat down slowly.

Ali of Ethiopia nodded. "The same consequences occurred in our country. Many indifferent and lethargic citizens now ask for Bibles."

"We understand," Rajah broke in. "Anticipating this possibility we have a special presentation for you. El Khader," he called out, "please respond."

A screen descended from the ceiling as the white-haired old Syrian secretary of state hurried forward. "Please observe." El Khader's voice cracked. He clicked a hand-held tuner and a picture of satellites circling the earth appeared. "We are now in position to broadcast much more than a thirty-minute TV walk down memory lane." A picture of one of the satellites came closer on the screen. "Through a new technological breakthrough, we can now pirate time on every satellite circling the globe. We will beam programs on the new religious perspective periodically throughout the day. We can preempt any program. Let them top this achievement!"

Khalil Hussein responded, "Excellent!"

"The breakthrough was achieved through an amazing new approach to research." El Khader clicked the tuner and a picture of a laboratory appeared. Scientists blindfolded and arms folded over their chests sat in front of tables and computers. "By applying the meditation techniques of ancient Babylon, we have been able to make unparalleled discoveries. Transcendental meditation is leading us far beyond anything achieved by experiments alone. We now call this method 'applied religion.'"

"Just a minute," Alexi Chardoff interrupted. "You don't have to sell us more of this polytheistic propaganda. Save it for the masses."

"With all due respect," the secretary of state answered, "I can sincerely tell you that spirit guides brought us to a new level of sight."

Rajah stood up again. "I can assure you El Khader is merely stating the facts. We will offer demonstrations and instruction in these techniques later this evening. May I invite you to participate, Mr. Prime Minister?"

Chardoff grumbled, his response muffled.

Rajah Abu Sita continued. "We will change the minds of the world's people by encouraging unbridled freedom and rampant individualism. I have asked an expert on the subject of social change to join us. An old childhood friend has become a significant leader at Hebrew University. Please welcome Dr. Zvilli Zemah."

As the group applauded the gray-haired teacher/student from Jerusalem walked forward. "Sociology and psychology have been my field of study for many years," Zvilli began. "I can tell you a basic fact about all human beings. No one likes to hear the word *no*. Human beings want no restraints. We are the last of the truly untamed animals." The instructor stopped and looked around the room. "Don't you hate obeying a monarch?"

The delegates looked at each other and nodded.

"We are making a religion out of personal freedom," Zvilli continued. "We will preach human rights without responsibilities." The pitch in his voice raised and he sounded shrill. "All restraint is the fault of Yeshua and the central government." Zemah waved his arms and pounded the podium. "Sexual license must be encouraged! We will brand all laws as manipulative tools of the religious oppressors. And I can promise you," he shouted, "the people will say yes!" His voice abruptly dropped to almost a whisper. "Because in their heart of hearts, they want to believe every word is true."

Silence fell over the room.

Zemah continued, "Polytheism will be explained in so many different and creative ways, that world citizenry will embrace the idea of many gods as the only intelligent alternative. We will give people a religious rationale for what they already *want* to do."

"Thank you, Dr. Zemah." Abu Sita patted his friend on the back. "We grew up together in a small town in Syria." The king laughed. "Zvilli was known as our village renegade." They shook hands again. "The cleverest part of our plan is that Zvilli will be coordinating this work from inside Jerusalem. He is already strategically placed to feed us information on how our plan is affecting the central government."

"How soon will the television assault begin?" Ali of Ethiopia asked.

"The first programs will be ready within a week," Rajah Abu Sita answered. "Once they start, other formats will follow quickly. We are ready to start the onslaught immediately."

Khalil Hussein rose to his feet. "I am impressed by these

reports. Let us give a vote of confidence." He began to clap and the rest joined in.

"Thank you." Ziad Atrash took center stage once more. "Now we take a break to allow informal discussion among ourselves. In one hour, we will convene behind closed doors to plan military procedure. Please accept our hospitality." He clapped his hands and dancing girls whirled into the room. Music blared in from musicians strolling and playing behind the dancers. Behind them servers brought in lavish trays of fruit, cakes, and sweets.

Chardoff sidled up to Fong. "Can you hear me over the noise?"

"Not well."

"Perhaps they want us to talk . . . but not too much," Chardoff answered and walked away.

At the other end of the hall, Claudine Toulouse nodded to Maria Marchino and the two women slipped out the front door. The hot desert winds swished Claudine's long hair around her neck. "They've had famine in this region since Feast of Tabernacles," she said. "It's always unbearably hot now, especially in Egypt and Iraq."

Maria shrugged. "You get hot air outside; you get hot air inside."

Claudine laughed. "Are we both reading these guys the same way?"

"I don't hear anyone asking our opinions." The Italian leader raised her eyebrows. "I have the distinct impression we're the third stringers in this operation."

"Exactly." The French leader shook her fist. "We are being taken along for the ride by the sheik and his buddies.

"I'm sure Atrash is clever enough to know the coalition can't pull off his coup without us, but I doubt if he finds much pleasure in our presence. We will be used as long as we serve that arrogant bull's purposes."

"My exact conclusions. I don't trust any of them. We

must hang together," Maria answered firmly, "lest someone try to hang us separately. Let us agree to watch each other's back."

"You are a woman after my own heart." Claudine Toulouse extended her hand.

Maria Marchino squeezed the woman's hand. "Agreed. We have our own pact."

"We will give them no hint of our understanding, but when the right time comes we will be in a position to act."

When the leaders reconvened, all other personnel were excluded. The room was restructured with a conference table in the center. Notepads and files were placed in front of each dignitary.

Atrash called the group to order by rapping the table with his knuckles. "I now pass the chairmanship to our esteemed brother from Russia, Alexi Chardoff."

The Russian nodded politely. "Our next item on the agenda is the development of a master plan of attack. We must coordinate movement of troops, set military targets, develop precise actions for an assault on Jerusalem, and agree on a definite timetable. Are we ready to proceed?"

Each leader nodded.

"We have every reason to believe that within one month every nation surrounding Israel will have significant strike capacity," Chardoff reported. "The People's Army of China must travel the furthest. If the Chinese are ready for large-scale troop movements to march south at this same time, we would quickly be poised to sweep across Israel with little opposition."

Fong smiled. "We have a plan to train our army while it marches. Since there has not been any form of military preparation for centuries, even our young men will not suspect what is occurring. The movement will be clandestine and without fanfare. Troops will not know what they are about until we are quite close to the jumping-off point. This approach will minimalize security leaks."

"Excellent!" Chardoff beamed. "Each of these factors suggests we will be ready for the final stage to begin during the month of Tammuz. Even though mid-summer is quite hot, there are strategic reasons to believe this an appropriate time to strike."

"The gods suggest so," Rajah interrupted. "We consulted Marduk and received this message." He read from a note in his file: "As the sun comes down, the flames shall go up. Use the heat of the summer to dissolve your adversary's courage like the furnace melts lead. Strike in the final days of summertime and the gods will be with you."

Fong looked straight into Chardoff's eyes. His stone-faced, emotionless glance was sufficient comment.

"Well," Chardoff pursed his fat lips, "we seem to agree either the month of Tammuz or Av is the right time for the assault."

"Jews observe a festival on Tammuz 17," Hussein commented. "This would be a clever time to start the first movement of troops as they would certainly be distracted."

"Exactly," Abu Sita agreed. "I calculate it will take about three weeks before the final assault."

"The date of Av 9 would fit," Atrash blurted out. "I don't know why, but I suddenly feel strongly that this could be a very productive time to go for the throat!"

The discussion continued for another fifteen minutes, wrapping up the final loose ends of the battle plan. Ziad Atrash finally called for adjournment and the group dispersed.

Khalil Hussein, a tall man with piercing black eyes and long black hair, was the last to gather his papers together and stuff them in a briefcase. The black goatee added an air of mystery to the king of Jordan. He was by far the youngest leader in the group. Although Khalil traced his ancestry back to the twentieth century, little was known about him because he seldom expressed his personal opinions. His reservations only added to the air of intrigue that hovered around his head like a desert kaffiyeh. Khalil snapped the case shut and hurried after the rest of the group.

Just as the king turned the corner, Claudine Toulouse scurried back into the room. The French head of state rushed right into Hussein's arms, knocking his briefcase to the floor. For an awkward moment, the king found himself with his arms around the woman.

"Oh excuse me!" Hussein tried to take a quick step backward, but Claudine was still coming forward.

"My, my." Claudine stopped inches from his face. "We all seem to be in a hurry." She did not step back.

"I hope I didn't hurt you." The king suddenly had a hold on Claudine's arm.

"Quite to the contrary." The woman breathed heavily. "The pleasure is all mine." Claudine looked straight into his eyes and smiled demurely. "We need to take more time to *really* get acquainted."

Khalil searched her eyes, unsure of what he was seeing.

Claudine raised one eyebrow and reached up gently, running her finger across the king's chest. "I think you would like to get to know me as a woman." She touched his lips and slipped on past.

Khalil didn't move for several seconds and then tripped over his briefcase before bending down to pick it up.

Deborah Murphy paced nervously in the Los Angeles teleport terminal, waiting for Isaiah to arrive. She kept glancing at the fax he sent the night before. "Be there at 8:30 A.M. Meet you at Gate 58. Love Isaiah."

The arrival notification lights began blinking. In several

minutes the gate silently opened and passengers began deplaning. Several dozen people walked past before Isaiah hurried through the door.

"Great to see you, dear." He bent down and kissed his wife. He put his mouth close to her ear. "Start walking with me and don't say much." Isaiah took her hand and pulled her along.

"Had a great time in New York City," Isaiah spoke very loudly. Multitudes of people walked past the couple. "Really enjoyed hitting the museums." He picked up the pace.

Deborah stared up at the tall black man. "I'm not quite sure I understand what's happening."

"You'd love the exhibition of the new three-dimensional paintings done with computers," Isaiah chattered and pointed straight ahead to where the corridors split in two different directions. "Never seen anything quite so real. The paintings actually have the capacity to exude emotion. As you watch you feel joy, peace, or even anger." He swung his wife around the corner and stopped. Isaiah silently watched the people pass.

"What is going on?" Deborah sounded exasperated. "You disappear for several weeks to who-knows-where and then show up . . ."

Isaiah gently put his hand over her mouth. "Directional microphones could pick us up. Wait until we get in the shuttle." He watched for thirty more seconds and then pulled his wife back into the flow of traffic.

The Murphys silently hurried through the terminal and into the parking lot. Isaiah threw the black duffel bag in the backseat and quickly sped through the parking area.

"I'm going to ask you again," Deborah sounded irritated. "What's going on here?"

"I'm very sure I was followed back from Ethiopia."

"Ethiopia?" Deborah's mouth dropped.

"I've gone virtually around the world since I left." Isaiah

pushed the shuttle into glide and lifted straight up from the end of the parking lot. He punched in his code for home and the automatic pilot immediately turned the shuttle south.

"Dear," Deborah pleaded, "p-l-e-a-s-e let your wife in on this little adventure. The last time I saw you, you were still limping around and should have been in bed recovering."

Isaiah looked thoughtfully out the window into the black night dotted with a million lights. "Remember when I was trying to get a lead on a cure for AIDS?"

"Weeks ago?" Deborah answered sarcastically.

"I was cross-referencing medicines because nothing else seemed to work," Isaiah continued. "I was even checking medical information for Africa. And then the computer slipped into chemical compounds. Remember?"

"Vaguely." Deborah shrugged.

"My computer picked up a very strange bit of information. The graphic printouts indicated unprecedented movement of sulphur, sodium nitrate, mercury, nitric acid, and ammonium nitrates from Ethiopia to Egypt and Russia." Isaiah paused. "Do you understand?"

"Absolutely. Since I know totally nothing about any of this."

"When I indexed these materials through another program, I found similar amounts of the same chemicals were being shipped from China to Russia. Because sudden large shipments of these chemicals was strange, I referenced an analysis program to identify how these materials might be used separately or in conjunction with each other."

Deborah nodded slowly. "Yes, but where in the world are you going with this?"

"To my astonishment, the analysis prioritized the possible uses of the materials. At the top of the list was the production of explosives now illegal and forbidden in every country in the world."

"Isaiah," Deborah said slowly, "this is beginning to sound dangerous."

"I figured I'd have the best chance of being anonymous in Ethiopia. So that's where I went . . . first."

"First?" Deborah's eyes widened. "Where else have you been?"

"Russia."

"Wait a minute. . . . What does any of this have to do with AIDS?"

"I have no idea," Isaiah answered. "That's the strange thing. I don't understand the relationship of where I started and where I ended up. Regardless," he paused, "I've hit something very big."

"Just what have you found?"

"Egypt and Russia have become staging areas for the development of explosives."

"The bombing in Jerusalem . . ."

Isaiah nodded his head. "Exactly."

"And you think you were followed?"

"Possibly."

"They might . . . bomb . . . us?" Deborah gasped.

"Anything is possible." Isaiah switched off the automatic pilot and suddenly swung the craft back to the north. "We're going to fly a diversion pattern and stop by the county building before going home. I might even be bugged and not know it. I'll go in and do a quick electronic scan."

Deborah reached over and squeezed her husband's hand. "I've been so worried about you. You should have told me where you were going."

"I didn't want you to be in any jeopardy, Deborah. I don't know where all the pieces in this puzzle fit, but I'm onto something much larger than I could have imagined."

"We need to get in touch with Jimmy and Ben," Deborah concluded.

"Absolutely."

# CHAPTER
# 11

Jimmy Harrison and the Feinbergs flew straight back from Petra to Ben and Cindy's home. Jimmy followed Ben and Cindy into the central area with the wall-screen television. Ben paused in front of the environmental control system and quickly punched in the numbers for "atmosphere of calm and tranquility." Lights on the control panel blinked several times and immediately the sounds of a gentle stream and winds blowing through a forest filled the house. A warm scent of wet pine needles and mountain breezes swept through the air. The overhead lights dimmed and a gentle blue light diffused throughout the entire house. Little was said until they plopped down around the dining room table.

"I'm overwhelmed," Jimmy confessed. "Whatever I thought Sam might tell us didn't even scratch the surface of what was on his mind!" His eyes nearly disappeared behind his eye folds.

"How could I have been so blind?" Cindy got up. "I'll fix some coffee."

"Dear, with your history of once being blind, that's a bit

of a humorous question," Ben teased. "But I certainly feel exactly the same way."

"Never have we needed the help of the Immortals so much." Jimmy thumped his cane on the floor.

"A day ago I put in calls to both Mayor David's and Saint Paul's offices," Ben added. "I couldn't even get the receptionist on the line. Paul wasn't kidding when he said everything was in our hands."

A red light flashed on the hologram telephone and a pleasant hum filled the air. "Ben, it's your office phone. We better get it." Cindy reached over and hit a button on the phone. A large picture of Wendy Kohn appeared on the TV screen.

"I know you told us not to interrupt you," Wendy explained. "Unfortunately, we are besieged by reporters with stories that you and Jimmy were critically injured. Without the Immortals, people are in a panic. The reporters want to see you alive."

"Us?" Ben rolled his eyes. "We're not celebrities."

"You certainly are now," Wendy shot back. "However, the really big story is happening on the streets and through the satellite broadcasts. You need to tune in this minute."

"What channel?" Jimmy asked.

"Doesn't make any difference," Wendy answered. "There's only one program every station!"

"H-m-m, strange." Ben reached for the clicker. "OK, Wendy, I'm shutting you off to take a look. I'll be back in touch."

Wendy's face faded as the program appeared. A collage of pictures of the ancient world whirled across the screen. The announcer's voice proclaimed, "Ancient mysteries are now being uncovered, revealing the wisdom of the past. In recent centuries we lost touch with the profound truths of our forefathers. Not so long ago, even *we* were considered to be gods."

"What?" Jimmy sat up in his chair. "I can't believe my ears."

A three-dimensional picture of a lion with a man's head leaped from the screen. "The people of antiquity lived without restraint. Complete freedom meant no moral inhibitions. Creativity and spontaneity were not squelched by laws and dogma. Wouldn't you like to recover the joys of primordial life?"

Ben hit the clicker but each channel was the same. "Wendy's right! Every station is controlled."

The announcer appeared on the screen dressed as an Egyptian priest in long, white filmy linens with a jeweled collar of red, yellow, and blue beads. From his waist dangled a gold belt with a center shield of multi-colored stones. "Look again on the colorful dress of the ancients. The time has come for us to recover the many-faceted values of our heritage. Each of these programs is presented to help you broaden your knowledge of the past. Do not be duped by those who want to repress the truth about our true heritage. Strike out *now* for a new and better tomorrow."

The picture faded to the sounds of powerful triumphant music.

Ben hit the clicker and Wendy reappeared. "You said something is also happening on the streets?"

"Yes, sir," the secretary answered. "Thousands of pamphlets are circulating throughout Jerusalem. The message is far more blatant than what was just on television." Wendy held up a pamphlet. "This material is similar to what appeared in Los Angeles but it's a much more pointed attack on Yeshua."

Ben drummed on the table with his fingertips. He shook his head and the white ponytail swung from side to side. "I see," he said slowly. "Our faith is directly under attack."

"There's no other way to describe what is happening,"

Wendy concluded. "We are being bombarded by an alternative religion."

"Just as I expected," Ben concluded. "We'll be back in touch shortly."

"But—," Wendy protested.

Ben clicked the phone off. The aroma of coffee filled the air.

"Let's go back to the television," Jimmy suggested. "I'd like to see if we can get any news reports from around the globe."

"Hey, the stations have returned to normal." Cindy set the tray of cups down. "Try the news channel."

" . . . No further explanation is now available on how the interruptions occurred," the announcer was saying. "However, worldwide communication is now restored. Authorities are investigating."

The scene changed to a view of Africa. "On other fronts a fast-breaking story reports an outbreak of a rare virus coming out of Africa and apparently breaking out in Los Angeles. The strain has been isolated and is much like the ancient AIDS epidemic, except it is moving faster and is proving to be more dangerous. No one in recent history has any memory of such a threat, and no cure exists. We are monitoring the situation and will report more results in the next hour."

"The story is out." Ben ran his hands nervously through his hair. "Everything I feared is now breaking loose."

The phone rang again. Ben sighed and pushed the button. Wendy's picture reappeared. "I'm sorry to interrupt again but I felt you should be aware of some news that is buzzing through the corridors of this building like a swarm of bees."

"What is it?" Ben sounded distant and professional.

"In addition to what happened in China some weeks ago, just moments ago the nations of Russia, France, Italy,

Egypt, Iran, Jordan, Syria, Iraq, and Ethiopia expelled their overseers and are pulling out of the world alliance of nations. No one has *ever* even intimated such an idea."

"Pulling out?" Ben's voice became almost a whisper.

"They are also calling on other nations to join them in rejecting the authority of Jerusalem," Wendy added. "Our people are very concerned and upset."

"They should be," Ben snapped. "These issues are serious. Thank you, Wendy. You did the right thing in calling me."

Ben stared at Jimmy and shook his head. "I think the real war is about to begin."

Cindy put her arm around Ben. "Don't worry, dear." She ran her hands through his hair and hugged him. "We've been here before and survived the onslaught. We can do it again."

The external security light began blinking. An intense disconcerting hum filled the house. Ben jumped up. "An intruder has gotten past the initial perimeters. That must mean someone has landed a shuttlecraft on the roof and has already gotten to the door."

"We may be under attack." Jimmy pushed back from the table. "We're not even prepared to defend ourselves."

"Hit the security system camera and see who's there," Cindy said.

Ben pressed the monitor button. A vague shape appeared.

"The guy's back is turned, and he's leaning on the door." Ben pressed his thick glasses near the monitor. "We can't see who it is."

"We have no choice but to protect ourselves," Ben answered. "Cindy, you take a mop handle from the closet and I'll get a skillet. Jimmy, use your cane. I don't know if we can do much, but at least we'll be ready for an attack."

Ben stood on one side of the door, watching Jimmy on

the other. "Hit the open button," he instructed Cindy. "As soon as the door slides open, we'll be ready to counter attack. Now!" He raised the skillet.

The door silently slid open. Isaiah Murphy nearly tumbled in. His eyes widened when he looked at his old friends, standing with mop handle, cane, and pan in hand. "You guys cleaning house?"

"Isaiah!" Cindy gasped. "What are you doing here?"

"Right now I can't remember."

Jimmy lowered the cane and shook his head. "Blue blazes, are we ever uptight. Come on in, Isaiah."

"You really know how to make a guy feel at home." Isaiah smiled mischievously.

Ben beckoned for the trio to follow him back to the kitchen table. "Things have gotten a little out of hand," he told Isaiah. "I suppose you know about the bombing."

"Frankly," Isaiah said, "I didn't let you know I was coming because I was concerned about security."

"You?" Ben frowned.

"I knew we had to talk face to face without any possible electronic eavesdropping. I've made some important discoveries that may have everything to do with the bombing."

"Sit down." Ben pointed to the chairs. "Whatever you have to tell us, I bet we can do you one better."

Isaiah stretched his long legs out under the table and began telling his friends about the strange movement of chemicals.

"Many years ago I worked with an Ethiopian named Hosni Gossos. I helped him solve some personal problems and we became close friends. In addition to working for the government, Hosni dabbled in politics. I flew to Addis Ababa to talk with him. Fortunately, Hosni thought I knew much more about the rebellion than I did. By playing it cool, I got him to admit that the Ethiopians were involved in an international intrigue."

Ben shook his head. "Excellent work, Isaiah."

"But I hit a brick wall and couldn't get Hosni to talk to me until the night of your television program. By providence, we had the TV on and saw your production. I was able to bear down on Hosni and he told me the rest of the story. Listen carefully."

Isaiah leaned forward and lowered his voice to nearly a whisper. "Right now a coalition of nations is uniting to attack Israel!" He looked deeply into his friends' eyes. "A war is brewing."

Each of the trio silently nodded.

Isaiah's forehead wrinkled. "You don't seem surprised."

"Keep rolling," Jimmy said.

Isaiah blinked. "Well . . . I . . . uh . . . got Hosni to fly with me to Russia and Egypt. Using his contacts, I was able to access warehouses and supply depots. Tons of sulphur and nitrates are now being shipped into these countries. Hosni introduced me as a colleague and I talked with soldiers in charge of making bombs and bullets. I learned names of conspirators and places where armaments are being manufactured and assembled. I know who the people are behind the bombing."

"Fits with the picture we have," Jimmy concluded. "We didn't know the source of the explosives, but we've got the big picture."

"Do we ever!" Ben shook his head.

Isaiah scratched his head. "Obviously I'm the one in the dark. Now, why don't you fill your old buddy in on *your* secrets?"

Cindy brought in a Bible and laid it on the table. Ben thumbed through the pages in the Book of Revelation "Jimmy's always been the Bible scholar. I'll let him tell you the whole story." Ben pushed the twentieth chapter of Revelation in front of Isaiah.

"The answer is so obvious," Jimmy began. "I guess our first mistake was taking the Bible for granted and not reading it. If you don't keep up on the content, the message slips from your mind."

Isaiah looked down at the page. "I haven't looked at Revelation in maybe a century or more."

"Fortunately Sam Eisenberg has. We flew to Petra to study the Bible with him. He helped us carefully evaluate the whole chapter. Verses seven through nine tell the story. Read the passage."

Isaiah started reading at verse one: "Then I saw an angel coming down from heaven, having the key to the bottom-less pit and a great chain in his hand. He laid hold of the dragon, that serpent of old, who is the Devil and Satan, and bound him for a thousand years; and he cast him into the bottomless pit, and shut him up, and set a seal on him, so that he should deceive the nations no more till the thousand years were finished. But after these things he must be released for a little while." Isaiah stopped. He rubbed his forehead and looked at his friends in bewilder-ment.

"On God's time clock a thousand years are up," Jimmy said. "We were here when the Evil One was chained, and we are still here when he is loosed."

Isaiah blinked and exhaled deeply.

"All these years we've been living out the promise in verse four," Cindy added. "Listen." Her small voice took on new authority. "And I saw thrones, and they sat on them, and judgement was committed to them. Then I saw the souls of those who had been beheaded for their witness to Jesus and for the word of God, who had not worshiped the beast or his image, and had not received his mark on their foreheads or their hands. And they lived and reigned with Christ for a thousand years. But the rest of the dead did not live again until the thousand years were finished. This is the first resurrection."

"This prophecy was fulfilled after the return of Yeshua when the Immortals came back to bring order to the world," Ben said. "The Immortals have already experienced the first resurrection."

"We *really* understand verse six," Cindy continued reading, "Blessed and holy is he who has part in the first resurrection. Over such the second death has no power, but they shall be priests of God and of Christ, and shall reign with Him a thousand years." Cindy smiled. "There's the good news. In this period King David and Paul, as well as Ruth, Jimmy's son, Jimmy's parents, and many others, governed the nations of the world."

"Certainly," Isaiah answered. "I understand about the Immortals."

"Here's the jackpot." Jimmy pointed to verse seven. "Now when the thousand years have expired, Satan will be released from his prison," Jimmy read slowly, "and will go out to deceive the nations which are in the four corners of the earth, Gog and Magog, to gather them together to battle, whose number is as the sand of the sea. They went up on the breadth of the earth and surrounded the camp of the saints and the beloved city." Jimmy stopped. "Got the picture, Isaiah?"

"So that's the meaning of what I saw in those warehouses in Russia and Egypt!"

"I'm afraid so," Ben said. "You've discovered the launch pad. The war is already on."

"But who would believe us?" Cindy mused. "Everything we've just said will sound crazy to most people."

"Cindy's right," Isaiah said. "We know the meaning of sin in Los Angeles but everyone has forgotten what Evil can do. We don't even have a point of reference."

Ben leaned back in his chair and stared at the blank TV screen. "At least we now see the common thread in the chaos we've uncovered. Satan is the source of illness and is behind the AIDS epidemic. Human lust and sin simply played into his hands."

"Exactly," Cindy agreed. "The rebellion of the nations and the attack on Yeshua are simply another dimension of Satan's plan. He is the author and father of all deceit and destruction."

Isaiah buried his head in his hands and slumped against the table. "What are we going to do?"

Ben looked at Jimmy. "That's the ultimate question!"

Zvilli Zemah was deeply tanned by the relentless June sunlight. Wearing the short-sleeved, casual shirt of the students, Zvilli was looking out of his small office in Hebrew University on Mt. Scopus when someone knocked on the door. "Come in," he called out without turning around.

"Dr. Zemah?" the gentle voice asked.

"Ah, Miss Zachary. I've been expecting you."

"I received your notice in my computer mail this morning." Rivka stood pensively in the doorway. The small woman's jet black hair was pulled back behind her head.

"Please sit down." Dr. Zemah pointed to a chair and leaned against the window. He had the tall, slender build of so many natives of the north. The striking appearance of his white hair against the sun-tanned complexion gave the professor an aura of great wisdom.

"Is there a problem with my work?" Rivka smiled apprehensively. Her large black eyes widened.

"Quite the contrary. You are clearly one of our very best students." Zemah picked up a file from the desk and opened it.

"Oh, good." Rivka settled back in the chair. The afternoon sun highlighted her dark, flawless skin, giving her a subtle glow. "I thought I had done something wrong."

"In fact, your excellent scores caused me to go back in your records to better understand your background. I was surprised to discover your family heritage is of both Jewish and Arab ancestry."

Rivka squirmed. "Well . . . uh . . . I don't exactly advertise the fact. You see, there have been some problems."

"Ah, but I do understand, dear. I would like to share a secret with you if you will keep my confidence."

"Of course." Rivka shrugged.

"I, too, have a similar background. My father was an Arab. In fact, I grew up in an Arab village. Because my mother was Jewish, I am considered to be a Jew. We are both aware that it is much better to present the Jewish side of our heritage here in Jerusalem." Zemah looked back out the window. "We are certainly surrounded by a *very* Jewish world."

"Yes," Rivka said slowly, "but I've never experienced any prejudice toward the Arabs. Actually my problem was with the—"

"You are young," Zemah's voice hardened. "In time you will come to see the problem clearly."

"Problem?" Rivka tilted her head slightly and frowned. "I'm sorry but I don't—"

"Oppression comes in many forms." Zemah cut her off. "My father was mistreated and slighted by my mother's people. Even from my earliest years I have seen the arrogance of the Jews."

Rivka rubbed her hands together nervously. "I guess I've been spared such an experience."

"You are fortunate," Zemah sounded bitter. "But I am glad for your friendship. I thought if you had been caught in the middle of the Isaac and Ishmael tug-of-war I might be of help."

"You are an excellent lecturer and teacher," Rivka said. "All the students admire you. I am flattered that you would take such a personal interest in me."

Zvilli smiled broadly. "Since you are now in my political science class on nationalism, I felt I could help you reflect on how the struggles of the Arab peoples have unfolded through the centuries."

"I would be grateful for any assistance you might offer, Dr. Zemah."

"Let me see if I can help you fully understand *our* problem." The professor walked around his small desk and sat in the chair next to Rivka. "Please, call me Zvilli."

# 12

The Feinbergs' shuttlecraft flew swiftly from Jerusalem to Jordan, then swooped low over the wide clearing along the edge of Al-Khubtha Mountain and swept past the Urn Tomb on toward Petra. Isaiah kept his face pressed to the window.

"Sam will think we're nuts," Jimmy quipped. "He doesn't see us for decades and then the next day we're back again."

"I have a hunch Sam assumed we'd return fairly quickly after we digested the facts he gave us," Cindy answered.

Ben guided the craft close to the tops of the rugged rocky peaks and swung around to sail above the colonnaded street running away from Ad-Deir, the monastery. "He wasn't dismayed when I told him we were on our way," Ben added. "Sort of took the call rather casually."

Isaiah pointed out of the window as the imposing intrusions of red, gray, and black granite whizzed by. "Never seen any place quite like this," he muttered. "The valleys and mountains look like the desert and the Grand Canyon rolled into one."

The hot morning sun baked the sandy areas around the

foot of the mountains and sent long shadows across the steep canyons. The towering carved columns of pink granite rose majestically in front of the monastery, glistening in the dazzling sunlight.

"Here we are." Ben brought the shuttle down to the small landing strip in front of the monastery. "Safe and sound." Dust blew as the vehicle came to a halt.

Sam and Angie Eisenberg waved from the huge entranceway. The four friends hurried out of the shuttle and into Ad-Deir, quickly reassembling in the Eisenbergs' living room.

"Couldn't get enough of the old place?" Sam joked. "This pile of rocks does offer an ambiance of security when the rest of the world is falling apart."

"I'm impressed," Isaiah confessed. "And a little speechless. Your house feels like the Rock of Ages."

Angie offered cups of hot tea from a serving tray. "After centuries of peace and tranquility, no one is prepared for what's happened lately. It takes a little while to realize how startling Sam's insights are."

"You really think the Devil is unleashed?" Isaiah asked.

"Afraid so." Sam settled back in his large overstuffed chair. "What is now happening points to a new intrusion of Evil; sin has always created chaos, but those problems were generally ones of broken relationships or serious consequences for the individual. The avalanche of social disasters and the physical illnesses we're now discovering are an intrusion from the outside, an attack on the human race. The new spiritual deception of the masses is the work of that diabolical old deceiver himself."

"Indeed!" Isaiah rubbed his gray hair and shook his head. "Never thought I'd see the problem again."

"People always take God's goodness for granted," Sam added. "Self-centeredness and arrogance seem to be built-in flaws in the human character. Even with Yeshua in our midst, we slipped back into patterns of indifference. Our mind-set is a ready-made invitation for Satan's work."

"But why is the attack happening *now?*" Isaiah asked.

"The Scriptures don't tell us much," Sam continued, "except that a thousand-year period is about up."

"I've been thinking about some clues my father and Ruth gave us when they helped us escape from Los Angeles," Jimmy added. "The Immortals seemed to imply we were facing a test of some sort. Maybe God is taking us through one last time of sifting for the final perfecting of our character."

"Very insightful," Angie added. "What better way to purge the last vestige of self-centeredness from the faithful?"

"Big thought." Isaiah sighed. "Wish I could avoid the sifting."

"Don't we all?" Sam agreed. "Unfortunately, we don't recognize our problems except in retrospect."

"Well, another piece of the puzzle is coming together for me." Cindy sighed. "I can see at least one reason why Yeshua hasn't made any appearances lately. He's withdrawn to leave the leadership responsibility to people like us."

"Looks like you're right," Ben said. "The time has come for us to get busy. Sam, we need your help in putting some of the pieces of the last puzzle together. Isaiah made a frightening discovery that Egypt, Russia, and Ethiopia are manufacturing bombs and bullets in violation of the decree of the central government. We already know China has been belligerent. Just before we left Jerusalem, we also received the news that other governments are joining in open rebellion."

Sam folded his hands across his chest and nodded his head slowly. "The pattern makes sense. Prophecy was clear about the forces joining with the Antichrist a thousand years ago. However, Scripture indicates far more than a few nations will combine in the last rebellion and a final assault on Jerusalem."

"You mean . . . *many?*" Isaiah's eyes widened.

"I'm afraid so," Sam responded.

"But we just started a worldwide revival," Jimmy protested.

"The problem lies with the leaders of the nations," Sam countered. "Heads of state can manipulate citizens against their wishes."

"But why would Yeshua allow evil people to gain control?" Cindy asked.

"I'm not entirely sure." Sam peered off into space. "But God has never limited individual freedom. The ability to love demands the capacity to make bad choices. At one time every world leader could have been the source of great good. I'm sure Yeshua saw significant potential in the leaders of the rebelling nations. Obviously, Satan recognized the same capacity. Remember, Yeshua once chose a man named Judas."

"So, you think the entire world is going to swing behind a group of rebel governments," Cindy said.

Isaiah shivered. "We've got to find a way to warn the nations!"

"But who would listen to us?" Ben threw his hands up in the air. "Look at us? We're minor functionaries in the great scheme of things."

"I'm afraid that's the essence of our dilemma," Sam agreed. "People are likely to think our interpretation of the present state of affairs rather strange. We're likely to come off as a bunch of old kooks."

Ben got up and began pacing slowly. "Why not try an attack on the problem from a different direction? Try thinking about what the other side is likely to do. During the Great Tribulation the Bible gave us all kinds of clues of what to expect. The twenty-one judgments of the Book of Revelation were all listed in sequence. Once we started paying attention to the times and dates, we were in a position to anticipate what was coming next. Sam, can you help us make some intelligent guesses about timetables?"

Angie laughed. "Sam's been sitting around here for days working with his computer on that exact question. He thought no one would ever ask."

"Two dates immediately come to mind." Sam opened his Bible. "From biblical indications and as a result of everything that has happened in the past, I have a premonition that a confederation of nations will begin to move their armies this year around the seventeenth of Tammuz. The date is not far away. Of course, there's one time you can bank on to be the day of the final attack."

Jimmy stared at Ben and Cindy. He slowly turned to Sam. "The ninth of Av?" His voice dropped to a whisper.

Silence fell over the room. Sam slowly nodded his head.

Angie spoke first. "The Devil always had a propensity for that particular day. Just think of all the disasters visited on the Jewish people on Av 9 through the centuries!"

"The first Temple was destroyed on Av 9," Cindy observed.

"And the second one also," Jimmy added.

"Hitler formalized his plans to destroy Jews worldwide on Av 9 too," Ben said. "Satan is using evil rulers now just like he used Hitler and the Antichrist over a thousand years ago."

"Many major events of the Tribulation were connected to Av 9," Isaiah added.

"We could never forget the significance of that date."

"There you have it!" Sam slid forward to the edge of his chair. "I would suggest you get ready for a period of intense struggle beginning on the seventeenth of Tammuz and culminating on Av 9."

"We don't have much time left," Ben concluded. "We must move quickly."

"I think I ought to go back to Los Angeles," Isaiah said. "I can organize our old friends to be ready for the struggle."

"Maybe you should take a side trip and go through Ethiopia," Jimmy suggested. "Talk to your old friend Hosni Gossos and see what else you can find out about their war plans. We need some insight into how they will use weapons."

"H-m-m-m," Isaiah mused. "I might be able to do some first-class spying."

Ben covered his mouth with his hand and slowly rubbed his chin. "I don't know if we can make much of an impact but at least I can get my office staff organized to be ready for the onslaught."

Sam nodded. "Our heavenly Father never expects us to do more than we can. But we are examples that believers can accomplish more than they often dream possible."

"Why don't you come back to Jerusalem with us, Sam?" Cindy said. "You and Angie could help us organize the troops."

Sam shook his head. "Our work is out here where we can keep our minds and spirits clear. I think the heavenly Father wants us to intercede for you. Intercessors energize activists. We're the unseen power behind the scenes. You can count on us to pray continually for you."

"What a reassuring thought!" Ben offered his hand to his old friend. "We'll be calling on your counsel in the days ahead."

"We'll be here at work on our knees," Sam answered.

"Our time in the desert taught us the incredible power of prayer," Cindy added. "The heart of God is particularly attuned to pain. I think the most important place to start preparation for what lies ahead is through intercession.

Before we take one step into this battle, we must be saturated with prayer."

"Cindy's absolutely right," Sam agreed. "Once we've prayed, the heavenly Father has the most amazing ability to slip in the insights and discoveries we need. Prayer is always the right place to begin."

"Then let's get busy," Jimmy answered and slipped from his chair to the floor. The others silently knelt with him.

For the next hour the group prayed fervently for guidance. Finally, Ben opened his eyes and put his thick glasses back on. "I feel prayed up! I think I'm ready to go on."

"Stay close to the Father," Sam added, "and you'll be ready."

"Let's go!" Ben stood up forcefully. "We've got work to do." The group followed him out to the shuttlecraft and the foursome piled inside for the trip back to Jerusalem.

Jimmy waved from the window as Ben guided the craft up from the ground. Sam and Angie waved back as it slowly rose above the monastery and turned back toward Jerusalem.

"I'm extremely glad we came," Isaiah said. "My next step is to get in touch with Hosni Gossos. I must explore that connection to the fullest before I go back to Los Angeles."

"Wendy Kohn and Mrs. Netanyahu will probably think the desert has fried my brain," Ben concluded. "But they are the people I must start with if we're going to make a dent in the problem."

Cindy settled back into the seat. "Who knows where all of this is going to take us? I'm certainly apprehensive."

"I think I'll take an evasive course," Ben thought out-loud. "I don't want to call any more attention than is necessary to our friends in Petra. I'll swing along the wilderness area bordering the Dead Sea and then shoot back to Jerusalem from another direction." The compact, shiny black shuttle glided quietly like a guided missile. Without wings, the anti-gravity capacity gave the craft total maneuverability, swinging and turning at the slightest touch of the controls. The bubble top gave the group a complete view of the area.

"Look!" Isaiah pointed out the window. "I've always wanted to see the desalination plant at work. I understand they siphon off the bromides and chlorides from the Dead Sea and use the remaining water for irrigation."

"The oranges grown here are as large as bowling balls," Jimmy said. "And the tomatoes are larger than grapefruits. The recycling process really works. Look around. The desert is truly blooming."

Suddenly the craft veered wildly to the left and dropped several hundred feet. Ben fought to lift the nose before they hit a rock peak. Isaiah bounced into Cindy, and Jimmy nearly sprawled on the floor.

"What's happening?" Cindy cried. "Make sure your seat belts are fastened tightly."

"I . . . I . . . just don't know." Ben kept pulling on the wheel. Red lights flashed on the guidance system. "This has never happened before. I can't seem to control anything."

The craft swung wildly out over the Dead Sea and then veered back straight into the rock cliffs. "Brace yourselves!" Jimmy yelled. "We're going to crash!"

Suddenly the craft shot straight up and sailed over a rough, broken valley. "The entire guidance system's gone crazy." Ben kept hitting buttons. "Nothing is responding."

The craft dropped into the grove between the walls of the valley and then maintained a height of a hundred feet above the ground. "Part of the time the altitude guidance is on," Ben called out. "Then it suddenly cuts out. I can't control our speed either."

Abruptly the craft pulled straight up toward the sun. In

seconds, it was several thousand feet above the wilderness before slowing down. Without warning the shuttle stalled. For a moment the small capsule hung in space before tipping backward and plunging toward the earth.

"Hit the anti-gravity system!" Jimmy cried. "That's our only chance!"

The pressure of the terrifying descent froze Ben's hand to the console. At the last possible moment his finger hit the button marked AG. The craft came to a terrifying halt just feet above the ground, shaking everything in it loose. The foursome jerked wildly, their seat belts cutting into their bodies as the shuttle skidded across desert rubble toward a boulder. The craft lifted slightly and then plowed into the ground, spraying sand and dirt in every direction. Silence and dust settled around the shattered shuttle.

For several seconds no one moved. Pieces of the broken windshield tumbled out. Broken metal clanked against rocks. Finally quiet settled over the winding valley. The silence of the barren desert became deafening.

"Cindy?" Ben finally called out feebly. "Are you OK?"

"I don't seem to have any pain. I'm alive . . . is about all I can say for sure."

"Isaiah?" Jimmy shook his friend. "Isaiah!"

Isaiah opened one eye. He slowly pushed his other eyelid open. "I'm afraid to look. What in the world happened?"

"Only the grace of God saved us," Jimmy concluded. "That's the only way we came out of that alive. I thought the force of the fall would devour us."

"I can't believe it." Ben fumbled to get his glasses back on while trying to unfasten his seat belt. "Never, never have I heard of one of these machines going crazy."

"The technology was perfected long ago." Jimmy tried to push away from his seat. "The automatic guidance

system alone should have compensated for any maladjust-
ment. There simply is no way for one of these things to go
out of control."

"Obviously it can!" Cindy pushed hard on the door.
"Now the locks won't open."

Ben threw all of his weight against the emergency lever
and suddenly all the doors lifted up. The hot air of the
desert immediately surged into the cabin. "Clearly the
climate control was working." He climbed out the side.
"We'll miss that small comfort in the desert."

Cindy stepped out on the barren hill. "My stomach really
hurts, but I'm able to walk. My legs are unusually fine for
an old lady." She looked up at the area towering above her.
"Do we have any idea where we are?"

"We were over the Dead Sea before everything snapped.
However, the craft was navigating up the ravines at a high
rate of speed when we crashed, so we could have made up
a lot of the distance between us and Jerusalem."

"Any idea what that means?" Isaiah looked around in
bewilderment and rubbed his back.

"None," Ben answered. "At worst, we are miles off
course. At best, we're only a short distance from Jerusalem."

"Anybody live out here?" Isaiah stared at the barren
terrain.

"Centuries of advancement haven't changed the bedouins much," Jimmy answered. "They're still around—somewhere. But the chances of running into one is about the
same as just happening to take the right gorge and ending
up in Jerusalem in a few minutes. We're a long way from
nowhere. Even the bedouins stay closer to the beaten
paths."

"The only good thing is that we started back late enough
in the day that nightfall will give us a reprieve of sorts from
the heat of the sun," Ben added.

"Ever walk around out here when the cold sets in?" Jimmy pointed with his cane.

"That's the bad news," Ben answered and wiped the sweat from his forehead.

"I think we'd better start walking in the best direction the sun offers." Cindy pointed in a northeasterly arch. "People dehydrate in this weather very quickly."

Ben shook his head. "We didn't even bring any emergency supplies. We'd do better to stay with the craft in hopes someone would find us."

"But no one knows we took this trip," Jimmy added. "To make matters worse, our evasive action would probably have not been noted by telaport radar as anything more than a tourist trip. We've broken every rule in the book."

"The craft offers some shelter," Ben argued. "And it might be spotted from the air."

"We'd simply shrivel up and blow away if we waited inside that wreck," Cindy shook her head. "Maybe Jerusalem isn't so far away. I think it would be better to try to get out than sit here and roast."

"Cindy has a point," Jimmy added. "We might be closer to getting out of the wilderness than we know."

"I don't think so." Ben shook his head. "But I'll go with what the majority says. How many vote to walk?"

All hands went up.

"That settles the matter." Ben turned around and looked carefully. "I think we'd better walk up the side of this valley as best we can and see if we can get our bearings. At least that's a start."

A swirl of hot air kicked up the sand and stung the group with the sharp grit. "At our age we must keep our heads covered," Cindy worried. "But we don't have anything to use for shade."

"I'll rip out some of the seat covers." Isaiah pulled out a

pocket knife and returned to the craft. "I can cut off enough material to shade us."

Ben covered his eyes and looked up the steep embankment. "God help us," he muttered. "I don't see how we'll ever make it."

They locked arms with each other and started up the winding ravine. Within a few yards their stumbling made it clear they wouldn't be of much help to each other. Each fared better alone. Several times Cindy nearly fell. Near the top they grabbed at a few surviving scrubby bushes to pull themselves onto the ridge. However, once they reached level ground there was nothing before them except the endless winding cracks in the earth.

The deep valleys had been eroded by eons of spring rains interspersed between endless months of complete dryness before sparse cloudbursts returned for momentary seasonal visits. Lizards scurried away as the foursome trudged by but there was no other sign of life. No one spoke much to preserve all the moisture they could. Their throats quickly became uncomfortably dry. They clung to each other, fighting the sand and the treacherous terrain.

By walking the top, the foursome moved along the crest of other valleys but soon came to the end of the ridge and had to cut across another deep gorge to keep going. They were sweating profusely and draped their shuttle seat coverings low over their faces to ward off occasional sprays of sand.

After an hour of walking, Cindy slumped to the ground and held her stomach. The back of her jersey top was soaked with perspiration. "I don't think I can go on much longer," she mumbled to herself. "Maybe we should have stayed with the craft."

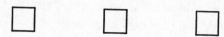

Back in Jerusalem, Rivka Zachary was finishing another private tutoring session with Dr. Zvilli Zemah in his office at the library. She smiled and turned nervously in her chair. "But, Dr. Zemah, the reign of Yeshua has brought nothing but good."

"Just make it Zvilli," he said for the third time that afternoon. "Rivka, you have ignored the Arab side of your nature. As long as you allow the Isaac portion of your heredity to dominate your mind, you can only see through eyes controlled by Jewish influences. You have no idea how much repression the people from the other side suffer."

Rivka shook her head. Her jet-black hair swung back and forth. "I'm sorry, Zvilli. My experience has been so different. Jews have always been good to me."

"You must realize compliance naturally brings reward. The central government continually panders to those who obey them, creating a type of conditioned reflex. We obey. We get rewarded. We feel good. We obey. So on and so forth, forever."

The raven-haired beauty crossed her arms over her chest. "I don't feel like an automaton. No one treats me badly or coerces me to do anything. I like following my leaders."

"That's because you've never released your desert impulses. You have a natural wildness in your soul, just waiting for expression. My social experiments during the last several years have opened my mind to see the larger truth. We have all been duped by the Jerusalem system. Rivka, you must throw off the shackles of mind and body to truly understand total fulfillment. Believe me." Zvilli's voice became low and intense.

"How can I be sure?" Rivka asked innocently.

"Because I've done it!" Zemah stared deep into her eyes. "I've cast aside the impositions of authority to enjoy unrestrained ecstasy. Listen to me!" He leaned forward and took her hand. "I can take you to a place of capacity and passion beyond your dreams. Give me your mind and I will open your eyes to see beyond even the confines of these mountains that surround Jerusalem."

Rivka tried to shake her head but his eyes had taken control of her thoughts. She swallowed hard. "Really?"

Zemah smiled. "Absolutely, my dear." He squeezed Rivka's hand; his hypnotic eyes held her captive.

# CHAPTER

# 13

Maria Marchino, the president of Italy, had said little during the confederation strategy sessions. Although she had been the leader of Italy for four decades, it was not her nature to be demonstrative or intrusive. The Marchino technique was to listen silently in the background while carefully plotting her own course.

When Maria Marchino entered a room everyone observed. The tall, imposing head of state had been a fashion model in her youth. She had learned the secrets of presence and beauty well. The influence of that early period continued in her elaborate wardrobe, which defied the worldwide generally accepted code of dress. Whereas most leaders wore the usual knit jersey uniform, Maria's more exotic dresses and pantsuits called attention to her striking beauty. Clothes did the talking for Maria Marchino.

The head of state sat down at her desk and punched in the code for the state palace where Claudine Toulouse, the head of France, awaited her call. Just before hitting the last number, she paused to look at her government's crest on the wall in front of her.

When the Italian state reformed after the Great Tribulation, the nation avoided any indication of its role in the previously re-constituted Roman Empire of Damian Gianardo. The Antichrist had commandeered Rome as the final seat of power, leaving a historically embarrassing stigma on the city. The new emblem of government was a straightforward shield with the colors of the national flag decorating the quadrants of the crest. Maria never liked the plainness of the design. She preferred something more glorious.

Although no one wished to evoke that unfortunate image, the idea of a Holy Roman Empire had always captured Maria Marchino's imagination. Her earliest studies of the ancient world fascinated her with the role Rome once played on the world stage. The thought of re-creating a new worldwide empire held a secret fascination for Maria. In fact, her concealed ambition had been an important factor in propelling her into politics.

The president of Italy punched in the final digit and waited for the hologram phone to respond. Maria knew she was a striking beauty compared to the plain leader of France; she enjoyed the contrast. Maria kept her hair dyed black and lined her eyes with an iridescent gray to increase their piercing quality. In a few moments the form of Claudine Toulouse materialized in front of Maria's desk.

"Peace to you." Maria offered the usual diplomatic greeting. "How good to see you, my dear."

Claudine Toulouse bowed her head ceremoniously. "Peace to you, great leader of the Italians." The French head of state wore the usual jersey pullover. She was small and the brightness of her blonde hair had long been washed out with wide swaths of gray. "You are gracious to call," she said.

Maria reached for another button. "Let us lock privacy into our conversation for security's sake."

"Exactly," Toulouse responded and pushed a similar tab on her hologram system. "Some matters are best kept only for our ears."

"We've not talked since our private conversations in Egypt," Maria began. "I'm wondering how your reflections have gone."

"I believe your initial assessments were quite accurate." Claudine Toulouse settled back into a large blue velvet-covered gold-leaf chair. "If this restored world order comes to pass, Arab influence will dominate the rest of the nations, leaving us with second-class status. I see their aims demonstrated clearly in every word coming out of Atrash's mouth. Abu Sita is merely his shadow.

"My sister," the French head of state continued, "we must stand together. You are right. These particular Arabs still hold all women in an inferior position. They are not comfortable with our presence in planning sessions. I, too, noticed their avoidance of our responses to many of their comments."

"Then we are in one accord," Marchino concluded. "We must find our own way in the midst of this treachery."

"I still believe we can become free of the control of the central government in Jerusalem." Claudine folded her hands and tapped the edge of her chin. "I'm not sure what I make of this spirit guide talk of Atrash and Abu Sita's, but the government of Yeshua does seem to have lost control. The time appears to be ripe for us to strike out in our own direction."

Maria Marchino nodded her agreement. "Hard to tell whether old El Khader is a schizophrenic or epileptic." She laughed at her own joke. "At least he puts on quite a show. Who knows?"

"I was once a very religious person," Claudine said. "I would have been deeply offended by all this gibberish about other gods, but I suppose I've changed a great deal." She paused, raised her eyebrows, and shrugged. "Maybe the pressures of running a government, the worries, the distractions of everyday problems changed me."

"We change as we age," Maria congealed. "Just part of the nature of things."

"I am much more concerned with this manifesto Atrash sent." Claudine Toulouse held up a sheet of paper. "He really has a hate for the Jews. Such emotionalism and madness can confuse one's thinking."

Maria held up her own copy of the document and started to read. "The Restored World Order swears to conduct a holy war against Jerusalem and every and all Jews until victory is achieved." She looked up from the document. "This language must be changed or other world leaders will not respond. Atrash sounds like a racist fanatic. Listen to this, 'by command of the gods, we must fight and kill Jews wherever they are.'

"Claudine, I suggest we lodge a formal complaint."

"I agree. Listen to this." Claudine read further. "Only a jihad, a holy war waged as a religious duty, can cleanse the earth of the influence of subversive religion and free us of the oppressive hand of Yeshua." The French leader shrugged. "The government of Yeshua has been strict prior to this past year, but never oppressive. Everyone knows that. We simply intend now to develop our countries as we please—without yielding to anyone's intervention."

"I would suggest a larger picture to you, my sister." Maria stopped and studied the hologram image carefully, measuring her counterpart. "Should Jerusalem topple, we must be aware of the possibility of considerable instability for a long period of time. Atrash and Abu Sita probably have other plans for us."

Claudine Toulouse sat up and leaned forward. "What are you suggesting?"

"Is it not to our advantage to be prepared to reform and create our own alliance?"

The French leader stared. "Our own coalition?"

"I would humbly suggest the boys from Baghdad could turn on us as easily as they have on the central government. Where would we be then?"

Toulouse settled back in the gold chair, folded her hands once more, and resumed tapping her chin. "Exactly what are you suggesting?"

"Perhaps the time has come to develop our own contingency plans. Maybe we should be ready for our own counterattack at the end of this war."

"How?"

Maria Marchino laid Atrash's manifesto down and picked up another piece of paper. "I've been making a few notes. First, I would suggest we secretly stockpile every form of armament we can. We must develop a private stash known only to us. Second, as soon as the attack plans are formulated, we must outline a secret military response for counteraction as the battle unfolds. Third, we should conclude with a secret agreement to bind our nations together. Our accord can form the basis for negotiations with other governments to bring them into our sphere of influence once matters start to unravel with Atrash and Abu Sita."

Claudine stared straight ahead for what seemed like an indefinite period of time. Finally, she reached out and offered her hand. "My sister! You are a true descendant of the Caesars."

For a long time after Claudine terminated the call from Italy, the beautiful face of Maria burned in her mind like an image of personal failure. Claudine's plainness had been one of the reasons she had doggedly pursued politics rather than what she painfully referred to as a "normal life." She knew men only as formidable adversaries—never as passionate lovers. That had been fine with her until Khalil Hussein came to power in Jordan. Known as the "boy genius" of politics, Hussein's meteoric rise had been admired across the world, and Claudine had instantly been physically drawn to this much younger man. But he hadn't responded to her invitation at the conference.

"I want him," Claudine murmured aloud. "Whatever it takes . . ." the words trailed away.

She thought of the promises Abu Sita had pushed at every meeting. "Meditations and prayers to Marduk will bring you new power and authority over others," he had claimed.

Claudine closed her eyes and tried to let her mind shift into complete neutral. After ten minutes of struggling to clear her mind, Claudine started the chant. "Come, Lord Marduk, come spirits of the past, come spirits of the dead. Come to me." She repeated the phrase over and over, slipping further and further into a trancelike state. "I will serve you . . . serve you," she muttered.

Suddenly Claudine stopped. An intense feeling of lust and desire shot through her mind. She felt an insatiable desire for Khalil. Her body burned and her mouth was dry.

Claudine began breathing heavily. "What . . . what's happening to me?" she sputtered.

As the hot afternoon faded, Ziad Atrash stood at his command post in Cairo, carefully inspecting the new surveillance equipment being installed around the war room. Workmen busily connected wires and hooked up both television monitors and hologram devices.

"How soon until everything is complete?" he barked at a general.

"We expect most of the work to be finished by this time tomorrow," the aide advised.

"Tell them to hurry up," Atrash ordered. "Everything is taking far too long." The general saluted and began mingling with the technicians and shouting orders.

Ziad had chosen this particular bunker near the Red Sea because of the ancient defeat Egypt suffered there at the hands of Moses centuries earlier. He had every intention of reversing the disaster and named the outpost Rameses in honor of the pharaoh of the Exodus.

Atrash flipped on a portable telephone. "What is the status of the arrangement for international satellite transmission of the heads of state? I want the information now."

"Details are falling into place quickly," the aide answered briskly. "However, we have received one communique you will want to review immediately."

"What?" Atrash snapped.

"The leaders of Italy and France just sent in a response to your manifesto. I can place it on your television monitor, channel 3."

"Do it." Ziad turned on the screen in front of him and hit the correct channel. The message filled the screen.

To:     President Ziad Atrash
From: Presidents Maria Marchino & Claudine Toulouse

After careful study we believe your manifesto states very clearly the objectives we have agreed upon for immediate military pursuit. As always you are clear and erudite.

Atrash laughed and pulled at his black moustache. "Of course, I am the master of all languages!" He continued to chuckle as he read further:

However, aspects of the manifesto may be misunderstood in some world capitals. Your attack on the Jews seems particularly vitriolic and racist. We suggest all language about divine direction be dropped. A simple call to liberation and freedom will be sufficient to enlist other nations in our campaign. We respectfully suggest immediate revision before release.

Ziad's eyes narrowed and his neck turned red. "How dare those old bags tell me what to say!" he shouted. "Who are they to even make comment on *my* manifesto?" Atrash shook his fist at the screen. "Their impertinence will not be tolerated!" He stormed out of the room and walked outside.

The sun was setting over the Red Sea and the heat of the day subsiding. *Unfortunately*, he thought, *I need those nations in the alliance. I have no choice but to respond positively to their arrogance. At the right time I will send those two sows sailing across the River of the Dead.* Atrash kicked at a pile of sand. *I will keep them off balance by treating them with more respect than they deserve.* He paced back toward the bunker. *Possibly, I should let Abu Sita respond and not even acknowledge the issue.* Atrash slammed the door behind him and stormed down the hall. *Whatever Abu Sita works out will be acceptable— if he has the brains to know what to say to them. Maybe I'd better do it myself.*

Atrash marched down the hall into the communications command post and flipped on a portable phone. "Return this message to Italy and France," he ordered the aide. "Your ideas and thoughts are always of the highest value to our cause. Please send your suggested revisions and adjustments. With highest regards, Supreme General Ziad Atrash. He clicked off the phone. "That will keep the old bags happy."

"Excellency," an aide carrying papers entered the room. "I made further inquiries about the international television hook-up. We have now reached agreement with the other leaders to apportion each head of state equal space on the screen during the announcement of the attack on the

Jerusalem government. However, without mentioning the fact, I have arranged for your picture to always appear first. Our people believe that projecting the images of the pyramids and the tombs of the kings behind you, we will create the preeminent image of ultimate authority."

"Excellent." Atrash smiled for the first time that afternoon. "Good planning. How is the training of our soldiers going?"

The general's demeanor changed. "Well, the men have no previous history of military training. Their skills are not good, but they are being pushed hard."

"What you mean is, they are behind schedule."

"We are now practicing twelve hours a day, Excellency."

"Don't let up," Ziad growled. "Time is of the essence."

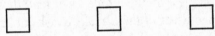

The setting sun cast haunting and foreboding shadows over the wilderness chasms that wound seemingly nowhere. Cindy clung to Ben as they inched up the side of a gorge. Their white hair hung down in their eyes. Isaiah and Jimmy waited at the top.

"I'm drying out," Jimmy called down. "Thank goodness the sun is disappearing. We will preserve moisture and get some of our energy back."

"I don't know," Cindy answered from the side of the bank. "I'm not sure how much further I can go—even in the next few minutes—much less tomorrow."

Ben pulled her up to the top and dropped into the sand. "I'm almost spent." He sprawled out on the ridge.

Jimmy shielded his eyes and looked around. "We have a reprieve between now and sunset. But if we don't find some form of shelter, we may be even worse off when night comes."

"I hate to say it," Isaiah stood up and rubbed his sore legs, "but we need to keep tracking. The sun offers us a compass of sorts; in the dark we could end up just going around in circles."

"Isaiah's right," Jimmy said. "We'll help you." He offered his hand to Cindy.

Ben rolled over and tried to stand. His bulbous shape made getting to his feet difficult. "I know you're right. I just don't know if I can keep on."

"We must," Cindy urged. "We don't have any choice. Too much depends on us getting back." She struggled to her feet.

Jimmy cupped his hand over his eyes and studied the terrain. "Let's go for that high point. Maybe if we can get on top of the bluff we'll see something." He stuck his cane into the sand like a walking stick.

The group slowly trudged forward, pushing on across the jagged side of the valley. The winds began to pick up, making the trek even more difficult. Cindy hung on Ben's arm, her steps becoming more halting the closer they came to the top.

"I think we must stop," Ben called out. "Cindy and I will rest here. The two of you go on by yourselves. We'll catch up later."

Isaiah shook his head. "We must not get beyond visual contact. We'd never find each other again."

Jimmy kept walking but called over his shoulder. "Isaiah's right. We've got to stay together. I'll get up here on the ridge and see if I can find a better direction, but we must stay within shouting distance."

Isaiah dropped to his knees and watched the Feinbergs below him. He kept looking up to observe Jimmy's progress in reaching the plateau. Finally, his old friend disappeared over the top. The sun was quickly setting.

"I can't see Jimmy anymore," Ben called.

Isaiah nodded but he looked apprehensively toward the

bluff. Time was passing and nothing seemed to be happening. Ben finally helped Cindy up to where Isaiah was sitting.

"I'm worried about Jimmy," Ben said. "He should have returned by now."

"We're all exhausted," Cindy sighed. "Our strength is gone."

"He could have slipped and fallen into another canyon," Ben concluded. "We've got to get up there and find out."

Isaiah painfully pushed himself up to his feet. Ben and Cindy followed behind struggling to move forward. At the top of the bluff, Jimmy was nowhere in sight. A gale bore down, sweeping away the dirt like a giant wind-driven broom.

"J-i-m-m-y," Isaiah called out but no reply followed.

"God help us!" Cindy clung to Ben. "Jimmy's fallen off the edge somewhere."

"H-a-r-r-i-s-o-n," Ben yelled at the top of his lungs, "where are you?"

"He could be trapped at the bottom of one of these pits." Cindy pointed to the blackness filling the ravines. "He wouldn't be able to hear us. We'll never find him." She started to cry.

Suddenly from the direction of the setting sun, a voice answered. "Over here! I'm over here. Hurry up."

"Where?" Isaiah looked around. "I can't see you."

Cindy pointed toward a rise. "The sound had to come from just behind that incline."

"Jimmy?" Ben hollered. "Direct us to where you are."

"Over here" echoed across the canyon.

"Yes." Cindy pointed. "He's definitely just over the hill."

"Jimmy, you okay?" Isaiah tried again but got no response.

"I don't understand." Cindy struggled to walk faster. "You'd think he'd answer us."

"He didn't sound bad," Isaiah puffed. "In fact, his voice was rather strong."

With their last ounce of energy, the threesome cleared the final hill on the bluff. Straight ahead they could see the shape of an old building. A figure was lying on the ground at the doorway.

"There's Jimmy!" Isaiah pointed. "He's not moving!"

"Hurry!" Ben led the way. "We've got to help him." Ben limped more than ran but he beckoned the others to follow him.

"Jimmy!" he kept calling. "Can you hear us?"

"It's an old abandoned army outpost," Isaiah exclaimed. "Even the tin roof is intact. The arid climate preserved the place." He huffed as he trotted.

"Jimmy," Ben dropped beside the limp form, "are you OK?"

Jimmy groaned but didn't move.

"He must have passed out." Ben rolled his friend over. "Exhaustion finally got him."

Isaiah fell next to Jimmy. "Come on, partner. Don't check out on us now." He gently shook Jimmy's face.

The old man slowly opened his eyes. "Where am I?" he moaned.

"You're a hero!" Ben laughed in relief. "You saved us." He helped Jimmy sit up.

Cindy trudged up from behind. "Thank God he's alive!"

"What happened to me?" Jimmy kept blinking his eyes.

"You've found us a hotel for the night, old buddy," Isaiah answered. "Not bad accommodations, considering."

Cindy peered inside the dilapidated building. "The army must have used this as a reconnaissance post centuries ago." She stepped inside. "Look!" Cindy pointed at plastic containers still stacked along the wall. "Supplies are still here!"

"I thought it was a mirage," Jimmy mumbled. "The last thing I can remember is thinking I was going mad."

"You hit the jackpot," Isaiah exclaimed. "You pulled us out."

"Ben," Cindy called from inside the shack, "you won't believe this. There's still water in these containers! Smells stale but it still feels like heaven to me!"

"Praise God!" Ben proclaimed.

"I thought I was hearing voices." Jimmy's voice was still very weak. "I kept hearing someone calling, 'Over here.' That's why I kept going. I knew I was delirious, but the voice sounded so clear."

"We heard *you* calling," Isaiah said. "Sure saved us."

Jimmy looked puzzled. "I didn't call."

"I'm bringing some water out for Jimmy," Cindy called out. "It will help revive him."

"But we heard you directing us this way," Ben insisted.

"Couldn't have been." Jimmy shook his head. "My mouth has been almost too dry to speak!"

# 14

The cold night and the unforgiving hard ground inside the desert hut were severe punishment to human body and soul. As the sun rose Cindy snuggled closer to Ben to try to keep warm. Jimmy curled in a tight ball against the back of the shed to preserve all the body heat possible.

Isaiah was the first to awake. For a long time he stared through a crack in the dilapidated building, looking out across the empty wilderness. Isaiah found it difficult to sit because of his excruciating back pain. He tried not to move.

Jimmy eventually stirred. He rolled over on his side, slowly curled his knees under him, and tried to push himself up. Only with great difficulty did he get to his feet. He quietly looked around at the rest of the sleepers.

When Ben stretched, Cindy woke up. "What time is it?" Cindy's voice was dry and raspy.

"About six in the morning," Jimmy answered.

Ben opened his eyes slowly and stared at the corrugated metal roof above him. "Where am I?" He fumbled around searching for his glasses.

Jimmy shuffled around. "I wish I knew the answer myself. Everything always looks the same out here."

"I don't think I can go on," Isaiah muttered. "My tired old body is simply too battered. I don't have it in me anymore."

"I agree," Cindy answered. "Yesterday I didn't realize what the strain against the seat belts did to me. But this morning my abdomen is so sore. I'm wracked with pain."

Ben reached for Cindy's hand. "We've got to get you medical attention. I should have insisted you stay with the shuttlecraft."

"No," she said softly. "We took the right course. The water saved us."

Jimmy peered out the door at the barren terrain. "Yesterday the wilderness seemed crossable. Today, the journey looks impossible. We're just too old and tired to make it."

"I'm starving," Isaiah rubbed his stomach. "We expended a lot of energy tramping around out there."

Jimmy slumped down close to the door. "Wouldn't it be ironic if this shelter became our final death trap?"

Ben kept looking at the roof. "Last night the tin saved us from the cold but I suspect in a few hours this metal building will become an oven."

"You're right," Cindy said. "Unless there's an unlikely breeze, we will be like chickens roasting in an oven."

"Won't take long," Isaiah said. "Probably in an hour the heat will really start to work on this place. Two hours and you could fry an egg on the roof."

Ben finally got to his feet. "Here we are in the midst of what might be the most important task of our lives and we're lost in the middle of nowhere." He ran his hands through his disarrayed hair. "Time is running out and we can't even find first base."

"I'm afraid we're not even in the ball park," Jimmy

answered. "I don't think any of us can live through another day like yesterday."

Cindy started to weep. "We're going to die out here. There's no hope." She buried her face in her hands. Her body shook as she wept.

Ben dropped to his knees by her side. "I'm sorry. I've run out of ideas. I just don't know what to do."

"We thought we were going to take on the world powers, the Evil One himself," Isaiah smirked. "We couldn't even fly home. That's just how effective *we* are!"

Jimmy threw a handful of sand toward the door and dropped to his knees. "We're a bunch of old 'has beens.' The truth is we're old fools who should have stayed out of the way of the traffic before we got run over by the cars."

No one answered. Defeat hung in the air like the desert heat.

"Hello?" a voice called from outside the building.

Jimmy jumped and toppled over.

"W-h-a-t!" Isaiah shouted.

"We've been found!" Ben exclaimed. "Thank God. A bedouin has found us."

"You have lost your way?" the voice answered.

"Who is it?" Jimmy rushed to the door.

"Don't you recognize me?" The handsome young man stepped into the doorway. "I thought by now you'd know my voice."

"Son!" Jimmy threw his arms around the Immortal. "My son, you're here."

"Didn't think I'd let you become pot roast for the vultures, did you, Dad?"

"Thank heavens you were watching over us." Ben hobbled forward. "We are fairly well spent."

"We had a wreck!" Cindy blurted out. "Crashed out there somewhere." Cindy pointed out the window.

"We thought we were goners." Jimmy hugged his son a second time. "We didn't think anyone could find us."

"Few people ever come this way," Jim Jr. explained. "You found an old security post left from the days before the Great Tribulation. You obviously need to get out of this place."

"The truth is," Jimmy agreed, "we're really spent and rather beat up. Cindy may have injuries."

Ben explained, "We need you to get us back to Jerusalem as quickly as possible. You see, our craft went berserk and . . ."

"I know. You must realize that these days nothing happens to you by chance or accident. You must be attuned with the ears of a fox."

"Not an accident?" Jimmy immediately queried. "Are you suggesting that the shuttle wreck was planned?"

"Your landing was cushioned by grace," Jim Jr. answered simply. "You might have plowed straight into the ground or you could have hit the final boulder head on. Remember?"

"You were there!" Cindy declared.

"The battle has already begun, my dear ones, but you have not fully appreciated the dimensions of the conflict. Do you think the Evil One is unaware of everything you've been doing? In the past month you have proclaimed the truth to billions and brought many back from the brink of destruction. Do you believe such heroics would go unnoted by your enemy? The war is on but you are treating the engagement like a slight tiff."

Ben's eyes widened and his lips parted before he spoke. "You had something to do with us surviving the bomb attack . . ."

Jimmy Jr. nodded his head. "For reasons you do not yet fully understand, our role in these latter days has become very limited. Yes, I saw the spy drop an electronic timing device into my father's pocket when he entered the Internal Affairs Building and I delayed the opening of the elevator door. But you must not assume further intervention after today. Each of you must fight the battle through your own integrity."

"What should we do?" Cindy asked.

"Have you forgotten the principles of spiritual warfare? Have you let every lesson from the past escape you?"

"Please, Jim," his father implored, "be more specific."

"Where is the *real* battleground?"

Cindy brightened. "In our hearts!"

"Exactly, child. You remember well. Fear and doubt are always the Enemy's initial weapons of war. Your lack of faith and courage are an invitation for attack. Once the door is open, the Devil will flog you with your own anxiety and hound you through your personal worries. The greatest threat has not been the dangers of the desert but your loss of confidence in the heavenly Father's ability to provide for you."

"What's the next step, Jim?"

"Your friend Sam instructed you well. Your journey must be bathed in prayer. You must continually seek the Holy Spirit's guidance. Whatever assistance I give is minor compared to the value of asking for the hand of God to guide you directly."

"Thank you, good friend," Cindy answered. "We've been fighting this war in our own strength."

"And none of you is big enough to spar with the Devil," the Immortal added. "Never forget that even in His crucifixion, Yeshua proved the weakness of God to be far more efficacious than the worst Evil could offer."

"So what should we do?" Isaiah asked.

"You are already on your knees," Jim Jr. observed. "Is not kneeling a posture of impotence? Can you think of a better place to begin to turn your weakness into strength?"

"Jim Junior," Cindy answered, "we shouldn't need you to remind us to pray. We won't make the same mistake again." She closed her eyes and bowed her head.

Ben began spontaneously, "O gracious Father, forgive us of our self-serving arrogance in trying to do everything in our own strength and not through your power . . ."

The group joined in the prayer and responded one by one. Conversational prayer moved back and forth in a gentle dialogue with the unseen Presence of life Himself. Finally, Ben closed with an "Amen."

"That was wonderful," Cindy stretched. "I already feel more energized. Jim . . . Jim Junior?"

"Where is that boy?" Jimmy jumped to his feet.

"He's gone!" Isaiah reached out into the empty space around him.

"But Jim Junior said he would get us out of here." Ben ran to the door. "Where'd he go?"

"He *said* we wouldn't be abandoned," Isaiah followed.

"Why would my boy come and then leave?" Jimmy asked.

"Look!" Cindy pointed through the door behind the shed. "There's a road! We have found a road out of this place."

"No," Ben said soberly. "We didn't find a road. God provided a way."

"Wendy," Ben spoke into his office portable phone, "I wanted you to know I'm back at my house now."

"Where have you been?" the secretary sounded irritated. "We've tried to locate you all over the world."

"I had to take a trip to sort things out."

"Let me call you on the hologram phone so we can speak more directly," Wendy Kohn answered.

Ben glanced around the room. Isaiah was slumped over

a chair sound asleep. Jimmy and Cindy sat next to him listening but they looked like they had been run over by an avalanche. "I don't think so." Ben glanced in the mirror. His white hair stuck out like a porcupine and dark circles lined his eyes. "It would take unnecessary time. Just tell me what's happening."

"You must have been on the other side of the pyramids not to have picked up on the fast-breaking news."

"Something of that order," Ben mumbled.

"Just after we last talked, the chairman of China, Fong, came on television and made a scathing attack on the central government. He declared Jerusalem had suppressed information on the outbreaks of an AIDS epidemic in Africa and America. Fong said this was only another sign of the impotence of our leadership. He called for a worldwide revolt against Yeshua."

"I see."

"Six hours later the president of the United States appeared on international television and confirmed Fong's discoveries about AIDS. Unlike AIDS in the twentieth century, this mutant develops full-blown AIDS in its victims shortly after they become HIV positive. He said the entire Los Angeles area was in an epidemic of the virus and Yeshua's leadership had failed his country." Wendy Kohn stopped and caught her breath. "I couldn't believe my ears. Apparently thousands of people are dying in the southern California region and people are rioting. The American president sounded frightened and off balance. He said he would no longer take directives from Jerusalem."

"Events are moving very fast." Ben was sober but not shaken.

"We've done everything possible to contact King David's office and the Immortals." She paused. "I hope you won't mind. We even used your name to ask for an audience directly with Yeshua."

"And nothing happened," Ben answered.

"Why . . . yes!" Wendy sputtered. "How did you know?"

"You will not be able to get any response from our leadership," Ben began speaking rapidly. "We are in a state of crisis and in a few hours the rest of the world will be plunged into addition turmoil."

"Are you serious?"

"Deadly," Ben shot back. "Listen to me carefully. Wendy, you are to immediately order maximum security around all offices. Yes, use my name to get action. You must be prepared for dangerous attacks and espionage. Anything is possible."

"Oh, my!" Wendy's voice faded.

"Things are going to get much, much worse before they get better but you are to show no signs of fear or panic. Be calm and stay in control until I arrive."

"Look," Wendy sounded apprehensive, "level with me. You obviously know more about what is going on than you're saying."

"Wendy, do you still have a Bible around?"

"Of course, but I haven't looked at it for a long time."

"I would suggest you start reading the Book of Revelation and praying a lot," Ben concluded. "You'd be surprised how much that will help. I'll be there as quickly as I can."

"I got the picture from just this side of the conversation," Jimmy said.

"My secretary was about to panic. I've got to get to the office immediately. Cindy, are you OK?"

"I'm tired but the short walk out of the wilderness to the road helped my stomach pains. Nothing a little rest and a couple of days won't cure. Who would have believed we were so close to the old highway?"

"You know, that old dump truck showed up very quickly after we got to the road," Jimmy observed. "In fact, I haven't seen one of those things around for years."

"I hate to wake Isaiah." Ben looked at his sleeping friend. "He may not be able to find out anything. On the other hand, I wouldn't have dreamed he could have made the other discoveries. Isaiah might come up with another breakthrough. Who wants to wake up the slumbering giant?"

Cindy laid her head on the table and closed her eyes.

"I was just leaving." Jimmy started toward the kitchen.

Ben shook his head. "You can wake up now, Cindy. I'll get Isaiah up before I leave."

Cindy opened one eye and smiled.

Ben took a quick look at the other numbers registered on his message recorder. Few people had access to the Feinbergs' private phone. He punched a separate button that deciphered each number, indicating the source. Most of the numbers were Wendy Kohn's repeated calls. A number near the end flashed an unexpected name. Ben looked a second time. The small display window read, "Rivka Zachary."

Ben hit the play button and the message began. "Dr. Feinberg, you may not remember me but I spoke to you some time ago when you lectured at Hebrew University. You said I might call if I needed your help." After a long pause, Rivka sounded like she was crying. "I have become very confused. I need your guidance badly. I know you are a very busy man. If you could ever spare a moment, I would be most grateful." The phone clicked off.

*How strange,* Ben thought. *I've got to get to the office.* He picked up a small electronic reminder and dictated her telephone number and name into the machine. *I'll call her as I fly down.*

"Good grief!" Ben spoke more to himself. "I don't have a shuttle anymore. My craft is a pile of junk out there in the wilderness. Esther Netanyahu will have to requisition me a new one immediately." He punched in her private phone number.

☐          ☐          ☐

Rajah Abu Sita listened intently in his planning room under the palace in New Babylon as Ziad Atrash spoke in Arabic on the hologram phone. He nodded but said little. "So, there is no question of at least ten more countries joining our alliance?" he finally asked.

"None," the Egyptian leader confirmed. "The reports keep pouring into our central office in Cairo. Our religious propaganda is having an extraordinary result. We've touched a nerve and our campaign is working. Fong's declaration certainly had its affect."

"And the explosive devices?" Abu Sita asked.

"All of the attacking nations are fully armed now. The military campaign is virtually ready to begin. I don't expect any more television appearances from those two old fools who popped up the last go around."

"Your men perfected the sabotage mechanisms?" the Assyrian leader asked.

"I have been able to infiltrate the Jerusalem area with selected spies who know how to use electronic and explosive devices," Ziad boasted. "The central government is totally unprepared for our attacks. The attack will come so quickly every Jew in sight will be totally demoralized."

"What about those two old jerks?"

"Before long I expect to receive an international communique mourning one or both of their deaths in an unexplained shuttlecraft crash. Just more evidence of the central government falling apart."

"How'd you do it?"

"A timing device hooked to an altimeter. When the shuttle gets high enough for a crash to be fatal, the craft will become unmanageable. Clever, no?"

"Excellent." Abu Sita shook his head whimsically. "Strange thing happening here with El Khader. He's really gotten into these meditations and believes he's the voice of Marduk all the time."

"Hmmm," Atrash mused. "What do you mean?"

"It's almost like El Khader is being swallowed by these seances and is losing touch with everyday reality," Rajah explained. "Occasionally, he will order me around as if he has become the supreme power."

"Cut him off at the knees," Ziad scowled. "Don't put up with his nonsense."

"The strange thing is that what he says is profound half the time. He has developed an uncanny knowledge of the future. He seems to read minds. The staff and the guards are afraid of him."

"What do you make of it?" Atrash asked.

"I don't know. I just don't know."

# 15

Ben paced back and forth across his office, firing off instructions with the explosive staccato of a machine gun while Wendy Kohn and Esther Netanyahu listened intently. The women periodically scribbled notes on their electronic notepads.

"Dr. Harrison," Wendy interrupted, "people in the government offices are looking to you for leadership. Since we no longer have access to the Immortals, people see you as the only source of dependable guidance. We need to send your instructions to every office in the entire government complex."

"I suppose so," Ben mumbled to himself. "I don't want to be in such a prominent role but perhaps . . ."

"Absolutely," Esther Netanyahu insisted. "You are the first person to make any sense of this information."

"Let me stress," Ben repeated his earlier dictation, "we must be keenly aware that the enemy is quite capable of using destructive devices on us and our offices. We must be prepared for a concentrated attack on Jerusalem."

"I will send out memos under your signature," Wendy answered.

A gray-haired man burst into the office. "Please turn on your telescreen," he requested nervously. "Several important communiques are being received."

Ben quickly pushed the buttons on the command module on his desk. The screen lowered and messages began appearing.

The United States, Mexico, Canada, and the Union of South Africa have declared, as of this day, their solidarity with the coalition identifying themselves as "The Restored Order" and are in the process of signing treaties of support and confederation. While military intentions have not been defined at this time, official statements imply defense agreements are imminent.

Ben shook his head. "Just what we anticipated. You can bet more bad news is on the way." He kept staring at the screen.

Ziad Atrash, president and supreme general of the sovereign state of Egypt, has demanded the central government in Jerusalem cease and desist from further intervention in the affairs of his and other nations. If this demand is not met within the next twenty-four hours, President Atrash will declare war on Yeshua.

A flashing red light at the bottom of the screen signaled the need to switch to the special security channel. Ben hit the control module. A number of symbols marched across the screen. Ben pushed the clicker again and the symbols became Hebrew. He read aloud, "The source of all pirated television interruptions has now been identified. The nefarious religious programming is produced and channeled from the tourist site called New Babylon, located in Assyria. In addition, some input seems to be coming from Jerusalem." Ben stared at the screen.

"What!" Wendy's mouth dropped. "Here in Jerusalem?"

"We have a most cunning enemy," Ben answered. "Anything is possible when one is dealing with the father of all lies."

Wendy rubbed her forehead nervously. "I'm terrified."

"No!" Ben snapped. "You mustn't be afraid. The enemy feeds on fear like fish feed on plankton. Faith in God is the most important weapon we have in this battle."

"Yes, sir," Wendy answered sheepishly.

"Esther, I want you to draw up a list of the nations opposing our government. Go back a year and start forward, arranging the nations by date of confrontation. We will be in a position to get a hard, cold look at who is leading this parade."

"Immediately." The secretary scribbled on her pad.

"Until someone who really knows what he is doing comes along," Ben said, "we will make this office a command post for defense of the city. Please send that order out at once."

"Sir," the white-haired aide interrupted, "I hesitate to give you this message at a time like this but we keep getting repeated urgent requests from a student at Hebrew University to speak with you."

"Rivka?" Ben asked. "Rivka Zachary?"

"Why, yes, exactly."

"Thank you." Ben nodded. "I meant to call her earlier, but I've been swamped. Just leave the number."

The secretaries and aide quickly left to return to their posts. Ben settled behind his desk and stared at Rivka's number. *Urgent? How strange.*

Rajah Abu Sita stood at the bottom of the steps in the Marduk Temple watching El Khader sway back and forth before the huge statue. The old man muttered sounds of

ecstasy and threw handfuls of incense into the huge brass
brazier at the top of the steps. Flames and great clouds of
smoke shot up toward the ceiling. The sweet smell of
frankincense saturated the air as the foglike clouds slowly
drifted down the stairs.

"I want to talk to you," Rajah demanded. "Come down
here at once!"

The secretary of state raised his bony arms over his head
and waved them back and forth mechanically. Low, guttural moans of ecstasy spilled out of his mouth.

"I said," Abu Sita yelled, "stop and come down here!"

El Khader turned slowly and stared contemptuously at
Rajah. The old man's bloodshot eyes were fiery red. His
disarrayed hair stuck out in every direction. Drool ran
down his matted beard. El Khader pointed at Rajah's face
and screamed, "Be gone, fool!"

"How dare you address *me*, your lord and master, in those
words! I am the ruler of Syria and Iraq!"

"I have but one master." The old man's voice crackled
with disdain. "I serve none but my Lord Marduk!" He again
shook his fist toward the ceiling.

"You're mad," Abu Sita shot back. "Psychotic."

"Would you call the divine voice of the gods crazy?" El
Khader rubbed his hands together. "You, a puny, conniving
little creature of the desert, accuse me, the divine expresser
of the mystery of the ages?"

Abu Sita stared half terrified, half entranced. He started
to take a step backward but checked himself. "Stop this
nonsense at once!"

"Stop? *Stop?*" El Khader laughed like a maniac. "No one
touched by the glory of Marduk can ever again settle for
the mundane. I will no longer be the servant of the likes of
you. I, El Khader, have been called by the gods to rule the
universe." He threw his head back and laughed like a wild
hyena.

"I'm going to call the guards." Rajah stepped back. "I will have you locked up."

El Khader slowly walked down the steps, pointing his finger straight in the face of the monarch. "None will touch me. My power is too great. Hear my prophecy!" He stopped on the bottom step and closed his eyes. "The armies shall gather from east and west like the vultures circling over corpses in the desert. Lightning will split the sky and blood will drip like the falling rain. As you battle over the bones of Yeshua's servants, I will again ascend to my rightful place on the throne of the heavens. None can stand in the way of omnipotent Evil!" The old man screamed aloud and ran out of the temple.

Rajah Abu Sita staggered backward and hurried after his mad secretary of state.

Isaiah Murphy's previous trip to Addis Ababa left him with a good working knowledge of the city. Once he cleared customs, Isaiah quickly left the airport and took a taxi shuttle into the heart of the city. He used his own portable phone to inform Hosni Gossos of his arrival. The Ethiopian sounded distant and evasive but agreed to meet him at a well-known downtown restaurant. Isaiah got out in front of the El Carbre.

For centuries the El Carbre had been an internationally known nightspot in the center of Addis Ababa. The restaurant's interior was decorated in African motifs, including stuffed lions and cheetahs. Famous people often conducted business there. The setting seemed an excellent place to make what would appear as casual contact. Thirty minutes later, Hosni arrived.

"Good to see you, old friend." Isaiah stood and offered his hand.

"Sorry, I can't say the same." Hosni quickly settled into the chair opposite Isaiah. "You shouldn't have come back."

Isaiah studied the black man across from him. Hosni looked tired and nervous. His gaze kept shifting across the room. "You look worried," Isaiah concluded.

"Are you sure you weren't followed?"

"Not a chance," Isaiah answered. "I came here straight from the airport. Tell me what's happened."

Gossos leaned across the table and whispered. "Don't you understand? The world is about to be plunged into war. The carefree attitude you see in this place is a facade. You've come to the center of the tornado."

"Look, Hosni. I need more specific information on what's ahead. We can't sit idly by and let mayhem be loosened on the world without doing our best to stop this avalanche of terror. You've got to help me."

"What exactly do you want?"

"Hosni, I need to know dates, times, places. When is the attack going to happen?" Isaiah cupped his hand over his mouth. "I need to have a more complete picture of the explosives being manufactured to get some sense of how this war might be fought."

"The last time you were here your presence was observed. Everyone is being watched. Directional microphones may even be picking up this conversation right now."

"What about your house? Wouldn't we be safe there?"

"Only if *you* weren't observed entering."

"Got any ideas?"

Gossos looked around the restaurant carefully. "In just a minute I will leave the entry card for my solar car on the table. It's parked just across the street, a big green eight-passenger job. Once inside, push 1 on the computer to lock you into the electrical guide wires under the street. Once you get moving, lie down in the seat. The automatic guidance system will drive you straight to my house and into the garage. Anyone seeing the vehicle enter the garage will just assume the car's been out on courier service. I'll get home another way."

"I'm putting you into jeopardy," Isaiah concluded. "We can call the whole thing off right now, and I'll go back to the telaport."

"Too late." Hosni shook his head. "Since you're here we might as well do everything possible to stop the madness breaking out around us." He slipped a small rectangular card onto the table. "I'm going to leave now. Give me ten minutes lead." He quickly got up and hurried toward the front door.

When the waiter returned, Isaiah explained that his friend had become ill. In light of the problem, Isaiah excused himself and left the astonished waiter staring.

The sleek solar-powered car was exactly where Gossos said it would be. Isaiah slipped the card in the slot on the side. The side of the vehicle raised straight up and Isaiah slipped inside. Because accidents were virtually impossible with both the internal guidance system and the traffic-controlled computerized response, the car's body was made of a very light alloy, allowing it to reach one hundred miles an hour in seconds. Isaiah slipped the card into the dashboard and the computer lights lit up. When he pushed the 1 button, the steering mechanism receded into the control panel and the side door dropped and locked into place as the silent engine effortlessly propelled the car forward. In a matter of seconds, the car swung into the express lane shooting through downtown at speeds between 80 and 90 miles per hour. He was soon traveling quickly through the suburbs. He slipped down into the seat and stretched out his long frame.

After several minutes, the solar car slowed down and began turning corners at more modest rates of speed.

Overhead, a mechanical voice advised the garage door was now open and the journey would be completed in twenty seconds. Before Isaiah could decide what to do, the car stopped as effortlessly and silently as it started. The garage door closed and the side door raised automatically.

"I'm never quite prepared for these automated gadgets," Isaiah said to himself as he got out of the car. "Just too confounding for an old codger like me."

"Come on in," Hosni called from an open door. "I just got here."

Isaiah followed his friend down the dim corridor into Gossos's living room.

"Sorry to be so blunt at the restaurant." Hosni pointed to a chair. "But I'm very concerned. People have gone stark raving nuts and you never know who is a government agent." He sat down across from Isaiah. "Everything is starting to feel like those ancient films of the Nazis taking over Berlin. Remember those old spy thrillers?

"I try to practice the faith I know I should have but I'm terrified most of the time. I don't think you realize how serious these matters are."

"Oh, I s-u-r-e do now." Isaiah rubbed his white curly hair. "Yes sir-e-e-e. I am a believer."

Hosni looked intensely into his friend's eyes. "We are just days away from the beginning of hostilities. As best I can tell, Tammuz 17 is the date troops start to march toward Jerusalem. Martial arts experts will be mixed in with armed soldiers. The final assault begins on Av 9."

"I see," Isaiah said slowly. "I'm not surprised."

"In the last few weeks, old manuals on how to make a wide assortment of bombs surfaced. I really fear what's ahead. The devices are primitive but effective."

"Give me some examples," Isaiah asked.

"Mercury fulminate crystals will explode by either shock or heat. They can be used by themselves or with other substances to cause explosions. Large quantities of nitric acid, sodium bicarbonate, and glycerine are being turned into nitroglycerine. Oxidizable materials are being treated with perchloric acid to make low-order explosives. Some of these materials will create sufficient shock waves to set off larger amounts of tri-nitro-toluene, TNT. Getting the picture?"

"Yes, rather clearly." Isaiah's eyes widened. "Anything else?"

"Anfos are being developed on a large scale basis," Gossos continued. "That's an old acronym for ammonium nitrate plus fuel oil solution. The whole thing has to be detonated but it makes quite a boom. Same result is possible by mixing potassium chlorate with Vaseline."

"I discovered the shipment of these chemicals weeks ago. That's how I got into the whole business." Isaiah scratched his head. "I didn't know that much about explosives then but I figured something big was coming down."

"Ever hear of nitrogen trichloride?" Gossos asked. "It's an oily yellow liquid that explodes when heated above 60 degrees celsius or ignited by a spark. Summer's a great time to use the stuff."

"I suppose they have developed delays and delay fuses?"

"Yes," Hosni said slowly, "but the plan is for straight-forward assault tactics. There won't be many delays on any front."

"Is there anything else I should know?"

"One other thing would be very important . . ."

Suddenly the front door shattered. Splinters of wood flew in every direction. Three men broke into the room. Isaiah leaped to his feet, but the first man whirled around and smashed his shoe against the side of Isaiah's head. The black man flew backward, slamming into the wall and then bouncing face down onto the floor.

The other two intruders grabbed Hosni and slung him

against the opposite wall. The attackers pinned Gossos's head against the wall.

"You vile traitor!" the larger of the two thugs hissed in Gossos's ear. "Did you think you had tricked the government?" He brought his elbow down sharply into Hosni's solar plexus, doubling him in pain.

The second man pulled Hosni back up against the wall. "No longer will the likes of you be tolerated!" With one powerful blow he smashed the black man in the mouth, knocking him senseless.

Isaiah didn't move or open his eyes, but he could hear faintly.

"Sure the delay fuse is set right?" one of the men asked. A different voice answered, "This crazy thing is no different from the timer on a VCR." Another man grumbled, "Don't distract me." The first man insisted, "I still think we should have used a lightbulb bomb and turned all the lights out. They would have eventually destroyed themselves." The third man barked, "Shut up and hook these wires together. We've got four minutes before this house blows." The three men ran through the open door.

Isaiah tried to push himself up on his knees. He quickly saw the explosive device was locked in a box snapped shut as the assailants left. Hosni was slumped on the floor in a heap. As quickly as possible, Isaiah crawled to the side of his friend.

Gossos was totally unconscious. Isaiah pulled Hosni's arm over his shoulder but he could barely budge his friend. "I don't think I can get him out of here in time," he moaned.

Isaiah's stomach churned and his vision kept blurring. The blow to his head caused him to fade in and out. Inhaling as deeply as possible, he pulled Hosni behind him out of the living room. Precious seconds ticked away as he strained with everything left in him.

☐　　　☐　　　☐

Ben quickly surveyed the list Esther Netanyahu just handed him. "I would conclude the Chinese are right at the front of this rebellion. The core of the coalition seems to be composed of Ethiopia, Iran, Jordan, Syria, Iraq, Egypt, and Russia. Looks like France and Italy are key players, too." Ben looked up at his secretary. "Who would you guess is the leader of the pack?"

"Egypt," Esther answered immediately. "From all of his statements, Ziad Atrash sounds like he's the mastermind."

"What do we *really* know of this man?"

"Anticipated your question." Esther smiled and pointed to the control module. "I have programmed in a great deal of information on the leader of the Egyptians."

"Excellent." Ben brought the screen up to full operation.

Instantly biographical data detailing the educational and political development of the Egyptian president streamed before their eyes.

"You've got just about everything down to the size of his underwear," Ben noted. "Job well done."

"If I might be presumptuous," the secretary added, "I would suggest we scroll down to a special section on his psychological development."

"Oh?" Ben hit the clicker several times. "What have you learned?"

"Stop on page 62," Esther instructed.

Ben ran the report forward. He read with rapt interest.

Yeshua saw great promise for Ziad Atrash because of his unusual physical capacities and bright mind. However, the young man had to overcome the severe limitations of dyslexia. His early failures in school created a fiercely competitive personality and profoundly deep need to prove his worth by exceeding his contemporaries. One must be aware of the unpredictable aspects of Atrash's personality. He can be quite deceptive and deceitful when threatened.

"Could we be running for our lives because this guy couldn't get his act together?" Ben asked.

"Certainly looks like it, chief."

Ben read the rest of the report.

> Atrash was given the spiritual task of transforming his deceptive tendencies into spiritual integrity and honesty. However, he often lost interest in the demands of spiritual direction and retreated from the discipline of bringing his thought life captive to moral definition. One must always be aware that Atrash has large reservoirs of hostility. His anger can be explosive and destructive, making him treacherous when threatened. If he develops the necessary character traits to compensate for these problems, Ziad could make an exceptional national ruler

"Says it all," Ben observed. "Not a pretty picture."

"Apparently, Atrash flunked the psychological exam. At least, we know something about what makes our enemy tick."

"Yes," Ben thought outloud. "We are faced with a very angry adversary who will stop at nothing to get his way. Obviously, a pawn of Satan's now."

Once Isaiah had pulled his friend into the garage, he was relieved to see the side of the car was still up. The computer card stuck out of the dash board.

*If I can get Hosni in the vehicle,* Isaiah thought, *maybe I can drop the doors and we'll have some protection against the blast.*

Isaiah pushed Gossos into the backseat and pulled himself into the driver's seat. He pushed the computer card deeply into the slot. The sides of the car dropped at once and the computer came on. Isaiah stared at the numbers without any idea what to hit.

"The 1 button got me here," he muttered. "Surely the 2 will take me somewhere else. What have I got to loose?"

He hit the switch. Instantly the garage door opened and the car went backward down the driveway into the street. The vehicle whirled around and started down the street.

"Thank you, Lord!" Ben said aloud.

Suddenly the car was rocked by a shock wave followed by a roaring boom. Isaiah hit the windshield and bounced back into the seat. The solar vehicle jerked to a stop for a moment and then started up again, speeding away. When Isaiah looked out the back window, he could see a nasty cloud of black smoke rising above the roof of Gossos's house.

"Where am I?" the voice in the back seat asked. "How did I get here?"

"It's a long story." Isaiah slumped. "The real question is where in the world are we going?"

The solar car swung wildly through the suburbs of Addis Ababa. Isaiah watched, trying to digest emotionally what had just transpired. Hosni sat up in the seat and held his swollen jaw.

"We'd best get you to the telaport and out of the country," Hosni finally said. "Our only hope is to put you on the next flight before they discover you're still alive."

"Who are *they*?"

"Government officials. No one else would have the explosives to blow up a house. You got a taste of what's coming to Jerusalem."

"You will have to go with me," Isaiah concluded. "They will be after you too."

"No." Hosni shook his head. "I belong in my own land. Who knows? I may yet prove to be of some help in the struggle ahead. I can hide out in the mountain country for the time being."

"I wish you'd go with me."

"Believe me, the offer is tempting. But I have family responsibilities here." Hosni looked around at the buildings flying past. "We're far enough away from the house to start back to the telaport. Punch in 6 and we'll be there in a few minutes."

The vehicle swung to the left and shifted into high, nearly flying at an oblique angle from the direction they had been going. "Hosni, you started to tell me one other important secret just as the assailants broke in. Remember?"

Gossos rubbed his jaw and blinked his eyes. "Nothing is coming back. My mind still feels like mush."

"Think hard."

The telaport loomed ahead. The solar car automatically turned toward the departure gates and slowed. Isaiah adjusted his clothes so they would not look so rumpled and prepared to leap out.

As the car pulled to a stop, Hosni reached for his friend's shoulder. "Now I remember. I don't know the details, but Jerusalem is vulnerable to sabotage from within. As hard as it is to believe, you have a traitor in your midst."

# 16

On July 15, the nine leaders of the coalition against Israel assembled at the Red Sea command center outside of Cairo. The blistering sun was intolerable, the air was unbearably dry. The traditional dress of the past had been replaced by general's uniforms and military attire. Even Maria Marchino looked like a battle commander. Aides and assistants hurried in and out of the central conference room. Atrash's command center was fully operational with the satellite transmission capability completed.

President Ziad Atrash convened the meeting at noon to give all leaders ample time to arrive. Each of the heads of state gave brief reports of the readiness of their troops. The next item on the agenda was a survey of efforts to bring every possible nation into the political alliance.

"I have firm commitments from the United Kingdom and America," Maria Marchino reported. "New countries include Canada and Mexico. I have established direct connections with the Scandinavians including Norway and Sweden."

Fong rose to his feet. "We now have mutual defense

treaties with Japan, Korea, Indonesia, and India. Each country has agreed to commit troops in the event of unexpected counterattack."

"The African nations are firmly with us," Ali of Ethiopia reported. "Five new countries will stand behind us."

"Excellent!" Atrash shook his fist in the air. "The world is moving with us."

"You must appreciate," Marchino interjected, "that we have political commitments that do not necessarily reflect the consensus of the national populations. No one is sure exactly where the sentiments of the people are."

"When you've got the power and the control, plebiscites don't matter," Atrash snapped. "Bombs and bullets make the difference."

"We simply must be aware many people are still firmly committed to Yeshua," the Italian leader countered. "No one knows how significant the impact of their faith may be."

Ziad shrugged indifferently. "Come the night of Av 9, the world will be in the palm of our hands. That *fact* will change their minds."

Abu Sita rose to his feet. "We have divine assurance of victory. The gods have spoken in our midst."

Claudine Toulouse looked at Maria and rolled her eyes. Fong and Chardoff exchanged brief glances before turning their heads. The room became silent.

Abu Sita cleared his throat. "We continue to receive divine encouragement. In fact, Marduk has spoken of a great cosmic battle. . . ."

"Is it true your secretary of state is now completely insane?" the French leader broke in.

"El Khader . . . is . . . has been profoundly affected by his meditations," Rajah explained hesitantly. "The effect of such seances has occasionally been overpowering . . . but . . ."

"I hear he's gone stark raving nuts," Chardoff asserted bluntly.

"Unfortunately, he could not attend this meeting," Rajah spoke rapidly. "If he were here you would be reassured."

Leaders looked back and forward around the room but no one spoke.

"Let us move on to the review of our battle plan." Ziad beamed a laser pointer at the maps overhead. For the next five minutes, Atrash carefully detailed the attack plans, tracing the convergence of armies toward the Israeli border. The march of Chinese troops across Kazakhstan and Iran was complete. Soldiers were poised to link up with the Assyrians in their drive into Israel. Jordan and Iran were ready for a similar merger. Russian soldiers were massed for a quick sweep through Turkey into Assyria to join the Chinese. Atrash concluded, "Gentlemen, we are ready to begin the final overthrow of the central government."

Claudine Toulouse arose and pointed at the map of Europe. "You, *gentlemen,* will be glad to know that the joint command of Europe is poised for shuttle craft transport of troops leaving from Rome and Marseille simultaneously."

"Joint command?" Atrash interrupted. "We operate from one consolidated supreme command center in Cairo."

"With all due respect." Maria Marchino stood. "The European forces allied with us are organized under a sub-command to ensure absolute synchronization of timing."

"Such intervention is clumsy and unnecessary," the Egyptian barked. "*We* will maintain complete control from this base."

"Should our plans be intercepted," Marchino continued with cool detachment, "the European joint command will ensure continuity. No one knows for sure how the Immortals might intervene."

"No!" Ziad crossed his arms over his chest. "The battle

command must remain consolidated under my . . . er . . . our central control."

"Just a moment," Chardoff spoke out, "the women have a point. We should take every necessary precaution. I believe the Russians and Chinese must have a similar system as a secondary security check. We will operate as the Europeans do."

"No!" Atrash's voice rose even louder. "We must not fragment control or we expose ourselves to misunderstanding, inner divisions."

"I object!" Rajah Abu Sita waved a hand in the air. "We must stay with the basis on which the attack has already been defined."

"Why?" Claudine Toulouse shrugged. "Are you afraid of a better idea?"

"Women bother you?" Maria asked sardonically.

Atrash's bull neck turned deep red and the veins on his temple protruded. "Stop this distraction at once!" he bellowed.

"Don't try to intimidate me," Claudine snapped. "I'm not impressed by your macho charades."

"Women know *nothing* of war," Abu Sita hissed. "Shut up and listen to the experts."

"Experts?" Claudine laughed. "Not one of you chauvinists has even seen a battle much less fought in one. We know as much about warfare as any of you."

Suddenly the conference exploded in an uproar of cat calls and shouting. "Give her a broom to fight with," someone yelled. "I am in charge," Ziad bellowed back. "Arrogant chauvinist," a feminine voice hissed. Fong stomped his foot and asserted, "We will not be ignored." For ten minutes leaders screamed at each other like angry children.

"All right, all right," Atrash held up his hand in concession. "We can't go forward without total unity. I concede to the demands for an intermediate level command system." His face was red and he was trembling. "Abu Sita will now review the readiness of troops in his region." Ziad slid down in his chair, trying to regain composure.

The Assyrian leader carefully traced proposed battlefield lines and reviewed how the final march would begin. The rest of the afternoon was spent in fine tuning the strategy. Once consensus was achieved, the master plan was approved and the timetable for launching the invasion was complete. The coalition broke to prepare for supper.

Atrash pulled Rajah aside. "I don't like this sudden intervention of those two whining sows. During the first meetings, they said nothing!"

Abu Sita shrugged. "They're not smart enough to make much difference. Blow them off."

"I still don't like it."

"Who would listen to them once the war gets started?"

Ziad rubbed his chin. "Of course, we can always send them only the information we choose to release. Such a tactic would render their intermediate command useless."

Abu Sita leered cynically. "I knew you'd find a way to sack those old bags." He shifted to the other foot. "You did not mention the terrorist attack on the government buildings."

"Only the Ethiopians are aware of the broad guidelines of this plot. Even Ali doesn't know the details. You and I must have some secrets no one else knows, Rajah. The unexpected assures we stay in control. I don't trust these people."

At the same moment, the prime minister of Russia was slipping into Fong's room. The Chinese head of state pointed at the ceiling and shook his head. "Never know who is listening."

Alexi Chardoff knocked and winked. "We must discuss this 'new' intermediate command idea further."

"Everything is already in place." Fong's voice was flat, without emotion. "We could implement the approach immediately by using secondary means of communication."

"I would assume the other Asians will find this connection reassuring."

"Very," Fong answered.

Chardoff scribbled in Russian on his computer note pad, pushed the translation button, and the message appeared in Chinese. Fong read, "Once Jerusalem falls we will be in position to counter-attack the Arabs immediately."

"My friends are ready to move," Fong said solemnly.

Down the hall Claudine Toulouse quickly slipped past the guards at the end of the opposite corridor and hurried toward the suite at the far end. She didn't hesitate at the door but entered immediately.

Khalil Hussein was standing by the bar in the center of the room, wearing a bathrobe. For a moment he looked surprised when Claudine entered without knocking.

"I thought knocking would be too conspicuous." Claudine stood pensively by the closed door.

The king set the glass down and looked intensely at her. "Of course," he said. "Of course."

"Matters got a little tense today." Claudine took several steps forward. "I thought we might have a little talk about where we are."

"You want to talk politics?" Hussein let the robe slip open. He was only wearing a swimming suit underneath.

"Not really." Claudine stared at his hairy chest. Each time she meditated as Abu Sita instructed, the primitive urges became stronger. Suddenly, the power of raw lust surged through her veins. "I thought we might relax," Hussein suggested.

"I didn't bring a suit."

"Do you need one?" Hussein's question sounded innocuous, almost misleadingly innocent.

Claudine smiled but suddenly wasn't sure how to respond. Khalil was living up to his reputation for not committing himself. His face appeared quite passive. Claudine took a deep breath. "I want you." The words rushed out of her mouth.

"I'm not into sex," the king's voice was flat, emotionless. "Power is my game."

Claudine flinched and her face flushed. The words stung. She felt very old.

The king tossed the bathrobe aside. "Power is my aphrodisiac," the king continued. "Nothing turns me on like a touch of strength." He extended his hand. "That's why I find you so incredibly appealing. You feel like the most powerful woman I've ever known. I saw that capacity in you the first time we were in the same room."

Claudine swallowed hard and blinked, stunned.

"I see I've caught you off guard now." Khalil laughed uncharacteristically. "I love it when a woman is overwhelmed by me." He pulled her forward. "Particularly a powerful woman." Before Claudine could speak, the Jordanian king swept her into his arms and kissed her forcefully on the mouth. She knew the blood was rushing to her head and felt lightheaded. Claudine could barely breathe. The moment was beyond her wildest expectations.

Khalil let Claudine gently slip from his embrace, breathing on her face. "Now . . . who's in control?" He laughed.

Wendy Kohn buzzed Ben's office. "Dr. Feinberg, you have an urgent call from Isaiah Murphy. He says time is of the essence. Do you want to take it on your hologram phone?"

"Yes," Ben spoke into his wristwatch intercom phone.

"But we must lock in top security. I don't want this call monitored."

"Everything will be ready when you are." Wendy clicked off.

Ben immediately switched to the new hologram equipment. In moments Isaiah materialized in front of his desk. The third dimension image was so clear and sharp, Isaiah appeared to be present in the room. "Welcome back to Jerusalem," Ben joked.

"I must talk quickly," Isaiah sounded nervous. "We won't have much time."

"Where are you?" Ben's demeanor changed.

"I must not disclose my location," Isaiah spoke rapidly. "Suffice it to say I was identified in the Addis Ababa airport and had to flee before I got a flight out. I'm hiding out in the country."

"What can I do to help you?" Ben began reaching for computer and switch buttons.

"Record what I'm about to say. Jerusalem's government buildings are going to be bombed. The explosive materials are rather primitive but the detonating devices have all the electronic sophistication of today's technology. Watch out for anything unexpected that comes in large quantities."

"What should we do?"

"Expect the terrorists to attack sometime between Tammuz 17 and Av 9. They want to cripple you before the final assault on Av 9." Isaiah slowed down and spoke very deliberately. "Remember. Most of these bombs can be detonated either by heat or electric charge. The devices will not be particularly stable."

"We will be ready."

Isaiah's voice became more intense. "I don't know if you can protect yourselves. You have a traitor in your midst. I can't find out but some Jew will turn Judas. You won't have any way of knowing this person is lying."

"I am going to send a shuttle in to rescue you, Isaiah. You mustn't continue to be exposed to danger."

"Hosni's got to come out as well if I can locate him."

"Since I can't call you, contact me in exactly twenty-four hours and I'll have a plan ready."

"I'll do my best." Isaiah clicked off.

"Wendy," Ben yelled into his wristwatch phone, "get in here. Get Jimmy on the phone. He'll know about transportation. Get me a security person over here on the double."

"Of course, of course," the secretary answered. "Remember the appointment you made yesterday? Do you want me to reschedule the girl?"

"Rivka? I forgot about her." Ben thought for a moment. "No, don't send her away. I'll call Harrison myself and then talk to her."

For the next five minutes, Ben laid out plans for a special shuttle to deploy inside Ethiopia to pick up Isaiah. Jimmy agreed to find a pilot quickly to make the secret trip and took over the mission to rescue their friend. With that problem out of the way, Ben was ready to talk to Rivka Zachary.

The young woman hurried into his office. The black-haired beauty looked troubled and nervous. "Thank you for working me into your busy schedule, Dr. Feinberg." She awkwardly wrung her hands.

Ben pointed to a chair in front of his desk and sat down. He studied Rivka carefully. She was smaller than he remembered but certainly had the Zachary family eyes. "My assistants said you knew something about security problems," he came straight to the point.

"Y-e-s," Rivka pulled at her handkerchief. "I'm afraid ..." her voice trailed away. "I've made a very big mistake." She began to cry.

"Please go on," Ben urged.

"Perhaps you remember Zvilli Zemah?" Rivka sniffed.

"No," Ben shook his head.

"When you lectured at the university, Zvilli heckled you."

"Oh yes," Ben nodded. "A rather arrogant student as I recall."

"He's both a student and a lecturer. Please understand." Rivka bit her lip. "I don't know how I ever got into this mess. I really have always been a good person."

Ben stared, trying to understand.

"You see . . . Zvilli was fascinating, very attractive. He is a very brilliant man, you know. I suppose I was just too immature."

"What are you suggesting, Rivka?"

"I was swept off my feet. He was so self-assured."

Ben crossed his arms over his chest and pulled at his beard. "Why are you telling me this story? Shouldn't you be talking with a religious counselor?"

"Oh, Dr. Feinberg. My family has always spoken so highly of you. I just knew I could trust you."

"You can."

"Then you must know what is being planned."

"Planned?"

"Because Zvilli and I became . . . involved . . . he was able to recruit me to be part of a plot to attack the government. Terrible things are underway." Rivka began to speak more rapidly, "People will be killed, property will be destroyed. I'm terrified that I am caught in the middle of the whole crazy thing."

Ben leaned forward, his eyes intense. "Tell me exactly what this Zvilli is up to."

"I'm not sure, but he seems to be an Arab agent in charge of sabotage in this city. He wants me to help him blow up buildings." Rivka began crying again.

Ben got up and walked around his desk. "I must ask you once more. Why are you telling me this information?"

"I can't go through with these terrible plans, no matter how I've come to feel about Zvilli. I don't want to hurt him, but I can't be part of destroying anyone else. I must stop this horrible plan."

"You want me to help you get away from him?"

"Well . . . no . . . I really want to keep him from doing something violent. And I don't want to be part of any diabolical scheme."

"You are willing to work with me and do what I tell you?"

"Yes, Dr. Feinberg. Yes, I'll do anything to make things right."

"Will you tell the date, time, and place of the first attack?"

"Of course," Rivka pleaded. "I will tell you everything you want to know."

Ben stared at her. *What a perfect way to set me up*, he thought. *She gets my sympathy and sucks me into this plot up to my eyeballs.* Ben bit his lip and looked carefully at her pleading eyes. *What a perfect traitor this descendent of Dr. Zachary makes. Like Judas, she can betray her friend with a kiss. They must think I am a complete fool.*

"The attack is set for tomorrow morning, Tammuz 17," Rivka began. "All I know is that the first bombing will occur in this building. Dr. Feinberg, you might be able to stop the disaster if you are here."

Ben put his hand on her shoulder. "Rivka, how do I know you are telling me the truth?"

As the sun set over New Babylon, Rajah Abu Sita stood in the Temple of Marduk, watching his secretary of state performing rituals before the giant statue of the god. The Syrian king slowly walked up the steps to get closer to El Khader to observe him more closely. At the back of the Temple, guards lurked behind the pillars.

El Khader wore the ancient robes of the Babylonian priests with the domed hat perched above his white hair. He moved back and forth from the statue to the bronze brazier throwing handfuls of incense into the fire. The old man stopped periodically and lifted his hands above his head making unintelligible incantations. The huge sleeves of the robe fell down past his elbows.

Rajah stopped on the top step, only feet away from El Khader and watched carefully. For all of his complaints, Abu Sita had great affection for this strange man. He had been a family friend forever, one of the faces Rajah remembered from his childhood. In fact, El Khader had been an adviser to Rajah's father during the years he was king. Abu Sita could not allow harm to come to the old man.

El Khader lowered his hands and turned toward the head of state. His eyes were bloodshot and his vision unfocused. Even though he looked at Rajah, there was no recognition. The secretary of state kept on turning toward the brazier with slow, mechanical, zombie-like movements.

"El Khader," Rajah commanded sharply. "Speak to me."

Saying nothing, the secretary of state dropped more incense into the flaming brazier. The smoke bellowed up into his face, but El Khader did not flinch.

Abu Sita ran his hands nervously through his hair and crossed his arms over his chest. For several moments, he paced back and forth while the prayers continued. Finally he reached out and gently touched the old man's shoulder. "Please just speak to me," he said quietly.

El Khader turned slowly and blinked several times. "I must be about my work. My Lord commands I serve him day and night."

"I am your master, your king," Rajah spoke compassionately, "not this statue."

"No," the old man drawled, "not anymore. My thoughts

have been taken captive by him who is the Lord of the underworld."

"Please," Rajah begged, "you are not well. The strain of these meditations has overtaken you."

El Khader looked puzzled and nodded knowingly.

"I don't know what's happened, but this thing has gotten way out of control. Something has gone wrong."

"Do not doubt what you see. We have come to the greater truth."

"Please." Rajah held up his hands in supplication. "You must let me help you. You need rest, medication, treatment."

"Yes . . . I . . . do," El Khader spoke more coherently. "But all of that must come later. Now is the time for you, too, to worship the great Marduk. The final battle is about to begin, and our praise makes the lord of the dark world stronger. We must call the peoples of the world to adore our god as he goes forth tomorrow into this final battle in the heavenlies."

"No." Rajah shook his head. "You have been swallowed by this thing I've started. I want it stopped."

"Far too late." El Khader's voice seemed to come from some other place. "Far, far too late now."

"I will help you." The Syrian king took El Khader's arm and gently pulled him back from the statue.

The old man jerked away with extraordinary strength. "No!" El Khader's voice dropped to a threatening guttural sound. "I will help you! Beware! All is not as it appears. The spirits send you their warning. *You* are being betrayed."

"What?" Rajah's eyes widened.

"Our plans are in jeopardy!" For a moment the old man sounded coherent.

Abu Sita shook his head as if trying to clear his mind. "Please repeat what you said."

El Khader took a deep breath and opened his mouth. Suddenly his body convulsed. He swallowed hard and grabbed his chest. His eyes rolled back in their sockets; the color drained from his face. The old man slowly sank to the floor. Like the final spark in a burned-out ember turning to smoke, his life ebbed away.

# CHAPTER

# 17

As the sun rose over the desert on the morning of Tammuz 17, Ziad Atrash moved into place at his Red Sea command post. During the night every system had been tested and retested for instant communication. Television monitors flashed images of troop convergence, recording every detail of the historic linkup.

Not far away at a reconstructed shrine erected before the pyramid of Cheops, priests of Osiris performed the ancient rites of the pharaohs. At Lexor in the Valley of the Kings, other priests had begun the same rituals, calling on the gods to arise and lead Egypt to the glory of the past.

The Russian and Chinese troops completed their double-time march across the Caucasus Mountains through Georgia and swept down into Azerbaijan. The combined armies were poised on the Iranian border at Zhdanovsk. Iran and Jordan were linking up with the Syrian army in the desert at Ar Rutbah. Near this town, Cyrus had defeated Belshazzar at Opis in 539 B.C., fulfilling the prophecy Daniel deciphered from the palace wall: *mene, mene, tekel, parsin*. Each army moved into place with precision.

The European television monitor flashed pictures of French troops loading at the Paris International Telaport. At the same time Italian troops marched across the runways toward large shuttles waiting for them to board.

*Everything is unfolding according to plan,* Ziad said to himself. *The rest of my scheme should be taking shape in just a few hours.*

At 9:30 A.M. Rivka Zachary left her apartment and walked through the back streets of Jerusalem. The rest of the city was relatively quiet as citizens observed the religious holiday.

The 17th of Tammuz had been a significant day of mourning throughout the history of Israel. Jews traditionally stayed in their homes and reflected on the past. Just as the prophet Zechariah predicted thousands of years earlier, the holy day was still observed in the millennial kingdom. Even though all days of fasting had become feasts during the reign of Yeshua, the occasion retained a grave and serious character. Moses broke the first tablets of the Law on this day because of the rebellion of the Israelites. In 587 B.C., the Babylonians broke through the walls of Jerusalem on this date. Twenty-one days later, they destroyed the Temple on Av 9. History repeated itself in A.D. 70. The Roman General Titus catapulted large stones into Jerusalem, killing many priests and stopping all temple sacrifices on the 17th of Tammuz. Again, twenty-one days later, on Av 9, the second temple was destroyed. The remembrance of the date could not but cause sober reflection.

At 10:00 A.M. Rivka Zachary arrived at a warehouse three blocks from Zvilli Zemah's apartment. Rivka shut the door quietly behind her and looked around the large room. A very dilapidated solar-powered van was parked in the center near the work area. Zemah was already at work, poring over a small box on a long mechanic's bench. Bottles of acid, strands of wire, and empty boxes littered the table.

"Ah, my love! You are here." Zemah laid down a wrench and opened his arms. "Come to me."

Rivka hurried across the cement floor and opened her arms. The white-haired man kissed her passionately.

"Today's the big day." Zvilli pulled her toward the table. "We are almost ready to leave as soon as the other men arrive."

"Other men?" Rivka jumped. "You never mentioned others."

"Didn't want you to have information that could put you in jeopardy." Zvilli pushed two small wires into place in the box and snapped the lid shut. "Three helpers are coming in from Egypt."

"Oh, no!" Rivka held her face with both hands. "I wanted to be just with you."

"Don't worry, darling. They don't know you either."

"Zvilli . . ." Rivka pulled on his arm. "This whole thing has gotten completely out of hand, we must—"

Zemah gripped her arm firmly. "We are fulfilling our destiny. Be who you are."

"We still have time to turn back."

"What?" Zvilli shook her slightly. "Don't say such a thing."

Suddenly the front door opened again and three large men hurried inside.

"You're here," Zvilli called out. "Good. Let's load. The battle is about to begin."

"In that thing?" One of the men pointed to the solar-powered van and grumbled, "Where'd you get that dinosaur?"

"We will use the engine to help detonate the Anfos mix in the back," Zemah explained. "Plus, the shape is just right. Your boss assured me this is how terrorists operated in the 'good ole days.' So few people will be out on the streets, the old crate won't make much difference today."

Rivka watched in bewilderment as the men silently went to work. They obviously knew exactly what to do.

After a couple of minutes Zvilli said firmly, "Get in the van and don't talk. I don't want anyone to be distracted. The time has come to act."

"But—" Rivka reached out, but the driver revved up the engine and the van drowned out her voice.

No one was on the streets as the rickety old van lumbered slowly toward the Knesset. The distance was short and the trip did not take long.

"Turn left," Zemah grunted to the Egyptian driver. "We're not far from the Knesset. Just keep a nice slow pace."

"Zvilli..." Rivka reached over the seat and put her hand on his shoulder. "I need to tell you—"

"Don't talk," Zemah snapped. His entire demeanor had changed during the trip from the warehouse. His eyes were cold and black.

"Circle around to the back and pull up in front of the Internal Affairs building," Zemah spoke rapidly. "We will park between it and the Knesset. When the van explodes, we can hit both buildings."

The driver pulled off the main thoroughfare and headed up the street between the two government office complexes. He slowed, pulled toward the empty curb, and shut the engine off.

Zemah turned around in his seat. "We're going to take care of some unfinished business for my friends before we set off the big firecracker in back. The last blast didn't accomplish what was intended and our leaders weren't happy. This time I will personally make certain we don't have any slip-ups. To make sure the Internal Affairs building is out of commission, we will wire it first before we explode the van."

"Okay. What's first?" the driver asked.

"Get those pyrotechnic bombs out," Zemah instructed. "I want all of us out of the van. We will plant bombs on several floors. We need to get these explosives in place quickly."

One of the Arabs opened the side panel of the van while another hooked wires from the engine to wires leading out of the piles of explosives in the back. Zemah and the third man quickly pulled out other crates and boxes of materials and set them on the sidewalk.

"The incline up to those steps is steep," Zemah noted. "Watch out for the stepped flower beds. We're going to have a hill and steps to climb, so hurry. Assemble the stuff up there on the plaza at the base of the steps into the building.

"I've *got* to talk to you," Rivka confronted Zvilli. "If anything that has happened between us is real and enduring, we must face the truth together."

"Stop it!" Zemah shook her violently. "I've waited my whole life for a moment like this. Now shut your mouth and get on with it." He forced a heavy box into her hands and slung a bag over his shoulder. "You should consider yourself lucky I even gave you the time of day." Zvilli pushed her ahead of him toward the steps of the Internal Affairs building. "You're too deep in this plot even to have the right to a second thought. Faster!" he shouted at her, hurrying forward.

"Why do you do this thing?" the voice came from the steps.

Zvilli looked up and to his astonishment, two white-haired men stood resolutely with their hands on their hips at the bottom of the steps. "Feinberg?" he gasped.

"You still have time to repent and change your course," Ben Feinberg answered.

"How . . . did you get here?" Zvilli sputtered. The three Egyptians ran to his side. "How did you find out?"

"The more important question is, what will *you* do now?" Jimmy Harrison asked.

"I tried to tell you." Rivka set the box on the ground and pushed it aside. "All of this is terribly, terribly wrong."

Zemah turned slowly, his eyes narrowing in anger. "You told them?"

"It was for our good, darling. We couldn't start a life together on such a wicked basis."

In one wild swing Zemah hit Rivka in the face, knocking her senseless into a flower bed. She rolled across the flowers and dropped down into the next terraced garden on the level below.

"Get them!" one of the Egyptians yelled.

"No!" Zemah dropped to one knee and whipped open the bag over his shoulder. He pulled out two bottles of yellow liquid and handed one to an Egyptian. "Perfect opportunity for us."

"What you do will be a judgment on your own head," Ben warned.

"Oh yeah?" Zvilli crept forward. "Ever hear of picric acid? Tri-nitro-pheno? TNP? A little sulfuric acid, a little nitric acid, and it's amazing what is possible." He raised his arm over his head. "Getting rid of you two creeps is a real bonus."

"Don't!" Ben held up his hand. His eyes filled the thick glasses to the rims, his ponytail swung back and forth. "Don't come any closer. I warn you."

"You warn me?" Zvilli laughed. He spoke out of the side of his mouth to the Egyptian, "Get close enough to throw the stuff and hit the ground."

"Stop where you are!" Jimmy shook his cane in the air.

"Now!" Zemah yelled and charged forward.

Suddenly the entire plaza was engulfed in a ball of fire, the attackers incinerated on the spot. The explosion sent the other two Egyptians rolling down the incline wrapped in flames. Clouds of black oily smoke shot up the front of the building. No one was left on the steps. Jimmy and Ben were gone.

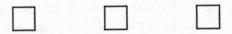

Ziad Atrash studied each TV monitor carefully. Cameras panned the three field generals' headquarters while the coalition's new national flags were raised. Troops stood at attention and saluted. The red banner speckled with nine stars in colors of green, blue, orange, and brown were raised simultaneously across the Middle East. "Will the nine flag raisings be shown together as a collage on viewers' screens?" Atrash asked his aide.

"Yes sir! The segment will be ready for insertion when we roll the footage of the nine leaders' declaration of war. We will intersperse these pictures while you read your intention of war."

"Excellent." Ziad smiled broadly. "Everything is on schedule." He looked to the monitor at the far end of the room; shuttles from Italy and France arrived and unloaded at the Damascus telaport. "The last piece in the puzzle is in place." He chuckled to himself. "The noose is about to be placed around the neck of Israel."

Another monitor flashed the prerecorded clip of Ziad's call for world rebellion. According to Atrash's instructions, he was in the most prominent position among the national leaders. Ziad listened carefully to his own speech. Pictures of the other eight conspirators clustered around his oversized image. "The time has come for the entire world to proclaim freedom from the tyranny of Jewish oppressors. "

A wicked smile crossed the Egyptian leader's face. *The*

*French and Italian broads didn't like the word 'tyranny.'*
*Thought they overruled me!* He snorted defiantly. *In the final*
*days ahead, they will learn who is running the world!*

"Today our armies have joined in one single great effort
on behalf of all humanity. We call on the nations of the
world to link arms with us and join our armies." The
Egyptian general's voice sounded fervent and inspiring.
"For weeks satellite programming has given you religious
instruction to set you free from fear of the Immortals. The
gods are now with us! Have no fear of retribution for our
efforts are undergirded by supernatural power."

"Everything is in place, pending your approval," the aide
interjected.

"Yes," Ziad said slowly. "I am satisfied." He glanced at a
special monitor at the far end of the room. "We will add
one more piece of footage. I want the unexpected explosion
in Jerusalem to come immediately after the pictures of the
flag raisings."

"Explosion?" The aide glanced at his electronic notepad.
"I don't have any indication—"

"Of course not," Ziad snapped. "The explosion was a
state secret. I want to see the footage now."

"But sir . . ." The aide bit at his lip. "Nothing of that sort
has come in from the satellites."

Ziad glanced at the clock. "Of course it has. The explosions were set to go off ten minutes ago. The agents know
I will not tolerate any deviation from the plan."

"With all due respect." The aide took a step backward.
"We do not show any TV transmission or seismographic
data of a significant explosion."

Ziad stared at the screen. "Roll the tapes backward and
restore zoom capacity. We should have clear pictures of
the government buildings going up in smoke."

The aide quickly spoke into his wristwatch and commanded a reset to 11:00. The satellite pictures automat-

ically enlarged, pinpointing three square blocks around the Knesset, but nothing unusual appeared.

"I don't understand." Ziad frowned and hit the table. "Rewind further!"

Just as the timer hit 10:45, a puff of smoke arose from the front of the Internal Affairs Building.

"Is that what you're looking for?" The aide spoke hesitantly. "That burst couldn't have been more than a small bomb. Doesn't look like any damage was done."

"Closer!" Atrash demanded. "Replay it slowly."

The images enlarged again. A van pulled to the curb. Small figures could be seen moving across the plaza. A fireball flashed and smoke obscured the area. When the cloud cleared, the van stood by itself.

Ziad cursed. "Those idiots have bungled everything! I wanted those pictures of destruction on the air! The world must see that revolution is already underway in Jerusalem itself!" He slung a chair across the room and into the wall. "I won't stand for incompetence!"

Aides snapped to attention. The Egyptian leader stormed around the room cursing. "How could they do this to *me*?!" He stared at the empty monitor.

"Uh . . . uh . . . sir," the aide squirmed. "An emergency call is waiting on the reserved security line from New Babylon."

Ziad glared. "Can't those idiots do anything right?" He snatched the receiver from the man's hand. "Hello."

Rajah Abu Sita cleared his throat nervously. "The bombing didn't happen. We've been monitoring from here. In fact, all contact with Zemah has been lost."

"I know," Ziad barked. "He was *your* friend. What happened?"

"Something went wrong."

"Obviously." Atrash sneered.

"I have other concerns," Rajah hesitated. "There . . . is . . . another problem."

"Can't it wait?"

"Uh . . . no. El Khader died last night during an incantation."

"*Died?*"

"It was bizarre, eerie . . . like something consumed him."

"What are you suggesting?"

"Just before he died," Rajah stopped and caught his breath, "he warned me we were being betrayed. And then he toppled over."

Ziad blinked rapidly and ran his hand through his hair. "Betrayed?" his voice lowered.

"I couldn't tell whether El Khader was giving me a message from the gods or if he had gone crazy."

"I don't understand," Ziad spoke slowly and deliberately.

"I had the feeling El Khader had seen some kind of vision. Listen, this business of contacting the spirits is more dangerous than we thought."

"The old frog just croaked, that's all."

"He was one of my best friends," Rajah warned.

"Of course, of course. Don't get excited."

"I've told you all that I know."

"Then pay attention to every detail you see anywhere," Ziad Atrash demanded. "Let me know if anything suspicious turns up. I've got to get back to the command post." He clicked off the receiver and returned to the monitors.

"Transmission of the international telecast is almost ready to begin," an aide advised.

Ziad cursed again. "I wanted those pictures of the Knesset in flames." He crossed his arms over his chest and shook his head. "Are all channels being monitored?"

"With the exception of the two intermediate command channels in Europe and Russia."

"Cut into them," Atrash demanded. "I want every international communique tapped and recorded."

The aide took a step back. "I'm sorry. We can't. Both transmissions are jammed with a code we can't break."

The Egyptian leader's glance darted back and forth. "When was this exception discovered?"

"Just this morning, excellency."

Atrash turned away and stared blankly at the bank of televisions. *What are they trying to pull? Was El Khader on to something?* He snapped his fingers and beckoned for the aide. "Record what you don't understand. Do everything necessary to intercept the messages on those two channels."

"At once." The aide bowed and hurried out of the room.

Atrash turned back to the two monitors of European and Asian troops assembling. He listened to the strange garbled sounds of the European leaders talking to each other. "Surely those two old bags couldn't be up to anything of much significance, but those Russians . . ."

In Rome, Maria Marchino listened carefully to the secret transmission as her field general reported the state of preparations. "Are all personnel unloaded and situated in Damascus?" she asked.

"Yes, Madam President," the general answered. "Our joint command center with the French has been consolidated and integrated. Everything is in place."

"Excellent. How is morale?"

The general hesitated. "Our troops will do as they are ordered. I am confident of my men."

"But their state of mind?"

"From their youth they were taught to obey the authorities as unto the Lord. We must believe that in some way we don't quite understand your directives are linked to the purposes of the Almighty."

"Well spoken, general. But you don't sound very convinced."

"Frankly . . ." He cleared his throat. "Many soldiers are confused. I have no way of knowing how many remain committed to the traditional faith. Of course, no one knows what could happen if the Immortals show up."

"Do not be afraid to speak freely, General," Maria spoke earnestly. "I want to know your mind on this matter."

After a long pause, the general answered. "What if we are wrong in our calculations? How do you rationalize what we are about to do?"

"If we are wrong," Maria said slowly, "we can take comfort in remembering the Immortals have always acted benevolently. We will plead for mercy and explain we were deceived by the Egyptian leaders. Does that answer bring you comfort?"

"Some."

"Then I offer you more assurance. When we reach a strategic place in the battle, you may be ordered to turn on the Egyptians. We will claim to have always been acting on behalf of Yeshua's government and be exonerated. If the Immortals don't appear and Atrash is right about these other gods, we can keep the Egyptians from becoming the supreme power."

"Amazing!" the field general gasped. "Brilliant."

"You will read the secret instructions to be opened following this phone call The code is 666. At the right moment I will give you our alternative plan and tell you where to strike. The most important fact is not to trust the Egyptians."

"Your wish is my command!"

"My great and fearless general doesn't sound so intimidated now," Maria chided. "Let's get on with the war. We have no choice but to hit them with all the firepower we have."

"We're ready."

"And what happens if you receive orders that I have not confirmed?"

"I will ignore them."

Maria laughed. "Keep steady, old boy. You're about to make history. Ciao."

The general punched in the code necessary to open the courier's pouch lying on the table before him. He took out the large envelope marked Top Secret: Operation Scorpion, and tore open the top. The general dumped out a military map and several typed pages. On the map a semicircle was drawn from Damascus to Al Mawsil in northern Iraq back down to New Babylon over to Ar Rutbah and on to Amman, Jordan. The tip of the line at Damascus was sharpened like a stinger.

He read the instructions aloud. "Like the tail of a scorpion uncoiling, we will strike as our troops close the noose around Jerusalem. The final assault will come down from the north out of Damascus. Should any Jews escape, they will be driven south toward the Dead Sea and the desert.

"Due to distance, methodical placement of troops, and the time needed to solidify world opinion behind the coalition, we can anticipate the final assembling of troops will occur on the evening of Av 8. By this date a solid wall of soldiers will have formed to the east, west, and north of Jerusalem. The first violence will come like poison from the scorpion's tail."

The general traced the line carefully with his fingertip and looked at the day-by-day schedule for troop movements. He began reading again, "Should Immortals emerge and attempt to disrupt troop movement, do not hesitate or wait for command central authorization to use bombs. Even Immortals will not be able to withstand the explosion."

The general put the paper down and looked out the window at the troops going through their paces. He pursed his lips and scratched his head. "We certainly better hope somebody knows what he is talking about."

# CHAPTER
# 18

Rivka Zachary slowly crawled out of the flower bed and onto the steep, sloping sidewalk. The stench of burning flesh hung in the air. She still felt woozy and her vision wasn't yet clear. A terrible ringing noise in her ears slowly subsided. With some difficulty, Rivka got to her feet and wiped the blood from her mouth.

She slowly looked around the plaza. Stains of black smoke covered the front of the building and windows were blown out. Not far away, lying in the shrubs, were the smoldering remains of two bodies. Near the van two other bodies were still burning.

"God help us." Rivka moaned and rubbed her eyes. "They killed Dr. Feinberg and his friend!" She ran toward the front stairs into the Internal Affairs Building. "Where are their bodies?" She hurried up the steps in despair. "I am responsible for their deaths," she sobbed.

"Not so, my child," a man's voice answered from behind the broken glass door at the top of the stairs.

Rivka froze in place.

Ben Feinberg and Jimmy Harrison stepped out of the glass door. "Do not fear, we are quite fine."

Rivka gasped and pointed but couldn't speak.

"I must apologize," Ben said as he walked down the steps. "I really wasn't sure if you were telling me the truth. I'm sorry I doubted you."

"But . . . I . . . was sure . . . the bomb got you."

"Actually, my distrust saved our lives," Ben explained. "Since I suspected a trap, Jimmy helped me make some unusual preparations for our visit from Zemah."

"But I saw you standing on the steps—" Rivka protested.

"No," Jimmy answered. "What you saw were carefully placed hologram images. Ben and I were inside talking to Zemah on the phone."

"Thank God," Rivka held her cheeks with both hands.

"In order to create the effect," Ben added, "we had to use the most powerful laser equipment available. It took an enormous amount of energy. The hologram was actually a very intense stream of hot light."

"Zvilli made a great mistake running at the images," Jimmy continued. "We warned him but he wouldn't stop. The heat from the lasers triggered his bombs. The rest of the story is scattered around the plaza."

Rivka slowly sank down on the steps and cried. "How could I ever have been so stupid? I jeopardized everyone . . . and I've been totally unfaithful. . . to God and myself."

Jimmy sat down beside the young woman and put his arm around her shoulder. "Rivka, your heart overwhelmed your head, but in the end you did the right thing. God is gracious to forgive and restore us when we confess and repent. In contrast, Zemah was destroyed by his own obstinacy."

"I really loved him," Rivka cried. "I would never, never have believed he could strike me."

"I am sorry." Jimmy patted her on the shoulder.

"I must do something to right the wrong I have done."

Rivka clung to him. "Surely, I can make some amends for the problems I have caused. Tell me what I can do."

"Hmmm...what an interesting thought." Ben sat down on the step on the other side of the young woman. "I think you could be of *significant* assistance if you are really serious."

"Oh, yes. Yes!"

"Rivka, you could go back to the university and spread the word about Zemah to the students. We are going to need their help in defending the city. Could you help organize a resistance movement?"

"We only have twenty days to get ready for a terrible assault," Ben added.

"I would do anything," Rivka assured. "Anything."

Jimmy leaned back on his cane and smiled. "We were just about your age at a very similar time in history. The place was Los Angeles and the attack of evil was coming at us full tilt. We were young but we made a tremendous difference. Maybe just such a moment has come again."

"Whatever you tell me, I will do," Rivka answered.

"Good!" Ben patted her on the back. "From now on, Rivka, we'll be a team just as we were with your ancestor, Dr. Zachary long ago in Bozrah and Petra during the Great Tribulation period."

Late that night Isaiah and Deborah Murphy sat glued to their television in their Los Angeles home, listening in silent dread to Egyptian President Atrash's declaration of war. Wearing a general's uniform bedecked with medals, the Egyptian's barrel chest looked massive.

"Arise, peoples of the globe!" the voice boomed over the television. "Join our righteous cause and strike out to realize your own destiny. Throw off the bonds of oppression now!"

Deborah reached for Isaiah's hand. "Thank God Jimmy was able to get you back home before the war began."

"Our armies are gathering today," Ziad hammered away. "Nations that stand with us now will reap the greatest rewards. Peoples of the world, demand your leaders lock arms with us." Pictures of flags rising over armies filled the screen. The exhilarating music of a military band blared in the background.

"What do you think?" Isaiah asked his wife.

"I'm terrified! We know all too well how people can be stampeded by political leaders into doing crazy, irresponsible things. The recent riots at the L.A. Courthouse are a sober reminder of how unstable this population is."

"You're right, Deborah. There is no way to predict public response. Much will depend on what the president of this country does."

"Want to make any predictions?"

Isaiah studied the television screen as he thought. Pictures of troops marching with weapons in hand flashed by. The faces of the nine leaders of the rebellion kept appearing on the screen. "The heart is deceitful and desperately wicked," he quoted aloud. "Who can know it?"

"So?"

"I think the odds are high the politicians will do whatever they think is expedient. So, get ready for a national call to join the war."

"We've got to get the old gang together and consider what we can do," Deborah concluded. She shook her finger at him. "This is no time to sit idly by and observe."

Isaiah scratched his head and rolled his eyes. "Didn't seem to me like I've been doing much sitting around lately."

☐          ☐          ☐

As the day drew to a close in the Middle East, coalition leaders linked up in a satellite joint conference on the day's progress. The hologram images created an appearance of nine people sitting in a circle speaking to each other. Each wore a military uniform.

Ziad Atrash opened the meeting, calling for a report on the status of the army. Abu Sita responded with a detailed accounting of where all troops were located. "We are in place and have met our initial schedule," he concluded.

"Excellent," the Egyptian leader answered. "Do we have any pressing concerns?"

Ali of Ethiopia spoke up. "As has been reported, the joint forces of Ethiopia and Egypt will shortly be consolidated just outside of Elath on the Gulf of Aqaba. We are ready to march up the Jordanian side of Wadi al 'Arabah and on past the Dead Sea on our way to Jerusalem to complete the tail of the scorpion." He cleared his throat. "Nevertheless, many of our men are secretly afraid of what the Immortals may do."

The leaders solemnly looked at each other and turned to Atrash.

"No one has seen those creatures for months," the Egyptian said disdainfully. "We have received no interference. Why should we worry now?"

"What if it's a trap?" Fong asked.

"We are prepared to blast them with everything from fire bombs to dynamite," Ziad snapped. "Remember, we have the guns. No one remembers what incredible damage these devices can inflict."

"Still . . ." Fong's eyes narrowed even further. "We do not know where they are and why they've vanished."

Ziad turned to Rajah Abu Sita. "The time has come to share a communique received some time ago by El Khader from the gods."

"The urgency of war preparations delayed the report

until now," Abu Sita sounded nervous. He pulled a file from a briefcase at his feet and thumbed through several pages. "The god Marduk is preparing for a great heavenly battle. As we fight in the framework of earthly time, a war will begin in eternity. Our visible forces fight alongside the heavenly hosts of the gods. We can conclude the Immortals will be too busy with their own problems to deal with us."

"Where'd you get that non-s-e-n . . . stuff?" Chardoff grunted.

"During one of El Khader's midnight incantations," the Syrian king answered.

Khalil Hussein and Claudine Toulouse stared at each other but said nothing.

"Look," Atrash said harshly, "the time has come to decide where we stand. We are either with the gods or not.

"This whole crusade began because I discovered the power of Yeshua was not only waning but could be displaced by other gods. Now, are we polytheistic or not?" he scowled. "Decide!"

For several moments there was a long, awkward pause.

"We are already committed to the conflict," Fong spoke in emotionless tones that betrayed no hint of true feeling. "The issue is whether we are vulnerable to forces we do not fully understand."

"Only if we are divided," the Egyptian president shot back. He slowly looked around the circle. "Our only danger is division from within."

The leaders froze in place and no one spoke. Finally the Jordanian king said, "The day has been most successful. We have much to celebrate. The only significant question before us is how the rest of the world has perceived our actions."

"The reports will start coming in tomorrow," Atrash

answered quickly. "We are scheduled to reconvene at the same hour tomorrow afternoon. Is that agreeable?"

Heads nodded and the images faded from the hologram system.

Atrash immediately reconnected with the Syrian leader. "Rajah, I don't like the smell of any of this."

Rajah Abu Sita shook his head. "We have not been able to crack the code the Europeans and the Russians are using to contact their people. We have no alternative but to go through the leaders with our communiques."

Atrash sneered. "We have a blind spot and I don't like it. After we take Jerusalem and attack the Europeans, we have no way of knowing how they will respond without a line inside their communications. We must work harder to crack the code."

"We are," Rajah assured the Egyptian. "Don't worry. We'll have the answer by the time the counterattack begins."

"You better!" Atrash flipped the switch and the Syrian's image disappeared. Ziad sat for several minutes staring at the wall. Finally he rang for his first assistant to come in.

The aide walked briskly into the room. "At your service." The young general snapped to attention.

"I want a special monitor attached to all calls coming in and out of Abu Sita's headquarters. I want to know everything he says to anyone. Understood?"

The aide looked surprised. "You are speaking of the leader of Syria and Iraq?"

"Exactly! The order is top secret. But I want to know even when he snores."

"Of course." The aide frowned and hurried from the room.

Atrash cursed. "I control all of the world's communication systems and the only existing army, and yet I can't trust *one* of them."

□          □          □

"I'm glad Ben brought you to our house." Cindy scurried around her kitchen as she talked to Rivka. "I think it's time for us girls to have a chat." She stopped and looked out the window as the last light of day completely faded into total blackness. "Yes, the night is coming."

"I feel like such a fool." Rivka buried her face in her hands. "I have betrayed everything that was important in my life."

Cindy put her arm around the girl. "You trusted someone who deceived you. I know your pain is very deep."

"My ancestors would be so disappointed in me."

"The important thing is that you *did* wake up." Cindy gently pulled the young woman's head to her shoulder. "You tried to make things right, but no one could stop Zvilli."

"What's worse, I don't have the slightest idea what to do next." Rivka squeezed Cindy's hand. "How could anyone follow me?"

"Oh, quite to the contrary, Rivka. We don't have to reveal the secret of your sin to let people know you've been a very effective agent in uncovering the plot to destroy our government buildings. You have great credibility."

"Do you *really* think so?" Rivka dried her eyes.

"Absolutely."

"But what do I know about getting the students prepared to protect Jerusalem? I hate war and violence."

"All the better." Cindy beamed. "I am going to help you use your natural aversion to conflict as one of our most effective weapons of battle."

"I don't understand."

"I am going to teach you one of the greatest secrets Yeshua embodied during his earthly ministry three thousand years ago. Even Ben and Jimmy have forgotten the real secret of how to overcome both the world and our Enemy."

Rivka blinked several times. "I don't get it."

Cindy sat down opposite the raven-haired beauty. "I had almost forgotten that I had this little piece of jewelry." She reached around her neck and unfastened a tiny gold chain. "We haven't worn these emblems for centuries, but the time has come to once again proclaim the power of this symbol." Cindy slipped the chain away and put the gold piece in Rivka's palm. "We shall overcome by this sign."

Rivka looked down into her palm at a small gold crucifix.

# 19

Ben stared through his thick glasses at the international communication screen in his office; dark circles ringed his eyes. Slumped down in his desk chair, Ben's large bulbous shape spilled over the leather chair. He read each line of the satellite report once again.

Jimmy sat on the other side of the desk with his hands perched on top of his cane. His head was tilted back with the resoluteness and confidence of a head of state. Jimmy's aquiline nose and sharp profile easily gave him the air of a person in complete control, regardless of the circumstances.

Wendy Kohn finally broke the silence. "The world is certainly in total turmoil but I can't see where there is any consensus among the nation's peoples about supporting the coalition of traitors.

"Your television appeal for renewed faith wasn't for naught!" Esther Netanyahu added.

"Things are up for grabs," Jimmy countered.

Ben shook his head and his white ponytail swished from side to side. "Ten days have passed since Tammuz 17 and only one thing is definite. The troops of the enemy are slowly but relentlessly circling us without any opposition."

Jimmy thumped his cane on the floor. "It doesn't make a lot of difference what people think! The national leaders are in control and no one is backing off."

"Afraid so," Wendy agreed.

"What is your wife up to with the students?" Esther Netanyahu asked.

"We've been so busy I haven't even had time to inquire," Ben said. "I know she and Rivka are working day and night to get students prepared and positioned before the final attack comes."

"Prior to the millennial kingdom, Av 9 had never been a good day for us Jews." Wendy looked down at the floor. "I can't but be apprehensive."

"The Immortals have left everything up to us. I guess we can take that sign as a vote of divine confidence."

"I've studied the Bible day and night," Jimmy added, "and I've come to the conclusion God is forcing the entire world to one last moment of decision. No assistance is going to be forthcoming. Everyone's faith is being tested and we're going to have to demonstrate what we're made of. So buckle up, ladies! It's time to get tough."

"Yes sir," Wendy said timidly. She stood up and the two secretaries left the room.

"I think we ought to see how Isaiah is faring about now." Ben began punching in Isaiah Murphy's personal code to locate him. "Let's see what too-tall Murphy thinks."

The picture cleared and for several moments only static lines crossed the screen. Slowly two shapes came into focus. Isaiah and Deborah were sitting in their living room in Los Angeles, dressed casually with their feet up on hassocks.

"Don't you guys ever knock?" Isaiah said. "I'm sitting here with my lovely wife enjoying the evening news and suddenly I get the Hardy boys from Jerusalem."

Ben laughed. "What a lucky man you are."

Deborah waved. "You can bet the James Bond of the Christian world is not sitting here *leisurely* enjoying himself. At least he's home and not somewhere over there about to get killed."

"How are things in L.A.?" Jimmy asked.

"Bad." Isaiah shook his head. "As you know our president has thrown his weight behind the coalition and is even proposing to send American troops to join the fight. People are completely confused."

"How many are standing with us?" Ben asked.

"I don't know," Isaiah answered. "I truly am not sure. We've become a lightning rod for opposition in this area. The old gang is hard at work trying to help people see through the smokescreen the Devil and his cohorts have created, but the government has turned on us, calling us unpatriotic."

"We are being attacked in the papers," Deborah added, "and on the news reports. I can't help but believe matters are going to get violent soon."

"How can we help?" Ben leaned forward in his chair.

"I think our job is to help *you*," Isaiah answered. "The problem is that television constantly encourages people to do whatever feels good. Unbridled freedom is the new message of the day. Lots of citizens are buying into it. Irresponsibility is rather intoxicating."

"I'll tell you what I think," Deborah broke in. "Here's what I think is going to—"

Suddenly the screen went dead. Ben feverishly began hitting buttons but nothing came up. Finally the earlier news report scrolled up on the screen. Ben grabbed a phone with a special line and tapped in his priority code. "What's going on in our transmission?" he barked.

The voice on the speaker phone answered, "We can't figure the problem out, sir. But it appears all worldwide communication has been commandeered. Every channel is jammed except the propaganda lines coming out of Egypt. We seem to be cut off from the world."

"See if you can get this corrected at once!" Ben ordered. "We mustn't lose touch with what is happening around the globe."

"We're doing everything we can but nothing is working. We'll not stop trying."

Ben lowered his voice. "Thank you." He hung up.

"We're cut off, aren't we?" Jimmy asked.

Ben slouched down further in his chair. "I'm afraid so. We have the best technology in the world. If our people can't fix the problem, it can't be done."

"They're closing in on us."

"Yes, Jimmy. They are."

Alexi Chardoff and Fong stood in their makeshift command post in the city of Al Mawsil. At one time the dusty little town was part of the Iraqi empire. During the ancient reign of Sennacherib, Al Mawsil was the king's sanctuary, but the royal city's demise was predicted by the prophet Nahum. The Medes and Persians fulfilled Nahum's prediction. Chardoff had chosen the city as a natural rendezvous point when the Chinese and Russian armies converged. The two men talked and watched the TV monitors of their troops moving out across the fertile countryside.

"Our men are cautiously reassured," Fong observed. "Each step forward further dispels their fear of the Immortals' intervention. By the time we get to the walls of Jerusalem, they'll be ready to charge."

Charoff nodded his head. "The Arabs don't seem to have even a hint of collusion on our part. I think they are almost more obsessed with getting rid of Toulouse and Marchino than taking the city. They have no idea we've read their intentions."

Fong's eyes narrowed. "Our loyal allies are nothing more than a traitorous pack." His voice betrayed no hint of emotion. "Their religious nonsense has left the world in total confusion. It will be up to us to pick up the pieces and restore order. By the time this war is over, people will again welcome a strong central government."

"Exactly!" Chardoff thumped the table.

Fong leaned back and crossed his arms over his chest. "I'll be honest. I got into this intrigue because I've never liked the Western world. I don't trust white and black people much, but I dislike Jews most of all. I'm here for a little revenge, pure and simple. But you, Alexi . . . what's your angle? You've never really told me."

Chardoff pushed his greasy hair out of his eyes. "About a hundred years ago, I started to think about what it all meant. Life just didn't add up for me anymore and I needed better answers than I had." Alexi gestured aimlessly in the air. "For a long time I wandered around trying to find a better way to understand the purpose of existence. One night I stumbled on to a completely different way of thinking about everything. I began to realize that the ultimate reality is *power*."

Fong stared for awhile and then nodded his head.

Chardoff grinned cynically. "I slowly began to see that the only significant truth about Yeshua and the rulers in Jerusalem was that they possessed the power. Take away their omnipotence and nothing is left."

"You don't believe in God?" Fong asked.

Chardoff shrugged. "God is only a symbol for what is ultimate. When you dig down to the center of everything, there is no personality hiding in there . . . only sheer force. My god is power."

"But what about the Immortals? Yeshua's miraculous abilities?"

The Russian leader laughed. "Superstition! Just as big a fraud as Abu Sita's garbage about this Marduk charade. The jerks call it prayer but they're doing nothing but talking to themselves."

Fong pursed his lips. "You're quite satisfied the Immortals won't show up?"

"Listen to me." Chardoff shook his finger in Fong's face. "When we have power, we are gods! The more we use power, the stronger we become! No, I don't know how these Immortals come and go but I am prepared to put a bullet in the brain of any who show up. One shot will level the playing field." Alexi shook his first in the air. "Exercise power and you are divine!"

Fong's eyes narrowed to bare slits. "I'm not sure I understand."

"Let me show you." Chardoff stood up and beckoned the Chinaman to follow him from the room. "Let me teach you what I've been practicing." He walked into the alley behind the building.

"You have a new insight?"

Chardoff pointed to three Arabs working at the end of the alley. "Let me demonstrate my new skill." The Russian pulled a pistol from beneath his uniform. "We found this little jewel in our stash. Gives one a wonderful sense of power. I've been practicing." He raised the pistol slowly and pointed it at the men. "Watch," he said coolly.

The explosion of Chardoff's first shot echoed off the buildings. One Arab tumbled forward on the ground. The other startled men looked up uncomprehendingly. Chardoff fired off two other shots in rapid order. The other two men crumpled to the ground.

"I've gotten quite good with this thing." Chardoff watched the thin trail of smoke rise from the barrel.

Fong stared, his mouth agape.

"Let's just say a Russian brought the first casualties of the war." He stuck the gun back inside his coat. "What a feeling! That's what power feels like." Chardoff grinned. "You ought to try it, Fong."

Fong stared in shock.

"We don't have much time to talk," Claudine Toulouse spoke quickly into the hologram speaker in her Damascus hotel. Even though Maria Marchino was on the other side of Damascus, she appeared to be standing in the French leader's large bedroom. A separate dining area opened to the side. "Everything is in place for a little midnight champagne supper," the French leader said. "Khalil will be here in minutes."

"You look ravishing, darling," Maria purred. "I really didn't know you had it in you."

"Rather different image for me." Claudine swirled her filmy gown around her waist. The unusually low-cut dress was made of red silk. Her hair was piled high on top of her head in a provocative twist. "I think Khalil will like what he sees."

"Just remember, I'm only blocks away if you need help." Maria laughed at her own little joke. "Are you sure Hussein knows nothing about our alliance?"

"Nothing. He thinks only of me and what we will have together."

"You have our agreement for him to sign?"

Claudine held up an official document. "Right here. At the right moment after he is . . . well . . . in a more passive mood I will put our accords before our little king of Jordan. Don't worry. We've got this one in the bag."

The Italian leader smiled. "Claudine, I have to admit you really surprised me with this ploy. Brilliant stroke on your part." Maria held up two other pieces of paper. "I have the agreements which Chardoff and Fong prepared. At the right time, we will be ready to offer them a separate peace with us. We will be able to move quickly and wrap up *our* new alliance."

"No time for further discussion," Claudine said. "Khalil will be here any minute."

"Ciao, darling." Maria waved. Her image faded.

Several minutes later an aide knocked on the door. "The king of Jordan is here, madam."

"Bring him up at once and begin serving the dinner."

Claudine took one final look in the mirror and carefully massaged her hair into place. She took a deep breath and hurried across the room. Just as she opened the door, the king appeared only feet away.

Before she could speak, the king of Jordan dropped to one knee and kissed her hand. "*Ma cherie,*" he cooed, "I am overwhelmed by your beauty." His light-colored suit gave his dark skin an intoxicating glow. The king's black eyes were mysterious and deep. His lips felt warm and gentle.

Claudine knew blood was rushing to her cheeks and she fought to keep a demure composure. "Come here, you handsome devil," she said impulsively and giggled. Claudine ran her hands through his dark black hair and then suddenly kissed him passionately on the mouth. "Oh, but you are good," she said and stepped back. Out of the corner of her eye, Claudine saw an aide bringing a cart with food. "Like a little something to take the edge off your hunger?" She beckoned Khalil into her room.

The aide quickly rolled the cart into the side room.

"Some hors d'oeuvres will whet your appetite. We can start with the soupe a l'aignon. I thought you would enjoy a special coq au vin prepared by my private cook from Paris. The chicken in wine sauce is exquisite. If that is not to your taste, I also have included boeuf bourguignonne." Claudine pointed to the elegant china on the table. "We have choix de legumes. I had the vegetables flown in tonight just for us." She led Khalil by the hand to the two chairs seated across the candlelit table. Claudine snapped her fingers at the aide. "Pour the Dom Perignon." The aide filled the crystal glasses then hurried out of the room.

The Jordanian king kissed her on the hand again. "Never have I met a woman as fascinating as you." He seated her at the table.

As they bantered, Claudine felt her usual facade of political professionalism melt like the candle wax. She found herself giggling like a school girl.

"A-a-a-h," Khalil sighed, "the wine sauce is superb. People just don't cook like this in our country."

Claudine studied his sparkling black eyes, while doodling with her food. He seemed to be the most handsome man she had ever seen.

"Your combination of style, taste, and magnificent strength is like an aphrodisiac to me," Khalil's voice was low and sultry. "My heart has become like the restless sea."

Claudine took a deep breath. Her pulse pounded and her hands trembled. "And we also have crêpes suzette. Perhaps, a little cognac to blend the taste? I also have crème de menthe should you desire."

"I crave the taste of *you*." Hussein tossed the napkin aside and suddenly leaned over the table, kissing Claudine passionately. "You are what I desire." He pulled Claudine to her feet and kissed up and down her neck.

For a moment, Claudine felt so lightheaded she thought she might faint. The French woman clung to the Arab's coat for fear her knees would buckle. She felt him lift her off her feet and sweep her toward the bedroom. The silk bedspread soothed her skin and felt wondrously sensual.

When the dawn sunlight broke through the windows,

the first rays struck Claudine's face. She blinked several times, trying to remember where she was. Her hand fell across a hairy chest and she jumped. Only then did the night before come back into focus. She stared at the sleeping figure next to her.

*Good grief! What have I done? I didn't even get the agreement signed. I let my emotions run away with me.*

Hussein stirred and rolled over. "Ma cherie." He kissed her again. "We were made for each other."

"Indeed," Claudine purred. "We were meant to rule together, like Anthony and Cleopatra."

Hussein propped himself up on an elbow and laughed. "Shall we take over Egypt so I can give you the Sphinx?"

"Why not?" She ran her hand through his ruffled black hair. "Who knows what we might do if our armies merged?"

"Merged?"

"Look!" Claudine cuddled near the Arab. "I can get Maria Marchino to join us. Our three nations could tilt the balance of power and we could overwhelm Atrash's lock on control."

"The three of us?" Khalil frowned. "We don't need her. We're enough." Hussein grabbed the back of Claudine's neck and kissed her passionately again.

The warmth of Khalil's breath sent shivers up her spine. Her usual cold-hearted logic blurred and for the first time in years Claudine felt indecisive.

"You and I will be more than sufficient," Khalil insisted. "Just us . . . together . . . think about it!"

Claudine looked up into his all-engulfing eyes. Suddenly Khalil was all she wanted in the world. "Do you really think we . . . just us . . . could pull it off?"

Khalil lowered his face until the tips of their noses barely touched. "We can do anything." He kissed her so passionately Claudine could hardly breath.

Much later in the day the French leader finally got

around to calling her Italian counterpart. "Sorry for the delay," she began.

"Must have been some evening," Maria joked. "I thought maybe you had drowned in the champagne."

Claudine pursed her lips searching for the right words. "He turned out to be much more difficult than I thought," she said slowly. "He is actually quite . . . resistant . . . to political change."

"What do you mean?" The Italian leader frowned.

"He seems to like me . . . just . . . for my own sake." Claudine suddenly brightened. "Actually, the whole thing is turning out to be more of a romance than a political intrigue."

"The point was to get him into our coalition," Maria sounded impatient.

"It will take more time."

"We don't have much time left," Maria's voice raised. "Av 9 is just around the corner."

"Obviously," Claudine said defensively. "I'll be seeing Khalil later in the day. I will try to talk to him again."

"Just keep your mind on business," Marchino snapped. "I'll be back in touch." Her picture faded.

Claudine tossed her undone hair over her shoulder and looked pensively at a single rose in the bud vase in front of her. "Maybe there is something more significant than politics after all."

# 20

Select student leaders filed into the large lecture hall at Hebrew University where only months before Ben had spoken to the students. The earlier atmosphere of casual indifference had been transformed into a new serious and sober intent. Cindy and Rivka watched the students closely.

"They are the key leaders?" Cindy asked

"We've checked all the files, records, and test results to identify people with real leadership capacity," Rivka answered quietly. "But I also know the outstanding students who naturally shape public opinion. They're all here."

The students sat respectfully. No one spoke.

Rivka walked to the microphone. "I'm sure by now everyone has read or heard my statement broadcast electronically through all the dormitories and across the campus. You know about the sedition and sabotage planned and executed by Dr. Zvilli Zemah. Dr. Zemah was a . . . special friend." Her voice faltered. "Of course, we are all disappointed." Rivka stopped and cleared her throat.

"You also know that in a very few days we are going to

be attacked by the first army assembled in virtually a thousand years," Rivka continued. "We have no choice but to help defend our city. You have been chosen to help organize our student body to face the fight."

The silence was broken as the students turned to each other and mumbled in consternation.

Rivka punched in buttons on the speaker's podium and the screen behind her filled with pictures of troops marching across the desert. "We have just learned our satellite communication with the world is now blocked and Jerusalem is virtually isolated."

The students became deathly quiet.

"Our only source of information on our enemy's armies is from shuttlecraft flying surveillance missions." Rivka pushed the enlargement button and the picture of a smashed vehicle appeared. "Tragically, the coalition troops have the ability to shoot us down. Two lives were lost in this crash."

The picture changed and a wide sweep of the desert appeared.

Rivka continued to explain. "Egyptian and Ethiopian forces are working their way up the Wadi al 'Arabah area across the Negev. These soldiers are quite accustomed to desert life, so they aren't bothered by this hottest time of summer. They are clearly preparing to stage an attack on Jerusalem from the south. The Jordanian army is quietly waiting in Amman for a quick dash at our city from the west. Are there questions?"

No one moved. The students stared at the scenes of men moving across the barren terrain of the wilderness.

Rivka changed the picture and the land became fertile and green. "Russian and Chinese armies," she continued, "are marching forward across the Euphrates River. As best as reconnaissance can tell, these two armies seem to be headed for a rendezvous with European forces that are waiting for them in the area around Damascus in Syria. Our experts believe they will converge on Jerusalem on Av 9." Rivka paused for emphasis. "They are the only people in the world with armaments that shoot and kill. In addition, we have reason to believe they will attack, first with troops trained in martial arts. We are virtually at their mercy."

Many students put their hands over their faces as if praying. Others looked stunned and immobile. Finally one young man stood up.

"Where are the Immortals, the protection of God Almighty?" the student implored. "We have always depended on Yeshua to lead and guide us. Where is He at this critical hour?"

Rivka turned to Cindy and raised her hands in consternation.

Cindy slowly stood and walked to the podium. Her wrinkled oriental skin and stark white hair made a striking contrast with Rivka's jet-black hair and olive complexion. Age had diminished Cindy's small size to a stature nearly that of a child. "I lived through the Great Tribulation," Cindy began. "Some days during this terrible time it seemed our heavenly Father had forgotten about us." She shook her head. "But we learned that sometimes God's seeming absence is the strategy He has chosen to actually be present with us. Though paradoxical, our God even uses emptiness."

Praying students opened their eyes and stared. The young man sat down.

Cindy continued, "At different times God expects different things of us. Now is a time of testing. All these years of divine intervention were meant to make us a mighty people for His service. Now, the time is come to see if we learned our lessons. The only significant question is, are you ready?"

Someone clapped. A student shouted, "Yes!" Another person clapped. Other students leaped to their feet and began clapping. "Yes!" rang through the air again and again. "We are ready!" one girl shouted over the uproar.

Cindy smiled and nodded again before motioning for the students to sit down. "I have a plan," she continued, "and we don't have much time left. If we organize well, we will be ready."

For the first time Rivka smiled. "My friends," she began, "Mrs. Feinberg and I have worked out a careful strategy for how you can help train other students. Each of you has been selected to be a centurion, in charge of a hundred other students. We will teach you what to do and in turn you will pass the instruction on to the others. Is this agreeable?"

Once more the students applauded enthusiastically.

"We are calling our plan 'Opposite Cheek.'" Cindy added. "I think you will be quite surprised." Cindy talked more rapidly as she explained the strategy.

Several hours later across town Jimmy Harrison was still sitting in Ben's office, studying the reports coming in from the shuttlecrafts. He pulled at the paunch beneath his chin and mumbled to himself.

"What do you think?" Ben asked.

"Because the Russians and Chinese have the greatest distance to go, I conclude once they are in place the attack will be set. No question but Av 9 is the day of destiny."

"You're worried."

Jim doubled his fists over the cap of his cane and rested his chin on top. "You have to meet force with force," he sighed. "And we sure don't have an ounce of capacity. It was one thing to trick Zemah with a hologram gimmick but stopping an army is another matter." He straightened up and bounced his cane off the floor. "Blue blazes! Do you think those students are of any value? I don't even know what Cindy's planning, but three times the number of that student body won't be any more than canon fodder for those guns. Nonsense!"

Ben's white ponytail swung from side to side. "You're right. I shudder every time I read Isaiah's report on this martial arts business he discovered in Ethiopia. Those desert apes will kick the living daylights out of our kids. All we're going to do is get people hurt and killed." Ben suddenly stood up and threw his hands up. "Look at us! We're a couple of old jokes without the slightest idea how to really defend this city or meet this crisis."

Jim shook his head despairingly. "I think we need to send a shuttle out to Petra to pick up our friends before they are surrounded by the army."

Ben shrugged. "Maybe they would be better off out there than in the city. I think the only objective of the coalition is to destroy Jerusalem."

"Perhaps, you're right." Jimmy stood up. "I wonder if want to burn this place completely to the ground."

They'll undoubtedly do everything possible to humiliate us. I think we can count on total destruction."

Suddenly the office door opened. Cindy and Rivka hurried in. "Things went tremendously well with the students." Cindy bubbled over with enthusiasm. "Operation Opposite Cheek is going to work!"

Jimmy and Ben looked at each other.

"We've got the right answer!" Rivka added.

"Wait, wait." Ben waved her away. "We've just been thinking how futile it would be to send hapless students into the midst of this battle. We can only get people killed and hurt. They don't have any weapons of war—"

"Oh, but they do!" Cindy shook both fists in the air. "We're not worried about those silly guns. Our battle is not with flesh and blood anyway."

Ben's eyebrows raised. "I beg your pardon?"

"Our approach is going to be nonviolent," Rivka interjected. "We are going to use the weapons of love."

"I'm teaching the students to turn the other cheek."

Ben turned to Jimmy and shook his head. "When she gets like this, there's no point in even talking. Let's go for a walk."

Jimmy nodded.

"Now just a minute!" Cindy protested. "I expect you to hear me out."

"Sure." Ben kept walking to the door. "Later."

"I want you to hear about Operation Opposite Cheek right *now*," Cindy insisted.

"I think we all need to give it a rest " Ben pulled Jimmy toward the door. "We've gone on overload." He gave a slight wave of the hand. "We'll be back later." He pushed Jimmy ahead of him out the door and closed it behind him.

"How dare you walk out on me, Ben Feinberg!" Cindy called after him.

"They've all gone nuts," Ben whispered to Jimmy. "Let's get some fresh air before it completely gets to us."

Jimmy and Ben walked up the street in front of the Knesset for a long time without saying anything. The hot sun of late summer wasn't pleasant but seemed appropriate to the mood of the moment. A new and disconcerting atmosphere of fear hovered over the city. People walking down the street didn't speak, preoccupied with their own fears. The two men trudged on without any sense of direction.

"We should have at least listened to Cindy," Jimmy finally said as he wiped his forehead.

"Yeah," Ben rolled his eyes. "Boy, will I catch it when I get home, but I just couldn't take it anymore. I feel too overwhelmed."

Jimmy shook his head. "I think we're in so far over our

heads that we are drowning. We need something to give us a completely different perspective."

"Like a little talk with Moses and Elijah," Ben added. "Boy, were they ever a tremendous help the last time Jerusalem was under the gun."

Jimmy stopped. "What an idea!"

"Idea?"

"Great idea, old man." Jimmy slapped Ben on the back. "As you suggested, let's go back to the old city. I haven't been there in ages. You know all the tourists flock there. Let's just go down and look at the great old stuff."

Ben shrugged and pulled his special taxi computer card from his pocket. He punched in several numbers. "It's too far to walk. I'll get us a ride."

In about thirty seconds an automated vehicle pulled up to the curb, the side door raised up, and the two men got in. "The old city," Ben spoke into a microphone in front of them. "Jaffa gate." Instantly the cab sped into the traffic. In a few minutes the car silently pulled up to the curb before the ancient entrance.

Jimmy got out, stretched his long legs, and looked around. To his right, he could see the Citadel and beyond the tower to the road to Bethlehem. He tapped his cane on the old cobblestone pavement, took a deep breath, and started toward the Street of the Chain.

"I'll never forget that awesome day when Moses and Elijah appeared on the Mount of Olives," Ben reminisced. "Wow, did they ever terrify the news media. Remember how they stopped President Gianardo out there on the Kidron Valley Road? Elijah told him the breaking of the Fourth Seal was at hand and a pale horse called Death would ride the skies by Passover. Happened, too. What a day!"

"And I remember what he said would happen by Tammuz 17 of that year," Jimmy added. "Just as he warned, one and a half billion people were slain." He turned at the corner and trudged down the narrow street between the tall limestone-and-granite buildings. "How could anyone forget those days?"

Ben rubbed his pudgy nose and readjusted his thick glasses in place on his bridge. "Someone said it somewhere, When people forget the lessons of history, they are doomed to repeat the mistakes of the past. What we've seen with our eyes, the mob treats like old fairy tales. But truth remains the truth."

"I can still see Moses and Elijah sitting there by the Western Wall." Jimmy stopped and smiled. "Way over there in Los Angeles we'd tune in that picture and just wait to see what would happen next."

"I came here with Sam Eisenberg in April of the year 2000," Ben said thoughtfully. "We had to sneak past the soldiers to get close enough to see the awesome sight. That afternoon Elijah prophesied that on the fifteenth of Nisan, God would bring vengeance on Babylon for her sins. On that exact day, the exodus of the Jews from Egypt began under Moses and that was the date when the last defenders of the Temple retreated to Masada and the Romans destroyed Jerusalem. I can still see Elijah pointing up the street to the Church of the Holy Sepulcher and proclaiming that on this very same day Yeshua died for the sins of the world."

Jimmy jerked at Ben's arm and pointed with his cane straight ahead. "That's a great idea!"

"What idea?"

"To go visit the Church of the Holy Sepulcher."

"I didn't say that." Ben rolled his eyes.

"Yes, you did!" Jimmy insisted. "I am always inspired to walk around inside that great dome and see where the empty tomb was and to climb up those steps to the top of Mount Calvary. That's just the lift we need!" Jimmy poked

Ben in the side. "I wonder if anything is still going on there."

"I just make the suggestions. I don't keep up on museum hours." Ben rolled his eyes again in mock consternation.

"Well, let's go find out." Jimmy hurried on.

The open-air vendors still plied their ancient trades along the narrow street. Tourist business had always made it lucrative to keep up the appearances of the ancient ways. Vegetable markets and spice shops operated next to little stores selling mementos of the old city. The smells of food and village life filled the two men's nostrils.

"I feel better just getting a whiff of this place," Ben said. He stopped and pointed. "Look! There's the gateway into the courtyard in front of the church. Let's go in."

The two old friends slipped through the entrance and found themselves in the place where Helena, the mother of Constantine, came 2,700 years earlier to restore the most precious site in Christendom. During the period of rebuilding after the Second Coming of Yeshua, the walls of the original church had been covered and reinforced by new stone facements but time had even turned these blocks of stone into artifacts. Nothing had changed the worn cobblestones covering the plaza leading into the door of the church.

"Feels like we have stepped into a time machine," Jimmy muttered. "Surely, we are standing on holy ground."

An old man in a black cassock pushed open the huge wooden door to the church and fastened it against the wall. The sound of music and chanting floated out on the evening breeze.

"Excuse me," Ben asked. "Are there *still* services going on in here after all these centuries?"

"Of course!" The man raised his white shaggy eyebrows in surprise at the question. "Every day."

"How interesting." Ben turned to Jimmy. "Let's see what is happening now."

"The Greek Orthodox are finishing afternoon prayers before the holy altar atop Calvary," the doorman answered. "Shortly, a Western rite service of Holy Communion will begin in the chapel in front of the empty tomb."

"I had no idea such worship continued until now." Ben beckoned his friend onward. "I suppose I've been so close to the government leaders I haven't thought much about these ancient customs."

Inside the church the high domed ceiling covered the remains of the past with sweeping arches and lingering shadows. The Stone of Unction, where by tradition the body of Christ was anointed for burial, was still a place washed by the tears and kisses of faithful mourners. The pitted rock was a reminder of the pain of death. Long ago the smell of incense saturated even the masonry between the stones, forever leaving a hint of the aroma of frankincense and myrrh. The pathways down steps and corridors were worn slick from millions of pilgrims walking the final steps of the Via Dolorosa.

Seemingly lost to the world but preserved in this place alone, a Latin chant began somewhere far off in a dark corridor and began coming closer. A priest singing and swinging incense appeared in a dark green chasuble, walking slowly at the end of a procession of other priests carrying candles behind a large cross.

"*Laudate, pueri,*" rang down the corridor. "*Laudate dominum.*"

"Let's follow them." Ben pulled at Jimmy's arm.

The procession wound its way into the chapel as the chanting continued. Clergy bowed to the altar and moved to their stations on the chancel. Ben and Jim slipped into a back pew and watched in rapt attention. Hymns were sung and Scripture read. A profound sense of awe and reverence settled over the two men.

The priests walked to the altar and began preparing the chalice for Communion. Altar assistants offered cruets of wine and water. The ancient rite of the Western Church continued as it had for nearly three millennia.

Ben leaned closer to Jimmy and whispered very quietly. "I had forgotten . . . just forgotten . . . that the real battle is never with flesh and blood. Cindy was right. I needed to be touched by transcendence. Worship is so important in restoring balance in the midst of the storm."

Jimmy nodded his head and both men slid from the pews to their knees.

The priest continued his prayers, finally lifting the chalice high in the air. He kneeled before the altar and then drank from the gold cup. The old man moved to the kneeling rail to await people coming forward.

Although such was not his regular custom, Ben felt an irresistible desire to receive the Holy Elements. He quickly slipped out of the pew, walked down the aisle, and dropped on the small pad before the wooden rail, polished to a soft glow from the touch of a million hands. Ben held out his palms for the bread and then waited for the priest to bring the chalice.

"*Deus noster refugium.*" The priest stopped before Ben. Then in excellent English said again, "God is our refuge and strength, a very present help in trouble." He offered the chalice.

Ben's memory supplied the next line of the Psalm: "Therefore we will not fear, even though the earth be removed, and though the mountains be carried into the midst of the sea. . . ."

For a brief moment their eyes met. Ben felt as if he were looking into the wisdom of the ages. In turn, he sensed the priest was reading the deepest need of his soul. He reached for the gold cup.

"The Blood of Christ, the cup of salvation . . . the body of our Lord Jesus Christ keep you in everlasting life," the priest again said in English and placed the chalice on Ben's lips.

Ben drank deeply and lowered his head onto the kneeling rail. The warmth of the wine burned as it settled in his stomach and then a profound sense of Presence arose within him and he felt overwhelmed. Where the fear and misgivings had been lodged in his soul, Ben discovered new joy. The moment of ecstasy was so wondrous, he feared he would cry out loud.

Just as he stood, a voice seemed to speak within his mind like a thought arising from beyond himself. "When you have done this to the least of these, you have done so unto me." Ben stood rigid, immovable. The message continued to race through his mind. "Your concern for the lost, the deceived, the wayward, is a concern for me. I have not only heard your prayers but read the sincerity and integrity of your heart. Rejoice my son; the dark night is almost finished."

Ben found his way back to the pew and dropped to his knees once more. As the final prayers were said, Ben wept. He was only slightly aware that the procession was preparing to leave the chapel. As the priest passed Ben's pew, the old man put his hand on Ben's shoulder and said simply, "*Non nobis, Domine.*" *Not to us, O Lord, but to your name give glory.* And then he was gone.

Ben stood up and shook his head signaling to Jimmy he didn't want to speak. Jimmy nodded back and the two old friends found their way out of the church.

Little was said on their way back to the Knesset office complex. Dusk was falling over Jerusalem and most of the staff had gone home by the time they got back to Ben's office. To their surprise, Cindy and Rivka were still there.

"Well, Mr. High and Mighty has come back," Cindy said to Rivka. "I'm sure he doesn't have time to listen to anything as mundane as what we've been doing with students all day."

"I'm sorry," Ben acknowledged. "I apologize for being so insensitive."

Cindy still had fire in her eyes. "Well, we've been just as busy," she snapped.

"I'm sure you have." Ben kept nodding his head. "We will try to do better."

Cindy looked away but winked at Rivka out of the corner of her eye.

Ben plopped down in his chair and ran his hand through his hair. "We've had quite an experience. I need to talk about it. I just seem to keep forgetting what this battle is really all about." Ben's head dropped down on his chest. He stared at the floor.

Cindy put her arms around her husband's shoulders and hugged him. "It's okay, dear. The truth is, you're doing a great job. Just tell me about it."

For the next several minutes Ben shared the trip to the old city and his experience of receiving Holy Communion. Rivka listened carefully. Jimmy kept nodding as Ben spoke.

"As I reflected on the meaning of the blood of Christ, I was reminded that our Lord's ultimate victory was won on a cross, the symbol of death and defeat." Ben stared out of his office window into the night. "In the darkest hour when everything seemed to be lost, the triumph of our God was actually closest at hand." Ben shook his finger in the air like a teacher instructing students. "But no human being caused the ultimate victory. Salvation is always God's gift acquired by nothing more or less than His decision of love. Everything is always in God's hands and His hands *alone*."

Jimmy looked up at the ceiling. For a moment his dignified profile gave him the regal look of a patriarch. "Ben was touched by the Holy Spirit today. We must remember that our God reigns, and we don't have to do anything more than be faithful servants. In the end, the victory isn't ours but His."

Cindy squeezed Ben's shoulder. "That's exactly what I wanted to tell you this afternoon. We are training the students to act on that very truth."

"Really?" Ben's eye's widened.

"Operation Opposite Cheek is simply applying Yeshua's teaching from the Sermon on the Mount." Rivka bubbled with enthusiasm as she talked. "What Yeshua did on the cross was actually the ultimate example of turning the other cheek. Yeshua showed us from the cross that the weakness of God is supremely more powerful than the power of men."

"How are you going to do *that?*" Ben asked.

Cindy looked thoughtful for several moments. "Don't forget," she began, "those foot soldiers of the coalition have been raised on the truth about our God and the reign of Yeshua. They are following orders from the generals, but no one knows what is truly in their hearts. Their lifetime of training is on our side."

Jimmy nodded in agreement. "But what does turning the other cheek have to do with the attack on our city?"

"Aggression begets aggression," Cindy continued. "Yeshua knows that an angry counterattack always escalates conflict. On the other hand, love calls forth love. If we refuse to fight and offer them compassion, we will appeal to the best in their hearts. I believe they will refuse to hurt us."

"The martial arts were meant for self-defense," Rivka added. "When we offer no resistance, these judo experts won't have anything to attack. Rather than a fight, we will offer our enemies the gift of love. The students will come out of the city bearing offerings of compassion to our enemies."

Ben stared at Jimmy. Finally he raised his hands as if to protest but dropped them on his desk. "This is the way of the cross," Ben concluded.

# 21

Once the initial troop movements were completed, Ziad Atrash no longer needed his original command post in Egypt. Lack of opposition from the Immortals ended any worry about a retreat and confirmed his projections. By the dawn of Av 8, Ziad had moved his headquarters from the edge of the Red Sea to Masada. Rajah Abu Sita flew in from Syria to assume joint command.

TV screens lined the makeshift building and monitored every side of Jerusalem. Satellite dishes were scattered across the flat top of the ancient desert fortress. Pictures of the troops of the many nations were constantly flashing across other screens.

Even though the late summer heat scorched the Dead Sea basin, the air-conditioning barely kept the room comfortable. The Egyptian leader insisted on wearing a military uniform with medals. "We are poised for a quick flight into Jerusalem as soon as our troops take the Knesset," Atrash explained to Abu Sita. He traced lines across the electronic map in front of the men. "By being the first to take control inside the Knesset itself, we can send our images as supreme conquerors across the world."

Rajah wore the lightweight jersey uniform of soldiers on desert detail. He watched soberly. "Our secret plan to stop the Europeans will make our inability to crack their communications code superfluous. We will create so much confusion in their ranks no counterattack will be possible."

Atrash grinned and ground his huge fist in the palm of his hand. "In one stroke, those obstacles will be gone! But we must be sure the Russians and Chinese don't overreact."

"I have a shuttle prepared to fly to their headquarters once the attack begins," Abu Sita said. "Talking to them in person should alleviate any possible fears."

Atrash grunted and pushed another button on the electronic map. The picture shifted from the political center of Jerusalem to the perimeters around the city showing the placement of the troops. He pointed to the south and traced a line from the Valley of Hinnom up through the Valley of Kidron. "The Ethiopians are assembled on the far end of the Mount of Olives and our Egyptian troops are strung along the rest of the valley to allow us to take the Old City quickly. Your people are next to the Italians. The Jordanians are wedged between the Italians and the French. We've put our martial arts people in the fore of this effort. We want to preserve the Old City from damage, and their attack will ensure nothing will be destroyed."

Rajah said dryly. "I have our priests of Marduk just behind the lines, poised to rush into the Temple Mount and begin polytheistic worship the instant the Temple grounds are clear. Cameras will be ready to flash the pictures around the world."

"*That* sight ought to finish off any resistance from abroad." Atrash grinned. "We have the Europeans set to our immediate left around the tops of the hills to the east, and on the other side of them, the Jordanian army is in place. We will be able to turn our guns on the Italians and the French the moment the attack begins. All our firepower will be concentrated on *them*. In the chaos, they will have no idea how to respond. One quick blow should be enough."

"I will simply tell the Russians and Chinese the two women were preparing to attack them, and we have saved their troops from surprise assault," Abu Sita said.

"The rest of the allies will be ringed on the right side of the city, waiting for our signal to enter the city shooting at and bombing everything that moves. We won't worry about damage to the newer parts of the city." Atrash stepped back and defiantly crossed his arms over his chest. "What are the gods saying?"

The Syrian leader looked quite thoughtful. "Our priests worship before the altars of Marduk and Osiris day and night, constantly chanting and burning incense. We have commanded our soldiers to meditate every day using the prayers El Khader wrote." He paused and inhaled deeply. "Strange things happen the longer one immerses oneself in that atmosphere."

"Are you drunk yet?" Atrash chided.

Abu Sita shook his head. "I backed off after I saw what happened to El Khader. He definitely went crazy."

"He was crazy to begin with."

"You speak of my lifelong friend," Rajah snapped.

"No offense." Ziad tossed the comment aside. "Who knows what goes on inside anyone's head when you get a mixture of smoke and chants floating through the brain?"

"Something *more* goes on with people who sincerely pursue the gods," Rajah insisted. "They are touched by a power—a spiritual reality—that takes control of their minds. Something . . . a spirit . . . seems to attach itself."

"I have learned to use this power for my personal advantage." Ziad sneered. "All that counts is that we are the last people standing when everyone else is on the ground."

"You don't take any of this seriously, do you?"

Atrash laughed. "The bottom line is I am marching at the front of the army that will control the world in twenty-four hours."

"Listen!" Abu Sita pointed his finger in the Egyptian's face. "I watched my childhood mentor become consumed by whatever is on the other side of silence. I've spent enough time trying these meditations and prayers to know we have been playing with fire. You *better* pay attention to your own preaching!"

Atrash smiled. "Don't get so heated. I just don't let myself get hooked on superstition. Understand?"

"No." Rajah shook his head angrily. "You don't understand. We have called up something . . . someone . . . that has been dormant for a long time." He nervously ran his hands through his hair. "We're walking around with a lot more than dynamite in our hands. I warn you that we have a tiger by the tail."

"Listen!" Atrash poked him forcefully on the chest. "When you're talking to me, you've got a lion in your face. Now cut out the 'things-that-go-bump-in-the-night' speech and get ready to go to war."

"I'm sorry." Abu Sita shook his head. "Really sorry I ever went through this door." He turned toward the exit. "None of us will escape easily from this thing." He walked away.

"Have you gone nuts?" Atrash called after him. "Get a grip on yourself." Ziad watched the Syrian walk out across the top of the huge mesa. "Rajah's gotten as goofy as that quack he called a secretary of state."

In the Italian headquarters perched on the ridge along the back side of the Valley of Hinnom, Maria Marchino angrily kept punching in the code for contact with Claudine Toulouse. "Where is she?" Maria said aloud. "Time is running out." Just as she was about to give up, a signal light blinked. Maria hit the hologram button, but no image appeared.

"Claudine Toulouse," the voice said.

"Where in the name of the gods are you!" Maria barked. "And how come I'm only getting a voice signal? Where's your picture?"

"I can't talk right now."

"Can't talk!" Maria was indignant. "Don't you know we're about to go to war? What's happening with this agreement with the Syrians?" She pulled at the collar on her military uniform and mopped her forehead.

"We're talking right now. I need to call you later."

"Later! I've delivered the terms of agreement to the Chinese and the Russians. We've got to have the Jordanians. Cut out the champagne dinners and get business done."

"I said, *later*." Claudine clicked the phone off.

The Italian leader stared at the silent speakerphone and kicked her chair.

Only five miles away, Claudine Toulouse flipped the silence switch to kill all incoming calls. "I've got to tell her something," she turned to Khalil Hussein. Her silk robe was tied loosely about her waist. She leaned against the bedroom wall, her bare leg propped up against a small end table.

The king laughed and abruptly pulled her close. "Tell her how good I am." He kissed her forcefully.

Claudine hung on to his neck and sighed. "I should tell Maria how wicked you are." She smiled and stepped back. "The truth is . . . what am I going to say? 'Sorry, the deal's off. I've got a better one.'" She whirled around like a dancer. "Too bad, Maria dear, but Khalil and I are sailing down the Nile to find Cleopatra's old throne. We worked out something on the side with the Russians and Chinese and I forgot to tell you."

Hussein shrugged. "Just keep telling her that I'm uncertain but I will offer no resistance to your previous plans. We mean Maria no harm. She just doesn't fit into what we have planned for the future." He began rubbing Claudine's neck. "I want you to spend the night with me. We can call Marchino in the morning with a good story."

"You make me feel so young," Claudine purred. "I keep forgetting how much difference there is in our ages."

"I prefer wines mellowed and seasoned with age. Claudine, you are a superb vintage."

The French leader breathed deeply. "I'll call her back later in the day and tell her something. Khalil, you are the consummate man. Are you sure Chardoff and Fong will sign with us?"

"How could you ever doubt me?" He kissed her again

Jimmy, Ben, Cindy, and Rivka sat in the command office in the Internal Affairs building, studying their wall screen filled with pictures of the armies positioned around Jerusalem. Each was dressed in the traditional jersey uniforms of government officials and even Rivka was newly outfitted to look like a government leader.

"We have a shuttlecraft flying as high as possible, beaming these pictures to us." Ben explained. "I pray they don't get shot. I think we've identified where all segments of the opposition are located. At this time, the top of the Mount of Olives is completely occupied by the Egyptians with the Ethiopians on one end and the Syrians on the other. Obviously, these troops will dash down the mountainside toward the Old City walls."

"What do you make of this tragedy?" Cindy asked Jimmy.

"I think they have two major objectives: take control of the Knesset building and occupy the Temple Mount. They want possession of the religious center of the city."

Ben nodded. "Jimmy's right. My guess is that they will send their martial arts people over the walls first. After they have taken the show places, their troops will start shooting."

"Then our students should line the walls of the Old City," Rivka observed.

"And that's where we need to be, too," Jimmy concluded. "If I'm going to go down, I want it to be in the same place where all the ancient sacrifices were made."

Ben nodded his head soberly. "I have asked all of our citizens to stay in their homes and pray. Resistance makes no sense. I have no idea what will follow, but if we must walk the way of the Cross, we have to be prepared to be slaughtered in the onslaught."

Cindy took her husband's hand. "The last time we faced such terror we were huddled together in an old farmhouse in California. On that dark night, God brought His light." She squeezed his fingers. "I am honored to stand with you again."

Ben took off his thick glasses and wiped his eyes. "Thank you, dear." He hugged her.

Jimmy pulled himself up to his full height. He brought his cane up under his arm and stood erect, like a general with a swagger stick. "I, too, am honored and humbled to march shoulder to shoulder with my friends. If we go down, we will do so together."

Ben reached out for Rivka's hand. "Your grandfather would be very proud of you, child. Never look back. Only forward. Our God is leading us to a victory we can't see. We trust it will come to pass."

Rivka bit her lip and nodded. "I will have our students in place tonight. We will sleep on the walls so as to be ready whenever the charge comes."

"The ancient pilgrims to Jerusalem once slept in the Church of the Holy Sepulcher to be close to the place of the crucifixion," Ben said. "I think I'd like to do the same. Would you all join me? I have nothing to offer but a stone mattress."

"Indeed!" Jimmy smiled for the first time.

Ben shook his old friend's hand. "I know that God has a plan in all of this confusion. I just don't know what it is."

"I wonder if Yeshua might intend to redeem everything after the city is totally destroyed," Cindy said pensively. "Maybe all of that dynamite and all of those bombs will be used to burn everything to the ground."

"We have to be prepared for the worst."

As the late summer sun sank behind the rugged terrain of the wilderness, Ziad Atrash and Rajah Abu Sita stood before the transmission camera to review the final plans for the attack the next morning with the other leaders. Atrash concluded, "Colleagues, we are poised for the ultimate victory. Nothing can stop us now. As the sun rises we will march to our destinies. The time of unified attack is precisely 7:00 A.M. We shall launch the assault while it is still cool. Good night and good luck." The leaders waved and their pictures faded.

"Everything is set," Rajah said resolutely.

Ziad reset the code and began again. "Brothers of the desert, you have just viewed the message heard by all coalition commanders and heads of state. Only you are receiving this final word of instruction. Your call to attack is one hour earlier, when no one is prepared. Six o'clock is the moment of decision for us. Do not issue assault orders until fifteen minutes before the strike. Surprise is of the utmost importance. Show no mercy. Are there any questions?"

No electronic response followed.

"Our final contact is complete. You will hear nothing more from us until after the assault is underway." Atrash saluted and turned off the cameras. Abu Sita had already left the command center.

Ziad walked slowly out of the center and across the hot sand until he came to the edge of the plateau. He looked out across the deep blue waters of the salty Dead Sea. The last light of day and the coming shadows of night painted a constantly changing panorama of beauty on the eroded crags and valleys that emptied into the barren basin.

"I don't need a god," Ziad spoke more to the wind than to himself. "I am enough."

Images floated across his mind. Friends laughing at him in school. His parents' displeasure with his lack of progress. Hiding in the closet filled with shame. The years of painful struggle to overcome the limitations of dyslexia. Each image left Ziad feeling diminished. He ground his teeth and clinched his fist.

"By the time the sun sets tomorrow evening, I will have made a mark all history will remember. No one will ever say again that I was insignificant!"

# CHAPTER

## 22

The bedroom was totally dark. Dawn was starting to break but the curtains were still drawn. "Wake her up," the Jordanian king commanded his aides.

Two soldiers shook Claudine Toulouse several times before she opened her eyes. "Time to start the war?" she said drowsily.

"Afraid so." The king smiled sardonically.

Claudine sat up in bed and rubbed her eyes. "Who's in here?"

"Special soldiers selected to get things under way." Khalil Hussein punched a clicker and all the lights in the room went on. Behind the two soldiers were four other men standing with rifles in hand. "They have come to escort you."

Claudine pulled the sheet up and blinked uncomprehendingly. "I don't understand."

"I forgot to tell you a number of things yesterday." The king sat down on a silk padded chair in the center of the room. "We've made a number of changes in our original strategy."

"Get these men out of here," Claudine ordered, searching across the top of the bed for a robe. "I don't talk with subordinates around."

Khalil ignored her. "At first, we really had no idea that you and the Italian had some sort of plot going. It wasn't until you tried to pull me into your scheme that we really understood what was under way."

"What in the name of the gods is going on?" Claudine pushed her hair back out of her eyes. "I said, *get these men out of here!*"

Khalil laughed. "To think all this nonsense began because we just wanted to get two women out of the picture."

"We?" Claudine shook her head. "Stop talking in riddles."

"Oh, yes." The king settled back in the chair and crossed his arms over his chest. "I suppose I should tell you all the details. We, of course, is Atrash, Abu Sit , and myself."

Claudine swung her legs out of bed, pulling the sheet around her. She struggled to stand. "I . . . I . . . don't get any of this." She steadied herself against a night stand next to the bed.

"You offended Ziad one too many times. He sent me to simply distract you and make you vulnerable. We had no idea you were trying to work something out with the Russians and Chinese. How fortunate you confided everything to me."

"What?" Claudine's eyes widened in horror. She looked desperately around the room into the sea of stoic faces. "You . . . you . . ." She grabbed a rock statue from the bed stand and lunged forward. Before Claudine could raise the statue above her shoulders, the two soldiers grabbed the object and knocked her to the floor.

"You must understand," Khalil continued. "Arabs are brothers. I could never betray my kin over a silly little affair."

"No, no!" Claudine pounded on the floor. "No!"

Hussein looked at the clock on the far wall. "In two hours your friend Maria thinks the war will begin. In one hour we will begin our attack on *her.*"

Claudine screamed a long, guttural cry and clenched her fists tightly. "N-o-o-o!"

"You will excuse me now." The king stood up. "Unfortunately, we have a war to attend to. Take her away."

The two soldiers jerked the French leader to her feet and shook her roughly. She tried to resist, but they held her tightly. "I thought you loved me!" she cried out.

"No," Khalil answered. "I said I found you very attractive. Your way of handling power was quite appealing. Lust, yes. Love, no."

"You betrayed me!" Claudine screamed at him.

"Oh no." Khalil smiled. "You betrayed yourself."

The soldiers pulled Claudine toward the door. "Where am I going?" she yelled over her shoulder.

"Someplace where you will be safe," the king answered.

Three soldiers with rifles fell in behind the aides dragging the French leader out. Her cries and protests could be heard far down the hallway. Only one aide stayed behind.

"I don't want her body ever found," Hussein said factually. "Stand her against the basement wall and shoot her on the spot. Bury the body underneath the stone floor in the basement. When it's done, I want you personally to shoot the five soldiers who observed everything." The king pointed his finger in the aide's face. "I don't want any eyewitnesses left!"

The aide saluted and turned on his heels.

"Khalil walked quickly down the stairs and across the courtyard in the center of the building. Once inside the command center he found a technician waiting for him.

"We have her recordings cued into the voice translator." The man began throwing switches. "Whatever you say into the transmitter will sound identical to the French woman's voice. We can transmit in French, Hebrew, or English."

"Go to English," the king commanded. "You also have her secret communique numbers in the system?"

"Yes, sir."

"Ok! Let's wake up the Italian sleeping beauty. Keep the hologram off."

Maria Marchino answered on the first beep. "Where are you?" she barked.

"I've got the agreement signed," Hussein said.

"Took you long enough, Claudine," Maria snapped.

"Forget the Jordanians. They are on our side now."

"Good. It was long overdue."

"What about the Russians and Chinese?"

"Once I tell them of Hussein's agreement, they will quickly align with us."

"I will not talk with you again, Maria, until after the attacks begin."

"At 7:00 A.M., we crush the Arabs. Ciao. See you inside the city." The Italian leader clicked off.

Hussein smiled. "Indeed! Perhaps, I won't ever see you again, my little pigeon." He turned to the technician. "Get me the Masada command post. I must speak with Ziad Atrash immediately."

The sky over Jerusalem was already light by 5:30 A.M. Although the sun had not yet appeared, darkness was fading quickly. Av 9 had come once again to the Holy City.

Ben, Cindy, and Jimmy had already left the Church of the Holy Sepulcher and were walking slowly toward the Temple Mount and the Eastern Wall where some of the students were still sleeping.

"Are you scared?" Ben asked his wife.

"No." Cindy shook her head. "Every time I woke up, I

could hear people singing or praying somewhere in the church. I'm tired, but I feel wonderfully reassured."

Ben took his wife's hand. "At least we will have this opportunity to stand together one last time."

Jimmy walked unusually bent over, poking at the cobblestones with his cane. "I don't mind telling you that my back is killing me. If we're going to get slaughtered, I'm ready for it to come quickly."

"Little pessimistic there, James?" Ben asked. "You don't fool me. You are one tough old buzzard."

Jimmy's eyes were swollen and the paunch under his narrow chin shook. He ran his hands through his thin white hair. "I'm just way too old for this sort of adventure," he groused.

"You always were a bundle of cheer in the morning," Ben chided. He opened a wrought iron gate into the Temple area and let the other two pass by him. "Let's cut through the Court of the Gentiles and see how fast we can find Rivka."

"She said she'd be in the area by the Golden Gate." Cindy hung on Ben's arm. "You boys can walk a little slower, you know."

"Glorious summer morning," Ben observed. "A great day to face death if necessary."

"Over here!" someone called from the wall.

"Look!" Cindy pointed. "There's Rivka!"

"What's all this stuff?" Jim poked at crates scattered in front of the wall. "Looks like fruit."

Cindy answered, "When the attackers come, the students will go out of the gates with offerings of fruit, bread, and vegetables. We will welcome them as children of God."

"Sure hope you're right." Jimmy shook his head.

"Join us on the wall." Rivka kept waving.

Some students were still getting out of bedrolls. Several crews had already assembled in front of the wall to prepare coffee, juice, and bagels. Others were opening the crates and placing oranges, grapefruits, and strawberries in small baskets. They waved in respect as the trio passed.

Ben, Cindy, and Jimmy climbed the last stairs to the top of the wall where they could see out across the Kidron Valley. They saw the ancient path of the Palm Sunday procession down the Mount of Olives. The Basilica of the Agony and the Garden of Gethsemane were obvious at the bottom of the valley. Along the top of the mountain line to the east the coalition troops were obviously moving into place. Shuttles swooped over the ridge and troop carriers sped along the streets.

"I wouldn't think they would waste much time," Ben observed "There's no need for their men to wait to attack us."

"As soon as troops start coming up from the valley," Cindy pointed as she talked, "the students will start walking down the hill with gifts in hand. We will know quickly if our plan is going to work."

Jimmy drew himself up to his full height. "Ours will be the noblest of efforts, regardless."

"I left instructions with Mrs. Netanyahu at the office," Ben added. "Should we fail, there is a recorded statement for release declaring our allegiance to Yahweh to the end."

A formation of twenty coalition shuttles suddenly lifted off the top of the Mount of Olives. The v-shaped formation flew straight up and then silently nosedived toward the Old City.

"Here they come!" Ben yelled. "Get ready!"

The shuttles shot barely fifty feet over the heads of the students but kept flying straight across the city.

"I expected them to bomb us!" Ben pointed after the craft. "Must have been an initial reconnaissance."

The shuttles maintained formation until they reached the city limits and then broke into separate directions, flying directly over the coalition soldiers on the other side of the ridge. Each shuttlecraft again veered straight up into the sky before executing a barrel roll and diving straight toward the ground. Suddenly the ground shook as explosion followed explosion. The far ridge erupted in bursts of flame and bellows of smoke. Immediately, the echo of gunfire filled the valley. The crackle of hundreds of rifles sounded like strings of firecrackers going off in every direction.

"What's happening?" Jimmy shook Ben's arm. "What in the world are they doing?"

"I...I...just don't know. Looks like they are shooting at each other."

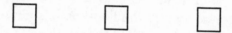

Ziad Atrash stood glued to his monitors, watching the bombing. Across the entire length of the European troop placements, bombs blew large holes in the soldiers' ranks. Bodies flew through the air like debris in a tornado. Buildings burst into flames and timbers scattered like toothpicks.

"Excellent!" Ziad pounded on the desk. "We are dead center on target." He turned to his command radio transmitter. "Give me a closeup of the Italian's command headquarters."

The picture zoomed into larger focus. The flat roof of the building was collapsed and fire poured out of the windows. Only the far end of the complex was still standing.

"Hit that command building again!" Ziad bellowed. "I don't want anything standing. Now!"

A shuttlecraft zoomed across the TV screen and dropped low over the damaged structure. The plane slowed to hover speed and then shot straight up. Immediately the top of the remaining building burst into flame.

"Excellent!" Ziad radioed the pilots. "Now get out of the

way so the infantry can move in." He turned to his other command system. "Troops of the New Order! Attack now. Kill everything in sight."

On the top of the ridge beyond the Hinnom Valley, the Egyptian troops charged. Beneath them in the valley, the Syrian troops began their advance forward. The two-pronged attack caught the Europeans off guard on both fronts. At that moment, the Jordanians stationed to the north turned their guns on the remaining flank of the Italians. Arab troops ran down alleys and up side streets, shooting like wild men at everything that moved.

The top of what remained of the Italian command post was engulfed in flames. Underneath the burning ceiling, men lay strewn around the floor. Smoke poured in from both above the ceiling and below the floor.

Maria Marchino tried to stand up but couldn't move the large table off her back. "Help!" she cried. "Somebody help me."

An aide struggled to his feet and hobbled across the room. He pushed with his last ounce of strength and the table slowly slid off her body. With a final sigh, the man rolled over on his side on the floor.

Maria tried to stand but her left leg wouldn't move. "What's happened?" She started to pull herself across the floor but could only move inches at a time, pushing herself forward by her elbows. The heat was increasing in intensity. "Somebody get me out!"

The sound of gunfire grew steadily louder. Men were hollering in the streets. The noise of chaos was nearly deafening.

Maria looked up at the scattered electronic receivers and broken screens. "I've got to find out what has happened."

Suddenly two men with rifles appeared in the door.

"That's her!" one soldier cried out. "We've found Marchino!"

"Get me out of here!" Maria cried.

Shots tore through the air. The Italian leader's body pulsated, jerking back and forth as the bullets blew her life away.

From his Masada compound, Atrash carefully studied the shuttlecraft's transmission. "It's safe to assume the European command is destroyed," he said to Abu Sita. "I think it's time for your trip to see Chardoff and Fong."

Rajah nodded. "I suppose so."

"For the time being, we won't let them know that Hussein knew about the attempts to bring their countries into the Europeans' camp. We only need them to sit still."

Rajah nodded his head and left the room without comment. His two-person shuttlecraft was ready in the center of Masada's landing strip. Within minutes, he was flying across the eroded wilderness to the west of the battle. Abu Sita's first pass went far north of Jerusalem across the fertile plain around Tel Aviv and then dropped low to glide into the area behind the lines held by the Russians and Chinese. Troops were running in every direction, obviously confused by the fighting to the west of their units.

The Syrian head of state landed on the street in front of the large hotel commandeered for the Russian and Chinese military command. He hurried out of the craft and into the hotel.

Coalition troops immediately recognized him and stood at attention as Abu Sita passed. "Take me to your leaders," he told a guard at the end of the first corridor.

Chardoff and Fong were standing at the window of the eighth floor, staring out at the fires burning on the other side of their eastern flank. They turned when Abu Sita entered but didn't seem surprised to see him.

Abu Sita began talking the moment he walked through

the door. "I came at once to alert you personally to what is happening. We discovered a most serious plot to defraud all of us. The Italian and French commanders intended to betray our alliance. We had no alternative but to protect you."

"Sit down." Chardoff pointed to a chair. Fong stood beside the Russian. "Tell us more."

Rajah nodded and dropped into the large chair. "For some time, we suspected an attempt to form a separate front in case the battle failed, but we soon found reason to believe the two women were plotting against all of us. We have maintained spies in the midst of their camp." He stopped and looked carefully at the impassive heads of state. "You do understand?"

Both men nodded but said nothing.

"We know that Toulouse is now dead and believe Marchino has met the same fate. We believe that we will have the rest of the quislings in line by the time we kick off our joint attack at 7:00 A.M. We should not experience any delays in our original projections."

"Such expert planning," Chardoff began. "But one would think you would have let your allies in on the details much earlier."

"We weren't quite sure of—"

"Of who all the players were," Fong interrupted. "Perhaps, you did not trust *us*."

"Oh! Nothing of the sort!" Abu Sita jumped from his chair. "We simply didn't want to create undue suspicion until we were sure of the facts."

"Or had us in a position to attack next," Chardoff added coldly.

"Next?" The Syrian's eyes widened. "Never!"

"Let me show you a little something that came in early this morning." Chardoff pointed to the screen on the opposite wall.

Maria Marchino's picture appeared. "Gentlemen, we have every reason to believe the Egyptians and Syrians will attack us first in the guise of assaulting the city. Once Europeans are out of the way, the Arabs will turn to your armies. Even Khalil Hussein has joined us out of concern for his future. Unless we have a mutual defense treaty, we will end up the slaves of Atrash. Jerusalem is no obstacle to world conquest for this Egyptian tyrant but we are. We must stand together or fall separately."

"No!" Abu Sita's mouth dropped. "It can't be! Hussein didn't mean that was his intention."

"Appears Miss Marchino was somewhat of a prophet," Chardoff said dryly.

"And even without the help of your god Marduk," Fong added.

"Don't jump to the wrong conclusions," Abu Sita said, gesturing frantically. "Her little speech is just part of their plot."

"Plot?" Chardoff turned to Fong. "Yes, but not the one you're trying to sell us, Rajah."

"Did you think us to be such fools that we wouldn't see through this little subterfuge of yours?" Fong's eyes narrowed. "However, we didn't expect you to come walking in here so easily. No, my friend, neither the Russians nor the Chinese have any intention of building bricks for you and your mad empire-building Egyptian despot."

"I tell you . . ." Rajah stopped and swallowed hard. "You've read all the signs wrong. Completely wrong."

"I liked you, Rajah." Chardoff unbuttoned his uniform. "You were so much more humane than that thick-headed bull. Unfortunately, the two of you were simply cut from the same cloth."

Chardoff drew his pistol from under his coat and pointed the gun straight at Rajah. His first shot struck the Syrian square in the forehead, knocking him over the back of the chair.

"The Arabs struck much earlier than we calculated." Chardoff put the gun back in his shoulder holster. "We have no choice but to hurl our men into the center of their lines. We must charge down the Hinnon Valley and wait until they finish with the Europeans."

"Undoubtedly, the Arabs will sustain casualties," Fong mused. "We will be able to take advantage of their losses as well as the fact they don't expect our attack."

"Our shuttles are loaded with explosives." Chardoff turned back to the window. "They've already spent their supply. We will soften them up with bombs before our men finish them off."

"Let us go instruct our commanders about the dash down the valley." Fong pointed to the door. "After you, Mr. Prime Minister.

The Russian laughed and the two men hurried out without looking back at Abu Sita's body.

At the other end of the military circle around Jerusalem, Ali of Ethiopia frantically watched his TV monitor's pictures of the battle raging on the other side of the city. He stared incongruously at the screen.

"What do you make of it, General Ali?" the aide asked. "Should we not call Ziad Atrash for information?"

"Something has gone completely wrong." Ali rubbed his chin with his long thin fingers. We must be careful not to get caught in the middle."

"Coalition troops appear to be fighting with each other."

"Yes," Ali said slowly, "or maybe . . . possibly . . . they are fighting against an enemy in their midst."

"I don't understand." The aide shook his head.

"What if the Immortals have finally reappeared?" Ali asked.

"We could never defeat them!" The soldier gasped.

"Exactly!" The Ethiopian leader exclaimed. "We have been lured into a trap set by the Immortals. They waited until we were massed in one place and then attacked. They are killing us!"

"We must contact Atrash for direction."

"No!" Ali barked. "Heavens no! We must not walk into the same trap!"

"What shall we do?" the officer begged.

Ali paced back and forth. "We must maintain radio silence, lest we be lured into a trap." He stopped and snapped his fingers. "We must make the Immortals believe we were always on their side."

"How?" The aide held up his hands in bewilderment.

"We must attack the Russians and Chinese . . . or anyone left standing! Order our soldiers to destroy all coalition flags and run up the colors of Yeshua's government. Tell our men we are on Yeshua's side and order the fighting to begin at once."

"Excellent!" The aide breathed deeply. "A brilliant stroke. We can still extricate ourselves."

"At once!" Ali ordered the solider out of his room.

Back on top of Masada, Ziad listened carefully to the communique that Marchino's body had been found. From the pictures he could tell his men were overwhelming her bewildered troops. The French were in total disarray as Hussein kept issuing confusing instructions over the voice translator.

"Much better than I thought," Ziad mumbled to himself. He pushed the buttons for special transmission to the field generals. "We are ahead of schedule. Send the martial arts people down the hill. I want to take the Temple compound as quickly as possible. Unlock the worldwide satellite transmission so these pictures can go through normal channels. There is no longer any need to block communication."

Ziad stepped back from the monitors. He rubbed the

back of his neck, realizing how tense he had been through the entire attack. "I need some fresh air," he said to his aides. "Don't bother me. I'm going to take a walk."

*Who knows,* he thought to himself, *by the time I get back this whole campaign could be over.*

# 23

Ben kept pointing up and down the valley. "I can't believe my eyes! Our enemies are killing each other! And look at how strange the sky is. Weird color everywhere!"

Explosions along the ridge sent large balls of fire up into the sky. Columns of smoke were turning the western sky black. The rapid staccato of gunfire continued unabated. Dark clouds of smoke drifted overhead.

"This scenario is just what happened to King Hezekiah," Jimmy shouted above the uproar. "We're sitting here watching the enemy kill themselves."

The students cheered and applauded. Rivka ran up and down the ramparts to encourage her troops. "We are winning," she shouted over and over. "Get ready for their attack."

Ben's wristwatch communicator abruptly buzzed. "Yes," he shouted into the receiver. "Who is it?"

Mrs. Netanyahu's familiar voice answered. "Ben, I didn't know whether to contact you under the circumstances, but I thought you'd want to know immediately. The international satellite system has started to work again. We have a message waiting from Isaiah Murphy."

"Wonderful! Can you beam it to us?"

"Hang on. I'll patch in the picture and audio."

Ben waved for Cindy and Jimmy to gather around. He shielded the small screen from the light and the pre-recorded picture emerged. "We're back!" Isaiah's familiar face filled the small viewer. "We've tried everything to get through and couldn't. But we recorded this message and set our transmitters to send the communique as soon as the channels opened."

"Isaiah really is clever," Jimmy said. "Doesn't miss a lick."

Isaiah pointed to a map on the wall behind him. "We have organized resistance groups up and down the coast. Just wanted you to know that multitudes of people are remaining faithful. No matter what happens over there, the Believers aren't throwing in the towel. The president of this country can say anything he chooses but the majority is not with him."

"We aren't alone!" Jimmy shook his cane toward the sky.

"Just remember one little story," Isaiah continued. "A scorpion asked a frog to let him ride on his back across a river. The frog said, 'If I do, you'll sting me, and I'll die.' The scorpion assured the frog no such thing would happen as they would both drown. The frog let the scorpion on and started across the river. Halfway to the other side, the scorpion unleashed his venomous tail and stung the frog. 'Why?' the dying frog cried. 'Now, we will both die.' The scorpion shrugged. 'I am a scorpion and it is my nature to sting frogs. Sorry.'"

"I don't get it." Jimmy grunted.

"Remember that the Evil One is stuck on who he is," Isaiah continued. "He's clever but not shrewd enough to keep from outwitting himself. The Devil will not prevail." Isaiah waved and the picture faded.

The trio looked across the valley once more.

"Is not the scorpion stinging the frog?" Cindy asked.

Suddenly new cries filled the air. Men in black jersey uniforms charged across the creek at the bottom of the Kidron Valley and up toward the walls. A sea of black shapes swept across the field like locusts devouring everything in their path.

"Here they come!" Rivka called to the students. "Open the gates. Let us go forth in the name of our God!"

Cindy rushed down the steps. "I have to help my troops," she called over her shoulder.

"What do you think?" Ben asked Jimmy.

Jimmy peered over the edge. "They're not far away and coming fast. The hour of reckoning is at hand."

"Are we going to stand up here and watch?"

"You're right, Ben! We can't stay here. We have to join them."

"What?"

"No, I won't argue with you. Let's go." Jimmy started down the steps, testing each one with his cane.

Ben shook his head. "Here we go again." He hurried after his friend.

A few students pushed the Golden Gates wide open while others poured out along the front of the wall. Each person carried a basket of fruit or bread. The attackers were no more than a hundred yards away.

"Remember your instructions," Rivka called up and down the line. "Take what they give and give what they take." Rivka hurried to the center of the line of students to lead the group forward.

The soldiers stopped when the students walked slowly toward them. Students began waving as if greeting old friends. The attackers looked at each other uncomprehendingly. Some men assumed defensive positions, others began making slow circular motions with their hands. The students edged forward, offering their baskets of fruit and loaves of bread. The soldiers looked around for someone to give directions. They appeared confused.

"We are your friends," Rivka called out. "Our hands are extended in friendship. Are we not one people under Yeshua?"

Several attackers broke ranks and charged forward. A young man bore down on Rivka, stopping only a few feet in front of her. The soldier immediately spun around backward and swung his foot high over his shoulder. The man's foot caught Rivka across the side of her face. The basket of oranges spilled over the ground, as Rivka fell sideways and bounced on the hard rocks. The soldier settled back into a judo-defense stance. Both lines stopped and watched.

Rivka rolled on the ground writhing in pain. Immediately, another young woman stepped into her place and extended a loaf of bread. "We wish you no harm. Are we not your friends?" As the young woman took a step forward, the attacker backed away as if uncertain of what to do next.

Three other soldiers rushed at the defense line. Students opened their arms, offering no resistance, which gave the martial arts fighters an unprotected target shot. The soldiers made menacing jabs and slashes with their hands but the students smiled and didn't move. Suddenly an attacker lunged for the mid-section of one of the young men. When the boy doubled in pain, the solider struck him on the back of the neck with the side of his hand. The student crumbled to the ground. The judo fighter dropped back into a defensive stance ready for a counterattack. None came.

Soldiers kept looking around, trying to find someone to give them orders. Bombs were still exploding on the far ridges, but no one seemed to be in charge of directing military operations. The martial arts fighters looked like an isolated line of attackers.

Students began humming a popular hymn of the day. "Glor-or-ia, Glor-or-ia," their song continued, "Glory to the Lamb. For He is our peace." Others waved good-naturedly and kept smiling. "We are your brothers and sisters!" Some kids cried out, "We come armed only with love. We are one family of God." A voice called over the rest, "Come home to your people."

Cindy emerged from the ranks of the young people and stood near Rivka. Her snow-white hair and Oriental face made a sharp contrast with the black hair and dark complexions of most of the young people. She held both hands above her head as if petitioning in prayer. "Let's end all hostilities," Cindy called to the attackers. "Even now your leaders are in retreat. Don't be duped any longer."

"Blue blazes!" Ben gasped. "She's out there by herself. They'll strike her just like they did Rivka." Ben bolted forward, pushing his way through the students.

"You're right!" Jimmy shook his cane in the air. "We must protect her at all costs. Cindy's too old and frail to survive an attack."

The two men broke through the line of students and ran toward Cindy. "Don't you dare touch my wife!" Ben shook his fist in the air.

Two soldiers had cautiously crept toward Cindy. The men kept moving with their hands in front of them in slow circling movements. Cindy walked forward calling to the men to join her.

Ben rushed past Cindy and pointed his finger at the first soldier. "You wouldn't dare attack an old lady!" Jimmy was at his heels, swinging his cane through the air.

The soldier grabbed Ben's outstretched arm and swung the old man behind him. For a second Ben looked like he was flying a few feet above the ground. He landed with a hard, dull thud.

Jimmy swung his cane at the head of the second soldier.

With a simple pivot at the waist, the soldier used the cane to gain leverage, sending Jimmy head over heels in a somersault. Jimmy fell on his back in a clump of bushes.

Ben kept gasping for air. His face was white. He could barely breathe, his glasses smashed on the ground. Jimmy sprawled defenselessly staring at the sky, equally stunned. The soldiers dropped into their judo stance and started circling Cindy.

Cindy looked troubled but managed a smile. "You see," she addressed the soldiers, "my husband is only trying to protect me. He doesn't wish you harm. Can you gain anything by hurting old people?"

The soldiers took a step backward and glanced at Ben and Jimmy. Both men were barely able to move.

"We offer you nothing but love," Cindy continued. "We forgive you for any pain caused us."

"Hey, I know those men!" a soldier yelled. "They are the two leaders, the TV guys!"

"Take them into custody," the man in front of Cindy instructed. "Get them back to our command."

Cindy bit her lip but didn't move as Ben and Jimmy were dragged away. "Remember your training from the days of your youth," she shouted to them. "What did your parents teach you? Look into your hearts and recognize what is true." Cindy watched the coalition soldiers hustling Jimmy and Ben toward the creek. They were obviously calling someone for instructions. "Help us, Lord," she prayed aloud.

The students close to the soldiers inched onward and then dropped to the ground at the feet of their attackers. They pushed the fruit and bread forward. Only then did other students rush over to help Rivka. They carried her back to the city gate.

Finally a soldier bent down and picked up an apple. Another started to eat a peach. The men relaxed and gave up their judo stances. Conversations broke out and the atmosphere of tension eased.

Cindy kept looking up and down the line as the air of confrontation dissipated. She watched nervously as her husband and friend were dragged farther and farther away. By the time they reached the bottom of the valley, Jimmy and Ben were surrounded by many soldiers. Cindy kept her place, trying to smile and stay calm.

In a few minutes, it was clear Cindy and Rivka's strategy was working. The students and soldiers were about the same age. They looked into each other's faces and no longer saw an enemy. Students invited the attackers in to see the city. With no one to attack, the soldiers' sense of purpose was broken.

From the top of the Mount of Olives, a shuttlecraft flew up into the sky before swooping down into the valley and landing just at the edge of the creek. Cindy watched in horror as Jimmy and Ben were loaded into the craft. The plane lifted and sped down the valley, lifting up over the ridge of the mountains.

For the last twenty minutes, chaos had consumed the leaders in the Masada command center on the plateau high above the Dead Sea. Ziad Atrash lurched from monitor to monitor trying to grasp what was happening. He kept returning to the picture of the Ethiopian army marching under the banner of the Jerusalem government.

"I told you to get Ali on the intercom immediately!" Ziad bellowed at his aide.

The man gestured nervously. "They . . just won't answer. Nothing gets a response."

"These idiots are attacking the Russians and the Chinese!" Atrash kept pointing at the TV screen. "What's that worthless flag doing up there?"

Another general dashed into the room. "Abu Sita can't be found anywhere. His staff has not heard from him since he landed in Jerusalem. His shuttlecraft is still there, but he's disappeared."

Atrash cursed violently. "Can't be! It just can't be. Get me Hussein on the phone."

Another monitor flashed pictures of Egyptian troops falling in the face of terrible explosions. Men were scattered about the streets and lying in heaps in the gutter.

"I can't believe my eyes!" Atrash screamed.

"We've just picked up a communique from the Ethiopian command that a statement is forthcoming." The aide hit buttons and the screens cleared. Ali's picture appeared.

"Peoples of the world," the Ethiopian spoke rapidly, "be aware that we are working with the Immortals to restore normalcy in Jerusalem."

"The *Immortals!*" Atrash grabbed the edge of the table.

"Obviously, our glorious leaders have returned and are now destroying your enemies. The Immortals have decimated the European armies and are now attacking the Arab coalition. We are offering support by assailing the flanks of these renegades. Order should be restored shortly. Rest assured, our efforts have always been with our glorious leader, Yeshua."

"The stupid fool has mistaken *our* attack as the work of the Immortals. That conniving idiot!" Atrash cursed again.

"What if he's right?" an aide asked.

"What do you mean?" Ziad screamed.

"Maybe the Immortals have led us into a trap." Color drained from the man's face as he spoke. "Maybe Ali is right."

Ziad glanced around the room. Every man in the command center was staring at the aide in shock, their eyes filled with consternation and misgiving. Atrash grabbed a rifle from the man at the door and swung the wooden butt into the face of the aide. The hapless man smashed into the wall and crumpled to the floor. With another staggering blow, Ziad cracked the unconscious man's head against the cement floor. He threw the gun back through the door.

"Anyone else got any other traitorous suggestions?" Atrash looked around the room. No one moved. "Let's get on with business. What's the current status of our troops?"

No one spoke.

Atrash pointed to the aide seated before the Egyptian monitor. "Speak up!" he demanded.

"We . . . lost . . . men . . . many men . . . hitting the Europeans. The Russians and Chinese are chewing up our troops." The aide inhaled and raised his arm slightly as if to protect his face. "Their bombs have ripped us to pieces."

"I've got to find Abu Sita." Atrash wrung his hands. "Where is he?"

No one answered. The only sounds in the room were the messages coming from the monitors.

"Get him out of here." Atrash pointed to the body of his aide. "The only squadron unaccounted for is our martial arts outfit. Get them on the line."

The soldier at the last monitor heaved a sigh of relief. "Good news!" He smiled broadly. "Our men have captured two of the opposition leaders—Harrison and Feinberg. They are being flown in here right now."

"A breakthrough!" Ziad shook both fists in the air. "Now, we will turn this thing around."

A general from the central screening area stepped forward. "Regardless of the cost to me, I must tell you some bad news. The Egyptian and Syrian armies are, for all practical purposes, destroyed." He stood at attention as if expecting a firing squad. "We knocked out the Europeans, but the Russians and Chinese prevailed. They are currently locked in mortal combat with the Jordanians."

Atrash ground his teeth and clenched his fist. "They will pay!" He could barely speak.

"I have just been able to get Hussein on the line," an aide interrupted.

"Khalil," Ziad spoke into the monitor, "are you all right?"

"No." The transmission was poor and without a picture. "The Ethiopians attacked me. They got inside our command center before we knew they had turned against us." Hussein's voice sounded weak. "We had a violent shootout . . . a bomb went off. Not much is left. The fighting is moving from house to house. They are eating us alive."

"Hang on," Atrash demanded. "Don't stop now! We still have a chance."

"For what?" Hussein choked. "I've been shot. The whole thing is going up in smoke." The receiver went silent.

Aides glanced at each other but said nothing. Atrash looked from man to man with hate and suspicion in his eyes. The men avoided eye contact.

"They're arriving!" the aide in charge of the martial arts platoon said confidently. "We have the enemy leaders in custody."

"Well!" Atrash ran his hands through his hair and pulled his uniform down tightly. "Let us greet our adversaries with all due hospitality." He stomped out of the building with his top aides following.

A strange cast covered the entire sky. Even though nothing could shield the unforgiving heat of the summer sun, the clouds grew dark and it looked as if a terrible storm was brewing. The craft came straight in from the north, breaking through a bank of red-lined thunderheads. The shuttle glided quietly to a halt on the runway in the center of the ancient fortress. The bubble top lifted and two soldiers in black uniforms got out. The men helped Jimmy and Ben down. Without his glasses, Ben had a hard time making out what was happening around him. Jimmy ap-

peared equally helpless without his cane. For several moments they held to the side of the craft, trying to get their
bearings.

"Bring them to me," Ziad commanded. "I want them
over here by the ruins of Herod's palace."

The soldiers led the two men to the ancient terrazzo floor
of what had once been a dining room for the infamous King
Herod. The morning sun was now climbing high into the
sky and the suffocating heat of summer was returning. Ben
kept squinting and shielding his eyes, desperately trying to
see.

"Latch them together to that column." Atrash pointed
to the remnant of a granite support that once had held a
massive roof. "I want them stretched tightly around the
stone. Put them back to back and tie their hands together.
If one falls, they'll both feel the pain!"

Jimmy and Ben's aged appearance contrasted strongly
with the youthful martial arts experts who looked like mere
boys. Ben gave no resistance but Jimmy jerked himself free
from their grip and stood unusually erect against the stone
support.

"Sir," a general spoke to Atrash. "Is there any value in
harming these old men? Nothing can change what has
happened."

Atrash's eyes widened and his face twisted in hate. He
reached up toward the aide's throat. "You want to take
their place?"

The young general hung his head and stepped back. He
proceeded to tie Jimmy to the column.

Atrash cursed and began walking around the two helpless prisoners of war. Then he stepped back to take full
measure of his captives. "As I live and breathe, the boys
from Jerusalem. Yeshua's right hand men!" Ziad pulled a
pistol from his waist and held the barrel inches from Ben's

eyes. "Take a good look! I don't know whether to beat you to death or just shoot off an ear or a nose, a piece at a time."

Ziad stepped back and chuckled. "You perpetuated the legend of having lived through the so-called Great Tribulation, which, of course, none of us ever witnessed except on your doctored TV tapes. At the very least, history will record you didn't live longer than I did." Ziad put the gun back in his belt and started walking silently around the column.

An aide emerged from the door of the command center and called to the commander-in-chief. "I have the latest update from the martial arts unit. The news is not good."

Atrash looked annoyed but didn't reply. He kept walking.

Another general ran from the command center and walked onto the terrazzo floor. "Sir," he spoke forcefully, "the martial arts unit appears to have surrendered. Nothing is left of the attack."

Ziad appeared not to hear. He walked to a sign explaining the significance of the site and suddenly smashed it into splinters with his hand. With a swift kick, he knocked one of the support poles to the ground and picked up the long piece of wood.

"We could let you two old geezers just roast out in the sun." Ziad thumped the palm of his hand with the jagged stick. "Dehydration comes quickly in the month of Av. But you boys are hard to put away. I tried to blow you up in front of the Knesset and you escaped. I even sabotaged your shuttle and you walked away. My, my, you're an elusive pair!"

Ziad suddenly rammed the stick into Ben's stomach. Ben screamed and doubled forward. Atrash brought a counter blow to the side of his face and blood ran out of his mouth.

"The trouble is," Ziad continued to talk in a matter-of-fact tone, "I depended on others to do what I should have done myself. Big mistake!" Ziad stopped and whacked Jimmy across the nose. "I'm a generous man." He leaned into Jimmy's face. "Tell me the secret of how you do the appearing and disappearing act, and I'll let you live." Off in the distance a great bolt of lightning flashed across the purple sky.

"You are a fool!" Jimmy spit blood out of his mouth. "Even without divine intervention, we are more clever than you."

Atrash swung the heavy pole to smash Jimmy's chest and collarbone. Jimmy's shoulder sagged from the blow and his knees buckled pulling Ben even more tightly into the back of the column.

"You just don't seem to understand, Harrison! This information is your last bargaining chip. I need this technology to recover from what has happened today," Atrash barked in his face. "I still have guns and bombs in a world without armaments. I'm not through by any means. I have defense treaties with many other nations. Now talk!"

# CHAPTER
## 24

The pain in Jimmy's shoulder and chest was excruciating. No matter how he moved, there was no escaping an additional burning rub when Ben's sagging body pulled the rope tighter on Jimmy's wrist. The increasingly hot sun was becoming unbearable. Burning sweat rolled down Jimmy's forehead and dripped into his eyes.

Each time Jimmy blinked to clear his eyes, Ziad was there. The Egyptian's eyes were wild and frantic. His red-blotched neck kept expanding like a puffing adder. The Egyptian general's hands shook but his rage was paradoxically controlled. Clearly he and Ben had become the focus of Atrash's frustration.

Jimmy's agony made it difficult to focus on what Atrash was saying. The despot's words rolled around in his head as if they were coming from across a great chasm or from a distant loud speaker. Jimmy blinked to clear his eyes. From high up on Masada, he could see far out across the Dead Sea basin. For a moment, the vast panorama seemed unexpectedly beautiful.

Atrash's hot breath on Jimmy's face was sour. Jimmy

tried to turn his head, fearing he was about to faint. He struggled to clear his mind. Only then did an image emerge. Jimmy remembered the inside of the Church of the Holy Sepulcher where they had slept the night before. During his first visit, Jimmy had not noticed the large icon of the crucified Christ, hanging in the Greek Orthodox section of the church. That night the picture had seemed to come to life and almost leap off the wall at him. Once more, Jimmy felt himself standing before the depiction of the crucifixion. The mental image seemed larger than life and three dimensional. As he looked the pain in his broken body diminished.

From somewhere deep within Jimmy an answer to Atrash spilled out. "I am not worthy to be crucified as was my Lord. But I would count it an honor to die at the hands of the likes of you."

Jimmy was surprised by his own words. Each syllable seemed to arise from a place that he had never known. An extraordinary sense of peace swept over him and pain wasn't important anymore.

Once again Ziad was shouting but the words didn't register. Jimmy's reprieve was so all-encompassing, little else mattered. His legs felt stronger and he could support himself better. Jimmy tried again to comprehend the words screamed in his face.

"After I crack your ribs, I'm going to crush your limbs before I break your head." Ziad's face was crimson and his eyes looked red. He raised the club above his head like an executioner preparing to deliver the final blow. "Say good-bye to this world, old man."

*I must show absolutely no fear,* Jimmy thought. *I will give God the glory regardless.* He forced a smile and tried to stand as erect as possible. *Let the final countenance on my face be a witness to my faith,* he prayed silently. *No man will be able to doubt where my trust and confidence were always placed.* He opened his eyes and looked at Ziad with total defiance.

The dictator rose on his toes to put the full force of his large body behind the terrible blow. His eyes widened, he ground his teeth. Suddenly a shot rang out. Ziad froze in place. His hate-filled look changed to surprise. A second shot rang out. The general's body sagged, the club rolled from his hand, and he grabbed his chest. Atrash turned slowly and a third shot exploded. He dropped to his knees and fell facedown on the terrazzo floor.

The general directly behind Atrash held a small smoking revolver. The rest of the military leaders stood silent, frozen in place.

Jimmy swallowed hard. *Am I dead? Hallucinating?* He blinked frantically trying to keep the sweat from blurring his vision. *I am finally losing it.*

"Untie them," the man with the gun said quietly. "The war is over." Only then did the soldiers move as if a magic spell had been broken.

When the bonds were cut, Ben tumbled forward. Jimmy began sliding toward the ground but a soldier held him up. The rest of the military gathered around the column.

"There is no atoning for our mistakes," the general with the gun said, dropping the weapon to the ground. "We must help you with your wounds."

"Help my friend," Jimmy said as he leaned on the stone column. "I'm worried about the blow to his head."

Immediately soldiers began attending to Ben.

"Your shoulder looks bad." The general pointed to Jimmy's sagging arm. "We must get you into a splint as quickly as possible."

"I need to get out of the sun," Jimmy answered. He held his arm against his chest.

"Let's get both of you inside," the solider answered.

"Help us carry him in," the general called to those around him and pointed at Ben. "Follow me."

"I want to look out over the Dead Sea just for a second," Jimmy answered. "A few moments ago, I didn't expect to be alive right now. I just need to get my bearings again. The sky has a strange cast." He pointed to the sun. Hues of violet and blue from strangely contorted clouds washed across the brilliant sunlight. Along the mountains the deep purple of a terrible approaching storm rolled over the jagged horizon line.

"We were raised to respect authority as unto the Lord," the young general continued. "No one knew quite what to do when the whole plot started to unfold. We had been taught to respect the chain of command between us and the government in Jerusalem." The general stopped and raised his eyebrows. "I know everything I say sounds like poor excuses, but I'm not trying to avoid responsibility. We are guilty of great error."

Jimmy only nodded his head. "Why don't you give me that piece of wood Atrash was swinging. It will make a good cane."

"Atrash was impossible to confront," another aide added. "The man simply overpowered all of us."

Again Jimmy nodded. "Boys, I'm not the one with whom you have to square things. The issue is between you and the Lord." Lightning crashed and crackled, and thunder rolled up from the far mountains. Violet clouds around the sun turned an ominous black.

"I suppose you want to get back to Jerusalem," the young general suggested as they walked to the edge of the cliff overlooking the Dead Sea. "We will fly you and your friend there as soon as you are ready."

Jimmy looked out over the broken terrain. "What a sight! Three thousand years ago the final remnant of Israel died right here . . . but the people survived. Today, the story was reversed. The enemy died on this ancient battle-field."

"Look at the clouds." The aide pointed at the sky. "They seem to be racing across the sky and yet there is almost no wind. The sun is disappearing behind those black thunder-heads."

A rumble began far off to the west. The ground trembled. Jimmy grabbed for the general's arm.

"Earthquake!" the young man shouted. "Hang on!"

The top of Masada shook with disconcerting vibrations. Soldiers tried to run for cover; others fell to the ground. The shuttlecraft waiting on the runway bumped up and down. The general lost his balance and fell backward. Jimmy grabbed a guardrail to keep from going over the edge.

The rumble became a frightening roar. Rocks broke loose and boulders tumbled down the steep banks of Masada, crushing the ground hundreds of feet below. Far across the valley avalanches of rocks and dirt slid down into the Dead Sea. Huge waves sloshed against the banks. The wavy surface bounced and swayed like water in a washtub.

Jimmy fell to his knees and clung to the metal pole for dear life. The roar was deafening. The ground shook harder and the few remaining buildings tumbled in. To the south, a terrible cracking sound pierced the morning sky. A whole canyon split open like a boulder breaking in two monstrous halves. The earth pulled apart, and in an awesome shift the entire base of Masada moved sideways. The movement crushed the ancient Roman causeway, built for Rome's final assault on the Jewish survivors. The huge, long mound split in a thousand pieces.

The soldier grabbed Jimmy's leg and pointed south. "That Valley runs up to Beersheba and on to the ocean. It's turning into the Grand Canyon! God help us!"

The crackling noise reached a deafening level, while the Dead Sea began to dry up. Like a sink emptying, the gigantic vortex of a whirlpool sent the salty ocean to the center of the earth.

"The bottom has fallen out of the world," Jimmy gasped. "The whole sea is disappearing!"

Suddenly, an all-engulfing cloud of steam exploded and sent huge boulders flying upward in every direction. Masada shook again as megaliths smashed into the top. Helpless soldiers cowered in trenches.

"The wrath of God has fallen on us for our evil deeds!" The general kept saying over and over. "Forgive us! Forgive us!"

Jimmy tried to peer into the bottomless lake that now looked like the center of a large volcano. As far down as he could see, there was nothing but black emptiness and boiling steam.

Another staggering, roaring sound rolled up the south end of the basin. The newly formed canyon split, then dropped again, as whole mountains spilled into the bottomless pit that had once been the Dead Sea. Farther to the west the rushing water grew louder and louder as if mountains were being washed away by a great tidal wave. Instantaneously, a torrent of water flooded through the valley and emptied into the vast hole. Behind the first onslaught came a tidal wave that looked at least a thousand feet high. The sea of water was so vast that it first filled the complete Dead Sea basin before dropping away as it poured into the gigantic hole.

Once again another eruption of steam sent dirt, rocks, and debris thousands of feet into the air. The first wave of boulders gave way to much smaller pieces of gravel raining down like hail. Bits of mud pelted Jimmy. He could see nothing but the mist covering everything like a heavy fog. Jimmy shielded his head but the stone pellets stung. The roar of a thousand oceans filled the air with the sound of terrifying power. Jimmy cowered next to the metal railing while the whole mountain swayed like a tree in the wind.

Jimmy stared again into the whirling abyss of water, steam, and smoke. A passage from the Book of Revelation came back to mind. "There shall be no sea." He thought to himself, *The Bible promises the new creation will have no oceans. Am I seeing the fulfillment of this promise? The oceans of the world emptying into the lowest point on the earth? Could it really be? But where else could such an endless amount of water come from?*

The terrible shaking and earthquakes subsided but the relentless flood only increased. Bellows of streams continued to shoot upward. Jimmy could no longer see anything inside the vast hole. He felt a tug on his coat. Jimmy turned and to his amazement found Ben groping across the ground.

"Ben! You're conscious!"

"What in tarnation is going on?" Ben shouted as loud as possible. "My glasses are gone! I can't see anything. What's happening?"

Jimmy locked his legs around the railing and reached out with his good arm. "Hang on to me."

"I can't see anything. When I regained consciousness, everything was covered by a cloud! What's going on?"

Jimmy hugged his old friend. "Unless I miss my guess, Yeshua is calling in all the cards. I think we're seeing the final wrap-up of history."

"Praise God!"

Slowly, the sound of rushing water receded and the clouds of steam diminished. A deep gurgling sound bubbled up from the vast hole in the earth. The smell of sulphur hung in the air. What had been the Dead Sea was now a vast gorge. Powerful sweeping winds roared down the empty valleys blowing the smoke and foglike clouds out to the south. The sky appeared blood red and the remaining clouds twinged with purple blackness. Streaks of light kept shooting overhead, leaving thin trails of smoke. Once again the two men could hear each other

"Look!" Ben pointed around the top of Masada. "Our captors are dead!"

Soldiers were piled in a heap as if trying to save themselves by massing together. Other men lay alone, covered with pieces of rock. The general who freed Jimmy and Ben was the only soldier left and was on his knees, thanking Yeshua for forgiveness.

"I still can't see anything very clearly without my glasses," Ben answered.

"There's not much going on now," Jimmy answered, "but I've got a feeling the fireworks are just about to start up there in the heavens."

"I wish I could see it."

"If what I think is happening," Jimmy said, "I've got a hunch you'll have a pretty fair idea of what's coming down."

"Describe what you're seeing."

Jimmy pointed to the clouds, then his finger dropped to the horizon line. "A great beam of light is splitting the sky now. Must be coming from some point far out in space."

As Jimmy watched, the dark clouds disappeared and a terrible calm settled, resembling the hush before a devastating storm. Streaks of fiery light began shooting across the sky like laser beams. Some of the luminous objects collided and exploded in a burst of red and blue energy.

"I can't believe it!" Jimmy began to shake Ben. "The sky is vibrating, just like an earthquake, but it's above us. Stars suddenly appear in broad daylight and then are gone. It makes me dizzy just watching."

"The sky is falling?"

"Some . . . thing . . . of . . . that order, I think."

Sprays of color filled the sky. The spectacle was like galaxies smashing together. The great beam of light slowly lowered until it cut straight across the earth. The light was like fire but the beam became, not flames, but dancing discharges of electric energy. The electronic fire devoured whatever it touched and surrounded every object with a golden glow. As pure energy popped and crackled, the electric discharges leaped from rock to tree to plant like a raging forest fire.

"What is it?" Ben pulled on Jimmy's arm.

"I don't know but everything is being transformed. And it's coming this way!"

The yellow light danced over the far edge of the barren wilderness. As it traveled down the sides of the stark terrain, even the ground changed. Sand turned into grass, dry ravines ran with streams. Plants appeared on the hillside and the scrubby little dwarf bushes filled with flowers. The desert bloomed.

"Ben, this thing is coming straight for *us*." The light split on both sides of what had been the Dead Sea, leaping past the gaping hole in the earth and sweeping over Masada. "Hang on!" Jimmy yelled. "Here it comes."

A staggering jolt of electricity shot through Jimmy's body as if he had stuck his finger in a light socket. His thoughts scrambled and every nerve in his body jumped. His muscles tingled and jerked in involuntary spasms. When his mind cleared, Jimmy was on the ground, on his knees. Perception returned slowly. Once again he could hear Ben's voice.

"Look!" Ben pointed across the top of the ancient fortress. "They're all gone! The dead soldiers have disappeared!"

Jimmy looked at Ben's outstretched finger. The skin was no longer wrinkled and blotched with liver spots. His hand was smooth and his skin glowed.

"Over there!" Ben jumped to his feet. "The mountains are covered with new trees!"

Jimmy looked into his friend's face. Every wrinkle was gone. His white hair had turned dark brown and Ben's cloudy eyes had cleared. He was once again a strapping two-hundred-pound young man.

"I can see!" Ben kept pointing toward the wilderness that had become a botanical garden. "I don't need glasses!"

Jimmy was speechless as he watched the miracle dancing before his eyes. In the twinkling of an eye, Ben was totally transformed.

Ben twirled around and froze in place. His mouth dropped. "J-i-m-m-y . . . unbelievable! . . . Is . . . that really you?"

For the first time, Jimmy looked at his own hands. They too were smooth, the fingers no longer crooked. His back wasn't stiff or bent. As he straightened up, Jimmy felt inches taller.

"You've become that six-foot-four blond Nordic weight-lifter that used to go with my sister!" Ben exclaimed.

Angels flying in formation shot across the sky and collided with the strange creatures of light, causing explosions of energy and smoke. One after another, disintegrating fire balls fell toward earth, streaking the Masada.

"We're going to get hit again!" Jimmy warned.

To his consternation, Jimmy watched the strange entities fly past him into the bottomless pit that had been the Dead Sea. Like a storm of meteors, thousands of the flaming substances descended over the edge and down to the boiling center of the earth.

"Demons!" Jimmy exclaimed. "Yeshua's angels are banishing evil spirits to hell forever!" He peered into the frightening hole. "I guess we now know where the Lake of Fire is."

Jimmy pointed to one last huge ball of light being surrounded and descended upon by a multitude of angels. "Satan is disguised as a messenger of light. I think our problems are just about completely and eternally over."

The ball of angry red light suddenly plunged toward the earth, zigging and zagging to avoid the ring of angels corralling its nebulous form. A hundred feet above Masada the glowing object stopped and hung in space.

"Look, Ben. The thing is changing form."

"It's becoming shaped like a . . . a . . . giant . . . human being."

"We always knew the devil could take on many disguises," Jimmy answered, "but I really had *no idea* how powerfully until now."

The light became a tangible form. A face of great beauty appeared. The giant red angel darted back and forward as if gesturing to the attacking angels to join him, but the perimeters of the angels circling him together forced him ever downward.

"These angels aren't buying it this time." Ben kept pointing at the multitude of flying hosts. "Can you believe your eyes?"

A swooping attack of angels with flaming swords sent the red angel tumbling backward nearly on top of Masada. When he swooped past Jimmy and Ben, the devil's countenance changed. His face contorted into pure hate and his eyes were filled with unrelenting rage.

Jimmy grabbed Ben's arm.

The angelic host made one final lunge with their flaming swords and the devil fell backward into the terrible pit. Jimmy and Ben peered into the vast crevasse. Wispy thin trails of smoke drifted upward. The world was filled with divine silence.

"I can't believe it's over," Ben said.

"Glory to God!" Jimmy shouted. "Yeshua has prevailed!"

"And so have you," a familiar voice answered from behind.

Jimmy spun around to find Ruth standing with her hands extended. "Never have I been as proud of you as in these days, my beloved. You have proven to be a man of God without measure." His former wife hugged him. "You have always been my heartbeat," the Immortal said.

Jimmy gasped and held Ruth tightly. Her hair felt like silk and her skin was wondrous to the touch. "I know there's supposed to be no tears in eternity," he choked back the words. "I am just so happy to see you I can't help myself."

"What a guy you proved to be, Dad."

To Ben's left Jim Jr. appeared. "Son! You wouldn't believe what we've been through."

"I've watched every minute of your battle, Dad. In fact, they had to restrain me a couple of times. Wow, did you ever prove to be a man of God!"

"Just did what we had to," Jimmy shrugged.

"Oh, no," another voice spoke from the other side "You were a hero."

Jimmy turned around and his mother and father stood beside Ruth. "A thousand years ago when I was a preacher back in Dallas, Texas, I prayed my son would be a great spiritual warrior." Reverend Harrison still spoke with a Southwestern drawl. "Never in my wildest dreams could I have guessed how those prayers would be fulfilled centuries later."

"The Immortals are back!" Ben said. "What a relief."

"Cindy's not here," Ben exclaimed. "She's still in Jerusalem."

"No, Ben." Cindy answered. "I'm with you, too." A tiny, dainty young woman with skin like porcelain held out her hands. All the wrinkles were gone. Her heart-shaped mouth was once again perfect. "We're all Immortals now."

"Cindy, you're gorgeous!" Ben laughed. "But how did you get here?"

"You've been so busy watching everything happen, you haven't gotten in touch with what this divine metamorphosis has done for you," Cindy explained. "Time and space no longer have any meaning. We are truly spiritual beings now. We can travel by thinking. Just imagine where you want to be and you're there!"

"*Really?*"

Jimmy held Ruth's hand. "How . . . how . . . do we relate?"

"With pure love," Ruth answered. "When we were married our relationships revolved around our needs. Now we relate to each other completely and totally through God's love. Nothing selfish will ever get in the way. We don't have exclusive and limiting bonds." Ruth pointed around her. "My parents, your parents, our ancestors, and our children comprise one great family of God."

"I'm just so glad to be able to see you when I want to," Jimmy answered, hugging his wife affectionately.

"And don't forget us," a bass voice rumbled. "You know we've been trying to get out of L.A. for years."

"Isaiah and Deborah!" Ben exclaimed. "You're here. The circle is complete."

Ben looked around at the desert that had become a paradise. He saw the sea of faces filling the top of Masada. His parents waved. His grandparents were there. Dr. Ann Woodbridge was waving. The old gang from California stood together. Joe and Jennifer McCoy, Erica and Joe Jr. were all part of the crowd. Everything Ben saw, heard, thought, and felt was in complete harmony.

## A Concluding Postscript from Michael,
## Guardian Angel
## Compiler of the History of the Third Millennium

The many years I served as the Feinbergs' guarding angel were filled with great satisfaction. To be associated with human beings who played such a significant part in Yeshua's ultimate victory over the minions of the devil was a great honor. In the beginning they had no more idea of their purpose than they did of my existence and constant care. Standing behind the curtain of time, watching them make discoveries about the intentions and designs of God was especially fascinating.

Once eternity began I had the additional joy of being the Feinbergs' servant. We angels have always served humanity, anticipating our role as their attendants throughout the endless ages. Becoming the Feinbergs' liegeman compounded my joy.

As everyone knows, Yeshua returned with the hosts of heaven, the Immortals, and all the saints for the final wrap-up of all human history. I watched the Great White Throne and Him seated upon it appear above the earth in the center of space itself. The Father judged no one, but all judgment was given to the honor of the Son. The dead, great and small, stood before the throne and the awesome Book of Life was unlocked. The sea and Hades gave up their dead and each person was judged according to what he had done.

With a rod of iron the Messiah cleansed the earth of every vestige of sin and rebellion. The Devil and his legions were forever banished, having rejected the one-thousand-year opportunity to repent and worship God. They forever remain a sign to us of the terrible power of pride, rebellion, and sin to ruin God's good gifts. Death, itself, was finally cast into the abyss of destruction.

I saw the Holy City, the New Jerusalem, come down out of heaven prepared as a bride adorned for her husband. Totally different from the old Jerusalem, the new city was in every respect the center of the universe. During the millennial reign of Christ, the new city had hovered above the earth as the home of the Immortals from whence they went back and forth to the planet. Far up above, heaven was also renewed and completed with its many mansions accommodating the blessings of God.

Once the transforming fires spread over the world, the earth was perfected and balance completely established. With the end of sin, the Garden of Eden was restored in the midst of Jerusalem. The Tree of Life once again flourished. All creation blended together like a perfectly scored symphony.

The New Jerusalem descended from the sky in the awesome shape of a pyramid of twelve floors with twelve great gates and an angel by each entrance. Every gate was a pearl of awesome size. Over each gate was the name of one of the twelve tribes of Israel. Four gates were on the north, south, east, and west. The vast city was 1,400 miles in length, width, and height, making it the largest city on earth and open to all tribes and races. Pure streets of gold were of such purity the pavement appeared transparent.

The city of gold had walls of jasper as clear as glass. The first foundation was jasper, the second sapphire, the third chalcedony, the fourth emerald, the fifth sardonyx, the sixth carnelian, the seventh chrysolite, the eight beryl, the ninth topaz, the tenth chrysoprase, the eleventh jacinth, and the twelfth amethyst. The blending brilliance of pure color revealed the indescribable beauty of God's grace in glory never seen before in creation. The redeemed were moved to complete ecstasy at the mere sight of such majesty.

In the very center of the New Jerusalem was the restored Temple of our God where He dwells forever. The light of the bright Morning Star, the Son of David, filled the city with a constant wondrous promise of tomorrows without beginning or end. The glory of the city sparkled with Light Eternal. From the Throne of God out through the center of the city flowed the sparkling River of Life.

Every living creature heard the supreme final summons. "The Spirit and the bride say, 'Come! Come! Whoever is thirsty, let him come; and whoever wishes, let them take the free gift of the water of life.'"

# BEYOND THE Millennium

# BEYOND
## THE
# Millennium

# PAUL MEIER
# AND ROBERT WISE

THOMAS NELSON PUBLISHERS
Nashville
Printed in the United States of America

# DEDICATION

*For our newest angel*
*Robert L. Wise II*

*"They finally named one right"*

# MEMORANDUM

**TO:** **Michael, Guardian Angel**
**RE:** **Records in the Archives of the Hosts of Heaven**

Further clarification is sought for the final years of planet Earth. Your original report, filed under the heading, *The Third Millennium,* left a number of issues unresolved. Please give additional information on how the ultimate scenario played out from your personal perspective.

We wish to preserve the heavenly view of the final struggle and to chronicle the strategy of the demonic forces; therefore, we require a more detailed description of how you personally conducted spiritual warfare. Now that the legions of Evil are banished, we want a record of their role in the constant disruption of human events.

Specifically, our records do not reflect the role played by Guardian Angel Seradim. We wish to record his service and activities. Please give us the inside story.

# CHAPTER
# 1

**M**ichael listened and knew this call was different. The angel understood the summons was personal, particular to him. Other angels might observe, but none could do so out of the totality of their being. This singular expression of Logos was for him.

The Great Light churned and boiled, rolling forth in brilliant dispersion of pure energy. Then the Creator spoke one word: "Seradim."

Michael turned toward the Center of all things and was instantly in the presence of glorious light, encompassed by a rainbow of incalculable hues. The angel both saw the sounds and heard the colors. The blending of sight, sound, and perception into a wondrous whole was all absorbing and completely fulfilling. As did all the angels, Michael basked in the moment, each moment, as the essence of all eternity, an encounter without beginning or end.

In an instant, the Father's will surged through Michael's mind with complete and total clarity. Seradim, a member of the Seraphim, was being reassigned as a guardian angel.

Michael suddenly knew his personal assignment: to be a tutor and mentor until the angel was ready to fulfill his destiny. "The burning ones," the Seraphim, were expressions of pure love and their affections so brilliant, they came forth like holy fire.

"Seradim," Michael thought, and the angel heard. "I am your companion and teacher. I have been called to instruct you about the coming battle on the other side."

"Battle?" Seradim puzzled. "I do not comprehend."

"Your whole existence has been to stand nearest to the heart of God, responding in love, praise, and worship," Michael explained. "The very purity of your vocation makes such a notion virtually impossible to understand." Michael pointed out beyond the reaches of heaven. "You have been reassigned to my order of guardian angels. Our job is to fight and work for human beings. You've been called to leave the very heights of heaven and travel to the dark depths named Earth."

"Earth?" The angel absorbed the instruction. "And I will intervene as light in that place?"

"No. As strange as it now sounds, you will become tangible in more solid terms," Michael continued. "A great war is just ahead in a place very different from ours. We will go there after I teach you something of this realm."

Seradim looked across eternity and saw no beginning or end, no limits or boundaries. Completeness was all he knew.

Michael understood at once. "You cannot yet imagine a place where there is something called time, limitation, dying. Of course, it will be painful for you to experience a world of incompleteness and finality, but this is where you will intervene."

For the first time in his existence, Seradim felt the sensation of not knowing. He frowned.

"Good!" Michael answered. "Now you are beginning. You must apprehend the nature of that other world. Trapped in finitude, those creatures must learn the meaning of eternity—a far more pleasant task than yours: to discover the nature of time and the dimensions of space. But that will come later, after other matters are sorted out."

"Earlier? Later?"

Michael nodded. "At this moment, you can only know sequence, but when we cross into that other place, distance and time will be added."

Seradim looked puzzled. "A battle?" he thought. "What is a battle? Sounds pleasant to me."

Michael frowned. "It is not pleasant. Let us learn of war." He took the angel's hand, gazing deeply into his being. "Let me tell you of strife." Michael remembered the beginning.

Immediately Seradim saw two brothers standing before a stone altar. One seethed with anger; the other was serene. Suddenly the angry brother picked up a stone and struck the other on the head. When his brother slumped, the attacker beat his head again and again with the pointed rock. The attacker hit repeatedly, until the life was pounded from his victim.

Seradim flinched and tried to push the image from his mind, but Michael would not allow it. New images filled his awareness. Seradim saw warriors racing toward each other, hurling spears and shooting arrows. Cries of hate rang through Seradim's consciousness; he tried to shake the thoughts away.

"I am sorry," Michael answered, "but you cannot intervene in what you do not understand. The world to which we must go is filled with far worse than what you have seen. War is an ugliness none should know. Yet the Holy One called you forth from the highest realm of heaven to send you into the strife. You are needed during Earth's final hours."

Seradim held his head in bewilderment. Another wave of images emerged. Great balls of fire exploded and hot metal showered down on combatants. Bodies were torn into pieces and limbs fell to the ground, cropped from the torsos of soldiers. The carnage filled Seradim with an unidentifiable sensation, making the wonder around him fade.

Michael responded, "Pain is also part of your instruction. Unless you understand its function, you cannot help. Do not worry. You will not be consumed, but you must know of the forces driving this world we will visit."

"You keep saying, 'world,'" Seradim wondered.

"Yes. Another place of unreality. It will be hard for you to understand separateness, but this is the very essence of the realm beyond."

"Why?"

"The Creator made it for Himself, but because the place is of another order, the world had to be of a different nature from heaven."

"Where is . . . the place?"

"On the other side of the wall of time."

Seradim quickly looked in every direction.

"You can't see the partition, my friend. We must experience it as a dramatic transition beyond eternity. I will teach you how to cross over."

"I'm prepared for whatever is ahead."

"No, not yet." Michael shook his head. "You must understand our enemy. We have an adversary on the other side, waiting to destroy us."

For the first time in Seradim's existence, fear shook his entire being. "An . . . enemy?" his thoughts scrambled.

"Never forget it. We have a nemesis bent upon our total annihilation."

"Enemy?" Seradim kept thinking over and over. "Enemy."

"Since you have never known anything but love, you cannot yet grasp the meaning of hate. I must teach you."

Seradim's consciousness slowly filled with a sense of pride and inordinate self-centeredness. The emotion expanded into greed and a desire to possess. The angel staggered backward, clutching at his throat. Without an immediate object to seize, his feelings twisted into anger, and black hatred spread across Seradim's awareness. He cried out in horror.

Michael immediately stopped his instruction. "Forgive me for causing you such severe pain, but the enemy has bathed the good creation of the Father in this kind of brokenness. The creatures of that world become infected with these same feelings and soon accept them as normal. We call such an experience sin. When left unchecked, the disease soon controls them. Unless intervention occurs, the creatures are hopelessly mired into the chaos that slowly destroys them. Only an outside force can set them free."

"That's our task?" Seradim shuddered again.

"Not exactly. The Father Himself has already offered a solution. Long ago the Creator struck our enemy with a fatal blow, but he still is able to work his diabolical schemes. We are part of God's plan to establish the final and total victory."

Seradim worried for the first time. "How do we face this enemy?"

"Our weapon is love, and you are already quite well equipped, for that is your very nature. You burn with love. Our task is to remain grounded in charity while fighting against the onslaught of evil."

"Why haven't I known about this world before?" Seradim thought.

"Because you've stood at the top of heaven's hierarchy," Michael responded, "doing nothing but worshiping the Most High. You've never really been in touch with what some of the other orders of angels do."

Seradim looked around. Multitudes of beings swept across the expanse of heaven. Some were huge, almost filling all the space above and below them; others were quite petite. Many seemed to be swirling creatures of energy, moving through space like meteors, leaving trailing trains of fire. The sound of singing swelled from small tones of simple concord then quickly expanded into multiple chords of perfect harmony. Pure worship swept in from the flying hosts with a gentleness that still had the impact of an overwhelming force. The vast diversity settled into a singular expression of praise.

"Holy, holy, holy, Lord God of hosts. Heaven and earth are filled with your glory." The words resonated into the deepest regions of the angel's being, and automatically Seradim joined in singing, "Holy, holy, holy is the Lord God Almighty."

A great golden throne encircled by a rainbow emerged from the center of worship. The One seated there had an appearance of jasper and carnelian. Seradim saw other lesser thrones around the great throne. Lightning and peals of thunder exploded and seven lamps of fire came forth.

Four strange creatures covered with eyes in front and back flew back and forth, crying again and again, "Holy, holy, holy is the Lord God Almighty, who was, who is, and who is to come." Sacred love burned in Seradim like a holy, incandescent light, and he became immersed in the praises of the highest hosts of heaven.

"Sorry," Michael interrupted, "but I must draw your attention away to the lower levels. You know, of course, the highest choirs of angels: the Seraphim, Cherubim, and Thrones, the juridical powers who contemplate the divine judgments. But you have never fully experienced the downward dimension of the work of our angelic hosts."

"I've always known they were there," Seradim mused, "but just didn't think about their assignments. . . ."

"The task of the next three choirs of angels is more related to the universe we are to visit," Michael instructed. "The Dominions carry the commands from the throne to those under them, the lesser angels. The Virtues help the universe operate according to the directives of the Dominions. Understand?"

Seradim nodded enthusiastically.

"Then the Powers fight the evil influences that would oppose the instructions of the Virtues. As you can surmise, we are getting closer to our enemy."

The new trainee rubbed his chin and frowned. "I can guess that trouble is just ahead."

"Now we are almost to the point where we connect with the earth. The last three choirs of angels are directly involved in human affairs. We are the Warriors or Guardians."

"We?" Seradim thought.

"Every single person in that world has a guardian angel to look after him or her. You're going to watch after some very special people during the final days of human history. I have been working at that job for what people call centuries."

"Really?" Seradim was amazed. "What is a century?"

"Time is a dimension of their world. Because we are eternal, time has no meaning for us; but on Earth they measure events in days, months, years, and finally, centuries. Understand?"

Seradim shook his head.

"Of course not." Michael smiled. "You have to go to Earth to get the idea. As a matter of fact, humans are now in their last seven-year period, a period that the Bible calls 'Daniel's Seventieth Week.' We are going to enter time and space at the start of the fifth year before the end."

Seradim smiled without comprehension.

"We work with the last two orders of angels—the Archangels, who carry the big messages to humanity; and the Principalities, who oversee the well-being of cities, nations, and empires. Together we help humans stand against the onslaughts of the Evil One."

Seradim pondered his new instruction for a few moments. "Awesome," he concluded.

■ ■ ■

Far across the galaxies from Michael and Seradim, another conversation was unfolding. Not in eternity but just beyond time, two other beings of similar but twisted nature stood behind the sweep of human affairs, looking in on unfolding history.

"Events are escalating," Malafidus thought.

"Exactly," Homelas added. "Remember when humans could only move with the speed of beasts, riding horses?"

"Their machines have made them travel almost as fast as we do. The fools only rush to their own destruction."

"I find it to be much more fun than it once was," Homelas reflected. "Remember when people only killed one at a time? Now the numbers are incredibly encouraging.

For a while, I thought they might blow up the whole planet with the big bomb."

"Those fool Russians spoiled it when they catered to the United States," Malafidus erupted. "If they'd just hung on another decade or two. . . ."

Homelas added, "All those evil prayers for peace and conversion spoiled everything. Consider how many souls could have been siphoned off into the fire with just one good exchange of missiles." The demon swore.

"Nevertheless," Malafidus reminded his comrade, "the final great battle cannot be very far ahead. All the pieces in the puzzle are coming together. The Man of Lawlessness is now in place: Damian Gianardo, the president of the United States. Just the man we've been expecting for centuries. We surely don't have long to wait."

"I believe our immediate assignment is related to the Great Plan. We are to use some young man for the devil's purposes. Who is this Jimmy Harrison we are supposed to corrupt?"

Malafidus pointed toward the West and the coast of California came into focus. "A fallen son of a Christian minister has been picked out as the vehicle for our main concern. Look, there he is."

Homelas thought and immediately saw Jimmy Harrison walking from a bar toward a shiny classic Corvette. He had the swagger and arrogance of a self-assured young man bent on nothing but his own pleasure. After draining a can of beer, Harrison crumpled the aluminum in his hands, threw the can at the curb, and leaped into the Corvette. His car shot into the oncoming traffic, causing several people to swerve, barely avoiding a wreck. Jimmy glanced in his side mirror and swore at the fools getting in his way.

Moments later the Corvette was on the freeway, flying down the coast.

"What do we need that slug for?" Homelas wondered.

"We want to help him corrupt a young Jewish girl. The message I got was that headquarters wants us to bring this girl down as the first step toward destroying her family."

"No problem. I've been doing Jews in since the Romans ran the scurvy lot out of Jerusalem when they burned the city. Why so much interest in this girl?"

"His infernal majesty, our leader, fears her family might have some strategic role in the final struggle. They must be eliminated before the war starts."

Homelas frowned. "Her old man is a general? They're Messianic Jews?"

"No," Malafidus answered, "Larry Feinberg is a psychiatrist with zip interest in any Messiah. They are basically a nonobservant Jewish family."

"So, why waste energy on them?" Homelas shook his head. "I'd much rather be back on assignment in Washington, D.C., influencing legislation to kill babies or push assisted suicides. We can harvest far more souls through bad laws or promoting a culture of death."

"You know better than to question headquarters. Nothing makes our leader angrier than being defied or second guessed. Anyway something big is already working in the White House and fully covered by our boys. If the assignment is only destroying one kid or knocking off a family . . . then that's all there is to it."

"Okay," Homelas shrugged, "what's the angle? Where's the opening?"

"Currently, the girl is in a rather typical teenage-rebellion frame of mind. Her name is Ruth Feinberg, and she's willing to lie a little, which gives us plenty to work on. She's already got a lust going for Harrison, so we have the usual perfect entry point. I think our boy Jimmy will be a good bet to get to her on all counts. Just needs a little encouragement from us."

"Who knows?" Homelas smiled wickedly. "We might get a quick pregnancy out of this one. An extra abortion. Might even be able to drive her to a suicide."

"Put your mind to it, pal. Maybe we can get you back to work in Washington in six months to a year. We're scheduled to hit her on New Year's Day. Let's go for it!"

# CHAPTER

## 2

We have a difficult battle ahead. Now is the time to tell you more about our foe." Michael settled back, resting against space. "He was once one of us. Called the Light Bearer, the enemy held the very highest rank, second only to the Triune God. As incomprehensible as it sounds, the Light Bearer is the ultimate enemy of this entire realm."

Seradim seemed mystified. "How could any creature be opposed to the Almighty? Isn't every emanation from the Center a complete expression of love? I don't think it is possible to—"

"You are not listening," Michael interrupted. "Hear my heart. I want you to receive an image. Every past moment still exists in the eternal now. We simply bring it before us again. You must be there and experience the explosion just as I did."

Seradim frowned and blinked rapidly, unsure of what was unfolding.

"We called the Light Bearer, the greatest of us all, Lucifer. His beauty and magnificence were awesome, the splendor of pure light. But that was not enough for him."

"How could anyone want more?"

"Lucifer desired the place of the Creator."

Seradim immediately started to protest.

"Of course, the very idea sounds like absurdity, but pride and ambition created their own form of insanity. Sin is madness deliberately chosen over sanity and health. Tragically, Lucifer's decision spawned a plague that immediately infected other angels."

"Us?"

Michael shook his head. "Lucifer's distemper contaminated many of them. In a single choice of their free will, they joined his rebellion, and the war was on. You must see the explosion."

Seradim's mind filled with images of great clashes of pure energy and discharges of vast light. Then the shape of a great hideous dragon breathing fire and belching smoke appeared. The dragon's enormous tail swung left and right, knocking angels aside.

The guardian angel directed Seradim's attention toward an image flying through his consciousness. "That angel is the other Michael, the Lord's chief warrior. Watch!" The great Archangel Michael drew a magnificent sword of light and attacked the dragon. The collision shook heaven.

Lucifer's army lined up behind him and the rest of the hosts of heaven moved into rank with Michael. A third of the angelic hosts charged forward with Lucifer. Angels tore at each other with the force of mountains splitting and continents colliding. The foundations of eternity shook, but slowly the dragon was forced into inevitable retreat. The angel who had presumed to displace God Almighty could not even stand against one of his own kind. Suddenly the hosts of Evil flew backward, hurling out into the vastness of eternal space.

"God expelled the dragon and his followers from heaven," Michael explained. "They were cast down to Earth, and that poor planet became a place of unending warfare. The sin of Lucifer was his inane desire to be the head of something lesser rather than to remain the servant of the Greater."

"But why would one of *us* even conceive such a preposterous thought?"

Michael nodded gravely. "As the Father was laying out His plans for all eternity, He confided in the inner circle of angels. His intention was to create a totally different race called humanity, and to eventually incarnate Himself as one of them, so they might be made complete in love."

"Humanity?" Seradim puzzled.

"They inhabit the earth," Michael continued. "Lucifer considered such an idea too undignified and smacking of weakness. He was appalled by the idea of the Almighty taking on the terms of flesh and blood. From that one conclusion, his leap of arrogance and pride was only a small step."

The newest Guardian slumped, putting his face in his hands. "My mind is spinning, and I feel very strange. I don't understand what is happening, but I feel disconnected."

"Earth people call the sensation craziness. When truth is bent, distorted into deception and delusion, we feel disconnected. Sin does that to people, because it's basically a form of insanity. Lucifer was eternity's first expression of madness."

Seradim shook his head. "To exchange heavenliness for hellishness, how could such be?"

Michael agreed. "Unfortunately, humans do it all the time. That's why the Father sends us to help them overcome."

"If I could help one person escape this problem, I would be the happiest angel in heaven."

Michael laughed. "You will help far more than one person. By the time we are finished, you will see Lucifer's entire scheme vanish like fog at dawn."

"Fog?"

"The time has come to take you to the frontier between us and them. Think with me, and we will travel to the edge."

Seradim locked his mind to Michael's and they whirled toward the boundaries of heaven. While the journey was accomplished in an instant, Michael's instruction made it feel as if they were traveling over a boundless amount of time.

"Heaven represents the very inner domain of God, the extension of the omnipresent Creator's mind," Michael explained. "We travel in Him, by Him, with Him, through Him, and yet the Almighty remains distinct from us. We always remain apart from Him, lesser than Him."

"Of course," Seradim understood.

"But humans are actually superior to us," Michael continued. "Because the Almighty came among them as Yeshua, the God–Man, they were able to receive divine life. Human beings who accept this wonderful gift become a part of the very being of the Creator. They can become the family of the Messiah, His brothers and sisters."

Seradim marveled at what he could not truly grasp as he became aware of a barrier arising before him. Like a vapor, the curtain of many layers moved from pure energy into substance. At the far end was the amorphous shape of a vast universe of whirling galaxies, asteroids, planets, the incredible beauty of physical space filled with countless objects.

Michael pointed at the nebulous veil. "The creatures on the other side will not be able to see us unless we assume their shape. We appear only as pure energy to them."

"Then how do we make contact?"

"Because we are energy, we can put our thoughts into their thought processes," Michael explained. "And we can also disguise ourselves as one of them. We can put on their skin like they wear a coat. You shall see."

"I can just walk through?" Seradim winced. "The enemy might be waiting to attack."

Michael extended his hand. "Take my hand and follow me. Lucifer can no longer return to eternity, so he stays away from the veil. Besides, he's too busy trying to run Earth to pay much attention to who comes across. Ready for the plunge?"

# CHAPTER

## 3

**N**ew Year's Day broke across America with the traditional promise of every new beginning. On the eastern seaboard, howling blizzard winds hurled sleet and snow against the White House. The president of the United States silently studied the bleak winter scene from a window in the Oval Office. Damian Gianardo appeared to need little rest and observed no holidays. No one stood in the way of the man with the deep scar on the side of his head.

A tall man of commanding presence, President Gianardo had the uncanny capacity to accurately read the intentions of his opponents. His ability to intimidate was legendary. Yet he felt completely at ease with his vice president, Jacob Rathmarker, a man cut from the same cloth and one of the few people Gianardo trusted.

"Unusual to do business on New Year's Day." Gianardo continued to stare out of the window into the dawn breaking over the country. "But I wanted a totally confidential environment."

"I'm your servant." Rathmarker sat on the edge of his leather chair. "When you need me, I'm here."

Gianardo smiled. "That's what I like about you, Jacob." The president turned and then pushed a file across his desk. "You'll notice most of this material is in my handwriting to ensure total secrecy. I've identified ten countries, mostly in Europe, that I intend to force into a new alliance with us. We've discussed the plan previously, but now I want you to head the negotiations to weld these nations into a union. They will be the cornerstone for my move to world domination."

Rathmarker opened up the file and thumbed through it quickly. "Yes," he mumbled, "just as you indicated earlier. The ten most significant nations in the world." The vice president closed the file. "Brilliant strategy."

"I intend to go for the jugular." The president picked up a dagger-style letter opener from the top of his desk and twirled the point slowly on a memo pad. "They will never know what hit them," he sneered. "By the time we've worked out the details of the political union, I'll have our military power in place. No one can stop us from being able to control the world." He smiled and suddenly plunged the dagger into the memo pad.

■ ■ ■

On the other side of the country, seventy-two-degree weather and bright sunlight bathed the residents of Southern California in warmth and hope. Joggers and families strolling their pets patrolled the beaches. Hordes of RVs and multitudes of tourists headed toward Pasadena and Disneyland. With the Rose Bowl parade starting later in the day, the southland was a vast theme park of entertainment and celebration. Birds-of-paradise, geraniums, ice plants, and rose bushes covered the landscape. The possibilities of the coming year seemed boundless.

In Newport Beach, Joe and Jennifer McCoy did not get up until well past 9 A.M. Joe Jr. and Erica were already watching the parades on TV with the family dog, Barkley, curled up in front of the set. Like the rest of the families in the tract-home neighborhood, their stucco house with its manicured front yard embodied the American dream of affluence and security. Inside and outside the Spanish-style two-story, the McCoys had it made.

"Great party last night." Joe yawned and pulled Jennifer closer. "We shouldn't have stayed till one o'clock." He blinked his bloodshot eyes and stared at the silk canopy above the four-poster bed.

"You shouldn't have drunk those three extra glasses of champagne. A little libation and you're ready to dance all night."

Joe chuckled. "Well, it was a great party." He rubbed his eyes. "But I guess I did overdo it a bit."

"You guess?" Jennifer asked playfully. "You were doing great until that last drop kicked in, and then you nearly went to sleep at the table. I had to drive us home."

"Oh, yeah." Joe grinned. "Well, in spite of the pounding in my head today, I believe this is going to be a great new year. The nation is in good shape. The president is a powerful leader and will keep the economy strong. People keep pouring into Southern California. The value of our house *has* to go up. Who could ask for anything more?"

"Yeah, we've got it all. Great house. Great kids." She nudged Joe in the ribs. "As long as you keep the bucks rolling in."

Joe stretched. "This is certainly the right time and place to be the comptroller for a growing computer company."

Jennifer threw the covers back. "I guess I ought to go downstairs and make some breakfast. I'm sure the kids are hungry." She stopped to brush her hair, taking a long look in the mirror. New wrinkles were forming around her mouth and lips. Pouches of skin bulged under her eyes. She felt the side of her cheek. Her skin was no longer velvety soft.

"You know," Joe called from the bed, "we ought to make some New Year's resolutions today. That's the traditional thing to do."

"And I'll fix black-eyed peas for good luck." Jennifer frowned and new lines rippled across her forehead. She was quickly leaving any appearance of her thirties behind.

■ ■ ■

Several hours later Joe and Jennifer McCoy sat at their dining room table. Jennifer held a pad and paper. "I guess your New Year's Day resolutions have to do with finance."

Joe grinned. "You do know me well, dear. But everything I do is for the family."

"Sure." Jennifer patted his hand thoughtfully. "I just worry that sometimes you work too hard for us. You drive yourself with such long hours at the office."

"That's the American way." Joe shrugged. "Let's get the kids in on this." He turned toward the den. "Erica? Joe Jr.? Where are you?"

"I'm in here," a soft feminine voice answered.

"Get your brother and come in," the mother called.

In a few moments Erica appeared in the doorway. The gangly fifteen year old had the awkward look of a typical teen. She kept her lips tightly closed to hide her braces. "Yes?"

"Where's Joe? We want to talk with you and your brother," the father answered. "Go get him."

"I can't." Erica rolled her eyes.

"And just why not?" Jennifer asked.

"Well, I'm not supposed to tell." Erica looked down.

Joe pushed his chair back. "I insist on knowing this second!"

"He, uh, slipped out to go to the video arcade."

"I have forbidden him to go to that place!" Jennifer stood up. "I will snatch him baldheaded when I find him."

"No, no." Joe shook his head. "You're going to the movies with Sharon Feinberg. I'll go get him." He turned to Erica. "We'll talk with you later. Right now your mom and I need to have a little talk."

Jennifer waited until Erica had left the room. "You want New Year's resolutions? Well, maybe this year we ought to think about the spiritual side of life more often."

"Spiritual?" Joe grimaced. "Are you serious?"

"Our kids have never even been in a church. At least we attended when we were their age."

Joe smiled. "Life was certainly different in the Midwest. Your parents took you to the Methodist church and mine made sure I was in the Presbyterian Sunday school every week. Do you realize we've been going together since we were sixteen?"

"We're sure not in Peoria, Illinois, anymore," Jennifer said thoughtfully. "I know we didn't take the teaching and preaching too seriously, but at least we picked up some values here and there. Values I wish our kids would pick up."

"Yeah." Joe frowned. "Wouldn't hurt Joe Jr. to learn a few Bible stories. Maybe it'd give him some perspective on those sadistic, violent video games he chooses."

Jennifer turned around and faced her husband. "And after all, Erica is fifteen. We've had the mother-and-daughter sex talk, but . . . well . . . I know her friends influence her. Kids today are just more loose than we were."

"Have to be." Joe nudged his wife. "You thought you were the Virgin Mary. Remember?"

Jennifer blushed. "I did learn something about morality in that little country church. The same lessons wouldn't hurt Joe and Erica."

"You've got a point." Joe kissed his wife on the cheek. "Okay, we'll add a spiritual dimension to our resolutions."

"I'll talk to Jane McGill this week. She and her husband are big church people."

"And I'll go get that wayward son of mine."

■ ■ ■

In Lake Forest, fifteen miles to the south, New Year's Day began at the crack of dawn for Frank and Jessica Wong. Business at the Golden Dragon was always good; few other restaurants stayed open on this day, and the immigrant family always put the dollar ahead of any other considerations.

Carrying a tray of lettuce, cabbages, and bean sprouts from the cooler, Frank hurried through the large kitchen in the back of the restaurant. "Jessica, it is almost ten o'clock," he said in Mandarin Chinese. "We must be open in an hour."

His wife laid down her dicing knife and wiped beads of perspiration from her brow. "We will be ready, good husband. We always are."

Frank set the tray down and checked one of the steaming kettles of rice simmering on the big stove. "Is it possible we have lived here for nearly twenty years?"

Jessica stared out the small window opening into the alley. "Twenty years . . . and we never speak of our parents or our relatives anymore."

Frank looked pained. "I try to put them out of my mind. The memories are . . . too . . . torturous . . . still."

"Do you think any of them escaped?"

Frank sat down on the stool next to his wife. Uncharacteristically, he searched her face as if seeking some hint of emotion. "We were Chinese in a Vietnamese country. I just don't know. Maybe the family migrated back to China. After all, the clan came south because we hoped for a better political climate. Once everything turned Communist, what choice did any of us have?"

Jessica's inscrutable face offered no hints of her feelings. She picked up a large silver knife and began dicing water chestnuts. Jessica recited the lines she'd said a thousand times before. "We only did what we had to do. The boat was the last chance to escape. We couldn't wait for the others. There was no alternative but to get on and hope the family made it." She chopped the vegetables with increasing fury. "I am only glad my father, Chin Lee, died before this terrible time."

"Yes." Frank clenched his jaw, his head tilted back in a pose of steely resignation. "There was no room left on the boat. Remember? Capacity was supposed to be for fifty. One hundred and fifty of us got on." He put his hand on Jessica's waist to slow down the pace of her chopping.

"And most of them died at sea. . . ." Jessica's voice trailed away. "I didn't think we'd survive the refugee camp." She quickly scooped the chestnuts in a pan and hurried to the sink to wash them.

"And now another year has come around. We are older, and honorable family is farther from us."

"At least we have Cindy." Jessica looked at their daughter's high school picture in the center wall of the kitchen. "She is all we have left."

Frank turned slowly toward the picture. His daughter's skin was smooth like porcelain china—a warm olive tint with a blush of color in her cheeks. Her heart-shaped mouth was perfect. Except for a slightly unfocused look, her sightless brown eyes looked completely normal. "If only she could see . . . if there was a cure for her blindness. I so often worry about what we did wrong." He trudged back to the cooler to pick up another tray of vegetables.

"What more could we do?" Jessica beat the drain pan against the sink. "We have made hundreds of offerings to our ancestors for her well-being. Cindy was just born blind. Is there a Daoist or Buddhist temple in this state in which we have not burned incense for her? You paid the monks well to pray constantly for our daughter." Jessica dropped the pan into the sink, and a dull thud echoed across the room.

Frank clutched his fists. "Our religion was for the old world. It does not work here. Maybe this year we find a new way."

Abruptly the swinging doors opened and Cindy shuffled into the kitchen behind Sam, her guide dog. "I have wrapped all the silverware in napkins," she said in English. "I think we have enough sets to take us through the evening." She laid a book on the counter.

"Excellent, good daughter," Frank answered in English. "You are a most dutiful child. A joy to your parents."

"I'm sure you would rather be celebrating the holiday with your friends," Jessica added.

"No." Cindy felt her way to the wooden chopping block. "I would rather be with my parents than anyone."

"You make our hearts full," Frank answered.

Cindy placed her braille book on the counter. "Maybe I will read for a while."

"Of course," Jessica insisted. "We have an hour before the doors are open."

Cindy's nimble fingers glided across the myriad of raised dots but her mind slipped away. The voice of Ben Feinberg floated through her thoughts. Never had a boy given her so much attention.

*Ben is different,* she thought. *He's sensitive and seems to care about me. Heaven's sake, I can't imagine what the boy would see in me. Of course, I can't imagine what anyone can see. I must guard my feelings. After all, I have so little to offer. I don't want any boy feeling sorry for me . . . or toying with my emotions.*

"You are reading?" Jessica asked. "I don't see your fingers moving."

"Giving them a little rest, Mama."

"What are you reading?" Frank Wong asked in Chinese.

"Last year in my discussion group at the library, this book was recommended. It is called the Bible." Cindy's fingers again ran across the raised dots of the braille.

"Bible?" Jessica Wong began stirring herbs into the special sauce she was making.

"Christians believe this is a holy book," Cindy explained. Her small voice matched the petite features of her lovely face.

"Indeed." Frank continued to speak in Chinese, his eyes so narrow they were barely slits. Most of his hair was gone, and he was slightly humped forward. "We must always respect such things."

"Especially because we are in a country where the majority are Christians," Jessica added. "We must offend no one."

"Are the teachings like those of the Buddha?" Frank stared down at the blank page filled with the raised dots.

"The first part is the history of the Jews," Cindy told her parents. "But the teaching of Jesus is in the second section."

"Jesus is like the Buddha?" Frank asked.

"Sort of," Cindy puzzled. "He was a Jew also. I really don't understand a lot of the story."

"Maybe you should talk to a Jew," Jessica observed. "Do you know any?"

Cindy smiled. "As a matter of fact, I do know a Jewish boy. He is one of our best customers."

"Really?" Frank began sorting the bean sprouts.

Cindy's grin widened. "In fact, you've not been too happy about the time I've spent talking with him when he was here. Remember Ben Feinberg?" Cindy bit her lip to keep from being too obvious.

"The big boy?" Frank looked at his wife. "The one who eats the Kung Pao Squid every time?"

"Exactly." Cindy nodded.

"For heaven's sake!" Jessica threw up her hands. "Why didn't you tell us that you were discussing religion?"

"Indeed!" Frank shook his finger at Cindy. "We highly respect such discussion. After all, we can learn from all religions."

"A Jewish boy," Jessica mused. "How interesting."

"Does Jewish boy understand the Bible?" Frank asked.

"I must have more conversation with him." Cindy tried to cover the widening grin with her hand. "I hope you will not worry if we have more discussion times."

"Of course not." Frank picked up a handful of mushrooms. "We want our daughter to be as well informed as any American."

"Then I will continue my religious meetings," Cindy said with a straight face.

One of the waiters burst through the kitchen door. "A young man ask for Miss Cindy. Very large boy."

"His name?" Frank's voice became stern.

"Something like Fine . . ."

Frank nodded his head to one side in deference. "A fortuitous moment. You must continue the religious talk with the Jewish boy."

"If you insist." Cindy bowed in respect to her father. Her guide dog led Cindy out of the kitchen.

# CHAPTER

## 4

Piercing the veil of time left Seradim disconcerted and disoriented. The endlessness of eternity turned into a universe of boundaries and finitude, confining and restricting. Although he was invisible to the world of animals and people, Seradim stared at the endless variety of tangible shapes everywhere. Time left him feeling chained, inhibited by an unseen force that hung around his very essence like a ponderous weight.

"The earth is really quite a beautiful place," Michael said. "Don't let the limitations confuse you. Water, mountains, trees, humans of infinite variety—the place can be quite intoxicating. The Creator does all things well."

Seradim saw the earth both kaleidoscopically and in particular at the same time, like a television screen within a television screen. "Yes, it is a wondrous and good place, though very strange to me. How could there be warfare in a place like this?"

"Let me show you something else before we cover that dimension." Michael pointed toward the continent of Africa.

"Follow me." In an instant Seradim stood in the heart of the Serengeti Plain around Mount Kilimanjaro. "Watch." Michael gestured toward a herd of giraffes loping through the trees.

Seradim shook with laughter. "What strange creatures! Absolutely amazing."

"Now, look toward the mountains."

A family of gorillas lumbered out of the rain forest, babies swinging from beneath their parents' chests. They chomped on bamboo and tree limbs, serenely unaware of their observers.

"These are humans?" Seradim marveled.

"No, no, gorillas and giraffes are animals, another aspect of creation."

"I'm very confused," the reassigned angel confessed. "Where do humans fit in?"

Michael nodded understandingly. "The earth is made up of three orders. Plants cover the planet with greenery and provide food. The beasts live off the plants and each other and roam the forests and plains. But humans are the highest order, living off both plants and animals." Michael pointed toward the north and snapped his fingers.

The ancient city of Cairo appeared before them. Teeming multitudes milled through the streets and marketplaces. People of many races drove wagons and cars through town. Children played on the sidewalks. Babies nestled against their mothers' breasts.

Seradim was speechless and could only point in wonder.

"Quite something, aren't they?" Michael beckoned for Seradim to follow him into the city. "Humans are a part of the physical world like the beasts." He pointed at a man walking a dog down the street. "But they also have the capacity to be spiritual, to touch and experience our dimension."

"Never could I have imagined such a thing!"

"Frankly, I envy them," Michael confided. "They have the ability to enjoy the best of both worlds, heaven and earth. We don't have the same capacity."

"We can't become like them?"

"Nor they like us," Michael answered. "The Father plans eventually to give them fully completed and glorified bodies, looking something like what they already have. But we're really only their eternal servants. We look in on their world but can never experience the earth as they do. In a spiritual sense, humans were actually made in the very image of God."

Seradim stared at the people. "So what am I doing here?"

"The Father is giving you the opportunity to help these creatures endure the final great tribulation period that is coming soon."

"All of them?"

"No, we are only responsible for a particular family. The Larry Feinberg family are Jews and have a very important role to play in the impending tribulation events. We will guard them."

"These people are in danger?"

"As a matter of fact, we're just in time to meet them and their enemies at the same moment." Michael looked toward the West. "We're going to a place called California. We'll stand a safe distance just above their house in order to watch what's going on. Ready?"

Seradim attuned his mind to Michael's thoughts. "I'm hanging on."

Instantly the two angels hovered just beyond the Feinbergs' living room in Newport Beach, looking down on the scene unfolding below.

"Ruth?" Ben Feinberg called to his sister. "The football game is about to start. Ruth?" The young man turned on the television.

"There's one of our charges," Michael pointed out. "You're going to find Ben to be quite a courageous and remarkable young man."

Seradim studied Ben's eyes for a moment. "Obviously, he has a very good heart."

"We must protect him."

"Look." Seradim pointed to the fireplace. "What are those ugly, knurled things? They don't look like animals or people, but they're certainly not one of us."

Michael nodded. "They're demons, fallen angels. They're part of the answer to your question about how warfare happens on this planet. Because you are seeing them through moral vision, their ugliness is particularly pronounced."

"What grotesque creatures! Surely, they're not like us!" Seradim protested.

"Yes and no. They can take on quite handsome forms when they want to, but you are seeing them from an angel's point of view. They are really no more tangible to humans than we are. Yet they are more like us than them."

Seradim studied the wrinkled creatures with shrunken red eyes and twisted bodies. Their arms were thin projections sticking out of their bulbous greenish-black bodies; on the end of their skinny fingers were sharp, protruding spikes. Each face was a convoluted expression of pure malice and envy.

"Who are they?" Seradim asked.

"A couple of ancient manifestations of malice," Michael explained. "Homelas's specialty is subverting young women. He has always fed on lust like people eat food. His insatiable desires turned into a hatred for what he can never completely consume. Consequently, Homelas enjoys trying to destroy beautiful women. No end to what he's willing to do, either!"

"The other . . . thing?" Seraphim pointed at Malafidus.

"He fell along with the lower angels that came down with Lucifer, but he never quite got the memory of the goodness of heaven out of his system. When the mindless wretch encounters a good person, he feels a deep twinge of guilt. His warped mind reasons that destroying the virtuous will set him free from his pain. Malafidus is the embodiment of misery created by acting against one's higher self."

"How could creatures of light have become such expressions of repulsion?"

"Sin infects creatures," Michael explained. "Utterly destroys. Frightening, isn't it?"

"Let's get him!" Seradim doubled his fist. "I'll wring that ugly snake's neck and—"

"No!" Michael restrained his charge. "Don't be impulsive. You have too much to learn before you start mixing it up. Just listen until you get a much better feel for what the world is like."

Michael thought into Seraphim's consciousness. "The demons have no idea we are listening. Their infernal arrogance causes them to be so self-absorbed, they seldom notice until we are within striking distance. Thinking themselves to be omniscient, they end up being quite stupid."

"Do we attack now?"

Michael smiled broadly. "No, we bide our time. We know a secret that Evil can never grasp. Lucifer and his minions only exist because the Father allows it. Even their schemes and attacks can be used in the plan of God. We give them plenty of rope, and eventually they hang themselves."

Ben sat down beside his father. "I thought maybe Ruth would watch the game with us since UCLA is playing."

"Maybe Ruth took a stroll down to the ocean," Larry Feinberg observed.

Seradim looked confused. "Where is the girl?"

"She lied to her family and went out the back door to meet a young man," Michael answered. "Ruth is putting herself in jeopardy."

"Then let's go help!"

"Not yet, Seradim. Ruth is one of those creatures who learns best through pain. We'll simply stand back and let those two rotten characters turn up the heat. When the time is right, we'll do what we can."

■ ■ ■

The two demons listened carefully to Larry Feinberg and his son discuss Ruth's disappearance.

Homelas laughed coarsely. "There we have it! Just the right beginning. A few lies to start the adventure rolling. Let's cut out of the family scene and see what sweet little Ruthie is really up to."

Being essentially energy without physical substance, Homelas and Malafidus could stand in the midst of human history and watch events unfold while remaining invisible to people. Yet the two demons operated with the same intention and sense of physical presence as any other person in the world. As angels did in heaven, they simply "thought" themselves to wherever they wished to be.

"I'll locate her." Malafidus closed his eyes tightly to access the central gathering focus of evil intelligence. Instantly, the interconnection of diabolic awareness scanned the world for information. The response came with the speed of light. "Well, well, sweet innocent Miss Feinberg is off being a naughty girl with our old hero Jimmy Harrison. Where better to have a secret rendezvous than the amusement park out there in the bay? Let's go to Balboa Island." Instantly, the two evil emanations reappeared in the center of the amusement park.

"Are you slick or what?" Jimmy Harrison pulled Ruth closer to him as the Ferris wheel made its final turn.

Ruth looked out over the park and the ocean surrounding the island. "Most fun place in Southern California." As the wheel settled toward the ground, she watched people getting off other rides and entering the little amusement shops around the island. "But I think I like you better."

Homelas and Malafidus perched on the edge of the bucket seat behind Jimmy and Ruth and watched over the couple's shoulders. "Going to be a piece of cake." Homelas chuckled.

Jimmy laughed. "How did you shake free of your family on New Year's Day without them blowing a gasket?" He slid his hand down her arm and into her palm, nestling against her.

"They think I'm at the movies with my college roommates, Heather and Amy. The old man would blow his mind if he knew I was taking a spin with the guy who sold us my car last week."

Jimmy smiled and bit her ear teasingly, but he didn't like the implication. From the moment the Feinbergs wheeled their big black Mercedes into the car lot, he knew his place in this rich family's scheme of things. Obviously, the mother and father saw him as a cut beneath them and certainly beneath their lovely, indulged daughter. To Jimmy the challenge of seducing Ruth was as intriguing as wringing the top dollar from their eel-skin wallets.

Homelas leaned over and whispered in Jimmy's ear. "You're just as good as the Feinbergs. Teach those pretentious snobs a lesson. Get the girl. She's insecure. . . . Make her feel important. Call her a real woman."

"You're my kind of woman." Jimmy grinned and watched Ruth's eyes light up when he put a heavy emphasis on *woman*.

The Ferris wheel came to a stop and the happy couple got out and started across the park. The two demons fell in at their side.

"Just what is your old man's line of work?" Jimmy put his arm around Ruth's waist.

"He's a shrink. Thinks he's God when it comes to sizing up people. Can you imagine, we were barely out of your car lot when he told us you were some kind of character disorder, a con-man type."

Jimmy's smile hardened. The psychiatrist's diagnosis cut through his facade and made him nervous. He felt uncomfortable, inferior, being only a twenty-five-year-old, dishonest used-car salesman.

Homelas concentrated intensely to push an image into the front of Jimmy's mind. He imagined a little boy sitting on the front pew of his father's church, feeling small, obvious, and insignificant. People were staring at the child and increasing his sense of being an outsider. The little boy desperately wanted to be important but was sure he wasn't.

For a few moments Jimmy forgot where he was and stumbled into an empty baby stroller parked on the midway. "Oh!" He grabbed his shin. "Some idiot left the wheels in my way."

"You all right?"

"Sure." Jimmy hobbled forward, trying not to swear in front of Ruth. "Let's truck over to my car. I've got a couple of joints hidden under the seat of my Corvette. How about a little grass to loosen us up?"

Ruth caught her breath. She had never used drugs before. The idea frightened her.

Malafidus watched Ruth's eyes drop toward the ground. Although tall, she easily tended toward the heavy side. Her weight had always been an issue. The demon instantly pushed an impulse toward her mind. "You won't get many chances like this one. Don't blow the promise by being a prude. The last thing a real man like Jimmy wants is an uptight little prig. After all, everyone smokes dope today. Just go with the flow."

"Sure." Her voice oozed hesitancy.

Instantly, Jimmy knew Ruth hadn't done marijuana and might get high quickly. "Well, let's give it a try."

The couple cut across the park, winding their way past popcorn vendors and men selling balloons. Straight ahead the ferry was bringing another load of cars across.

"My father's a real pain!" Ruth suddenly blurted out. "He's so self-confident all the time!"

"Tell me about it," Jimmy sneered. "I hate my old man. What a big-time jerk."

"What does he do?"

Jimmy froze. That was the one question he hadn't expected, and the answer might blow everything. Jimmy gazed into Ruth's innocent, all-accepting gaze. She was really on the hook, but Ruth was Jewish.

"Come on, honey," Ruth cooed. "There isn't anything you can't share with me."

Jimmy's eyes narrowed. He let "honey" roll around a moment. No question Ruth was going for him. "He's a Christian minister," Jimmy answered haltingly. "Has a big church in Dallas, Texas. My old man's a big daddy in Big D."

"Seriously?" Ruth asked incredulously.

"Turns you off, doesn't it?"

"No, no." A sly grin crossed Ruth's face. "I've just never been around preacher types."

"I avoid him at all costs. . . . The fanatic spent his whole life saving souls at the expense of me and my four brothers. He was so busy making God happy, Mr. Holy wouldn't even take in one of our baseball games. Don't worry. Reverend Big-Time has taken care of any interest I'll ever have in God or religion. I don't buy anything the old creep is preaching."

Homelas quickly whispered in Ruth's mind, "Your head-shrinking father didn't spend enough time with you growing up either!"

Ruth stopped and abruptly kissed Jimmy passionately on the mouth. She reached up and ran her hands through his hair, breathing heavily. "I like everything about you. Don't worry about some family hang-up. My world's not any different."

"Wow!" Homelas rolled his eyes. "I thought we were going to be in trouble. Slid past that sticky wicket just in time."

"Great turn of events." Malafidus's black eyes danced. "I was only counting on a little teenage rebellion mixed with good old-fashioned lust, but we've got some deep layers of emotional pain here. Maybe we'll be able to wreck the life of the seducer himself. Two for the price of one."

# CHAPTER

## 5

O ur immediate task," Michael said, "is to help you understand how evil operates. Only then will you become effective in combating the enemy."

Strolling along the edge of the ocean, Michael pointed out across the deep blue. "Demons fear water. It reminds them on a subconscious level of the depths of their own depraved thoughts, feelings, and motives. Water also suggests cleansing, healing. Demons avoid both like the plague."

"So we're not likely to run into the adversary down here?"

Michael laughed, "Not probable." Michael motioned toward the horizon. "Too wholesome. . . . You can enjoy the glorious beauty of the coast while I instruct. God didn't give people any better gift than the ocean."

Seradim watched the endlessly changing pattern of waves breaking over each other. Brilliant orange sunlight blended into the blue sea and suddenly changed colors, becoming a sparkling mass of red, purple, and aquamarine constantly drifting apart, then the dark blue-green of the deep broke through the whitecaps again.

"Water makes me feel peaceful," Seradim thought. "No pattern or rhythm exists in the endless changes, and yet the movement is completely with order."

Michael completed Seradim's thought. "And such is how God's plan operates. Often events do not appear to be part of any ultimate scheme, and yet everything occurs within the parameters of the Father's grand design. Even those ugly instigators of chaos cannot escape the divine context."

Seradim pondered the explanation. "Since the Father is orderly, such consequence would follow. Tell me more about how these evil creatures work on humans, causing them so much trouble."

"Demons use several basic strategies. Those two conniving creeps are undoubtedly employing one of their most common and successful methods right now. Manipulating human beings' feelings and imaginations, they will try to tempt the girl and her boyfriend to act on lustful images the demons conjure up in their minds. Couples often make the mistake of assuming that inner emotional tugs are real and not merely a momentary device to create imbalance or distort perspective. Unfortunately, the approach works quite well."

"What else is possible?"

"They create unfounded fear or use anxiety in exaggerated doses to panic the frightened into a self-protecting course of action at the expense of others. Fear is as effective a prod as thunder is in stampeding cattle."

"Humans overreact?"

"Most of the time." Michael watched the waves crash against the breakers just ahead. "Their survival instinct turns into apprehension when they are threatened. Children have to develop the ability to trust and have faith. Some never do and are constantly targets for chaos. Unfortunately, a few are permanently infected with paranoia and live their entire lives diseased with dread. The only remedy for fear is to learn to have constant confidence in God's provision. Fear will either make or break a human!"

"Simply describing dread gives me a tingling sensation of apprehension." Seradim shivered.

"Lucifer often uses another method on the more devout," Michael continued. "One of the Evil One's favorite disguises is to appear as an angel of light, deceiving people through false revelations. Church folks tumble for that old scheme all the time."

"Church people?"

"Some humans are already committed to the love of the Father and are His personal possessions. Remember? The people who have the life of God in them?"

"Oh, yes. The blessed ones."

"Periodically, Evil will detour these folks off on a tangent. They'll think some surge of enthusiasm is a divine revelation. Much like a runaway imagination, spiritual deception can create even more havoc than plain old temptation."

"Our enemy is quite crafty and capable."

"Seradim, never doubt his tenacity. Lucifer's brilliance often turns into stupidity and his intelligence into madness, but he doesn't stop. If given the opportunity, Lucifer will invade and completely take over a human life. At other times, people don't even realize they are being sucked into the vortex of his intentions."

The new Guardian watched the waves creeping up the beach. "Like the tides pulled in by an invisible force?"

Michael nodded his head. "Evil is sometimes subtle, like gentle waves, and other times as obvious as a hurricane. Lucifer's diabolical storms work on three levels. Of course, everyone is tempted. That's just part of the human condition. But when demonic forces find a really effective good person, they attempt to oppress the individual. Their assault creates depression and overwhelming sorrow, especially if they can generate some bitterness in that person toward himself or toward others."

"That's when we step in?"

"We are called on to help drive Lucifer's forces out," Michael explained, "but the spirits only look for new territory. Because demons never die, they have a way of hanging around for centuries, just waiting for a new opportunity to attack again. The worst kind are the most persistent and destructive."

"Give me an example."

"Molech is a good case study. The demon hated children. After centuries of spiritual intrusion in weak and perverse people, he finally got himself recognized for several centuries as a false god in Canaan. The ancient Canaanites practiced child sacrifice to Molech.

"When the Jews entered the land, they destroyed the idols and put an end to appeasing Molech, but the diabolical creature's pursuit of death was relentless. The demon moved over to Tenochtitlán in Mexico, and got a similar system going with the Aztecs, using young maidens as sacrifices to satisfy his appetite. The Spanish conquerors stamped out the practice, and Molech went north to bide his time. For a while, Molech's spirit worked overtime in the Nazi death camps. Today the demon is behind the abortion mills across America. Get the picture?"

Indignation welled up in Seradim as only righteous wrath can in the innocent. "I will seize Molech by the throat. By all that is holy, I will bring an end to his influence!" The angel kicked a spray of sand across the beach. "Bring on this vile thing!"

"All in due time, Seradim," Michael said, laying a hand on his young charge's shoulder. "The important thing is to make sure *we* are part of God's divine plan and don't go off on our own ill-conceived tangents. As angels we must remember that we are part of something much larger than our own sense of outrage. We are members of an army and must stay under our commander."

"But you're always by yourself, Michael."

"Oh, far from it! Most of the time I've battled as one of the Lord's legion. . . . Let me show you a story." Michael recalled the era of Elisha, the prophet of Israel. Once again he saw Elisha's servant standing at dawn in the ancient city of Dothan. Seradim immediately experienced the scene as if it were happening for the first time. The high walls of the city rose above the horizon. Palm trees swayed in the hot summer breeze.

Seradim pointed at images dancing in his imagination. Rank upon rank of chariots driven by armed soldiers bore down on the city gates. Archers put arrows to their bows. Men with spears were poised. "A war is about to begin," Seradim exclaimed. "The people in the city are in great jeopardy."

"Listen carefully," Michael instructed, "and simply watch."

Elisha's servant burst into his master's simple room in a watchtower perched high above the fortress city. "Wake up!" he shouted. "The city is surrounded by chariots, horses, men with spears. They have come for you. We can't escape. What shall we do?" He wrung his hands and pulled his dark brown robe tightly around his shoulders.

Throwing the sheet back, Elisha calmly walked to the window and looked down on the city walls. "As you say, we are outnumbered."

"Oh, my Lord, the king of Aram hates you. The Arameans will slay you. All hope is lost!" The servant put his hands to his face and wept.

"Now, now." Elisha put his arm around the young man. "There's no reason for panic. We are more than they who are with them."

The servant looked out the window again and then down at the emptying streets as people ran for protection. *Fear has affected his mind,* he reasoned. *Elisha retreats into madness.*

The prophet pointed to the hills. "Son, you must learn to trust the angels." Elisha bowed his head and prayed. "O Lord, open my servant's eyes, so he may see."

As the scene flashed through Seradim's mind, he saw the prophet's servant begin to blink rapidly and then look over the walls again. To his amazement, countless chariots of fire appeared, standing behind the enemy soldiers' lines. Suddenly, the hosts of the Lord raced down the slopes toward the Arameans. Seradim instantly recognized the lead charioteer.

"That's you, Michael! You're leading the Lord's army."

"One of my finest hours. We struck the king of Aram's men blind and Elisha led them like helpless babies to the King of Samaria. The result was so dramatic, the meandering bands of Aram never returned again."

"Wonderful!" Seradim applauded.

"But did you see how many angels were there? Keep looking! Quite an army. Don't ever forget that we outnumber the grains of sand on the seashore. Don't forget it! Our job is to help humans remember."

# CHAPTER
## 6

Follow me." Michael's thoughts guided Seradim toward Balboa Island. "I'm going to give you some field experience in how the demons influence humans. We'll check in on those two fiends, Homelas and Malafidus. By now they're already hard at work on Jimmy Harrison and Ruth Feinberg."

Seradim and Michael saw the couple walking lazily through the crowds at Balboa Park. Homelas and Malafidus hovered at their side, oblivious to the surveillance going on just above them.

Michael pointed to the two young people and the ghouls following them. "Let me explain a few things about what you are seeing. You need to understand perception.

"Humans fundamentally perceive through their five senses. Of course, they are capable of spiritual vision, but often only the poets and artists use the ability very well. Consequently, Jimmy and Ruth don't know we are here." He pointed at the demons. "You and I see moral reality.

The despicableness you see in the devil's errand boys is a true reflection of their very essence."

"Why don't they see us?"

"Creatures of evil have a natural aversion to goodness. Basically they avoid looking in our direction much like humans turn away from bad odors. If they perceived our presence, the vile perverts would quickly discover we're here and see us as bright shining lights. In due time, they'll discover we are on their trail. Right now we need to concentrate on the young couple."

Ruth took Jimmy's hand. "My parents have got some rich Jewish doctor or lawyer staked out for me." She paused and tossed her long black hair. "But a long time ago, I realized that my father lives his life by the book. All I ever get out of him is what the latest psychiatric party line is. I figure out what he wants to hear, and I just feed it back." Ruth's eyes snapped with fire. "I'm sick of being analyzed by him every time something goes wrong." She thought for a moment. "I'm going to have to go to the movies to cover my tracks. I think I'd better not do a joint today. Maybe next time."

Jimmy smiled.

"Watch carefully," Michael instructed. "Our bad boys are pushing images into each of their minds. While the demons can't read their thoughts, those two jerks can impress ideas on them in response to what they see going on. Right now they're pushing lust."

Jimmy squeezed Ruth tightly and kissed her neck. "Next time, we'll make sure that we have plenty of uninterrupted time. I'll call you at your apartment at the university."

"You bet." Ruth put her arms around his neck. "I hate to run, but if I don't, I'm going to get into problems with the traffic." Ruth started for her own car and then turned back. "I can't wait for us to be together again. Just maybe I'm falling in love with you, Jimmy Harrison." Ruth ran back, kissed him passionately again, and then ran for her car.

Jimmy stood beside his highly polished red Corvette and watched her drive away. He wore a self-satisfied grin.

"Our adversaries have scored points," Michael noted. "Ruth's rebellious attitude toward her parents prepared the way. Jimmy's current lascivious attraction to anything in skirts set the stage. The two young people might as well have sent an engraved invitation to attack."

"Our charges are in danger?"

"In a limited way. Right now their emotions are spinning. Unfortunately, that's how the first step is taken. Things can quickly go from bad to worse."

"Then we must charge in!"

"And do what?" Michael's question betrayed his amusement.

"Well . . . I . . . don't . . . exactly know."

The senior angel laughed. "My young friend, you're going to prove to be a great warrior, but you do need a little more preparation. No, Ruth and Jimmy don't need us just this moment. They will have to face a number of truths about themselves. Let's follow our two corrupt adversaries. If you listen intently, you can pick up what they are saying. You will naturally want to censor out much of their conversation, but fight the impulse. Everything you see and hear will be repugnant, but this is necessary to our task. Ready?"

The junior angel apprehensively shook his head. "I hadn't bargained for a walk through the mud."

Homelas and Malafidus watched Ruth drive away, and then the two demons slowly ascended above the earth.

"Piece of cake," Homelas boasted to his colleague. "This one is already in the bag."

"Don't be so sure," Malafidus warned. "Our nemesis has this weird thing about protecting Jews. They won't let the girl go easily. We must pay attention."

"Okay. But they won't pick up on the caper until we've been able to do real damage. Look. The girl's a virgin and she's got the hots for him. If we set it up right, Harrison ought to be able to get her in bed on the next go-around."

"Possibly. But I've had angels discover one of these operations and just appear out of nowhere." Malafidus swore. "After all, the girl has been raised with strong moral values."

"Forget it." Homelas pointed toward the north. "Let's take a break and really enjoy ourselves for a while."

"Where to?"

"Let's cruise up toward the Brentwood and North Hollywood area. Great porno shops up there." The sun was slowly sinking over the ocean. Shadows fell across the streets.

"I'm with you."

The two demons slowly rose above Balboa beach and then leisurely floated toward the north. Michael and Seradim ascended with them and moved back, giving the demons plenty of distance. Like feathers in the breeze, the two drifted along the freeways and over the endless rows of buildings until they settled around the Northridge area.

"Let's swoop down over the Sunset Boulevard area," Malafidus suggested and pointed south.

"Sure. Lots of action around there."

The two demons dropped down over the busy thoroughfare. A woman in an extremely tight short skirt was standing on a street corner. Her high leather boots came up to her knees, and the low-cut red blouse was sheer and skimpy.

"Look at that!" Homelas pointed at the woman. "A really good sign."

A sports car slowed at the curb. The driver made quick obscene remarks to the woman. She smiled and got in. The car sped away as she snuggled closer to the man.

"A-h-h-h," Malafidus sighed. "Makes me feel warm all over."

"Look!" Homelas pointed toward a low building with a bright neon sign flashing *Strip Joint.* "Let's try it."

The two demons shot through the walls into the topless bar. The lights were low and dim. Smoke hung heavy in the air. Men and women sat around small circular tables, watching naked women writhe in endless contortions to the loud, thumping drumbeat of the disco music. Strobe lights flashed in bright blues and greens. Men laughed crudely and hollered suggestive directions to the dancers. Wearing virtually nothing, women mingled among the customers, talking, buying drinks, laughing, and enticing.

"This *is* the place." Malafidus giggled in glee. "I've been working in and out of here for two decades. Feels like home."

"N-a-a-w," Homelas shook his head. "I didn't come up here to work. I just want to relax and absorb the atmosphere. Recharge my batteries. All this unbridled lust makes me feel s-o-o-o good."

"Yeah, sure, but it's hard for me not to zero in on somebody."

"Do what makes you happy." Homelas tossed the suggestion aside indifferently.

Far above the scene, Seradim turned away. "Let's destroy them now!" Seradim's thoughts were twinged with disgust.

"All things must run their course until the Holy One's plan is fulfilled." Michael motioned toward the boundaries of eternity. "Watch," Michael instructed Seradim. Endless scenes of past human history raced by the new Guardian like in a fast-forward motion picture, playing out the entire history of humanity in a matter of seconds.

"The Heavenly Father gave humans great promise and they have made great strides. You will be surprised to know the Father also allowed extraordinary latitude to the Evil One. Lucifer has never understood that he still has a place in the plan of God. Don't worry. The day of the final great battle will come, and then we will have our revenge. Homelas, Malafidus, and all the rest will receive their due."

Seradim stared in awe as the images of history slowly dissolved. "I can stand no more."

"My friend," Michael said in a heavy voice, "you have certainly not seen the worst."

"But I have seen all I can stand for now. Please, I want away from here."

"We can leave them," Michael concluded. "This place will keep the demons occupied for a while. I am sorry to expose you to the battle so quickly, but we don't have much time. The final conflict is not far away."

■ ■ ■

Customers poured into the Golden Dragon up to the moment of closing. "Happy New Year," Frank greeted the last patrons paying their checks. "Prosperity to you!" He waved good-bye and turned on the neon *Closed* sign. "Must have said that one thousand times! Not say again for twelve months!" He hurried back to the cash register.

The busboys quickly cleared the dishes in a frantic effort to get home or to the last party of the season. Frank cleared out the cash drawer, cramming the wad of bills into a bank deposit bag.

"Wonderful!" He chuckled. "We do very, very well tonight." He slammed the drawer shut and hustled to the private office in the rear of the kitchen.

Jessica sat just inside with her back to the door.

"Look," Frank held up the bulging money bag. "What a haul!"

Jessica slowly turned around, her eyes filled with tears.

Frank stopped, stunned. "What . . . what has happened to my honorable wife?"

Jessica buried her face in her hands.

"Please. Please speak to me."

The Chinese woman finally looked up. "I try not to think of our family. I push their faces and memory out of my mind . . . but they wouldn't stay gone today. Oh, Frank. I am so lonely. We have no friends here. Only Cindy. And I worry if any of them survived." She sobbed. "Or if they died terrible deaths."

Frank put his arm around his wife and for the first time in a very long time tears rolled down his cheeks. "Yes," he answered slowly. "We are so very alone in this land. No one stands with us." His voice trailed away. "No person, no god."

# CHAPTER
## 7

**M**ichael lifted Seradim up and out of the corruption on Sunset Boulevard and whisked him away. "Let me show you another method Lucifer uses to deceive the gullible and the grieving. We are going to visit a family that will have future importance to the Feinbergs. Think with me about a town called Lake Forest, California. We are going to visit a Chinese family."

The pair of angels envisioned, and were instantly transported to, a small house several blocks from the Golden Dragon restaurant. Seradim studied the simple stucco structure with a sign on the front door: Your Fortune Told Immediately. He noticed the symbols of the zodiac hung in a window and a placard on the wall that promised, "Contact your lost loved ones again!"

"Frank and Jessica Wong are inside," Michael explained. "They are Chinese immigrants. Their parents were Daoist, ancestor worshipers. The Wongs' daughter, Cindy, is the apple of Ben Feinberg's eye. Right now, Frank and Jessica are trying to get in touch with Jessica's father, Chin Lee, who died just before they came to America. She hopes to talk with him this evening."

"Talk to the dead?"

Michael nodded gravely. "Let's perch on top of the house and watch."

Seradim looked down on the Wongs, who were seated at a circular table with a bowl of green incense in the center. Gray smoke curled upward. Their eyes closed, the Wongs' fingertips touched those of a middle-aged Chinese woman across the table. Behind her were statues of dragon-headed people with frightening faces. Burning candles filled the room with the smell of hot wax and pungent incense.

"Help us, Yong Lou," Jessica Wong begged, tears running down her wrinkled and worn face. Her hair was still jet black, pulled back in a tight knot behind her head, making her plain face look severe. "Please bring back my honorable father, Chin Lee."

Her eyes tightly closed, the fortune-teller gripped the table fiercely. "Your father is coming now," Yong Lou said. "His spirit is returning to us."

Michael tapped Seradim gently and pointed knowingly at the woman's face. "Here it comes."

Yong Lou's expression slowly changed. The pleasant smile gave way to a contorted grimace. She caught her breath and rocked back in the chair. Yong Lou's lips moved mechanically, but nothing came out. Then a low guttural sound like a growling man slowly slipped through her parted lips. "My child," the new voice drawled, "I am here with you."

"Father?" Jessica Wong clenched her eyes even more tightly. "Honorable father are you among us?"

"I have come back to speak to you," the rumbling voice continued. "To tell you of my happiness where I am."

"Oh, Father," Jessica cried out, "where do you dwell?"

"In the abode of your ancestors where the great spirits rule. I have found the blessedness of which Buddha spoke, the place of complete enlightenment."

"Wonderful! Wonderful!" Jessica clamped her hands to the table. "I am so relieved. I knew you were a good man."

"I offered incense in the temples," the voice continued. "I drank the blood of the sacred snakes and always placed rice on our ancestors' graves. I have been rewarded."

"Thank you, thank you," Frank Wong joined in. "Chin Lee, we need direction to know what to believe in this new and strange land. Help us see the truth."

Yong Lou's body became rigid, and she caught her breath. The incense continued to rise from the bowl in front of her face.

Michael thought softly, "Seradim, I want you to look very carefully at the fortune-teller. Look inward through the layers of her being and see what is dwelling at the center."

To Seradim's amazement, he began to see a form within the woman's body, as if another person were wearing her body. The inner shape was ugly and gnarled like Homelas and Malafidus.

"The woman is possessed," Michael explained. "Many times séances are charades, just magic tricks made to look like something is happening when the whole thing is a hoax. Not this time."

"She can't be talking to the dead!"

"Of course not! Necromancy is an old trick of Lucifer's. He uses master ventriloquist demons to slip into the minds of fools who toy with evil. Yong Lou's family has been possessed for centuries. They have a long tradition of fortune-telling and calling up the dead. What she thought was an inheritance, a gift from her grandmother, was simply the demon moving from grandmother to grandchild."

"And now the Wongs are victims."

"Not yet, but they are being deceived. We must stop this exploitation lest they really get hooked into this calamity."

"Aren't there any warnings for such good people?"

"Unfortunately, the Wongs never read the Bible. If they had, they would know such practices are an anathema to the Holy One. The law of God forbids divination, horoscopes, psychic enchanters, witches, charmers, wizards, and necromancers. The Bible warned that these practices are condemned . . . forever!"

"We must teach the Wongs," Seradim interrupted.

"They have already heard some of the truth when their daughter introduced them to the Bible a few nights ago. . . . Now we're going to do something about this current situation." Michael pointed at the fortune-teller. "Follow me."

Michael gently descended behind the Chinese woman. For a moment he concentrated on the meaning of love. The harder he pondered, the brighter his personal radiance became. The demon inside Yong Lou slowly turned, as if distracted from his task. At the sight of the radiance of pure light, the creature recoiled and the woman shook violently.

"Away from me!" the demon protested.

The demonic words came out of Yong Lou's mouth in an explosion of agony. Frank and Jessica jumped. Their eyes popped open in a terrified stare.

"You can't touch me," the demon threatened. "Leave me, or I will destroy you!"

Frank and Jessica leaped up, their chairs hitting the floor. Yong Lou's eyes were fixed, and drool ran down the corner of her mouth.

As Michael stretched forth his arm like a sword of light, an increasing aura of goodness settled around the room.

"I have the power of death!" the demon cried. "Evil must triumph." Suddenly the demon gagged. "I can't stand the smell." The grotesque thing backed out of Yong Lou's body, and she fell face forward on the table.

Frank Wong grabbed his wife's hand. "Run! We are about to be attacked!" They bolted for the door.

The demon writhed and twisted in pain but finally detached from the fortune-teller. Michael advanced, driving the spirit in front of him.

"A-h-h-h!" the creature screamed. "I can't stand any more goodness." He shot through the walls into the darkness outside.

After a few moments, Yong Lou opened her eyes. She wiped her mouth and looked around the room. She saw the two overturned chairs on the floor. The front door was wide open.

"Oh, my." She stared at the mess. "What happened here?"

Yong Lou slowly stood up. With halting steps, she walked around the table and uprighted the chairs. "How strange. I remember the Wongs coming but not leaving." She looked around the dim room. "I need more light," she decided and switched on an overhead lamp. "Yes, what this house needs is much more light!"

# CHAPTER
# 8

**M**ichael pointed south of Highway 5, toward Irvine. "I want to teach you more about what humans call psychology, the dynamics behind human behavior. At the same time, I'll give you some insight into Larry Feinberg. Let's go down and watch the good doctor at work."

Seradim followed Michael's lead and zoomed down toward the Physicians Medical Building just blocks away from the Orange County John Wayne Airport. Michael led his charge down the pastel colored corridor on the fifth floor. Potted palm trees and flowering shrubs lined the hall.

"Doctor Feinberg's in session. He's seen this young woman a couple of times before. Her parents are long-term missionaries in New Guinea, where they translated the Bible into a new language.

"Unfortunately, their daughter struggles with some severe mental and emotional problems. You will notice that Larry does not have a very charitable view of Christianity. The freethinker's mind-set only applies to socially approved causes." The two angels walked through the wall.

Bookcases filled with leather-bound volumes lined the walls of the exquisite office. Above a red leather couch hung an oil painting of the surging ocean coastline. Larry sat in a large overstuffed chair across from a distraught young woman.

"Look, Dr. Feinberg." Louise wrung her hands as she struggled to choose her words. "I think about suicide all the time. I just can't get the thought out of my mind."

Dr. Feinberg nodded sympathetically. "Feels like you're trapped under a huge black cloud, doesn't it?"

"Yes!" The black-haired, twenty-six-year-old woman brightened for the first time.

"It's like morning never comes. You live in a perpetual night."

"Exactly. Oh, yes, I can't get away from the darkness."

"Louise, you're struggling with depression. You don't really want to kill yourself. Your feelings create those thoughts."

"But I've prayed for help so often."

Larry almost sneered, but instantly recovered his demeanor. "I've always found mood brighteners do a whole lot more for people than prayer," he chided. "The real need is for us to get to the bottom of your depression."

Michael nudged his young charge. "Of course, the psychiatrist is right about the cause of her self-destructive inclinations, but all humans need to feel important. They have a great vulnerability in this area. One of the reasons Larry likes being a psychiatrist is that he can be the expert for everyone. He's had lots of trouble with his kids because of this tendency."

Seradim nodded. "Obviously, a target area for the demons."

"Exactly," Michael confirmed. "Louise's problems started in her need to feel important. The need is easily manipulated. Keep watching Larry as he works."

"Seems like I've been depressed forever," Louise moaned. "Since my parents went back to the mission field six months ago, the gloom has been impenetrable."

"Did you want them to go back?"

"Of course. Their work is very, very important."

"More important than you?"

Louise looked shocked. "Well . . . my goodness . . . I never thought about . . ."

"Yes, I think you have. I think you've resented always being left behind by your parents."

"Absolutely not!" Louise's brown eyes snapped. "How could I possibly stand in the way of the work of the gospel?"

"Yes, how could you stand in their way without being a bad person?" Larry spoke gently. "But you still resent being pushed aside."

"Never!" Louise clenched her fist. "I'm not that kind of person. You're making me sound . . . selfish . . . my parents insensitive."

"You're hurt, Louise, and you're very angry with them as well as with yourself."

"No!" Louise's voice raised with more than a hint of agitation. "No! I tell you . . . I mean, I want you to know that . . ." The woman began shaking. "I can't be angry," her tone took on the feel of pain. "What kind of a person gets angry at godly parents?"

"A normal human being," Dr. Feinberg answered sympathetically. "A good, sensitive, caring person."

Louise choked and grimaced. "Good?" Tears ran down her cheeks. "How could I possibly be good?" Suddenly

Louise began sobbing so violently, Larry worried that she might slide from the chair.

As the flood of tears ebbed, he commented, "You've been very angry for a long time, Louise. Your suicidal thoughts are only one symptom of an inability to deal with your anger toward your parents."

"But I shouldn't be angry," Louise protested and dabbed at her eyes.

"*Should* and *ought* don't have a place in the world of our emotions," Dr. Feinberg explained. "We feel what we feel. It's just that simple, except we must admit to ourselves what's going on. Otherwise, we become prisoners of our past."

Michael nudged his colleague. "Larry's actually a very good psychiatrist in spite of himself."

Louise began crying again, but the sound had changed. The weeping was gentle, pleading.

"As you set the pain free, your anger will subside and the suicidal thoughts will disappear," the psychiatrist advised. "Don't worry. You won't kill yourself if you release your rage."

"I've just never felt I could admit how much I resented my father leaving me."

"Men struggle with Oedipus complexes and women face similar Electra complexes." Dr. Feinberg sounded professorial. "Or to put it another way, you've had a father vacuum."

"A what?" Louise dried her eyes.

Michael laughed. "Our boy's trying a little razzle-dazzle on his client. Freud talk. Nevertheless, he's on to something. Pay attention, Seradim."

"Your father worked alone in the jungle a great deal of the time while you were a child, didn't he?" Larry asked.

Louise nodded.

"You probably didn't feel like you had much control over your life in those days?"

Louise looked shocked. "How did you know?"

"You've been trying to control these sessions from the moment you walked through the door." Larry smiled. "It's okay, but I immediately noticed your need to stay in the driver's seat."

"Am I so transparent?"

"My job is to read the signs, Louise, and to help you accept the fact that anyone growing up under your circumstances would feel the same way."

Seradim looked at Michael. "A father vacuum?"

"A big problem in American society," Michael said, "caused more frequently by people chasing money than those helping the lost in primitive jungles. But Larry hasn't learned about the biggest emptiness of all. The God vacuum. We're going to have to help him with that one."

"But my behavior is far from normal." Louise choked her words.

"Especially when it comes to men."

Louise froze, and the color left her face.

"I have a hunch you're also depressed about your sexual behavior."

Louise began breathing rapidly, as if her heart were pounding out of control.

"Everything said in this room is kept completely confidential. You have to be able to let me help you deal with your secrets."

"You know about the men in my life?" Louise could barely speak.

"Only theoretically. But I do know that girls with a father vacuum are sitting ducks for men's sexual advances."

"I . . . just can't . . . seem to say no . . . often enough." Louise's voice trailed away. "But I try to be a good Christian girl."

"The Christian stuff doesn't interest me, but I know that every time you violate your own moral code, you pay a heavy price in guilt and self-condemnation."

"Oh, I do. I do."

"And every time you succumb, you're really trying to fill the father vacuum with a man. Once you see what you're doing, you'll be able to get your life under control again."

Seradim turned to Michael. "I bet the demons have a field day tempting women who have that tendency!"

"Important insight," the senior angel said. "The inability to understand this need has shipwrecked legions of young people."

"Where do I begin?" Louise asked.

"Accept the fact that it's normal to resent the absence of your parents even if they are doing a good thing. Recognize anger as a normal emotion. Allow yourself to experience the pain that's behind the resentment. Then you can truly forgive. The healing comes by forgiving, but you'll never be able to forgive your parents or anyone else if you don't even know that you are angry and bitter."

Louise settled back and leaned against the chair. She stared at the ceiling for a long time.

Michael explained to Seradim, "Men have similar problems with the father vacuum. They get into homosexual relationships, trying to find the masculine image lost in their childhood. Very tragic consequences follow. When fathers neglect their sons, they set them up for a lifetime of painful struggle. Make careful note. The demons never miss that one either."

After five minutes of silence, Louise spoke. "I can't believe it. I don't feel as depressed!"

"Good," Larry affirmed. "Those dark moments will probably be back to some extent, but now you will know what to do. We'll keep working until they're gone. Remember, Louise, listen to your own feelings, admit what they are, share them with a friend, forgive, and fill those parental vacuums by connecting more on a deep personal level with good people. Then you won't be so vulnerable to men taking advantage of you sexually."

Michael tugged at Seradim. "Enough of the psychiatric couch talk for one day. Larry doesn't even know his advice works because it's biblical. Let's go across town. I want you to watch a far less therapeutic meeting going on right now. Think yourself to the Community Church three blocks from here."

When the two angels arrived in the fellowship hall of the highly successful church, four people were gathered around a small serving area at the far end of a row of tables being prepared for a Wednesday night dinner.

A tall, thin woman was speaking in a low voice. "Ed, you're the chairman of the pastoral relations committee. I think you've got to get the committee together and lower the boom."

The overweight accountant shook his head. "I don't know, Dorothy. We're playing with fire here. A lot of people really admire the pastor. He's got a large following."

A chunky middle-aged woman with frosted hair pushed her finger in the accountant's face. "I don't care, Ed." Sylvia Springer, head of the church's social committee continued, "We can't have a minister who's got trouble at home. Everyone knows Pastor Reynolds is facing the possibility of an unwanted divorce. We need to sack him before word gets out around town."

"And everyone thinks his wife is a nut," Dr. Stanton Young, a distinguished-looking man, interjected. "The woman is unfriendly and distant—and only heaven knows what she's into."

Michael motioned for Seradim to sit next to him on the edge of a small stage behind the group. "What we have going on here is an old-fashioned unofficial board meeting. You don't need demons when you've got a crew like this one at work in the church. You're going to learn one of the reasons people like the Feinbergs don't take the Christian message seriously. These church members are a bigger problem than our old buddies Malafidus and Homelas."

"Dr. Young, I always respect your opinions," Ed Parker continued. "But starting an assault on the pastor could result in a church war we might well lose."

Dorothy smiled faintly. "I've been at this a long time." The elderly woman looked as if she'd been to the plastic surgeon once too often. "I've been in many church scraps, and we'll be here long after the Reynolds family is gone." Dorothy's voice became sharp. "It's better to bite the bullet and get it over with quickly."

"Agreed!" Dr. Young said.

Michael nudged Seradim. "Remember the human need to be important? Here it is again, causing strife and dissention. Sex, power, and money. Those are the big three. Louise tried illicit sex to fill her father vacuum. But these church folks are definitely into power to feel important."

"Yes, Michael, it seems the whole bunch are on a power trip," Seradim concluded.

Michael pointed toward Dorothy James and Stanton Young. "We've got a couple of obsessive-compulsive personalities on our hands. Legalists are usually cut from this cloth. You get the nice-guy types—neat, orderly, hard working—but behind the perfect facade is a dangerous need for control. Usually these people are big into hoarding money. Unfortunately, this church is filled with money-chasing social climbers. They will listen to Dorothy and the doctor spin their yarns."

Dorothy pointed a long bony finger at Ed. "The first step is to get the facts out. Let people know what's going on at the Reynoldses' house. Once the pastor's popularity is undercut, the rest is a downhill slide."

Ed Parker's eyes narrowed. "The truth is, we're the most influential people in the church. People will listen to us."

The chunky woman smiled. "I talk to people on the phone all the time, making calls on the inactive members. A few well-placed comments can turn the tide in a hurry." Sylvia Springer glared. "I never really trusted the pastor from the start."

Michael nodded knowingly. "Sylvia is more than a tad paranoid. Had alcoholic parents that set her up to not trust any authority figure. She's a controller as well. Because Sylvia is so filled with anger, she assumes everyone else is angry with her. She sees the speck in her brother's eye instead of the log in her own eye. No matter what the pastor did for her, Sylvia couldn't trust him because she is projecting her anger onto the good man. She'll feel completely righteous trying to hang the pastor because underneath it all, Sylvia is trying to get back at her parents who failed her."

"The biggest problem will be the McCoys," the doctor noted. "Since they've joined the church, Jennifer and Joe think Reynolds hung the moon."

"We can't win them all." Dorothy shrugged. "They're new. If they don't like what's happening, let them go to another church. The town's full of 'em."

"Where do we start?" Ed rolled his eyes.

Sylvia smiled. "I've seen the pastor come early to his office to counsel a woman. He says it's the only time she can come because of her work schedule. Sounds fishy to me."

"Reynolds has left himself wide open," Dr. Young continued. "Over our objections he let that Alcoholics Anonymous group meet here. They try to keep the lid on it, but everyone knows his wife drinks too much. Well, of course, that's a rumor. But I say we start the ball rolling by letting people know the moral laxness of the man."

"Okay. Okay," Ed agreed. "You people make the phone calls, and in a week I'll call the pastoral relations committee together."

Michael sighed. "Pastor Reynolds is a very good man. . . . God has really used him, but that won't make any difference now. His real error was failing to see that all the adulation and praise heaped on him by these people was only a form of projection. They wanted the pastor to be the perfect parent they never had. Of course, no one can fill that role. As they discovered his humanity, these members started sharpening their knives. Pastor Reynolds is too good-hearted a man to see what's coming."

"Ed, that's sound thinking," Dorothy said condescendingly. "The attack must be swift and to the point. When the pastor sees the handwriting on the wall, he'll slip out the back door."

"And the AA group goes as well!" Dr. Young insisted.

"But what if Reynolds doesn't go quietly?" Sylvia asked. "The pastor can be quite obstinate." The chunky woman bit her lip. "After all, he didn't listen to us in the past."

Dorothy's eyes narrowed. "If we throw enough dirt, some will stick."

"I just worry about the McCoys." Ed looked away. "They just started attending church recently."

"Oh, well." Dr. Young smiled. "The last time we were involved in a church split there was some fallout. Just part of the process."

Seradim stared in shock. "What a terrifying scenario!"

"The actions of this small group of people will have big repercussions in the future. The Scripture warns Christians to be respectful of their leaders. Because of their opposition to the pastor, these dissidents will destroy their spiritual covering and open the door for Evil to strike their church. Their personal needs for importance, control, and domination will be the downfall of many."

"Should we do anything?"

"Not yet, Seradim. Humans have freedom. Once they invite attack, the opposition has a right to respond."

"I fear for the McCoys. They're not true believers yet."

Michael hung his head. "When you see such travesties, you know the church has to have been preserved through the centuries only by the grace of God. Any other organization would have turned to dust long ago.

"Well, Seradim, we have work to do. The world is coming to an end, and these foolish, vain people want to fight a war over who controls the keys to the clubhouse!"

# C H A P T E R
## 9

**B**lack clouds boiled and spirit winds blew fiercely toward the eastern seaboard of the United States. At the imperial summons, demons from across the globe instantly responded. New orders were about to be issued and demonic forces repositioned. Specialists in fear management and deception swooped down on Washington, D.C. Such a gathering of evil had not occurred since Adolf Hitler's Munich putsch or Joseph Stalin's political purges, which resulted in the deaths of twenty million people.

"Something big's coming down," a huge black troll told the comrade flying at his side. "Maybe a world war is in the making. Anybody who is anybody is being called in."

"I love a great military explosion," his yellow-greenish companion answered. "Civil wars are particularly good. Relatives kill each other, and the hate lasts for centuries. Of course, chemical warfare is excellent for maiming children. Genetic defects even produce kids without arms and legs. The pain just won't quit. I hope they start slinging around some nasty viral concoction."

"Perhaps we're going to get an atomic explosion out of this one. Maybe hit Damascus or Jerusalem. What a blast!" The demon laughed at his own pun.

"Whatever. Let's hunker down to the war room and see what's cooking."

The two demons merged into a multitude of ugly creatures pouring into an enormous smoke-filled chamber. The swarm quickly blended together in a semblance of order in front of a huge opening similar to a gigantic television screen where Earth scenes were magnified for the legions of hell to watch.

A gargantuan form overshadowed the congregation of malefactors. "Pay close attention." His deep, ominous voice rumbled through the assembly. "You must carefully observe what is unfolding. We are now positioned for a major opportunity to create chaos and revolution everywhere. Millions can be destroyed!" A sound akin to thunder erupted in an orgasmic explosion of raw emotion, sending shock waves across the gathering.

"For the first time in a decade, we may be able to foment a world war and unbounding carnage! We are going to watch the president of the United States give instructions, which will set these possibilities in motion. You must be ready to give him every assistance." His hideous laughter rocked the gathering.

The inner office of the American president came into focus in the gigantic viewing area. Damian Gianardo and his vice president, Jacob Rathmarker, stood side by side in the Oval Office, listening to the secretary of state report. Occasionally, they looked knowingly at each other.

"In summary," the secretary said as he turned the final page and cleared his throat, "your suggestion to the European heads of state for a federation of ten nations has been received with total consternation. The idea of a new common market and new trade agreements with us was welcomed. However, the notion that we develop a joint military, combining all land and sea forces, was met by bewilderment. And when I talked of governmental linkage, they ran."

"Thank you, Mr. Clark." The president smiled condescendingly. "Did you bring it to their attention that we have the nuclear attack capacity to make compliance advantageous?"

Secretary Clark pulled at his collar. "Sir, they would have seen such a suggestion as an implied threat. I didn't feel that such a course was helpful."

"Not at this time . . . at least." Rathmarker smiled cunningly. "I trust all discussions have been completely and totally confidential."

"Absolutely. I spoke only with my counterparts at the top level of government. No one wanted a word of these discussions leaked."

Gianardo turned and walked to the opposite end of the office. He crossed his arms and paced back and forth. "Something is needed. Some extraordinary event must happen that will cause each of these nations to realize how much it needs my leadership. The world needs a good shaking."

"I don't understand what you are suggesting," the secretary said nervously.

The president stood with his right side to the wall. "Obviously, I am changing the political face of our country very quickly. People have learned that my leadership is flawless. On the domestic scene, we are creating complete dependence on me. We need a good worldwide disaster to accomplish the same thing abroad."

"A *good* disaster?" The secretary swallowed hard.

"Come now, Clark." Damian Gianardo laughed. "Be a little imaginative. Surely we can create a nice little crisis that will demonstrate a demand for my proposed alliance."

"I . . . I'm not sure how to proceed, sir."

Gianardo leaned over the desk, jabbing at the secretary of state with his index finger. "Assemble a top secret think tank of military experts to work on this problem. I want every aspect of international terrorism and deception explored. Study everything from the sinking of the *Lusitania* to Lyndon Johnson's Gulf of Tonkin manipulation of the Vietnam War. What would it mean if we caused the economy of a country like Italy or France to collapse? And then brought overnight restoration?"

"Frankly, Mr. President, some heads of state suggested that we seem to be trying to re-create the old Roman Empire. As absurd as it seems, they—"

"Significant choice of words, Mr. Secretary." Gianardo cut him off. "Why not?"

The secretary of state's eyes widened in dismay. Clark nodded his head mechanically. "Let me . . . uh . . . give it . . . some thought." He hurried from the room.

The scene faded from the viewing area; demons frantically communicated with each other. Steam and foul vapors arose from the heated discussions, which sounded as abrasive as a drill grinding on a tooth.

"Get the idea?" the singular massive voice echoed over the gathering. His awesome shape overshadowed the assemblage. "See the potential?"

The demonic assembly squirmed and writhed in increasing agitation. Explosions of energy sent fireballs in every direction. The swarm was clearly building to a frenzy.

"I want us to create a massive, worldwide sense of fear, dread, and apprehension," the oppressive voice continued. "We must create a climate of panic around the globe."

"Yes! Yes! Certainly!" the group echoed. "At once!"

"Give me a report from the major principalities," the supreme voice ordered. "I want an update on the social climate you are creating in the American scene."

A monstrous shape floated up from the group and drifted toward center stage. The brownish, amorphous figure changed form as the demon hovered in space. "We have successfully captured the entertainment industry," it explained. "Hollywood is the spiritual Babylon of our era. Christian beliefs and values are consistently belittled. Cherished symbols of faith are put to blasphemous use in both television and movies. Whenever a Christian character appears in a film, we make sure the person is portrayed as a fool, a liar, a cheat, a murderer, or a crazy person. Media bias promotes intolerance and materialism. Yes, we are winning the culture war."

The convocation exploded in enthusiastic approval.

"We have created a significant wall of separation between God and the screen," the head of the Hollywood principality continued. "The common Judeo-Christian values that shaped the founding of America have been replaced with moral relativism, which often celebrates the degrading."

"Give us examples," an evil enthusiast yelled.

"Back in the 1990s we had great success with a film titled *The People vs. Larry Flynt*. We were able to slip in total nudity and complete degradation under the heading of 'art.' We made the fundamentalist minister Jerry Falwell look like an idiot while portraying the porno publisher as courageous and progressive. Shortly after that event, we got a grotesque episode aired on the Fox network, portraying a series of clergy murders. Splattered dead priests' blood all over America!"

The conclave again erupted in approval.

"We have been able to suppress the fact that Hollywood has two thousand committed Christian employees. The believers never think to pray for them, so we continue to rule virtually unopposed. All we need is to make one change in a script, distort one idea in a movie, and we reshape what millions of people think and believe."

The leader of the council pointed to the opposite side of the gathering. "Tell us about the European principality," his ominously deep voice invited and demanded all at the same time.

A knurled, ancient-looking demon with great claws arose. "We've had our ups and downs over the centuries," he began slowly. "The high Victorian culture of a hundred and fifty years ago was a problem, but with the help of Sigmund Freud, we were able to portray morality as repressive and unhealthy. World Wars I and II provided the maximum opportunity to destroy restraint and propriety. Consequently, Europe is now filled with morally adrift parents and kids without any sense of spiritual direction.

"Many have found an affluent lifestyle beyond anything their ancestors could have dreamed. All we will need to do is shake their faith in the economic underpinnings that feed them and they'll fall for anything. Accept the lie. Embrace a dictator. Riot. Steal. Believe me, the world is filled with soulless rabble whose consumerist mentality leaves them totally vulnerable to the least threat to their affluence."

"But will the churches be a menace?" another demon shouted.

"They could be," an anonymous demon answered. "But most groups are so preoccupied with ski trips and basket weaving for the old folks, they never get around to the message. And many ministers are busy building their own personal empires and chasing after everything under the sun except sharing the Christian story. As long as they stay distracted with monkey business, we don't have to worry."

"In addition," a green creature said, "we've been able to profit from the national climate of disillusionment with TV evangelists. In thousands of local churches, we've incited distrust and disrespect for religious leaders. Members whisper rumors and spread stories of deceit, enabling us to discredit the clergy. Never have pastors had as difficult a time leading their flocks."

The Evil One applauded slowly and then more forcefully until the entire chamber rocked with the sound of raucous applause. Demons hissed and spit. The stench rose like the smell of manure on a hot summer day.

Another scene appeared before the conclave. Damian Gianardo continued talking to his vice president, Jacob Rathmarker, after the secretary of state had left. Gianardo was a tall, distinguished man of commanding presence. Long before the presidency fell into his hands, he had acquired the art of walking into any room in a way that demanded attention. His intimidating black eyes and penetrating stare always produced a disconcerting feeling that he knew what others were thinking. He had an uncanny capacity to accurately read the intentions and motives of his opponents. Once he grasped the other person's position, Gianardo had no restraint in the pursuit of his own ends.

"Jacob, I have little confidence in Clark's ability to do what needs to be done. He's of the old school. Ethical

behavior and honorable intent. The man's out of touch
with today's world. He'd be terrified even to order the CIA
to assemble a hit squad and bring an enemy down."

The president's graying hair was carefully combed over
the right side of his head, down across his temple and toward
his neck. Even hair transplants could not conceal the
reminder of the near-fatal head injury. His vanity caused
him to keep the damaged side of his head toward the wall
as he spoke.

Rathmarker shook his head. "I agree. We may have to
take things in our own hands. Bumping Clark aside now
could raise questions later."

"Yes, we must be quite prudent." The president rubbed
his hands together. His perfectly manicured fingers were
long, tapered, and unusually thin. Though they might have
been the hands of an artist or a surgeon, the fingers had
the disconcerting look of a stereotypical undertaker in a
horror movie. "Perhaps history will yet play into our hands.
If not, we will seize the nations by the throat and shake
them until they fall into line."

Rathmarker laughed coarsely. "I admire you for many
reasons, Damian. But most of all, your ruthlessness is an
inspiration."

As the scene faded, the exhilaration of the hordes of evil
climbed to an elevated stage of euphoric ecstasy.

"Yes! We've found our man," a voice echoed from a far
corner of the conclave.

"He can lead them into the great war," another harmful
creature shouted over the din.

The Evil One, the personification of every diabolical
intent, ascended even higher above his legions, extending
his arms into the air. "The Beast is ready," it exclaimed. "The
unbridled evil of uncontrollable governmental authority is

about to be made manifest. Don't let me down," it threatened. "I've waited since the beginning of time for just such a moment! We've had an antichrist in the wings in every era since Yeshua's death and resurrection. Gianardo is our man for the third millennium. No doubt about it!"

# CHAPTER

## 10

Michael beckoned Seradim to follow as he rose aloft over Community Church and its conspiratorial committee members. He pointed toward the amorphous veil separating time and eternity. "We're going back across the great barrier. We need to let some time pass."

The two angels shot through the vaporous curtain covering the entrance into eternity. Immediately a sense of profound and ultimate completeness wrapped around them like an all-sufficient mantle of peace.

Seradim sighed deeply. "I had lost touch with the impeccability of heaven. The quintessence, the *ne plus ultra* that feels so inexpressibly awesome."

"In the mind of God, everything is in the now," Michael began. "All moments are immediately present to the Holy One because eternity is only an aspect of His Being. Time on Earth will race forward while we talk."

Seradim absorbed the instruction. "Time moves on while we are stationary in eternity?"

"A number of events must happen before we return. For one thing, Sharon Feinberg caught on to her daughter's little rendezvous with Jimmy Harrison. She didn't need our help to put the clamps on Ruth's behavior. The entire family is going for counseling with a therapist named Dr. Ann Woodbridge, an associate of Larry's who happens to be a Christian. Things are moving along right on schedule."

"Oh," Seradim nodded approvingly. "Good."

"Moreover, we must give Lucifer ample room to put a few more pieces in place for the grand scheme the devil thinks he is creating. Remember Gianardo, the president of the United States?"

"Certainly."

"During the next several months, Gianardo and his vice president, Rathmarker, will be looking for a worldwide crisis to catapult them to unprecedented power. Little do they know that heaven itself will give them their opportunity. With no idea that the Creator is working, Lucifer is actually fulfilling God's sovereign plan."

"I don't grasp what you are describing," Seradim said. "Perhaps . . . I—"

"No," Michael interrupted, "you must not think with the same patterns humans use or you won't ever be able to understand. Mortal insight is called syllogistic thinking. People attempt to figure out the world, nature, events, even the mind of God, as if reality is a path of stepping stones leading logically from one idea to the next. People fail to see the difference eternity makes in understanding existence." He chuckled. "Lucifer has also forgotten. As a result, the most brilliant minds often skip down the path of logic and end up with conclusions worse than ones drawn by humans of greatly limited capacity. Geniuses have ended up not even believing the Father exists. Now that is arrogance!"

"People are exceedingly strange," Seradim concluded. "They have such awesome potential, and yet they come to such peculiar ends as if their capacities were even lower than the animals."

"Such always follows when they ignore the divine factor in their equations." Michael pointed across heaven. "In our world all things come together. What appears to be contradictory on Earth coalesces here. Heaven is not only the place of harmony of relationships, but of ideas. Ours is the realm of paradox."

"The place where contradictions meet and kiss?"

"Excellent, Seradim. A paradox is two ideas that appear to be in collision but are actually both true. Human behavior is quite paradoxical. The best of people can do the worst of things. The most dangerous humans are capable of very altruistic thoughts and actions. Get it?"

The new trainee nodded. "And that is how even Lucifer serves the Father?"

"Lucifer's actions seem to be the result of utter contempt for the Creator, and they are. Yet he is acting right now in accord with prophecy given by the Holy Spirit millennia ago. With no insight whatsoever, the demons are performing right on schedule. Quite a paradox!"

Seradim lowered himself until he lay prone toward the throne of the Father. Spontaneous words and melody rolled out of his soul. "Holy, holy, holy, Lord God Almighty, before Your throne of glory our songs arise to Thee. Holy, holy, holy, wondrous and mighty, God in Three Persons, blessed Trinity." The words poured out in heartfelt praise and tribute.

Michael could not resist being swept into Seradim's praise. He sang a completely different melody, blending with the young angel like the countermelody in a fugue. The two angels' songs rose and ascended to the heights, blending into a mighty chorus of adoration.

Other angelic voices spontaneously joined the hymn. Seradim's simple song became a canticle of heaven, total and original yet resonate with all the glorious sounds of continuous praise and love that circulated around the Father's throne like the massive movement of clouds constantly in motion over the earth.

When they came to the end, both angels felt even greater exhilaration than in the beginning. Slowly, Seradim's melody lowered into a singular song within his own heart.

"I find it difficult to stop," Seradim confessed to Michael.

"It is truly glorious. But we must stop now because we have other work to do. Someday nothing will interrupt us.

"During our song, several months have passed on Earth and Lucifer's plan has progressed. It will soon be time for us to return. The Satanic trinity has been hard at work."

"Satanic trinity?"

"Lucifer attempts to counterfeit everything in heaven," Michael explained. "Ultimately, no originality exists except that which mirrors the mind of the Father."

Seradim's soul sighed deeply, still enraptured with the lingering melody of praise. "I have a difficult time shifting my attention to such contrary thoughts, but I know it is important for me to understand these matters. Explain the Satanic trinity to me, please."

"As the Father is the center of all things, so Lucifer is the source of all destruction, the unity behind and within all evil." Michael projected into Seradim's mind a collage of pain-filled scenes from Earth.

In an instant, the new Guardian envisioned airplanes crashing, children dying, diseases devouring healthy people, thousands starving, and people betraying each other with endless schemes of deception. Seradim put his hands to his eyes. "Stop! Please stop. I can't stand it."

"Very different situations," Michael continued, "but tied together with one strand: Lucifer."

Seradim nodded hesitantly.

"The second person in the diabolical scheme is 'the lamb with the voice of the dragon.' The devil is constantly working to create a system of apostate religion as his alternative to the work of Yeshua on the cross. Often the same biblical words are used, but Satan redefines the meanings to serve his worst purposes. See the possibilities?"

"No," Seradim puzzled. "No, I don't."

"Watch." Once again Michael recalled scenes from the past. He thought of teenage Moonies standing on a street corner, selling flowers to raise money for their cause. "Seradim, look into those young faces so innocently working for the Moon that pretends to be the Son." Michael next remembered Jim Jones and the masses who followed the preacher to Guyana and died at Jonestown. Immediately, Seradim experienced hundreds of people lying dead on the jungle floor with cups of Kool-Aid in their hands.

"Apostate religion can be deadly," Michael added. "Jesus redeemed the lost. The lamb with the voice of a dragon condemns the deceived."

"Father and Son," Seradim repeated aloud. "Lucifer and religion."

"The third person in the devil's trinity is 'the Beast,' a system of governmental power." Michael quickly switched images in Seradim's mind, unfolding the panoramic story of the evolution of the kingdoms of the world. Pictures of tribal chieftains, kings, and tyrannical despots flashed past. The concept of government expanded and Seradim saw

Caesars dispatching legions to annihilate innocent people. He saw the city-states of Europe spring up into the emerging nations of medieval times. Kingdoms turned into democracies, and kings were replaced by committees and security councils. The czars of Russia became the prime ministers of communism, and millions died in labor camps and before firing squads.

"What you are seeing," Michael instructed, "is the way in which political power can take on a life of its own. The system becomes like a train run amok without any hand at the switch. The Beast is the metaphor for corrupt state agencies and armies that have actually slipped into Lucifer's hand. Regardless of nameplates on governmental doors of authority, he alone has become the true master behind the thrones of power. At this moment the devil is turning Damian Gianardo, the American president, into the final manifestation, the incarnation of the Beast."

"Astonishing!" the reassigned angel gasped.

"But we both know the secret of how the final victory arises from what seemed to be the ultimate defeat," Michael said. Instantly he recalled the darkest day in human history. Black clouds rolled up from the deep and covered the city of Jerusalem. Tornadic winds abruptly swept across the ancient city, over the high stone walls, and down on a limestone quarry where men were hanging from cross beams tied to massive poles sticking out of the ground. Soldiers with iron spears milled about watching the crowd cowering in grief before the monstrous scene of three men having life slowly drained from them.

"A-a-a-a-h!" Seradim writhed in torment. "I can't stand to revisit this sight."

Michael kept remembering. One lone figure towered above the grotesque executions. Blood ran down His face, and bones protruded from His distended chest drooping beneath arms nailed to the rough cross-member beam. His head hung low as if no capacity for movement was left. Above the thorn-crowned head, a crude sign proclaimed in Greek, Latin, and Hebrew, "This is the King of the Jews." The Rabbi slightly raised His head and cried out, *"Eli, Eli, lama sabach-thani.* My God, My God, why have You forsaken Me?"

Seradim wept.

The image expanded in Michael's memory. Yeshua's head and body finally sagged out of control, limp and dead. Michael could hear the sounds of the great Temple curtain tearing in two pieces. An earthquake shook the earth and great boulders exploded in half. Thunder roared over the city. Lightning split trees into splinters. Michael could recall the scene no longer.

Seradim turned and stared into eternity. Slowly, far off in the distance, another image arose before his vision. A wondrous glorious shape appeared between the throne and the flying Cherubim and Seraphim. A slain Lamb, standing triumphant.

The Lamb reached out and took a great scroll. Immediately the elders of the tribes of Israel and the twelve apostles fell down before the Lamb. Angels swooped low in obeisance. The elders and apostles took up harps and golden bowls of incense, and smoke arose in the form of prayers.

The mighty chorus burst into song, "Worthy are You to take the scroll and to open its seals, for Your blood did ransom humanity for God from every tribe and tongue and people and nation. You have made them a kingdom and priests to our God, and they shall reign on earth."

Suddenly myriads of myriads and thousands of thousands of angelic voices rang out, "Worthy is the Lamb who was slain, to receive power and wealth and wisdom and might and honor and blessing!" Blending into the incredible chorus came other voices, voices of earth and sea singing, "To Him who sits on the throne and to the Lamb be blessing and honor and glory and might for ever and ever!" The elders worshiped by crying out again and again, "Amen, Amen, Amen."

Seradim smiled. "We have only to remember, the victory is already His."

# CHAPTER
## 11

The time is right for us to reenter the universe," Michael instructed his charge. "We're going back on one of my favorite days."

"Rosh Hashanah!" Seradim caught the thought before it was completely expressed. "Yes, I can see how special holy days are for angelic intervention."

"High holidays help us keep our bearings as we move between time and eternity. I'm particularly moved by this day, Rosh Hashanah, the beginning of the Jewish New Year. Many times I've hovered above synagogues and listened for the shofar's sound, the blast of the ram horn that tells the world Jehovah Rafah has called another year into being."

Seradim looked around heaven, noticing a great change in the usual patterns of worship and the offerings of the incense prayers of the saints. A flurry of activity was building. Cherubim and Seraphim continued their usual ministries of praise, but the Thrones had shifted their major focus to directing the work of the angels under their authority. Juridical angels who constantly contemplate the divine judgment were in a high state of animation. Dominions rushed back and forth across heaven, delivering special messages and instructing the Virtues on special assignments.

"Some very unusual preparation is underway," Seradim observed. "Warrior angels are charging across the time barrier as if they are preparing for an all-out war and Principalities left even earlier. A completely new alignment seems to be taking place within heaven itself."

"For eons, we've waited for this moment to arrive," Michael answered. "Heaven is about to swell dramatically, and we will be needed on Earth as never before." Michael pointed to the barrier. "We must depart quickly; the hour is at hand. The great event will coincide with the celebration of Rosh Hashanah."

In an instant, the two angels burst through the barrier and plunged rapidly into the hectic pace of life in Southern California. Larry and Sharon Feinberg were speeding toward the counseling office of Dr. Ann Woodbridge in Newport Beach. Heading south from the other direction on Highway 5, Jimmy Harrison and Ruth Feinberg were just about at the parking lot in front of Dr. Woodbridge's building, the New Life Clinic.

"Since our departure, much has happened." Michael pointed to the scene unfolding beneath them. "The Feinberg family is trying to come to grips with a number of their problems. Ruth and Jimmy's flirtation took on a new depth of meaning. Homelas and Malafidus blew their assignment when youthful lust and rebellion turned into love and caring. We really wouldn't have had much to do but observe." Michael pointed to the five-story building. "The demons won't be around here today. Rosh Hashanah makes them nervous and the atmosphere inside the office is too

Christian. Let's go down and watch. The fireworks are about to begin."

The two angels flew above the packed 405 Freeway, gliding toward Irvine. "Let's check in on the McCoys quickly before we join the Feinbergs in their little showdown. Think yourself to Joe's office."

Joe McCoy pointed to the chart behind him. The twenty employees in the room listened carefully to his instruction.

"We must reprogram how computer routing is occurring," Joe continued. "We need to have a more efficient system for quicker response to the customer."

One of the employees laughed. "We've already got the quickest draw in the West. Our company is the original 'Billy the Kid' of the defense industry." Others laughed.

Joe shook his head. "Well," he drawled, "you just never know when the unexpected can happen. Our job is to make sure the national security radar and response systems can't be fooled. In that spirit, we have to make sure the customers buying our products have an absolute sense of instant response."

"Is anyone more up on their toes than old Joe McCoy?" another employee asked. "Go get 'em tiger." The group laughed again.

Michael beckoned for Seraphim to follow him. "Before the morning is out, the laugh will be on Joe's colleagues. Time to check in on Larry and company. Let's think ourselves over to the counselor's office."

The Feinbergs were already waiting to enter the conference room on the fourth floor when Jimmy and Ruth rounded the corner. Ben was with his parents. Their greetings were stilted and stiff. Dr. Woodbridge stood at the door, ushering the group inside.

"Watch the father," Michael said. "He'll automatically go for a chair in the center of the room to claim the power position and his wife is going to tell Ruth and Jimmy where to sit. Real controllers."

Dr. Woodbridge opened the session. "Why don't we put our expectations on the table? Let's explore the agendas that we brought with us today."

"I'll start," Ruth blurted out. "After all, the meeting is somewhat at my instigation. No one thinks Jimmy is good enough for me!"

"Oh, come now!" Larry protested. "We are very accepting."

"Absolutely," Sharon agreed. "We have friends from all walks of life." Her dark brown suit seemed unusually severe.

"I pride myself on openness." Larry shook his head. In contrast to his usual Southern California casualness, he wore a tie and sport coat.

"How do you feel about what you just heard?" Dr. Woodbridge asked Jimmy.

"I know you mean well." Jimmy tried to smile. "But you sound like I'm the gardener you invite in for a sandwich every Christmas."

Sharon's jaw tightened and Ben rolled his eyes.

Larry sat upright with his chin stuck out. "If I have any hidden agenda, it's shaped by what I know professionally. The statistics just aren't good. Ruth's dated only one boy in her life. The odds are even worse for a Jewish girl and a Baptist boy making it work."

"And what are the dangers of a girl who hopes to get a Ph.D. marrying a used-car salesman with a high school education?" Ruth added, defiantly tossing her hair sideways.

Larry shrugged. "You know as well as I do. That's strike three."

Dr. Woodbridge kept trying to smile. "At least, we're getting it out quickly."

Sharon cleared her throat. "I don't like what I need to say. I don't even know how it makes me feel to speak up, but I can't be honest if I'm not forthright." She scooted to the edge of her chair. "Maybe it's totally selfish, but I am self-conscious about how my Newport Beach friends will view any future son-in-law who is a used-car salesman. After all, we're professional people."

The room became intensely quiet. Jimmy looked down at his feet and Ruth grimaced.

Sharon broke the silence. "Yes, and I feel guilty because I didn't contribute enough of our family background to help Ruth make sure she stayed within our race when she was looking for a spouse."

"I'd like to add a word." Ben pulled himself up to his full height in his chair. "We've always been a close-knit family. We have our little rituals and ways of doing things. It's not easy to bring someone into the inner circle." Ben stopped and smiled unexpectedly at Jimmy. "But I appreciate how it feels to be an outsider. Ethnic differences shouldn't matter if we're as liberal as we profess. All of us need to get over thinking we're better than other people."

"I didn't say that." Sharon bristled.

"In fact, we did." Larry fidgeted in his chair. "It's not flattering, but that's about the sum of what we've said so far."

Michael pulled Seradim aside. "The activity you saw in heaven has great significance for what will transpire in a few minutes. For centuries, prophets and teachers attempted to help human beings recognize what's coming. Ironically, Jimmy's father is a highly respected minister who understood the scenario and tried many times to warn his son about the coming Rapture. The Feinbergs have no idea the heavenly Father is about to execute His special plan for believers. Watch."

Jimmy raised his hand. "I know it doesn't sound like much to your family," Jimmy winced as he spoke, "but I really like selling cars. Sure, it doesn't take much education to be a salesman, but I'm good at what I do. Ruth has motivated me to become honest, and I am building an excellent reputation in Laguna Hills. I've done so well, I've saved $12,000. The boss said that he plans for me to manage our new place in Laguna Niguel, and I'll get 10 percent of the profits."

Jimmy smiled weakly. "Can't your Newport friends simply think of me as a businessman? Maybe someday I'll own a chain of car lots."

"Jimmy has been very good for me." Ruth reached out for his hand. "He's the best friend I've ever had."

Ann Woodbridge seemed distracted. Her usually rapt attention faded as if she were hearing something that no one else heard. She turned her head slightly and began staring at the ceiling almost as if she saw Michael and Seradim looking down on her.

"That sound!" Seradim grabbed Michael's arm. "It's an irresistible summons calling us home to the Father. It's the last trump, blowing on the Feast of Trumpets. We must leave."

"No." Michael held Seradim's hand tightly. "Hang on. The call is not for us. The heavenly Creator is calling home an army of people like Ann Woodbridge."

"Ann?" Larry Feinberg tried to get the therapist's attention. "Ann? Are you with us?"

In the twinkling of an eye, Dr. Ann Woodbridge was gone.

"Look!" Seradim pointed as Dr. Woodbridge passed the angels. "She's going toward the time barrier! What's happening?"

Michael pointed across the face of the globe as multitudes of humans rose from the earth, flying toward the same place. "The Rapture is occurring," he explained. "God's people are being pulled out of the world before the final battle occurs. Dark days are ahead for the entire planet."

"Shouldn't we help them enter eternity?"

"No, Seradim, our assignment is to help the people left behind. We must protect the Feinbergs and Jimmy. They are important players in the final confrontation with evil."

"Oh, no!" Jimmy was the first to break the stunned silence. "No! NO!"

Ruth slid to the edge of her chair. "Ann? Ann! Is this a joke?"

"This better not be some kind of crazy psychodrama experiment." Larry stood up.

"It's happened," Jimmy gasped. "Just like Dad said it would. He preached about the Rapture."

Larry took several steps toward the vacant seat. "She was right there." He reached out to touch the arm of the chair.

"Mom was right." Jimmy moaned. "The time is at hand."

Larry spun on his heels and raced toward the offices. Ben followed but found only empty desks and chairs, with clothing and jewelry scattered across the floor. The receptionist's headset was lying on the desk next to her phone. On the other desks, pencils and papers were scattered about as if everyone had abruptly left on a coffee break.

Jimmy held to the doorjamb and stared at the floor. "My father preached this exit would happen someday. He must have figured out that Rosh Hashanah was the key to the timing of the Rapture."

"Rosh Hashanah?" Larry spun around. "Stop it. Don't add to the confusion. We've got to keep our heads."

"But they've disappeared," Sharon said. "Gone . . . just vanished into thin air."

After several heated exchanges, Larry demanded they leave and rendezvous at the Feinberg home to make some sense out of what had happened. Ruth and Jimmy took the stairs and left through a side door. Once in the parking lot, they sped off in his red Corvette without waiting for the rest of the family to catch up. Vacant cars were smashed and burning all along the way.

"Jimmy?" Ruth grasped his arm. "What were you talking about up there? What's a Rapture?"

"If I'm right, my parents will have disappeared. There won't be anybody at their usually busy church in Dallas." He veered off the street into the driveway of a convenience store with an outside drive-up telephone. An empty pickup truck had smashed into the store itself, and people were screaming in panic. Jimmy grabbed the phone and punched in a set of numbers followed by his credit card number. No one answered.

"Let's help some of these folks," Ruth said tearfully as Jimmy stared into space, totally stunned by this strange turn of events.

Michael watched the growing consternation on Ruth and Jimmy's faces. "Seradim, the chaos has just begun," he concluded. "Get ready."

■ ■ ■

Joe McCoy braced himself against the wall, his face white. He kept his hand over his mouth. Twelve of the remaining

employees raced from chair to chair. Two women were crying.

"I . . . I . . . I *saw* them . . . just disappear!" Joe stuttered.
"Poof! They were gone!"

The division manager kept slapping the back of one of
the empty chairs. "No one disintegrates into thin air!"

"Is this a trick?" one of the secretaries asked. "Are we
being put through one of those contrived security examinations? A psychology grilling to see if we will come unglued?"

"Yeah," a male programmer growled, "this whole thing
smacks of a military stunt to check us out. I don't like it
one bit."

Joe shook his head in disbelief. "No. No one could stage
what we just saw. I was looking straight in the face of Sally
Vaca. I've known her for years. She was an outstanding person. She wouldn't be part of some government plot. In an
instant Sally was simply . . . gone . . . gone, I tell you."

■ ■ ■

Frank Wong held Jessica's hand in a vice grip. He kept
pointing across the dining room, which had erupted in
complete chaos. Couples had been split apart. Whole tables
were empty. Waiters had disappeared.

"I tell you, Jessica, one minute every table was full, and
in a matter of seconds, lots of these people were gone!
Gone! Do you understand?"

Jessica stared. "Is not possible!"

"Even three of best waiters vanish. Best servers. Never
steal."

Cindy patted her father's arm. "I can only hear what you
say, good father, but it sounds like many people were upset."

"Oh, Cindy." Jessica clutched her daughter. "Stay close to us. World gone completely crazy. Nothing predictable. Stay close. We must not lose you. Ever!"

"Think of all money I didn't get!" Frank shook his head, and he looked out the window. The parking lot was snarled by cars that had crashed into each other. People were screaming.

"Oh, help us!" Jessica implored, speaking more to the empty space above her head than to any specific place. "I fear I go crazy."

# CHAPTER
## 12

Jimmy and Ruth stared at the evening newscast. The anchorman sounded urgent. "Apparently, about 25 percent of the population has simply vanished." A picture of the Notre Dame Cathedral in Paris appeared on the screen. "Europe reports about 5 percent losses, while virtually no one is missing from Muslim, Hindu, or Buddhist nations. This factor is forcing an analysis of a possible religious component in the disappearances."

"Yeah," Jimmy drawled, running his hand nervously through his hair, "maybe they would like to factor in the disappearance of my parents and their entire congregation! Let Mr. Nightly News explain that one."

A picture of an empty podium with the seal of the president of the United States flashed across the screen. "Please stand by," the broadcaster said. "We have a live statement from the president."

Damian Gianardo walked briskly to the stand, appearing nervous and edgy. "My fellow Americans, tonight we are facing one of the strangest crises in national history.

There is no current explanation for the disappearance of millions of our citizens. Key military and police personnel are absent without reason. To ensure order and security, I am now declaring a state of emergency. National Guard and reserve units will patrol our streets until further notice."

Jimmy squeezed Ruth's hand. "For years, my parents tried to prepare me for this moment, and I didn't listen." Gianardo's voice rumbled on in the background.

"I know most of what I'm saying doesn't make much sense to you, Ruth. Give me time and I'll help you get everything into perspective. I need to retrace my steps and get back in touch with what my father taught."

"You can rely on me and my government to protect your interests and guide you through this difficult time." The president jutted his chin out and spoke defiantly. "In the name of human goodness, we will gain the inevitable victory!"

"He's wrong," Jimmy quietly answered as the picture faded. "This time the head man is completely deceived."

Ruth squeezed Jimmy's hand and grimaced.

■ ■ ■

Homelas and Malafidus intently watched the same news conference from the back of the State Department auditorium. Other demons hovered around the room or were perched on the walls.

"A couple of African nations lost nearly half of their populations," Homelas quipped. "Russia and some Eastern European nations also lost large numbers. What do you make of it?"

"An old legend once floated around about a rupture or rapture or something of the sort." Malafidus squinted his deeply shrunken red eyes and lowered his voice. "All the Christians were supposed to bail out before the big war. I don't know. Always thought it was nonsense."

"Where would we find out more about the idea?"

Malafidus pointed his skinny arms, which jutted out of his bulbous body, and jabbed his spearlike finger in Homelas's face. "Don't you dare go looking around in one of their Bibles for insight. Headquarters would clamp you down like locking up a bank vault on a holiday! No sir! Keep your mouth shut and wait for instructions from the source himself!"

"Okay! Okay, I'm not looking for trouble. But you've got to admit these disappearances are a strange turn of events."

Malafidus snorted, discounting the question. "Actually, the departures are to our advantage. Think how many problems were jettisoned out of our way. We won't have interference from all those prayer fanatics who kept messing up the airwaves. Half the time, I couldn't think straight, trying to sort out instructions from headquarters while those blasted intercessors kept breaking in. I hated them. Maybe the exodus is a sign we are winning."

"Time to get to work." Homelas pointed to the president. "Right now, Damian is a might shook up. He's always at his best when apprehension makes him mean-spirited. We need to apply pressure at his fear points to gear him up a tad more."

■ ■ ■

Seradim and Michael watched Ben Feinberg pace the floor in front of Cindy Wong. The reception area in her dormitory was empty except for them. The usually crowded sidewalks to the classrooms were sparse. The blind Chinese girl patiently listened as Ben rambled almost incoherently.

"The whole thing must have been an attack from outer space," Ben muttered. "People don't just disappear. I mean that doctor . . . counselor . . . whatever . . . that woman my parents took Ruth to just went up in smoke! I mean, you talk about weird!"

"Please, Ben. Be calm." Cindy reached out but couldn't touch him. "Yes, I'm sure my blindness saved me from the shock you are feeling, but we've got to stay calm and keep ourselves together."

"I just don't know." Ben wrung his hands as he paced. "I feel like I've gone nuts." Ben walked to the door. "Cindy, I've got to get some air. I'm going to the ocean to think. Sorry, but I need to be by myself for a while. I'll call you this evening."

"I understand, Ben. I want to go to the library and study anyway. I'm going to listen to my cassette recordings of the last lectures in biology. Keeping my mind on science for a while will help me get my mind off of all the crazy and painful things going on in the world right now! I'd rather not sort it all out yet.

"I guess that's a difference between me and you, Ben. I feel pain and confusion, so I want to escape from it—to stay 'blind' to reality until later. But you want to go straight to your emotions and dive into the truth headlong. I admire that."

Ben touched her hand as he left, then hurried toward the parking lot.

"Seradim, your hour is at hand." Michael pointed at Ben and instructed his charge. "Ben and Cindy are going to need a great amount of oversight to fulfill their destinies. The spiritual warfare is about to heat up."

"Where will the attack come?"

"It's already started. The real battleground is always the human soul. The ultimate struggle is over control of the precious ground in the center of each human life where connectedness to God begins and ends, the place where the highest affections and deepest commitments are held. If the demons can disrupt and destroy the divine linkage, they've captured the person. We have to make sure they don't win."

Seradim observed Ben carefully. "I can't read his thoughts," the angel concluded, "but I certainly sense what his demeanor indicates. Ben doesn't know who his heavenly Father is."

"Exactly."

"We must help Ben get connected."

"Very good. You make me look like an excellent teacher."

Seradim studied the young man carefully. "Ben is a good person. Lots of integrity there. Where can we expect evil to attack?"

"Not all evil comes directly from demons," Michael explained. "Most doesn't. The flesh is quite capable of an amazing assortment of delightful expressions of wickedness. Demons often play off of these themes and employ them like fishermen use worms. Of course, the world system also comes into play."

"How so?

"Greed, lust, power, immorality, enmity, strife, divisiveness, selfishness, and a host of equally destructive tendencies form webs of intrigue and seduction, trapping people much as spiders catch flies. The demons help set the ambush, so we've got to help Ben, his family, and his friends escape the snares by giving them a vision of the greater spiritual realities."

"Tell me how to make sure our charges do the right thing," Seradim urged.

"Sorry, friend. Human beings are endowed with an awesome capacity. Like the Creator, they have free will. Each person must make up his own mind to do the right thing. Even God Himself will not force the human race to do His supreme will. We do everything we can to help, but the choice is theirs."

"Then, what *can* we do?"

"Watch over them carefully! I am constantly making sure Cindy doesn't get in trouble. Blindness makes her physically vulnerable. What do you see right now, Seradim?"

The junior angel thought himself to the street corner across from the library. The sounds of traffic filled his mind, but one sound prevailed. A block and a half away, a teenager roared up the street in a red Pontiac Firebird. Going far beyond the speed limit, the car veered toward the curb. Within seconds, Cindy would be standing where the vehicle was aimed. Sam, her guide dog, unable to sense the approaching danger, kept leading Cindy toward the street.

Michael instantly placed himself in front of the guide dog. Although Sam couldn't see the invisible angel, he sensed the unexpected presence and started backing away, pulling Cindy with him. A second later, the red Pontiac's right front tire hit the curb and bounced over the sidewalk. The teenager instantly jerked the steering wheel, sending the car back into traffic. Swerving to miss a parked car just ahead, the Pontiac barely managed to keep from sideswiping a car in the second lane of traffic. People honked and shouted, but the boy only increased his speed.

"Sam!" Cindy jerked the handle on the dog harness. "What was that? Did we nearly get hit?" She listened to the sound of the car speeding away and the honking. "Is someone there?" she called, but no one answered. "Felt like a person was close," she said to herself. The noise subsided. "It certainly sounded like we were at the racetrack for a moment, and someone special was here." She urged Sam to take her across the street.

Seradim moved to Michael's side, observing Cindy as she crossed the street and went up the steps of the library. "Intuitive intelligence is everything," Michael instructed. "Trust what you 'just know' and contemplate what pulsates from the mind of God. You'll automatically know what to do."

"That miss was too close for comfort!" Seradim said. "I was really frightened."

"That's because we profoundly care for them," Michael replied. "The Creator built that capacity into us. Our love naturally flows from what we know. Humans tend to feel love. We *will* love. We choose it! The instant I saw Cindy's dilemma, everything in me moved according to the dictates of love. Don't worry, Seradim. You'll get the hang of it quickly enough."

# CHAPTER
## 13

The disappearance of millions of people sent shock waves of chaos across the world. The catastrophe hit hard at Frank Wong's restaurant in Lake Forest, California. The Golden Dragon lost many customers and a number of its best employees. With no explanation for the disappearances, the Wongs worried and fretted constantly. Most of the time Frank and Jessica spoke Chinese and avoided unnecessary conversations with Caucasians.

The sun was going down as Frank turned off El Toro Road into the parking lot in front of a large apartment complex clubhouse. "Jessica, I . . . very . . . uh . . . glad we prepare for initiation into Transcendental Meditation before all craziness happen." He turned off the ignition and got out of the car. "We must find serenity in midst of confusion. Most difficult time."

"Honorable husband, I agree." Jessica joined Frank on the walk leading to the long, flat-topped building. She carried a small plastic sack. "T.M. promise prosperity if only follow teaching of the Maharishi Mahesh Yogi. Obviously, many people agree with us."

"After bad experience with séance, we need something more in this world than talking to our ancestors." Frank took his wife's hand at the door. "Mr. Penny is good instructor. He say reaching fourth state of consciousness is answer to our worries. News reports only make everything worse."

The Wongs cautiously entered the spacious club room filled with people. Chairs lined the back, the main area covered only by a thick rug. In the front of the room, an altar-like table featured a picture of an Indian guru. Flickering candles placed around the room threw long shadows across the walls. The smell of incense was heavy and stale. Many of the initiates were sitting on the floor.

"You have special offerings?" Frank asked.

"Yes. Teacher say bring six flowers, three pieces of fruit, and white handkerchief." Jessica held up the plastic bag. "We are ready for the offerings of life and for cleansing."

After removing their shoes, the Wongs found a place near the altar. Like others seated on the floor, they assumed lotus positions. Their teacher entered from the back of the room, smiling and nodding to the group.

Jim Penny lit a candle beside the picture and began singing a Sanskrit hymn. The Wongs bowed their heads in respect. Michael and Seradim hovered above the scene.

"We cannot be concerned for Cindy without experiencing the same love for her parents," Michael said. "Keeping Frank and Jessica out of trouble is nearly a full-time job."

"What's happening?" Seradim wondered.

"After the Wongs got the bejabbers scared out of them talking to the dead, they turned to this old Hindu hoax and paid a considerable initiation fee. Their instructor told them T.M. wasn't a religion. Little did they know the teacher was leading them into the Shankara Hindu tradition. The origin of everything they've learned is in the texts of the Hindu sacred writings—the Vedas and Upanishads—and particularly the Bhagavad-Gita. Frank and Jessica are dangerously close to connecting with the principalities and powers of this world."

Michael pointed at the picture. "The T.M. people tried to sell their system to the American schools as nonreligious, but the lawyers caught them at it. The Federal Courts consistently ruled T.M. a religion." Michael laughed. "One of the few things the Supreme Court did right during the last decade."

Seradim listened to the chanting for a moment. "I don't think anyone in the group has any idea what the words mean."

"Frank and Jessica think it's a nice chant. The Vedic hymn, the *puja,* is actually worship of Hindu deities. In the first part of the song, Penny is calling out the names of the gods. Through the mantra the people receive, the gods will be worshiped. Listen. He is saying, 'I bow down.' Scary stuff indeed!"

"Who's the guy in the picture?"

"Sri Guru Dev was the Maharishi's teacher. In just a moment, Penny is going to worship the guru because he is identified with the Trimurti—the Hindu triad: Brahma, Vishnu, and Siva. Dev was declared a personified fullness of Brahma."

A strange sensation inched up Seradim's body. He felt agitated, and an eerie sense of foreboding settled around his thoughts. "Something weird is happening. . . . I don't understand. . . ."

"Watch!" Michael pointed toward the candles. In the shape of curling smoke, convoluted forms began emerging out of the flames.

Seradim stared at their evil faces as the disembodied creatures floated up like greasy smoke.

"The Hindu gods are only the facade for demons, each name the result of centuries of seduction." Michael made a slight gesture, parting the smoke and incense rising to the ceiling. "Although the initiates don't know it, they are being prepared to worship and make contact with these demons. Sri Dev actually became the name used by a demon known to us as Dungetius, a vile creature thriving on rotten thoughts."

People stood, came forward, and knelt before the altar. The teacher bent down, whispering a mantra into each person's ear.

"These people think they are receiving a harmless sound to repeat," Michael explained. "Actually, the mantras are the names of demons. As they repeat the word over and over, the vibrations invoke the presence of the spirit."

Seradim choked at the thought.

"Look!" Michael pointed at the candles again. More spirits emerged as each person received a mantra. The ethereal horde increased, blending together in a whirling mass above the group. Like storm clouds forming a tornado, the black minions writhed together like snakes slithering over each other in a den of venomous death. Periodically, a single demon's face surfaced above the horde. Poised to strike, the horde waited for the signal to attack.

"As soon as the group starts mass meditation, the demons will hit them. Seradim, prepare yourself for battle. We must strike first!"

"H . . . H . . . How?" Seradim stuttered.

Michael dived into the center of the demonic mass. A great burst of light exploded in a brilliant flash. Demons momentarily evaporated like a campfire dissolving in a gust of wind. The stunned horde tumbled backward out across the boundless expanse of space separating earth and heaven. Unaware of the spiritual warfare exploding above them, the Wongs continued the ritual of initiation.

The demons surged back toward the room in an attempt to regroup. Seradim saw the pack returning and immediately flew down to protect Michael's back. "I'm with you!"

"Let my thoughts guide you," Michael instructed. "We must scatter this scum quickly." He paused until the scourge was nearly upon them. "Jesus is Lord!" Michael exclaimed. "You are completely defeated!"

Like a squadron of tanks screeching to a halt before a cliff, the demons stopped in consternation. A thundering voice arose out of the mass. "Who are you?"

"Angels of the Most High!" Michael shouted. "Come forth and meet your fate." Michael began glowing in an increasing aura of light.

"Our time is not yet," a demon's voice rumbled back.

As Seradim thought on the light of God, he reflected the celestial glory. The splendor of brilliant color merged into the light already emanating from Michael.

"The Light of the world has appeared," Michael answered the demon. "The darkness is overcome."

For a moment, the evil pack paused in bewilderment. Then slowly the demons backed away, moving toward the dark edges at the end of time. One by one the mass dissolved, the black energy dissipated.

"Wow!" Seradim gulped. "What happened?"

"They're gone." Michael smiled mischievously. "You did good."

Seradim looked into the empty space in amazement. "What . . . did . . . I . . . actually do?"

"Darkness cannot traffic with light. You blasted our adversaries with the splendor of God. These vile creatures can't stand the impact."

"Will they return?"

"Not tonight! However, if these new T.M. initiates continue the practice of calling forth the Hindu deities and the demons behind them, then yes, they will return to infest the people."

"What about the Wongs?"

"Seradim, let's go down and stand beside them. I think we can quickly get them out of this snare. Follow me." Michael immediately thought himself next to Frank.

Frank turned to his wife and opened his eyes. "It working?"

Jessica shrugged her shoulders. "Just making strange sound but nothing happening."

The instructor looked around the room and frowned. People were not connecting as he had anticipated. "Concentrate," Penny urged. "Let your mind go into neutral while you say the mantra over and over."

Frank closed his eyes again and started repeating the name in a low hum.

Michael looked knowingly at Seradim. "Think with Jessica while I do the same with Frank. Concentrate on the love of God. Remember how the Father wants a real and genuine relationship with all of His creatures. Help the Wongs realize the true nature of their spiritual hunger."

Michael steadily emanated the profound love of the Heavenly Father. His thoughts hung in the air like the sweet smell of spring flowers. The angel leaned near Frank's ear, sending his thoughts like beautiful music traveling through a special frequency to an inner receiver. Seradim did the same thing with Jessica.

Frank abruptly opened his eyes and looked around the room. He shook his head and looked perturbed. Jessica opened one eye. "I don't think this what we need," Frank whispered. The instructor checked the thermostat on the air conditioner.

"Atmosphere seems stale," Penny announced. "Just keep repeating your mantra and soon you will enter your new level of consciousness. Please, don't stop," Penny urged nervously.

Michael smiled. "The teacher can't make the system work tonight because we have broken the spell of the spirits. Penny doesn't know why but he knows something is missing."

"Look at him." Seradim pointed. "The teacher appears to be wrapped in a film."

"Unfortunately, the instructor is sealed," Michael explained. "Penny dabbled with the satanic elements one too many times, granting them possession of his life. In ancient times, people used a seal stamped in wax to indicate ownership. You are seeing the spiritual sign of Satan's possession. Just as Christians are sealed and protected in the baptism of the Spirit at salvation, this man is marked by the devil."

"Can't we break the bondage?"

"No, the teacher has free will. We cannot cross that boundary. Even the heavenly Father honors his right to choose. Only as the man repents and renounces evil can he be set free. In the meantime, the demon controlling him is protected from us. People who own Ouija boards, tarot cards, or dabble with astrology, Scientology, witchcraft, or visit fortune-tellers are in the same danger. They become cursed as this poor man is."

"Is there no hope?"

"There's always hope, Seradim, because Jesus Himself became a curse through His crucifixion to break all bonds of evil. But until this man accepts the gift of salvation, he is trapped like a lion in a zoo. What he thinks is freedom is nothing but a cage with invisible bars."

Jessica poked Frank in the side. "I want to go home. This is not at all what I expected."

Frank nodded toward the door. "Let's slip out." He stooped over for several feet before standing up. To his surprise several other couples joined them.

"Please," the instructor begged, "we've just begun."

"Don't look back," Michael whispered in Frank's ear. "Keep walking."

Frank and Jessica hurried through the door and toward their car. "Strange. We just can't seem to find anything that works," Jessica concluded. "Cindy is so much more satisfied with the Bible lessons she discusses with her friends. Maybe we should listen to her."

"Yes, holy book not like this silly business with candles and funny words."

Jessica nodded her head and slid into the car.

As Michael felt profound satisfaction, the feeling immediately registered with Seradim. "We did well tonight, Seradim. Very well. Now it's time to get back to Cindy."

# CHAPTER
## 14

While the Wongs terminated their foray into the world of T.M. at the Lake Forest clubhouse, Ben Feinberg finished supper at the Golden Dragon. Cindy's questions about the Bible encouraged him to reconsider his skepticism about the Scriptures.

"An amazing number of people are converting to evangelical Christianity," Cindy told Ben as he consumed Hunan chicken. The smell of simmering vegetables and roast duck hung in the air.

"So it seems." Ben ate without looking up. Guests walked past him. Most of the tables in the popular restaurant were already taken.

"I heard one report that thousands of people in Eastern Europe and parts of Africa are accepting the ancient faith," Cindy added. "The strange disappearance of Christians has certainly left everyone in consternation."

Ben put his chopsticks down and sat back in the black ivory chair. "Apparently thousands of Orthodox Jews have suddenly embraced the idea that Jesus is the Messiah," he added. "Some discovery from a just-released portion of the Dead Sea Scrolls convinced them. The Essenes, who collected the Dead Sea Scrolls, had eight copies of the book of Daniel, a book that predicts some of the things that seem to be happening right now. They thought the events would happen in their era." He took a long drink of iced tea.

Cindy swallowed hard. "We've got to recognize something incredible is going on."

"Some Jewish converts have also come to an additional conclusion," Ben said. "They expect there will soon be another worldwide persecution of Jews, which will be worse than Hitler's holocaust."

"Oh, Ben!" Cindy stiffened. "That is too horrible to think about. Don't say such a thing."

Ben looked up at the elegant ceiling. The long figure of a dragon wound its way across the top of the dining room. "We once thought smog was the worst thing in the air. Now a little pollution seems innocuous." Ben finished eating silently and laid his chopsticks down for the last time. "Got to run, Cindy. See you tomorrow morning."

"Drive carefully, Ben."

He impulsively leaned over the table and kissed Cindy on the lips. "*Ciao!*" the youth called over his shoulder.

Cindy sat stunned for several moments before a sly smile finally inched across her face. "Well, for goodness' sake! *Ciao* to you, too, Mr. Ben Feinberg."

Tapping with her white walking stick, Cindy found her way back to the kitchen. The afterglow of Ben's romantic gesture sent her mind spinning in other directions.

*A breath of fresh air is what I need,* Cindy said to herself. *Ben has an amazing effect on me. Just can't think straight around him.*

Leaving Sam curled up next to the stove, Cindy used the cane to guide herself toward the back door. She stepped out into the evening alone. *The cool air means it must be dark.* Her fingers glided over the top of her braille wristwatch. *Ah, my parents should be home by now,* she concluded. She felt her way along the side of the building leading into the alley-way where trash containers were kept.

Fifteen feet away a large figure lurked behind one of the dumpsters. A man crept out, hovering close to the building. He crouched down with his hands outstretched, open, and aimed at the blind girl carefully tapping against the brick.

"Good evening," Michael abruptly barked from behind the thug, where the angel had suddenly appeared in human form.

The startled attacker slipped and fell into the wall, sprawling on the cement.

"Hello," Cindy answered timidly. "I didn't know anyone was out here."

Struggling to his feet, the assailant leaped toward Michael, only to discover him towering nearly a foot above his head. The culprit froze, stared for a second, and then charged toward a hedge at the back of the shopping center.

Cindy tilted her head, listening to the man run. "Don't leave."

"I'm still here," Michael answered.

"There's two of you?"

"No, just me. I scared off a man about to harm you."

"Oh, my goodness." Cindy braced herself against the wall. "Who are you?"

"Just a friend. Call me Michael."

"We've met?"

"Not formally." The angel chuckled. "But I've been around. I'd suggest you be more careful walking around in the dark by yourself. After all, most of the spiritual people are gone from the face of the earth. Why don't you get a quick breath of fresh air and go back inside?"

Cindy swallowed hard. "Well, I . . . uh . . . think so. I really should keep my guide dog with me all the time." She turned toward the restaurant's back door. "You said you're a friend named Michael?"

"Yes," the angel answered. "I'll be around."

"Thank you." Cindy opened the door. "We need to get better acquainted."

"Certainly," Michael answered and promptly stepped out of time into eternity, reappearing next to Seradim.

"You became one of them!" the trainee angel exclaimed. "How did you do that?"

"We have the capacity to assume bodies by thinking ourselves into them," Michael explained. "Guardians can put on a human form like people wear costumes. The shape we take is like wearing a mask. Because angels aren't born, we don't have anatomy like humans. We never breathe or eat. Of course, you can munch on a cookie if you choose . . . taste is quite an adventure, but you never get used to the feeling. Sense perception and appetite are only a vehicle to achieve our purposes."

"I can't believe it!" Seradim shook his head. "You looked exactly like one of them."

"I could have assumed any height or weight I wished." Michael shrugged. "You just think yourself into the condition. Being confined in space is an interesting experience."

"Hmmm," Seradim pondered the thought. "The idea of physical space is amazing. Strange."

"Humans have an equally difficult time understanding how place doesn't confine us. Centuries ago medieval philosophers debated how many angels could dance on the head of a pin." Michael laughed. "Not a dumb question at all! Since place cannot confine spirit, an infinite number of us could think ourselves in any one place at any time. Locality doesn't surround us as space does a human body. We can encompass an area as I did by entering into a body."

"When you saved Cindy from getting run over at the stoplight, people couldn't see you. Right? But the attacker saw you a few moments ago?"

"Exactly. On the first occasion I enabled Cindy's dog to sense my presence, so I didn't need to materialize. Actually, I can speak directly with Cindy more often because she's blind and won't realize I haven't taken on a human form."

"Why don't we just appear as we are, Michael?"

"Humans can't see or comprehend pure spirit. And people have nothing in nature to compare with our appearance; we have a beauty beyond human imagination. In the same way, people's souls are more beautiful than their bodies."

"I certainly have an incredible amount to learn," Seradim concluded. "How do you always stay on top of things?"

"While humans sleep, we watch. Often the Father directly dispatches us to fulfill His will. Of course, prayer helps us stay aware. Hear the supplications?"

Seradim frowned and shook his head.

"You are accustomed to hearing the heavenly praise. Now you must learn to tune into the special frequency that lifts the needs of people to the throne of God. A heavenly network is poised to maintain an unbroken line of communication. No prayer ever goes unnoticed."

"I'm missing something," the younger angel concluded. "I don't hear anything."

"Tune in the praises of the Cherubim and Seraphim. Now, shift your perception a little farther down and tune in the worship of Christians in this world."

Seradim concentrated with everything in his being. "I . . . think. . . . Yes, I am getting the sound. In fact, I can *see* it happening. I perceive faces of many people in small groups, large sanctuaries, and lone prayer warriors, praising God and asking for divine help, pleading assistance for people in need. Incredible!"

"Excellent, Seradim! Often we respond to those very prayers, as the Holy Spirit guides us."

Listening to the myriad of intercessions rising up to heaven, Seradim was completely distracted. "I had no idea," he said. "I never heard them before."

"As each prayer goes up, the need comes before the Throne of Grace. The twenty-four elders constantly offer up prayers in golden bowls as overtures of pure incense." Michael pointed toward heaven. "Prayers are the one human thing that can cross time and penetrate eternity."

"People are the only creatures who can pray?"

"Yes, in their minds they have a wonderful spiritual frequency transmitter capable of breaking through the limitations of the physical world. Unfortunately, most don't know they have the ability, and few of those who do work to develop their full capacities. If people knew what their prayers accomplished, they would be on their knees day and night."

Seradim nodded. "With their feet on the earth, their souls can roam the realms of heaven!"

Michael tilted his head and pointed toward California. "I want you to listen to one specific prayer going up right now. Eventually you'll become accustomed to staying attuned to prayer for our charges. Pay attention to a prayer on behalf of the Feinbergs. Hear it?"

Seradim looked mystified and shook his head.

"Joe and Jennifer McCoy are old acquaintances of the Feinberg family. The good doctor and his wife have no idea Joe and Jennifer pray for them. Before the Rapture, the McCoys knew what God expected, but didn't know Him personally. The McCoys simply didn't embrace Yeshua into their hearts. After the Rapture, at a Christian fellowship, the McCoys accepted Jesus as their Savior and Lord, so from now on they will have the presence of the Holy Spirit who is sealed within them until they get their new bodies in heaven someday. They returned to the spiritual roots of their parents. Follow my mind and I'll help you pick up their prayers."

Steadily and with increasing clarity, words filled the space between the two angels. Seradim listened carefully, and the sound became louder.

"Bless Larry and Sharon, Father. . . . We have no hope in this world without you. Please forgive us that we didn't listen all those years. But please, please, help the Feinbergs. We know they are closed to their Jewish heritage, but please help them understand how Jesus is their Messiah too. . . ."

"Hear them praying?" Michael asked.

"Amazing!" Seradim replied. "It's like I'm right in the room with them."

"Sure. If we pay close attention, the McCoys' prayers can be a wake-up call to alert us to the Feinbergs' need."

"Then the Holy Spirit uses angels and other means to answer those prayers?"

"Exactly. The Holy Spirit translates their prayers into heavenly groanings that cannot be uttered by humans. Then the Father tells Yeshua and some chosen angelic creatures, and the prayer becomes a symphony of action—divine action. Then angels deliver suggestions to other humans to help fulfill the original prayer request. An amazing process! Those prayers return to Earth with the power to touch the souls of people like the Feinbergs. The intercessions are change agents, influencing a new mind-set. Prayer creates a sense of need. Humans are deeply affected by their environment. Teenagers want loud music on the radio so they won't feel alone. Adults like the thermostats set just right to feel comfortable. Lovers try to create romantic moods. Understand? Prayers release spiritual energy, the power of the omnipresent Holy Spirit. Prayer surrounds people with the aura of God's love and compassion. Hearts are turned and inclined to the Father."

Seradim nodded slowly. "They return to the persons in need?"

"And with all the power of heaven added. . . . Let me show you." Michael thought himself and the young angel into the Feinbergs' living room. Larry was adjusting the TV, and Sharon was reading a novel.

Sharon laid her book down. "Larry, maybe we ought to turn the TV off. Since the Rapture there's nothing but violence, crime, and sex left on the screen. I didn't think much of TV before, but now the content is simply ridiculous."

"You're certainly right about that!"

"I'm concerned that we have, well . . . for lack of a better term . . . no spiritual direction in our lives." Sharon sounded apologetic. "Know what I mean?"

Larry frowned but paused a moment before answering. "I . . . started . . . to tune you out, but maybe you're right, dear. I guess . . . I . . . I just don't know . . . where to turn for help. We were never observant. The synagogue doesn't seem to be the right place now."

"I don't know why, but I feel that Jennifer McCoy might offer some help. I've known her forever. And recently she told me she'd found some spiritual answers. Maybe we ought to talk to the McCoys about this."

Larry shrugged. "Couldn't hurt anything. Who knows? Might help."

"I'll make the time to talk with her."

Michael smiled. "See how the system operates? The power of prayer really works! The Holy Spirit answers prayers with compassionate conviction, and the Holy Spirit uses us and spiritual humans as His messengers."

■ ■ ■

A week later Sharon ran into Jennifer in the grocery store and invited the couple over for dessert. Joe and Jennifer came prepared to tell their story. The Feinbergs stared in rapt attention as Joe and Jennifer McCoy answered their questions. Sharon Feinberg had been amazed at how quickly the McCoys wanted to meet with them, as if they had just been waiting for an opportunity like this.

Jennifer placed her cup on the coffee table in the Feinbergs' den. "Many Christians are meeting frequently for fellowship. Once a week on Sundays just doesn't seem enough with so much turmoil in the world after the Rapture—the disapperance of so many millions of believers. So people are getting together in their homes for fellowship and prayer."

"One of the leaders taught a short Bible study," Joe continued. "He talked about Jesus being the light of the world and how much we needed illumination in these dark times. He explained the disappearances, and it made tremendous sense."

"Yes." Jennifer nodded her head. "Joe and I had discussed our family's need for spiritual guidance for a long time. We could see the terrible moral dangers our children faced and knew we deeply wanted the hand of God in our family. The moment was right for us to say yes."

Joe smiled. "The leader said that we could have Jesus in our lives all the time. He suggested that if we didn't know that decision was an already accomplished fact, we should settle the matter at that exact moment."

"Our eyes met," Jennifer continued. "We both knew what the other was thinking. I put my hand in Joe's, and while the group prayed, we asked Jesus to be the light of our family."

"By the time we left, Jennifer and I knew something tremendous had happened. Everything about the future would be new and exciting. We haven't been disappointed."

Larry rolled his tongue around in his mouth and forced a smile. "Quite a story," he mumbled.

"But we are Jews," Sharon protested.

"Jesus was a Jew," Jennifer answered. "His name in Hebrew was Yeshua, and many Messianic Jews use that name."

"Well, yes," Larry agreed. "But for us it's more difficult." He rubbed his chin nervously. "To be honest, we don't know much of anything about what Christians really think or what the Bible says, Old Testament or New Testament."

"Hey, we were no different." Joe picked up a cookie. "We were as spiritually blind as a bat in a church belfry. But we've had an incredible time simply studying the Scriptures and going to Bible studies." He reached for a sack. "We've brought you a Bible and some study materials."

"I prepared a list of Scriptures that have really been helpful to us," Jennifer added. "You'll love making your own discoveries."

"Thank you for the thoughtfulness." Sharon slowly accepted the material from Joe. "I promise we'll take a look."

"It will take time," Larry hesitated.

"Whenever you have questions, we're as close as the phone," Joe assured. "We won't push you . . . just be available to answer questions."

"Simply let us know." Jennifer beamed.

# CHAPTER
## 15

The national security adviser's eyes flashed with anger. "Any second now we will have to walk into his office and talk with the president," he said to his top-ranking staff member. "We don't have the answers we promised. Do you understand the seriousness of our plight?"

"He's a harsh man." The staffer looked grim. "But we've been unable to find anything but religious explanations."

"God help us if you bring that up!" Further comment ended when the president's chief of staff opened the door to the Oval Office and motioned for the two men to enter.

"Good morning, gentlemen." Damian Gianardo stood and offered his hand. "Excuse me for a lack of pleasantries. We must get right to business. We are facing an increasing financial crisis across the world. I must quiet public fears. Time is running out. Please give me the report of your investigation of the disappearance of millions of people."

"Sir," the national security chief said haltingly, "we really don't have a written report."

"A verbal explanation is sufficient for now," the president answered sourly. "I promised the world an answer before the end of the year. A quick synopsis will do."

"The problem is . . ." The security chief stopped and turned to his assistant. "You tell him, Ralph."

"Mr. President, we have found no rational explanation. We have been unable—"

"You've what?" Gianardo's neck began turning red. "I promised the world that I would have an answer. You had best not make me appear to be a fool." His black eyes narrowed, glaring as if he could burn holes through the assistant's face.

"Our only explanations are religious," the staffer blurted out. The national security chief covered his face.

"Religious!" the president shouted. "You expect me to make a sectarian pronouncement about this disaster? Financial markets are collapsing everywhere, and you want me to offer superstition to assure the masses?"

"It's all we have." The assistant held up his empty hands.

Damian Gianardo turned slowly to his national security head, his gaze so fierce the man was forced to look down. "I would suggest two things. First, you fire this incompetent fool before sunset. Second, you have a plausible answer for me in one week or prepare yourself for new employment immediately thereafter. Good day, gentlemen." The president turned back to a letter on his desk and continued reading without looking up; the two bewildered men scurried from the Oval Office with the chief of staff hurrying after the two aides.

Gianardo had no idea he was actually the subject of intense scrutiny. From the dimension existing behind time and beyond space, the demonic war council continued their ongoing examination of the president of the United

States. "What do you wish us to do, O Great One?" Dungetius humbly asked the leader. The host of demons genuflected before the Lord of Hate.

Radiating with the brilliance of the morning star, their leader brushed the question aside. "This one is my chosen man. He is almost prepared to do my total bidding." The Evil One towered above the other demons like a mountain eclipses a valley, his radiance beyond theirs as the sun is brighter than the moon. "He does not yet understand the destiny I have placed at his feet, but Damian is learning." Lucifer thought of his future intentions, and his vision instantly rippled through the hierarchy of iniquity, causing a gasp of awe and amazement. "We must help him grasp the meaning of this moment."

Lucifer's voice bristled with pure spite. "Help Damian see his options," he snarled. "I want him to throb with the same motivation and drive that worked in the bones of Nebuchadnezzar before his conversion to God. Make him pulsate with the same greed we put in the heart of Nero. My son Damian has a right to enjoy the intoxication that comes only from the joy of fulfilled hunger for power." The Evil One pointed his finger through the curtain of time straight at the president still sitting behind his desk. "Dungetius, get down there and work on expanding the possibilities of the religious explanation the aide offered. Damian needs to know what excellent opportunities are his through the politics of counterfeit religion. Get on with it!"

"Excellent, majesty!" Dungetius kept bowing and rubbing his hands together. "I can help him understand the value of the partnership between 'the beast' and the 'lamb that speaks with the voice of the dragon.' Fortunately, the Christians are gone, except for the post-Rapture converts, so we don't have to contend with much prayer opposition. Nothing is left to push our Regional Overseers out of place."

"Dungetius will require assistance!" The devil's response rumbled across timelessness. "I want the Principalities and Powers controlling Washington, D.C., to increase fortification over the entire area. We cannot tolerate a counterattack to break our grip on the capital. Work on the entire presidential staff. Mingle greed with fear! Now is the moment to send Rathmarker into the president with the book we placed in front of his face." Lucifer clapped his hands; thunder roared through eternity. "Do it now!"

Principality demons controlling the eastern seaboard surged into place. Demonic princes immediately began securing the space above the national capital to avoid a counterattack from any angels circulating in the area. Dungetius and his pack thought themselves into the White House. They found the fear and distrust permeating the staff, offering them additional leverage for their work.

Dungetius instantly found Vice President Jacob Rathmarker reading in his office. The demon stood beside the politician and bombarded his mind with intense thoughts. "Tell Gianardo about this book you are reading. Share your conclusions. Get in there and speak to him. Do it now!" Repeating it like a mantra, Dungetius kept saying over and over, "Now, now, now, now, now, now ..."

Rathmarker put his book down and stared at the wall for several moments. He finally reached for his phone and rang the Oval Office.

"Yes," Gianardo answered sharply.

"Mr. President," Jacob began, "I think I'm on to something that might help us out of this crisis."

"Then you're the only one who's got any brains," Gianardo carped. "The rest of these idiots are completely hung up on religious answers. I am surrounded by a pack of idiots!"

"Interestingly enough, we might be able to use this nonsense to our advantage. If there's one thing we can count on these days, it's that people are incurably religious because of the turn of the millennium and the disappearance of more than half a billion people. We simply need to manipulate their tendencies."

"Come on over, Jacob," the president's voice softened. "I've been about half distracted for the last hour. Don't know why but I can't seem to concentrate."

"I'll be there in a moment."

Rathmarker quickly walked from his office into the inner office. He laid a book before the president. "I've been reading poems written by Lenin. Very interesting."

"What?" Gianardo did not hide his irritation. "Poetry at a time like this?"

Rathmarker smiled slyly. "Lenin taught me something. What the world needs at this moment is a messiah, a new Christ, a quasi-religious hero. Every major leader of the twentieth century had an inkling of this need. Think about it, Damian. Stalin, Hitler, Mao. Every one of them was fundamentally a religious figure pursuing a bigger, better hope than the churches offered. We've come to another opportune moment for a charismatic leader to take the place of God. After all, the evangelical Christians seem to be gone so we don't have to contend with their Jesus-talk nonsense to confuse people."

"What are you driving at?" Gianardo laid his pen down.

Rathmarker picked up the book of poems. "Lenin called this one 'Oulanem.' The title is the inversion of the Russian name for Emmanuel, meaning 'God is with us.' The satanists have been turning Christian words and symbols around and upside down forever. Lenin once was an enthusiastic Christian, but he became involved with the occult. That's when he wrote the following: 'If there is something which devours, I'll leap within it, though I bring the world to ruins. The world which bulks between me and the abyss, I will smash it to pieces with my enduring curses. I'll throw my arms around its harsh reality. Embracing me, the world will humbly pass away. And then sink down to utter nothingness. Perished, with no existence; that would be really living.'"

Gianardo got out of his chair and walked around to the front of his desk. "Those words strangely resonate with me. I don't know why, but it feels as if I have been waiting all morning for this moment. Bizarre! My ancestors were, like Lenin's, very religious, and I have always wanted to depart from the faith of my fathers."

"Here's one Lenin called 'The Fiddler.'" Rathmarker cleared his throat and read in low threatening tones. "The hellish vapors rise and fill the brain, till I go mad and my heart is utterly changed. See this sword? The prince of darkness sold it to me.'" Rathmarker closed the book. "Get his drift?"

Gianardo frowned and shook his head.

"Lenin wasn't an atheist. He was a God-hater! The man learned the secret of becoming an antichrist, a messiah of this world!"

Gianardo's eyes widened. The president slowly shook his head as if suddenly possessed by an idea of monumental portions.

"Look!" Rathmarker's eyes narrowed. "What if all those Christians were swallowed up by the devil? Expelled from the world! What if the deity the Christians called 'God' was actually a weak contender for control of the universe? What if the figure Lenin called the prince of darkness finally won the war?"

"Incredible idea, Jacob. Remarkable."

"Lenin, Stalin, Hitler, all knew how to manipulate the religious needs of their subjects, and obviously they had help. Just maybe Satan is waiting to empower and guide anyone willing to follow his leading." Rathmarker grinned. "Why not you, Damian? You fit the criteria for a worldwide antichrist. You can become the god of this world, and I will gladly serve as your prophet."

Gianardo rubbed his forehead and let the weight of his body down on the top of his desk. "I was always impressed that communism, fascism, and Nazism were pseudo-religions. For years, many Americans turned patriotism into a religion of sorts." He snapped his fingers. "Of course. That's exactly what this country needs right now. A strong popular patriotic faith! A United Nations—'We Are the World'—type feeling of unity with me as leader."

"It's what the whole world needs," Rathmarker corrected the president. "You're the person to fill the job. Just stop thinking of yourself as president and get used to the title Caesar."

A smile inched across Damian's face. "What a tremendous thought!" He grinned like a child contemplating Christmas.

"People already see you as the sole leader of the country and the most powerful leader in the world." Jacob pointed to the presidential seal. "In this time of crisis, people will naturally turn to you as the hero, the great man. We must take this tendency on to the next step. They must see you as the incarnated spirit of the nation. From there, it's only a short step for them to focus all of their religious needs on you."

The president clenched his fist. "Exactly! Get me on television surrounded with quasi-religious symbols. I must assume the posture of the ruler of this world."

Jacob laughed. "Fools think modern people aren't religious. The truth is they remain fervently devout; they've just changed their focus. People are looking for something in *this* world to worship, not beyond it."

"And I'm it!" Gianardo boasted. "I can turn those religious explanations upside down and inside out." He walked with new confidence around to the back of his desk. "The first step is to assemble a think tank of advisers to consider and formulate new policy for world domination. We'll start immediately." The president hit the buttons on his telephone. "Get me the chairman of the joint chiefs, the secretary of state, and the treasury secretary! I want the chairman of the Fed in here too." Damian clicked the phone off. "Jacob, I want you to convene the meeting so I won't look self-serving. At the right moment, you will persuade me to accept the course destiny intends."

"I will serve you well, sir."

Damian sat down in his chair and settled back against the leather upholstery. "What do you think Lenin really meant in his poem? 'The prince of darkness sold him the sword'?"

"I believe evil is a personified reality," Rathmarker concluded. "In fact, I'm willing to bet Satan annihilated those trouble-making Christians. We don't have to tell people that's our conclusion. Just ignore their disappearance and cut a deal with the devil."

"But Stalin, Hitler, Mao didn't last. Mao and Stalin died. Hitler committed suicide."

"The times weren't right." Rathmarker shrugged. "For some reason, things are in place now. Think of the greats like Engels, Marx, Himmler, Khrushchev, Idi Amin, as preparing the way for you."

Gianardo pulled at his chin and squinted. "The prince of darkness sold it to me," he mused. "Do you think Lenin meant those words literally?"

"My research confirms a strong satanist link in Lenin's past. Many political leaders talked with the other side as easily as they phoned down the street."

"I want to know how it's done," Gianardo pressed. "Find out how I can get in touch with what you call 'the Evil One.' I'm going to need all the help I can get."

"Consider it done, Mr. President. I will be your prophet, and the Evil One will be your source of worldwide power. A new age is dawning!"

# CHAPTER
## 16

Over the next several days, events moved quickly. Specialists in foreign affairs, international finance, and military strategy streamed through the White House day and night. Pressed in between the marathon planning sessions, the president met with occult practitioners, fortune-tellers, witches, New Agers, clairvoyants, scientologists, and satanists.

The special envoy from Assyria intrigued Gianardo the most. "Sir," the leader of the ancient cult of Zoroastrianism instructed, "are you aware that your name carries the sacred number?"

"I don't understand," the president said.

"The ancient Babylonians assigned a number to every letter in the alphabet. For example, A is equal to six, B to twelve, C to eighteen, and so forth. With this method we were able to assign a special meaning to everyone's name." The gnarled old man grinned a toothy smile. "You, most high one, have a name with a numerical value of 666, the sacred number of the ultimate world emperor. We highly revere such a man."

"Damian Gianardo adds up to 666 using this Babylonian method?" Damian grinned. "666. I am astonished."

The strange little man bowed from the waist. "Yes, it does, therefore, your wish, sir, is my command."

Gianardo slapped him on the back. "My good fellow, we shall yet see what this number means."

The old Assyrian kept bowing as he exited from the room.

Emergency trips and midnight sessions continued into the early hours of the morning. Slowly but steadily, a new national and international policy emerged.

During demonstrations of clairvoyance, ESP, and automatic writing, the president sat spellbound, paying rapt attention to explanations for contacting the devil. Warlocks offered incantations and white witches danced. Repeated incense and spice offerings made the Oval Office smell like frankincense and aromatic gums.

On December 30, the grand scheme was finished and in place. Many politicians and even some cabinet members resigned because of the radical changes: Gianardo's grip on the government was total, exceeding the authority of any president in the history of the country. Even the design of the American flag was changed to show six stars, six stripes, and a special set of six new stars to indicate 666.

As the nation celebrated New Year's Eve, the White House prepared for a very different observance. Aides placed candles around the president's office. Lavers filled with incense sent wispy curls of smoke up toward the ceiling. On the president's desk a skull rested in the center of a red circle. A quill pen, a feather extracted from a raven, waited in front of the bleached, toothless jaw. Knudiaon, the high priest of an ancient Egyptian satanic cult, flew from Cairo the night before for the ceremony. Only Jacob Rathmarker was allowed to watch the president's initiation.

"Notice the amulet around his neck," Rathmarker told the president. "In the center is the ancient Egyptian 'evil eye,' a demonic eye above the pyramid. The image is the seal of the cult."

"Hmmm, sounds like the symbol we Masons use in the lodge meetings." Damian laughed. "Americans have no idea what we slipped in on the back of their dollar bills scores of years ago. Do you realize I am the sixth straight Masonic president? But I am the only one to understand the full meaning of all of the symbolism."

"We must be silent now as we await the priest's coming," Rathmarker remarked. "He told me we must be mentally prepared."

As midnight approached, Gianardo and Rathmarker took their places in two carved chairs placed in the center of the Oval Office. Military guards stood at attention outside the doors. Knudiaon, the senior surviving member of the secret society, entered through a side door used only by the president and his personal staff. He did not acknowledge the two dignitaries waiting for him. His thick black robe could not conceal a hunched back and massive beard. White eyebrows exploded from his forehead like wiry puffs of wool. Knudiaon carried a smoke-stained bowl. The skin on his bony hands was paper thin; the priest's long, unkempt fingernails were yellow and dirty.

With the demeanor of a solitary sphinx lost in the Sahara, Knudiaon walked to the desk and began chanting. After several minutes, he called in English, "Come, Osiris." The black-robed priest walked around the room holding a ceramic dish with a small candle in the middle of some sand. "Come, Isis," he continued. Knudiaon held the hieroglyphics-covered dish above his head while curls of white smoke hung in the air. "Spirits from the land of the dead join us in this hour. Oh, great Lucifer, do not tarry beyond the river of death. Come to us." He lapsed into Egyptian phrases and Arabic words.

Gianardo watched in amazement as the smoke thickened, becoming more like fog, the gathering of a thick mist that took on a life of its own. The temperature in the room dropped. The high priest slowly slumped to his knees, letting the dish of sand slide to the floor and spill over the carpet; the candle bounced and went out. Knudiaon crumpled into a heap as if slain by a hallucinogenic drug.

"It's working!" Gianardo whispered to his vice president. "Just as you said. The master teacher is becoming possessed."

Rathmarker assured him, "The old man is our conduit to the devil. You can trust the prophet."

After a few moments, the priest recovered and stood up, his passive countenance changed. Knudiaon's eyes looked angry and aggressive. "Absolute devotion is demanded!" The priest's voice turned harsh and hard. His face was strangely immobile and void of emotion. "I demand complete fidelity. Are you prepared?"

"Stand up," Rathmarker whispered in the president's ears. "He's ready."

Gianardo rose to his feet, clasping his hands together in front of his coat. He nodded his agreement.

Knudiaon pulled the pointed hood on his black robe down, enveloping his face in shadows. Nothing was visible except his mouth, barely moving in the center of the white beard that dangled down to the base of his neck. The priest reached inside his robe and produced a parchment. He unrolled it and laid it in front of the skull.

Gianardo inched forward with unaccustomed timidity. He took off his coat and handed the jacket to his vice president. The president quickly unfastened a presidential cuff link on his right sleeve and dropped the gold piece in his pocket. Gianardo looked over his shoulder for reassurance. Rathmarker nodded encouragement.

Knudiaon began translating the Sanskrit message written on the parchment immediately below the symbolic pyramid with the evil eye. "My Lord and Master Satan, I acknowledge you as my God and Prince, and promise to serve and obey you while I live. And I renounce the other God and Jesus Christ, the saints, and the church and its sacraments, and I promise to do whatever evil I can. I renounce all the merits of Jesus Christ, and if I fail to serve and adore you, paying homage to you daily, I give you my life as your own. This pact is made on the thirty-first day of December." The old priest stopped and looked Gianardo directly in the eye. His voice dropped nearly an octave lower, rumbling like the sound of chains dragged over stones in a dungeon floor. "Do you intend so?"

"Yes," Damian began hesitantly. "Certainly," he repeated more decisively.

"Give me your hand," the priest demanded.

Damian offered his perspiring palm.

Knudiaon abruptly pulled a jewel-handled dagger from behind the black robe. Before Gianardo could respond, the priest made a surgical slice across his palm; blood instantly filled the president's hand. The old priest laughed diabolically. Gianardo tried to pull away, but the old man held the president's arm with a vice grip.

"The time has come to sign," the priest's cracking voice rumbled. "With your signature, the pact is sealed. Do you agree?"

The president nodded his head mechanically but leaned backward.

Knudiaon picked up the quill in front of the skull. Dipping it in the blood-filled palm, he commanded, "Sign the document!"

The president had to steady his hand against the desk. Blood spilled on the wood and splattered across his shirt sleeve. He breathed deeply but signed with a flourish. Once done, Gianardo straightened and closed his bloody fist.

The old priest smiled slyly. "In the past, the other God has tried to communicate with you through your dreams, but now only the great Evil One will speak to you in your sleep. Should his grace wish to speak with you more directly, Lucifer will have no trouble making contact. Listen to the voices you hear in your head." Knudiaon quickly melted sealing wax with the candle. A blob dropped onto the parchment and Knudiaon plunged his signet ring into the red ooze. "The matter is sealed. You have a new lord. Do not disappoint him. You belong to the devil!" With a flourish the old priest turned and disappeared through the side door.

Damian Gianardo stared at his bleeding hand, unaware blood had already stained his pants and dripped onto his Bruno Magli shoes. He turned to walk away, leaving bloody footprints on the presidential carpet.

■ ■ ■

In accordance with his strict instructions, President Gianardo was not awakened the following morning until late, allowing ample time for dreams to appear. New Year's Day was normally an uneventful time at the White House, but nothing was any longer routine. A week of feverish planning was about to come to full fruition.

Three hours later, Gianardo stepped before the television cameras, opened the file containing his carefully prepared speech, and began at once. "My fellow Americans, we start this new year with grave problems confronting us. I am taking the unusual step of speaking on New Year's Day because I am proposing a new, dramatic path to recovery. I want you to sleep well tonight, knowing your president is about to turn our deficits into assets. Congress has just completed an emergency session that I called two days ago." He stared hard at the camera. "All foreign assets have been frozen. We will hold hundreds of billions of dollars in assets for a period of six months. The nations that agree to become states of the U.S.A. will receive their assets back, while the obstinate will lose their holdings. I would never have done this in the past, but the disappearance of millions of Americans last September has brought on an economic crisis and marks a new, spiritual era. We must do this now to survive."

The president stopped and nodded to the technician. Pictures of European countries filled the screen. Cathedrals and shots of the Vatican emerged. Gianardo waited for a scene of Paris and Notre Dame to appear. "During the past week, Vice President Jacob Rathmarker and I flew secretly to the major capitals of the world with leaders of Congress accompanying us. In secret negotiations, I proposed the creation of a New Roman Empire, resulting in a new world order. Though there was some initial resistance, my explanation of the mutual benefits brought some degree of compliance." Gianardo stopped and smiled wickedly at the screen. "Particularly, if they wanted their moneys back and wanted to avoid nuclear warfare."

Jacob Rathmarker stood in the wings listening. "Masterful stroke," he said to McAbee, his confidential aide. "Because we are the supreme military power in the world, no one can really resist us. Our plan not only eliminates any government debt but instantly makes us the strongest financial nation as well. We've taken a worldwide crisis and turned it into a national asset."

The aide nodded enthusiastically. "But what about the Muslims? Are they really buying in?"

"Even as we speak, we are finalizing negotiations with the consortium that is reconstructing and reorganizing Babylon as the capital of the United Muslim League. Gianardo will link their new Babylonian Empire with our Neo-Roman–American government. As a result, we will have more oil resources than we can ever use. We've got the world by the neck!" The vice president laughed cynically.

"Amazing!" McAbee beamed.

Gianardo cleared his throat and continued. "An international computerized banking system will be located in Rome for our central banking system. While the dollar remains current, I propose an exciting breakthrough. Cash will soon no longer be needed across the empire. Multipurpose credit cards will offer speedy business transactions. You will receive a universal social security number along with our fellow citizens in Japan, Italy, and Great Britain. With laser technology we can painlessly place a computer chip with the invisible number under the skin of your right hand. The chip could also be placed in the forehead, at the hairline, and no one could ever see it. You wave at a cash register, and the computer will deduct the purchase from your bank account. A completely fair line of credit will be established based on your record of the past three years. A new chapter in economic history is being written. We will finally have a cashless society."

Rathmarker lowered his voice and spoke directly into the aide's ear. "McAbee, universal identification has unlimited possibilities. Total surveillance is just one aspect. We will be able to extend instant control over the worldwide citizenry. Resistance can be crushed in a few hours."

The aide blinked several times. "Why . . . the president . . . will become more like . . . a . . . a . . . world emperor . . ." McAbee's voice trailed off into a whisper.

President Gianardo continued his speech. "As a concession to the United Muslim League, we will be using the ancient Babylonian system for numbering names." Gianardo shared what he had recently learned. "Common denominations by six will be employed, since six is the number for humanity. For example, A would be equal to six; B equals twelve; C equals eighteen; and so forth. Using this system produces a numerical equivalent for my name, Damian Gianardo, of 666. Since I am founding this system, I am asking that all universal social security numbers be preceded by 666, despite the silly superstitions surrounding that number." The president shook his fist in the air. "Let us affirm the power of humanity; 666 is a triple way of asserting the capacities of a human race set free from the old religious superstitions."

Rathmarker's aide turned away from the address. "Can we really get away with freezing the assets of another country?" McAbee grimaced. "A rather bold and, if I may say so, illegal step."

Rathmarker clenched his jaw defiantly. "Who's going to stop us? Congress buckled out of fear and intimidation. The nations of the world will do the same." His eyes flashed. "We have learned the secret of absolute authority, omnipotence, control!" He slapped the aide on the back. "Get on the train, Mac. Gianardo is now the embodiment of sheer power!"

# CHAPTER

## 17

**N**ational and international events unfolding over a period of weeks flashed past Michael and Seradim at the pace humans watch the evening news report on television. Each additional episode left Seradim in profound consternation and distress.

"Why doesn't the Almighty stop this nonsense?" Seradim agonized. "I can see where the entire scenario is going."

Michael nodded. "Of course." He pointed at Damian Gianardo. The president was pressing Japanese diplomats to agree to the terms of the treaty his government was imposing on them. The officials looked haggard and tired. "The world has not yet seen a dictator with the mind and finesse of this man. Gianardo's talents and disposition equip him to be both the most winsome and cruelest despot of the entire sweep of history. Moreover, the power of evil is with him."

"Then the Holy One of Israel must intervene!"

"Do not make the same mistake Lucifer made," Michael cautioned. "A host of well-meaning Christians have slipped into the same error, thinking the devil is capable of standing on equal terms with the Lord and posing a genuine threat to God. Lucifer always swings from the end of a rope held by the Holy One."

"A rope?"

"Figure of speech, my friend. Lucifer made the error of thinking it was possible to exist outside the sphere of divine influence." Michael pointed toward the glowing perimeters of heaven in the distance behind them. "Impossible! The Almighty's seeming absence is only the opportunity for His creatures to have the freedom to grow in love. Truth is, the mercy of God is so total and extensive that the Father waits and waits and waits, hoping that His love will be returned to Him. But the day will come when He reels in the rope, and Lucifer will finally realize he has only hung himself by misusing the independence granted from the beginning of eternity."

Using his moral sight, Seradim looked down on the world spinning beneath clouds of moral decadence, and his angelic eyes allowed him to see morality as people view scenery. From the slums of inner cities, smokestacks belched corruption and spilled the black soot of hate across the urban terrain. The junior angel could see millions of aborted babies, rising up toward heaven from bloody graves inside and outside abortion clinics.

"I can't stand it," Seradim cried out. "The pain is more than I can endure."

"Yes. The great surprise both humans and the devil can never grasp is that the Father feels the same pain but to an infinite degree. Lucifer does not value human life and has no capacity for love. When the Holy One finally smashes the devil and his minions, the Father will still feel loss. Amazing grace, indeed!"

The two angels watched Gianardo as humans would view a movie. The president didn't seem to need sleep. Like an aphrodisiac, the lust for power energized him. Gianardo ordered his subordinates around like a chess player moving expendable pawns.

Michael pointed within the president. The angel's moral sensitivity was like an X ray, exposing Gianardo's soul. Michael could see ghostlike spirits moving in, out, and through the president as worms work through a corpse. "His thoughts are not yet completely possessed by the devil, but the demons control him spiritually," Michael explained. "Moreover, evil has permeated the social and political structures around the president so effectively, the man simply functions as an extension of the corrupt world system. Long ago, Gianardo's Italian immigrant parents started worshiping the American way of life. Even though they were originally devout Roman Catholics, "America" became their true idol. Damian thus departed from the faith of his parents and grandparents and became a natural product of the pervasive seduction of his own society. Thinking himself omnipotent, this foolish man has become the ultimate expression of the devil's heart's desire."

"Terrible days are ahead," Seradim concluded.

"Damian Gianardo isn't our charge. We need to help the Feinbergs get ready for the consequences of his decisions. As Jews, the family naturally fears that persecution is coming. Because they are deeply disturbed, the Feinbergs are now spiritually open, and we can help them take the next step. We need to sit in on their meeting with the McCoys. Follow me. We will join them in the Feinbergs' living room. Since Jimmy Harrison began examining his father's writings, he has become amazingly astute about what is going on. Reverend Harrison had a profound grasp of prophecy, and Jimmy has accepted Jesus as Savior as a result of his father's studies. I want you to watch carefully what is happening to Doctor Feinberg; obviously, we can't read Larry's mind, but we can pick up on the spiritual undercurrents."

Larry paced up and down in front of a large oil painting of a castle on the Rhine River. He kept running his hand through his hair as he talked. "I tell you, Joe, we are standing on top of a political San Andreas Fault! The president can wipe any of us out any time he chooses."

"I truly understand." Joe put his arm around Jennifer. "I came to the same conclusion the moment I heard that Gianardo renamed the presidential jet, *The White Horse*. Revelation chapter six says the Antichrist will conquer nations without war, using a bow without arrows, and riding on a symbolic 'white horse.' Once we knew he had assembled a ten-nation confederation in Europe, we could read the handwriting on the wall. That's when we knew how important it was to recognize Jesus as the Messiah."

Jennifer slid forward on the expensive brocade-covered couch. "Here's a sheet listing the prophecies fulfilled in the first coming of the Messiah. On the back is a list of Scriptures yet to be fulfilled." She put the sheet in Larry's hands. "You can see that many of these yet-to-be-completed prophecies are being fulfilled right before our eyes."

Jimmy looked over Larry's shoulder and nodded his head enthusiastically. "Right on the money."

Joe pointed to key verses describing the Antichrist. "The Bible is the only information we have that can make sense out of what we're watching on our televisions."

"We believe the next major event will happen on July 25," Jennifer continued. "If the next phase begins on this day, there will be no question that we are racing toward the Great Tribulation at breakneck speed."

"You are exactly right," Jimmy broke in. "My reading clarifies that July 25 will be the ninth of Av in the traditional Jewish calendar, their next religious holiday."

"Jewish holiday?" Larry frowned. "I've never heard of a summer holiday."

"The Feast of Tishah b'Av," Jimmy confirmed.

"Never heard of it." Larry sounded condescending.

"I have!" Sharon corrected her husband. "I'd forgotten about Tishah b'Av, but my father kept the day. Solomon's Temple was burned by the Babylonians on Av 9 in 587 B.C."

"Really?" Larry's eyes widened.

"Few days in Jewish history have been as significant as this one," Jimmy continued. "My father was big on the meaning of this holiday."

Joe slid to the edge of his chair. "Centuries before the temple fell, the twelve spies sneaked into Canaan and returned in terror on Av 9. The faithlessness of ten of those spies caused another forty years of wandering in the wilderness. Joshua and Caleb were the only two spies who had faith, so God spared their lives."

Jimmy smiled knowingly. "Titus and the Roman legions destroyed the second temple in A.D. 70 on Av 9. A year later the Romans plowed Jerusalem under, and it was on the same day."

"I've been reading Jimmy's books," Ruth joined in. "Because Reverend Harrison underlined so much, it's easy for me to get the high points. Simon Bar-Kochba led the last Jewish uprising against Rome, and his army was destroyed on Av 9, 135. Here, Dad, look for yourself." Ruth handed a book to her father.

Larry turned uncomfortably in his chair. "Are you sure that your information is correct?" he mumbled.

Jimmy opened his Bible on the table. "We've barely scraped the surface. On July 18, 1290, England expelled all its Jews on this same day. France expelled all its Jews in 1306 on Av 9, and later Spain repeated the same injustice. Anyone want to guess what the year was?"

"It was 1492," Ben immediately answered.

"Exactly," Jimmy said. "The year Columbus left Spain, the Spanish Empire expelled eight hundred thousand Jews by August 2 and killed many others. Care to guess what day August 2 coincided with that year on the Jewish calendar?

Larry shook his head. "Av 9."

Jennifer continued, "Our Bible teacher taught us that World War I and Russia's renewed killing of Jews began on August 9, 1914. Want to guess what day that was?"

"I don't need to," Sharon answered. "My great-grandparents were driven from their village in eastern Russia on Av 9."

"And Hitler and his henchmen made their final plans to kill Jews worldwide on Av 9, 1942," Jimmy added. "The gas chambers of Treblinka began the holocaust officially on that fateful day."

"Do you have any idea of the mathematical chance of such a thing occurring?" Joe asked. "As a comptroller and accountant, numbers are my world. I'd guess that the odds are about 1 in 265 to the eighth power. Literally 1 chance in 863 zillion . . . that's 863 with 15 zeros after it!"

Michael nudged his protégé. "Watch Larry's eyes. His defenses against the truth are crumbling. Even though that old psychiatrist doesn't want to admit the fact, Larry likes being in control. Right now, his world is wobbling like a top about to fall over. He can't control anything!"

"He's rubbing his temples and breathing harder," Seradim observed. "Our boy's obviously frightened as well."

Jennifer reached out to Larry. "When we put all the numbers together, the first thing we thought of was your family. Jews haven't fared very well on Av 9. We love you and want to make sure that nothing bad happens this year. We are ready to protect your family from any form of anti-Semitism."

Seradim looked at Michael and exclaimed, "I can sense Larry's response! He is deeply touched. The McCoys' love has broken through his facade."

"Exactly! The spiritual barriers are tumbling quickly." Michael beamed. "Larry Feinberg is very close to accepting the gospel. Our task now is to allow the Holy Spirit to use us in any way possible to finish the job and see Larry enter the kingdom of God."

"What do we do?" Seradim asked.

"Intercede and call for Larry and Sharon to feel the Spirit of God draw them close." Michael retreated within himself and began praying, "Come Holy Spirit . . . come fire divine."

Seradim's voice blended into the plea, "Omnipresent Spirit of God, come and fill Larry's heart. Come now."

Instantly, Michael knew what he should do. "The Spirit of God is directing me to protect our charges. Seradim, look carefully and see what must be done." He stared at the living room scene again. "Something big is about to happen."

"I pride myself on being a scientist," Larry told Joe and Jennifer. "I have to take facts seriously. It's all coming so quickly. I just don't know. I feel like I've been hit by an avalanche. I just can't put it all together this fast. I guess I need some time to think."

Seradim asked, "Why is Larry losing focus, Michael?"

"Look!" Michael pointed on the other side of the living room. Two evil figures emerged through the wall.

"Malafidus and Homelas! They're back!"

"We must act quickly." Michael clenched his fist. "We cannot allow the demons to confuse our friends. Now's the time to blow our cover and take those two head-on. Attack!"

Michael dived into the living room scene in an explosion of spiritual light, blasting the two demons with pure radiance and knocking them back through the walls. "After them!" Michael beckoned Seradim to follow.

The glare momentarily threw the evil pair off balance. Michael locked his mind onto their essence and violently flung them backward. The battle scene shifted away from the space around the Feinbergs' living room, continuing in the eternal void between heaven and earth.

"What's going on?" Homelas called out in confusion. "What's happened?"

"You've just met the God squad," Seradim answered. "Try taking an angel on for size." The junior angel spiritually lunged at Homelas only to tumble off into the emptiness.

"Let's destroy that naive toad." Homelas clawed at the angel. "Get him!"

Malafidus grabbed Seradim from the back, immobilizing him. "Something as puny as you created all this confusion?"

"No," a voice thundered from behind the struggle. "He's got a friend." With a great swipe of his mighty arm, Michael knocked Homelas into space. "You boys are about to get a real taste of godly power." With a burst of the same energy used to begin creation, Michael unleashed the cosmic radiation of the authority of the Word. As the angel spoke, the force of divine speech shattered the demons' ability to think, to respond, to react. In seconds, the pair shot out across the cosmos, light years away from the Feinbergs' house.

"Eventually, they'll find each other again," Michael explained, picking Seradim up. "By then Larry will have come to the right conclusions." Michael laughed at his charge. "They roughed you up a bit. Taking on the two of them at once was no small act of courage . . . but you might be a bit more prudent next time."

Seradim looked sheepish and shrugged apologetically.

"You've got great heart, my friend. Nothing to make amends for in this battle. We kept Larry from being bombarded by doubt. Look." Michael pointed into the living room.

"Thank you." Larry stood up and offered his hand to the McCoys. "I'm sure we'll give this entire matter our undivided attention."

Ben Feinberg turned to Jimmy Harrison. "You've been studying a lot more than the *Blue Book* on used cars lately. A lot more."

"There's much more at stake," Jimmy answered. "Money's one thing. Eternity is another."

"Jimmy, I've badly underestimated you," Larry said. "You have an excellent mind and a very good heart. Let's talk more, son. I want you to help me understand your father's teaching."

Jimmy's eye's watered. "I'd be honored."

"You'll certainly be in our prayers," Jennifer added. "God is obviously at work at the Feinberg house."

# CHAPTER
## 18

During the following weeks, Larry and Sharon diligently studied everything the McCoys gave them. They also talked with Jimmy Harrison. No matter what they read, they remained tentative while waiting for Av 9 to arrive. The Feast of Tishah b'Av would fall on July 25 this year. The Feinbergs sensed the day might be the pivotal event in their lives.

When the day finally arrived, the Feinbergs attempted to follow their normal routine. Larry and Sharon sat down for breakfast as usual. "You're okay?" Larry asked.

"No," Sharon said, breaking a two-decade-old pattern. "I'm not."

Larry really looked at her for the first time that day. "I love you," he said and turned on the TV.

The screen exploded with images of soldiers on horseback riding over rough terrain. The anchorman said, "Last night's report of large-scale movements of Syrian and Russian troops on horseback now makes sense. Continuing economic troubles apparently have some bearing on this unusual approach of horse brigades for combat. At this hour, Russian and Syrian troops are in control of the mountains of Lebanon and are bearing down on the state of Israel."

"It's happening!" Larry leaned toward the television. "Israel's under attack! The war predicted in chapters thirty-eight and thirty-nine of Ezekiel is beginning, just like Jimmy and Joe said it would."

Columns of troops lumbered down a dusty road. "Libya and Iran have dropped paratroopers on Israel," the reporter continued. "Ethiopian soldiers are reported moving toward Jerusalem at this hour." The news broadcast showed images of an Arab despot dressed in women's clothing, making psychotic, fist-shaking statements about Jews worldwide. "Some small nuclear weapons were just fired into Israel," the reporter added, "apparently by artillerymen in the Pisgah mountain range in Jordan, near Petra. Intelligence sources say the missiles were fired from shoulder-held artillery sold by China to Libya. Palestinian terrorists are said to be the mastermind behind the whole Russian invasion. Jordan continues to claim neutrality."

Another reporter appeared on the screen. "The State Department is now releasing its assessment of this attack. The Israeli prime minister has been assassinated. Many have already died in Israel. Hard-liner Russian President Ivan Smirkoff apparently concluded that the current anti-Israeli sentiment would permit a quick strike. Using allies in Iran, Libya, and Ethiopia, Russia evidently has designs on Israel's new oil and gold discoveries, as well as Dead Sea minerals.

"However, world leaders are now expressing their shock. The report of the sudden and unexpected invasion is rocking capitals around the world. The responses point to a serious miscalculation on the part of the invaders. Fear is mounting that Israel will respond with nuclear weapons of its own, since nuclear weapons have already fallen in Israel. We switch you now to a live statement by President Gianardo, who went to Spain two days ago for unexplainable consultations with European leaders."

"Spain!" Sharon gasped. "Oh, no!"

"Fits exactly what Jimmy said." Larry's eyes widened. "He said that Ezekiel predicted that the people of Tarshish, or Spain, would be surprised by the invasion of Israel."

"And Ezekiel said the Russian army will be destroyed by fire and brimstone!" Sharon put both hands to her cheeks. "We have already studied what the reporters are going to tell us."

Larry rushed out of the room and returned with the McCoys' list of Scriptures and a Bible. He quickly turned to Ezekiel. "The Bible says here that Israel will take seven months to bury all the dead Russian and allied soldiers." Larry thumbed the pages. "Let's try this part from the prophet Joel."

Sharon put her finger on the page and started reading. "I will remove far from you the northern army, and will drive him away into a barren and desolate land, with his face toward the eastern sea and his back toward the western sea—"

"That description would fit the Dead Sea and the Mediterranean Sea perfectly," Larry interjected.

"His stench will come up, and his foul odor will rise, because he has done monstrous things," Sharon kept reading.

"All Israel has to do," Larry said as he looked up at the ceiling, "is to nuke them and leave their radioactive bodies to decay if this twenty-six-hundred-year-old prophecy is to be fulfilled."

"And who's the father of that weapon?" Sharon slowly sank down in a kitchen chair. "A Jew! Albert Einstein! Larry everything fits."

"We heard every bit of today's headlines last night. Today is the ninth of Av. Right on schedule."

"What can we do?" Sharon clutched her husband's arm. "We must do something."

Larry searched Sharon's face, his eyes darting back and forth. "I really don't know how . . . but I think we need to pray."

"You start," Sharon pleaded. "I'll just repeat silently whatever you say."

Larry lowered his head into his hands and closed his eyes. *"Shema Israel."* He recited the words he heard at the synagogue as a boy. *"Adonai elohenu Adonai echad.* God of our fathers, Abraham, Isaac, and Jacob, please hear us today. Whoever You are, I believe in You. Forgive my arrogance in ignoring You. I must believe that You intervene in history and that You are sovereign over all things. Whoever You are, please make Yourself known to us."

"Yes," Sharon said softly.

"If Jesus is the Messiah, please show us what to believe. Even if I don't like the truth, I want to see it before my eyes. Help us to know how to help our fellow Jews in Israel and around the world. Please help us find our way out of this confusion. Amen." Larry blinked his eyes but didn't move. Sharon squeezed his hand.

Michael embraced Seradim. "He's done it! We've fulfilled our first purpose. The Feinbergs have crossed the line."

Seradim held his hands up. "Praise God!"

"Listen." Michael looked upward. "Heaven is jubilant."

The rejoicing of the nine angelic choirs flooded the void between time and eternity. Dominions sent to the angels beneath them sang their song of joy. Archangels answered with antiphonal responses of celebration: "The lost has been found!"

■ ■ ■

At the opposite end of the realm dividing heaven and earth, another court assembled. While hordes of demons watched the pair cautiously approaching the seat of all Evil, Homelas and Malafidus inched forward. Blackness hung over the pair like an approaching hailstorm. The awesome silence was as stifling as the eerie calm before a tornado. Homelas and Malafidus looked nervously at the glaring horde. All they saw was frightening contempt.

Lucifer shook his fist. "You have failed," he charged. "We trusted you with the two lives we might have totally destroyed." Fire flashed from his eyes; his fangs were bared. "The children will eventually follow the parents. You let the Feinbergs get away! How dare you!" The devil's rage thundered. "You two fools have failed! Failed!"

Homelas and Malafidus crowded together, looking down, trying to avoid Lucifer's red eyes.

"You know how much I hate Jews! From the very beginning, those worthless God-loving sons of Abraham have been His secret weapon in heaven's battle with me! I have tried relentlessly to destroy Jews for centuries. And you two idiots let an entire family slip through my hands!"

"We were attacked," Malafidus offered timidly. "Just as we were about to intervene, an angel dive-bombed us."

"Not *an* angel," Homelas interrupted. "We were hit by a whole squadron. Must have been several hundred. We were simply outnumbered."

"You couldn't have called for backup?" The devil's voice changed and was now beguilingly sympathetic. "We wouldn't have responded with help?"

"The assault came out of nowhere," Homelas pleaded. "Before we could even consult each other, they got us from behind."

"Poor things," Lucifer cooed. "With four thousand years of training, you two fools couldn't smell an attack coming." The Evil One suddenly screamed, bellowing fire, smoke, and ash. "Angels are always hanging around when humans talk about spiritual things! You completely mindless hunks of snot! There is no excuse for your failure!"

"Mercy!" Malafidus begged. "Mercy!"

Satan arose. "Mercy? Where did you learn that word? I don't have such a useless term in my vocabulary. Been talking to the enemy?" the devil asked condescendingly.

Malafidus covered his head and tried to hide his eyes.

"I don't think you two slime-sucking swamp bottoms deserve to exist. Returning you to hell is too good for you."

"No!" Homelas pleaded. "Hell is too terrifying even to contemplate. Please!" He held up his hands in petition.

"Yes, the lake of fire." Satan pointed to the center of the earth where a lake of molten lava seethed with smoke and fire. Like an enormous volcano, the vast cauldron of fury boiled and bubbled molten brimstone. "A perfect place to roast the likes of you two buffoons."

"A-h-h-h," the pair screamed and wilted in a heap, writhing together in agonizing terror.

"I warn you." The devil pointed at the pair. "If you ever slip up again I'll make you an eternal example." Satan's words belched hate. "You had best rectify this incompetence in some significant way or I will assign you to the abyss."

"Oh, thank you." Malafidus backed away. "Thank you. Yes, we will bring you a trophy of victory. Count on it." The demons kept receding from the devil. "We'll do it quickly."

"It better be good!" Satan roared with a blast of pure malice, blowing the pair completely out of the demonic assembly.

Malafidus looked around the void where they landed. "At least we still exist on the surface of the earth rather than within it!" He could barely communicate. "We survived." The demon cursed. "Man, am I ever glad to be out of there."

Homelas kept shaking but couldn't speak.

"The last time anyone got a dressing down like that was when all those drug-using hippies became Jesus freaks." Malafidus brushed himself off. "A whole legion of demons disappeared from the surface of the earth over that faux pas."

Homelas rubbed his neck and hugged himself to stop the trembling. "I . . . I . . . think . . . we ought to kill someone." He thought for a moment. "Murder would put us back in good graces."

Malafidus nodded slowly. "Excellent idea. Nothing pleases his infernal majesty like a good homicide. Who do you have in mind?"

Homelas thought for a moment. "I know exactly who we should get! They caused this whole mess to happen."

# CHAPTER
## 19

Michael and Seradim watched Ben Feinberg talk to Cindy in front of the UCLA library. Cindy sat on the front steps with her German shepherd guide dog, Sam, at her feet. Ben held the latest newspaper.

"When Israel used atomic weapons on the Russians, one of the prophecies we studied was fulfilled." Ben pointed at the headlines. "The enormous earthquake that followed cracked the earth open and swallowed most of the remainder of the Russian army. It must have been an act of God, along with the fact that the nuclear missiles fired by Libyan artillerymen from the Pisgah mountain range 'accidentally' landed on the Palestinian guerrillas surrounding Jerusalem instead of killing the Jews they were intended to kill."

Michael observed, "Ben is shaken because he understands the spiritual implications of what's happened in the Holy Land. Reality is setting in."

Seradim smiled. "Maybe the son is about to follow in the footsteps of the father. The prophet Ezekiel said this war would show Jews everywhere that the God who loves and delivers Israel is alive and well. Ben is certainly examining the headlines with unusual intensity. Let's get closer."

"Sure. We'll stand next to them. I need to give Ben a special encouragement."

"Ben, we've carefully studied the Scriptures Joe McCoy gave you." Cindy's voice was grave and serious. "Everything is just as the Bible said it would be. We can't ignore the implications."

"I know. I know." Ben folded the paper. "For the first time in my life I've asked God to show me the truth. I don't want to accept what the McCoys have been telling us, but the handwriting sure seems to be on the wall."

"I've been trying to teach my parents." Cindy patted her dog on the head. "They listen, but they are more terrified than anything else. Nothing in their background prepares them to understand. Half the time the news reports frighten them, and my Bible lessons leave Mom and Dad in complete consternation the other half. I feel that nothing is like it was."

"Certainly not for the Russians." Ben rolled his eyes. "And not for my family, either. No one has said it out loud yet, but I think we've already thrown in the towel on the last of our doubts. How can we ignore the meaning of the total defeat of Russia and her allies?"

"Ben." Cindy looked toward the sky as if her sightless eyes seemed to see something she couldn't quite perceive. "I've been trying to pray like the Bible suggests. What I ask, I ask in Jesus' name, with very interesting results."

Ben frowned. "In what way?"

"I have the strangest sense that Someone is there, that I'm being heard. I think it's working."

"I thought the issue is what we believe . . . having the right ideas."

"Maybe it's much more," Cindy pondered. "What if this whole business is about making contact? A personal relationship with Jesus?"

"That's a new wrinkle."

"Here's another one for you." Cindy smiled mischievously. "I've been having these unusual intuitions. Hunches if you like."

"And? . . . And?"

"I think the issue is even bigger than you've thought. I think that God has something very important for you to do in the days ahead."

Ben jerked. "You've got to be kidding."

Cindy's smile faded, and she became very serious. "I can't tell you why, but I feel a strong inner sense of guidance. You have a special task that God wants you to do."

Ben stared. "Cindy, this is getting way too far out for me."

Michael nudged Seradim. "Now's the time for me to give Ben a little encouragement." The angel pointed. "You can read confusion in Ben's face. He's going to need our help to put this moment in the right perspective. I will intervene in the parking lot."

"See you at lunch," Ben called one last time, running toward his car. He mumbled under his breath, "This whole thing gives me the willies. I hope Cindy is not going to get weird on me."

"Now's the right moment," Michael told his colleague. "I'm going to use the same body I put on last time. Watch me give Ben something to think about." Michael stepped out of eternity and into the UCLA parking lot.

"Consider what I said," Cindy hollered after Ben.

He put his key in the car door, acting as if he hadn't heard her.

"Take her seriously," Michael said from behind Ben.

Ben spun around and flattened himself against the car. "Who are you?"

"Michael. I am your friend, Ben." The angel towered above the young man.

"I don't know you." Ben inched back toward the street.

"But I know you. I have known you since the day you were born. Do not be afraid. I bring you good tidings."

"What?" Ben squinted. "What are you talking about?"

"You asked for guidance." Michael stared deeply into Ben's eyes. "Do not be afraid to receive it."

Ben pulled away from the all-revealing stare and started running down the sidewalk. Michael stepped back out of time. When Ben looked over his shoulder, the figure had disappeared, causing Ben to run all the harder for the library.

"Ben?" Cindy was still sitting on the library steps. "Sounds like your footsteps. Back so soon?" Sam watched the approaching figure and barked.

"Cindy," he panted. "I just had the living daylights scared out of me. A big guy . . . a strange man appeared out of nowhere. And then he was gone. Disappeared."

"What are you talking about?"

"The guy said he'd known me all my life. I swear I've never seen him before. Maybe I really am going nuts. He called himself Michael."

"Michael? I know a Michael. Did he have an unusually deep bass voice?"

"Why, yes. Exactly."

"Talk sort of strange?"

"Yes, yes. You've seen him?"

Cindy laughed. "Not hardly. But I have met Michael on a number of occasions. I always thought he was a student. Sort of shows up at very opportune moments."

"Listen, Cindy. This guy is big. Strange. Terrifying."

"Come now, Ben. I've always found him to be extremely considerate."

"You know anything about him?" Ben sounded skeptical.

"Actually nothing. When I've tried to ask questions, he changes the subject. But he's been no problem. Really, Michael has a knack for appearing when I really need help."

"I don't know." Ben kept shaking his head. "Weirdest thing I've seen since the Rapture."

Seradim moved into place next to the couple.

Michael turned to the young angel. "We have to be strategic about making physical appearances. The best time to appear is on the anniversary of the Jewish festivals and feasts. Often, we are especially sent to make a special announcement of God's intentions and plans, but our job is always to encourage people without taking away or destroying their freedom of choice. We help them in their uphill struggles, but we must not remove obstacles from their path that are needed for developing integrity. Moral exercise is imperative for their spiritual development."

"I understand." Seradim nodded. "Endurance helps develop character. And godly character produces unfailing hope."

"Exactly. We want people to come to the place where even suffering doesn't stifle their optimism and capacity to overcome. We must make sure our appearances don't hinder the inner battle that produces victors. That's called 'putting on the full armor of God.'"

Seradim watched Ben return to the parking lot. "You certainly stretched his imagination. Ben's got plenty to think about today!"

"We need to go back to heaven for more training and allow some time to roll by on Earth. Gianardo will soon be creating a security apparatus capable of doing great harm to our wards. By contrast, heaven is also preparing for its own invasion."

"More angels are coming down?"

"No, Elijah and Moses will shortly return to Jerusalem as the big battle in Israel starts to take shape."

"They're not angels?"

Michael shook his head. "No. When people die, they don't turn into angels. We are a completely different species from them. In heaven, people become like us, but they have temporary bodies. After Satan is defeated and time has played out, people will be resurrected to new physical bodies. Understand?"

"Amazing! They'll always be superior to us?"

"Exactly."

"Moses and Elijah?" Seradim pondered and immediately his mind was filled with the knowledge of who the two great biblical heroes were . . . and would be.

"We will help prepare for those great heroes' return to the Mount of Olives on the Feast of Purim. While we work on their project, we'll give Ben a little more time."

■ ■ ■

Throughout the hot summer, the papers and television news reports were filled with stories of radical political change in America and across the world. The new Israeli prime minister was very careful in his public appearances not to offend Gianardo. No one seemed to be able to resist any plan Damian Gianardo proposed. With uncanny skill, the president was always a step ahead of his opposition.

Units of his personal secret surveillance police sprang up in every town.

Seradim's training took him to a new level as he grew to understand the extraordinary appearances coming in the immediate future. As fall approached, the time came for the two angels to get back in touch with Ben and Cindy. Everyone in the Feinberg family was making great spiritual progress . . . except Ben.

As he often did, Ben walked Cindy from her dormitory to the library. "Hope your classes are easy this morning."

"Big day for you!" Cindy beamed.

"Huh?" Ben puzzled.

"Come on," Cindy chided. "You're not paying attention to the calendar. A girl down the hall is Jewish. She said today is Yom Kippur, the Day of Atonement. Your big day for repentance."

"Yom Kippur! I forgot all about it."

"Naughty boy," Cindy teased. "Now you will have to make double confession."

"Wow!" Ben slapped his forehead. "Today is Yom Kippur. All the strange things started happening just over a year ago on Rosh Hashanah. I should have paid more attention to the calendar!"

"Yom Kippur is a time for getting right with God, isn't it?"

"Something like that, Cindy. Unfortunately, my family didn't pay much attention to our traditions."

Michael nudged Seradim. "That's the clue I need. It's time to give Ben a bit more to think about."

"Can I go with you this time?"

"No. I'm all Ben can handle for the moment." Michael stepped into time, standing behind the couple.

"I'm still trying to put everything together," Ben confessed.

"There are times and seasons appointed for all things," Michael spoke over Ben's shoulder.

"What?" Cindy turned toward the voice. Sam looked nonchalantly toward the sound.

"You!" Ben jerked.

"These days are your special times," Michael said.

"Michael?" Cindy asked. "Is that you?" Sam wagged his tail.

"Where did you come from?" Ben stared. "You weren't there a moment ago."

"You are very important people. I am honored to be a comrade."

Cindy reached out and took Michael's hand.

"Look!" Ben trembled. "We haven't done anything to you. What do you want with us?"

"The issue is what I can do *for* you." Michael smiled. "You are part of a great plan, and I will help you execute your part."

"Why do you keep coming and going?" Cindy asked.

"I have special work to do."

"Who do you work for?" Ben held up his hands defensively. "You're an extraterrestrial? A spaceman?"

"I come from the center of reality itself, but I know your world exceedingly well, Ben. I have been watching your people from the beginning."

"My people?"

"Are you Jewish?" Cindy asked.

"No. But I do work for a Jewish carpenter," Michael said. Then he stepped back into eternity.

Cindy's fingers collapsed on themselves. "He's gone."

"My gosh!" Ben choked.

"Where did he go?" Cindy groped around.

"Right before my eyes! Boom!" Ben stared at the empty sidewalk.

"Ben, we're not crazy. This isn't a hallucination. Michael was *here!*"

"Let me sit down . . . for a few minutes. I must get myself together."

# CHAPTER
## 20

Cindy shook Ben's shoulders. "Quit running from the obvious. From reading the Bible I know enough to understand what it means that a 'Jewish carpenter' is Michael's boss."

Ben rubbed his eyes and looked carefully around the UCLA campus. "What are you driving at?"

"In the Bible there is another person named Michael. I don't know if this guy is the same one or what . . . but I do know that the Michael in the Bible was an angel."

"An angel!" Ben sputtered.

"Well." Cindy held up her hands and shrugged her shoulders. "It makes a lot more sense than that spaceman talk."

"An . . . angel?"

"I read one place in the Bible where it said that many people had entertained angels unaware." Cindy sounded defensive. "Why not us?"

Ben stared.

"Working for a Jewish carpenter?" Cindy beamed. "He had to mean Jesus. The whole thing fits together."

Ben ran his fingers through his hair. "Maybe we're both getting caught up in the mass hysteria sweeping the country after all of the strange experiences. Maybe—"

"Stop it," Cindy said firmly. "I'm not crazy, Ben, and neither are you. Maybe my blindness is an asset. I have to depend on far more than my eyes to make sense out of things. I know that we have been talking to a real person regardless of how he comes and goes. Let's be scientific about this encounter. If Michael is for real, he'll be back. And if he is an angel, Michael wants the best for us."

"How in the world can we set up an experiment with an angel?"

"Doesn't Michael seem to show up around Jewish holidays? After all, today is Yom Kippur!"

Ben rubbed his chin and bit his lip. "Seems so," he said reluctantly.

"When's the next special day? Come on, Ben. Think."

"I think," Ben said slowly, "yes, it's the Feast of Tabernacles! I would have to check, but it's probably coming in a week or less."

"Let's have a date that night!" Cindy's voice rang with enthusiasm. "If we're on to something, we ought to be able to make contact with Michael then!"

"If I had told my father about this six months ago, he'd have thought I'd gone nuts! Psychiatrists tend to think spiritual beliefs about God and angels are a psychological crutch. Are they right, Cindy, or are they just spiritually blind and using the massive denial they accuse their patients of? I'm beginning to think the pot is calling the kettle black."

"I won't tell anyone if you don't," Cindy replied. "It's our secret." She reached over and hugged Ben.

■ ■ ■

Several miles away in downtown Los Angeles a contingent of special agents marched up the stairs to the district attorney's office. Brownish smog hung in the air. Cars buzzed by, indifferent to the drama unfolding in front of the halls of justice. Rod Galligher was looking out his second-story window apprehensively, watching the Washington-based investigation crew arrive. He could not see Homelas and Malafidus floating behind the federal officers.

At forty-five, Galligher was relatively young for such a prominent political position. Graying temples imparted dignity and bearing. An ex-Marine, he was known for staying in top physical condition. Galligher was also known for maintaining a no-nonsense posture toward law enforcement. Whatever Rod Galligher did to get elected, he had staunchly maintained his integrity since taking office.

Galligher turned away from the dirty window and spoke to his assistant, Helen Fortier. "Don't like any of it, and I am concerned. We have no choice in the matter, but these agents really bother me. I feel like we're being invaded."

The attractive young woman nodded her head. "I understand." Helen Fortier stood on tiptoe to watch over the attorney's shoulder. "On the phone they sounded more like hit men for the Mafia." Dressed like an ad from *Style* magazine, Helen was both a secretary and a paralegal as well as a good friend. Her black eyes snapped. "Arrogant bunch of jerks." She walked around the desk and plopped down in a desk chair. "Are you ready?"

Galligher clenched his jaw. "Law and order don't seem to mean much to Washington these days. When the attorney general called about this investigation, he brushed aside all questions about due process. I was ordered to follow without question all instructions these men bring with them."

"Real Bad News Bears." Helen Fortier clicked open her briefcase. "I'll try to take careful notes." She laid a small recorder on the table. "We'll keep everything for the record."

"I've got a terrible feeling that I am going to be ordered to take actions that have always been illegal. We want to leave a paper trail."

Helen shrugged. "Certainly, but Damian Gianardo is in complete control these days. I don't think you have much choice anymore."

"No." Galligher pounded on his desk. "We *always* have a choice. The Nuremberg Trials proved that fact. I don't care who these thugs represent, I will not be forced into acquiescing with illegal and immoral directives!"

"It's none of my business, Rod, but I wouldn't try to stand against the tide. People have changed. Everyone's scared to death. The masses don't look at the presidency like citizens did in the past. Gianardo's viewed like a god or superpower. What he says goes . . . without any opposition."

"Not around here while I'm the DA," Galligher snapped.

The door opened, and six men in black suits walked quickly into the inner office. The agents fanned out around the room as if they were taking over. The two demons following them slithered across the room, stopping next to the district attorney and his assistant.

"Agent Adams, representing the president of the United States." The stocky man extended his hand. In his midthirties, Gerald Adams's hair was cropped short, his dark eyes deep-set and hard. "Pleasure to be working with you." He pointed at the men behind him. "Meet agents Miller, Toomey, Pike, Randolph, and Abrams. Each an expert in his field. Computers, forensics, surveillance, research, so forth and so on."

Standing like statues, the men nodded sullenly.

"We must go to work immediately, accessing your entire computer system and particularly all personnel files on police officers. Code names and passwords for all computers are necessary. We need to review psychological profiles to know who will follow instruction without question or reservation."

"Gentlemen," Galligher smiled thinly as he spoke, "we cannot allow public scrutiny of such confidential material. While I understand the priority given your investigation, I must insist we follow the legal procedures of the state of—"

"Excuse me." Agent Adams cut him off. "International legislation now supersedes all state statutes. We are operating on a global level within the framework of the new federation of nations. Nothing is allowed to stand in our way."

"You must understand." Galligher hesitated, biting his lip. "I am responsible for maintaining confidentiality and setting proper standards that—"

Gerald Adams stuck his finger in the DA's face. "You are responsible to do what I tell you! Understand?"

The district attorney's neck and cheeks turned red. "I don't care who you are. I will not have anyone come into the good offices of the people of California and order us around like pawns in some political chess game."

Without answering, Adams brushed past Galligher and strolled behind the DA's desk. Adams raised his eyebrows, a mock frown crossing his lips. "Really?" He dropped down in Galligher's chair. "In about five seconds, I can have you hauled downstairs on a charge of obstruction of justice. If need be, I can take over this entire building with force. I have the armed services of this country at my disposal. Am I communicating?"

Galligher's eyes widened. His jaw dropped.

"I'm not asking permission." Adams leaned over the desk. "I'm giving instructions. Get it?"

Confusing images interrupted Galligher's thinking. A bolt of fear shot down his back. Menacing faces popped into his mind. His usual bold demeanor crumpled. For reasons he couldn't define, the attorney felt weak and incapable.

"Don't toy with me," Adams warned. "I never make idle threats."

Galligher tried to speak but his mouth was dry, his mind addled. Unseen by Rod, Helen, and the federal agents, another conversation was going on in the room.

"I nuked the DA," Homelas boasted to Malafidus. "I touched Galligher's frightening childhood memories of authority figures. He's overpowered. His hard-nosed-attorney front is only a defense against anxieties created by child abuse. Once old Rod's cover is blown, Mr. Tough Guy turns into a quivering four-year-old child again."

"You're next," Malafidus cooed in Helen Fortier's ear. "They are coming to lock you up and throw away the key." The demon bore down. "All this big-time status you've acquired with this high-profile job will vanish in an instant! Why fight the inevitable?"

Agent Adams got up from the district attorney's desk and walked back around to the front. "We will require special assistance." He put his hand on Helen's shoulder. "I'm sure you can expedite matters for us." Gerald Adams smiled salaciously. "Can I depend on you?"

Helen swallowed hard and looked helplessly at the district attorney. "Rod?" her voice was weak and shallow. "What do you suggest?"

Adams picked up the tape recorder lying on the desk. "Rodney would be delighted to have you help me." The agent clicked the machine off. "Any problems there, Rod, old pal?"

Homelas nudged his comrade. "We've picked the right team to get the job done. In short order, we'll be able to reap our revenge. If we play our cards right, we may be able to bag even more scalps than we thought possible."

■ ■ ■

Five days had passed since Ben and Cindy encountered Michael. As the Feast of Tabernacles approached, the words *Jewish carpenter* kept rolling around in Ben's head with disconcerting frequency. When the big night came, the couple settled on a little corner pizza place two blocks from the women's dormitory. As always, Ben and Cindy laughed, kidded, and joked their way through a large pizza and endless refills of soda.

"I guess our little experiment failed," Cindy finally said. "But the evening has still been the best of my life."

Ben did not turn away from Cindy's sightless eyes in the self-conscious way he usually did. Instead he studied Cindy's lovely olive-colored skin and beautifully contoured face.

"You're the most beautiful girl I've ever seen in my life."

Cindy's cheeks turned pink, and she lowered her head.

"I've never known anyone like you." Ben's voice filled with emotion. "I don't want to ever be away from you, Cindy."

"We . . . ah . . . better go." Cindy's voice became softer, lower, more hesitant.

"Don't retreat from me." Ben took her hand.

"Please," Cindy's voice cracked, "don't toy with me. I am a very lonely person, Ben. I've learned to accept the fact, but I can't live with false expectations. It would be too painful."

"Oh, Cindy!" Ben took her hand in both of his. "I would never mislead or use you."

Cindy nodded her head as a tear ran down her cheek.

"You make me very happy." Ben leaned over and kissed her tenderly on her hand. "You can trust me."

"May . . . maybe we should go." Cindy sniffed.

"Yeah," Ben said. "I'm starting to sound like someone on a soap opera."

Laughing, the couple walked out of the restaurant arm-in-arm. Sam trotted along beside Cindy.

Michael turned to Seradim. "Watch carefully. The timing is perfect," Michael concluded. "We'll let them get some distance from the crowd and in an isolated stretch close to the dormitory. Then I'll show up. Let's give our boy a bit more rope."

Ben stopped behind a tree near the door to the dorm. He pulled Cindy back into the shadow and kissed her forcefully.

"You turned out to be my angel tonight, Ben." Cindy ran her hand down the side of his face.

"You really got shortchanged!" Ben kissed her again.

"I've got to give Ben a break," Michael confided. "Let's not completely ruin the moonlight and romance. I'll give them a hint I'm coming." The angel materialized ten feet behind the couple. Sam immediately picked up the sound and barked.

"Someone there?" Cindy called out.

"*Shalom,*" Michael answered.

"It's you!" Ben gasped.

"*Shalom aleichem,*" Michael responded.

"You did come!" Cindy clapped her hands. "I was right. You are an angel!"

"No." Ben shook his head. "I refuse to believe my eyes."

"I want you to meet a friend of mine someday." Michael sounded sincere and serious. "You will enjoy Doubting Thomas. He had a problem similar to yours."

"Why are you here?" Cindy was nearly dancing with glee.

"You're a fraternity prank. I know it!" Ben sounded defensive.

"My Master has a wonderful sense of humor, but I assure you that my reasons for following you are very serious. In fact, it has been my total preoccupation since the day you were conceived."

"If you're really an angel, you should be able to answer questions that no one can know anything about," Ben said critically.

"Sure," Michael answered smugly. "Want to try me?"

"What was my favorite toy as a child?" Ben crossed his arms over his chest.

"You expect me to say a football," Michael said. "You worked hard at convincing everyone you were going to be an athlete because you knew that would please your father. However, your favorite toy was the stuffed bear you secretly slept with until you were well into grade school."

Ben turned white and his mouth fell open. His arms dropped listless at his sides.

"Good question, but not too tough. Cindy, do you have a difficult request for me?"

Cindy thought a moment, obviously enjoying what terrified Ben. "I once had a family keepsake locket that I lost. It was my mother's, and she was very upset when I couldn't find her treasure. It's been years ago, but I would like to have it back. Do you know where it is?"

"Your parents had just started the Golden Dragon, and you helped them put napkins in the holders. You were quite small. Remember?"

Cindy nodded enthusiastically.

"You reached out to find more napkins in the storage cabinet but could not touch anything. When you stretched forward, the necklace fell down inside the cabinet and through a crack in the bottom. If you will move the cabinet, the treasure will be on the floor underneath."

"Wonderful! Wonderful!" Cindy clapped.

"Can you . . . can you read our minds?" Ben's eyes were filled with fear.

"I am your best friend, Ben. You do not have to worry. No, I cannot read your mind. Angels do not do that sort of thing, but we can affect the way you see things. You might say that we nudge you in the right direction."

"Please help us." Cindy said. "We want to believe the right things. We just can't sort it all out. If you work for a Jewish carpenter, then you must know the truth about who Jesus was."

"'Was'?" Michael smiled. "Try 'is.' Ready to find out, Ben?" Ben could only nod.

"His Hebrew name is Yeshua. That's what we call Him in heaven. Angels know that He always existed. When He died on the cross, He had both of you in mind. He has a most special plan for your lives and has sent me to help you find your place in that destiny."

"This is why you have appeared to us?" Ben asked weakly.

"I have important secrets that I cannot yet disclose, but the hour is coming. You will not see me again until Passover next spring, but I will be guiding you toward that time."

"What are we to do now?" Cindy reached out for Michael's hand.

The angel clasped Cindy's palm tenderly. "Keep yourselves pure. Love each other profoundly but chastely. In the days ahead you will need great moral strength."

"Hard time coming?" Ben asked meekly.

"Next year's Passover will be a terrible day for the descendants of Abraham. Cindy, your life will be spent well, and Ben, you shall see the glory of the Lord revealed. Learn now what the love of Yeshua offers, for His love will be your salvation."

Michael held up his hand in a blessing and then was gone.

Ben and Cindy began to weep. They held each other and swayed back and forth as the darkness of night settled over them. Periodically, they said something, but most of the time, they huddled together in silence.

Finally Ben said, "I think I want to pray. I've never really done that . . . I mean in a personal way."

"Me too. You say the words, and I'll follow."

"Jesus . . . Yeshua, we're still very confused, but we must place our faith in You. We want a personal relationship with You, Yeshua, and we also want to believe the right things and get ready for whatever is ahead. Thank You for sending Michael to warn us. I know I've done a lot of selfish things, and I need Your help. Please forgive me where I've messed up in the past . . . today . . . in the future. Thank You for remembering us on Your cross. We now offer You our lives."

After a long silence, Cindy said, "Amen. Thank You, Yeshua."

Michael wept in sheer joy. Seradim lifted his arms toward heaven. The angels immediately tuned in the sounds of eternity. Cherubim and Seraphim were singing in endless praise. "You are God: we praise you. You are the Lord: we acclaim you; You are the eternal Father: All creation worships you." Seradim suddenly joined with the heavenly chorus singing, "Holy, holy, holy Lord, God of power and might.

Heaven and earth are full of Your glory. Thank You for a life saved."

Michael looked toward heaven. He could hear the glorious company of apostles praising God, the noble fellowship of prophets in worship, the white-robed army of martyrs singing. The words of praise thrilled the angel's soul.

He reached out to contact the mind of God. "Come then, Lord, and help all of Your people, bought with the price of Your Own Son's blood, and bring all Your saints to glory everlasting."

# CHAPTER

## 21

The intimidating aura of the White House settled around Agent Gerald Adams like a suffocating blanket of authority. He stood at rigid attention. Secret Service
agents and secretaries hurried down the corridors leading
to and from the Oval Office. Adams stared at the pictures
of the president shaking hands with numerous world dignitaries. Finally the inner door opened and a familiar face
beckoned him to enter.

Agent Adams saluted Jacob Rathmarker as the vice president held the door to the Oval Office open for him. Adams
marched across the bright blue carpet until he stood in
military form in front of the president's desk, waiting
acknowledgment. Damian Gianardo stared out the window
and did not turn around.

"I've followed your work in Los Angeles," Gianardo spoke
without emotion. "Is it true you kept the district attorney
behind bars for several days?"

"Yes, sir." Adams answered hesitantly.

"I understand you took command of the police system in the entire L.A. area." Gianardo turned slowly. "And you did so in my name?"

"Yes, sir!" the agent acknowledged slowly.

"They're screaming from Sacramento to Washington, D.C." The president sounded cool, detached. "Congressional leaders complain you and your men have become more powerful than the FBI. Quite a charge." Gianardo turned around, leaned on his desk, and stared coldly at the special agent. "Do you have any reservations about the accuracy of these reports?"

Agent Adams briskly shook his head. "No, sir."

A twisted smile crossed the president's face. He strolled around his desk and extended his hand. "Congratulations, Agent Adams. Well done."

For the first time the stocky security officer relaxed and smiled. "Why, thank you, Mr. President."

"I'm very pleased with your progress. Set a standard for the rest of the country, Adams. Excellent work!"

"I can report that we have secured essential control of the L.A. police department and they will now do as we order them."

Gianardo nodded. "In perilous and unpredictable times we must keep the population under control . . ." He paused as if carefully framing his words. ". . . to protect our people from radical and divisive elements. Understand?"

"Absolutely."

"I am particularly concerned about future opposition arising from religious elements. Fanatics have always been a threat to social stability and cannot be tolerated in the current climate created by these bizarre disappearances."

"I agree completely." Adams kept nodding his head enthusiastically. "We will soon have infiltrated the entire country with agents trained to identify the nut fringe."

Gianardo pursed his lips thoughtfully. "Southern California has long been a hotbed of religious ferment. Jesus freaks, Eastern religions, drug experimenters, suicide cults, heaven knows what else . . . the smog seems to spawn screwball agitators. I consider Christians to be the most dangerous element of all. They have a long history of creating dissent and turmoil. Remember those disruptive abortion protesters?"

"I will make Southern California an illustration to the nation. Young people can be particularly dangerous. We will target the universities and infiltrate on all levels."

"Excellent!" The president pointed at a chair. "Sit down, please."

Adams settled into a leather chair. "Millions of Christians have disappeared during this strange episode some people call the Rapture. I suspect a plot. Perhaps someone figured out a way to transport them, like getting beamed up in an old *Star Trek* movie. And perhaps the absentees are secretly regrouping for an attack on the government."

Gianardo's eyes narrowed. "An insurrection?"

"Be a perfect setup for a self-made pope."

"Hmmm. Very interesting explanation. In fact, the most insightful answer I've had to date explaining this phenomenon. But could this many people really be in hiding? Where could they have disappeared?"

"Multitudes change their identity every day." Adams's countenance took on an air of smug self-assurance and importance. "In medieval times, the pope and his legions controlled many nations. Why not a new strategy for world domination secretly controlled by some leader we've not yet identified?"

The president stared hard. "Stranger things than I would ever guess happen today." Gianardo looked at the picture of himself and the Egyptian satanist priest, Knudiaon, now hanging on his wall. "The freakish and grotesque seem to have become common. Yes, I suspected some such scheme could be behind these disappearances." The president clenched his fist and pounded his palm. "I want these people crushed, wiped out, and I am giving you the personal authority to do what it takes."

"Thank you for your confidence, Mr. President."

Gianardo curled his lip and jutted his chin forward. Standing with his hands on his hips Mussolini-style, he glared at the agent. "Do this right, Adams, and I'll make you the head of a national secret police bureau to rival anything Stalin ever thought possible."

"Yes, sir!" Adams jumped up and extended his hand. "Consider the job done."

Gianardo shook the agent's hand. "I will be carefully following your progress."

■ ■ ■

The leadership of Community Church gathered in the living room of Ed Parker's rambling ranch-style home. Coffee cups and cookies cluttered the large walnut-inlaid coffee table. The overweight accountant listened carefully to Sylvia Springer lecture the group.

"I know the pastor's wife has moved into an apartment of her own, and they are hiding the fact from the public. She has to be running around with some man. Obviously, the good parson cannot control his own home."

"You're certain?" Ed squinted and grimaced.

"I have it on good authority!" Sylvia tossed her frosted hair as her puffy neck turned pink. "How could you doubt my word? I just can't divulge my sources."

Dr. Stanton Young looked wise and knowing. "No one is doubting you, Sylvia. We just need to be sure of the story. Don't want to be misled down any blind alleys."

Dorothy James pointed her bony finger at the chairman of the pastoral relations committee. "I've been talking to people at all levels of the church. When I explain the facts, no one doubts the seriousness of the problem. Ed, we should have gotten rid of Reynolds two years ago when we first talked about it!"

"Yeah. What are we waiting for?" Sylvia reached for another cookie. "We have more than enough support—everyone thinks Reynolds is wrong for the church."

"Not everyone," Parker cautioned. "I received a concerned call from Joe McCoy. He's standing solidly with the pastor and believes we've started a vendetta to get the man. The McCoys could be trouble."

"Well," Dr. Young drawled as he smiled broadly, "we can't win them all. I think the McCoys' influence can be isolated. After all, they are very new to the church. Not really one of us. I've thought for some time they're just a little too pious for Community Church.

Ed scratched his head and smiled nervously. "I'm worried that Reynolds could really upset the applecart with what he's been preaching lately. Since this Rapture thing, the pastor seems to have radically changed what he believes. Keeps talking about how wrong he's been in the past. I get the feeling his wife really moved out because the preacher has gotten too religious for her."

"He's become quite the fundamentalist," Sylvia agreed.

"Fear!" Dr. Young interjected. "Our pastoral leader has succumbed to fear, like so many have done since this strange disappearance of people, and he's started sounding like a Bible-thumping revivalist. I find that behavior to be as offensive as any of the rest of what we suspect might be true."

Ed nodded. "He's got many other frightened people listening to him. If we get some sort of emotionalism going, the hysteria could overturn the control we now have of the church."

Sylvia Springer defiantly crossed her arms over her rotund stomach. "Now is the time to get this business over with. I vote that we immediately sink Pastor Reynolds's boat and find another preacher at once. Delay only works in his favor."

"Hear! Hear!" Dr. Young applauded.

Ed hesitated. "There is one other matter." He pursed his lips. "I had a strange contact from a government official seeking information on Reynolds. I think you should be aware of this situation."

"Really?" Stanton Young raised his eyebrows. "What's that all about?"

"I don't know, but the man asked questions about whether the pastor really supported the government and the president in particular. I didn't know what to say. He insisted I take his phone number and call him if anything suspicious happened."

"Tell him the truth." Sylvia snorted. "The pastor has said some harsh things about the direction the country is going, and last week he questioned Damian Gianardo's religious values. Made me right mad."

Dr. Young chuckled. "Maybe the government can do the job for us. Possibly Reynolds hasn't been paying his taxes."

"Yeah," Dorothy added. "Tell them the McCoys are with the pastor. Let the government haul the whole bunch of them away."

The group laughed and Ed stood up. "More coffee anyone? Got a fresh pot in the kitchen. No one?" He stretched and looked around his luxurious living room. "Well, I think the more realistic approach is to begin taking concrete steps in the next board meeting to officially remove Reynolds. Sylvia, you may want to raise objections to what he said about the president in his last sermon."

"Sure. And I'd like the phone number of that government agent. I want to know more about what's going on."

■ ■ ■

Frank and Jessica Wong hurried around the kitchen of the Golden Dragon, trying to complete the final cleanup before closing for the evening. Frank put the last crates of vegetables back in the cooler. Cindy sat by the chopping block, quietly patting her dog, Sam. She seemed to be waiting for just the right moment to speak.

"Just about done." Frank stopped and wiped the sweat from his brow. "Not much waste tonight. Good for additional profit. We can leave in only a few more minutes."

Jessica looked up from the large battered and blackened pot she was scrubbing. "You are most quiet tonight, daughter. Are you okay?"

"I have something important to tell you," Cindy said quietly, "when you have time to listen."

"Always have time for honorable daughter." Frank pulled up a stool. "You must be learning great things in your university. Have special insight to tell us?"

"Yes. . . ." Cindy hesitated. "But the most important dis-coveries I've been making lately are . . . religious."

"Religious?" Jessica looked alarmed. "Must be most care-ful. Religion can be very dangerous." She hung the pot on an overhead rack and stopped in front of Cindy.

"What you learn?" Frank scooted closer.

"I've been giving a great deal of attention to what hap-pened to all those people who disappeared. Ben and I study the Bible, and we now believe God took the true Christians out of the world because a terrible war is coming."

Frank's chin dropped. "Another war?" he gasped. "Good heavens!"

"Not just another war," Cindy explained. "A final, great war to end all wars."

Jessica's eyes widened in horror. "We have run from war all our lives. Go from country to country. This is terrible news."

"But there's so much more . . . and it's good. Actually a new day is coming when peace will cover the entire world and God will set up His king to bring harmony to all the nations."

"Amazing!" Frank shook his head in disbelief. "Where you and Ben hear such things?"

"The complete account is in the Bible. Everything we need to do to be ready for this battle is in the sacred Book."

Jessica wrung her hands. "What you say frightens me. I don't know what to say, daughter."

"Mother, I'm learning marvelous insights into who Jesus is."

"Jesus?" Jessica frowned.

"He's the person Christians follow and was the Messiah the Jews expected. I believe I have found the true way through Him."

"Honorable ancestors believe the Buddha taught the way," Frank answered. "But there is no reason we cannot learn from this Jesus. All religions can teach us something worthwhile."

"Father." Cindy nodded respectfully. "Jesus is much more than a teacher. He is God, and He brings God to us and can lead us into a personal relationship with our Creator."

"O—o—h." Frank's eyes widened in consternation. "Never hear of such a thing as meet God."

"How do you know this idea is true?" Jessica's voice took on a skeptical edge. "Sounds very, very strange to me."

"Ben and I studied the Bible and found it is full of predictions coming true today, right now! The Scriptures describe the events leading up to this great war, and the incidents are happening every day. I just turn on the news and the facts are in my face."

Jessica looked at her husband and scowled disapprovingly. Frank raised his eyebrows in consternation.

"But there is more," Cindy continued. "I know what I am telling you is true because . . ." She stopped, cleared her throat, and took a deep breath. "Because I have been visited by an angel."

"Angel!" Jessica's eyes widened in horror.

"An angel named Michael."

Frank stood up and grabbed his chest. "How you know? You can't see anything."

"Michael's been helping me for a long time, and I didn't know he was an angel until he appeared when I was with Ben. Ben saw him come and then disappear."

"An evil spirit!" Jessica screamed. "My daughter is being visited by demons!"

"Just as happened to us when we go to talk to dead ancestors. We are all doomed!" Frank covered his eyes.

"Stop it!" Cindy pounded the counter. Sam jumped. "I won't tell you any more unless you calm down."

Jessica and Frank huddled together, staring at their child. "You may go to college and read many books, but we know about such matters," Jessica whined. "Chinese people know about terrible reality of demons. Great harm comes from these evil creatures. You are mixed up in frightening business, good daughter."

Cindy took a deep breath. "Please, Mother. Just listen to me. Michael saved me from an attacker and has been the best bodyguard any person could ever have. Believe me, he is no demon."

Frank kept shaking his head. "This Christian business no better than the rest. Daughter now hovers over the brink of disaster. Oh, Buddha, help us!"

" P—l—e—a—s—e." Cindy shook her head in disgust. "I am trying to tell you of the most important discovery anyone can ever make and you're turning this conversation into Halloween time."

"We hear all we can take for one night." Jessica waved her daughter away. "Please no more tonight."

"I can't believe my ears." Cindy slid off the stool and pulled Sam's harness. "Okay. I won't tell you any more, but if a big guy named Michael shows up, don't mess with him. He's dynamite!"

"No more! No more!" Jessica hurried out of the kitchen with Frank scurrying behind.

"Come on, Sam. Let's walk home. You make more sense than they do."

# CHAPTER
## 22

Watching from the other side of time, Michael turned to Seradim. "What have you observed in these scenarios we have been watching?"

"Wickedness and ignorance," he responded instantly. He again conjured up images from inside the Oval Office and Ed Parker's home. "Obviously the Antichrist will manipulate the security agents into hurting and even killing many people. The church committee is going to crucify the pastor. But I am mystified and amazed at how reactionary the Wongs were."

Scenes of Jessica and Frank fleeing the kitchen reappeared. "They are not even hearing their daughter."

"People don't listen well," Michael commented. "Sounds bounce around in their ears, but they seldom focus their attention on what is truly happening around them. Preoccupation causes emotional and spiritual deafness. Emerged in constant noise and stimulation, human beings lose their capacity to tune in the music of nature and the resonance of eternity. They hear only the static of business."

"Tragic."

"Now what should we do, Seradim?"

"We must immediately plunge through the time barrier and straighten these messes out. I suggest we descend on this dangerous little demagogue, Agent Adams, and let him know how the L.A. district attorney felt when Adams dropped him in jail. Next, we clean house in Community Church before these supercilious busybodies hurt a good man. We know the truth about Pastor Reynolds and—"

"Stop there," Michael interrupted. "Why are you getting ready to go to battle?"

"Why?" Seradim looked shocked. "Because that's our job! We have to protect our friends."

"Someone told you to do this?"

The junior angel felt short-circuited. "Well, not exactly."

"You had some suggestion from somewhere to act?"

Seradim was speechless. "Well, no."

Michael bore down. "In some ways, we are very much like humans. Both angels and people have one supreme lesson to learn, and the time has come for you to grasp this basic principle."

Seradim blinked several times. "Am I not called to do the business of God?"

"And what is the business of God?"

Seradim went blank.

"People get into great trouble by assuming they know what God has in mind when they are only doing their own will. Community Church's 'hang-the-preacher club' are quite sure they are about the business of God. Crusaders and inquisitors were no less zealous for the intentions of God as they maimed and murdered their way across Europe."

Seradim shook his head in dismay. "I don't understand."

"Only one thing is needful, friend." Michael consoled his charge. "Obedience. We are called to find the mind of the Father first. Our business is not to do something *for* God; but what God *wants* done. There is a great difference."

The trainee squirmed, searching for some appropriate response.

"Our job isn't to do what we think *might* please the Father. Our responsibility is to listen first so we do *exactly* what the Almighty wills. And humans have the same task, although most go through an entire lifetime and never get the message."

"Obedience?"

"The difference between life and death is in that one simple concept. Disobedience began in Eden, and obedience was completed on Calvary. Lucifer and his followers fell because of rebellion. Eternal life came back to the world because of the submission of Jesus."

"But . . ."

"We must learn how to use our freedom," Michael instructed. "Angels and humans have the same capacity of choice. Our most basic task is to choose what the Father intends."

"But surely He would want us to stop those destructive people at the church."

"Really?" Michael smiled. "The Lord told you so?"

Seradim gestured aimlessly. "No."

"Then you must not presume on what is not given."

"I just don't understand."

"You must learn an important insight into how the will of God operates. Let's look in on how things have gone with Jimmy Harrison as the months and years have gone by. The Rapture and the loss of his parents brought Jimmy to his own crisis of faith, and he turned his life over to the Lord. Take a look."

Seradim watched as scenes from Jimmy's life flowed past like a VCR on fast speed. He watched Jimmy plod away at the car lot in Laguna Niguel, selling everything in sight. Jimmy quickly acquired 10 percent of the business and was doing well while he prospered spiritually. Seradim smiled, observing Jimmy's relationship with Ruth deepen into true and meaningful devotion.

Michael pointed to the scene. "There are laws of psychology, sociology, society, relationships, and human dynamics at work. Jimmy labors; he prospers. The young man turns to God; God turns to him. You are seeing the order God placed in the universe working."

"Yes," Seradim answered without fully comprehending.

"We don't interfere with God-ordained principles. We work in accord with the Creator's purposes. Angels respect what the Almighty started in the beginning."

"I think I understand."

Michael pointed through the veil of time. "Let's go down and watch what is happening." Seconds later the two angels were inside a Southern California restaurant.

Jimmy and Ruth were finishing a romantic Valentine's Day supper at the five-star Five Crowns restaurant in Corona del Mar. Cindy and Ben had joined them. The Tudor-style restaurant was elegant with its stucco-covered walls decorated with English coats of arms and hunting trumpets.

Cindy ran her sensitive fingers over the fine linen tablecloth. "We know that God is going to take care of us," she said quietly. "No matter what . . ."

"Things have completely changed." Ben passed the thick-sliced homemade bread around again. "In the past, I wouldn't have given much consideration to anything more serious than my next want. Now we're caught up in a great adventure. I know bad stuff is out there, but I feel alive and part of something very exhilarating. Sure, we have some very formidable enemies, but we're on the side that's ultimately going to win . . . although the Bible says that vast numbers of believers will die during the Great Tribulation."

"We have Michael watching over us." Cindy cut into her petite filet.

The senior angel turned to his charge. "Yes, we're watching," Michael said, "but we must not keep humans from the sovereign will of God or the natural consequences of their decisions. Our job is to fight off the demons when it is appropriate, but we must never take away the autonomy that is vital to human development."

Seradim rubbed his chin, pondering the scene carefully. "Why not?"

"People grow by overcoming obstacles. Struggle perfects their faith and character. If we remove barriers or make the struggle easier, we ultimately diminish what humans can become. Remember the attack on Pastor Reynolds? We can't pull people like the pastor out of the fire without cheating them of an important opportunity to become stronger."

Seradim nodded slowly. "So, I can't fight their battles for them?"

"Not the ones they must face to develop endurance, patience, additional strength, and the capacity to love."

Ben looked at his sister as he spoke. "Our lives used to be flat and overindulged. We were spoiled rich kids, but that's behind us. I wouldn't go back to the old days for anything."

"Me too!" Jimmy agreed. "I just didn't realize how important my father's ministry was. He was in the real battle every day of his life."

Michael nudged his charge. "See! Jimmy and Ben are getting the picture. They have become different people through turmoil."

Ruth reached out for Jimmy's hand. "I don't know how much time we have left together." Her voice was low and intense. "Who knows what tomorrow will bring? We have to make the most of every second."

"Yes," Jimmy said soberly. "I'm afraid you're right. Our great adventure is going to be filled with drastic uncertainties."

"I think we need to take advantage of this very moment," Ruth insisted. "I have the perfect idea for finishing the evening. What better time to get married than Valentine's Day?"

Jimmy started to laugh, but something in Ruth's decisiveness checked him. "You're not kidding."

"No, I'm not. Jimmy, I want to marry you tonight."

Ben and Cindy almost stopped breathing.

"To . . . tonight?" Jimmy stuttered.

"Why not? We love each other, and that's all that matters."

"But I thought you'd want a big wedding . . . the white dress . . . the walk down the aisle." Jimmy kept blinking his eyes.

"In a short while we may be dying." Ruth's voice became almost a whisper. "I don't want to face that moment alone. More important, I want us to be together through every step of the way into eternity. I say let's go for it tonight!"

"But . . . how?" Jimmy was uncharacteristically befuddled. "Where?"

"Mexico!" Cindy and Ruth said at the same time.

"Sure!" Ben clapped. "Mexico is only an hour and a half from here. For a couple of bucks anything's possible there. We could leave right now and have you married before midnight."

"Midnight?" Jimmy swallowed hard and then beamed. "Why not?"

"Let's go!" Ruth stood up. "I'm ready to become Mrs. Jimmy Harrison on Valentine's Day."

Seradim began slowly nodding. "Love wouldn't be possible without having free choice, would it? This scene couldn't have happened without the couple having the unencumbered ability to make their own decisions."

"You've got it, Seradim. Our job now is to protect the couples on their way to Tijuana. The world is filled with improbabilities—unexpected, random events. Accidents happen. We can help them over these intrusions so their own choices can blossom and come to full flower. But we must use discernment in recognizing what is the appropriate action at any moment."

Seradim and Michael gently ascended out of the restaurant and hovered above the couples' car as it sped south on Interstate 5 toward the Mexican border. The young angel turned to his mentor.

"How can I make sure I'm reading the signals right?"

"Always turn to the mind of God. Tune in His purposes. Only then will you know you are acting in obedience and not presumption."

"But don't the purposes of God override human decisions?"

"The purposes of God are final and ultimate. Only in the mystery of the mind of the Almighty are His plans fully comprehensible. One of the reasons we are here is to make sure the Evil One can't frustrate God's plan for Ben, Cindy, Ruth, and Jimmy. We must fight to keep the demons from interfering in those arrangements."

"I understand much better."

"Human existence is a complex interaction between the laws of the universe, random chance events, and the final purposes of God," Michael explained. "Our job is to help the process work and keep the devil's army from creating chaos. Lucifer never liked playing by the rules."

The angels watched the wedding and the return trip. The newlyweds were dropped off at Jimmy's apartment, and Ben took Cindy back to her dorm.

"What do you think is ahead for us?" Ben asked as he pulled in front of the dorm.

Cindy felt the window of the door as if rubbing a magic looking glass. "I don't know." She seemed to be peering out into the black night. "The angel said . . ." She stopped.

"I guess we can't get married." Ben was clearly pained. "I don't understand it. Michael seemed to be clear that we were to maintain a certain proper distance."

"Perhaps we are to develop a perfect love for each other." Cindy turned toward Ben. "Maybe in heaven . . ."

"I don't want to wait for heaven." Ben groaned. "I want now. I envy Jimmy tonight. Cindy, you'd be heaven enough for me."

"We must trust God to know best." Cindy leaned against Ben. "You have something important to do in the days ahead, and we must not do anything that could spoil your purpose."

Michael beamed. "Cindy has caught the vision. Only by allowing them the freedom to slip could we give Ben and Cindy the opportunity to develop such maturity. Let's follow Ben home."

By the time Ben returned to his room it was three o'clock. In spite of near exhaustion, he lay on the bed praying. "What is it You want from me?" he finally cried out. "I don't understand." Releasing the last grasp of frustration, Ben fell into a deep sleep.

Michael and Seradim listened intensely to both his silent and spoken prayers. "You will know soon enough," Michael answered. "Soon enough."

As the two angels left, the senior angel instructed his charge. "The couples are reaching out for the Father's highest purposes. They will not be disappointed! When we fall on the will of God, all trains arrive on schedule."

# CHAPTER
## 23

Jennifer watched her children glare at her from across the den. It was late, she was tired, and now exasperated. Jennifer caught her breath and tried another approach. "Your father and I are not trying to cram anything down your throats. We appreciate the pressure your friends are putting on you, but these matters are very serious. The government is investigating Christians. We could be in deep trouble very quickly. We need your cooperation."

Erica crossed her arms over her chest and rolled her eyes contemptuously. "O-o-o, James Bond stuff. Give me a break. R-e-a-l-ly!"

Family strife attracted the demons like the scent of fresh meat brought to wolves. Homelas and Malafidus immediately descended through the McCoys' roof and slipped through the walls. One demon inched next to Joe Jr. and the other cuddled close to Erica. Each of the apparitions began slowly breathing into the ears of the children.

Joe Jr. smirked at his mother. "What a pain! Everything was fine until you started going to that stupid church and turned into religious wombat freakos. Next, we got embroiled in all the stupid fighting with these church people who have the maturity of a bunch of monkeys in a zoo. Now, we have to pray before we eat. Pray before we sleep. Pray before we think. Bor—i—n—g."

"Stop it!" Jennifer bit her lip, trying not to explode. "You are two over-indulged, spoiled brats who can't see any farther than the latest MTV slice of immorality. I'm tired of your self-centered preoccupation with nothing more significant than the designer label on your clothes."

Homelas nudged Malafidus. "Olé! Mom's about to pop! If we can keep the pressure up, maybe we can create a real screaming fight. Let's really rattle Miss Pious in front of the kids."

"Gosh," Erica choked. "I've never heard you talk like *that* before."

"Yes, and that's part of the problem," Jennifer shot back. "I've let the two of you grow up as nothing more than a pale reflection of this spineless society. Now your father and I are paying the price."

Erica hesitantly looked at her brother and shrugged. "It's just that I think we have the right to choose our own religion and—"

"You don't have a religion," her mother interrupted. "And since when did you start choosing the important things in your life? You don't decide whether or not you're going to school or to a doctor when you're sick. So don't tell me about whether or not you're going to church."

Homelas flinched. "Stop the religion talk if you can. Head it off! We've got to keep a wedge between the children and the parents. It's essential this conversation turn nasty."

"You've got to admit there's a problem." Joe Jr. came off the couch shaking his finger like an attorney on cross examination. "The leaders of that stupid Community Church are after the preacher like a pack of wild dogs, and they're saying bad stuff about you and Dad. Why should we go some place we're not welcome?"

Jennifer took another deep breath. "I'm trying to tell you children how serious the issues are. It isn't a matter of going to this or that church. Evil has been unleashed in the world, and terrible things are ahead. Do you understand?"

Joe Jr. rolled his shoulders indifferently. "Sorry, Mom. Just can't see the problem. All this bizarre political stuff going on in Washington doesn't interest me any more than this squabble over the preacher and his wife. Count me out."

Erica stared at the floor. "It's getting late, Mom. I've still got some homework to finish, and I'm tired." She edged toward the door.

Malafidus sent a message to Joe Jr. "Cut out of here while the getting is good. Move on while your mother's not looking."

Jennifer rubbed her forehead and stared at her daughter. "Time is running out," she implored.

"That's exactly my point." Erica slipped into the hall and hurried for the stairs. "I'm going to bed."

When Jennifer turned back, Joe Jr. had disappeared down the hall. She sank into the overstuffed chair and buried her face in her hands.

"Excellent!" Malafidus applauded. "She not only has been defeated, but she feels the loss. Look at the pain in her face."

"Heavenly Father, help me." Jennifer's prayer rose from the depth of her soul. "Please help me to know how to witness to my children and offer them the new life we've found."

Jennifer prayed for nearly twenty minutes until she was finally interrupted by Joe Jr.'s return to the den. Avoiding her, he sat down in front of the large-screen TV and switched it on.

"I want to watch TV." He kept hitting the clicker. "You don't have to say anything. I won't even get near the MTV channel. At least not as long as you're here." He laughed at his little joke.

To Joe's amazement, every channel was preempted by a special news bulletin from Jerusalem, where it was already morning. The excited voices of announcers were explaining an amazing phenomenon that was occurring. The broadcasts kept repeating news clips of clouds boiling and swirling above the Mount of Olives. Two figures descended slowly out of the clouds toward the earth.

Joe's mouth dropped. "Is this science fiction," he finally stammered, "or is this for real?"

Jennifer blinked and moved closer to the TV. Brilliant light flooded the terrain as the two figures moved over the ground as if they were floating. The news anchor explained that the two figures kept changing languages, speaking flawless Russian, Arabic, Chinese, English, and Spanish.

"Man!" Joe Jr. cheered and shook his arms. "What a cool program."

Jennifer slowly rose to her feet. "I . . . I . . . I . . . know what's happening. Good grief. I read about this prediction in the Bible. It is the Jewish festival called Purim, and sacrifices will cease in Israel if Jimmy Harrison's predictions are right."

Joe turned around to his mother and frowned. "Come on, Mom. Please give it a rest. This is TV."

"Those two men are . . . are . . . Moses and Elijah. I just know it."

Joe laughed. "Mom, you're as big a weirdo as those two guys in long robes."

The CNN correspondent was visibly shaking. His assistant aimed his TV camera at the two giants. "In an early morning meeting on this day of Purim," the reporter announced, "Gianardo ordered Israel to halt animal sacrifices, and now this unbelievable duo from who knows where is descending from the sky. Are they space aliens? Are they two of the people who were beamed up two years ago?"

The larger of the two figures pointed his finger directly into the TV camera. His deep-set black eyes looked as if they could pierce steel. "Hear me!" he said in perfect English. "We have come that you might hear the final witness of the Holy One of Israel. Listen well, lest your own words become testimony against you. The hour of accounting is at hand!"

A correspondent inched forward holding a microphone at arm's length as if to protect himself. "Who . . . who might we . . . ah . . . be . . . ah . . . talking with?"

"Moses!" the huge man roared, his voice sounding as if it might shake the mountain. "I have come with my heavenly colleague. Behold, Elijah the Tishbite!"

The correspondent fell backward, and the two figures moved past him down the hill.

"It *is* Moses!" Jennifer's hand came to her mouth. "Just like the Bible predicted. Moses and Elijah have returned."

Joe's smile faded and bewilderment crossed his face. He stared at his mother. Terror filled his eyes.

Malafidus reached for Homelas. "What . . . what's . . . happening?"

The demon put his hands to his ears. "By the fires of hell itself! I've heard such a thing was predicted." Homelas retreated from the television set.

"We've got to get out of here," Malafidus choked. "Got to get to headquarters and find out what's going on."

"The Jews are always the source of the trouble," Homelas whined. "Someone should have nuked Jerusalem long ago. Nothing but trouble ever comes out of there."

The two demons disappeared into the blackness.

■ ■ ■

Very early the next morning, after phone calls from the McCoys and calls to Jimmy and Ruth, Larry and Sharon Feinberg replayed their video recording of the day's events in Jerusalem for the fifth time. Sharon stared at the Bible in her lap. "The whole event is right here." She put her finger in the book of Revelation. "We have watched eternal history in the making today."

"Jimmy is right in his conclusion," Larry answered. "We must leave this country and go to Israel before Passover if Jimmy's predictions are right. Bozrah is going to be the only divinely protected city of refuge for the Jewish people. As a Jew and a doctor, I have no choice but to be there to help our own."

Sharon nodded. "Ancient Bozrah is known as Petra now, and it's the place prepared for us in the wilderness, mentioned in Revelation and Isaiah and Obadiah. Jesus even alluded to it indirectly in Matthew 24."

"If we are anywhere else in the world after the Antichrist desecrates the temple, as Daniel warned, then we'll be

killed," Larry added. "Especially Jewish believers in Jesus."
He consulted the map in his Bible. "Petra is in Jordan, sixty
or seventy miles southeast of Jerusalem. We'll have to act
like tourists. Pack our necessities and get there before
Passover. Jimmy says Passover is when the worst Jewish holocaust in history will start and then Yeshua will return 1,260
days later."

Sharon looked around their luxurious home. "Hard to
leave all this behind."

"We had relatives in Europe before the Holocaust who
had the same choice," Larry concluded sadly. "Those who
decided not to leave paid for their reluctance with their
lives."

"Jimmy and Ruth will go with us, but I know Ben will stay
here and try to help the students he works with. He won't
leave Cindy and her family behind."

Larry shook his head. "I felt great pain when Jennifer
and Joe said they must stay because their kids are sucked
into the ideas Gianardo and his associates are putting out.
We must pray constantly for the conversion of those young
people."

Sharon took her husband's hands. "Events are going to
move very fast. We can expect Gianardo to seize all remaining power. Many will die."

A long silence fell between them. Only the sound of the
ticking of the hall clock filled the room.

"Everything we've held dear in this place will soon be
gone," Sharon finally spoke.

"We will be wanderers on the face of the earth once
again."

"Our people always have been." Tears ran down Sharon's
cheeks. She slipped to her knees in front of the couch.
Looking toward the ceiling, she prayed fervently. *"Shema*

*Israel Adonai elahonu echad.* "Tears filled her eyes. *"Echad ela-honu gadol Adonenu kadosh shmo."*

"Maranatha," Larry answered. "Come quickly, Lord Jesus."

# CHAPTER
## 24

As did the McCoys, Frank and Jessica Wong began each day by tuning in the events unfolding in Jerusalem. They watched the cameras panning the two white-bearded prophets. Crowds lined up to stare at the scene in front of the Western Wall where Moses and Elijah were sitting.

They found it nearly impossible to grasp what was occurring in this scene, which both intrigued and terrified them. Cindy tried to explain, but her parents inevitably were left confused and mystified.

"We have nowhere left to run." Frank winced. "How can we hide from such strange events?"

Jessica nodded frantically. "The world has gone crazy. People filled with madness. I fear for Cindy. She and Ben stand too close to the fire."

"I just don't understand who these two men really are. I can't comprehend their religion. Very strange."

The screen blurred and the scene shifted. The words *Fast-Breaking News Alert* covered the screen. An announcer declared, "An important series of statements is anticipated momentarily from the vice president of the United States and the prime minister of Israel." A picture of the hastily rebuilt Temple in Jerusalem appeared. Surrounded by troops, Gianardo and Rathmarker stood in front of the reconstructed edifice on the Temple Mount.

As the announcer continued, the president walked around the sacred precincts of the Temple as if there were no boundaries or limitations to visitors. The high priest followed Gianardo, frantically trying to wave him away. A microphone had been set up just outside the Holy of Holies. The presidential seal was being attached as the announcer said the prime minister of Israel was ready to make a statement.

The prime minister shuffled to the microphone and began reading from a crumpled sheet of paper. "The New Roman Empire called the Knesset into session this morning and demanded that control of all nuclear capacity be turned over to them. Failure to comply would bring immediate attack upon our country. We had no choice but to comply and have now done so. Mr. Gianardo has also demanded that we recognize him as the supreme ruling power in the world. Failure to do so would invite disaster. The president of the New Roman Empire obviously does have supreme authority." The old man stepped backward, staring at the ground.

In a hushed voice, the announcer said, "Vice President Jacob Rathmarker will now make a response."

Rathmarker moved quickly to the microphone. "Thank you, Mr. Prime Minister. We are gathered at this place as a matter of principle. Clearly, the New Roman Empire is uniting the globe in order to create a more just and decent world. We are the last hope for a peaceful order. The empire will insist on nonaggression even at the price of going to war in order to stop killing. However, global order demands recognition of our authority at every level. History records that religion has been a constant source of strife and conflict. As you know, immoral animal sacrifices were stopped a month ago. Today, on your Passover, we are going to put an end to further religious discord."

Rathmarker whirled around and jerked a section of the huge curtain open, letting outside light flood into the holiest place. The priest screamed and the Israeli prime minister dropped to his knees, but Rathmarker marched into the center of the sacred chamber, deliberately knocking aside a golden plate of incense. Calmly, the vice president returned to the microphone.

"No longer will Damian Gianardo be known as president. As of this moment, his title shall be world emperor, and I will be prime minister of the New Roman Empire. Our authority extends over matters of state *and* religion. As it is treason to resist the secular office, so shall it be sedition to oppose our religious authority. We will not allow anyone in the religious community to stand in the way of global peace. Those two impostors by the Western Wall who call themselves Moses and Elijah will submit to our rule or face the same penalty." Rathmarker stopped and glared at the Israeli prime minister. "No longer will religious charlatanism be tolerated in any form!"

An ominous quiet fell over the crowd. No one moved. People stared in terrified awe.

Rathmarker declared, "Today, I will place a life-size statue of Emperor Gianardo in the center of the Holy of Holies so no one forgets where ultimate control and authority lie."

Frank Wong turned to Jessica. "Honorable wife, do you understand? Did he say they kill the two holy men?"

Jessica shook her head. "Apparently, Mr. President now take over all religion. Very frightening."

"Reporters and priests seem very upset that president now walk around inside most holy room." Frank pulled closer to the screen. "Gianardo run everything now . . . everywhere. Such a man is greatly to be feared."

■ ■ ■

At that moment Michael and Seradim stood among the throngs of Guardians observing the same event. Behind them stood the Thrones. These angels, who conveyed the juridical power of God, standing in rapt attention, scrutinized Gianardo walking into the Holy of Holies. Anger seethed from the depths of their beings. Above the hosts of angels the Dominions and Virtues hovered, poised to attack. From out of the center of heaven, Gabriel led the archangels in a flurry of activity while the Principalities prepared for war in Jerusalem.

"Not yet," the Divine Voice rumbled from the very center of the essence of light itself. "Hold steady until the full measure of evil is fulfilled. The hour is close at hand, and the bowls of wrath will be poured out on those who kill My chosen ones; but the time is not yet."

Michael and Seradim instantly received their special instructions and knew what to do. The resonance of the voice of God continued to ring through their beings long after the content of His message was received.

Michael turned to his charge. "Ready?"

Seradim's countenance became intense. "I have learned much of waiting for the divine timing. Yes, I will be obedient to that which the Father speaks, and I am prepared to follow His word to the end."

"Then we are ready to return. We must visit Ben and Cindy immediately. We have a message to deliver. They are watching TV in the Feinbergs' living room."

Seradim paused. "Why would Ben and Cindy receive such special delivery when other people hear nothing?"

"In the economy of God," Michael explained, "special leaders are singled out for unique tasks. At those moments, the Father gives them specific and distinct direction. The Virgin Mary was instructed about the future. Saul was given the insight that would allow him to become the apostle Paul. Now the time has come to inform Ben and Cindy about their future assignments."

The angels instantly thought themselves through the time barrier and shot like heavenly rockets into the Feinberg home, settling just behind the couch where Ben and Cindy were talking. Michael slipped into human form and stepped toward them.

Sam looked up and barked.

"Someone's here!" Cindy jumped.

"Be not afraid." Michael's voice was hushed.

Ben leaped up from the couch. "Michael! You're here!"

"Yes." Michael walked in front of them. "The moment has arrived for me to give you complete instructions. Events are moving quickly. The next three and a half years will seem like both an eternity and a flash of time. Some days will feel totally unbearable, but in retrospect they will be a blur. Ben, I want you to know beyond any doubt that you can and will survive. Long ago you were chosen for these assignments because we knew that your family had the capacity and the ability to endure during these last times."

"My family?"

"The Feinbergs are from the tribe of Levi. Even though you have largely ignored your heritage, you come from the priestly lineage. You carry a godly capacity to stand before the heavenly Father on behalf of others. Once again your family will fulfill their call."

"We're not prepared for such a thing. . . ."

"To the contrary! Who has a better analytic mind than you, Ben? You're the family chess master. Your ability to strategize will serve your survival needs quite well, and we will protect you."

"But my parents?"

"The Holy Spirit is currently drawing multitudes of Jews to Petra–Bozrah where they are already safe. Many will need medical attention, but far more will be so traumatized by the catastrophes unfolding around them that their emotional care will be paramount. The members of your family are extremely well equipped for the work. The hand of God will protect the area, and no one will be able to hurt them there."

Cindy slowly raised her hand. "You said 'survive.' Sounds like Ben's going to be a general in a war. That's scary."

"Sit down, children. Listen well."

Ben picked up a pencil and a pad.

"Gianardo has committed the ancient sin of Babel, thinking he can stand tall enough to shoot an arrow into the heart of God. Even as we speak, secret security squads are already beginning to kill millions of Jews, especially Jews who believe in Jesus as predicted in Revelation chapter 12 two thousand years ago. Nothing is left to restrain this man's arrogance."

"What can we possibly do?" Cindy shook her head. "A blind Oriental girl and a Messianic Jew aren't going to make much difference."

"Yes, you will. Cindy, you are going to become a key helper in our counterintelligence operation. In some instances, you will automatically know what to do. At other times, I will direct you to the people you are to contact. You will be bringing hope and insight during these final days. The first point of contact will be your fellow students at UCLA."

"Amazing," Ben exclaimed.

"We know you have a heart for the task. Ben, you are one of the 144,000 chosen ones mentioned in the book of Revelation. No one can harm you in any way. Others will be killed, including believing Jews, but not you. Cindy, however, has no guarantees."

"Please tell us everything you can," Cindy pleaded. "We'll need all the insight you have for us."

"First, I want you, Ben, to move your operation to a more secluded place. I will lead you beyond Los Angeles to an obscure house in the country, which will become your center of ministry. Next, you need to share all of this information with the McCoys. They will assist you in your outreach."

Ben nodded but shot a worried look at Cindy. "We have shortwave contact with my parents in Petra–Bozrah. I can't wait to share your instructions with them."

"You must be very cautious, Ben. As soon as Gianardo's secret police are fully functional, they will have the capacity to monitor all radio contact."

For the next few minutes Ben and Cindy discussed with Michael the implications of his directions. The full scope of their involvement and the danger became more apparent as each detail fell into place. Finally Cindy asked, "What can we expect next?" She reached for Ben's hand.

"We saw the white horse of the Apocalypse when Giannardo seized world power after the Rapture. Russia's defeat last Av 9 in Israel was the red horse of the Apocalypse. The widespread famines throughout the lands of Africa and Russia and her allies was the black horse of Revelation chapter six.

"And now the pale horse of the Apocalypse, Death, has begun to ride, my children. War, famine, plagues, and wild animals will be used as vehicles of judgment. The alarm is being sounded, and none will be able to say that they were not warned. You will see great consternation everywhere. Twenty-five percent of the world population will die in the next few months, but fear not. The Lord Yeshua is with you to the very end of the age. I always stand in the shadows."

■ ■ ■

Across the city, the McCoys were engrossed in the special news program. As the last words of the emperor's speech faded, Joe turned the TV set off. "Now, children, do you see the truth? This is exactly what your mother and I have been saying would happen."

"Great guess, Dad." Joe Jr. shrugged. "But I had a hunch that religion was the next thing Gianardo would go for. After all, he's already picked up most of the chips."

Jennifer shook her hands at the ceiling. "Children! This is a life-and-death matter. Don't you understand what's ahead?"

"Sure," Joe Jr. said forcefully. "I'd shelve all that religion talk you've been having with the Feinbergs. You could get all of us into a lot of trouble."

"Please, Mom," Erica begged, "get rid of those Bibles. One of my friends might see them and think that Joe and I approve of what you're doing."

"Children," their father begged with tears in his eyes, "you've got to change your minds. We're not only trying to avoid trouble. Our eternal destiny is at stake. Don't you understand?"

# CHAPTER
## 25

Special Agent Gerald Adams looked around the dimly lit room at the strike force assembled in the commandeered Los Angeles district attorney's office. He knew each man fit the psychological profile of a sociopath. Suffering did not touch this crew; they could inflict pain without the slightest tinge of remorse. The agents were his kind of guys.

"We suspect treasonous activity throughout this entire area," Adams lectured the group. "A number of religious groups and churches are under surveillance. In fact, we have operatives in some local congregations already. However, we must infiltrate more churches, clubs, and college campuses until we have an ironclad grip on the entire state of California. Understand?"

Affirmation rippled across the room.

"We are also monitoring all radio signals and computer-generated transmissions—any form of international contact. By tracing these communiqués back to their origins, we'll be able to pinpoint the location of any troublemakers. Once we've got 'em in sight, we'll hit 'em hard."

A man in the back raised his hand. "Robert Schultz, sir. Just transferred in from Atlanta, Georgia. When we locate culprits, how long do we wait for due process? Are search warrants still necessary?"

Adams shook his head. "We're special forces, envoys of the president of the United States and world emperor." He chuckled. "Almost above and beyond the law. Seriously, let's not push our luck and hit some uninvolved citizen by mistake. Creates a backlash. But when we're on to the real thing, strike first and ask questions later."

"And if there's resistance?"

"Mr. Schultz, in the case of hard-core religious fanatics, we can also claim they attacked us first. Shoot 'em. We can control the press. Gianardo wants a high body count on the subversives."

The agents smiled at each other knowingly.

"We've been looking for this sort of climate for years," Adams continued. "An environment in which we can do our job without having to contend with meddling lawyers and bleeding heart judges. Let's do it right."

■ ■ ■

Ben and Cindy's student ministry on the UCLA campus proved to be extraordinarily successful. Explosive conditions around the world and political tyranny in the United States created a natural backlash among many intelligent students. Affiliating with Christians was a convenient way to oppose the government. Along the way, many of the students discovered the truth about Jesus. Student rebellion turned into personal conversions.

But the rebellion of the McCoy children continued no matter how hard the parents tried. Circumstances, however, were changing.

Adams's men showed up at Newport Union Harbor High School. In Erica McCoy's class, students were piling into their chairs and completely ignoring the teacher's attempts to call the class to order. Mary Higbie, Erica's arch rival, sat next to her. Erica kept talking to a boy beside her in order to ignore Mary.

"Please!" The teacher pounded on the desk. "We have a special speaker. I need your attention for an important announcement."

The students continued talking as if nothing had been said. Erica flipped a paper wad at a boy several rows over.

From the other side of time, Michael beckoned for Seradim to follow him. "Erica is going to need our encouragement. This could be an opportune moment for us to touch her life. Let's go."

The two angels settled on each side of the teenager. Michael instructed Seradim, "Concentrate on how much Erica's parents care for her."

"Stop it!" The teacher slammed a book on her desk. The boom echoed across the room. "What do I have to do to get your attention? Kill someone?" Students jeered and applauded the suggestion but quieted down.

"We have a representative of the office of education. Now listen carefully to what he's got to say. Please welcome Mr. Robert Schultz."

"Recognize him?" Michael asked.

"That's one of Adams's special agents!" Seradim declared. "He must be a plant in the education department."

The tall, lean man walked to the center of the room with an indifferent swagger. His voice was cold and hard. "I'm here to talk about abuse. As you know, the educational system takes all forms of abuse very seriously. Anyone who reports sexual, physical, or emotional abuse will receive immediate care and protection. We simply will not allow parents to take advantage of their children."

"Yippee!" A youth in the back row yelled. "Can you come out and work my old man over? He's been short on my allowance lately."

The class roared.

Schultz walked down the row until he stood in front of the teen. Suddenly the undercover agent lifted the boy completely out of his chair. "You have something to report?"

The astonished student's mouth dropped as he silently shook his head no.

"If you have nothing intelligent to say, then don't interrupt." Schultz let the student drop back into the chair. His notebook went flying off the desk.

"We're not out here playing games." Schultz continued walking through the desks. "Abuse is serious business, and we take it seriously."

The room was completely silent.

"Today we have identified a new form of abuse . . . religious abuse. Understand?"

No one spoke.

Michael breathed heavily on Erica. "Listen, child. Listen to the man's words. Notice what's really happening in this room. Listen to his threats."

Schultz leaned over the desk and stared at the kids on the front row. "The leader of our country is now the supreme authority on all religious matters. Noncompliance can be very deadly business. We will not allow rampant misrepresentation of religious truth to be disseminated through our society. Should your parents fail to comply, they could be putting you in jeopardy. Such action would constitute abuse."

"I don't understand." Erica held up her hand. "Please give me an example."

"If your parents try to force on you religious ideas that are not approved by Emperor Gianardo," Schultz spoke slowly, "or if they teach you that any power exceeds that of our leader, then you are being put in an abusive situation."

"Do Christian ideas count?" Erica asked hesitantly.

"If Christian principles are used to avoid obedience to the empire's rules, then they are immoral and illegal. We are increasingly suspect of Bibles. Let us know if anyone pushes biblical beliefs on you. That would be religious abuse. Good question, young lady."

Erica smiled back pleasantly, but her eyes were fixed wide open. As the man continued talking, Erica began scribbling violently on the notebook on her desk.

"Listen to your heart, Erica." Seradim concentrated intensely. "Tune in to your best self."

Erica did not even realize that Schultz had finished and sat down until Mary spoke softly in her ear.

"Didn't you say your parents are always putting fanatical stuff on you?"

Erica looked in horror at the smug grin on Mary's face. "Sure," Erica fumbled. "You know we all complain about our parents at home, but I didn't mean anything like this guy was describing."

"You said they were always studying the Bible," Mary insisted.

"Yes, but they read lots of porn too," Erica lied. "Just broad readers."

Mary smirked and looked the other way.

"Listen, Erica," Michael continued. "Listen carefully. Your life depends on it."

Erica stared at the blackboard as if in a trance. When the teacher sent reading material down the aisles, she mechanically put her handout inside her notebook but her expression did not change.

"What do you suspect she's thinking?" Seradim asked his companion.

"I don't know. I often wish we could read their minds. The best we can do is offer suggestions. Of course, demons can't get inside their minds either."

"We've got to do something," Seradim protested.

"A human soul cannot be forced, even spiritually," Michael explained. "The best we can do is to inspire a person."

Seradim pondered their dilemma. "What can I put into her thinking?"

"Push all the teenage garbage aside," Michael instructed. "What do you think is at the bottom of this tension between Erica and her parents?"

Seradim puzzled. "Rebellion?"

"Rebellion against what?"

The angel's face brightened. "Against how much she feels bound to her mother . . . because she loves her!"

"Touch that center of love. Jennifer McCoy has always been a very loving mother."

Seradim reached to where God's love resonated at the center of his being. An image rolled up in his mind. A young mother was stooping over her newborn child. The room was poor, meager, but the devotion in the woman's eyes was profound and constant. He saw the Virgin Mary holding the baby Jesus.

Michael tuned in on the scene and felt the mystery of incarnate divine love, enfleshed in and expressed through the child. The prototype, the archetype of all parental devotion, radiated its own aura of profound solicitude.

The two angels kept projecting the image of the Virgin's joy and devotion. Erica's distant stare focused. A gentle smile crossed her face. A tear ran down her cheek.

Shortly after Erica's scare at school, Ben had a scare of his own at a rented house. While sending a radio transmission to his parents in Petra–Bozrah, Adams's forces had uncovered and identified his late-night radio signal and honed in on the house. Providentially, Ben saw a shadow outside the window and immediately stashed the transmitter. When the police broke through the doors, he was able to sneak out through the kitchen and cut through the backyard. He escaped with only a few scratches, but the incident had been too close for comfort.

As he related his tale to Joe and Jennifer McCoy and some of the students at the McCoys' home, Cindy offered to stay behind at UCLA to minister to students there.

"I don't know" Ben hesitated. "I don't like the exposure."

"You sure don't need to be wandering around down there," one of the guys replied. "A quick computer check of your family background would reveal that your parents left with passports for Israel. They'd nail you in a minute."

"In addition, you may have accidentally left some clues back at our old meeting house," another student reasoned.

"I suppose so," Ben mused. "But Michael assured me I'd be safe. I'm just nervous about Cindy being pursued. Only my two very good eyes and the grace of God saved me the other night! I know Michael promised that no one could hurt me, but I'm still human. I get scared sometimes."

"We'll take good care of Cindy," the student assured Ben.

"Let's join hands and commit the plan to the Lord." Joe McCoy reached out for a tall black student and a Hispanic student next to him. "We need to pray for protection for us, our families, and all of our contacts."

After the heartfelt prayers had ended, the group prepared to disperse into the summer night. Some left by the back door while others waited before going down the front driveway so they would not appear to have been meeting. After all the other guests had gone, Ben, Cindy, and her dog, Sam, left.

"Drive carefully," Jennifer called after them. "Your lives are precious."

Ben and Cindy talked all the way back to the campus until they finally pulled in front of Cindy's dorm. Sam sat up in the backseat.

"The work is really going well." Ben smiled. "I'm amazed at how many students you have been able to reach. People seem to be especially attracted to your honesty."

"Perhaps my blindness is an asset, like Michael said. I'm easy to trust."

"Maybe so. I've also been amazed at the response from the people Michael sent me to contact. The results have been equally exciting. They were obviously ready for the gospel."

"I worry that the university will try to track you down."

"No, I'm just a person who dropped out of school for medical reasons." Ben opened the car door for Cindy. "I think my tracks are well covered. I don't see how they could possibly locate me unless I let myself get caught like I nearly did last night."

"Don't let that ever happen again!" Cindy mockingly scolded. "You're better at getting me around than my dog. You'd be hard to replace!"

They kissed each other good night, and Ben hurried back to his apartment.

# CHAPTER

## 26

**A**re you getting a feel for the battle?" Michael asked his charge.

"Amazing the difference a little practice makes," Seradim concluded. "In the beginning, I thought just having a few facts and the commission from on High was enough to be ready for the war. Obviously, I missed the mark rather badly. One certainly has to know the terrain."

"Since we stepped out of history, the enemy's fury has broken loose. In a power bluff, Gianardo set off a round of atomic exchanges with the Chinese. To his dismay, he discovered they had a much larger nuclear capacity than Gianardo dreamed possible. The world is in a terrible state, and things will get much worse. The power-mad dictator has unleashed great suffering on the innocent as well as the guilty. We have a few more tasks to do, and then I want you to handle a situation on your own."

Seradim smiled broadly. "I hope I'm ready."

"You're getting there. We need to go back and check in with Ben. Big Jewish commemorative day coming up. Time to give him an important message. Ready?"

Seradim agreed and they were immediately transported to Ben's house. Without a sound they slipped through the wall of time and into his room. After turning on the automatic coffeemaker, Michael sat down in a bedroom chair and waited for Ben to wake up. Soon he stirred and reached for the clock.

"Good morning, Ben."

The alarm clock hit the floor. Ben sat straight up in bed. "Who is it?" he shouted.

"I thought you'd recognize my voice by now."

"Don't you ever knock?" Ben looked disgusted. "You scared me silly."

"I apologize. I just wanted to get the morning started right for you. Important day, you know."

Ben frowned and reached down to pick up the alarm clock. "Why?"

"It is July 22nd. The Fast of Tammuz."

"Already?" Ben blinked. "How did it get here so fast?" He got out of bed and put his pants on. "Let me get a shirt. No telling what's next."

"Actually, nothing you can see today, Ben. Pour yourself a cup of coffee and I will explain."

"Coffee?" Ben stared uncomprehending at the coffee steaming in the pot.

"Today a new phase of the Tribulation begins. The Lord Jesus will break the fifth seal that John wrote about in the Revelation. The saints who have died so far during the persecutions have been kept under the heavenly altar. Today their cries to be avenged will be heard, and the next period of woes begins."

"So, we start again." Ben drank a sip of coffee and sat down at the kitchen table. "The police got very close the other night, Michael. I was really terrified."

"Yes, I know. Perhaps I should clarify some things about your situation. There is no place in the world that is completely protected except the Bozrah–Petra area. Even there, people are still subject to the normal bodily processes like heart attacks, strokes, or injuries. Here in California you are living in a genuine war zone. You must start now to get ready for what is ahead, and I want you to let your parents know about the next catastrophe. You must also understand what the atomic exchange has done to the world."

"We really *did* get hit? Can't trust the news reports anymore."

"Indeed. Skin diseases will multiply like a plague. You must wash your body often and carefully. Wear long-sleeved clothing and a hat. Expect problems. Crops will fail and food will be in short supply. Animals will go on savage rampages. Wild dogs will roam the streets. Take no chances."

"No kidding!"

"The nuclear explosions have produced large amounts of nitrogen oxides, which are quickly depleting the ozone layer. Nuclear fireballs have set many fires around the world. Hundreds of tons of smoke and soot have been released from the burning cities. The nuclear winter is coming, which will drop temperatures by an average of thirty degrees."

Ben took another long drink of coffee. "What will the results look like when it hits people . . . us?"

"People will feel nauseated and tired, and many will vomit. Then they will feel better for a while, but they will be developing fewer and fewer white blood cells, antibodies, and platelets. Infections will be hard to fight, and many people will lose their hair. Others will suffer severe weight loss and struggle with internal bleeding. Skin lesions and cancers will be quite common. The degree of injury will depend on how long people are exposed to concentrated radiation."

"And these effects will increase as the days go by?"

"Unfortunately, yes."

Ben set the cup down and looked out the window. "It's going to be a long summer. And what can we expect at the end of the period?"

"In about a month . . . on Tuesday, August 12 . . . Av 9 comes around again. At sunrise in Jerusalem, the sixth seal will be broken, and the most violent upheaval the world has ever known will shake the very foundations of creation."

"And I am to tell my parents everything you have said?"

"Yes. They must be prepared for the bad condition people seeking refuge will be in. You must be in a safe location when the earthquakes come, for nothing of this magnitude has ever befallen the globe."

"I'll get to the transmitter as soon as I can. By the way, Michael, any help you can give me along the way will be appreciated. Something simple would do fine . . . like a warning that the bad guys are coming."

"Fear not, Ben. Great is your reward in heaven."

■ ■ ■

As Michael had promised, he led Ben and his crew to a farm near the little town of Lancaster. As the summer progressed, the effects of the Chinese atomic attack caused by Gianardo's power grab became increasingly clear. Communication across the United States was in total chaos. Government problems mounted and citizens were captured by their fears. The world seemed paralyzed to respond. Only

Damian Gianardo appeared to have any sense of where events were leading.

The retreat at Lancaster quickly became a haven and escape for the youth in Ben's movement. The McCoys became the communication link between Cindy's UCLA ministry and the farm, and they kept the troops in food. The small living room was usually filled with college students laughing, teasing, praying, and devouring food. One day in August, Ben and Cindy gathered their team for an afternoon discussion.

"We've got the transmitter wired up," a student named Deborah told Ben. "I think we've found a good place to keep it protected when the big quake comes."

Deborah pointed upstairs. "We've got all the electronic equipment inside a metal box, and it's surrounded with foam rubber padding. If the house falls in, the equipment will make it."

"What a job you've done!" Ben beamed. "How can I ever thank you?"

"Thank us?" the group echoed.

"How can we ever thank you?" George, a Jewish student, answered. "You and Cindy have brought life itself to us. Without you, we would all be hopelessly entangled in the lies and destruction devouring the world. You have been our lifeline to eternal survival."

"We are just grateful that God chose to use us." Ben reached out and grabbed Cindy's hand. "The truth is that anyone who really desires to know the true God will find the way even if an angel has to be dispatched. We owe a great debt to our friend Michael. Actually, we found each of you because Michael directed us."

George pointed to several students. "We Jews came to the Lord through your witness, Ben. No matter what lies ahead we will live and die with the supreme satisfaction that we found what our ancestors prayed for. God has surely fulfilled our deepest longings and greatest hopes."

"And we've become great friends," Ben added. "I've found a friendship among you that I've never known before." He stopped and the room became very quiet.

Cindy squeezed his hand. "Why don't we try the radio out?" She broke the awkward silence. "Let's call Petra."

"Terrific idea." Deborah stood up. "We can show you our handiwork. Let's go upstairs."

The group fell in behind her and piled up the steps. Deborah led them to a sparsely furnished room with only a table and chair in one corner. At the bottom of one wall was a large metal grate covering the heating duct.

"Watch this!" Deborah dropped to one knee and pulled the cover off. She slid a metal box out of the wall. "Rather clever, I'd say." She opened the top and lifted the transmitter out. "We're ready to talk to the world."

"We've made a new hookup." George put a small speaker on the table and plugged in the wires. "You won't have to use a headset and we can hear."

"Excellent." Ben carefully fine-tuned the dials. "Calling the Woman in the Desert," he repeated several times. Static crackled over the speaker and humming filled the room. "Come in, Woman in the Desert."

"Hello . . . hello . . ." The voice sounded low, far away but familiar.

"Jimmy? Jimmy? Is that you?"

"Hey, Ben." Static broke in. "It's me. The old used-car salesman."

The group cheered. "You've got an audience here," Ben explained. "The whole gang of believers is with me."

"Can't sell you any cars today," Jimmy's voice crackled. "But I've got a couple of low-mileage camels with lots of tread left."

"Save us a couple. How's the family? Ruth? Mom?"

"Of course, it's night here in Petra, and Mom has turned in. Ruth is out at the hospital. Ought to be here shortly. Been a busy, hard day, but everyone's healthy. People just keep showing up. The pronouncements by Moses and Elijah are having their effect. More and more are believing."

"People in bad shape?"

"Yeah," Jimmy drawled with his Texas accent. "The world's falling apart and so are the people. Ruth and I work from sunup to sundown, but we love every minute of it. Wouldn't have missed this trip for the world."

"Ready for the earthquake?"

"We think so, but we're not sure what God's special protection will mean. We can only go by the quake earlier in the summer. We expect to feel the effects but not suffer damage. We are far more worried about you. Southern California is not a great place to be for a really big one."

"I know, I know," Ben sighed. "The whole group will be out here with us when it comes. At least we'll be away from L.A., where the big catastrophes will happen. We think we're prepared."

"We'll be praying for you."

"Better sign off," Ben concluded. "Don't want to stay on too long in case we've got any eavesdroppers. So long until the next visit."

"Peace!" Static filled the speaker, and Ben switched the set off. Everyone applauded.

"It worked!" Isaiah Murphy shouted. "We're beating the system!"

Someone clapped. "More lemonade for a toast," George demanded. The entourage rushed for the door and stampeded down the stairs.

"Cindy . . ." Jennifer McCoy stopped at the door. "Could I ask you for a favor?"

"Of course."

"We can't bring the children out here." Jennifer's face suddenly looked drawn and sober. "We would only endanger the whole mission. We will have to stay behind with them from now on."

"Oh, no!" Cindy protested.

"No. Joe and I have already discussed the matter. They could easily betray us because of their flippant attitude. Erica's improved some, but she has a long way to go. We will try to take them to another safe place. But I was hoping that you might at least witness to Erica before next Tuesday. It's almost our last hope."

Cindy's brow furrowed. "You know that I would do anything in the world for you and certainly to help the children. But . . . it . . . seems only the people that Michael directs us to or those who seek our help respond. And he warned that when we go beyond those boundaries we could be in serious jeopardy. I just wouldn't want to raise any false hopes. . . . But you are my dearest friends."

"Sure, I understand. I guess Joe and I are getting desperate."

Cindy hugged her friend. "I'll see her tomorrow if you'll set it up. Don't give it another thought."

"Well," Jennifer hedged, "maybe we ought not."

"Tomorrow," Cindy insisted. "I'll pray and do my best."

■ ■ ■

The next afternoon Jennifer drove Cindy to the McCoys' house. As she led Cindy up the walk, Jennifer explained, "Erica and a group of girls are working on cheerleading yells. They should be going home shortly. I'll let you know when I think Erica's friends are gone. There's quite a bunch of them."

"Why have your children been so resistant?"

"Painful question." Jennifer opened the front door. "I anguish over that issue, and I'm not sure I fully understand the answer yet. Joe and I were good parents even though we were gone a great deal of the time when Joe Jr. and Erica were small. We couldn't support a Southern California lifestyle on one salary. I guess today you'd label our children as affluent latchkey kids. Perhaps the lack of contact developed their tendency to give more credence to their friends. That's sure the way they are now."

Cindy felt for a chair. "Just pray that I can get through to her today." Sam lay down at her feet.

"I'm going to take you outside to the backyard and let you sit by the gate. A couple of comfortable chairs are there. When the squad leaves, I'll send Erica out with a glass of lemonade."

Noise echoed from fence to fence as the girls yelled, danced, and waved pompoms. Cindy sat in her obscure corner listening and praying silently. Sam watched the scene intently. After about twenty minutes the rehearsal ended, and the laughing voices drifted away.

Erica's familiar voice jolted Cindy out of her prayer. "Mother said to bring you this drink."

"Erica!" Cindy turned toward the sound. "Sit down. I haven't talked to you in weeks."

"Well . . ." Erica was hesitant and distant. "I have to leave with my friends. We're meeting some guys for pizza. I really can't stay."

Cindy felt the cold glass touch her hand. "Erica, we might never have the opportunity to speak together again. I've got to say several things to you. The hand of God is moving very quickly."

"Please," Erica begged, "we shouldn't be talking about religious stuff. I know you're sincere, but you and my parents are playing with fire."

Cindy set the glass down and took the teenager's hand. "In a few days the earth is going to be nearly shaken out of orbit. We're all going to slosh around like terrified fish in a bowl. Most of what you see around you will collapse."

"Look." Erica's voice was hushed. "I'm sure you believe these things, but some of these kids would turn us in to the authorities just for laughs. I have enough trouble making sure my parents' Bibles are well hidden when the girls are over here."

"I understand . . ." Cindy looked down. "I really *do* understand, but your eternal destiny is at stake. Even if something terrible happened to me, I would do everything I could to tell you about Jesus."

"You're a very good person, Cindy. Kind. Giving. I've watched you when you've been here with Ben. But the world doesn't have a place for people like you anymore, and I have to go on living with some of these creeps who call themselves my friends. I must leave religion alone for the good of everybody."

"Erica, no one has much time left. The days are numbered. In a very short while your friends and their opinions won't matter. They *will not* be here. But God has a plan for your life for today and for all of eternity."

Erica chewed her lip. "After next week, I'll listen. I've got to catch up with the gang now. But I'll talk more if you'll just wait until then."

"I'm going to be praying for you. I'll ask God to keep you through what's coming on Tuesday. There is no power on earth greater than the Lord Jesus."

Suddenly the back gate swung open. Mary Higbie stepped in and stared at both of them. "I wondered where the God talk was coming from."

"M . . . Mary! You . . . you've been listening!" Erica stammered.

"I came back to find you. The girls are waiting. I just happened to come in the back way."

"Mary?" Cindy asked uncomprehendingly.

"You Christian freaks!" Mary sneered at Cindy.

"I don't understand," Cindy answered vaguely. "Who are you?"

"Really weird conversation, Erica." Mary smirked. "I thought your family was straight. Next thing we know you'll be leading cheers for Jesus." The girl spun on her heels and ran toward the car waiting in the driveway.

"Mary!" Erica darted after her. "Mary! Stop it!" Her voice trailed away as she chased her old nemesis. "Please. Don't make something out of nothing."

Cindy heard the door slam and the car drive away. The backyard seemed intensely silent. "Michael warned me," she said to herself. "He cautioned me about just such a danger."

# CHAPTER
## 27

**H**ow's it going to happen?" Seradim asked.

"Let me show you. We have the capacity to look right through things," Michael answered. "You must learn to use inner sight and see through mountains and continents. It is possible to read earthquakes." Michael beckoned his charge to follow. "Concentrate on seeing beneath the surface of the earth."

Seradim struggled but slowly began to sense the strata of the earth.

"About sixty miles below the surface of the earth is the Eurasian Plate's base. The continents rest on these gigantic masses. If the Scotia Plate below South America and the Caribbean Plate move at the same time, the earth will shake like a bowl of jelly."

Seradim nodded. "Yes. Frightening for the humans."

"One man has figured it out, but no one is listening to him. Terbor L. Esiw knows the result of such movement would also push the Somali Plate off the coast of Africa and the Philippine Plate into a slide. Never has the world known the shaking that would follow such a collision. The Creator will use this shift to fulfill prophecy."

Seradim watched in rapt fascination. "Of course, the San Andreas fault would split open," he concluded. "Structures in California would tumble like a stack of children's building blocks."

"Gianardo is too big of an egomaniac to allow Esiw to warn the world. Disaster awaits for multitudes of people."

Seradim pondered. "Are the Principalities and Archangels prepared?"

"Of course. The human race has been given ample warnings, but they have ignored them. The heavenly Father is merciful beyond comprehension. When he finally acts, no one can say they were not offered every opportunity to choose the right and better course."

"The time has come," Seradim concluded. "I am ready."

The two angels turned toward the center of heaven. Angels swirled in magnificent arches around the throne of God. The hosts of heaven kept singing in angelic response, "Worthy art Thou to take the scroll and to open the seals." Michael and Seradim watched the Lamb of God, who was holding the scroll as the angels sang, "For You were slain and by Your blood did ransom humanity for God." Myriads of angels, numbering thousands of thousands kept repeating, "Worthy is the Lamb who was slain, to receive power and wealth and wisdom and might and honor and glory and blessing!"

The impulse to worship swept Michael and Seradim into the mighty response of the chorus, "To the Lamb be blessing and honor and glory and might for ever and ever." The four living creatures bowing before the throne of God began repeating, "Amen, Amen, Amen. . . ." The elders fell down in silent worship. The Lamb reached out and broke the sixth seal, and all heaven paused in awe.

Michael and Seradim turned toward Earth. As the sun rose over Jerusalem, a deafening rumble began rising from the ground. Like a rug shaking on a clothesline, the terrain of the entire globe began moving. Gigantic luminous flashes exploded in the sky, and meteorites plunged toward the earth. Huge clouds of black smoke moved across the globe.

Michael and Seradim watched in awe as the tremors roared and shook every continent. Slowly the planet returned to a state of stability as the ground stopped shifting. Wherever the two angels looked, skyscrapers had toppled and buildings were broken like matchboxes.

"We must return." Michael pointed toward California. "I have my assignment, and you have yours."

"I . . . I . . . do?" Seradim fumbled. "Yes. . . . But what is it?"

"You are to visit Frank and Jessica Wong. Help them get a grip on themselves and understand what to do next. Stay in tune with the will of the Father."

"Am I ready?" Seradim's eyes widened.

Michael chuckled. "Quite so."

Once the angels penetrated the time barrier, they descended in different directions over California. Seradim beamed in on Lake Forest, and Michael sped toward Lancaster. Michael found the students gathering up their blankets and trying to pull themselves together after the "great shake."

The time was right to appear physically and speak to the entire group. Once more Michael stepped into human history at a point about ten feet from the front porch of the farmhouse.

"Peace be unto you!"

"Michael!" Ben spun around. "We knew you'd be here!"

"I can see him!" Deborah exclaimed. "I'm actually seeing an angel!"

"It's really him," George pointed. "I can't believe my eyes."

"Today I come to all of you as a sign of favor. Behold, you have found a special place in the sight of God. Rejoice! For as this world passes away, you chose the better portion that is eternal."

"Michael, tell us what has happened." Ben took Cindy by the hand and led her forward. Sam strained on the harness behind her. "Petra . . . is everyone okay?"

"God's hand has more than protected. Your family and friends have endured very well, even as their enemies were being swallowed by the earth."

"Praise the Lord!" Ben shouted.

"What about the rest of the globe?" Deborah walked forward cautiously.

"Do not fear. Come close and listen."

The students huddled around the farmhouse steps.

"Many people will be ready to receive your witness now. I will send each of you to those who are hungry for hope. Yet be prepared for danger to increase! The times are becoming more desperate with every judgment."

"What's happened to California?" a student ventured.

"Judgment has engulfed San Francisco. Their wickedness has been called into accountability. The city is no more."

"L.A.?" George held up his hand.

"The city is in flames, and many sections have been leveled. Yet other portions in Orange County stand. Railways, overpasses, and bridges have buckled before the glance of the Lord."

"And our people?" Cindy asked. "The Christians? And my parents who are not Christians?"

"Your own parents are alive and well, my child. When you see them next, you will find new receptiveness to your message. But the last sixteen weeks have taken a great toll. Believers all over the world have become martyrs. Hundreds of thousands of Israelis who embraced Yeshua as Messiah have already paid with their lives. Those who have fled the persecutions of Gianardo compose a new diaspora. Petra–Bozrah has become a haven for these people of the truth."

"What are we to do now?" Ben asked.

"I will talk with each one of you separately. I have many assignments for you to fulfill in the coming months. You will find that the time flies as you complete your mission. Yet for the world, each day will seem an eternity of agony. As the end of this period approaches, you will know what to expect next. Watch the skies, for the next great judgment will come from above. Now come and receive your divine appointments."

The students lined up and Michael began giving instructions.

■ ■ ■

"Help! Help!" Frank Wong screamed at the top of his voice. "Wife is trapped. Please, someone come!" He turned to every corner of the smashed kitchen, looking for assistance. No one was there.

Patrons of the Golden Dragon pushed pieces of the roof aside and struggled to crawl out of the wrecked restaurant. Dust still hung heavy in the air and pieces of the walls kept dropping in. But no one paid any attention to the cries for help coming from the kitchen.

Frank yanked pieces of ceiling tile aside, but his effort was futile. The chopping block had fallen on top of Jessica, and he could not budge the heavy wooden table. She kept moaning until she lost consciousness.

Frank frantically rubbed her hand and wept. Her lips were turning blue. "Cannot live without wife. Oh, Jessica, don't leave me."

The door to the kitchen fell from its hinges. The massive plate glass in front of the restaurant was scattered in a thousand shards. Frank looked out and could see huge cracks in the parking lot. Some cars had fallen into the ground. Voices cried for help everywhere. People walked about in a daze, disconnected from the calls for help.

"O God of Cindy," Frank cried and held his hands up to the cracked ceiling. "If you help with honorable wife, we will give you our lives. As you protect our daughter, please, please, help us."

Seradim stepped into time a few feet behind Frank. "Let me serve you," he said simply.

Frank whirled around. "Where you come from?" He stared at the six-foot, red-haired young man of decidedly athletic proportions. "You not here just minute ago."

"We must get your wife out quickly," Seradim said. His blue eyes flashed.

"Table too big for three or four men," Frank lamented.

"Perhaps not." Seradim put his hands underneath the edge of the toppled table and lifted. He slowly set the chopping block back on its legs.

Frank gasped. "Such strength not possible!"

"She could barely breathe." Seradim bent over Jessica. "We must put more air back in her." He gave quick powerful blasts of air in her mouth. With his hands on her shoulders, Seradim concentrated. "Yes, her leg is fractured and will need to be in a cast for a while," he concluded, "but as soon as she gets enough oxygen circulating, she will be fine."

The old man stared. "Who are you?" he asked in awe.

"Your friend."

"Where did you come from?"

"From your prayer."

Jessica moaned and then opened her eyes. "I hurt. What happened?"

Frank reached out as if to touch Seradim but couldn't quite bring himself to do so. "My prayer?" He wept as he spoke.

"A terrible earthquake has shaken the whole world. You must understand this is a sign. God is calling the entire globe to turn to Him. The time has come for you to believe."

Jessica grabbed Seradim's forearm. "I was dying," she muttered. "Suffocating."

"Please, your name," Frank ventured.

"Seradim."

Frank shook his head. "Never hear of such a name."

"You saved me." Jessica looked into the deep blue eyes. "If you not come, I soon die."

"Life awaits you, Jessica. Do not be afraid to receive the One who gives you the life you cannot lose."

"Where can I find this life?" Jessica squeezed his arm. "Please?"

"Listen to your daughter. Cindy can tell you."

"You know Cindy?" Frank puzzled.

"Believe what she tells you." Seradim stood up and walked to the doorway. "I must go now."

"How you know Cindy?" Frank called after him.

"I'm a friend of Michael's," Seradim answered and then disappeared into the shambles of the once proud restaurant.

# CHAPTER

## 28

Sitting behind the former district attorney's desk, Gerald Adams studied the five special agents standing in front of him. Each man seemed poised for action, trustworthy of his complete confidence. Adams turned in his chair and looked out the window. Buildings were in shambles. Cars were still barely able to make their way down the cracked and debris-strewn streets. An ugly gray smog hung over the city.

"The word from the top," Adams said, "is that more disasters may be on the way." He tried to sound detached and unemotional. "We have been warned to expect a possible collision with some sort of asteroid capable of great damage. After the nuclear explosions and earthquake, people are rather unstable. No telling what another catastrophe might create."

Adams turned back to face the agents. They looked straight ahead and did not flinch.

"Frightened people get superstitious, crazy. Think they're seeing ghosts, angels, God, who knows what else. We've got to keep a lid on the religion thing. Gianardo believes a rampant religious revival is one of our major threats to national stability." Adams rocked back in his chair. "I'm concerned about what these college kids are doing. I don't like the tenor of what's being distributed on campuses. We think there's an organized ring working the streets. Any progress on what you're finding south of L.A., Schultz?"

Robert Schultz smiled. "I've made significant inroads and infiltrated all of the target churches. Yes, a number of adults are a part of a well-coordinated system. They have transmitters and international connections. But we're on to them."

"Good," Adams acknowledged coldly. "Same with the rest of you boys?"

The group nodded.

"Sir, I am about to interrogate a leader in one of the churches," Schultz said. "I have a lead on a group that may be one of our government's prime enemies. We have come close to catching their leaders and believe we are about to zero in on one of the major organizers."

"Really?" Adams raised his eyebrows. "I'd like to observe."

"Interrogation's going on right now." Schultz pointed toward the hall. "Come on down."

The group followed Schultz into the hall and down the corridor. At the far end, behind an unmarked door, three agents surrounded a heavy-set man seated in the center of the room. The agents circled their frightened prey, firing questions at him from all sides. The man's tie hung loose below his unbuttoned collar. Large damp spots dotted his shirt.

"I'll take over from here," Schultz instructed his men as Adams and the other four agents joined the interrogation. "I believe you're Mr. Ed Parker with the Community Church?"

Parker mopped his forehead with his handkerchief. "I don't understand why I'm here." He looked nervously around the room. "I've always been a good law-abiding citizen." His pudgy neck had turned red, his face flushed in pink blotches. "Honest. I'm only involved with that church because it's good for business."

"You're a shaker and a mover with the church, aren't you, Ed old boy?" Schultz paced in front of him.

"I'm just a member." Ed shrugged and dabbed at his neck.

"We understand you're a committee chairman. Local big shot." Schultz suddenly got two inches from Parker's face. "Helped can the pastor. Ran him off."

"Look." Ed bit his lip. "We felt the pastor's sermons were . . . well . . . just not what we should be hearing. That's not illegal."

"Not at all!" Schultz patted Ed on the back. "We couldn't agree more with what you did. The preacher was polluting the people."

The heavily perspiring man swallowed hard. "Really? You mean it?"

"Certainly, you helped get your church in line with the leadership of our exalted national and international leader. Excellent move." Schultz smiled and winked at Ed.

Parker heaved and exhaled. He mopped his forehead again. "Then . . . then why am I here?"

"We need information on some other people in that church." Schultz picked up a file from the agent originally interrogating Parker. "We'd like to know what you know about Joe and Jennifer McCoy."

"Them!" Ed rubbed his mouth. "Well, I'll tell you whatever you'd like to know. I'm no friend of the McCoys. No sirree. Those people are trouble."

"Yes." Schultz smiled broadly. "I understand they resisted the effort to remove the pastor."

"Caused me lots of problems." Ed raised his eyebrows. "Created deep divisions in our church. We're still trying to get rid of the McCoys."

"Maybe we can help you, Ed." Schultz sat on the edge of the table and smiled down at the overweight committee chairman. "Think these people would oppose the government by organizing subversives?"

Ed blinked several times uncomprehendingly. He looked carefully around the room at the sullen, staring faces. "You're saying the McCoys are in on an antigovernment plot?"

"I'm asking if you think they have the kind of fundamentalist faith that would make them capable of espionage?"

Ed's eyes widened. "Listen. I got nothing to do with those folks. They're screwball types. Real pious goody-goody phonies. Yeah, I can believe they'd be trouble."

"Then we want you to help us accumulate data on them." Schultz bore down. "We want to know about their influence on young people. We want you to keep tabs on what they're doing with people in their circle of influence. Can you do that?"

Ed's head bobbed up and down enthusiastically. "Whatever you say. I'm just a good law-abiding citizen. Never breaking any of the—"

"Good, Mr. Parker." Schultz ingratiatingly patted him on the back. "My associates will have some specific instructions for you. We will be in direct touch with you from time to time. Thanks for the assistance."

Adams and the other four agents followed Schultz out into the hall. Gerald Adams carefully measured the man in front of him. He liked everything he saw in Schultz.

"Excellent work. Shouldn't be long until you zero in on these McCoys, Robert."

"Got 'em in the crosshairs right now, boss."

Two other figures had observed the entire procedure. Lurking unseen in the shadows, Malafidus and Homelas carefully followed the conversations and inquisition.

"Do the police need any help?" Homelas pondered.

"Not when they've got a pansy like Ed on the hook. The McCoys' kids belong to us, and Ed's church buddies won't hesitate to do the parents in. I think we'll get this one wrapped up quickly and soon be back in the good graces of the front office."

"I don't want them to slip through our hands," Homelas fretted. "We're all spread too thin right now."

"No problem, I tell you. The government is taking care of the McCoys for us."

■ ■ ■

The atomic explosions and earthquake had changed the McCoys' house. Although their home fared better than most, windows were cracked and several had to be boarded up because of the shortage of glass. Water rationing made it impossible to care for the grass and plants. The heat turned everything an ugly brown. Barkley, the family dog, died. Death hung in the air.

Jennifer closed the door behind her when she entered her daughter's bedroom. Erica was stretched out on the bed, looking out the second-story window at the street below.

"Mind if I come in?" Jennifer asked.

Erica shook her head without looking up. "Our beautiful neighborhood looks like a war zone."

Jennifer sat down on the bed. "Grim, isn't it?"

Erica turned toward her mother. "I'm terribly afraid. I try to keep up appearances, but the truth is my friends are just about as disgusting as this neighborhood. The whole world seems trapped in some kind of monstrous evil plot." She suddenly sat up and threw her arms around Jennifer's neck. "Oh, Mother. I'm most afraid for you. Security police are floating around our school all the time. They ask questions about our family. What is going to become of us?" Erica began to sob.

"I know it's very hard for you to understand, but we must go on as if everything is normal." Jennifer hugged her daughter and then gently pushed her back so she could look straight into her eyes. "Erica, you must grow up very quickly and grasp what an important mission your father and I are involved in. Cindy Wong was trying to tell you the same thing. Even though you can't yet accept the idea, God has called us to work for Him. We are part of an eternal plan. Dear, God has a plan for your life as well."

Erica drew her legs up next to her chest in a tight ball. She buried her face in her knees; her hair fell around the side of her jeans. "I don't know what to believe anymore, Mother. But I am sure most of what I hear at school isn't right. I can't trust the people I know. There is nowhere to turn . . . except . . . to what you say . . . to what you believe."

Jennifer closed her eyes for a moment and inhaled deeply. A prayer raced through her mind. *Please, Lord, help me. Help me seize this moment.*

Instantly, Michael and Seradim were invisibly present. "I'll make sure we have no intrusions." Seradim began circling the mother and daughter. "No demonic influence is going to deter this moment!"

Michael moved next to Jennifer and put his hand on her head. "Come, Holy Spirit," the angel implored. "Come and inspire. Come and fill."

"Erica," Jennifer's voice was low and intense, "I can't force anything on you and wouldn't if I could. Only you can decide if you want to give yourself to the ugliness you see everywhere or whether you will entrust your soul to the beauty that only God can give. But, Jennifer, you *do* have control over what's inside you. If you invite Jesus to come into your life, it won't make any difference what anyone else says or thinks."

Erica suddenly grabbed her mother and held her tight. "But how do I do that? How does it happen?"

Jennifer whispered in her daughter's ear. "The Jews call Him Yeshua; we call Him Jesus. He's the key. He's here to help you find your way to God. All you have to do is ask Him to forgive your sins and come into your heart for an eternal relationship."

Michael called to Seradim. "Pray! She's almost there! This is the moment we've been waiting . . ." He stopped. Coming toward them from heaven was a glorious light, moving as if swept forward by gentle winds of subtle power. In the center of the brilliant splendor, the descending figure moved with one hand lifted as if in a benediction. Michael covered his face. The Light engulfed the angels with wondrous warmth. "He has come. . . . He has come!" Michael exclaimed. The angel fell prostrate before the pulsating luster of the all-encompassing resplendence.

Erica closed her eyes tightly. "Please, Jesus. Help me find out how to know You. I want to give You my life before someone in this crazy world takes it away from me. I surrender myself to You. Please forgive me for all my sins and enter my life."

Michael instantly sensed the Light had broken through their side of eternity and engulfed Erica's soul. The darkness inside her mind and spirit dissolved like a sunrise after a stormy night. The angel could see the spiritual transformation unfolding within the teenager.

Erica began to weep.

Jennifer stroked her head and prayed aloud, "Thank you, Lord. Oh, thank you."

As the brilliance receded, Michael heard words thunder through him. "The angel of the Lord encamps around those who fear Him, and He delivers them. Well done, faithful servant." The incandescent figure lifted heavenward.

"Something is very different," Erica whispered in her mother's ear. "I can feel something different inside me."

"Yes, dear. That's how it was with me. 'To as many as receive Him,' He gives the power, the capacity to become children of God."

Erica sat back and beamed. She pointed at her heart. "It's a new beginning! No matter how bad it is out there, in here, I'm starting over!"

# CHAPTER
## 29

During the following months, the secret police interrogated the McCoy children several times. Joe and Jennifer suspected there was a leak in their Bible study group, but no one could be sure. The children were making significant spiritual breakthroughs, but Joe Jr. had not yet trusted Jesus and was terrified whenever the police cornered him. Each time the interrogators were professional and polite. Their questions were vague and their demeanor nonthreatening. Mostly the investigators asked about Erica and her friends, and the possibility that Joe and Jennifer were pushing religious ideas on the kids.

Although Seradim and Michael remained invisible most of the time, they did not cease to watch over Ben and Cindy, and on several occasions Michael had to intervene. Seradim spent more and more time watching over the Wongs and encouraging them. Frank and Jessica listened to Cindy with new intensity.

In late March the secret police nearly cornered Ben and one of his friends in a UCLA dorm that had survived the great earthquake. Michael saw the police preparing to surround the building. Ben and George were in a sophomore's room sharing the gospel. They did not have much time to spare, so Michael materialized in the hallway and knocked on the young man's door.

"Can I help you?" the puzzled student said as he opened the door. "You're not the one I thought was coming."

"I believe there is a Mr. Ben Feinberg here."

"Yeah, sure." The sophomore answered uncomprehendingly.

"Michael?" Ben asked from across the room.

"Sounds like Michael," George chimed in.

"Yes. Some urgent business has just come up," Michael stated matter-of-factly.

"What?" Ben bounded across the room. "What in the world are you doing here?"

"We must run," Michael whispered. "Time is short, very short." He frowned.

Ben stared for a moment and blinked uncomprehendingly. Suddenly he understood. He grabbed his friend's arm. "Hey, we'll try to be back tomorrow." He jerked George past the startled student. "See you then." Ben pulled George into the hall and shut the door behind them.

"Michael! What are you doing here?"

"Police are closing in on the building. The student you have been talking to is a plant. The security agents will be here any minute."

"What can we do?" George looked panic-stricken.

"We're on the second floor!" Ben looked desperately up and down the hall.

The student's door flew open, and the sophomore ran down the hall toward the stairs at the opposite end.

"Quick! Ben . . . George . . . into the student's room. Lock the door and turn out the light. Get on the ledge outside his window. Give the police time to get in, and then drop into the bushes and run for it. I will be your decoy inside the dorm."

Ben and George slammed the door behind them, and Michael opened a janitor's closet and grabbed a broom. In less than thirty seconds the police were charging up the stairs and moving onto the floor.

"Stop!" the lead cop shouted. "Who are you?"

"Just cleaning up."

"Three men were here. Where did they go?"

"Three men?"

"Two college students and a big guy! About your size."

"Oh, I'm just cleaning up the mess they left."

"Let's check up the stairs at the other end."

The first wave of police disappeared, running up the exit stairs to the third floor.

"I'd recognize the other guy." The sophomore's voice was loud and nervous as he bounded up the stairs with the second detachment of police. "Sort of a strange-looking man."

Michael stepped into the little janitor's closet and back into eternity as the secret police ran up and down the halls.

"Where'd the janitor go?" The leader of the first group came back downstairs.

"What janitor?" one of the second group asked.

"The man sweeping the floor."

"The janitors aren't here at night," the sophomore interjected.

The security officer glared at the college student. "Don't mess with me. I'm not blind. I want to know where the janitor we talked to went." The man swung the closet door open and looked inside. "If this is a college prank . . ." He jerked the sophomore forward by the shirt.

"Hey, I don't know what you guys are talking about. I'm on your side, remember?"

"There's no one here," a policeman who returned from the top floor reported. "This thing smells like a little joke pulled on us by the boys' dorm."

"Where's the janitor?" the policeman growled in the sophomore's face. "We'll teach you to trifle with national security personnel."

"No . . . no . . . no." The student flattened against the wall. "Really, there were people here pushing religion on me. Honest. HONEST . . ."

"Try this room." One of the policemen reached for the door. "It's locked."

"Can't be." The student fumbled for his keys. He swung the door open. Curtains were blowing gently in the evening breeze.

The policeman ran to the window. "There they go!" He pointed across the campus. "Two guys are running into those trees."

Michael left the student to face the secret police's accusations and followed Ben and George to make sure they returned safely to the farm. Ben had made the mistake of going to a student who seemed open to the gospel, but he was not someone Michael had assigned for contact. Although he meant the best, Ben's mistake could have been deadly, at least for his friend George. Ben was quite ready to follow the rules in the future.

Their subsequent conversation allowed Michael the opportunity to warn of the approaching Doran asteroid, which would be the first sounding of God's trumpets of judgment. Michael prepared Ben for the Whiton asteroid

and comet Wormwood as the divine adjudication fell on
the earth. His charges were well prepared for the next catastrophe.

■ ■ ■

Weeks later the Doran asteroid flashed its bright red tail
in the predawn skies across the world, and after NASA fired
a nuclear missile at the asteroid, millions of burning rock
particles scattered over the earth's stratosphere. Alaska
shook when the remaining central chunk burned its way
into a small coastal island. In the following days, the night
skies were a constant display of showers of exploding and
falling stars, but their frequency lessened. By June most of
the unusual night displays had subsided and people were
back indoors. The sun was setting much later, and both the
public's fear and fascination were passing.

Erica McCoy took the bold step of inviting her closest
friends to listen to her parents explain what was happening in the world. The group of five girls gathered outside
around the McCoys' swimming pool.

Joe pointed to the sky. "I'm not trying to frighten you,
but these strange occurrences are warnings God is giving
the world. We still have another asteroid and a comet headed
toward the earth. Unless we repent, a great price will be
paid."

Erica's best friend, Melissa, interrupted. "My science
teacher says the odds have just caught up with the earth.
Sooner or later we were bound to get hit by something big
anyway."

"Sure." Joe walked back and forth in front of the group,
holding his Bible. "But the real issue is timing. Think. How
many things are happening right now that fit the Bible's

timetable for the final days of history? And why are so many happening on Jewish holy days? Is it really a coincidence? How can Moses and Elijah predict the precise times and dates so far in advance if God isn't telling them?"

Another classmate, named Paula, said, "My parents don't want us to speak about the possibilities at home. But I hear them talking when they think we are asleep. Mom and Dad went to church when they were children and know what you are teaching us is right."

"None of us would be here," Melissa added, "if Erica hadn't sworn us to secrecy. I know we're in danger, but I want to know the facts."

"My sister and I really rebelled against our parents for a long time," Joe Jr. said, "but the earthquake changed our minds. My parents told us for weeks that it was coming. It's taken me a while to say it out loud, but I know now that what the Bible says about Jesus is the truth, and I've put my faith in Him."

"We have a special Bible study group for parents," Jennifer McCoy said. "We help people like Paula's parents. I think your mothers and fathers would be more open than you think. The police system works by fear. Once you refuse to be intimidated, they've lost their hold over you.

"Girls, that's our story." Jennifer joined her husband and son in front of the group. "Our family has gone from being another Southern California wreck to a real unit that stands together. Sure, it's scary, but I wouldn't give anything for the joy that has been restored to us. Even if we were hauled in tomorrow, we have the joy of knowing that we will face eternity together."

"You probably have questions you'd like to ask," Joe added. "Erica, Joe, Jennifer, and I will be here for any response you have. If you don't have any questions, then grab a cola and we'll break up in a bit."

While the girls talked with the McCoys, three cars pulled up down the street. Plainclothes security police quietly shut the doors. A teenager got out of the last car and pointed to the McCoys' residence.

"How do you know they are there?" Robert Schultz asked.

"Because they didn't invite me," Mary Higbie answered indignantly.

"These are the people you told me about several months ago?"

The teenager smiled cynically. "I've overheard a number of conversations in the McCoys' backyard when the Chinese girl was pushing Christianity. I've seen Bibles lying around their house."

"And you'll testify to these facts?"

"Absolutely," Mary said defiantly.

"Got that on tape?" The leader turned to the man behind him.

"Every word of it. Fits exactly with the reports we have from Ed Parker."

"What?" Mary looked puzzled.

"We don't want you to back out," the man in charge grumbled. "We've been waiting quite a while to make a big bust, and we're going to hit these people hard. Your testimony makes it stick."

"Hit hard?" Mary retreated. "I just want them arrested. Humiliated like Erica treats me . . . but nothing more."

The police drew their weapons and began inserting the bullet clips. "This isn't some kind of game, kid." The agent began pointing in different directions and his men moved quickly. "We're going to make a real example of these fanatics."

"Well, sure," Mary said nervously. "But I don't want any-one to *really* get hurt."

"Hurt?" The security agent laughed. "Pain is our business. Let's get 'em, boys!"

Suddenly the men dispersed into the trees and shrubs. The first carload of agents charged the front door. One lone agent held Mary tightly by the arm. "Stay put. We want you to identify the suspects."

For a couple of minutes Mary and the security officer stood under a tree. They could hear distant shouts. Then an agent came out the front door and motioned for them to come in. They hurried through the house and out into the backyard. The teenagers were huddled together on the ground with police circling them and pointing their guns. Joe and Jennifer and their children stood together. Police aimed guns at them too.

"Identify the traitors," Schultz ordered Mary who stood at his side.

"Mary!" the girls echoed. "How could you?"

"Really," the terrified teen muttered, "I think I've made a mistake. . . . Yes. . . . This is all a big mistake."

"Identify the McCoys!" the agent demanded. "We already have your accusations on tape."

"I didn't mean for this to happen." Mary tried to pull away.

*"Identify them!"* the man exploded.

Mary pointed a trembling finger at the McCoys.

"Get the women first." A policeman grabbed Erica's wrist while another man reached for Jennifer.

Joe suddenly pushed the first man backward so force-fully that he fell in the shrubs. Pulling Erica and Jennifer with him, Joe darted toward the side gate. "Run!" he yelled to Joe Jr.

A policeman charged out of the shadows and swung the butt end of his Uzi into Joe's face, sending him sprawling in the grass. Two other agents rushed Erica and her mother. One man wrapped his arm around Jennifer's neck in a stranglehold. The other man hit Erica in the stomach with his fist. She doubled up with an agonizing groan.

"Get 'em over here." Schultz pointed toward the edge of the swimming pool. "Line 'em up."

The security agents dragged Joe through the grass and dropped him on the swimming pool tile. Erica was pushed down by his side. A big man held Joe Jr. by the edge of the water while another agent pushed Jennifer next to her family. The teenagers began screaming.

"Shut them up!" The man in charge motioned to the other police. "We don't need a bunch of crazy girls!"

"Please stop!" Mary pleaded. "I didn't want any of this."

"Shut up!" the policeman in charge yelled. "Or they'll get it right now!" Immediately the girls became silent.

"The man assaulted me." The agent with the Uzi kicked Joe's hand aside. "I should have shot him then. Let me finish them off now."

"We don't know about the status of the girls," another agent interjected. "Are they witnesses or victims?"

Schultz walked over to the terrified teenagers. "Do you believe what the McCoys were preaching here tonight? Are their ideas representative of your convictions?"

"No! No!" the girls whimpered and pleaded. "No! Never!"

"Okay," the leader snarled. "They're victims. Get their names, addresses, and parents' names, and then let them go. Photograph 'em as well as this backyard."

"And our criminals here?" The policeman pointed his Uzi at Joe's stirring figure on the ground. He tried to sit up but couldn't stabilize himself. Blood was running out of Joe's mouth, and his lips were extremely swollen.

"He tried to escape. So did the girl and her mother."

"You won't get away with this!" Joe Jr. strained against the man holding him. "God will judge you for what you are doing to us."

"You know our orders," the agent in charge grumbled. "Get these teenagers out of here and then shoot the family."

# CHAPTER
## 30

The secret police herded the McCoy family together on the grass bordering their swimming pool. Erica fell backward on top of her father's limp form; he struggled to speak but still could not clear his mind. Trembling, Jennifer hugged her son tightly. Joe Jr. clutched at his mother's waist and hid his eyes.

Schultz nodded and the agents cocked their weapons. The clicking sound of bullets sliding into metal chambers echoed into the black night.

Seradim wrung his hands in agitation. "We can't just watch. We have to *do* something."

Michael looked knowingly at his charge but said nothing.

"Yes. Yes. I know we haven't received orders from on High yet, but . . ."

"But?"

"They are going to kill the McCoys, Michael!"

Michael knelt down beside Joe and put his hand on the father's shoulder. The angel looked up into Erica's terrified eyes as if she could see him through the veil of time.

"Can't we do anything?" Seradim implored.

"Now comes your final lesson, my friend." Pathos inched its way across Michael's sad smile. "We have to recognize the final boundaries in any intervention. It is not given to us to stop the course nor block the path that human free will takes. The Father will not allow us to circumvent the devastation that sin and human rebellion bring."

Seradim reached out to stroke Erica's hair even though she could not feel his hand. "This poor child is horrified. I must find some way to comfort her."

"Lend her your spiritual strength," Michael advised. "Send love, but you must not keep her from this crossroads. This is Erica's moment of truth."

Seradim looked helplessly around the dark backyard. Agents stood poised with their loaded guns pointed at the family. The teenage girls' whimpering could still be heard in the front yard.

"Some things can never be fully grasped or comprehended either by us or by humans," Michael said. "Terrible events will come to pass and still be part of a plan yet to be seen. What the heavenly Father does not intend, He still uses."

The angels listened to Schultz instructing his agents on what to do with the bodies after the execution.

Seradim cringed and gnashed his teeth.

"You have come a long way, my friend," Michael concluded. "You have struggled and persevered when observing the suffering of the innocent. Nothing in this world is more powerful than suffering love that will not retreat in the face of brokenness."

"They will suffer." Seradim reached out for Joe Jr. as if he could shield him from the unrelenting path of the bullet. "I want . . . to . . . keep him from this moment."

"We always want to do the impossible," Michael reflected. "Yes, even after all of these centuries I still want to rip through the veil of time and smash these evil men. But I can't. I must not. I am first and last only a servant of the Most High. Not even we who stand so close to the throne can always understand the destiny of humans, but the sovereign intentions of God *will* prevail."

"But their pain?" Seradim protested.

"At this moment fear is like a noose around each of their necks, but their actual pain will be but an instant, and then the agony is over forever. Death is more merciful than it appears."

Seradim shook his head in consternation and looked away. "I don't think I can watch it happen."

Michael looked into the faces of the children. Joe Jr. cowered next to his mother like a whipped puppy. Erica buried her face in her father's chest. Joe was still having a hard time maintaining consciousness.

Schultz's men raised their weapons. Shots rang out in a rapid drumbeat. Shells flew in every direction, bouncing on the cement around the swimming pool. For a moment Agent Schultz looked at the bodies, then blanched and turned away.

■ ■ ■

"Where . . . where am I?" Joe Jr. reached out for something to hold on to.

"Mother?" Erica blinked several times. "Dad? Are you here?"

"Joe?" Jennifer looked around. "Joe?"

"My head doesn't hurt anymore." Joe rubbed his eyes. "There was that terrible noise, and then my head stopped throbbing."

"Everything looks so different," Joe Jr. gasped. "I feel like I'm almost floating."

"We're all here!" Jennifer exclaimed. "A moment ago we were over . . ." She turned and looked at the bodies behind her. "Oh, my goodness how horrible!" Jennifer looked away. "Who are those poor people?"

Erica shook her head. "Everything is so different. I remember being terrified and then . . ."

"I seem to have stepped through an invisible barrier," Joe said. "Like I closed one door and then walked through a gate."

Erica looked at her father. "Dad! The blood's all gone from your face. Your lip isn't swollen anymore."

"I can see the swimming pool." Joe Jr. pointed. "But I can't quite reach it. How strange. The backyard seems to have turned into a mural."

"I can't get over how quickly my pain disappeared." Joe kept feeling his face where the agent struck him with a weapon.

"Excuse me." Michael stepped from behind the family. "Let me help you."

"Michael!" Joe exclaimed. "We haven't seen you since your appearance at the farm at Lancaster."

"What are you doing here?" Jennifer asked.

"Is he the angel you told us about?" Joe Jr. asked in awe.

"Please meet my colleague, Seradim." Michael beckoned for the other angel to join him.

"Wow!" Erica beamed. "Two of 'em."

"Michael," Jennifer begged. "We must help those poor people on the ground. They've been badly hurt."

"We did." Michael smiled. "Now we must turn our attention elsewhere."

"We can't leave them," Jennifer urged.

"We already have," Michael answered. "I would suggest that none of you look back again. Actually, those people were you, your family."

"What?" Jennifer muttered.

"Seradim and I have come to welcome you to eternity. Your old bodies have been left behind, and you are now ready to receive your reward."

"We're dead?" Erica's eyes widened.

"No," Michael smiled. "For the first time, you are truly alive."

"This is heaven?" Joe Jr. probed. "No wonder Mom and Dad and Erica and I all look the same age now."

"We've come to take you to heaven," Michael answered.

Jennifer turned and looked at her home. "Strange. Seems so close and yet, yet, like a place from long ago."

"I am so glad to be out of that mess!" Erica beamed. "What a terrible time we had the last few months. What a bunch of traitors and crooks."

Joe Jr. looked up toward the stars in bewilderment. "We're going up there?"

"Well, yes and no." Michael laughed. "We're actually going to take you to another place beyond the stars. You'll quickly see that the world was a constantly deteriorating, changing scene. Now, we're going to take you to the place where everything is permanent."

"And you are martyrs," Seradim added. "Very special guests in the House of the Lord."

"Martyrs?" Erica puzzled.

"That's right!" Joe snapped his fingers. "They were about to kill us because we are Christians."

"As a matter of fact," Michael hesitated a moment. "They did kill you."

"Strange." Joe sounded perplexed. "I don't remember . . ."

"Happened awfully fast," Seradim added.

"Really, the perceived pain of death is one of the devil's tricks," Michael explained. "Christians usually fail to realize both how easy the crossing is and how instantly the struggles of the world are left behind."

"And now we are beyond time?" Jennifer asked in amazement.

"Exactly," Michael explained. "You'll notice you didn't bring any watches with you."

"Far out!" Erica shouted.

"Wait a minute," Joe Jr. said. "How did we get here so easy?"

Michael put his hand on the boy's shoulder. "Young man, you actually passed from death unto life a number of weeks ago."

"Huh? What do you mean?"

"Do you remember when you decided your folks were right? That their religious convictions were true?"

"Yes," the boy said slowly.

"Then what happened?"

"Well." Joe Jr. paused to remember. "I knew their faith was right and so I accepted Jesus like they had taught me."

"At that moment you were ready for eternity."

"I don't remember anything being all that different."

Michael laughed. "That's the problem with the earth. You seldom can see what is actually happening in eternity. Nevertheless, at the moment you invited Jesus into your life you passed from death to life. Your heart stopping was only a technicality."

"Is it that way for everybody?" Erica asked.

"Oh, no," Michael answered. "If people are spiritually dead, then when physical death comes they are swallowed in the terrifying blackness of hell. Their experience is quite the opposite of yours."

"I see," Erica said solemnly. "For the first time I am truly sorry for Mary Higbie. She must be dying in her guilt right now."

"Well put," Michael agreed. "At this moment Mary is one of the loneliest people in the world . . . and that's a form of death."

"But that's behind you now," Seradim chimed in. "The Lord Jesus is waiting to greet you personally and thank you for all you did."

"Us?" Joe choked.

"Yes," Michael answered. "To be absent from the body is to be present with the Lord."

"Your life's made quite an impact," Seradim congratulated the family. "You've come a very long way from that New Year's morning when you decided it was time to take your spiritual needs seriously."

"What do we do in heaven?" Erica asked.

"You will come into the fullness of everything you had hoped to be." Michael pointed upward. "We will first get you ready to return in the great victory march of the reappearing King of kings. You will experience this preparation as only a short span, but during this period a significant amount of time will pass on Earth, wrapping up all history. Your friends the Feinbergs and Jimmy Harrison will live through the final tribulation and then you'll see them again, but some of your friends may also become martyrs and join you here."

"Follow me," Seradim beckoned. "You now are capable of a new mode of travel. We think ourselves places. Just think about flying with us and you will ascend quite naturally."

"I can do it!" Joe Jr. exclaimed. "Look at me! I'm really flying!"

The family rose upward with the angels, ascending above the housetops and beyond the flashing lights in the street in front of their house.

"This is far out, absolutely awesome," Erica squealed. "Way beyond the other side of cool!"

"Far out?" Michael laughed. "You're on your way 'far up.'" The undertakers will bury your old bodies, but Seradim and I are your 'uppertakers,' and we're quite pleased to take you to your new eternal home."

Seradim pointed ahead. "The time has come to cross the veil and leave this place behind."

"I don't see anything," Joe puzzled.

"You will grasp where this crossing is only once you've been on the other side," Michael explained. "Ready?"

The angels and the family shot through the great barrier. Instantly brilliant splendor engulfed them in a blaze of glory.

"What's that sound?" Erica choked.

Around, above, below, and beyond the family, countless multitudes of angels applauded. The reverberation was more like the harmony of a great symphony that produced not music, but a choral hymn attuned to the deepest yearnings of the soul.

"The angelic hosts are saying thank you. Your reputation precedes you." Michael beamed.

From the center of the Great Throne emerged an eminent shimmer of brilliance that shone with colors never seen by the human eye. A singular orb of glorious light advanced toward the McCoys. Both one and indivisible from the original Light and yet separate and distinct, the circle of luminous splendor descended toward the family. The closer the Shekinah glory came, the more discernible was the Figure in the center.

Joe pointed but could not speak. Jennifer grabbed his hand, and the children huddled close, staring in total amazement.

The exalted figure held one scarred hand in the air in a magnificent sign of benediction, and the other hand He extended to the family. The McCoys sank to their knees, overpowered and stupefied.

Thunder rolled across heaven and lightning flashed from the center of the Throne of Glory. The Voice from within the circle of light said simply, "Well done, good and faithful servants. Enter into your Master's glory. Welcome home."

# CHAPTER
# 31

Time to go back," Michael told Seradim. "We have much more to do before the end comes."

The other angel nodded. "I'll see how quickly I can help the Wongs cross the line. I want to be part of another homecoming."

"Makes everything worthwhile, doesn't it?"

Seradim sighed. "I will never forget what I saw happen in that backyard. I know who is behind such terror and tragedy. I am poised to find our enemies and do battle."

"You are ready. I must meet with Ben and the students and let them know what has happened."

Once more Michael stepped into history at about the same place on the porch that he had materialized on his last visit to the Lancaster farmhouse. The group of young people continued looking at the sky for several minutes, not realizing that he was present.

"I'm going to find out what the radio reports." George turned toward the house. "Look!" he pointed. "It's Michael!"

"Peace to you on this night of consternation."

"Michael!" Cindy turned toward the house. "I knew you'd be here soon. Tell us what is happening."

"Sit down and listen carefully."

The students quickly assembled around the porch steps.

"First, let me tell you about the condition of the world. The fires of the past months have seriously defoliated most of the forests. Reduced rainfall and rising temperatures last spring hampered crops. Fresh water is diminishing. You must be aware that the decreasing food supply will result in increased violence. Soon guns will be worth more than gold. People will kill for water."

"What's happening to the population?" Cindy asked.

"AIDS and drought have decimated the continent of Africa. Zimbabwe is nearly deserted. In Kenya the soil is baked clay. Drought has spread from the Cape of South Africa to Cairo. Starvation has taken a great toll."

"And South America?" a Hispanic student asked.

"El Niño winds have caused drought from South America to Australia. Except for Israel and Petra, the whole world is experiencing the full judgment for corrupting the atmosphere. The hand of God has been heavy while He waits patiently for the nations to turn to Yeshua as Messiah. However, in Israel and Petra, the land is being prepared for His return and rule."

"What's happening here?" Ben asked. "What is going on in Southern California?"

"You can feel the effects here tonight. Although air pollution has blocked one-third of the sunlight and moonlight, nothing is stopping the increase of ultraviolet radiation. Not only skin cancer but incidences of terrible cataracts are increasing. Respiratory illness is rampant. What is occurring in the skies is the fourth trumpet of judgment.

"Each of you has been affected in ways that have already begun to take their toll, even though you may not feel them. It is important that I pray for you and relieve the harmful effects. As our Lord did, I am going to lay hands on you that you may be healed of what has accumulated in your systems. Kneel and let me walk among you."

The students bowed on the ground. Some lay prostrate on the grass with their faces in their hands. Michael slowly moved among them, touching them on their heads prayerfully as the power of the Holy Spirit cleansed and renewed their eyes, revitalized their respiratory systems, and healed their skin lesions. The darkness of the night continued to be broken by thousands of intermediate bursts of meteoric explosions of light.

"Now, let me share with you the heavy words that I must bring for this hour."

The students gathered once more around the steps. "In the days ahead, the final woes will be visited on those who have rebelled and been disobedient. The Evil One prowls the earth; he knows that his final hour is at hand, but he is too obstinate to face the implications. You must understand that he is not alive and well but wounded and dying. His final weapon appears to be death, but it is not so. He can use only fear and anxiety to deceive you. Death will come, but you must not be dismayed. Dying is only part of the natural process that continues to work in this world. For the unbeliever, death is terror; but for you, it must be seen as the final means of transformation."

"Why are you giving us this instruction?" Ben interrupted. "Sounds rather ominous."

"You must remember that faithfulness does not exempt you from the consequences of life on this planet."

"Some of us are facing death?" George asked hesitantly.

"All of you have the potential to fall at any time, except Ben, who is one of the 144,000 and is absolutely protected."

"Michael, what are you suggesting?" Ben asked. "What lies ahead?"

"Remember, martyrdom is the mark of ultimate victory . . . not defeat."

"The McCoys!" Cindy gasped. "You're trying to tell us that something has happened to our friends."

The group became deathly quiet. Ben blinked apprehensively and reached for Cindy's hand.

"Yes. The McCoys have entered into their reward. Let your loss be tempered by the knowledge that they went as a family and now stand together before the throne of God. The faith and patience of the parents ultimately resulted in both children trusting Yeshua."

Cindy's often stoic features froze in place. Ben bit his lip and closed his eyes. Two of the students gathered around Ben and Cindy, putting their hands on their shoulders.

"They were faithful to the end. . . ." Cindy's voice broke uncharacteristically, and she began to weep.

"Such good people," Ben muttered. "Was . . . was the end terrible?"

"Swift and without lingering pain. The McCoy family left this troubled world together."

"We must hold some sort of memorial service for them." Ben pointed to a large oak tree next to the house. "The area beneath that tree would make a nice burial plot. We can't actually bury them, of course, but we could honor our friends with a memorial there."

"Yes," Deborah agreed. "Let's make crosses out of the old lumber behind the house. We can write their names on the crosses and stick them in the ground like grave markers."

Without anything more being said, the students started preparing a special site under the thick branches of the spreading oak. Some of the youths piled up rocks while others tied two-by-fours together with pieces of rope. Deborah wrote the McCoys' names with an indelible marker she found in her backpack. Soon the four crosses stuck out of the heap of rocks. After the students gathered around them, Ben began reading from the fourteenth chapter of John's Gospel: "'Let not your heart be troubled; you believe in God, believe also in Me. In My Father's house are many mansions; if it were not so, I would have told you. I go to prepare a place for you.'" Ben stopped and looked at the little group circled around the four crosses. "Would anyone like to say something?"

Deborah spoke softly. "Without Cindy's testimony, Erica would have perished in her sin. We don't have a choice about living or dying, but we make a decision about where we go. Cindy made that difference in Erica's life."

Silence settled over the group. Finally, Ben read again, "'I am the way, the truth, and the life. No one comes to the Father except through Me.'" He closed the Bible and the group started singing in hushed, broken tones. "Amazing grace! How sweet the sound that saved a wretch like me. . . ."

Their strong young voices filled the night air as they sang louder with each succeeding verse. Their hymn faded, and they stood quietly beneath the great oak tree, watching the thousands of meteors explode in the black sky.

To his surprise, Michael wept as he stepped back across the barrier of heaven and earth. As he moved away from the scene, his tears increased. Images of more friends dying filled his mind—the death of Ruth Feinberg and her unborn child in Bozrah. He looked back at the students, especially at Ben, and clenched his fist. *The end is coming,* he thought to himself. *And I will be ready to strike a blow like nothing Evil has ever known!*

# CHAPTER
## 32

Wincing in horror, Michael and Seradim stood at the other side of time and watched the nuclear exchange between Damian Gianardo and the Chinese prime minister tear the world apart. Even though the angels knew what was coming, their pain was still overwhelming. Innocent children were consumed by the same firestorm that devoured the wicked. By the time the two egomaniacs stopped, the world was in shambles, cities destroyed, and food sources contaminated. One-third of the remaining global population was wiped out. Suffering was vast and widespread.

"How much more can the world endure?" Seradim lamented.

"Time is growing very short indeed." Michael looked out toward the horizon where the sun was setting. "The final war is just ahead. Only a few pieces of the puzzle remain to be fitted into place. Our time is almost at hand."

Seradim looked intensely at the world beneath them. "The Chinese government gave Gianardo more than he dreamed possible. Obviously, he seriously miscalculated.

Even at this moment he is trying to shift all the blame for his aggressive and impulsive behavior on the Chinese people." Seradim looked carefully at Southern California. "I see Gianardo has started a counterattack on his own citizens. Anyone of Oriental descent is his target tonight. Look." The angel pointed toward Lake Forest. "The Wongs are in harm's way."

Michael studied three government vehicles speeding down Highway 5 from Los Angeles. The black automobiles turned off the freeway onto the exit ramp into the Lake Forest area. Within minutes the three undercover agents' cars pulled up in front of the Golden Dragon.

Michael pointed at the city. "Yes, Adams's men are arriving at the Wongs' restaurant even as we speak."

"May be my last and best opportunity to help Frank and Jessica," Seradim pondered. "This time I'm going to take a rather unique approach. Please forgive me, but time is too short for explanations."

"You've got to move fast. Adams and Schultz are almost at the door."

At that moment Cindy Wong was sitting on a stool in the back of the family restaurant, listening to her father read the newspaper aloud. Her mother continued to stir a boiling kettle on the stove, preparing for their evening customers.

"Say here that emperor make peace with Chinese premier three days after nuclear disaster. Now that one week pass, it clear that in addition to many millions who die, millions more injured." Frank put the paper down and shook his head. "Craziness. Gianardo is madman."

"The emperor's losing his grip," Cindy added. "We would never have seen such a story one year ago. He can't censor the press any longer."

"Empire is collapsing!" Jessica shook her finger in the air. "The evil man not stand forever."

The kitchen's swinging doors flew open, and a large man barged in. "Please follow me without saying a word," he commanded.

"Who are you?" Cindy's father dropped his paper.

"We must move quickly. Go out the back door now. Do not make a sound."

Jessica reached for a large chopping knife. "You not rob us tonight!"

"We only have seconds to leave before the security police arrest you."

Before Cindy could speak, the man pulled her off the stool and headed for the rear door. "Follow us," he demanded. "Secret police are coming in the front door this very minute."

"Hurry," Cindy yelled. "Trust him."

The Wongs ran silently behind their daughter and the stranger. The group darted down the alley behind the shopping center. Near the back fence line, the large man pushed a piece of the broken fence apart, and the Wongs slipped through.

"What happening?" Frank puffed.

"Get across the street!" The stranger took Cindy's hand and waded into the traffic, winding his way among the cars waiting for the stoplight to change. Only after they turned into the first street that ran into a residential area did he stop.

"Michael!" Cindy exploded. "What in the world are you doing? I recognized your voice in the restaurant. That's why I did just what you said."

"Michael?" the parents echoed.

"Listen carefully," the angel said. "The government is rounding up all Chinese-American citizens tonight. You must hide for several days. Within forty-eight hours confusion and chaos will be so great that the emperor's decision will have to be rescinded, and the government will be forced to release all prisoners. However, the police will be double-checking to find any Christians who might have been caught in the sweep. Cindy, they have your picture on file."

"Oh, Michael! You saved me again."

"We have no time to talk. Listen to what I want you to tell the students you are discipling. We have less than a year left. The Antichrist will become more desperate as his empire disintegrates. His inability to defeat China will result in other nations, such as Russia, the Ukraine, and the United Muslim League, defying his authority. He will be even more reckless and dangerous. If the police had taken you tonight, you would have been dead before morning."

Jessica grabbed her daughter. "Help us!"

"Quiet! Just listen to me. After the next couple of days pass, there will be a period of relative quiet. Governmental leaders will be so involved in trying to handle the disasters in the various nuked cities of the empire, they will leave the Christians and the Chinese alone."

"Cindy tell us about you, Mr. Angel." Frank's voice quivered. "We also meet another angel once. It difficult to believe . . . but we have heard your name often. We are old . . . foolish. But must believe in your Jesus now . . . tonight . . . this moment."

The shrill whining of sirens split the brisk night air. Police cars could be heard closing in from opposite directions. "They are arresting your Chinese employees right now, but do not worry. In three days they will be back to work. Catching Cindy would have been the deathblow to all of you."

Frank bowed up and down in the Oriental manner. "Mr. Michael, when workers come back, I tell them to believe in Jesus. I tell them angels never stop doing His work. Yes, we tell them we believe. They should believe too."

"Cindy, even though it is some distance away, you and your parents must get to the McCoys' house. No one has been there for months. The police will not be expecting anyone to hide in that place because of its reputation for harboring disloyal citizens. The back door is unlocked, and there are still canned goods in the pantry."

"Ben will be terrified," she pleaded. "I must let him know that we are okay."

"I will appear at the farmhouse after I leave you. Do not worry. I will put Ben's mind at peace. Now go!"

"We believe. We believe," Frank kept saying over his shoulder as the family scurried down the street.

Michael abruptly stepped into time and stood next to Seradim. Together they watched the Wongs disappear into one of the dark side streets. "Very clever," Michael said. "You took the form and voice I always use when appearing to Cindy. We look and sound like twins."

"Wasn't enough time left to chance her not following my instructions without questions. No point in explaining the switch. Might have further confused the Wongs. Praise God they have found the truth."

"You've truly learned to be a Guardian, my friend. You're ready to be a frontline solider in the final conflict."

Seradim smiled broadly. "Thank you. I already know who my targets will be."

■ ■ ■

As time passed, Seradim's predictions proved to be correct, and Gianardo backed down on his oppression of

Chinese citizens of the New Roman Empire. By early spring, the Wong family had closed the restaurant and moved into Ben's ministry headquarters, away from the roving gangs that had become an even greater threat than Gianardo's secret police. Frightened, hungry people roamed the streets like packs of wild animals. Anarchy and chaos reigned throughout California and across the nation.

Homelas and Malafidus were frantically responding to an unending array of opportunities. Easy marks distracted them from their old projects. Renewed confidence and expectation of final and total victory motivated all the legions of demons to work with frenzied fervor.

"Another new assignment!" Homelas shouted to his cohort. "Just came in. Killing the McCoys got us promoted. We've been attached to one of the new young generals in Gianardo's inner circle. We're getting near the heart of world control."

"Excellent!" Malafidus concentrated a moment, retrieving the complete files on their new target, General Calvin Browning. "Yes! Browning's a nuclear attack expert. He'll offer superb opportunities for action. Let's go."

When the demons descended on Washington, General Browning had just sat down at a small table next to four other military leaders in the center of a maximum security chamber. This room in the National Security Building was totally sequestered and free of possible electronic eavesdropping, but nothing could keep Homelas, Malafidus, and their comrades out. The two demons settled on each side of the young officer. Looking around the room, they acknowledged the other demons working the briefing.

Gianardo walked in and shut the door behind him, and the five generals immediately stood. "I am now surrounded by old fools and reactionary idiots," he mumbled to himself. The emperor flung a number of files down on the table and motioned for the group to sit down. "My New Roman Empire is being assaulted by the last vestiges of resistance to my complete control. We must now be ready to crush the enemy without fear of disobedience or resistance from within our own government."

Homelas and Malafidus could see the totally pervasive extent of Gianardo's degeneracy. Cruel conniving was etched in his being; deceit and malice in his eyes.

"Notice how his soul is yellowing," Malafidus said to the swarm of demons that hovered around the emperor. "You boys are doing an excellent job."

"Got the arrogant old fool under total control," Belial, the leader of the pack, shot back. "We've totally captured his imagination and dreams. We control his every intention."

Gianardo cleared his throat. "Your time of opportunity has come. General Smith thinks that I am not aware of his attempts to thwart me. We must be ready to stop his men at a moment's notice. When the final strike against the Chinese and the United Muslim League comes, each of you must be prepared to assassinate anyone who stands in our way. You may have only one shot. You must not miss."

"You can count on us." Browning saluted.

Malafidus concentrated on touching the burning ambition simmering at the center of Browning's heart and mind. He gently massaged the young man's sense of self-importance.

"When this period is past," Gianardo said with complete confidence, "you will not only be commanders in this empire but the first military leaders of the entire globe. I congratulate you on a very intelligent decision to stand by me."

A greenish ethereal fog emanated from the demonic swarm. The haze rolled out over the table and settled around the generals.

Gianardo pushed a file toward each person. "I have already appointed each of you to a new position that will take effect at the moment we strike. Askins will head security. Browning, you'll have the nuclear strike command. Jackson, I have selected you to coordinate all ground and attack forces. I want Imler to oversee domestic coordination of all legislative activities. Salino will handle the final details of surrender after we have humiliated our international enemies."

General Jackson smiled broadly. "We are your servants as together we write the history of the beginning of the third millennium. What can I do at this time?"

"Watch him," Malafidus whispered in Browning's ear. "Jackson's trying to upstage you. Don't let him get an edge with Gianardo."

The emperor–president pointed beyond the walls. "I want you to create a system that will circumvent the nuclear detonation device in this building. It must be portable since we will be taking it to Rome with us in a few months. We will reassemble our command post there. No one must be aware of what you have done except an expert that I will assign to you. Terbor Esiw will know what to do. He is the secret creator behind this effort."

"Speak up now!" Malafidus shouted in Browning's face. "Take the initiative."

General Browning immediately asked, "Who else is aware of this plan?"

"No one. You will note that the instructions are in my own handwriting. When we meet, you will tell your staff personnel that I have appointed you to an ad hoc task force preparing plans for the rebuilding of this country. Any other questions?"

"Can the world survive another war?" Imler probed. "I'm sure that you have covered this option."

"A world with less population will be much easier to manage." Gianardo smiled. "Yes, long ago I recognized the need to reduce population to a level that would be more controllable. In the future we will not have to worry with negative public response or the failure of any form of compliance. I will have completely united religion, politics, and all forms of philosophical thought. Gentlemen, we will be gods!"

Browning applauded loudly and the rest of the generals followed. He smiled ingratiatingly at the emperor, who appeared quite pleased at the young general's responses.

As the military leaders dispersed, several of the hovering demons lingered behind. Belial joined them. "Our infernal leader is pleased," the highest ranking demon confided. "Never have we had such unassailable control over the world. These presumptuous warmongers are mere pawns in our hands."

"When do we get to kill them off?" Malafidus asked. "Anyone know?"

Belial answered, "The indicators are clear that these fools will continue to precipitate worldwide crises. We think some can be nudged into killing each other, just as Gianardo is planning the assassination of General Smith. There will be more carnage than even our appetites can handle."

Homelas looked knowingly at Malafidus. "We've knocked off families, children, leaders for the other side. What a season of hope it's been."

"Headquarters keeps a running total of our assassinations," Belial hissed. "Don't worry, boys, they'll know when you suck your young general down into the blackness of the pit."

# CHAPTER

## 33

Standing at the edge of heaven, Michael and Seradim scrutinized Earth's final months as history spun out of control.

Gianardo became obsessed with establishing Rome as the geographic center for his reign. He took over the papal palace and chased the new pope out of the country. He halted all worship in St. Peter's Basilica. Periodically Gianardo strolled into the chancel and sat on the high altar, proclaiming himself omnipotent. Ironically, his so-called "total power" was not sufficient to stop the continuing disintegration of the United States.

In late August the emperor summoned the five young generals now controlling all military operations to the Sistine Chapel. Full-scale maps, drawings, and plans were laid out on long tables beneath the ceiling that was Michelangelo's greatest accomplishment. The junta planned their final battle strategy.

Near the end of the meeting, Gianardo placed his finger on a point on one of the maps. "I have personally planned every detail of what lies ahead." He thumped the map of Israel. "We are going to land on the beaches near the ancient city of Megiddo. I want to prepare for a drive down the Valley of Jezreel, called by some Armageddon. We will cut the country into two sections."

Browning leaned over and stared at the map. "Armageddon? Why there? In fact, why in the world are we going to Israel of all places?"

"Two reasons," the emperor snapped. "For some unexplainable cause, the Israelis are the only people who have escaped the ecological damage visited on the world by my enemies. They have the only real estate left where we can hope to escape the effects of pollution and radiation. We will govern from Jerusalem until the rest of the world cools off. In addition, their capital has religious significance. In the future, Jerusalem will be a more suitable place for my throne."

Browning stared at the map, the consequences of the action racing through his mind. *We are no match for the Chinese army,* he thought, *particularly since the Japanese and the Muslims have joined them. We will eventually have no recourse but to use atomic weapons. Then Israel will no longer be free of radiation effects. We are courting total global disaster.*

While Browning reflected, Gianardo explained exactly how he wanted the landing handled. The emperor abruptly turned and stared at the young man. "Some problem with my plan, General? You disagree?"

Every eye in the room trained on Browning. He shook his head; the blood drained from his face. He slowly slid down into his chair at the table. *Our days are truly numbered! We can never survive this assault.*

Gianardo's once brilliant ploys were now so paranoid that each new idea was more exaggerated and bizarre than the last. Because no one was left to moderate or restrain him, any balanced perspective was lost.

A month later a helicopter lowered the emperor down in front of the Western Wall in the old city of Jerusalem.

With television cameras offering the world a picture of his every movement, Gianardo marched to the spot where Moses and Elijah had been sitting unharmed for three and a half years, passing the judgments of God and foiling many attempts to kill them. Gianardo angrily confronted the two biblical giants, but they calmly stared at him.

"I have the power of life and death in my hands." The emperor's voice was menacing. "You nuisances have been allowed to stay only because of my choosing. Do you understand that in a moment I can dispatch you back into the mist from which you came?"

Across the plaza no one moved.

"Now let the world see who laughs last!" Gianardo screamed. He turned to a soldier behind him and jerked the man's pistol from his holster. The emperor cocked the gun and ran directly in front of the prophets. "Let every eye see who has the power." He fired rapidly, toppling Moses and Elijah from their thrones. Complete silence descended on the holy site. Disbelief and dismay covered people's faces.

Gianardo turned to the stunned multitude. His voice split the silence. "I am the most powerful force in the world," the emperor screamed. "Do you understand? I have exposed these frauds. I have done what even Pharaoh of Egypt could not accomplish." No one moved.

"The world thought some abstract idea called God was the power of life and death. I alone am this power. I am the supreme one! Throw away your superstitions! I decree these bodies be left in the city that the world may watch. No one touch them! Watch them rot!"

When no one moved, Gianardo threw the gun down and stomped back toward the steps. Soldiers fell in around him. The square emptied as his helicopter disappeared. Yet silence hung like an impenetrable fog over the temple mount.

■ ■ ■

For three days the two great leaders lay face down on the platform next to their thrones, jagged holes ripped open in the back of their robes where the bullets exited. No one dared to touch their bodies.

On the fourth day the sun broke over the mountaintops around Jerusalem. Light bathed the plaza in front of the Western Wall in a blaze of arid sunlight. Moses slowly got to his feet and Elijah reached for the arm of his chair, pulling himself up. The two prophets silently surveyed the strange scene before them; a ring of fully armed troops slept at their feet.

Moses thumped his staff on the wooden platform. The hollow sound echoed menacingly across the square. A soldier looked up and blinked. A second raised his head. Another leaped to his feet. "They're alive again!" He scrambled for his gun. "Look!"

"Call the CO!" another soldier in the back called.

"Do not fear us." Moses waved them back. "Rather fear him who would steal your soul. The time is short. Repent now, for the era draws to a close."

Clouds began boiling in the sky, just as they had on the day of their appearing. Moses and Elijah quickly retraced their steps up the Kidron Valley toward the Mount of Olives. The ground began shaking violently, and roaring noises filled Jerusalem.

On top of the mount at the site of Jesus' ascension, the two prophets disappeared gradually, ascending very slowly in sight of many in a swirl of cloud covering.

Within seconds the earth rocked even more violently and every building in Jerusalem rumbled. Crevasses opened across streets and entire buildings fell in. Seven thousand of Gianardo's men disappeared as the earth kept shifting, swallowing them alive. Throughout the rest of the day, aftershocks rocked not only the city but people across the world. Damian Gianardo was increasingly discredited because of the impact of the television pictures of the resurrection and ascension of Moses and Elijah—pictures which had been seen around the globe.

In the late afternoon General Calvin Browning barged into the emperor's office. "I have an update on how the troop landing is progressing. We believe that our units are moving at top speed to secure the entire area near the entrance to the Jezreel Valley." The building shook. He paused to catch his breath.

Although there had been no signs of a storm, a bolt of lightning flashed across the sky. A great explosion of light filled the room, followed by a deafening roar. Gianardo and Browning rushed to the window. A large tree across the street was now a smoldering, splintered stump. Streaks of lightning popped and crackled through the air. People outside dived for shelter in the nearest building.

"The earth is coming apart," Browning sputtered. The building shook again, and across the street large rocks bounced as another earthquake began. The general's eyes widened. "Everything is coming unglued."

"Get a grip on yourself, Browning! The environment's messed up from the pollution and A-bomb attacks. Don't go nuts on me."

A file cabinet toppled over and Gianardo's desk began sliding toward the opposite wall. The general lost his footing and nearly fell. Staggering like a drunk, he tried to reach the door. "I'll try to get some kind of report to you later." Browning ran, not even attempting to close the door behind him. He stumbled down the hall and staggered into a corner where he slumped, curling up in a ball.

"We've lost our control over him," Malafidus swore. "I didn't think he would crack."

"Headquarters will be livid if we don't reel him back in." Homelas groaned. "We've got to get inside his head."

Browning placed his hands to his ears and began whimpering. He pulled his knees tightly against his face.

"Fear has gone from being our tool to a barrier." Malafidus circled the general. "Oh, no, the idiot's starting to pray!"

"Dear God," whimpered Browning. "What have I done? It's all true, isn't it? This is Your doing. Is it too late . . . too late for me?"

Belial emerged through the wall. "What's going on here?" He stared at the general on the floor. "Not him!" the demon roared. "Don't tell me he's capitulated!"

Malafidus and Homelas exchanged nervous glances.

"We're working on the problem," Homelas answered. "Go on back to Gianardo. Everything will be okay in a moment."

Browning uncurled himself and kneeled, bowing his head down to the floor. "Sweet Jesus, only now do I see my father was right about You. I don't want to die . . . not without You."

The senior ranking demon inched toward Browning, listening intensely. "I swear! The man really is praying. Stop him!" Belial screamed. "He could contaminate the entire place."

The building shook again and big sections of the ceiling fell down. A support beam split and crashed. A piece of the paneling fell on Browning's head. The general slumped, blood running down his face.

"He's still alive!" Belial shrieked. "Better he die than repent of his sin! Fools! Idiots! Incompetents! I don't want Lucifer to know I was even in the vicinity!" The demon disappeared instantly.

"He'll turn us in!" Homelas grabbed his head. "Belial will show no mercy."

Malafidus listened intensely. "I can hear . . . yes . . . at this moment . . . that old devil *is* reporting us. . . . No . . . no . . ."

"What will they do to us?" Homelas agonized. "They won't let this failure stand." He stumbled backward and fell through the wall out into the streets.

Lightning fired through the sky in great streaks of brilliant fire. Thunder roared in deafening answer. Bowls of wrath were being poured out everywhere.

# CHAPTER
## 34

The final call went out. From across the expanse of the cosmos, the hordes of evil swarmed into the center of darkness. Like vultures landing on dead tree limbs, demons gathered for the assault. The legions of malice turned their undivided attention to the very heart of Perdition where cold emptiness reigned supreme. Homelas and Malafidus slipped into the back of the pack, trying to be obscure although nothing could be hidden in the realm beyond time.

Quiet settled. The silence of death permeated the assembly. No one moved, waiting for something not yet formed but surely coming like an eclipse at high noon. Satan waited in a grand pause as before the closing movement of the last symphony. After relishing the supreme moment of fulfillment, the Evil One appeared as the axis in their midst.

A clamor of awe arose like vapor from a steamer. Though Satan had appeared in many disguises, never had the multitude beheld their leader in such glory, sparkling like the brightest of stars. Ugliness was replaced by the magnetic aura of power and majesty.

Satan looked astonishingly like Damian Gianardo, suave and debonair. Yet, the eyes were dark and foreboding as if they contained the collected wisdom of the centuries, awful and frightening in their comprehensive insight. The Evil One slowly crossed his arms and genuinely smiled for the first time since the beginning of creation.

"I stand on the verge of total victory," he pronounced. "I battled to gain undisputed control of this realm because I always knew the power of the Creator was not omnipotent. Now I have proven myself correct."

The assembly writhed in delight and roared in endless waves of exhilaration until Lucifer again raised his hand. Silence was instantaneous.

"I have tried many approaches," Satan lectured. "In ancient times I offered humans the forms of Osiris and Isis of Egypt, Marduk of Babylon, and Molech of the Canaanites. Yes, they worshiped me in many shapes and guises . . . for a time . . . but our Nemesis would not stop. First this and then that. Sacrifices, prayers, prophets, and worst of all the angels." Satan paused and glared. "But for every one of His attempts I had a counterattack." He thought for a moment. "The offering of political domination, authority, strength was unparalleled. Power was always the best aphrodisiac. Caesar made a much better god than any alternative a fertility cult ever manufactured."

Homelas meditated carefully, offering Malafidus as gentle and quiet a thought as he was capable of extending. "I don't think Belial was able to do us in. Things are going to be okay."

Malafidus squinted out of the corner of his eye and shook his head despondently.

"Of course, the Christians' dying savior was a serious problem," Satan muttered. "His descent into death hurt. Confused people. Made Easter propaganda." The devil snorted. "Took away our best weapon," his voice trailed away for a moment.

"But we didn't stop!" Satan screamed. "We offered humans such awesome portions of pleasure that death's sting was swallowed by sheer mindless distractions. From Monte Carlo to Las Vegas, from the boardrooms of America to the power brokers of the Arab world, we made them forget any other world existed by polishing the veneer we laid over this one to an intoxicating luster!" Satan ground his fist into his palm.

"We offered them the lamb with the voice of a dragon." His voice dropped almost to a whisper. "Purposeless religion that was nothing but soothing, meaningless words." Satan ranted. "Words, words, words flowing endlessly like sewage to a cesspool. The false prophets were always our best allies!"

"We won!" a demon screamed. Again the hordes of hell broke into buoyant celebration. "You prevailed!" they screamed.

"We've made it." Homelas leered as he spun around his friend. "All is forgiven. We've prevailed!"

"The final battle is at hand," Satan intruded. "My pawn, Gianardo, thinks himself the supreme religious personage of the age. As soon as he is dead, I will fill the vacuum once and for all. The world will be united in their capacity to embrace my full disclosure. The Creator will retreat from further intrusion, and my kingdom will be established. The time has come to prepare for the final battle. Assemble yourselves!"

The unruly mob instantly formed into rank-and-file order, shaping into a multidimensional sphere, filling height, depth, breadth, and space with Satan at the center. Homelas and Malafidus settled into the reassembled Attack Command with Responsibility for Power Centers in the United States.

"As dawn breaks in their world," Lucifer continued his instruction, "armies will collide. When angelic interference occurs, attack with a vengeance! Be fearless. Your assignment is to create a bloodbath, drenching them up to their armpits. Feed on their fears and banquet on their anger. Tease them with power and terrify them with death. When it's done, I want a valley full of corpses to offer to the heavens! Let the Creator try and tell this world that death no longer reigns!"

No demon moved, each standing in rigid attention.

"The world is united for the first time in human history as one entity. Communications, electronics, and mass transportation provided the tools that the most ambitious dictators could only dream and hope for. I will show this race of contemptible idiots what *we* can do with their toys. Onward to Armageddon!"

The horde abruptly glided forward toward the great barrier into time. At that moment, only Malafidus and Homelas heard the same message simultaneously.

"Do you think I am not aware of the failure of you two incompetent, blundering oafs?"

The countenance dominating the two demon's awareness changed. Loathing and sordidness were etched in the lines of his face. The visage became a singular entity, blotting out everything else in their minds.

"Reward?" Satan's voice kept increasing. "When this day is done, you two are through forever. You are to stay out of the battle!" His command rang like explosions of fire. "Why should I reward you with the joy of observing death and disfigurement? You have one final assignment left."

The remainder of the devil's instructions rocked through them with a roar that blinded and destroyed all capacity for response. The two demons dropped from their ranks and floundered on the edge before tumbling into time, trying to regain composure.

■ ■ ■

Well before dawn, the eastern side of the Jezreel Valley exploded with staggering bursts of fire. Phosphoric pieces of smoldering debris sailed through the night. From out of the blackness, countless hordes of demons swarmed on, over, down, and around the battlefield. As day broke, waves of airplanes dumped endless forays of bombs while the sky filled with fighter jets locked in mortal combat. By ten o'clock, the fallout and dust were so thick that it was difficult to breathe even miles away along the coast.

The Chinese counterattacked with a simple strategy. Waves of human beings were hurled into the fray. Bodies were quickly strewn over the area like tree limbs after a tornado. Demons attacked again and again in an endless feeding frenzy. By late afternoon, the eastern slope and the terrain down the Armageddon Valley were completely filled with dead bodies of the Chinese and their allies. Gianardo's losses were even more staggering.

Malafidus and Homelas stood alone above the fray, isolated from the struggle. The two demons could only observe, nothing more.

"When do we know to begin our final task?" Homelas asked.

Malafidus hung his head. "I suppose some demon will let us know . . . at some point . . . maybe *he* will speak . . ."

"He did say 'final,' didn't he?"

"I think so." Malafidus's voice trailed away. "The shouting was so loud I didn't catch everything. At least we are to escort a load of these victims to the Pit and . . . then go in with them." He wrung his hands.

"Will we ever come out again?" Homelas's voice was barely a gasp. "What do you think?"

"I've never heard of anyone returning." Malafidus choked.

■ ■ ■

In his quarters in the concrete command bunker far beneath Megiddo, General Browning struggled to function. His head was tightly bandaged, but the pain of depression was a far more formidable distraction. By the time Gianardo summoned him and the four other generals to his bunker, Browning had found the resolve to do what he must.

The field command general quickly reviewed the losses and gains of the battle. Another general gave a five-minute summary of the current world situation. The news was devastating. Browning said nothing and stared at the floor. Silence settled over the room.

"What do you think?" Gianardo asked his grim-faced assembly, huddling together in his Megiddo communications center. "Where are we on this Friday night, September 28? If memory serves me right, tomorrow's the big Jewish Feast of Trumpets. Anyone requesting leave for the holidays?"

No one smiled at the feeble joke. Finally, Browning spoke up, "I have always prided myself on being a soldier, not a butcher. Never have I witnessed what happened out there today. Surely the carnage exceeds the worst ever seen by the human race."

The emperor dismissed the general's comments by not acknowledging them. Gianardo changed the subject and quickly detailed his final scheme to outflank the Chinese by proposing peace and then releasing a final nuclear attack while the opposition was preparing for a cease-fire.

"You offer peace while planing to totally destroy the Chinese and their allies!" Rathmarker declared proudly. "Very clever. This will be the war to end all wars. World domination with no opposition will finally be ours."

"Brilliant, is it not?" Gianardo smirked. "This is not the time to retreat."

"You are quite right." General Browning slowly rose to his feet, a look of determination and, strangely, peace on his face. "This is not the time to back off." He walked out of the room alone, the weight of his past finally lifted from his shoulders.

# CHAPTER
## 35

The blackness of that night exceeded anything previously known on Earth. The moon and stars were completely obliterated by smoke. Life was systematically being snuffed out. As dawn approached, an awesome stillness hovered over Jerusalem. The exhausted emperor and Rathmarker huddled together, ready to respond to any surprise move by the Chinese and their allies. Vultures hovered overhead, anticipating the feast of their lives.

At that exact moment the sun started to rise, the clouds over the Holy City broke, and a great shaft of light shot through the sky like a beacon in a stormy night. The spear of illumination cut through the murky smog and shot out toward the ends of the globe. To their utter surprise, the citizens of Jerusalem awoke to wonderful morning light streaming into their windows. They rubbed their eyes in amazement at the shimmering daybreak no one had seen for several years. Out in the streets, people looked awestruck toward the sky. The glorious aurora did not blind their eyes but felt soothing and healing. To their astonishment, the continuing glow seemed to swallow the smoke and pollution, imparting a renewed clarity to the sky.

Homelas and Malafidus stared incredulously at the brilliant light cutting through the smoke over the battlefield. The sunlight penetrated their own darkness with a glow of an uncanny dazzlement.

Malafidus blinked and put his arm over his eyes. "What . . . What's happening out there?"

"I . . . I . . . don't know." Homelas closed his eyes. "Headquarters didn't say anything about . . . blackness was supposed to prevail . . . death would reign. I thought the war was over."

"Bad intelligence, guys." A voice spoke from behind the demons.

"What?" Malafidus turned around.

"Who are you?" Homelas gawked at the awesome figure.

"Part of the God squad, remember?"

A look of recognition passed over the demons' faces, quickly replaced by looks of fear.

"Been following you boys around for several years," Seradim answered, towering above the evil creatures. "Cleaning up your messes."

"A-h-h-h," Malafidus shrieked. "They've turned us over to an angel to destroy us!"

"No! No!" Homelas begged. "We know you can obliterate us with a single blaze of celestial light. By all the devils in hell, we have no hope." He tried to hide his face.

Seradim held up his fist as if to smash the demons in a single blow. He looked intently into their cowering faces, dreading their imminent assignment to hell. From his face luminous radiance emanated outward in all directions. Incandescent love made the angel appear as a singular spotlight of splendor. Cleansing light wrapped around the two demons and traveled out across the endless expansion of eternity.

"Has the Master of Evil ever offered you any promise of joy . . . genuine joy?" Seradim said gently.

The two demons huddled together, shaking their heads, refusing to look up.

"You don't deserve grace . . . but then again no one ever does. Look straight at me!" Seradim commanded. "Open your eyes."

The demons retreated.

"Even now you would reject Him who is the Light, the Truth, the Way?"

"I think it's a trap!" Homelas balked defiantly. "A test to see if we'll cross over. The real angels were defeated in the battle. This one isn't for real." He pointed at Seradim. "The boss has come again disguised as an angel of light."

"Do I really look like Satan?" Seradim radiated the brilliance of divine love.

"The devil's seduced the best of 'em." Homelas remained recalcitrant. "I'm not about to throw in the towel after fighting against namby-pamby, bleeding-heart goodness for so many centuries. I'm standing with the front office. Even in the Pit, our side still holds the final power. Evil is stronger than goodness." Homelas cupped his hand to his mouth. "Hear me, Lucifer! Even if I flunk this last test, I know you'll bring me back from the depths. We're going to win in the end."

"Yes," Malafidus said resolutely. "This time we're not going to fail the test. We've been given another opportunity to redeem ourselves." The demon turned and looked at the expanding illumination lingering above the Mount of Olives. "I don't know what's going on, but I'm betting our boss has an alternative strategy at work."

"We're not fooled!" Homelas screamed. "The war is over and we've won!"

"No, warfare is not finished," Seradim answered gently but firmly. "The last battle has just begun."

At that moment a brilliant explosion of resplendence shot out from the Mount of Olives. The Source of the light broke through the clouds on a great white horse. Wearing a golden crown and holding a sharp sickle, the risen and exalted Yeshua once more rode into human history, this time as Lord of the Third Millennium. Across the dazzling white robe of the Messiah was emblazoned in Hebrew, "King of kings and Lord of lords."

His appearance sent shock waves backward into and across eternity. Like the force of an enormous invisible explosion, the imperishable winds of immortality swept over the three figures. Homelas and Malafidus were hurled backward into the receding darkness, disappearing in the expansive blackness and then pushed into the gigantic black hole at the end of all existence. Their screams echoed until endless silence swallowed them as they plunged down into the Pit.

Legions of angels swooped from the heavens onto the Armageddon battlefield, descending with unrelenting purity of cleansing light. The Seraphim choirs from highest heaven echoed their song above the last encounter. The Thrones released the full force of the judgments of God. Dominions issued instructions for attack and counterattack. Evil retreated in scattered disarray. The mouth of hell opened, and demons fell into the Pit. The Powers were relentless in their pursuit.

■ ■ ■

On the other side of the world, pitch black darkness was torn apart by the light. Brightness filled the room where Ben and the Wongs were sleeping. The moment each person was bathed in the light, the sallow color of their skin damaged by the environmental pollution, turned to a pink healthy glow.

"For goodness' sake!" Frank Wong looked around the room in bewilderment. "What happen?"

"He's returned." Ben's dry raspy voice was barely audible. "The Lord has returned! Today is a Feast of Trumpet's Day we will remember for eternity."

"We're saved," one of the students gasped. "We're going to survive."

"Praise Him!" Deborah raised her hands toward the ceiling. "Praise God! Praise Yeshua, His Son!"

The night had turned into a glorious sunrise. The usual murky gray sky changed to a brilliant blue. Even the trees and plants were visibly energized and revitalized. "Oh, thank You, Lord!" Ben ran to the window. "The whole of creation is coming into its own!"

"So *that's* you, Ben!" a small delicate voice said from behind him.

Ben turned. "What? Cindy?"

"You do have a beautiful face!"

"What are you saying?"

"I can see you, Ben. For the first time in my life, I can see."

At that moment Archangels and others in the heavenly ranks broke forth out of the stream of light covering Jerusalem. The heavenly hosts processed into the world, passing on both sides of the Messiah on His white horse. Vast multitudes flew forth over the face of the earth as the exalted Yeshua sat suspended in the air. A mighty chorus proclaimed together, "The kingdoms of this world have become the kingdoms of the Lord and of His Christ. And He shall reign forever and ever!"

When the Messiah's horse touched the place of His original ascension nearly two thousand years before, the Mount of Olives broke apart. A great quake split the earth to its center, and the shock wave reverberated to every fault line across the globe, opening a path from the Dead Sea through the Mount of Olives to the Mediterranean. Lightning flashed across the world, and the skies were filled with a staggering aerial display of color and energy.

■ ■ ■

Anticipating the Return at sunrise, Jimmy Harrison and Larry and Sharon Feinberg climbed to the top of the highest mountain in the area well before dawn. At their refuge in Petra–Bozrah, they had helped many thousands of Jews survive the continuing disasters. The physical and emotional toll had been enormous, especially the struggle to adjust to Ruth's death during childbirth the previous year. All trace of weariness was gone now as they waited in eager expectation for this glorious daybreak.

Below them in the valley, groups of Jimmy's students were kneeling in silent prayer even before the all-encompassing beam of light first shot across the sky. As the procession of angels began passing overhead, the new believers covered their faces. They knew from Scripture that whenever the Battle of Armageddon was won by Yeshua, He would personally come to Bozrah to gather His brothers and sisters and lead them through the East Gate of Jerusalem to begin the forty-five-day transition into the third millennium A.D.

Jimmy fell with his face to the ground. Larry and Sharon huddled together with their heads bowed. A great chorus of overpowering singing and heavenly praise encouraged them to look again to the sky. They watched awestruck as millions of angels appeared in the clouds. An ever-increasing army of martyrs and saints followed, spreading out in all directions. Many in the cavalcade paraded above them, sweeping closer and closer to the ground as they passed by. The group approached Bozrah–Petra.

White-robed saints waved to the citizens of Bozrah as if they knew them and were reunited with old friends they had been observing for a long time. In turn, the people began waving back. The Jews stood, clapped, held their hands to heaven, shouted, and prayed. They danced and waved to the hosts overhead, weeping for joy.

Jimmy Harrison stood mesmerized by the sound. He closed his eyes as his ears drank in the blissful music that exceeded any strain he had ever heard. "Jimmy." Sharon shook his arm. "Two people are waving at you. They are trying to get your attention."

"Jimmy! Jimmy!" Sharon began sobbing uncontrollably. "To your left. Look! In the white robe . . . it's Ruth!"

Open-mouthed, crying, Jimmy reached up on his tiptoes for the sky. The dark-haired beauty in the white robe extended her hand as she slowly descended.

"Ruth! Ruth!" Jimmy called. "It's really you!" The McCoys and Ruth steadily moved toward the trio standing on the mountaintop with their hands lifted as high as they could reach.

"A young man is holding on to Ruth's hand." Larry pointed to his daughter. "Jimmy! He must be one of your ancestors. He looks so much like you."

Jimmy found it nearly impossible to see through his tears. He danced from one foot to the other, waving, holding his arms outstretched. "Ruth . . . Mom . . . Dad . . . Joe and Jennifer . . . Erica and Joe Jr. . . . . we're here. . . . We've waited so long."

As they moved very close, Reverend Harrison opened his arms. His voice was loud and clear. "Oh, son, we've been so proud of you. How pleased we are with what you've done!" Jimmy's father took the other hand of the young man standing with Ruth. "We are bringing a very special person with us. Meet my grandson . . . your son."

■ ■ ■

The procession of angels passed beneath Seradim, continuing to march out across the globe and into the whole of the cosmos. From out of the millions of angels, one large Guardian stopped and beckoned. Instantly Seradim heard his call.

"Hail, conquering one," Michael summoned. "Join me. You've more than earned your place in our ranks, for you have overcome through the power, not of the sword, but of love. You are a brother to the Crucified One who always reigns from the cross. Come. I would be proud to have you stand by my side."

Seradim was overwhelmed with the joy of total fulfillment. "I am on my way!"

Michael beamed. "You have earned a special place in this procession. Your assignment is complete. You presided over the demise of the last two demons on Earth. Behold the dawn of every tomorrow."

A great voice thundered across creation, guiding the legions of angels forward. "Behold I make all things new.

It is done! I am the Alpha and the Omega, the beginning and the end." Another burst of splendorous light flooded across the creation and Seradim abruptly experienced a heavenly *déjà vu.*

"I know this exact experience of glory!" Seradim explained to Michael. "This is precisely where I began in the highest heaven, worshiping around the throne of God. The realm from above has descended to the world of human beings!"

"All the plans of eternity are fulfilled," Michael answered in awe.

Worship exploded from the deepest recesses of Seradim's being. He answered, "Amen and Amen."

# APPENDIX

■ *The Third Millennium* has remained a bestseller since it came out in early 1993. The partnership I began with Robert L. Wise in that book extended to *The Fourth Millennium,* which has been a steady best-seller as well. Using the backdrop of our travels together in Israel, we attempted to put the secrets of the Scripture in an exciting form to help people prepare spiritually for their struggles as the world becomes an increasingly difficult place to live.

We hit some amazing predictions right on the head. In *The Third Millennium,* our characters discovered a number of approaching turning points in history that have now happened around the world. Our book foresaw secret negotiations between Israel and their Arab enemies; in the summer of 1993, Israel and the PLO held secret meetings. Our book also forecast a treaty; an actual treaty was signed at the White House by the Israeli prime minister and Yasser Arafat in the fall of 1993.

If you've not read it, you will find the appendix in the back of *The Third Millennium* to be very helpful in understanding the mathematical and prophetic reasons for these projections and why we thought (and still do) that the year 2000 will be a significant turning point in Bible prophecy. The discovery of the importance of Av 9 in the Jewish calendar allowed me to develop other projections based on Israel's feast days. These events are definitely tied together in an amazing biblical system of prophecy that is the key to understanding the future.

The Feast of Trumpets is the Jewish New Year. For a variety of reasons, and using the prophecies in the book of Daniel concerning "Daniel's Seventieth Week," I counted back seven years from the Feast and landed in the fall of 1993. The calendar offered two options for the signing of the peace treaty (which will actually start Daniel's Seventieth Week some day in the future): November 6 (using the Hebrew calendar) or September 16 (using the Gregorian calendar). Because either date was possible, we compromised and picked the "fall of 1993." However, as a matter of fact, Yasser Arafat and Yitzhak Rabin really did sign a now famous treaty on the White House lawn with President Bill Clinton watching . . . on September 13, 1993, three days before the Feast of Trumpets that year.

To my pleasant surprise, Yitzhak Rabin returned to the United States, on November 6, to sign another yet-to-be-disclosed deal. While the details are secret, *The Jerusalem Post* suggested the U.S. government promised to protect Jerusalem if Rabin in turn would cooperate in signing more ridiculous "land for peace" deals with the nations surrounding Israel. (It sounds strangely reminiscent of Hitler's land-for-peace deals, which led to World War II.)

*The Third Millennium* also successfully predicted the formation of an economic union within the Arab world; we called it the United Muslim League in our book. In 1994 such a merger was accomplished. I do not claim to be a person with special prophetic insight but have simply memorized verses from every prophetic chapter in the Bible. I try to guess in accord with my best interpretation of the Scripture.

On this basis, we also anticipated that Russia's "flight into democracy" would end in anti-evangelical and anti-Semitic attitudes and laws; this came to pass in 1997 with new legislation that restricts religious organizations. In 1993, after the state had changed hands, I stood in Red Square with a soft drink in hand, toasting the new prime minister with Russian soldiers. I was chanting, "Yeltsin, Yeltsin." During this visit I taught Christian psychiatry at the state university in St. Petersburg. Since then, former communists have become the "black mafia," and they actually continue to control Russia in spite of its democratic window dressing. With great grief, I recognized from my study of Scripture that true freedom of religion would soon be gone in Russia.

No one knows the day or hour of the Rapture or the Second Coming. As a psychiatrist, I know that people who are dogmatic on these matters are both biblically and emotionally unsound. At the same time, the serious Bible student will not retreat from recognizing the nature of our era and the times in which we are living. While we can't hit the final date with the precision of a rocket launch, we still eagerly wait for Jesus' return and can live with an eternal perspective during tough times. Not knowing *the day* does not keep us from having a cause to live for as we look toward the end.

I have listened to the ongoing arguments about future timetables. Different groups predict a "pre-trib," a "mid-trib," or a "post-trib" Rapture. While we lean toward a "pre-trib" view, Robert Wise and I are officially "pan-trib," meaning only God knows when the end events will happen—but we believe it will all "pan out" in the end.

We have had to adjust our speculation about the Second Coming possibly happening in the year 2000. The desecration of the Temple Mount (predicted by Jesus in Matthew 24) would have to have occurred on Passover 1997 to meet that date. *It didn't happen.* A month before Passover, or Purim 1997, Orthodox Jews would have to have stopped animal sacrifices in Jerusalem, *which they haven't even started.* Yet unexpected pieces of the puzzle are coming together. The rare red heifers have now reappeared in Israel and will be available when the political climate allows sacrifices to start again (possibly in the year 2000).

Since the writing of *The Third Millennium,* we discovered another problem. Our first novel indicated a nuclear attack in Israel on July 25, 1996. That future war is predicted in Ezekiel 38 and 39. In the Hebrew calendar the date would have been Av 9. *It didn't happen.*

Why were we wrong? Allow me to reference some of the material I discuss in much greater detail in the appendix of *The Third Millennium.* First I will quickly survey the history of what happened on Av 9 through the centuries, and then I will look at what could have been anticipated on that one particular date in 1996.

Over 3,500 years ago on Av 9, ten spineless Hebrew spies entered Canaan in preparation for Israel's invasion. Because they were faithless, Israel wandered in the wilderness for forty more years. From that point on, the date of Av 9 became a day of infamy. Most of the horrible things that God, in His sovereignty, allowed to happen have occurred at this time. The Old Testament calls Av 9 an annual day of fasting and mourning.

The first temple fell on Av 9, 587 B.C. In A.D. 70 Titus and the Roman legions besieged Jerusalem, killing many priests and stopping sacrifices, finally destroying the rebuilt temple on the ninth of Av. Sixty-five years later, the last Jewish uprising against Rome, led by Simon Bar-Kochba, was crushed on Av 9.

Centuries later, the expulsion of Jews from England in 1290 and France in 1306 occurred on Av 9. In 1492, Jews were driven from Spain on . . . guess what day? The ninth of Av. The Holocaust officially began on that unspeakable Av 9, 1942, when Hitler began loading the crematoriums. As horrible as this review is, the entire catalogue has hardly been touched. This singular day should cause every Jew to shudder every year as it rolls round.

But we picked July 25, 1996, to be the special Av 9 predicted in Ezekiel 38 and 39. The prophet foresaw a future war during a time of false security based on a faulty peace treaty. Israel's enemies will be Iran, Ethiopia, and Libya, with a high probability of Syria, Russia, and several other nations joining them. The clash will probably be short-lived, because God will supernaturally deliver Israel. Ezekiel predicted dead enemy soldiers piled in such quantities that it would take seven months to pick them up and bury them.

We anticipated fulfillment of this prophecy on July 25, 1996, and everything was on schedule right up to this moment. What went wrong?

In the summer of 1997, Robert introduced me to an amazing book written by a secular Jewish reporter for *The New York Times*. Michael Drosnin's *The Bible Code* raced to the top of the charts as it revealed hidden messages encoded inside the Hebrew text thousands of years ago. These messages are now available to us because of the new capacities computers give us. Four years earlier, we had actually used one of these cryptic messages in *The Third Millennium's* chapter thirteen, but we barely touched the tip of an iceberg.

To our astonishment, we discovered Drosnin's *Bible Code* picked July 25, 1996, as a critical moment in Israel's life. On this date, Prime Minister Netanyahu was supposed to be assassinated in Amman, Jordan, triggering Ezekiel's nuclear holocaust in Israel. But this was only the first shock wave.

*The Bible Code* had another insight. Encoded in the same message were the words, "delayed, delayed, delayed." For some reason, known only in the economy of God, the date apparently was planned and then actually changed, postponed!

A coincidence? Could the Bible have predicted a modern event three and half millennia ago with the exact names and dates by accident? The chances are about one in who knows how many billion.

Michael Drosnin discovered in the hidden code, predicted 3,500 years earlier, the assassination of Yitzhak Rabin. He warned the prime minister a year before his death; Rabin ignored the message. The election of Benjamin Netanyahu was also detailed. In addition, a trip to Cairo was predicted, to be followed by Netanyahu's own assassination in Amman, Jordan, on Av 9, 1996. This prediction was modified by "delayed," the word used not once but three times.

As a matter of fact, Netanyahu *did* schedule a visit to Cairo and had another trip planned on July 25, 1996, to Amman—before Drosnin warned him of the consequences. But Netanyahu was determined to go anyway up to the last minute. Then Jordan's King Hussein became ill, and the trip was delayed until August 5.

Although World War III was postponed for that year, the Bible code indicates we're back on track for Av 9, 2006. We missed it, but we made a good guess (and I emphasize only an educated guess).

Why did we return with a third novel? In the September 1997 issue of *Christianity Today* magazine, *The Third Millennium* was called "the most biblical of the three prophetic novels under discussion." Their only suggestion was that we should have written more about spiritual warfare. We had already anticipated this need and were hard at work on this book. The first two novels were aimed primarily at a secular audience. This book is particularly for the Christian concerned with today's highly demanding spiritual and emotional battles. We have zeroed in on the issues that I, as a psychiatrist, and Robert, as a pastor, find people facing every day.

The book of Revelation warns that demonic activity will get worse and worse as Lucifer reads the signs of the times, knowing that his days on earth are numbered. Look around. Watch TV. What is the content of today's movies. Only the morally blind could miss the escalating assault on every front. Make no mistake: your children are the number one target on the demonic hit list.

We hope our three novels will give you the insight and motivation needed to "retire" from the vain human rat race. Our prayer is that you will get excited about serving God and people and sign on for the "kingdom team."

You'd be surprised to discover some of the people who are already suited up. Occasionally I do Bible studies for the Texas Rangers baseball squad and the Dallas Cowboys football team. One of these genuinely spiritual players is my friend Chad Hennings, defensive tackle for the Cowboys.

A week before the Cowboys beat Pittsburgh in the 1996 Super Bowl, Chad called me up for lunch. The Air Force academy graduate and jet pilot asked me to join him and Cowboys' chaplain John Weber. Trying to keep up with the lunch consumption of a six-foot-six, 290-pound athlete is an exciting experience.

I expected Chad to be nervous about the Super Bowl. Perhaps he was thinking that a Christian psychiatrist could give him some techniques for relaxing before the big game. To my surprise, Chad wanted to have lunch with me so I could give him an update on biblical prophecy. He said, "I love playing on a Super Bowl team, but I'm a lot more excited about being on the kingdom team." Chad's perspective was on target. He had his eye on what would last.

I hope this novel has the same effect on you. Writing it has reinforced those feelings and values in Robert Wise and me.

*Till He comes again,*
Paul Meier, M.D.
Dallas, Texas
Rosh Hashanah, 1997

# ABOUT THE AUTHORS

■ Paul Meier, M.D., is the cofounder and medical director of the New Life clinics, the largest provider of psychiatric services in the United States. He is the author of more than forty books including *The Third Millennium, The Fourth Millennium, Love Is a Choice,* and *Happiness Is a Choice for Teens.*

■ ■ ■

■ Robert L. Wise, Ph.D., is a noted teacher, lecturer, and author of fifteen books including *Quest for the Soul, The Fall of Jerusalem,* and *All That Remains.* He and Meier are the authors of *Windows of the Soul* and *The Fourth Millennium.*